SOCIAL CHANGE, INDUSTRIALIZATION, AND THE SERVICE ECONOMY IN SÃO PAULO, 1950–2020

SOCIAL SCIENCE HISTORY

Edited by

Stephen Haber and David W. Brady

SOCIAL CHANGE, INDUSTRIALIZATION, AND THE SERVICE ECONOMY IN SÃO PAULO, 1950–2020

FRANCISCO VIDAL LUNA
AND HERBERT S. KLEIN

STANFORD UNIVERSITY PRESS
Stanford, California

Stanford University Press
Stanford, California

Printed and bound by CPI Group (UK) Ltd,
Croydon, CR0 4YY

Cataloging-in-Publication Data available upon request.

Library of Congress Control Number: 2021051937

ISBN: 9781503631359 (cloth), 9781503631847 (ebook)

Cover photos: Central district of São Paulo, (foreground) Rua 25 de Março, (background) corner Ladeira Porto Geral, Francisco Vidal Luna.
Typeset by Newgen in 10.5/13 Bembo

To
Boris Fausto

TABLE OF CONTENTS

TABLES, FIGURES, AND MAPS

Tables

Figures

Maps

PREFACE

This represents the third volume of our economic and social history of the state of São Paulo, which begins in the middle of the eighteenth century and extends to the present day. Although São Paulo underwent major transformations until the middle of the nineteenth century, at that point it was still a province without prominence in the empire, with small urban centers and with little connection to international markets. Its population was composed of a mixture of poor whites, Indians, *caboclos* (mestizos), Africans, and Afro-Brazilians, and its agriculture supplied mainly local and regional markets. Despite the fertility of its lands, its lack of an adequate infrastructure meant that most land remained unexploited and it exported relatively few products. Its capital city was small, and even in the early stage of coffee production it was a secondary producer until the second half of the nineteenth century.

Coffee, virgin lands, railways, and slave and free immigrant workers made it possible to transform this relatively backward and modest province into a power of the empire and the republic. With the new entrepreneurial elite of coffee growers that emerged in the second half of the nineteenth century, local agriculture finally became competitive in national and international markets. Initially based on slave labor, the modern coffee plantations were able to shift to free wage labor in the 1880s with the wealth generated from the slave period, allowing the planters to attract millions of foreign and Brazilian immigrants, which in turn gave rise to a modern economy, based on wage labor. The local elite invested the profits obtained from coffee exports in domestic and foreign trade, in railroad construction, in financial institutions, and even in industry. Free wage workers, in turn, created an expanded market for food, clothing, and other consumer products, increasingly supplied by local production. The population grew rapidly; the railroad penetrated all regions of the state, and coffee expanded along with the railroads, so that by the beginning of the twentieth century, São Paulo had become one of the most dynamic regions of the Brazilian economy.

The economic and social transformations that took place in São Paulo were facilitated and supported by the evolution of an administrative structure and by a state government determined to invest in basic infrastructure. The São Paulo elite, whose influence during the empire had been restricted to a limited provincial government, strove so vigorously for autonomy that they eventually took control of the federal government during the Old Republic period and forged a powerful state government. Throughout the twentieth century, the state of São Paulo led the nation in such fundamental areas as health, education, science, and technology, in addition to being a model of administrative organization by the country's standards. It educated more people, had the best water and sanitation systems, and owned most of the nation's highways and the best secondary roads in the country.

All these changes were made possible by the reorganization of state finances after 1889. Under the new republic, the São Paulo government reorganized and expanded, with new and extensive fiscal and financial powers. The objective of this government was to forge a state that had a high degree of autonomy and would sustain and expand the economy and society. These objectives demanded increasing resources, financed by the growing tax revenues and by large loans obtained in the national and international credit markets.

While promoting growth, the São Paulo government in the twentieth century also actively intervened in the coffee economy and, finally, controlled production, buying stocks, and limited the supply in ports to protect coffee growers in times of international crises. It also had to deal with other economic, political, and fiscal crises. Among them were the financial bubble known as the *encilhamento*, the two world wars, periodic overproduction in the coffee market, and the economic depression that began in 1929 and which led to a major transformation in the structure of coffee production and forced the state to finally resort to federal government support. Although the Vargas revolution in 1930 reduced the power of the state government, even with less power and fewer resources the state was still able to provide basic economic support for the increasingly industrialized and complex São Paulo economy.

Another aspect of this dynamic growth of the state of São Paulo was the growth of the city of São Paulo, which went from a small town of 20,000 inhabitants in 1850 to a population of 2 million by 1950 and began to challenge the dominance of the federal capital, Rio de Janeiro. But it was in the period after 1950 that the city emerged as one of the largest metropolitan centers in the world. While the rest of the state progressively urbanized in this period, and its agriculture dramatically diversified, it was the capital city that would become a world metropolis with influence far beyond the borders of the state. Smaller than Rio, Mexico City, or even Buenos Aires in 1950, by 2020 it had become the leading urban center in Latin America and one of the largest cities in the world, with its influence spreading far beyond the borders of the country.

Until the middle decades of the twentieth century, coffee dominated agriculture and the exports of the state. But already by 1950, the slow evolution of a more complex agricultural and industrial economy had begun in the state. Even when coffee dominated exports, foodstuffs and commercial crops such as cotton were an important part of the agricultural sector. The state's agriculture led the nation in the use of machinery and fertilizers, and reached a new level of productivity in various traditional crops. But only after 1950 did the state become a modern producer of meat, sugar, oranges, and soybeans, with levels of productivity that allowed these products to replace coffee as the main agricultural exports of the state by the end of the twentieth century. The agricultural revolution that placed Brazil among the great countries of world agribusiness only happened in the last quarter of the century, and especially from the 1990s, with the opening of the economy and the impact of government-sponsored research in agriculture and livestock. There was also increasing productivity in traditional food products such as rice, corn, and beans—the basis of the Paulista food basket—that allowed local agriculture to support the ever growing urban population of the state. It was also local production that provided the raw material for the food industries that developed into an increasingly important part of the thriving manufacturing sector. Similarly, it was cotton produced in the state that supplied most of the raw material for the important São Paulo textile industry. By the late 1940s the frontier lands of the state had been mostly settled, and the middle decades of the century were therefore a transition period in which local agriculture stopped expanding through the exploration of virgin lands and started to depend on the systematic use of machines and fertilizers. From this base, Paulista agriculture in the second half of the twentieth century would emerge as the national leader in agricultural diversification. Not only were new products developed in agriculture but there was even a major revival of such traditional products as sugar along with a new milling and refining industry.

It was also in the second half of the twentieth century that the bases for the explosive growth of the São Paulo industry were consolidated, which transformed São Paulo from a secondary production center into the main industrial state of the country. From the end of the nineteenth century, São Paulo industry, which started mainly with the production of textiles and the processing of foodstuffs, grew at an impressive rate. Several factors explain this advance: the introduction of free labor (especially of European immigrants who immigrated to Brazil, the majority of whom arrived in this state), with their growing purchasing power in comparison with slave workers; the availability of resources thanks to coffee exports; the willingness of large coffee farmers to invest in urban and industrial projects; a growing agro-industrial integration; and a series of external shocks that limited international trade. This set of factors, to a greater or lesser extent, stimulated local production and allowed the consolidation of an industrial process even before the introduction of effective policies to protect industry, which only began in the second half of the twentieth century. When protectionist policies were implemented by the federal government, São Paulo had already consolidated its industry, which was based largely on local raw materials, and production expanded to meet regional and national demand.

But if the first volume dealt with slavery in São Paulo and the second volume focused on the transition from slave to free wage labor and the consolidation of the state as the main coffee-producing center in Brazil and the world, this third volume deals with the accelerated industrialization of the state as well as its growth into the dominant center of services in the nation. Brazil from the 1950s to the 1980s built one of the most advanced and integrated industrial structures among the so-called developing countries. This process was initially concentrated almost completely in the state of São Paulo, and more precisely in the metropolitan region of São Paulo, mainly in the area known as ABC Paulista. This metropolitan region showed rapid economic and population growth, centered on industrial expansion, which shaped the urban fabric.

But from the 1980s there began a process of decentralization of industry to other states, reducing the relative importance of the state in the country's industrial product. At the same time, there was a decentralization of industry within the state of São Paulo as industry left the capital for interior industrial centers, with a rapid loss of the relative importance of industry in the metropolitan region. Though the state was still the leading industrial state in the nation in 2020, its relative importance within Brazil declined. This in turn led to a slowing of internal migration as the local labor market matured and no longer provided expanding occupational opportunities. The rise of new industrial centers within the state was accompanied by the rapid growth of new metropolitan centers that competed with the capital and São Paulo metropolitan area and led to a relative decline in those latter two areas' industrial prominence within the state.

In turn the capital transformed itself from an industrial city to a primarily service city in the current century. It became the financial capital of the country as well as the headquarters of most of the national and international companies operating in Brazil. Its health and educational services were to become the most important in the nation. In this period it saw major growth in public and private universities, which quickly became among the most advanced in Latin America. This educational base, the most advanced in Brazil, in turn educated an ever larger class of liberal professionals, which quickly filled the expanding service workforce. So rapidly did the capital grow in income and importance that its influence soon spread well beyond the borders of Brazil. In its cultural institutions, its universities, its banking, and its corporate importance, the municipality of São Paulo with its 12 million people became a world metropolis. It is the largest city in the hemisphere, one of the largest in the world, and the single most important city in Latin America, attracting a large entrepreneurial class of natives and foreigners. It was in the sixty years after 1950 that São Paulo emerged as a global city, with all its splendor as well as its frailties and problems.

Given the rapidity of its growth from 2 million to 12 million in this period, the capital and its metropolitan region of satellite cities still exhibit problems of distribution, housing, and governance. The rise of an educated middle class and the decline of the premium of education as more well-educated persons entered the workforce seems to have had only a modest impact on overall income distribution, as both the state and the nation remained one of the most unequal societies in the world. As migration and growth slowed, the state and above all its capital city still were left with major problems regarding how to house the migrants who had come from all over Brazil. Though the capital built avenues, subways, and schools, it could not increase the housing stock and services at a rate equal to the size of the migration. The result was the expansion of illegal and unsafe settlements known as favelas. Favelas developed in the capital and its metropolitan region. They also appeared in almost all of the interior and littoral cities, with Santos having the largest favela on stilts in Brazil, and Campinas and other important urban centers of the state also containing these illegal and poorly built slums. Although electricity was brought into most of the favelas, sanitation facilities lagged and the transport system remained problematic. For the size of its working population, the metropolitan area of the capital had insufficient subway lines and an insufficient bus network, such that moving people from home to work became ever more difficult. Thus despite all the positive changes and the systematic growth of state and federal government funding, the state of

São Paulo and its cities still had serious problems providing for all its citizens even as late as 2020.

This study thus covers one of the most dynamic periods in the history of the state of São Paulo. It was in this period that the state and its capital became the unqualified leaders of the nation in industry, agriculture, and services. It was the period for which one can say that São Paulo really did become the locomotive of the train of Brazil. With all its problems, the city has modernized its infrastructure, developed a dynamic professional class, and created a modern service industry. It is this transformation that we will examine in this study

In order to assess the general transformations that occurred in the state of São Paulo in the seventy years studied in this volume, we begin by drawing a general picture of the state in the year of 1950. We then go on to examine industrial growth and relative decline and how industry has changed in the capital and the state. We next examine the very important changes in the state agricultural sector in this period, which saw the state not only maintain its lead as Brazil's richest agricultural producer but also diversify into a host of new crops as coffee moved into a position of lesser importance. Finally we examine the rise of services and trade and how they came to dominate the capital in this period, replacing the previously dominant industrial sector.

We then explore the dramatic demographic and social changes in the state in the next several chapters as the state became more urbanized, with a better-educated population, and passed through the modern demographic transition, which led to low birth rates, smaller families, and higher rates of education and labor participation for women. It also led to a change in female roles in all parts of Paulista society, from marriage and the family to work and education. There was also a very significant increase in life expectancy, and this combined with lower fertility resulted in an increasingly aged population in this period, as São Paulo and its southern neighboring states led the nation in this demographic and social transformation.

The section on social change also explores the variations in social mobility that occurred both in the early stages of industrialization as well as in what might be defined as the post-industrial phase of the state's development. Clearly the state has moved away from a very fluid system of mobility as occupations expanded dramatically and toward a more traditional circular pattern of movement both above and below parents' initial positions in the socioeconomic class system. We also deal with the question of race, a fundamental issue in any former American slave society. While this is a question of importance to all Brazilian society, it became a major theme in São Paulo as the migration of native-born Brazilians from other regions to the capital and the state created an ever more racially mixed society. We will try to assess how the rise of an industrialized and unionized labor force and a professional middle class influenced the role of Blacks and Browns in Paulista society.

Finally, we explore how the capital and its metropolitan area developed in this period and came to distinguish itself from the rest of the state despite the increasing urbanization of the state population. Our study ends with the transformations and problems created with the growth of the capital and its metropolitan region into a world metropolis.

In preparing this work, Judith C. Schiffner and Matiko Kume provided important editorial assistance. We owe a special debt to Eric Wakin for his general support of this and earlier projects. William Summerhill, Stuart Schwartz, Marta Grostein, Simon Schwartzman, Donald Treiman, and Sonia Rocha have often helped us to understand basic changes in this period. Renato Augusto Rosa Vidal, Bruno Teodoro Oliva, Roberta Fontan Pereira Galvão, and Renata Carvalho Silva provided support on data and analysis. Finally, we thank Steven Topik, who suggested that we do this third volume in a social and economic history of São Paulo.

SOCIAL CHANGE, INDUSTRIALIZATION, AND THE SERVICE ECONOMY IN SÃO PAULO, 1950–2020

Chapter 1

The State of São Paulo at Mid-Twentieth Century

In the four centuries before 1950 the province and state of São Paulo followed a well-defined path. Starting as a marginal area far from the sugar plantations of the Northeast, it progressively moved into the center of national development. The sixteenth- and seventeenth-century slaving, exploration, and mining expeditions were the first expressions of the polyglot original settlers' more than local impact. In the eighteenth century its food-producing centers reached out to the interior mining regions to help develop a regional market. The rise of a sugar plantation economy in Rio de Janeiro in the late eighteenth and early nineteenth centuries, which spilled over into the province, was another factor pushing the formerly marginal region into the international economy. But it was the rise of the modern coffee plantation system that finally placed the state in the center of national development in the late nineteenth and early twentieth centuries. With rich lands well adapted to coffee, São Paulo resolved problems of labor supply first with African slaves and then with European and Asian wage workers. It built a major railroad infrastructure that finally opened up Santos as the principal port for the state and the nation between 1850 and 1950. The wealth generated by coffee led to São Paulo becoming Brazil's richest, most populous state in the post-1950 era.

The phenomenal growth in coffee cultivation led to the strengthening of a substantial internal market within the state and the evolution of a major national market. An important impetus to the development of the agriculture, industry, transport, and service sectors in São Paulo in the late twentieth century was private and public investments. It was the income from the state's coffee exports that provided the financial resources to transition to a wage labor force to produce coffee and to build the basic infrastructure of railroads, highways, and roads.[1] The growth of a large free wage labor force in coffee farming promoted a significant domestic market in the state, and the arrival of a mass of more educated European and Asian immigrants laid the foundations for a modern industrial workforce. By the 1920s foreigners accounted for at least a quarter of the industrial workforce in the state. Capital for new industries came from the wealthier foreign immigrants attracted to the growing internal market, from the wealthier coffee growers, and from local importers transitioning into import substitution industries.[2] It was thus domestic and foreign capital, together with Brazilian and foreign workers, that made São Paulo into the largest and most dynamic industrial state in the country in the first half of the twentieth century. In the post–1950 period São Paulo would also become the first state to acquire a modern durable goods and capital goods industry, and it would be the largest in the nation.[3]

It was during the second half of the 1950s, under civilian and military governments, that an intense process of government-induced industrialization took place, creating a capital goods industry in Brazil. Taking the lead in this development would be the newly established motor industry, producing cars, trucks, and buses. Thanks to the government policy that promoted foreign investment, São Paulo would strengthen its role as an industrial leader of the nation when much of this new automotive industry with its complex supply chain was established in the state. The automobile industry would become the main dynamic driver of the Brazilian economy.[4] It would also generate new and powerful labor movements, which would have an impact on national politics.

These economic and industrial transformations in São Paulo were facilitated and supported by the evolution of a state government determined to invest in basic infrastructure. The Paulista elite, whose influence during the empire had been restricted to a limited provincial government, now took control of the state administration and assumed many tasks that had formerly been the purview of the imperial central government. Throughout the first half of the twentieth century, the state of São Paulo began to lead in key areas such as health, science, and technology, as well as being a model for administrative organization of government services. It educated more people, had the best water and sanitation systems, and eventually owned most of the country's highways and most of its best secondary roads, always with strong support from the state government. In addition, it was the state with the highest percentage of literate people in the country in 1950, having risen from eighth-most-literate province in 1872.

The population of the state was also growing at a very rapid pace in this period, due both to high natural growth rates and to increasing internal migration from other states. In 1940 the state's population was 7 million, and this increased to 9 million ten years later, for a very significant growth rate of 2.4% per annum. In turn, the city of São Paulo grew at the extraordinary rate of 5.2% per annum between 1940 and 1950, reaching almost 2.4 million persons.[5] At the 1940 census São Paulo had become Brazil's most populous state and by 1960 its capital city would become the largest metropolitan area in Brazil.[6]

The state was also one of the most urbanized regions in Brazil. Half of the state population, or 4.8 million persons, resided in cities by 1950. Using the mesoregion classification that is currently used to group the regions of the state, it is evident that a third of this urban population could be found in what would become the metropolitan region of São Paulo, with the metropolitan regions of Ribeirão Preto and São José do Rio Preto accounting for 8% each of the total state urban population, Bauru and Campinas at 7% each, and Presidente Prudente at 6%. These areas accounted for more than two-thirds of the total state population and 78% of the population living in metropolitan regions.

Except in the metropolitan region of São Paulo, which had a density of 299 inhabitants per km^2, in the other urban centers the population density was low. In the Ribeirão Preto region, the second-most-populous city, for example, the density was only 27 people per km^2. Nor was any other city close in size to the capital. The city of Santos had only 198,000 inhabitants, Campinas had 99,000, and Santo André just 97,000. The city of Guarulhos, which today has 1.3 million people, had only 16,000 people in the city core. Overall, only four Paulista cities had more than 100,000 inhabitants in 1950, twenty-two had more than 50,000 inhabitants, and 256 had less than 20,000 inhabitants each (see Table 1.1).

As with urban population, there was an uneven pattern of regional settlement in the state especially along the routes of the main railways, particularly the Mogiana, Paulista, and Norte lines. There was relatively light population density in the older western frontier regions, the coastal areas, and only moderate density in the expansion new coffee zones. The sole exception was the capital region, which grew dramatically and had the highest population densities (see Map 1.1).[7]

TABLE 1.1

Population of the State of São Paulo in 1950 (by 2010 Mesoregion) (1) Distributed in Regional Districts According to the Census of 2010

	POPULATION			PARTICIPATION				
Mesoregions	Area (km^2)	Municipalities (a)	(b) Cities	Area	Municipalities	Cities	(b) as % of (a)	Pop. density per km^2
Metropolitana de São Paulo	9,788	2,923,038	2,507,128	4%	32%	55%	86%	299
Ribeirão Preto	27,519	747,315	260,645	11%	8%	6%	35%	27
São José do Rio Preto	26,920	689,160	159,160	11%	8%	3%	23%	26
Bauru	27,554	667,602	217,774	11%	7%	5%	33%	24
Araraquara	9,478	241,955	97,333	4%	3%	2%	40%	26
Araçatuba	17,051	399,061	94,098	7%	4%	2%	24%	23
Campinas	14,044	645,556	271,424	6%	7%	6%	42%	46
Presidente Prudente	23,962	546,585	116,425	10%	6%	3%	21%	23
Vale do Paraíba Paulista	15,806	477,235	214,280	6%	5%	5%	45%	30
Macro Metropolitana Paulista	12,459	455,127	194,684	5%	5%	4%	43%	37
Piracicaba	8,810	332,478	160,056	4%	4%	4%	48%	38
Assis	13,238	319,621	82,429	5%	3%	2%	26%	24
Marília	7,182	318,708	90,598	3%	3%	2%	28%	44
Itapetininga	21,204	269,325	70,929	9%	3%	2%	26%	13
Litoral Sul Paulista	12,207	101,657	15,129	5%	1%	0%	15%	8
State Total	247,222	9,134,423	4,552,092	100%	100%	100%	50%	37

SOURCE: IBGE, Censo Demográfico 1950, Série Nacional, vol. 1: 193–197; Ipeadata, Regional.

NOTE: (1) Mesoregions adopted from IBGE censo demográfico de 2010, at https://censo2010.ibge.gov.br/sinopse/index.php?dados=4&uf=00, and Ipeadata, Regional.

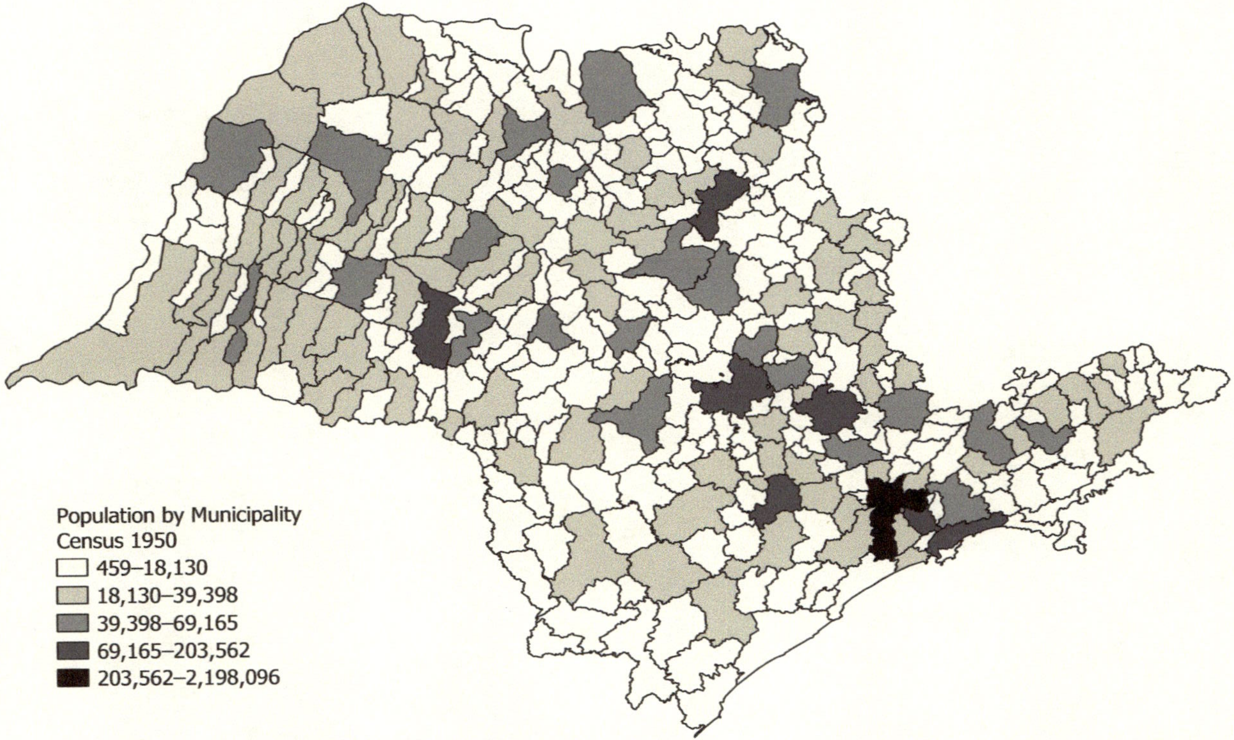

Map 1.1. Population Density by Municipality, São Paulo, 1950

SOURCE: IBGE, Censo Demográfico, 1950; NEPO, Base Cartográfica.

The importance of the state within the national economy in 1950 is clearly revealed in the national accounts. The state of São Paulo alone accounted for 47% of the national GDP in industry, a third of the GDP in services, and 29% of national GDP in agriculture. It was thus the leading state in all three sectors (see Table 1.2). No other state had such a high proportion of GDP in industry or agriculture. São Paulo even stood out from the other leading states in services. Rio de Janeiro, which competed with São Paulo at the beginning of the century, accounted for only 21% of the value of Brazil's industrial production by 1950.[8] In agriculture, São Paulo's importance was almost double that of the next leading state, Minas Gerais (see Table 1.2).

The importance of São Paulo in the national economy is also reflected in the distribution of employed persons.[9] The 6.7 million persons employed in the state represented 18% of the country's total employed workforce which was close to the state's share of participation in the national population.[10] But its manufacturing industry accounted for 36% of the total number of people working in manufacturing nationwide. The state also exceeded its share of national population in the percentage of people employed in services, who were 25% of all national service workers, and in commerce, where the state accounted for 26% of all Brazilian commerce employees. In 1950 there were 1.5 million people employed in agriculture in São Paulo, making up 22% of those employed in the state. But they represented only 15% of agricultural workers in the nation, even though São Paulo accounted for 29% of national agricultural production; this demonstrated the higher economic productivity of São Paulo agriculture (see Table 1.3).

The 25,000 industrial companies in the state accounted for 47% of the value of national production, and São Paulo's 488,000 factory workers (as defined by the industrial census) constituted 38% of all such workers in Brazil in 1950.[11] The state industrial sector represented 43% of the capital employed in industry, and 40% of the energy consumed in national industry. In terms of average production value, number of workers, and energy consumed, São Paulo and Rio de Janeiro, the second-largest industrial state, had similar figures, both far above those of other states (see Table 1.4).

The most representative sectors of São Paulo industry in terms of value of production were textiles (20%), food, chemicals, and pharmaceuticals (10% each). Accounting for a third of the industrial establishments in São Paulo, textiles also employed the most workers and used the most energy. In some industries, São Paulo totally dominated national production. Two-thirds of the value of industrial goods produced by the machinery and

TABLE I.2

Gross Domestic Product by Sector and Principal Economic States of the Federation, 1950

	PARTICIPATION OF THE ECONOMIC SECTOR IN THE GDP OF THE NATION AND THE STATES						
Sector	Brazil	São Paulo	Rio de Janeiro	Minas Gerais	Rio Grande do Sul	Pernambuco	Bahia
Industry (1)	20%	28%	23%	13%	18%	20%	9%
Services (2)	49%	46%	69%	39%	45%	49%	48%
Agriculture & Ranching (3)	31%	26%	8%	48%	36%	31%	43%
Total	100%	100%	100%	100%	100%	100%	100%

		SHARE OF STATE GDP IN NATIONAL SECTORAL GDP					
Sectors	% of the 6 States in GDP Sector Brazil	São Paulo	Rio de Janeiro	Minas Gerais	Rio Grande do Sul	Pernambuco	Bahia
Industry (1)	89%	47%	21%	7%	8%	4%	2%
Services (2)	84%	33%	27%	8%	8%	4%	4%
Agriculture & Ranching (3)	70%	29%	5%	16%	11%	4%	5%
% of National GDP (4)	82%	37%	21%	11%	8%	3%	2%

SOURCE: Ipeadata, Regional, http://www.ipeadata.gov.br/Default.aspx; PIB Estadual preços básicos.

NOTES (1) PIB Estadual—indústria—valor adicionado—preços básicos (1950).
(2) PIB Estadual—serviços—valor adicionado—preços básicos (1950).
(3) PIB Estadual—agropecuária—valor adicionado—preços básicos (1950).
(4) PIB Estadual a preços constantes—R$ de 2010 (mil)—IBGE—PIBE; obtained from Ipeadata.

TABLE I.3

Persons 10 Years of Age and Over, Employed During the Week of the Census and Not Attending School, 1950

Principal Activity	Brazil	São Paulo	Rio de Janeiro	Minas Gerais	Rio Grande do Sul	Pernambuco	Bahia
Agriculture	9,886,934	1,449,396	316,113	1,618,491	824,629	738,038	1,068,174
Mining	482,972	44,472	25,739	42,851	19,985	11,161	37,345
Industry	2,231,205	801,325	407,451	218,684	162,699	120,637	121,579
Commerce	958,509	248,293	171,227	97,468	81,240	62,561	68,286
Services	1,672,801	413,133	316,532	225,909	133,647	100,483	127,240
Transport and Communications	697,089	197,269	143,951	75,976	54,191	32,608	39,645
Total Persons employed	36,557,990	6,691,114	3,537,360	5,545,631	2,939,001	2,375,219	3,345,849
Total Population	51,944,397	9,134,423	4,584,645	7,717,792	4,164,821	3,395,185	4,834,575

SOURCE: IBGE, Censo Demográfico 1950, volume 1: 102–178.

TABLE I.4

Industrial Census of 1950: Various Indicators for Leading States (Value in Cr$, 1949/1950)

	Brazil	São Paulo	Rio de Janeiro	Minas Gerais	Rio Grande do Sul	Pernambuco	Bahia
PARTICIPATION IN EACH CATEGORY							
Firms	92,350	25,016	9,699	11,950	13,652	3,844	4,270
Capital Realized Cr$	41,396,736	18,457,928	11,099,807	2,886,593	3,396,397	1,393,369	488,269
Applied Capital Cr$	53,408,198	22,977,603	12,480,779	4,190,782	4,056,488	2,236,523	650,078
Workers	1,279,184	488,633	250,094	111,513	99,945	76,483	35,719
Energy Used hp	2,824,152	1,135,764	578,291	244,656	244,426	126,427	44,843
Value of Production Cr$	118,605,165	55,291,473	25,036,922	8,437,674	10,185,701	4,712,145	1,744,739
Industrial Aggregated Value Cr$	55,038,897	25,869,093	11,951,994	3,803,204	4,280,425	2,276,429	810,612
PARTICIPATION OF THE STATES							
Firms		27%	11%	13%	15%	4%	5%
Capital Realized		45%	27%	7%	8%	3%	1%
Applied Capital		43%	23%	8%	8%	4%	1%
Workers		38%	20%	9%	8%	6%	3%
Energy Used		40%	20%	9%	9%	4%	2%
Value of Production		47%	21%	7%	9%	4%	1%
Industrial Aggregated Value		47%	22%	7%	8%	4%	1%
AVERAGE PER FIRM							
Value of Production Cr$	1,284	2,210	2,581	706	746	1,226	409
Industrial Aggregated Value Cr$	596	1,034	1,232	318	314	592	190
Applied Capital Cr$	578	919	1,287	351	297	582	152
Workers	14	20	26	9	7	20	8
Energy Used hp	31	45	60	20	18	33	11

SOURCE: IBGE, Censo 1950, Série Nacional, volume III, tomo 1: 91–284.

TABLE 1.5

Industrial Census of 1950: Basic Indicators for Brazil and State of São Paulo (Value in Cr$ 1000, 1949/1950)

Industry	Firms	Workers	Energy Used c.v.	Value of Production Cr$	Added Value of Industrial Transformation Cr$
BRAZIL					
Non-Metallic Minerals	14%	9%	6%	4%	7%
Metallurgy	4%	9%	11%	8%	9%
Mechanics	2%	3%	2%	2%	3%
Transport Material	1%	2%	2%	3%	3%
Chemical and Pharmaceutical	3%	6%	10%	9%	10%
Textile	6%	29%	22%	21%	20%
Food	32%	9%	20%	23%	13%
Drinks	4%	2%	2%	2%	3%
Editorial and Graphic	4%	3%	1%	2%	3%
Construction	4%	5%	1%	5%	5%
Other	27%	23%	23%	20%	24%
Total	100%	100%	100%	100%	100%
N	92,350	1,279,184	2,824,152	118,605,165	55,038,897
SÃO PAULO					
Non-Metallic Minerals	14%	9%	6%	4%	7%
Metallurgy	4%	9%	11%	8%	9%
Mechanics	2%	3%	2%	2%	3%
Transport Material	1%	2%	2%	3%	3%
Chemical and Pharmaceutical	3%	6%	10%	9%	10%
Textile	6%	29%	22%	21%	20%
Food	32%	9%	20%	23%	13%
Drinks	4%	2%	2%	2%	3%
Editorial and Graphic	4%	3%	1%	2%	3%
Construction	4%	5%	1%	5%	5%
Other	27%	23%	23%	20%	24%
Total	100%	100%	100%	100%	100%
N	25,016	488,633	1,135,764	55,291,473	25,869,093

SOURCE: IBGE, Censo 1950, Série Nacional, volume III, tomo 1: 91–284.

transport materials groups in Brazil was accounted for by the state's firms (see Table 1.5).

Although industrial growth in São Paulo was impressive by 1950, the consumer goods industry was still primary, with little capital goods development. But changes in federal government policies would lead to a massive restructuring and expansion of the state's industrial sector. The first occurred during the government of Juscelino Kubitschek (1956–1961), when the foundation of the consumer durables industry in Brazil was established.

The second occurred during the period of military rule (1964–1985). It was then that a complete industrial complex was created with massive investments in both basic inputs and capital goods industries. In the first period, the state of São Paulo gained the most, since the entire auto industry—automakers and auto parts makers—was initially installed within its borders. But under the military government's industrial program, which initially promoted strong growth in São Paulo industry, a systematic policy of economic decentralization moved large industrial projects to other states.

Within the state there was initially a significant concentration of industrial production in what would become the capital metropolitan area. At midcentury, what was then called the Metropolitan Mesoregion of São Paulo included the capital and new industrial satellite towns that would be included in the future Metropolitan Region of São Paulo (created in 1973), such as Santo André, São Caetano, and São Bernardo do Campo.[12] The Metropolitan Mesoregion of São Paulo produced more than two-thirds of the value of industrial production in the state, with the city of São Paulo alone generating more than half of that value (and 20% of the value of national industrial production), with similar numbers for capital invested, employed personnel, and energy used (see Table 1.6).

Not only was São Paulo the dominant industrial state by 1950, but it was also the dominant agricultural state in the country. São Paulo agriculture remained as important to the local and national economies as it had been for most of the first half of the twentieth century. Data from the 1950 agricultural census shows that the state had 222,000 farms covering a total of

TABLE 1.6

Industrial Indicators for Brazil, the State, the Mesoregion Region, and the City of São Paulo, 1950 (Value in Cr$ 1000)

Brazil and São Paulo	Firms	Capital Employed Cr$	Personnel Employed Cr$	Energy Used (hp)	Value of Production Cr$
Mesoregion of São Paulo	9,139	15,465,262	366,508	672,517	36,079,944
Capital of São Paulo	7,374	10,946,805	299,513	497,675	28,565,661
Total for the State of São Paulo	24,068	22,547,627	546,847	1,100,095	52,715,952
Total for Brazil	92,350	53,408,196	1,522,844	2,824,152	118,605,165
City of São Paulo/Brazil	8%	20%	20%	18%	24%
City of São Paulo/State of São Paulo	31%	49%	55%	45%	54%

SOURCE: IBGE, Censo 1950, Série Nacional, vol. III, Indústrial, Comercial e Serviços: Data for Brazil in Tomo 1of III: 91-284; data for São Paulo, Censo 1950, Serie Regional, vol. XXV, Tomo 3: 91-98.

19 million hectares and employing 1.5 million people. Land dedicated to crops represented 4.2 million hectares, corresponding to 22% of Brazil's total cropland. Small farm properties predominated in the state, as in the rest of Brazil, with those up to 100 hectares accounting for 86% of all farms but only a quarter of the total land dedicated to agriculture.

Fertilizer usage in São Paulo agriculture was above the Brazilian norm, as can be seen in the high proportion of fertilizer expenditures in the state compared to the rest of Brazil. As for mechanization, 35% of disc plows and half of all tractors in Brazil were found in the state. Nevertheless, the relative underdevelopment of machinery use in agriculture in even this advanced state was reflected in the fact that less than 1% of farms in São Paulo had tractors (see Table 1.7). But mechanization would proceed rapidly in this decade; by 1960, the number of tractors in the state reached 27,000, out of 61,000 tractors in all of Brazil.

Although coffee production was now increasing in the states of Minas Gerais, Paraná, and Espírito Santo, São Paulo, with its output of 864,000 tons of coffee in 1950, still accounted for 44% of national production. Despite the diversification of domestic economic activities in Brazil and the creation of new export products, the country still depended primarily on coffee, which accounted for more than half the value of all Brazilian exports.

But other crops were also becoming important in the state at this time. São Paulo produced over half of the cotton grown in Brazil, which mainly supplied the Brazilian textile industry. It also dominated peanut production, English potatoes, and to a lesser extent rice, corn, sugarcane, oranges, and milk (see Figure 1.1). In terms of area cultivated and value of production, coffee was still the leading product, but cotton now occupied a large share of the state's lands, as did rice and corn (see Table 1.8). In this period it was evident that coffee was becoming less dominant; the state was developing a more diversified agricultural production, with new crops and pastures taking over fields originally used for coffee.

Agricultural activity was of course not uniform across the state. The mesoregions of Ribeirão Preto, São José do Rio Preto, and Bauru each had more than 2 million hectares of land devoted to both permanent and seasonal crops. This was followed by the mesoregions of Araçatuba, Campinas, Presidente Prudente, Vale do Paraíba Paulista, Assis, and Itapetininga, each with 1 million hectares under cultivation. The big three regions of Ribeirão Preto, São José do Rio Preto, and Bauru, along with Campinas and Presidente Prudente, each had over 100,000 people engaged in agricultural activities, which together accounted for just under half of those employed in São Paulo agriculture (see Table 1.9).

TABLE I.7

Agricultural Indicators for Brazil and Principal Agricultural States, 1950
(Value in Cr$ 1000, Area in Hectares)

			PERCENTAGE OF NATIONAL TOTAL					
Indicators	Brazil	São Paulo	São Paulo	Minas Gerais	Paraná	R.G. do Sul	Bahia	Pernambuco
Total Area	232,211,106	19,007,582	8%	16%	3%	10%	7%	2%
Farms	2,064,642	221,611	11%	13%	4%	14%	12%	8%
Crop Area	19,095,057	4,257,633	22%	15%	7%	13%	7%	5%
Pasture Area	107,633,043	8,647,935	8%	21%	2%	14%	4%	1%
Property Value	155,625,221	37,512,986	24%	16%	8%	18%	6%	3%
Personnel Employed	10,996,834	1,531,664	14%	17%	5%	10%	12%	8%
Fertilizer Expenses	1,303,691	675,918	52%	8%	4%	19%	2%	6%
Tenants (Renters)	186,949	53,122	28%	5%	2%	9%	4%	19%
Rented Area	12,946,538	994,957	8%	6%	1%	16%	1%	2%
Farms over 100 ha	301,151	31,830	11%	22%	4%	9%	9%	3%
Area in Farms over 100 ha	193,622,987	14,314,583	7%	16%	3%	8%	6%	2%
Farms less than 100 ha	1,763,491	189,781	11%	11%	4%	15%	13%	9%
Area in Farms less than 100 ha	38,588,119	4,692,999	12%	16%	6%	16%	11%	4%
Farms with Disc Plows	41,162	11,947	29%	13%	6%	24%	1%	1%
Number of Disc Plows	54,576	19,062	35%	13%	4%	23%	1%	1%
Farms with Moldboard Plows	442,248	104,779	24%	11%	6%	49%	1%	0%
Number of Moldboard Plows	659,683	205,885	31%	10%	4%	45%	1%	1%
Farms with Tractors up to 10 hp	1,086	537	49%	11%	4%	19%	1%	2%
Number of Tractors up to 10 hp	1,273	633	50%	10%	4%	21%	1%	2%
Farms with Tractors over 10 c.v.	4,851	2,112	44%	10%	3%	29%	1%	1%
Number of Tractors over 10 c.v.	7,099	3,186	45%	9%	3%	28%	1%	2%
Total Expenditure	14,856,785	5,212,122	35%	14%	7%	13%	5%	5%

SOURCE: IBGE, Censo 1950, Série Nacional, volume II: VI–IX and 27–111.

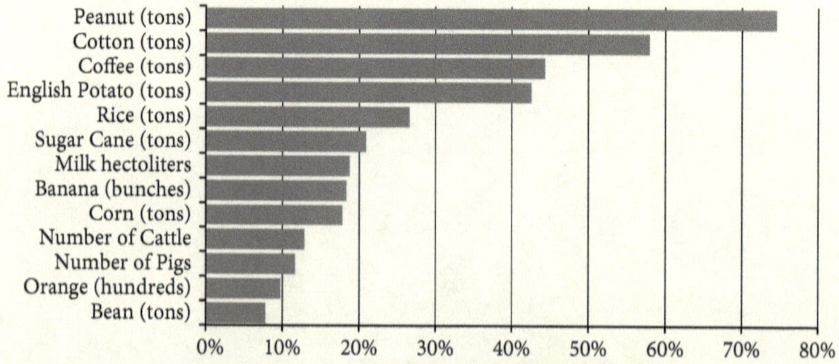

Figure 1.1. São Paulo Agrarian Production as a Share of National Total, 1950

SOURCE: IBGE, Censo Demográfico, 1950, Serie Nacional, volume II.

There were also important changes in the concentration of agricultural crops within the state. This can be seen especially with coffee. By 1950 the mesoregions of Bauru, São José do Rio Preto, and Marília were still major coffee producers. But in terms of young trees, Presidente Prudente was clearly the newest growing area, with its 44 million new trees representing 32% of the newly planted trees in the state. As for cotton, 40% of the production came from the Presidente Prudente mesoregion, followed by Araçatuba, Marília, and São José do Rio Preto. Sugarcane was also highly concentrated, in this case in the Piracicaba, Ribeirão Preto, and Campinas mesoregions, which together represented 75% of the state's sugarcane production. Corn was more generally distributed, with Ribeirão Preto, Itapetininga, Bauru, and São José do Rio Preto each accounting for less than 15% of the state's production. Like corn, cattle production was also more uniformly distributed in the state, with higher concentrations in the mesoregions of São José do Rio Preto, Ribeirão Preto, Bauru, and Araçatuba (see Table 1.10).

A better characterization of production in the state in 1950 comes from analyzing the data from municipalities. Marília was the most representative municipality, in terms of both employed personnel (17,000 people) and cultivated area (54,000 hectares). It was the largest coffee producer (3% of the state's total), and it also cultivated cotton, corn, and other crops. Marília along with Garça (both in the mesoregion of Marília), Lins, Pirajuí, Getulina, Cafelândia, and São Manuel (all in the mesoregion of Bauru), and Catanduva (in the mesoregion of São José do Rio Preto) all reported coffee production of over 15,000 tons in the 1950 census (see Map 1.2). Cotton was concentrated in the municipalities of Martinópolis, Presidente Prudente, Santo Anastácio, Regente Feijó, and Alfredo Marcondes. These

TABLE 1.8

Principal Products Cultivated in São Paulo, 1950 (Value in Cr$ 1000, Area in Hectares)

	BRAZIL				STATE OF SÃO PAULO			
Product	Area	Quantity	Quantity per Hectare	Value	Area	Quantity	Quantity per Hectare	Value
Coffee	2,663,117	1,071,437	402	15,884,691	1,406,613	469,229	334	7,971,029
Cotton	2,689,185	393,000		6,273,524	1,256,031	205,426		3,081,393
Dehusked Rice	1,964,158	3,217,690	1,638	5,399,028	648,150	997,772	1,539	1,917,740
Corn	4,681,827	6,023,549	1,287	5,581,366	873,089	1,262,481	1,446	1,257,753
Sugarcane	828,182	32,670,814	39,449	3,253,471	145,643	6,913,524	47,469	754,702
English potatoes	147,739	707,159	4,787	1,301,501	45,863	242,133	5,279	536,281
Beans	1,807,956	1,248,138	690	2,248,591	245,441	177,421	723	341,903
Manioc	957,493	12,532,482	13,089	3,138,657	45,007	812,453	18,052	238,308
Peanuts	127,428	118,192	928	259,753	106,710	97,685	915	216,603
Bananas (1000s of bunches)	110,126	162,874	1,479	1,012,735	21,778	29,236	1,342	185,387
Oranges (1000s of fruits)	77,018	6,015,129	78,100	625,516	16,859	965,798	57,287	99,344

NOTE: Quantity in metric tons, except bananas and oranges.
SOURCE: *Anuário Estatístico do Brasil,* Ano XII—1951: 85–113.

TABLE 1.9

Agriculture in the State of São Paulo, 1950 (Area in Hectares)

Mesoregion	Farms	TOTAL AREA AND TYPE OF CULTIVATION Total	Permanent	Annual	Personnel Employed
Metropolitan Region of São Paulo	7,300	332,850	10,246	25,182	34,754
Ribeirão Preto	15,032	2,402,611	178,504	378,358	146,446
São José do Rio Preto	28,235	2,432,452	233,689	286,030	153,432
Bauru	17,889	2,397,063	312,569	227,338	161,088
Araraquara	5,312	858,732	78,049	91,794	43,883
Araçatuba	17,713	1,419,702	124,739	205,133	85,771
Campinas	14,315	1,224,346	110,265	209,338	101,581
Presidente Prudente	32,776	1,663,467	140,190	389,346	133,193
Vale do Paraíba Paulista	9,662	1,089,508	12,600	78,604	53,927
Macro Metropolitana Paulista	11,313	767,228	45,011	106,425	61,853
Piracicaba	7,906	761,476	38,947	178,944	55,687
Assis	13,354	1,090,982	118,006	178,068	83,266
Marília	14,270	629,475	120,115	156,519	86,477
Itapetininga	17,658	1,418,968	8,800	153,614	66,071
Litoral Sul Paulista	8,876	518,722	32,586	28,624	29,932
State Total	221,611	19,007,582	1,564,316	2,693,317	1,297,361
Municípality (Mesoregion)	MOST REPRESENTATIVE MUNICIPALITIES BASED ON PERSONS EMPLOYED				
Marília (Marília)	2,779	128,829	23,681	30,570	17,285
Lins (Bauru)	1,032	96,190	24,329	12,344	14,054
Pompéia (Marília)	3,095	84,314	8,763	34,385	13,172
Garça (Marília)	741	70,627	25,429	9,376	12,879
Piracicaba (Piracicaba)	1,837	144,601	4,660	44,734	12,487
Tupã (Marília)	3,544	101,310	20,537	31,433	12,442
Olímpia (São José do Rio Preto)	892	125,201	16,516	12,617	12,174
Andradina (Araçatuba)	3,292	200,490	11,753	31,245	12,149

SOURCE: IBGE, Censo Agrícola 1950, Série Nacional, volume II, Agricultura: 298–305.

were all within the mesoregion of Presidente and were served by the Sorocabana Railway, which carried much of the cotton produced in the state. In the case of sugarcane production, Piracicaba, a traditional sugarcane producer since the nineteenth century, and other municipalities in the region such as Limeira, Araraquara, Campinas, and Capivari were now all actively producing sugar. These five municipalities accounted for 40% of the state's sugarcane production. Finally, in the case of cattle rearing, the municipalities of Araçatuba, Paulo de Faria, and Andradina stand out, each of the three with more than 90,000 cattle in 1950. But since cattle production was spread throughout the state, no locality accounted for more than 3% of the state's total cattle population (Table 1.11 and Map 1.2).

Along with its importance in industry and agriculture, the state of São Paulo was also the most populous state in the nation in 1950. There were

TABLE 1.10

Agriculture: Cattle Production and Main Crops, 1950 (Area in Hectares, Production in Metric Tons)

		PRODUCTION OF SOME CROPS			CULTIVATION AND PRODUCTION OF COFFEE				
Mesoregion	Number of Cattle	Cotton	Sugarcane	Corn	Farms	Production	Area	Trees in Production	New Trees
Metropolitan Region of São Paulo	25,847	74	36,284	13,844	135	55	98	72,979	34,236
Ribeirão Preto	744,486	31,246	1,103,978	170,167	5,915	76,063	155,406	126,370,337	7,043,386
São José do Rio Preto	1,017,910	42,479	44,534	127,427	10,241	126,520	197,813	161,957,264	20,873,918
Bauru	664,247	25,061	270,978	138,896	8,979	248,641	279,156	211,929,416	13,183,630
Araraquara	278,608	7,015	450,869	44,398	2,687	41,639	64,105	50,932,490	2,668,254
Araçatuba	713,940	54,938	82,788	62,969	5,831	65,047	84,476	67,395,339	16,507,510
Campinas	392,854	19,130	686,129	106,387	6,024	55,868	87,837	73,865,556	8,582,654
Presidente Prudente	424,866	177,870	3,755	70,316	8,542	41,001	66,771	53,018,589	44,577,135
Vale do Paraíba Paulista	384,851	-	58,803	43,083	859	2,245	4,805	3,619,357	961,560
Macro Metropolitana Paulista	153,714	5,144	132,157	69,367	2,354	18,410	33,954	27,717,141	2,329,682
Piracicaba	207,246	8,973	1,806,691	61,373	2,353	15,380	20,817	15,808,370	1,357,397
Assis	311,057	24,584	38,940	78,519	4,192	70,338	92,481	61,417,021	9,747,182
Marília	173,152	44,637	14,042	37,589	4,142	96,396	100,605	73,406,084	9,260,982
Itapetininga	220,033	4,408	39,937	148,910	1,622	5,896	6,613	5,066,255	635,172
Litoral Sul Paulista	9,166	-	13,286	10,275	1,238	1,363	991	767,988	173,488
State Total	5,721,977	445,559	4,783,171	1,183,520	65,114	864,862	1,195,928	933,344,186	137,936,186

SOURCE: IBGE, Censo 1950, Série Nacional, vol. II, "Agricultura."

TABLE I.II

Principal Municipalities in the Production of Cattle and Crops, 1950 (Area in Hectares, Production in Tons)

			PRODUCTION OF SOME CROPS			CULTIVATION AND PRODUCTION OF COFFEE				
Municipality	**Mesoregion**	**Number of Cattle**	**Cotton**	**Sugarcane**	**Corn**	**Farms**	**Production**	**Area**	**Trees in Production**	**New Trees**
State Total		5,721,977	445,559	4,783,171	1,183,520	65,114	864,862	1,195,928	933,344,186	137,936,186
			MUNICIPALITIES WITH LARGEST NUMBER OF CATTLE							
Araçatuba	Araçatuba	146,481	5,800	11,793	7,029	487	5,505	7,390	5,902,920	1,088,400
Paulo de Faria	São José do Rio Preto	96,317	154		2,989	14	26	41	28,800	46,830
Andradina	Araçatuba	91,104	8,065	630	3,024	832	3,349	6,155	5,084,150	3,335,192
Valparaíso	Araçatuba	73,502	3,103	158	1,832	114	5,203	5,560	4,161,150	756,060
Nhandeara	São José do Rio Preto	70,588	3,942	8	5,781	261	413	1,093	883,720	452,760
			LARGEST PRODUCERS OF COTTON							
Martinópolis	Presidente Prudente	23,693	29,656	2,028	3,726	174	1,803	2,165	1,606,056	466,185
Presidente Prudente	Presidente Prudente	33,068	16,084		11,084	750	5,398	9,088	7,279,100	390,900
Santo Anastácio	Presidente Prudente	36,124	15,012	1,167	2,910	350	1,140	2,247	1,745,922	603,480
Regente Feijó	Presidente Prudente	44,309	14,198		6,468	365	3,066	5,660	5,008,930	830,250
Alfredo Marcondes	Presidente Prudente	4,286	12,780		3,385	178	1,058	1,585	1,311,360	41,240

				LARGEST PRODUCERS OF SUGARCANE						
Piracicaba	Piracicaba	32,350	1,649	749,768	11,499	325	860	1,382	980,634	112,743
Limeira	Piracicaba	11,670	563	349,384	4,691	188	599	1,337	829,920	29,180
Araraquara	Araraquara	35,107	445	327,484	4,400	372	3,788	7,393	5,771,678	156,730
Santa Bárbara D'Oeste	Campinas	4,780	202	262,990	1,348	35	49	90	53,100	4,920
Capivari	Piracicaba	7,908	201	238,256	4,926	139	304	618	436,954	93,205
				LARGEST PRODUCERS OF CORN						
Barretos	Ribeirão Preto	51,976	2,520	35	18,970	74	403	1,217	992,814	94,500
Bragança Paulista	Macro Metr. Paulista	18,980	6	21,586	14,272	799	5,284	12,079	9,528,030	520,564
Itaporanga	Itapetininga	4,799	696	25	13,120	30	537	373	283,152	101,830
Itapeva	Itapetininga	18,791	115	1,313	12,396	99	41	27	13,105	1,661
Itapetininga	Itapetininga	33,776	627	9,175	11,998	30	242	159	133,840	19,016
				LARGEST PRODUCERS OF COFFEE						
Marília	Marília	36,051	7,608	64	7,682	677	25,084	20,089	14,864,410	1,163,417
Lins	Bauru	31,301	1,503	562	3,794	622	24,380	21,600	16,803,743	1,204,905
Pirajuí	Bauru	26,752	1,798	52,385	4,807	497	22,809	24,735	19,403,853	895,322
Garça	Marília	16,252	1,391	667	2,849	444	21,868	22,586	15,663,173	1,677,103
Getulina	Bauru	20,709	1,216	77	3,963	731	18,784	22,965	16,838,954	1,072,050
Cafelândia	Bauru	20,126	878	8	2,404	429	17,122	18,717	14,161,056	776,151
Catanduva	São José do Rio Preto	23,000	114	218	3,958	449	16,865	17,767	14,480,346	321,708
São Manuel	Bauru	14,510	1,050	22,534	5,424	556	15,795	21,924	16,977,001	1,108,635

SOURCE: IBGE, Censo 1950, Série Nacional, volume II, Agricultura.

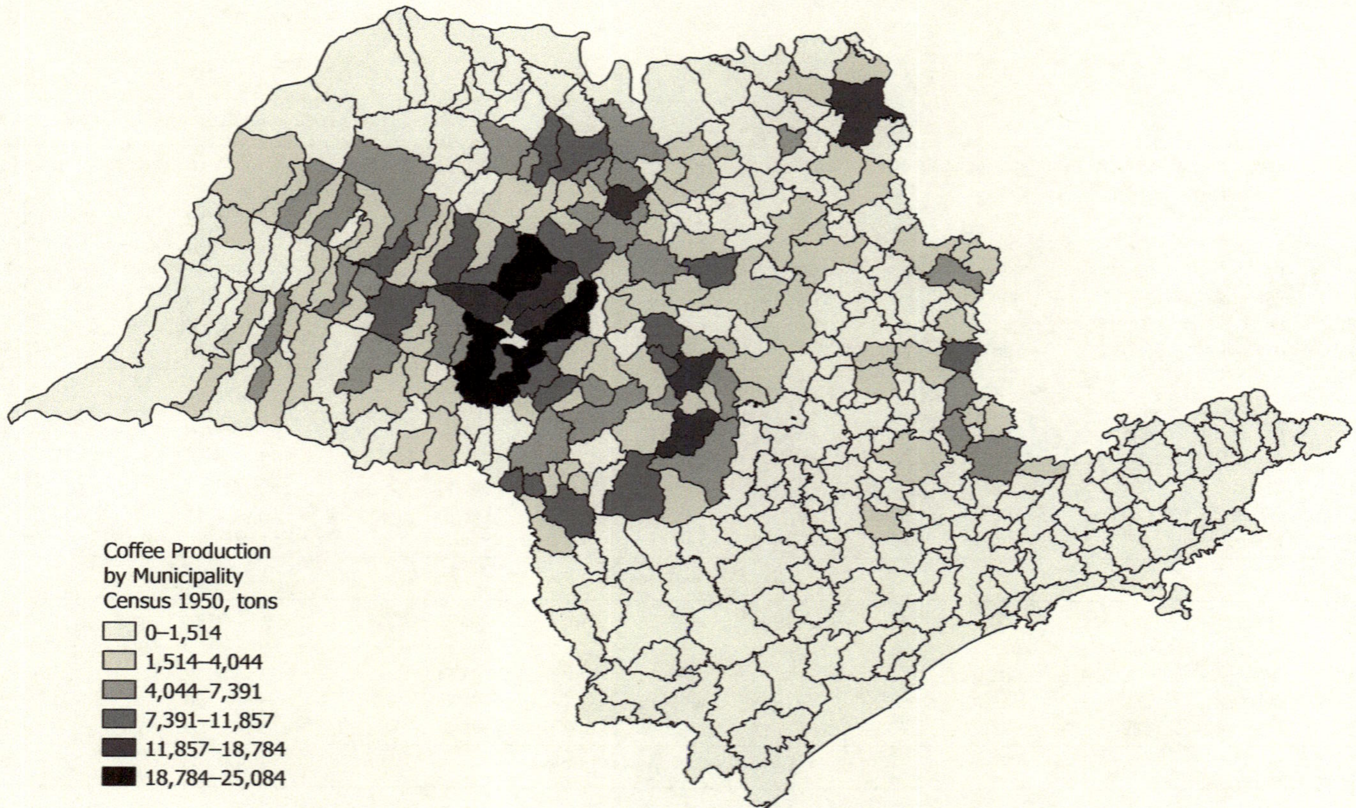

Map 1.2. Production of Coffee by Municipality, São Paulo, 1950

SOURCE: IBGE, Censo Agrícola, 1950; NEPO, Base Cartográfica.

9,134,423 people residing in the state in that year, and they accounted for 18% of the Brazilian population. São Paulo, with 40% of its population residing in urban areas, was Brazil's second-most-urbanized state. The state population also differed in significant ways from the rest of the nation in terms of color and origin. While in Brazil whites accounted for 62% of the population, in São Paulo this percentage was 86%, comparable only to Rio Grande do Sul. The massive European immigration to São Paulo that occurred in the late nineteenth and early twentieth centuries explains this result (in the case of Rio Grande do Sul, the high percentage of whites was due to earlier European immigration). São Paulo was also different in its high ratio of Asians, another group brought in to work the state's coffee fields. Of the 329,000 people classified as Asians in Brazil in 1950, 84% lived in São Paulo (see Table 1.12).

But the impact of the foreign-born population was declining by the mid-twentieth century. Although the state had 57% of Brazil's foreign-born population, those born outside the country (including those who had been naturalized) accounted for only 8% of the state's population. Nevertheless, migration still remained a major factor in the growth of the Paulista population at midcentury, but this time the source was native-born migrants from other states. That year's census showed that 1 million of the state's residents (12% of the population) were born in other states, with neighboring Minas Gerais accounting for almost half of these migrants. Small numbers of Northeastern natives were beginning to appear in São Paulo in this period, and they would become the dominant migrant force in future decades (see Table 1.13).

São Paulo was also unusual in the high literacy rate of its population. The state had a 59% literacy rate, compared to the national rate of just 43%. As in the rest of the nation, there was a significant difference in literacy by sex, with men in the state having a literacy rate of 65% and women just 54%. Although Paulista men were the second-most-literate group in Brazil, Paulista women were less literate than those living in Rio de Janeiro, the Federal District, and Rio Grande do Sul, and equal to women in Santa Catarina (see Table 1.14). This would change in subsequent years, with major state investments in education eventually leading to equality of literacy rates for women and men as the state became the leader in persons completing school as well as those who were literate.

Despite the distribution of population and economic activity across the state, the capital city of São Paulo still stands out as an exceptional place. In the capital there were 7,374 industrial establishments, which accounted for about half of the capital invested in the state's industrial activities, as well as

TABLE 1.12

Demographic and Social Characteristics of the Brazilian Population in Selected States, 1950

	Brazil	São Paulo	Pernambuco	Bahia	Minas Gerais	Rio de Janeiro (1)	Rio Grande do Sul
DISTRIBUTION OF RESIDENT POPULATION							
Total Population	51,944,683	9,134,423	3,395,185	4,831,575	7,717,792	4,674,644	4,164,831
Urban	12,957,543	3,647,804	499,033	944,447	1,429,894	2,710,364	1,015,868
Suburban	5,825,634	1,156,407	668,367	303,060	890,160	684,057	406,122
Rural	33,161,506	4,330,212	2,227,785	3,584,068	5,397,738	1,280,223	2,742,841
DISTRIBUTION OF RESIDENT POPULATION BY COLOR AND ETHNICITY							
Total	51,838,102	9,120,420	3,131,145	7,902,914	4,567,151	4,361,383	4,156,438
Whites	32,027,661	7,823,111	1,428,685	4,509,575	1,372,917	2,733,751	3,712,249
Blacks	5,692,657	727,789	316,122	926,075	1,122,940	699,660	217,520
Browns	13,788,742	292,669	1,386,255	2,467,108	2,069,037	924,456	226,174
Asians	329,042	276,851	83	156	2,257	3,516	495

SOURCE: Censo 1950, Série Nacional, volume 1 Brasil.

NOTE: (1) Includes the Federal District.

TABLE 1.13
Origin of the Resident Population of the State of São Paulo, 1950

RESIDENTS BORN IN BRAZIL		RESIDENTS BORN OUTSIDE BRAZIL	
Origin	Number	Origin	Number (1)
Native-born	8,440,763	Total	693,325
Born in São Paulo	7,360,340	Italy	173,652
Born in Other States	1,080,423	Portugal	151,320
Minas Gerais	512,736	Japan	108,912
Bahia	189,685	Spain	102,671
Pernambuco	62,745	USSR	27,089
Alagoas	56,788	Germany	24,473
Rio de Janeiro	56,076	Syria and Lebanon	22,225
Paraná	32,708	Poland	14,582
Ceara	29,054	Romania	11,482
Sergipe	25,033	Yugoslavia	11,294
Federal District	18,172	Austria	8,189
Santa Catarina	15,410	Argentina	7,625
Rio Grande do Sul	13,743	France	3,442
Mato Grosso	13,016	United States	2,789
Paraíba	10,712	Belgium	672
Others	44,545	Others	22,908

SOURCE: Censo 1950, Série Nacional, vol. 1 "Brasil." NOTE: (1) Includes those naturalized.

TABLE 1.14
Literacy by Sex of the Population of Brazil by Northeast Region and States of the South and Southeastern Regions, 1950

	Brazil	Northeast	São Paulo	Minas Gerais	Espirito Santos	Rio de Janeiro (1)	Paraná	Rio Grande do Sul	Santa Catarina
Literate Men	46%	27%	65%	42%	45%	66%	52%	61%	60%
Literate Women	39%	24%	54%	35%	36%	62%	40%	56%	54%
Total Literate	43%	26%	59%	38%	41%	64%	46%	59%	57%

SOURCE: Censo 1950, Série Nacional, volume 1: 90, quadro 47.
NOTE: (1) Includes Federal District.

half the workers, value of production, and energy consumed by industry in the state. Both the wholesale and retail trades were concentrated in the city of São Paulo, with the city accounting for 63% of the state's wholesale trade (see Table 1.15).

This high concentration of industry and commerce in the capital was reflected in the distribution of employment throughout the state. Half of the people engaged in the state's manufacturing industry resided in the capital, as did half the workers in the service sector, the liberal professions, and public administration. Only in agriculture was the capital of little importance (see Table 1.16).

TABLE I.15

Economic Activities in the State and Municipality of São Paulo, 1950

Economic Activities	State of São Paulo	City of São Paulo
Industry		
Establishments	25,016	7,374
Capital Employed Cr$[1]	22,977,603	10,946,805
Persons Employed	576,766	299,213
Workers	488,633	255,951
Energy Used (cv)	1,135,764	495,675
Total Salaries Cr$	7,446,448	4,525,331
Workers' Salaries Cr$	5,997,671	3,618,315
Company Expenses Cr$	29,422,380	13,996,850
Production Value Cr$	55,291,473	26,565,661
Retail Business		
Establishments	50,519	15,174
Capital Employed Cr$	2,239,533	966,379
Persons Employed	116,968	44,120
Revenue Cr$	20,424,169	9,133,234
Wholesale Business		
Establishments	6,659	3,929
Capital Employed Cr$	1,513,597	1,140,351
Persons Employed	58,040	43,805
Revenue Cr$	45,647,205	28,667,964

SOURCE: Censo 1950, Série Regional, volume XXV, tomo 3, "Estado de São Paulo," Censos Industrial, Comercial e dos Serviços.
NOTE: Revenue in Cr$ 1000.

TABLE I.16

Economic Activities of Residents 10 Years of Age and Older by Sector, State, and City of São Paulo, 1950

	STATE OF SÃO PAULO		CITY OF SÃO PAULO	
Economic Activity	Men	Women	Men	Women
Agricultural Activity	1,292,754	156,642	14,753	689
Mining Activity	43,645	827	4,180	95
Industrial Transformation	631,688	169,637	319,500	100,571
Commerce	224,442	23,954	107,741	14,688
Services	211,698	201,435	95,970	97,417
Liberal Professions	22,077	4,418	11,680	2,531
Public Administration	48,067	8,905	19,720	6,275
Public Security	34,419	853	18,292	657

SOURCE: Censo 1950, Série Regional, volume XXV, tomo 3, "Estado de São Paulo," Censos Industrial, Comercial e dos Serviços.

TABLE 1.17
Characteristics of Homes in the State and City of São Paulo, 1950

Households	Total	With Piped-in Water	With Electricity	With Sanitary Facilities
		STATE OF SÃO PAULO		
All Households	1,798,735	583,693	910,652	1,109,393
Urban	737,867	497,420	660,665	717,483
Suburban	236,472	54,163	145,233	212,402
Rural	824,396	32,110	104,754	179,508
		CITY OF SÃO PAULO		
All Households	455,917	263,096	385,497	434,063
Urban	337,042	252,644	320,602	331,462
Suburban	86,382	8,265	56,606	81,790
Rural	31,993	2,187	8,289	20,811

SOURCE: Censo 1950, Série Regional, volume XXV, tomo 1 "Estado de São Paulo."

The city's 2.1 million inhabitants represented about a quarter of the state's population, with similar proportions of men and women, and was composed mostly of whites (87%). The vast majority of the population could read and write (79%), a percentage much higher than the state average. Finally, the city was unusual in its abundance of services not readily available in the rest of Brazil: 96% of the capital's urban households were serviced by piped water, 83% had electricity, and 76% had sanitary facilities. These numbers were higher than for the state as a whole as well as for the nation (see Table 1.17).[13]

Both the capital and the state of São Paulo were in an ideal position to take advantage of any growth that would occur in the post-1950 period. São Paulo was already the leading agricultural and industrial state in the nation, with one of the best educated populations. Its communications infrastructure was already well developed, and it had Brazil's best rail, road, and even airline connections. It was the state with the largest service sector, and it had both a well-endowed capitalist class and a skilled labor force. The coffee elite, foreign investors, and immigrants were deeply involved in the industrial economy, and the local economy provided economies of scale to make investment in the industrial sector viable. When in the following decades the federal government decided to massively invest in the national economy, it was São Paulo that was the state best prepared to profit from this investment.

Chapter 2

Industrial Growth in São Paulo 1950–2020

Industrial expansion was the most significant change in the post-1950 period as São Paulo became the premier center of a modern industrial complex. The cause of the state's emergence as an industrial power is the subject of much debate and discussion.[1] Much of the initial debate was influenced by the post–World War II discussion of the viability of traditional comparative advantage models. Led by Latin American economists, a school of thought associated with the United Nations Research Center for Latin America (ECLAC), challenged the traditional comparative advantage model. They argued that in the long run states that produced primary products were at a disadvantage in their trade relations with states that were industrial producers, and only through industrialization could these primary producers develop and expand their economies. This, in turn, required direct government intervention to create protected markets; alternatively, it could occur through external shocks that forced primary producers to replace imports by developing local industries.

In the Brazilian case, industrialization began before formal protection was established. The Brazilian state had no coherent pro-industrialization program until the early 1940s, when the process of industrialization was already underway.[2] Celso Furtado and others claimed that the disruption in international trade stemming from World War I and the Great Depression established effective protection, allowing these pioneering industries to flourish.[3] Recently scholars have argued that industry was already developing before 1914, and that rather than protected markets, it is comparative costs, the emergence of a wider market, and the abundance of local capital that explain the initial development of industry in Brazil.[4] The cotton textile industry, producing popular cloth and clothes, would be the most important manufacturing activity at the early stage of industrialization due to the availability of locally produced cotton and to high transportation costs that burdened low-value-added products. At the same time, the food processing industry was developed to supply local consumption, and it too used products generated by local agriculture.

It was foreseeable that this local industry would evolve to supply the agricultural sector and its workers. The fundamental role of the agro-export sector as a driver of industrial activity can be seen both in the first products from Brazilian factories and in the association of industrial activity with cycles of the exporting economy. Prior to the 1929 crisis, industrial expansion corresponded to the most dynamic periods of the agro-export economy. For example, the textile industry emerged to provide slaves with cotton garments and jute bags to pack coffee for export. It expanded even faster with the arrival of European workers, who were employed in the coffee plantations after the abolition of slavery in 1889. This new wage labor force vastly expanded the internal market.[5] In turn, the food processing industry evolved to supply this growing free labor market, and the sugar refining industry made progress with the expansion of the revitalized sugarcane sector in the late nineteenth century. Finally, metallurgy progressed in parallel with the advance of railways in the second half of the century, a development that was linked to that of the coffee economy. All this growth benefited from the abundant and cheap supply of hydropower now coming online, on the cheaper transportation provided by the new railways, and on the lower costs of imported machinery during this period.[6]

The concentration of coffee activity in the state beginning in the late nineteenth century created the conditions for industrial development. The coffee planters and their capital were active agents of the dynamics of industrialization. As Wilson Cano has pointed out, even to finance its railways São Paulo used more local capital than any other province in the country. Also by the end of the century it was systematically generating large trade surpluses. With the end of the free coffee market in 1906 and subsequent restrictions on coffee planting, much of the capital intended for new plantings would be used for industrial development instead.[7]

The textile industry was the main industry for a long period in Brazil generally and in São Paulo in particular. The growing importance of the national textile industry was reflected in the decline in textile imports.

European fabrics had represented an important part of Brazilian imports in the nineteenth century but increasingly declined in the early twentieth century, with the replacement of imported fabrics by domestically produced ones.[8] As early as the 1907 industrial census, the domestic textile industry supplied two-thirds of the local market. There were also numerous areas of food production and light industry where Brazilian factories already met most of the national demand.[9]

Although the state of Rio de Janeiro and its Federal District were initially the most important industrial region in the nation, by the census of 1906 São Paulo represented the second-most-important industrial zone. The São Paulo textile industry mainly consumed cotton produced in the country, grown either in São Paulo itself or in Pernambuco and other Northeastern states. Its main imports from abroad were machinery. Moreover, the growth of this industry was so rapid that the fabrics produced in São Paulo not only supplied the local market and reduced dependence on imports, but also allowed São Paulo to export its production to other Brazilian states. By the 1920 industrial census São Paulo dominated national production in several major industries, with over 40% of national production in metallurgy, ceramics, transportation vehicles, and luxury goods. It also contained some pioneering industries that would later become of great importance in the state and in the country. São Paulo already had a significant paper industry in the 1920s, supplied by native and cultivated forests. It also had a glass manufacturing sector closely linked to the food and beverage industry, which not only met local needs but also produced enough to export to other states in Brazil. Most of the raw materials used in glass production were obtained in the region itself.[10] It was also significant in sugar milling. Brazilians were the dominant owners of these factories, but by 1920 Italians were second as factory owners, and Canadian and other foreign nationals had entered into industrial activity in the state.[11] In that year as well São Paulo passed Rio de Janeiro and DF in the total number of industrial workers.[12] The distribution by sex and age of employees in São Paulo industries was similar to those in other states. Cotton spinning and weaving factories and the garment industry, the largest employer of industrial workers, employed more women than men; two-thirds of their workforce was over 17 years of age, with only 4% under 7 years of age.[13]

The national government led by Getúlio Vargas after 1930 created a state structure that for the first time supported industrial activity through public investments in both infrastructure and basic industry and began the policy of import substitution to foster manufacturing growth in segments previously supplied by imported manufactures. The crisis in international trade generated by the 1929 economic crash was also a strong stimulus for local industrial production. But problems with foreign debt and trade would be a recurrent theme in the Brazilian economy and explain most of the economic policies implemented in Brazil until the first decade of the twenty-first century. The most-used instrument in the Brazilian economic policy was the exchange rate, and this, in addition to the interest rate, was used as a mechanism for attracting foreign capital and allowing balance-of-payments adjustments. The succession of measures in this area, such as fixed exchange rates, multiple rates, segmented exchange auctions, mini devaluations, and flexible exchange rates, are some of the many instruments used over the years, and they were supplemented by currency manipulations and customs restrictions. This is the world in which Brazilian industry has developed and still lives today.

The expansion of the electrical system was also a significant factor in industrial growth by providing cheap power. Between 1920 and 1950, the installed capacity of electricity-generating plants in Brazil grew from 367,018 kW to 1,883,007 kW. Similar growth occurred in the state of São Paulo, which had an installed capacity of 855.06 kW in 1950, representing 45% of the national total; in São Paulo, almost all this electricity was generated by hydropower.[14] This system continued to expand and evolve in the subsequent decades, providing local industry with a steady supply of cheap electricity.

In the 1930s and 1940s, São Paulo industries gained complexity, and traditional industries grew, so by the time of the 1950 census, the state held the leading economic position in the country. It now represented 37% of national GDP.[15] Industry represented 28% of São Paulo state GDP, surpassing the 26% represented by agriculture.[16] It accounted for just under half of both the value of Brazilian industrial production and total capital invested, and for 38% of all industrial workers, whose wages represented 47% of the total industrial wages in Brazil.[17]

In 1950, industry in São Paulo was still highly concentrated in the traditional sectors of textiles, clothing, food products, and beverages. These represented about half of the companies, workers, value of production, and capital realized by the manufacturing industry in the state of São Paulo. On average, companies in the textile industry were larger than companies in other segment—in contrast to the average of 92 workers per textile mill, food companies employed on average only 6 workers. Despite this huge difference in size, the difference in the value of production narrowed because the textile industry had an average output 4.7 times higher than the food industry, demonstrating that the former was more labor intensive.

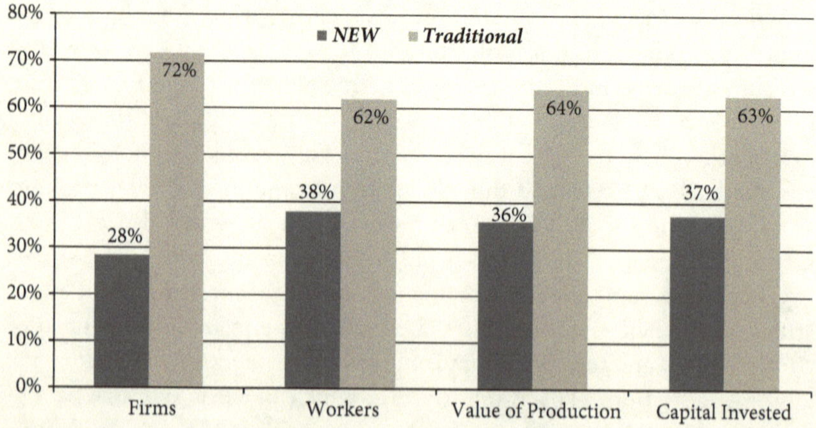

Figure 2.1. Participation of Traditional and New Industries in the São Paulo Manufacturing Sector, 1950

SOURCE: Censo Demográfico do Brasil, 1950, Série Nacional, Tomo 1, volume XXV: 1–27.

Although the more modern firms in metallurgy, chemicals, and Pharmaceuticals represented only a bit over a quarter of all firms, they had a much higher ratio of workers, value of production, and capital invested than the traditional firms (see Figure 2.1).[18]

Brazilian industry, besides being concentrated in São Paulo, also was highly concentrated within the state. The city of São Paulo and its metropolitan mesoregion had a majority of the state's industry, with more than 9,000 industrial establishments employing 366,000 workers and accounting for more than two-thirds of the state's production value. The city of São Paulo itself was at the time the main industrial core of the country. In this city alone there were 7,343 industrial establishments, with 299,000 industrial workers, who accounted for more than half of the state's production value. Within the metropolitan area around the city of São Paulo there emerged several satellite cities, such as Santo André, São Caetano, and São Bernardo, that would become the main automobile hub of Brazil in the following decades. Nevertheless, there were also several interior cities, such as Sorocaba, Campinas, Santos, Jundiaí, and Piracicaba, which had significant industries (see Table 2.1).

In 1952, during the second Vargas administration, the government presented a general industrial plan that proposed large investments in infrastructure as well as in the basic manufacturing industries. The role of the state in the industrial development process was more clearly defined, with

TABLE 2.1

Principal Indicators of Industry by Mesoregion, 1950 (Capital in Cr$ 1000)

Mesoregion	Firms	Capital Employed	Personnel Employed (1)	Workers (1)	Motor Force (C.V.)	Value of Production
Metropolitan São Paulo	9,139	15,465,262	366,508	313,109	672,517	36,079,944
Ribeirão Preto	2,027	707,439	16,092	12,308	60,223	1,862,028
São José do Rio Preto	1,392	257,893	5,678	3,719	19,781	907,612
Bauru	1,702	439,200	11,182	8,484	29,249	1,628,412
Araraquara	663	333,070	8,289	6,791	11,243	841,436
Araçatuba	687	299,370	4,189	2,976	16,587	811,413
Campinas	2,307	1,186,907	32,795	27,926	67,483	2,423,151
Presidente Prudente	632	259,844	4,454	3,379	14,755	1,098,432
Vale do Paraíba Paulista	797	862,525	20,829	19,197	37,897	1,389,002
Macro Metropolitana Paulista	1,337	1,401,909	42,550	36,845	76,821	2,469,881
Piracicaba	1,348	716,051	20,467	16,739	48,170	1,520,205
Assis	711	250,225	3,716	2,763	15,590	482,171
Marília	564	195,936	3,801	2,750	16,335	960,639
Itapetininga	591	130,992	5,426	4,562	11,149	200,400
Litoral Sul Paulista	171	41,004	871	672	2,295	41,226
State Total	24,068	22,547,627	546,847	462,220	1,100,095	52,715,952
MUNICIPALITIES WITH HIGHER INDUSTRIAL PRODUCTION VALUE						
Municipality (Mesoregion)						
City of São Paulo (Metropolitana São Paulo)	7,374	10,946,805	299,513	255,952	497,675	28,565,661
Santo André (Metropolitana São Paulo)	448	1,491,329	27,775	24,258	71,042	3,492,348
São Caetano Sul (Metropolitana São Paulo)	165	629,381	13,771	11,989	31,936	1,695,321
Sorocaba (Macrometropole)	238	633,001	16,624	15,245	31,645	1,078,179
Campinas (Campinas)	474	390,680	11,436	9,729	23,355	1,037,433
Santos (Metropolitana de São Paulo)	318	203,359	4,040	3,182	9,339	938,669
Jundial (Metropolitana de São Paulo)	235	276,348	10,481	8,515	16,147	585,596
São Bernardo Campo (Metropolitana São Paulo)	133	223,130	4,822	4,030	9,431	459,082
Piracicaba (Piracicaba)	359	227,488	6,809	5,275	16,351	456,042

SOURCE: IBGE, Censo 1950, Série Nacional, volume III, Indústrial, Comercial e Serviços.

NOTE: (1) Workers usually mean hourly wage or line workers and employees are all workers, including clerical personnel and management, as well as workers.

the creation of planning bodies and processes that would enable the implementation of government plans. During the second Vargas administration, the National Bank for Economic Development (BNDE, today BNDES) was established, which would become the fundamental institution for promoting industrialization. In 1953, Petrobras (Petróleo Brasileiro S.A.) was created, a company that would come to exercise a monopoly on the extraction, refining, and distribution of oil. In addition, the Vargas government founded a number of groups and institutions that effectively implemented the new industrial policies through the end of the century.[19]

These pro-industrialization policies were expanded under the Juscelino Kubitschek government (1956–1961). Faced with strong inflationary pressures, an increasing public deficit, and a serious balance-of-payments problem, a recurring phenomenon in the Brazilian economy, the new government decided to opt for an ambitious investment plan—the so called Targets Plan—which was the most coherent and well-developed policy to support industrialization to date. It gave priority to more complex segments of the industrial process, such as durable consumer goods, and basic input industries such as the chemical industry.[20] Even if the government had wanted to promote a stabilization policy, it would have encountered strong political opposition.[21] In opting for growth, the government coopted large social groups, including industrialists and workers. Even the opening of the economy to foreign capital, one of the fundamentals of the Targets Plan, was accepted by the main forces supporting it, including the military.[22]

This period of state-funded basic infrastructure construction was crucial for the industrialization process. The government's plan proposed private and public investments in the areas of basic industry, energy, transport, food, education, and even agriculture. But only some of these targets were met. The most successful was the expansion of national production in steel, cement, alkalis, pulp and paper, aluminum, non-ferrous metals, and rubber. The government significantly increased electricity production and oil refining,[23] with all investments directed mainly to public companies. In the state-dominated transport area, a rolling stock and permanent rail modernization program was set up that allowed the rail system to increase its load capacity by 21%. Road construction and paving resulted in a 75% increase in the federal road network and tripled the length of paved federal highways.[24] Together these select areas, along with the construction of the new capital, Brasília, received almost all the investments of the Targets Plan.

The most successful and ambitious program was the establishment of a national automobile industry funded by foreign capital.[25] Until then Brazil had only produced trucks and utility vehicles, but now it was able to produce automobiles. Automobile production in turn had a significant multiplier effect.[26] As the government demanded that a minimum percentage of parts (between 90 and 95%) be produced in the country, a private auto parts industry was quickly established, involving the mechanical, electrical, plastics, and rubber sectors, while at the same time a network of parts resellers, maintenance and replacement companies, and car dealerships was created.

The construction of Brasília, the new capital of the country in central Brazil, was the grand synthesis of all the government plans, and also had a major impact on the Brazilian economy by opening up new regions for development.[27] The size of the investments and the location of the new capital stimulated a displacement of activities from the coast, where the population and economic activities were concentrated, to the interior of the country. This displacement also required major road infrastructure expansion, which explains the investments in new highways.

The great transformation promoted by the Juscelino regime was the opening of Brazil to foreign capital, so much so that in 1955 it introduced the possibility of imports without foreign exchange hedging, which had an important impact on the internationalization of the Brazilian economy.[28] The first phase of Brazilian industrialization, based on traditional segments such as textiles, food, and beverages, was largely developed with national capital. But after World War II, it was foreign capital that became an important factor in the maturation of the industrial sector, promoting a new industrial expansion that allowed Brazil to enter the international market. In turn, an aggressive business state, which invested heavily in infrastructure and basic industries, became attractive to multinational companies.

The government manipulated a range of instruments—subsidies, credit, exchange, tariff protection, and direct investments in infrastructure or sectors in which the private sector, domestic or foreign, did not find it attractive to invest. Also, the BNDE played a key role in designing these projects and supporting them.[29] Thus, there were two basic sources of funding for this massive industrialization project: foreign direct investment and government fiscal resources. According to the Targets Plan, most of the resources would come from the public budget and the resources generated by the public companies themselves.

Given the ambitious nature of the Targets Plan, there was an extraordinary demand for public resources without the equivalent ability to generate tax revenues. This resulted in budget deficits, largely financed by Banco do Brasil in its dual role as commercial bank and central bank. There was not yet a public debt market in Brazil, partly because of the incompatibility between high inflation of 25% to 30% and the usury law, which limited interest rates to 12%.[30] The financing of the Treasury deficit was essentially by monetary expansion, generating inflationary pressures. But in that period, development was a priority, not fiscal and monetary stability.[31]

TABLE 2.2
Brazil's Automobile Industry: Financing, Investments, and Projects Approved by GEIA (1) as of 1960

Automotive Companies	Investments US$ 1000	Finances US$ 1000	Total US$ 1000	National Expenditures (2) Cr$ 1000
All Companies	**134,709**	**36,602**	**171,311**	**9,308,426**
FNM	2,600	15,691	18,291	659,000
Ford Motors do Brasil	30,000		30,000	1,338,000
GM do Brasil	21,550		21,550	1,800,000
International Harvester	4,500		4,500	121,989
Mercedes-Benz	21,939		21,939	892,628
Scania-Vabis	704	413	1,117	248,000
Toyota do Brasil	1,664		1,664	107,215
Simca do Brasil	4,478	6,183	10,661	723,971
Vemag do Brasil	2,312	3,010	5,322	282,000
Volkswagen	18,895	4,305	23,200	643,023
Willys Overland do Brasil	26,067	7,000	33,067	2,392,600
Auto Parts Companies	**116,078**	**45,066**	**161,144**	**8,095,597**
Total	**250,787**	**81,668**	**332,455**	**17,304,023**

SOURCE: Conselho do Desenvolvimento, *Relatório do Período 1956–1960*, tomo IV (RJ), December 1960, p. 6, cited in Limoncic (1997), p. 109.
NOTES: (1) GEIA is the Grupo Executivo da Industria Automobilística.
(2) Land, construction, and national equipment.

The relative aversion to foreign capital present in Vargas's second government was replaced by a policy that was frankly conducive to such investments in Juscelino's government, which attracted many multinational companies. Most of this capital came in the form of loans, but approximately one-fifth of the capital came as direct investments, the main beneficiaries of which were core industries, particularly the automotive industry, and to a lesser extent the pulp and paper and steel sectors. Total financing and direct investments totaled approximately US $2 billion, of which 31% went to the auto industry, 18% to the steel industry, 16% to electricity generation, and 13% to the rail sector.[32] In the case of the auto industry, there was a total of US $332 million in foreign direct investment or financing, about half directly from vehicle manufacturers and the other half from parts manufacturers (see Table 2.2).

Faced with the shortcomings of a public administration poorly equipped to cope with an ambitious Targets Plan, the Juscelino government preferred to create a structure supported by existing institutions, such as Banco do Brasil and BNDE, and new entities such as the Executive Groups. The Executive Groups operated primarily with the private sector, coordinating all institutions involved in sectoral policies. The BNDE in turn, centralized public activities, prioritizing projects in terms of both financing and the granting of guarantees for foreign loans. The results achieved by these new administrative structures were exceptional.

As the consumer market in Brazil was still limited, the main US auto companies were initially uninterested in developing production facilities, so the first automakers to set up in the country were the German firms Volkswagen and DKW (Vemag), the French firm Simca, and the American firm Willys Overland.[33] The other automobile companies soon followed these pioneers as the success of the Brazilian industrialization plan became evident. This project to establish an auto industry would involve mostly foreign capital, with the participation of American, European, and Japanese companies, along with a modest amount of national capital. The government also promoted the development of a national auto parts industry through a national content law.[34] By the mid-1960s all vehicles—automobiles, utility vehicles, and trucks—produced in Brazil contained 90% or more domestically produced components.[35] These industries originated either from large multinational companies, existing national companies that were already in this market, or small companies that emerged to serve a specific market niche. The auto industry also promoted other industries such as rubber, plastic, textiles, and chemicals. To be close to their clients, many of these companies built large-scale factories with thousands of workers in the metropolitan region of São Paulo.

The rail transport system, which had been the basis of the economy in the nineteenth century and still essential in the transport matrix in the first half of the twentieth century, would quickly be replaced by road transport, as the impact of the national automobile industry took hold (see Figure 2.2). In 1957, when the first automotive vehicles were produced in Brazil, there were only 13,000 km of paved roads in Brazil. Ten years later the asphalted grid had grown to about 50,000 km.[36] By the late 1960s the state of São Paulo already had 12,000 km of paved roads, 858,000 cars, and 203,000 trucks.[37]

Practically the entire auto industry—automakers and major auto parts companies—would be established in the state of São Paulo, especially in the metropolitan area of São Paulo and three of its cities, known as the ABC region (Santo André, São Bernardo, and São Caetano). But the industry first began elsewhere. The National Engine Factory (FNM) was the first automotive factory in Brazil, a state-owned company founded in 1942 in Rio de Janeiro. Its purpose was to manufacture aircraft engines, but it failed, and the government entered into an agreement with Alfa Romeo to produce trucks at that factory. In 1968 FNM was sold to Alfa Romeo and the factory remained productive until 1977.[38] VEMAG, a former distributor

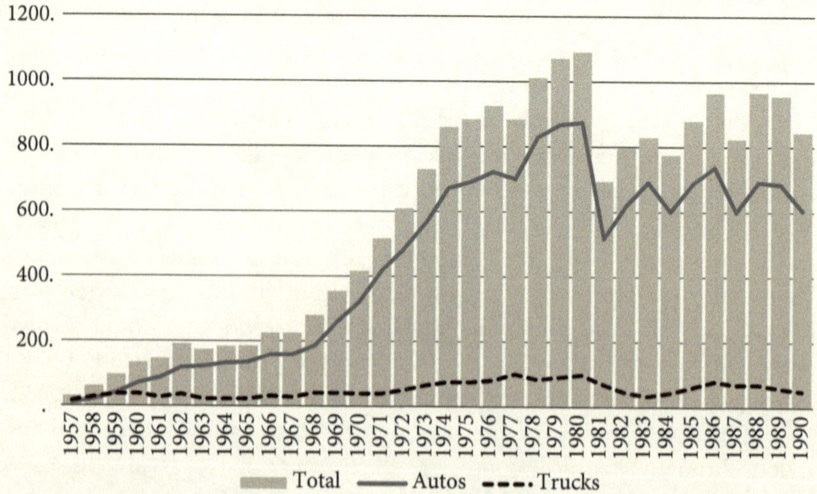

Figure 2.2. Auto and Truck Production in Brazil, 1957–1990 (in thousands of units)

SOURCE: Anfavea; IBGE, Anuário Estatistico; IBGE, Séries Históricas.

of imported vehicles, was another pioneer in the auto industry, created by national capital and the first to receive government incentives. VEMAG's factory was installed within the municipality of São Paulo. Its first car was launched in 1956.[39] In 1964 came Simca do Brasil, a subsidiary of Simca Francesa, which was founded in Belo Horizonte but for operational reasons moved to São Bernardo, where it set up its factory. In 1966 Simca do Brasil was sold to Chrysler do Brasil, which would start its operations in this São Bernardo do Campo plant.[40] In 1952 Willys Overland do Brasil was established in São Bernardo do Campo. Many of these early startups began with mixed Brazilian and foreign capital.[41]

Some American companies had a longer history in Brazil. Ford cars had been assembled in Brazil as early as 1919, but the company only began to manufacture its cars in Brazil in the 1960s. In 1953 a Ford factory was established in São Paulo, and by 1958 it was producing engines and started the production of trucks and tractors. In 1967 Ford launched its first Brazilian-made car, and it acquired Willys Overland do Brasil, with its line of jeeps, utility vehicles, and automobiles.[42] General Motors began operations in Brazil in 1925 and established its first manufacturing unit in São Caetano do Sul. In the 1930s the company produced the first bus bodies in Brazil and soon started to produce truck bodies as well in São Jose dos Campos.[43] In 1957 it launched the first Brazilian truck. Volkswagen began its operations in São Paulo in 1953. In 1959 it opened a new factory in São Bernardo do Campo, the first outside Germany, and started production of the Beetle, with over 3 million units sold by 1986. Volkswagen was the first automaker to inaugurate a center for development, research, and design in Brazil.[44] Toyota do Brasil began in 1958 in the city of São Paulo and eventually transferred to São Bernardo do Campo, and it represented the company's first operation outside of Japan.[45]

Mercedes-Benz do Brasil, founded in 1956, also established its factory in São Bernardo do Campo, producing 5-to-6-ton diesel-powered trucks.[46] Another major truck producer in Brazil was Scania-Vabis do Brasil, a Swedish company that in 1957 started production at Vemag's factory in São Paulo and moved its production unit to São Bernardo do Campo in 1962. This was Scania's first factory outside its country. International Harvester also installed a truck factory in Santo André, but the company stopped production in 1965

Almost all of these truck, automobile, and auto parts and input factories were located in either the capital or the municipalities of Santo Andre, São Bernardo do Campo, and São Caetano, along the principal railroad and road connections between the capital and the port of Santos. Between the Ford factory in São Paulo and the existing car and truck factories in São Bernardo, the distance was only about 20 km, with access by an excellent two-lane highway. The distance between Ford in São Paulo and General Motors in São Caetano was even shorter. In the 1960s, practically all the Brazilian automotive industry was concentrated in this limited territorial space.[47] Most of these factories were built with easy access to the Via Anchieta, a highway of exceptional quality for the time, which connected the plateau on which the city of São Paulo was situated to the port of Santos on the coast. Its construction, begun in 1939, was completed in two stages, with both lanes finally opening in 1953. The existence of the road caused a rapid transfer of cargo from the railway to the highway.[48] Most of the auto companies were concentrated on the first 20 kilometers of the 65 kilometers of the Via Anchieta (see Map 8.2).

Along with the growth of the automobile industry, São Paulo was the center of what has been called the new syndicalism. In the auto factories of the metropolitan region was born a new union movement and a powerful political party.[49] While not abolishing the unions, the military regimes of 1964–1985 intervened in union leadership, suspended the right to strike, implemented strict wage control, and abolished employment stability.[50] They also radically altered the system of retirement and pensions.[51] The impact on unions was severe, and it took more than a decade before labor mobilizations and strike movements effectively resumed.[52] At the end of the 1970s, workers' protests were revived, and the so-called new syndicalism emerged.[53] The strike of the ABC region's metallurgical workers in 1978 represents a milestone in this process of resurgence.[54] Luiz Inácio Lula da Silva, known as Lula, who would later become president of the republic, emerged as the leader of this new trade unionism. Strikes followed in 1979 that involved several professional categories and were repressed with violence by the police. The biggest demonstrations would be in São Bernardo do Campo and Diadema, where there was an extended strike sponsored by the local metalworkers' union, led by Lula. The Regional Electoral Court considered the strike illegal, and there was federal intervention in the union. There were protests on May Day in São Bernardo, which brought together thousands of workers. This strike and the demonstration were other milestones in the struggle for redemocratization in the state and the country.[55] The new syndicalism openly opposed the *unicidade sindical* model (which confined unions to one district) and the union tax, two features of the labor code that limited free union organizing and reinforced state interference. The new syndicalism acquired expressive political force when it allied with intellectuals, representatives of popular movements, and sectors of the Catholic Church to found the Workers Party (Partido dos Trabalhadores, PT) in São Paulo in 1980.[56]

Accelerating the industrial process in São Paulo required a sufficient supply of electricity. The abundance of rivers and waterfalls in the state eventually led to the use of hydropower.[57] The major expansion occurred when foreign capital entered the sector. The Canadian São Paulo Tramway Light & Power Company Limited (commonly referred to as Light) and the American Foreign Power Company (Amforp) invested heavily in major generating plants and played a leading role in power generation in the state until the mid-twentieth century.[58] São Paulo Tramway Light & Power Company built the Parnaiba plant, which required the construction of the Guarapiranga Dam.[59] Next came the construction of the Billings Generating Plant in Cubatão, which went into operation in 1954.[60] Even with this foreign investment, electricity was still in short supply. Thus the state government began to take an active role in the generation of electricity. In 1951 it created the Department of Water and Electric Energy (DAEE) and began to generate electricity and construct dams on major rivers within the state. In 1952 it created a mixed private-public company, Urubupunga Power Plants (Celusa),[61] and in the next year the Paranapenema Electric Power Plants (Uselpa), another mixed-capital company. In 1966, the state established the Centrais Elétrica de São Paulo (CESP), which was formed by the merger of five state-owned companies from São Paulo and six companies in public

TABLE 2.3
Installed Electric Energy, State of São Paulo, 1967

Company	Capacity (in 1000 kW)
Light	1,506
Cesp	628
CPFL (Amforp)	314
Outros	209
Total	2,627
CESP GENERATORS IN OPERATION	
Barra Bonita	122
Alvaro de Souza Lima	82
Armando A. Laydner	86
Lucas Nogueira Garcez	62
Euclides da Cunha	98
Armando de Salles Oliveira	28
Graminha	68
CESP GENERATORS UNDER CONSTRUCTION	
Álvaro de Souza	41
Ibitinga	114
Promissão	264
Chavantes	400
Jaguari	24
Paraibuna	50
Jupiá	1,400
Ilha Solteira	3,200
Total Under Construction	5,493

SOURCE: Iannone (2006): 103–105.

hands.[62] By the late 1960s CESP would become the largest energy company in the state, surpassing the capacity of Light (see Table 2.3).[63]

In addition to electricity, the federal government began to build oil pipelines from the port of Santos to the capital of São Paulo.[64] By 1951 a second oil pipeline was completed, and in 1974 both lines were acquired by Petrobras. In addition, the government built the Presidente Bernardes Oil Refinery in Cubatão.[65] The refinery began to function in 1955 and produced automotive and aviation gasoline, kerosene, and diesel as well as other petroleum products and was able to process heavy Venezuelan and lighter Arabian crude as well as oil from Bahia.[66] From its debut, the Presidente Bernardes Refinery would be responsible for more than half of the refined oil produced in Brazil until the early 1960s, when the opening of refineries in other states gradually reduced its importance to about 8% of national production.[67]

Another major state industry developed in this period was Companhia Siderúrgica Paulista (COSIPA). A group of engineers from São Paulo proposed building a steel mill on the coast.[68] In 1956, COSIPA was founded in Cubatão as a mixed private-public owned steel mill, with the BNDES holding half the shares and the state participating as well.[69] This steel mill, which went into production in 1965, would eventually become a totally state owned enterprise when Siderbrás took it over.[70] Blast Furnace 1, inaugurated in 1965, was considered the largest in Brazil and the second-largest integrated steelmaker in Latin America. It transformed ore into pig iron, pig iron into steel, and steel into flat products.[71]

In resolving the problems of energy, transport, and basic inputs with public and private capital, the federal and state governments were major agents in promoting industrialization in São Paulo. The state's industry was now growing faster than manufacturing in the other states of the nation. Thus between 1950 and 1960 the value of industrial production increased 120% in São Paulo, compared to just 80% in Brazil as a whole. By the time of the 1960 Industrial Census, there were some 36,000 industrial establishments in São Paulo, the state represented 46% of the country's industrial workforce and 52% of the energy used by industry, and it generated 55% of the value of all industrial production (see Table 2.4).

TABLE 2.4
Industrial Indicators for Brazil and São Paulo, 1960 (Value in R$ 1000)

				NUMBER OF FIRMS	
1960	Brazil	São Paulo	São Paulo as % Brazil	Brazil	São Paulo
Number of Establishments	110,771	36,254	33%		
Total Employed Personnel	1,799,376	831,339	46%	16	23
Workers	1,425,886	650,072	46%	13	18
Motor Force	5,145,225	2,677,865	52%	46	74
Total Salaries	145,123,339	78,589,310	54%	1,310	2,168
Workers' Salaries	102,802,744	53,335,323	52%	928	1,471
Industrial Production Value	1,194,784,551	658,067,422	55%	10,786	18,152
Industrial Value Added	553,918,842	301,914,041	55%	5,001	8,328
1950					
Industrial Value Added	118,605,165	55,291,473			
Total Employed Personnel	1,522,844	576,766			
Workers	1,279,184	488,633			
Motor Force	2,824,152	1,135,764			

SOURCE: Censo Industrial 1960, Série Nacional, volume III, p. 76.
NOTE: Values of 1949 and 1959, adjusted by the corresponding IGP-DI.

Although traditional industries such as textiles and food still were important in terms of the number of establishments, employees, and value of production in 1960, the sectors influenced by the automobile industry were now as important as these traditional industries in the state. These new industries included rubber, metallurgy, and machines. These new industries had fewer establishments but accounted for just under half of the employed workers, about half of the value of production, and over half of the value of industrial output, and their average value of production and value of industrial transformation was more than double that of the traditional sectors (Table 2.5).

By 1960, state-owned companies represented more than half of the total value of production and value of industrial transformation in Brazil. In some sectors, such as machines, electrical and communications equipment, transport equipment, and rubber, state participation was even higher. The state even accounted for over half of the national textile industry. In the decade of the 1950s the share of São Paulo's participation in national industry had increased in terms of the number of workers employed, the value of production, and the value of industrial transformation.

In this decade the concentration of industry in the capital and its neighboring towns increased. But there was also growth in new industrial centers within the state. Cubatão become a major chemical and petrochemical hub. Sorocaba, Campinas, and Jundiaí, also became significant industrial centers within the state, where a variety of medium and large industries were established (see Table 2.6).[72]

All this state investment in industrial development in the 1950s left the nation with serious economic problems, which included an annual inflation rate of around 50% and major imbalances in its public and current accounts. The country was also going through a new crisis in coffee, with low prices, large inventories, and production that exceeded the size of the foreign market. In this context came the political crisis of the 1960s, which ended with the 1964 military coup.

The first military regime identified serious distortions in the country's economic structure as the cause of inflation and economic crisis. It highlighted the productive sector and the excessive pressure on aggregate demand exerted by public deficits financed by monetary expansion. This led to excessive expansion of credit to the private sector, and to rising wages. The government resolved to change these structural impediments, and, given its authoritarian nature, it could carry out reforms unopposed, creating new taxes and indexing the economy through the creation of the monetary correction. The deficit was now funded mainly by the issuance of

TABLE 2.5

Industrial Indicators for the State of São Paulo by Sector, 1960 (Value in Cr$ 1000)

	Firms	Workers	Salaries Paid	Value of Production	Industrial Value Added	Average Number of Workers	Average Value of Production	% Workers	% of Industrial Value Added	% Firms
Non-Metallic Minerals	5,515	58,046	3,850,296	26,606,262	18,068,199	11	4,824	8%	6%	15%
Metallurgy	2,542	75,131	6,429,839	59,721,443	28,023,157	30	23,494	11%	9%	7%
Mechanics	1,132	35,883	3,284,638	26,531,348	14,554,856	32	23,438	5%	5%	3%
Electrical and Communications Equipment	709	35,024	3,066,929	37,360,397	16,770,587	49	52,694	5%	6%	2%
Transport Equipment	1,098	47,519	4,439,249	69,958,781	35,206,215	43	63,715	7%	12%	3%
Wood	1,931	12,517	872,714	7,038,505	3,592,522	6	3,645	2%	1%	5%
Furniture	2,844	24,152	1,854,486	12,966,789	6,964,318	8	4,559	4%	2%	8%
Paper and Cardboard	376	19,626	1,568,729	22,421,847	9,816,217	52	59,633	3%	3%	1%
Rubber	168	10,809	1,069,205	21,538,045	10,229,756	64	128,203	2%	3%	0%
Hides, Skins, and Their Products	548	6,165	408,109	4,231,620	1,756,104	11	7,722	1%	1%	2%
Chemistry	670	35,904	3,288,690	69,512,397	30,195,638	54	103,750	5%	10%	2%
Pharmaceutical and Medicinal Products	157	6,728	555,221	12,100,320	6,877,097	43	77,072	1%	2%	0%
Perfumery Products	283	3,828	255,903	8,570,353	3,602,051	14	30,284	1%	1%	1%
Plastic Materials	222	5,565	470,505	4,418,071	2,285,415	25	19,901	1%	1%	1%
Textiles	2,147	152,706	10,561,883	87,048,974	36,951,188	71	40,544	22%	12%	6%
Clothing and Footwear	3,274	38,399	2,541,500	22,686,395	10,506,784	12	6,929	6%	4%	9%
Food products	8,581	66,478	4,425,840	115,145,398	36,355,924	8	13,419	10%	12%	24%
Drinks	690	10,235	792,014	12,834,988	7,262,433	15	18,601	1%	2%	2%
Tobacco	19	2,619	219,641	4,490,291	2,695,781	138	236,331	0%	1%	0%
Editorial and Graphic	1,429	19,352	1,655,081	14,211,336	8,151,003	14	9,945	3%	3%	4%
Other	1,129	18,814	1,404,532	10,240,541	6,125,296	17	9,070	3%	2%	3%
Total Manufacturing	35,464	685,500	53,015,004	649,634,101	295,990,541	19	18,318	100%	100%	98%

SOURCE: IBGE, *Anuário Estatístico do Brasil, 1963*, 82.

TABLE 2.6

Industrial Production in the State and Municipality of São Paulo by Industrial Value Added, 1960 (Value in R$ 1000)

Municipality	Population	Firms	Motor Force (CV)	Total Workers (1)	Value of Production	Industrial Value Added	Worker Salaries	Participation In Value of Production	Participation In Value Added by Industry	Participation In Workers
São Paulo (capital)	3,825,351	14,546	1,044,764	377,832	335,998	162,467	31,746	55%	60%	55%
Santo André	245,147	455	200,382	32,088	45,068	18,221	2,981	6%	6%	5%
São Bernardo	82,411	284	93,355	21,688	34,466	16,936	1,965	6%	4%	3%
São Caetano	114,421	252	123,949	16,195	21,119	9,117	1,400	3%	3%	2%
Cubatão	25,166	50	106,856	2,461	20,067	9,499	381	3%	1%	0%
Sorocaba	138,323	267	44,494	17,538	11,271	5,316	1,193	2%	2%	3%
Campinas	219,303	520	53,387	12,328	10,855	4,504	847	2%	2%	2%
Jundiaí	118,874	365	55,330	14,094	8,453	4,048	991	1%	2%	2%
Mauá	28,924	84	19,070	4,211	8,330	3,456	344	1%	1%	1%
Santos	265,753	551	22,025	4,751	7,086	2,224	347	1%	1%	1%
Guarulhos	101,273	453	32,127	6,972	6,197	2,894	541	1%	1%	1%
Piracicaba	116,190	392	55,813	6,515	5,534	2,486	442	1%	1%	1%
State of São Paulo	12,974,699	36,129	2,621,109	687,982	650,752	297,752	53,175	100%	100%	100%

SOURCE: IBGE, Anuário Estatístico do Brasil, 1963, 118.

NOTE: (1) This total of workers is the average total employed for the year.

public debt securities, unlike the previous practice of financing it through printing money.[73] It also promoted a correction in the prices of public goods and services and adopted a policy of delaying (and thus reducing) wage adjustments to the inflation rate.

Industry suffered from these restrictions on credit, and industrial production declined. In 1967, when the second military regime took office, the economy showed signs of recession. But the authoritarian regime needed political legitimacy, and the only way to achieve that was through economic growth. Although this was the most politically repressive period of the military era, extending from 1967 to 1973, it was also the time of the "economic miracle," so named because of the high rates of growth achieved by the country. Benefiting from the stabilization reforms, the government established new incentives and subsidies, and took advantage of the idle capacity in the productive sector and favorable conditions in the international market to give a great impetus to industrial growth as well as to agriculture.

To avoid the traditional external bottleneck, the government introduced incentive mechanisms for the export of manufactured goods, which until then were unimportant in Brazilian exports. Exports now had a realistic and relatively stable exchange rate, thanks to a system of periodic minidevaluations linked to the differential between internal and external inflation, which protected exporters from strong relative price fluctuations. The federal government now provided credit, incentives, and subsidies to stimulate and direct private investment to priority areas, and it began to act more intensively through public companies. The federal government also sought to decentralize investments, not only to meet political demands but also to reduce the huge regional disparities that existed. This had a direct effect on São Paulo, which, despite its strong growth of industry in this period, gradually lost its importance within Brazilian industry as a whole.

Between 1967 and 1973, GDP grew at an average annual rate of 10% and industry at an even higher growth rate.[74] The economy was modernized, there was a significant incorporation of new workers into the formal employment market, and a large middle-class consumer class developed. But rapid growth largely financed by resources from the international credit market, along with imbalances accumulated in both state and external accounts, led to Brazil's growing indebtedness and an increase in the country's vulnerability to sudden changes in the international financial market. The first oil shock in 1973 was a clear sign of this fragility.

In 1974 the moderate wing of the military came to power. Its purpose was to open the political system. To legitimize such openness, it would need to achieve high rates of economic growth. Stabilization plans that produced recessions would not be politically acceptable. Most countries affected by the oil crisis adopted recessive programs, seeking to restrict domestic demand and adjust the economy to the new environment of expensive energy, and had to transfer a considerable part of their income to oil-exporting countries. In contrast, the Brazilian government followed a completely opposite path. It stimulated the economy and developed an ambitious investment program aimed at increasing the domestic supply of capital goods and basic consumer products, hoping to reduce its dependence on imports. The abundance of foreign capital from the resource recycling generated by oil-exporting countries enabled Brazil to follow this path through international lending, but at the cost of growing domestic and foreign debt.

In the 1974 Second National Development Plan, the military government proposed major investments in industry.[75] The industrial and infrastructure targets were ambitious, but most of these targets were achieved during the designated period.[76] There was also a new emphasis on decentralizing industry away from São Paulo, and large infrastructure projects were directed to other states.[77] The plan proposed that the Northeast would grow faster than the rest of the country to reduce existing regional disparities. It was in this period that Fiat established the first modern automobile factory to be built outside the state of São Paulo.[78]

In 1979 came the second oil shock, but this time the international financial market drastically reduced the supply of resources to debtor countries. This was the beginning of the decade-long so-called debt crisis that affected almost every country in Latin America in the 1980s, forcing governments to restructure their external debts and halting the long growth trajectories they had experienced beginning in the second half of the twentieth century. In August 1982, the Mexican crisis clearly exposed the seriousness of the situation, so much so that international banks closed their doors to Brazil and demanded that the country sign a formal agreement with the IMF. But the economic situation continued to worsen as the country kept on delaying its external debt payments. It also had difficulty honoring its agreements with the IMF, which required deep reductions in the economy, even though Brazil was already in recession. São Paulo was particularly affected, since industry was concentrated in São Paulo and industrial GDP growth turned negative. This was the economic scenario when the country was redemocratized in 1985.

The twenty years between 1960 and 1980 were ones of profound economic and social transformations in Brazil. The industrialization process was completed with the creation of new industries in the basic inputs

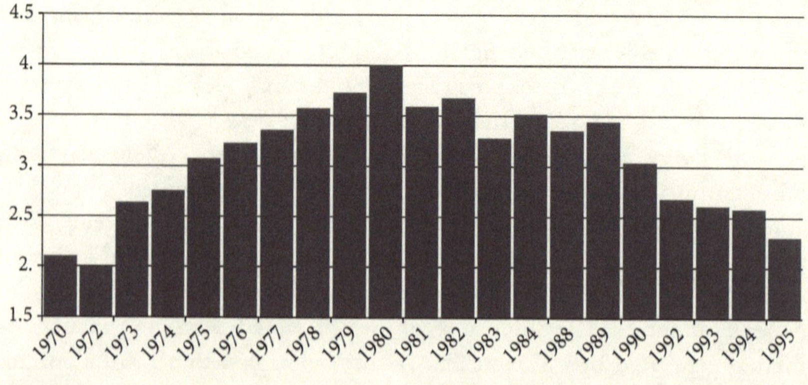

Figure 2.3. Number of Workers in Industries of Transformation, Brazil, 1970–1995 (in millions of persons)

SOURCE: IBGE, Séries Históricas, table IND04100.

sector, and a mature capital goods industry was created. Growth in all aspects of manufacturing was very rapid in this period, and in fact 1980 represented the peak in Brazilian industrial growth. This can be seen in manufacturing employment, which peaked at 4 million workers in 1980 and then began on a steady decline; by the mid-1990s, there were just half as many workers in manufacturing (see Figure 2.3). The 1980s would also see the peak in the industrial share of GDP, which reached 48% in 1985 and thereafter steadily declined to less than half that figure by 2018. The same occurred with industrial value-added GDP (see Table 2.7).

The state of São Paulo, like the rest of the country, experienced this rapid growth in the industrial sector in the period from 1950 to 1980. Personnel employed in the São Paulo industry increased from 831,000 to 2.2 million. Despite this growth, the basic size of industrial establishments in São Paulo remained the same as in 1950. Half of the 62,000 industrial establishments had fewer than 10 employed persons in 1980, but they accounted for just 6% of employment and 2% of the value of production. Those employing 100 or more accounted for about two-thirds of the number of workers employed, of the value of production, and of the value of industrial transformation (see Table 2.8).

But there was a significant change in this period in the weight of new and old industries, reflecting the increasing importance of basic or heavy industry. The industries classified as "new," those which provided basic inputs or capital goods, now accounted for the majority of the workers and of the value of industrial production (see Table 2.9).

TABLE 2.7

Annual Change in Industrial GDP and Industry's Share of National GDP, 1947–2018 (Percentage)

	% IN GDP		ANNUAL VARIATION			% IN GDP		ANNUAL VARIATION			% IN GDP		ANNUAL VARIATION	
Year	GDP Industrial	GDP Value Added by Industry	GDP	GDP Value Added by Industry	Year	GDP Industrial	GDP Value Added by Industry	GDP	GDP Value Added by Industry	Year	GDP Industrial	GDP Value Added by Industry	GDP	GDP Value Added by Industry
1947	26.0	19.9			1971	38.8	29.7	11.3	11.9	1995	27.0	16.8	4.2	2.0
1948	24.9	19.4	9.7	12.3	1972	39.5	30.4	11.9	14.0	1996	25.6	15.0	2.2	0.1
1949	25.4	19.3	7.7	11.0	1973	41.9	33.0	14.0	16.6	1997	25.7	14.8	3.4	2.5
1950	25.0	19.3	6.8	12.7	1974	43.2	33.8	8.2	7.8	1998	25.1	13.8	0.3	-4.8
1951	26.0	19.6	4.9	5.3	1975	43.3	33.6	5.2	3.8	1999	25.1	14.2	0.5	-1.9
1952	25.0	18.8	7.3	5.6	1976	43.0	33.4	10.3	12.1	2000	26.8	15.3	4.4	5.7
1953	26.3	19.7	4.7	9.3	1977	41.8	32.1	4.9	2.3	2001	26.6	15.4	1.4	0.7
1954	26.7	20.8	7.8	9.3	1978	43.1	33.1	5.0	6.1	2002	26.4	14.5	3.1	2.1
1955	26.6	21.2	8.8	11.1	1979	43.6	33.2	6.8	6.9	2003	27.0	16.9	1.1	2.7
1956	28.2	22.0	2.9	5.5	1980	44.1	33.7	9.2	9.1	2004	28.6	17.8	5.8	9.1
1957	28.9	22.4	7.7	5.4	1981	44.3	33.2	-4.3	-10.4	2005	28.5	17.4	3.2	2.2
1958	32.2	24.7	10.8	16.8	1982	45.8	34.4	0.8	-0.2	2006	27.7	16.6	4.0	1.2
1959	33.9	26.7	9.8	12.9	1983	44.4	33.1	-2.9	-5.8	2007	27.1	16.6	6.1	6.1
1960	33.2	26.3	9.4	10.6	1984	46.2	33.9	5.4	6.2	2008	27.3	16.5	5.1	4.2
1961	33.5	27.9	8.6	11.1	1985	48.0	35.9	7.8	8.4	2009	25.6	15.3	-0.1	-9.3
1962	33.6	27.1	6.6	8.1	1986	47.2	34.7	7.5	11.3	2010	27.4	15.0	7.5	9.2
1963	34.2	27.4	0.6	-0.2	1987	47.5	33.4	3.5	1.0	2011	27.2	13.9	4.0	2.3
1964	33.7	27.1	3.4	5.0	1988	46.8	33.4	-0.1	-3.4	2012	26.0	12.6	1.9	-2.4
1965	33.2	25.9	2.4	-4.7	1989	46.3	32.4	3.2	2.9	2013	24.9	12.3	3.0	3.0
1966	34.2	26.6	6.7	11.7	1990	38.7	26.5	-4.3	-9.5	2014	23.8	12.0	0.5	-4.7
1967	33.5	25.5	4.2	2.2	1991	36.2	24.9	1.0	0.2	2015	22.5	12.2	-3.8	-8.5
1968	36.3	27.8	9.8	14.2	1992	38.7	26.4	-0.5	-4.2	2016	21.2	12.5	-3.6	-4.8
1969	36.9	28.3	9.5	11.2	1993	41.6	29.1	4.9	8.3	2017	21.3	12.3	1.0	1.7
1970	38.3	29.3	10.4	11.9	1994	40.0	26.8	5.9	7.0	2018	21.6	11.3	1.1	1.4

SOURCE: Ipeadata. Dados originais: IBGE, Sistema de Contas Nacionais.

TABLE 2.8

Size of Industrial Firms in São Paulo by Personnel Employed, 1980 (Value in Cr$ 1000)

						PERCENTAGE			
Personnel Employed Grouped	Firms	Personnel Employed	Workers Employed	Value of Production	Value Added of Industrial Production	Firms	Workers Employed	Value of Production	Value Added of Industrial Production
1–4	15,867	43,941	16,259	31,533,538	13,347,643	26%	1%	1%	1%
5–9	14,730	96,878	57,634	79,480,724	30,990,107	24%	3%	2%	1%
10–19	11,842	160,608	120,449	204,292,391	80,660,811	19%	6%	4%	4%
20–49	10,258	319,322	262,594	527,630,160	217,228,776	17%	14%	11%	10%
50–99	4,498	314,978	269,334	591,328,351	257,194,622	7%	14%	12%	12%
100–249	3,147	482,513	423,024	1,041,416,454	440,731,047	5%	22%	21%	21%
250–499	1,076	365,679	332,644	1,073,759,863	444,983,069	2%	17%	21%	21%
500+	535	503,126	460,776	1,467,716,733	608,049,100	1%	24%	29%	29%
Total	61,953	2,287,045	1,942,714	5,017,158,214	2,093,185,175	100%	100%	100%	100%

SOURCE: Recenseamento Geral 1980, volume 3, tomo 2, parte 1, no. 19: 256–257.

TABLE 2.9

Basic Industrial Indicators in the State of São Paulo by Sector, 1980 (Value in Cr$ 1000)

Type of Industry	Firms	Total Workers (1)	Salaries Paid	Value of Production	Value Added of Industrial Production	Average Workers	Average Value of Production	% Workers	% Value of Production	% Value Added by Industry
Total All Industries	60,222	2,209,344	401,867,009	4,988,156,532	2,062,211,831	37	82,829	100%	100%	100%
Non-Metallic Minerals	8,147	141,988	19,175,601	158,692,877	91,057,109	17	19,479	6%	3%	4%
Metallurgy	6,251	300,531	58,379,346	679,102,285	244,522,124	48	108,639	13%	13%	12%
Mechanics	5,516	324,198	87,048,260	497,403,644	264,700,751	59	90,175	14%	10%	13%
Electrical equipment	2,110	165,038	32,758,899	331,434,439	161,328,539	78	157,078	7%	7%	8%
Transport equipment	1,504	172,765	39,915,100	563,288,474	203,510,657	115	374,527	8%	11%	10%
Paper and Cardboard	892	58,822	11,401,038	145,098,870	63,510,779	66	162,667	3%	3%	3%
Rubber	514	37,784	7,833,066	112,414,674	37,324,172	74	218,706	2%	2%	2%
Chemistry	1,553	80,351	21,338,243	906,593,580	312,904,827	52	583,769	4%	18%	15%
Pharmaceuticals and Medicines	222	19,030	4,037,209	68,715,420	42,051,069	86	309,529	1%	1%	2%
Perfumery products	309	13,547	2,454,974	53,735,425	23,721,339	44	173,901	1%	1%	1%
Plastic materials	1,721	75,230	11,160,828	117,694,548	57,017,744	44	68,387	3%	2%	3%
Subtotal "new"	28,739	1,389,284	295,502,564	3,634,174,236	1,501,649,110	48	126,454	61%	72%	71%
Wood	1,860	30,888	3,943,437	36,427,238	20,617,702	17	19,585	1%	1%	1%
Furniture	3,081	66,819	8,305,851	65,579,521	31,474,066	22	21,285	3%	1%	1%
Hides and Skins	357	11,867	1,347,722	13,145,413	5,040,627	33	36,822	1%	0%	0%
Textiles	3,194	186,506	26,224,152	320,038,356	135,087,496	58	100,200	8%	6%	6%
Clothing and Footwear	6,747	195,756	19,456,544	172,228,565	80,615,985	29	25,527	9%	3%	4%
Food Products	10,540	178,792	21,517,180	533,038,637	155,782,993	17	50,573	8%	11%	7%
Drinks	575	17,169	2,628,222	34,839,117	15,792,526	30	60,590	1%	1%	1%
Tobacco	6	1,895	520,736	8,667,687	5,912,322	316	1,444,615	0%	0%	0%
Editorial and Graphic	3,263	64,538	13,304,017	77,427,454	51,068,680	20	23,729	3%	2%	2%
Other	1,860	65,830	9,116,584	92,590,308	59,170,324	35	49,780	3%	2%	3%
Subtotal "Traditional"	31,483	820,060	106,364,445	1,353,982,296	560,562,721	26	43,007	36%	27%	27%

SOURCE: Recenseamento Geral 1980, volume 3, tomo 2, parte 1, no. 19: 2–3.
NOTE: (1) This total is the average of a firm's workforce for the year.

TABLE 2.10

Industrial Indicators for São Paulo and Brazil, 1960 and 1980 (Value in R$ 1000)

1980	Brazil	São Paulo	São Paulo as % of Brazil	NUMBER OF FIRMS Brazil	NUMBER OF FIRMS São Paulo
Number of Establishments	214,158	62,426	29%		
Total Employed Personnel	5,004,522	2,287,045	46%	23	37
Production Personnel	4,155,986	1,942,734	47%	19	31
Total Wages	704,568,557	399,651,315	57%	3,290	6,402
Production-Linked wages	450,740,675	337,061,664	75%	2,105	5,399
Value of Industrial Production	9,738,340,472	5,059,027,348	52%	45,473	81,040
Value Added of Industrial Production	4,017,104,045	2,105,850,014	52%	18,758	33,734
1960					
Number of Establishments	110,771	36,254	33%		
Total Employed Personnel	1,799,376	831,339	46%	16	23
Production personnel	1,425,886	650,072	46%	13	18
Total Wages	145,123,339	78,589,310	54%	1,310	2,168
Production-linked wages	102,802,744	53,335,323	52%	928	1,471
Value of Industrial Production	1,194,784,551	658,067,422	55%	10,786	18,152
Value Added of Industrial Production	553,918,842	301,914,041	55%	5,001	8,328

	1960	1980	VALUE ADDED INDUSTRIAL PRODUCTION IN % 1960	1980	Change 1960/1980
Brazil Total	553,918,842	4,017,104,045	100%	100%	7.3
North	6,140,083	103,294,760	1%	3%	16.8
Northeast	42,332,128	323,459,610	8%	8%	7.6
Southeast	432,811,470	2,899,419,316	78%	72%	6.7
South	68,819,226	628,357,602	12%	16%	9.1
Center-West	3,815,935	51,196,191	1%	1%	13.4

SOURCE: Censo Industrial 1960, Série Nacional, volume III, p. 76; Recenseamento Geral 1980, volume 3, tomo 2, parte 1, no. 1, table 2.

Even with the increasing decentralization of industry in this twenty-year period, the state's position in the context of national industry remained relatively stable. Of the five Brazilian regions, the fastest industrial growth was in the Northern region, helped by the creation of the Manaus Free Zone in 1967.[79] But São Paulo still accounted for roughly the same share of all factors as before, and had even increased significantly its share of production-linked wages (see Table 2.10).

But the relative weight of the capital's industrial sector within the state was changing in this period. The city of São Paulo, which accounted for

55% of the state's industrial employment and 60% of the value of industrial output in 1960, was now reduced to 40% of employment and 35% of industrial value added in 1980. Aside from textile plants and electrical generating facilities in other parts of the state, there was the major development at Cubatão on the coast near Santos, a new petrochemical and steel complex, and another petrochemical complex at Capuava. Finally, Petrobras's largest current refinery in Brazil was in the municipality of Paulínia (Table 2.11). But if the city itself was less industrially prominent, the metropolitan region still had a formidable industrial establishment. The newly created Metropolitan Region of São Paulo (RMSP), which comprised thirty-seven municipalities and the capital, still represented 64% of employment and 63% of value added in industry. The most important of these metropolitan municipalities were São Bernardo do Campo,[80] Santo André,[81] and the municipality of Guarulhos, in which a varied industrial sector was emerging.[82]

But all these developments peaked in the 1980s, and the history of Brazilian industry after 1990 was one of painful change and crisis. The new democratic government established in 1985 inherited a difficult economic situation, with rising inflation and fiscal imbalance of state finances. This pattern of external sector vulnerability, fiscal imbalance and rising inflation would be the norm throughout the 1980s and part of the 1990s. Nevertheless, the major reforms carried out by the new democratic governments of the late 1980s and early 1990s led to a major period of economic stability that lasted for at least two decades. The renegotiation of the foreign debt, the balance of state expenditures and income, and the establishment of the Real Plan, which finally brought inflation under control, were key elements in this fiscal reform. Although growth was stagnant or low in these two last decades of the twentieth century, these budget and foreign debt reforms provided the basis for a major period of economic stability in the early twenty-first century.

But there was a basic change in industrial policy that began in the government of Fernando Collor (1990–1992). In the 1990s it was decided to end tariff and quota protections for national industry and abandon state participation in this sector of the economy. The central idea of the so-called Washington Consensus was that the end of protectionism and the opening of national economies to the world market would promote a productive integration between international and domestic industry. It would thus result in technological improvements and increase productivity and economies of scale for Brazilian industry. It would allow the integration of Brazilian industry into global value chains and both increase the imported component in local industrial production and increase the proportion of exports of

TABLE 2.11

Industrial Production in the State and Municipalities of São Paulo by Industrial Value Added, 1980 (Value in R$ 1000)

							PERCENTAGE		
	Population	Firms	Number of Workers	Worker Salaries	Value of Production	Industrial Value Added	In Value of Production	In Value Added	In Workers
State of São Paulo	25,040,712	62,426	2,265,748	337,061,664	5,059,027,348	2,105,850,014	100%	100%	100%
Greater São Paulo (GSP)	12,588,725	33,369	1,455,812	227,826,666	2,963,594,590	1,322,721,474	59%	63%	64%
São Paulo (capital)	8,493,226	24,842	914,980	127,442,344	1,519,185,554	731,837,394	30%	35%	40%
São Bernardo (GSP, ABC)	425,602	1,099	124,711	28,990,174	461,433,071	166,470,329	9%	8%	6%
Santo André (GSP, ABC)	553,072	981	65,146	14,163,933	242,549,004	82,114,877	5%	4%	3%
Cubatão	68,233	126	18,347	8,779,211	325,582,099	75,222,098	6%	4%	1%
Guarulhos (GSP)	457,856	1,306	80,135	12,972,984	155,568,220	72,725,383	3%	3%	4%
Sorocaba	269,830	1,540	75,302	10,091,818	151,122,896	63,710,138	3%	3%	3%
Paulínia	17,835	62	4,294	1,623,737	147,971,116	59,435,025	3%	3%	0%
São José dos Campos	287,513	351	40,557	8,612,049	165,430,474	58,923,773	3%	3%	2%
Jundiaí	258,800	1,082	60,669	8,824,268	106,044,473	52,135,577	2%	2%	3%
Campinas	664,559	1,208	51,347	8,085,313	104,122,341	45,965,255	2%	2%	2%
São Caetano (GSP, ABC)	163,082	557	35,837	7,485,072	99,928,424	44,063,080	2%	2%	2%
Osasco (GSP)	409,547	512	36,843	7,662,153	81,501,608	40,548,857	2%	2%	2%
Mauá (GSP)	205,740	259	19,364	4,191,474	73,371,740	30,515,344	1%	1%	1%
Piracicaba	214,295	749	24,179	4,094,424	57,181,758	26,238,771	1%	1%	1%
Ribeirão Preto	318,496	1,284	26,962	3,310,589	61,752,652	21,879,395	1%	1%	1%
Santos	416,681	476	9,463	1,011,645	15,843,373	6,525,173	0%	0%	0%

SOURCE: Recenseamento Geral 1980, volume 1, tomo 3, no. 17: 2–68; volume 3, tomo 2, no. 19: 4–192.

industrial products. But for a variety of reasons this positive transformation did not occur. In fact, industrial growth slowed considerably in comparison with the rest of the economy, and foreign manufactured imports often reduced the role of Brazilian companies. By the beginning of the twenty-first century, the continuing weak performance of industry provoked an intense debate about whether Brazil was experiencing deindustrialization. Whatever the results of this ongoing debate, there is little doubt that the 1990s can be seen as the beginning of a new era in the history of industry in São Paulo and in the nation.

Collor inaugurated the liberal reforms of the Washington Consensus and took the first steps toward opening the Brazilian market to international competition, promoting foreign investment, privatizing state-owned production companies, and eliminating state monopolies on the production of goods and services. The complete protection of national industry against foreign competition, which had remained unchanged for forty years, was progressively dismantled.[83] Reforms were swift and intense: customs tariffs were drastically reduced, as were most bureaucratic restrictions on importers, and most import controls were eliminated. The tariff reduction program began in the capital goods and raw materials sectors and was extended to consumer goods. Another major factor reducing protection in this same period was the creation of Mercosur, a regional free trade market between Argentina, Brazil, Paraguay, and Uruguay, which promoted further tariff reductions. But Mercosur trade was often subject to a constant state of negotiation and adjustment and sometimes even led to import and export quotas.[84]

The other major reform of the 1990s was the successful implementation of a heterodox stabilization plan that finally broke the long period of high inflation. The 1980s and early 1990s saw rampant inflation, and the level of economic activity deteriorated, with several years of negative growth. Unemployment rose to 13% in 1993. The external debt was high and national reserves were limited, creating serious external instability—a pattern that had become the norm in the 1980s and early 1990s (see Table 2.12).

In May 1993, Fernando Henrique Cardoso took over the Ministry of Finance and led a stabilization plan that finally controlled inflation. Known as the Real Plan, named for the new currency adopted, it stopped the inflationary process that had persisted in the country for nearly half a century. The stability achieved with the Real Plan was based on three fundamental points: an exchange rate anchor, the maintenance of an overvalued real, and the broad opening of the economy. Unlike previous plans, it was possible to use the foreign exchange anchor because Brazil had renegotiated its

TABLE 2.12

Population and Basic Economic Indicators for Brazil, 1984–1993 (Value in US$ Billions)

	1984	1985	1986	1987	1988	1989	1990	1991	1992	1993
External Sector										
International Reserves	12.0	11.6	6.8	7.5	9.1	9.7	10.0	9.4	23.8	32.2
Balance of Current Transactions (% GDP)	0.1	-0.1	-2.1	-0.5	1.4	0.3	-0.8	-0.4	1.6	-0.2
Gross External Debt	102.1	105.2	111.2	121.2	113.5	115.5	123.4	123.9	135.9	145.7
Balance of Trade Balance	13.1	12.5	8.3	11.2	19.2	16.1	10.8	10.6	15.2	13.3
Exports	13.9	13.2	14.0	15.1	14.6	18.3	20.7	21.0	20.6	25.3
Imports	27.0	25.6	22.3	26.2	33.8	34.4	31.4	31.6	35.8	38.6
Fuel Imports	6.9	5.7	3.1	4.1	3.5	3.8	5.0	4.4	4.2	4.5
Manufactured Exports	15.1	14.1	12.4	14.8	19.2	18.6	17.0	17.8	20.8	23.4
Population										
Total	129.1	131.6	134.1	136.6	139.2	141.7	144.3	146.8	149.4	152.0
Urban	71%	71%	72%	73%	74%	74%	75%	76%	76%	77%
Rural	29%	29%	28%	27%	26%	26%	25%	24%	24%	23%
Variation in Basic Rates										
Change in GDP	5.4	7.8	7.5	3.5	-0.1	3.2	-4.3	1.0	-0.5	4.9
Change in Industrial GDP	6.2	8.4	11.3	1.0	-3.4	2.9	-9.5	0.2	-4.2	8.3
Unemployment rate	12.4	9.8	7.3	8.6	8.6	6.7	9.4	10.5	14.4	13.3
Inflation										
Inflation—IGP—annual rate	243	246	61	431	1,118	2,012	1,217	497	1,167	2,851
Inflation—IGP—Monthly average	11	11	4	15	23	29	24	16	24	32
Inflation—IGP—highest monthly rate	12	15	18	26	29	49	81	26	27	37

SOURCE: Ipeadata.

foreign debt, allowing it free access to the international financial market, which had abundant resources, high liquidity, and low interest rates.[85] At the same time, in the domestic market, real interest rates were extremely high, which attracted foreign capital, generating an abundance of dollars that also overvalued the national currency.[86]

The subsequent Cardoso presidential period continued with the process of privatization. It was one of the largest such privatizations in the world and encouraged the participation of foreign investors, who accounted for more than 50% of purchases, which helped the balance of payments. Electricity and telecommunications accounted for almost 30% of sales, followed by metallurgy and mining, with 8%; oil and gas, with approximately 6%; and the financial sector, with 5%. The privatizations involved emblematic companies that dated back as far as the Vargas era, and although Petrobras, the state oil company, was not privatized, its monopoly on oil exploration and telecommunications was broken.[87]

The rapid opening of the economy, its exposure to international competition, and the maintenance of an overvalued national currency had a positive effect on prices, which achieved stability after decades of rising inflation and even reaching levels that could be considered hyperinflationary. For the economy as a whole, the elimination of inflation and the reduction of prices due to cheaper foreign imports led to an explosion of demand. It also spurred consumer and corporate credit expansion. But these reforms were also supposed to help Brazilian industry integrate into the world market.[88] While this opening of the market increased competition, the continued maintenance of an overvalued national currency, intended to attract foreign capital, led to the deterioration of the trade balance: imports became cheaper, and national exports became more expensive and thus declined. Moreover, much of the foreign capital attracted was speculative, taking advantage of Brazil's high interest rates rather than being foreign direct investment.

Thus the price of all this expansion of demand and spending was a reversal in the trade balance, and new external shocks in the international economy would soon have a direct impact on Brazil. In response to the Mexican crisis, which led to capital flight, the government increased interest rates, significantly increased bank reserves, restricted consumer credit, raised taxes on numerous imported products, and set quotas for car imports. All these measures constrained liquidity and had a negative impact on economic activities. Foreign reserves did increase and domestic prices were held steady, but a policy of appreciation in the real, which was designed to attract foreign capital, would become the standard over the next twenty years. This policy constrained the country's growth, increased unemployment, and led to deterioration in public finances and a large increase in foreign debt.

In 2002 the first government of the Workers Party took advantage of the price stability achieved by the Real Plan, and the relative calm in the international financial markets, to promote major advances in social programs, especially though massive income transfers, which had a major impact in reducing poverty in the country. It also initially maintained the liberal trade and industrial policies of the previous government. But in Lula's second term, there was again a return toward traditional state interventionist industrial policy. Fiscal policy would play a key role in the process through public investment and support for private investment as well as in the form of financing, subsidies, and incentives.[89] The concept of the regulatory state was abandoned and replaced by the state's role in promoting economic development.[90]

The consolidation of this new developmental policy was reinforced when the new Workers Party government of Dilma Rousseff took advantage of the international crisis of 2008 to shift industrial policy back to a pre-1990 state interventionist model. Growth was to be promoted by the state using the BNDES to finance the public and private sectors. The bank provided credit and stimulus to domestic industry and began aggressively promoting the consolidation of private Brazilian industrial groups seeking to create competitive national companies in the international market. The new developmental policy was also intended to act on the supply side through massive public investments in the energy sector and infrastructure. There was a strong expansion of credit in general, particularly from public financial institutions, which included the Banco do Brasil and the Caixa Econômica Federal. The amount of credit made available to industrial production, consumers, and housing grew significantly. Public spending in general increased, particularly in social programs such as conditional income transfer programs and the popular public housing program Minha Casa Minha Vida.[91] The policy of systematic increases in the minimum wage also expanded demand among the poorest sections of the population.

But exchange rate policy discouraged national industrial production. Thus, between 2003 and 2010, while there was a cumulative GDP growth of 37%, industry expanded by only 27%. Nor was there a major resumption of private investment. Poorly executed and often corrupt infrastructure projects such as roads, railroads, and ports meant that there was no significant improvement in Brazil's major infrastructure bottlenecks despite massive public investment. The government even adopted protected markets, especially for purchases made by Petrobras.

To revive industrial growth the government launched the Greater Brazil Plan in 2011.[92] The government exempted a variety of building materials, capital goods, and vehicles from the industrialized products tax (IPI); it reduced the payroll tax for some industries; and the repayment of credits from the Social Integration Program (PIS) and the Construction for Social Security Financing (Cofins) accumulated in the production chain of the manufacturing sector. The tax relief measures, initially restricted to a few sectors, were soon expanded, reaching a large part of the industrial sector. The government believed that growth would occur through strong state intervention, which would promote public and private investment and in turn would stimulate consumption. The idea was that that demand would be the engine of industrial growth, but this did not happen. The tax relief measures did not attract much private capital, and most of the government projects were poorly designed and executed, with many never completed.[93]

After years of stability achieved under the Real Plan, the government again began managing the price index by manipulating public tariffs. There were also profound changes in how credit was financed and how it was distributed. Between 2007 and June 2015, total credit increased by about 20 percentage points, from 35% to 55% as a proportion of GDP. The largest growth occurred in earmarked resources, which are loans with rates or resources defined by government regulation.[94] Public banks increased their role in the credit market, and went from accounting for 34% of credit in 2007 to 54% by 2014. The BNDES financed the consolidation of large national business groups in sectors such as meat, mining, oil, and paper and pulp. But results were mixed.[95] Also, the government increasingly resorted to using tax resources to finance the bank's activities.[96] At the same time, the international market lost its previous dynamism with the gradual reduction in China's growth levels.

Brazil also lost competitiveness in industrial production due to the low productivity of labor in Brazilian industry. A study presented by the National Confederation of Industry showed that labor productivity in Brazilian industry grew on average only 0.6% per year between 2002 and 2012, compared to 6.7% in South Korea, 4.4% in the United States, 2.9% in Germany, and 1.3% in Australia.[97] This was due to the lack of capital investment during that period.

Although demand was stimulated by the new developmental policy, the multiplier effect of this demand was shifting abroad through increasing imports of manufactured goods, to the detriment of local production. In turn,

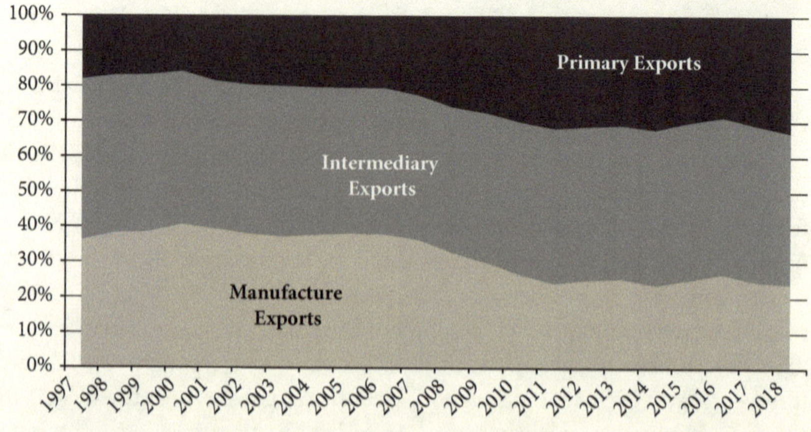

Figure 2.4. Exports of Primary, Intermediate, and Manufactured Goods, 1997–2018

SOURCE: Ipeadata.

manufactured goods saw a decline in their share of the country's exports, going from 36% in 1997 to less than 24% of exports in 2018. At the same time, the share of the manufacturing industry in GDP declined from 15% in 2000 to 11% in 2019.[98]

The fall of the Workers Party government in 2015 led to the abandonment of this aggressive development program, and the previous liberal program again become the norm in government industrial policy. But growth of industrial exports has continued to decline (see Figure 2.4). Industrial activity fell from 8.4% to 4.8% in 2015 and showed only a small amount of growth in the following two years.[99]

The economic evolution of Brazil from the 1980s helps explain the evolution of industry in São Paulo in this new phase of its development. Until the 1980s the industrialization process in Brazil depended on the direct government intervention. By the time the industrialization process was completed, in the late 1980s, Brazilian industry was one of the most vertically integrated and closed systems in the world. In this first phase, much of the development of Brazilian industry occurred within the boundaries of the state of São Paulo, which came to account for more than half of the value of national industrial output. Even after the military government implanted large industrial complexes outside the state, São Paulo still maintained its relative participation in national industry.

But in the last two decades the importance of the state's industry in the national economy has steadily declined. São Paulo, though remaining the leading industrial state of the nation, no longer dominates the industrial landscape as it did before 1990. Its own evolution now follows closely that of national industry as a whole, which in turn depends on world market conditions.

The fragmentation and globalization of industrial processing, the privatization of the main controlled industries, and the so-called fiscal war among Brazil's states to attract industry through tax subsidies have been powerful factors in the continued decentralization of national industry and the decline in the relative status of São Paulo industry.[100] The tax reform of 1967 created the State Tax on Circulation of Goods (ICM), which had the characteristics of a value-added tax (VAT).[101] Under the 1988 Constitution, the ICM was expanded to include services such as electricity, transport, and telecommunications, and the name of the tax itself was changed to ICMS (Tax on Circulation of Goods and Services). Rates for transactions within states vary but range from 17 to 19 percent.[102] When there are interstate transactions, the tax is paid at the source of the product, with differentiated rates depending on the destination. Products sent to the North, Northeast, and Center West regions and to the state of Espírito Santo pay 7% at the origin; for the other regions they pay 12%. The manipulation of this interstate taxation is what allows for the tax war. Let's assume that a car produced in São Paulo and sold in São Paulo will be taxed at 18%. A state that wants to attract a car plant can provide a fiscal stimulus that reduces this tax or offers other support. This is characterized as fiscal warfare.[103] There are numerous ways, not always totally legal, to make the manufacturer's cost lower by reducing the portion of the ICMS that would be charged at the product's origin. This is an important competitive advantage for directing new investments to states that offer this advantage. In general, the most industrialized states, such as São Paulo, suffer the effects of this fiscal war because they cannot offer such tax advantages. They cannot only grant such exemptions to new plants, because if they did, they would be creating a differential between "new" and "old" production units already existing in the state.[104] And it would be impracticable to grant it to all manufacturers of that product subject to the tax because of the impact it would have on the state tax collections. Although states have other sources of revenue, the ICMS is the most important.[105]

The state receiving the new plant is giving up some tax revenue, but it would not have received any tax revenue at all if there was no plant built, and thus the state has little to lose from a tax point of view by offering such subsidies. But there are other advantages as well. The new plant creates jobs, there are other taxes levied, and the subsidies to some companies can create externalities for other companies. Most automobile plants built in the last twenty years have received these tax benefits, which explains their distribution throughout Brazil.[106] Even within states there is strong competition between municipalities to attract new productive investments, but in this case the subsidies offered are smaller, usually limited to donating land and offering to pay infrastructure costs.[107] But there were also other factors that played a role in the dispersion of industry, such as the cost of land in densely urbanized areas, the difficulties of setting up large industrial plants in such areas, and the desire to escape the strong unions in the São Paulo metropolitan region.

The opening of the economy in the early 1990s was a mixed blessing for industry. There was healthy competition between local and international production. Some segments, particularly those controlled by multinationals, integrated Brazilian industry into their global value chains. Other companies closed, and some industrial segments reduced their participation in the domestic market, unable to withstand international competition. Also, the level of vertical integration of the domestic industry was reduced.

Initially the opening process seemed to increase productivity and competitiveness.[108] But it has been suggested that these initial productivity gains were achieved through what is called "labor-shedding" rather than investment and the expansion of employment. That means that the newly privatized manufacturing plants simply reduced the size of the previous public company's labor force, which led to productivity increases.[109] Another study has argued that changes in the industrial structure caused by the opening to world trade led to capital flows to resource-intensive industries. In this Brazil was not unique, as such flows also occurred in Argentina and Peru.[110] Furthermore, industrial competitiveness was undermined by currency appreciations, which made Brazilian products less competitive on world markets. Brazil was able to preserve a much broader and more complete industrial structure than most other nations of the continent, and this structure still include a fairly large sector of capital goods, machinery, and equipment.[111] But growth has slowed so significantly compared to other parts of the economy that the influence of industry has systematically declined decade after decade, as has its role in international exports.

The theme of deindustrialization, which some have suggested has been occurring in Brazil since 1990, has merited countless studies. In the rich countries there is clearly a downward trend in the importance of industry, which has been replaced by the systematic growth of services.[112] In general, in these countries there is a relationship between a certain level of income and the reduction of the relative participation of industry in GDP.

The causes are many, such as changes in income, changing composition of demand, the fragmentation of the production process, and the change in relative prices.[113]

In Brazil, the fall in the relative share of industry in GDP is evident. But this process has been interpreted in several different ways.[114] Was it a natural process, similar to what happened in rich countries? Or is Brazil, for internal reasons, a case in which industrialization occurred before adequate development standards were reached? One recent study has created a series of the real value added by the manufacturing sectors that covers the Brazilian GDP from 1970 to 2016. The peak of the degree of industrialization as measured by its importance in GDP would have occurred in 1973 and was maintained at this level until 1980, when manufacturing still accounted for approximately 20% of national GDP. By 1980 Brazil was manufacturing all the intermediate products and inputs that were produced in the mature industrialized countries, but did not produce them with the same efficiency because domestic industry was protected, technological development was weak and the export coefficient low. Thus, export performance by Brazilian manufacturing companies was relatively limited compared to the countries with mature industrialization (United States, Japan, and Germany).[115]

From 1981 until today, Brazil has regressed in its industrialization trajectory, and Brazilian manufacturing is no longer the engine of growth that it was before. There has been a relative stagnation in the evolution of the real manufacturing product and a significant relative decline in the importance of manufacturing. Since 1980, there has been a downward trend in the value added by manufacturing in GDP, which decreased from 19.5% to 11.3% by 2018 (see Figures 2.5a and 2.5b). This indicates either stagnation or a significant drop in manufacturing, depending on the sector.

Brazilian industry has declined at both constant and current prices and much further than industry in most other industrial nations, even excluding China.[116] The pace of decline has differed by industry. Clothing, leather, footwear, and the textile sector began to lose share in the early 1970s; machinery and equipment in the mid-1970s; metallurgy, metal products, and non-metallic minerals in the early 1980s; and chemistry and petrochemicals in the mid-1980s. However, a few manufacturing sectors, such as electronics, computers and electronic materials, and paper, pulp, and printing, seem to have held up well. Sectoral decline is also not homogeneous in its intensity; for example, clothing, leather, and footwear recorded a much more intense decline than non-metallic minerals.[117] And the food and beverage sector diverged from the expected pattern, only beginning to show a clear downward trend in the mid-2000s.

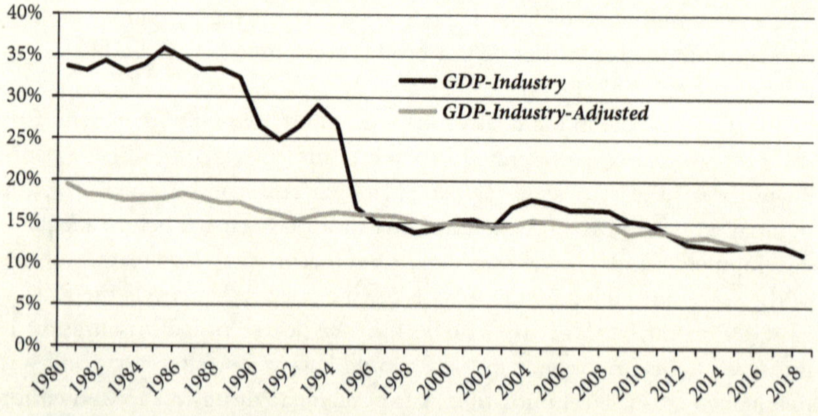

Figure 2.5a. Industry as Percentage of National GDP, 1980–2015, Original Series Adjusted by Morceiro

SOURCE: Morceiro (2018): 186; Ipeadata.

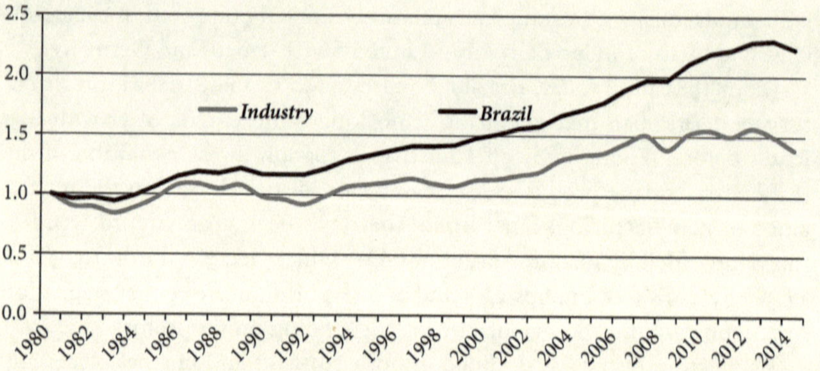

Figure 2.5b. Change in Brazilian GDP 1980–2015, Adjusted by Morceiro

SOURCE: Morceiro (2018): 186; Ipeadata.

Why have these industries declined so quickly? One factor is the lack of national innovation. Despite government efforts in science and technology programs, industrial innovation has been limited. A recent study indicates that from the late 1990s to the early 2000s, the country made progress in consolidating R&D institutions, in designing financing policies, and in adopting a broad incentive legislation for science, technology, and innovation.[118] These advances should have been reflected in the growth of some key indicators, such as numbers of global publications, development of research centers, and companies claiming innovations. But these indicators, such as innovation rates or patent filings, have not led to significant technological development.[119] Overall, Brazil spends little on research and development compared to mature countries and especially compared to countries that have promoted national industries and become major competitors in the world market for high-tech manufactures, such as Korea, China, and Israel. Although Brazil has increased its research investments to 1.6% of GDP, it still spends little compared to Korea, which spends 4.6% of its GDP on R&D; China, which spends 2.1%; Israel, which spends 3.2%; and the United States, which spends 2.8%. Moreover, most of the expenditure in this area in Brazil is done by the government. Less than half corresponds to investment by businesses, and even then a significant portion of "private" investment came from large state-owned companies, such as Petrobras and Eletrobrás.[120] Between 2002 and 2006, Brazil occupied seventeenth position in terms of technical and science publications, far behind the United States, Japan, and major EU countries such as Germany, England, France, Italy, and Spain. It was also behind several of the BRICS countries such as China, Russia, and India.[121]

Brazil ranks low globally in terms of ease of doing business in the country.[122] It is also low in productivity. Using output per worker in constant 2011 international dollars in PPP (purchasing power parity), Brazil's productivity increased by only 16% between 2000 and 2018, against 51% in the world, 356% in China, 172% in India, and 62% in Korea. Countries that already have high output per worker, such as the United States, Japan, and countries in the European Union, also showed higher rates of increase than Brazil, widening the labor productivity differential between these countries and Brazil.[123]

Industry in the state of São Paulo suffered in this period. São Paulo industry did see significant increases in the number of industrial workers, in the value of industrial production, and in industrial value added from 1996 to 2017. But its relative importance in national industry progressively declined in this same period as industry expanded more rapidly elsewhere in the country (see Table 2.13).

São Paulo industry has had some unique advantages compared to the rest of Brazil. It was the national leader in innovation in technology. A government survey on industrial innovation (PINTEC) sampled 117,000 companies, of which 42,000 indicated that they implemented some kind of innovation: 4,500 implemented an innovation in the domestic market, 493 implemented new products in the international market, and 302 implemented new processes in the world market. São Paulo led on all these

TABLE 2.13

Industrial Indicators for São Paulo and Brazil, 1996–2017 (Value in R$ 1000)

	BRAZIL				SÃO PAULO				SÃO PAULO AS % OF BRAZIL	
Years	Firms	Personnel Employed	Value of Production	Industrial Value Added	Firms	Personnel Employed	Value of Production	Industrial Value Added	Personnel Employed	Industrial Value Added
1996	120,217	4,939,816	331,973,199	155,053,516	46,699	2,105,589	163,618,601	78,927,752	43%	51%
1997	118,819	4,804,577	366,853,963	167,270,375	45,569	2,013,935	180,767,699	85,523,642	42%	51%
1998	125,537	4,702,114	371,169,134	167,061,829	46,561	1,915,348	183,761,019	85,414,993	41%	51%
1999	129,211	4,812,166	440,814,587	198,869,795	45,592	1,916,518	210,201,310	96,950,879	40%	49%
2000	136,219	5,121,301	542,555,521	240,319,531	47,919	1,999,905	252,316,620	113,487,330	39%	47%
2001	142,596	5,260,075	630,685,237	273,582,708	49,686	2,019,234	289,329,238	127,418,038	38%	47%
2002	146,246	5,366,324	724,893,897	313,847,803	50,682	2,017,247	321,073,887	141,816,509	38%	45%
2003	150,706	5,769,621	900,056,461	379,544,345	50,766	2,124,698	388,641,964	166,239,949	37%	44%
2004	157,022	6,182,585	1,080,902,806	444,369,405	52,869	2,274,846	456,807,995	191,630,567	37%	43%
2005	160,574	6,215,189	1,125,675,188	464,065,678	54,315	2,297,130	481,204,216	202,549,391	37%	44%
2006	168,422	6,527,106	1,202,240,081	505,869,100	54,762	2,375,912	510,767,909	216,595,482	36%	43%
2007	168,313	6,816,749	1,329,006,849	546,378,905	56,299	2,497,932	557,922,409	232,062,858	37%	42%
2008	177,979	7,142,147	1,553,032,318	645,366,982	58,800	2,639,426	636,966,825	266,690,773	37%	41%
2009	181,332	7,197,977	1,427,350,146	604,484,096	58,277	2,597,713	584,880,506	251,662,648	36%	42%
2010	185,299	7,722,295	1,680,745,068	726,670,935	57,031	2,777,277	680,539,654	296,310,558	36%	41%
2011	194,337	7,937,126	1,848,072,089	798,638,373	60,126	2,816,739	740,888,366	325,765,500	35%	41%
2012	188,033	8,002,244	1,984,081,396	840,399,533	58,656	2,846,426	776,842,697	335,681,186	36%	40%
2013	199,154	8,197,536	2,202,682,172	923,127,855	59,453	2,815,574	849,062,342	361,906,160	34%	39%
2014	204,441	8,059,082	2,296,588,544	947,513,047	62,013	2,736,408	860,525,327	359,357,410	34%	38%
2015	196,026	7,412,700	2,303,115,508	955,173,440	57,921	2,502,329	848,682,717	355,476,972	34%	37%
2016	189,986	7,059,501	2,330,548,591	968,617,748	57,883	2,396,747	854,481,038	363,454,213	34%	38%
2017	184,320	7,011,215	2,436,520,929	1,018,870,321	54,519	2,359,516	884,423,710	381,665,143	34%	37%

SOURCE: IBGE, SIDRA, Pia Empresas, https://sidra.ibge.gov.br/pesquisa/pia-empresa/tabelas.

indicators: the state's companies accounted for 48% of the amount spent, and for 44% of companies that launched new products in either the national or international markets or implemented new processes.[124]

The state of São Paulo was also a leader in the process of creating science and technology. The SCIE and SSCI citation databases show that of the top four Brazilian academic institutions, three are universities from São Paulo: Universidade de São Paulo (25.5%), Universidade Estadual de Campinas (10.1%) and Universidade Estadual Paulista (7.3%). Other institutions in the state are also among the most significant, such as the Federal University of São Paulo (4%) and the Federal University of São Carlos (3%). In other words, almost half of the university scientific production in Brazil was generated in the state of São Paulo, mostly from public institutions maintained by the state government of São Paulo.[125]

Nevertheless, from 1996 to 2107, there was a gradual but systematic decrease in the participation of São Paulo in the transformation value of Brazilian industry, which went from 51% to 37%. The reductions occurred in virtually all sectors, with greater or lesser technological intensity. Moreover, competition from the Manaus Free Zone, which assembled foreign-made electronic and communications products, had a significant negative influence on the national manufactures of these products. In the case of chemical manufacturing, there is less shrinkage; the state of São Paulo still accounts for more than half of national production. But there has been a drop in coke manufacturing, oil refining, nuclear fuels, and alcohol production.

While the relative importance of state industry has changed over time, there has not been a significant change in the structure of industry within the state. There has been some increase in the relative share of food products, which is the sector with the highest position in the 2017 industrial census, and only a slight downturn in the chemicals sector. There was a significant increase in the coke, oil refining, nuclear fuels, and alcohol sector, which increased from 6% to 10%, possibly due to the growth of ethanol production in the state. Despite decentralization, the automobile industry remains highly represented in the state of São Paulo. The segments with the highest technological intensity always maintained a share of over 50% in the São Paulo manufacturing industry (see Figure 2.6).

Within the state, the São Paulo Metropolitan Region remained important, and even added to a few more municipalities such as Guarulhos, Osasco, and Mogi das Cruzes which have recently developed industries. The second most important industrial nucleus within the state is now the Campinas Metropolitan Region, which includes the city, as well as some highly industrialized municipalities such as Paulínia (for oil refining),

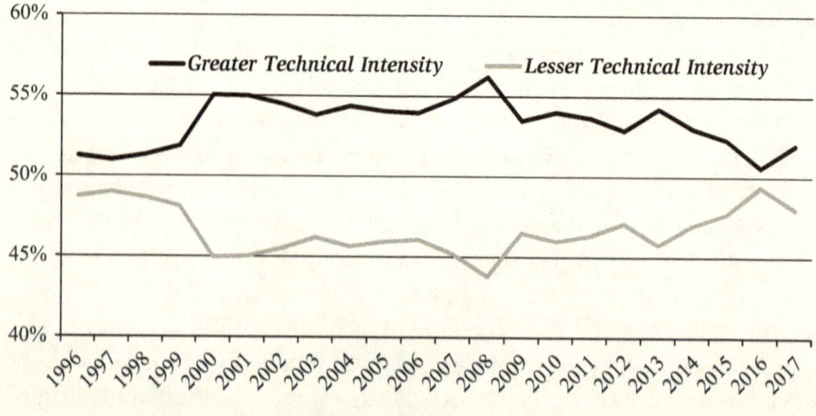

Figure 2.6. Sector Participation by Technological Intensity, State of São Paulo, 1996–2017

SOURCE: IBGE, SIDRA, 1848 (using definition of Morceiro [2018]).

Sumaré, and Indaiatuba (both for automobile plants). The extensive metropolitan region of the Paraíba Valley and the North Coast extends along the Via Dutra axis and includes major cities such as São José dos Campos (the location of Embraer headquarters and a General Motors factory), Taubaté (with a Volkswagen factory), and Jacareí. The Sorocaba Metropolitan Region has a varied industrial park, including one of Toyota's plants. While most of the state's industry was located in these larger groupings, there were several municipalities outside metropolitan regions that also had factories (see Table 2.14 and Map 2.1).

The one exception to the lack of innovation and international competence was the São Paulo aviation company known as Embraer. It became a major internationally competitive and highly productive manufacturer in one of the world's most fiercely competitive industries. Created by the Brazilian government in 1969, it was headquartered in the São Paulo municipality of São José dos Campos. This was the municipality that also housed a government-funded technical university, the Aeronautical Technology Institute (ITA), which was created in 1946 and run by the Brazilian Air Force. Among Embraer's founders were many ITA graduates. Embraer initially launched with the Bandeirantes plane, totally designed and built in Brazil. Gradually, the company expanded its product range in the agricultural, commercial, and executive aviation segments. In the 1980s, new aircraft were launched in the commercial and defense markets. In the commercial area it became a dominant world player in small regional jet aircraft.

TABLE 2.14
Industrial Value Added by Region in the State of São Paulo, 2016

	Total Added Value	Industrial Value Added	Services Value Added	Agriculture Value Added
Total for State of São Paulo (in current R$ 1000)	1,724,554,931	369,304,807	1,319,422,467	35,827,657
Metropolitan Regions and Urban Agglomerations		Ratio of State Total		
Metropolitan Region of Baixada Santista	3%	4%	3%	0%
Metropolitan Region of Campinas	9%	13%	7%	5%
Metropolitan Region of Ribeirão Preto	3%	3%	3%	8%
Metropolitan Region of São Paulo	53%	36%	59%	4%
Metropolitan Region of Sorocaba	4%	6%	3%	6%
Metropolitan Region of Vale do Paraíba e Litoral Norte	5%	8%	4%	1%
Aglomeração Urbana de Jundiaí	3%	4%	3%	1%
Aglomeração Urbana de Piracicaba	3%	4%	3%	3%

SOURCE: SEADE, http://www.imp.seade.gov.br/frontend/#/tabelas.

Following the launch of new commercial airplanes in the early 2000s, it created a family of business jets, one of which became the world's best-selling executive jet. In 2001 Embraer inaugurated a new production unit in Gavião Peixoto, also in the state of São Paulo.[126] The company was privatized in 1994 and was unquestionably the most successful company in the history of Brazilian industrialization. It was developed with national technology and was integrated into the main value chains of the international aviation sector. In addition to supplying the local market with a variety of civil and military aircraft, Embraer is a major contributor to the Brazilian export agenda.[127]

The huge auto industry, in contrast, tended to rely on design and advanced technology created outside of Brazil. Products from their Brazilian factories only entered the international market when it was convenient to do so because it fit the changing needs of multinational companies. Brazilian factories mostly exported parts or engines and less often entire automobiles. Moreover, most of these exports went to the regional market, especially the Mercosul countries, with products specifically destined for

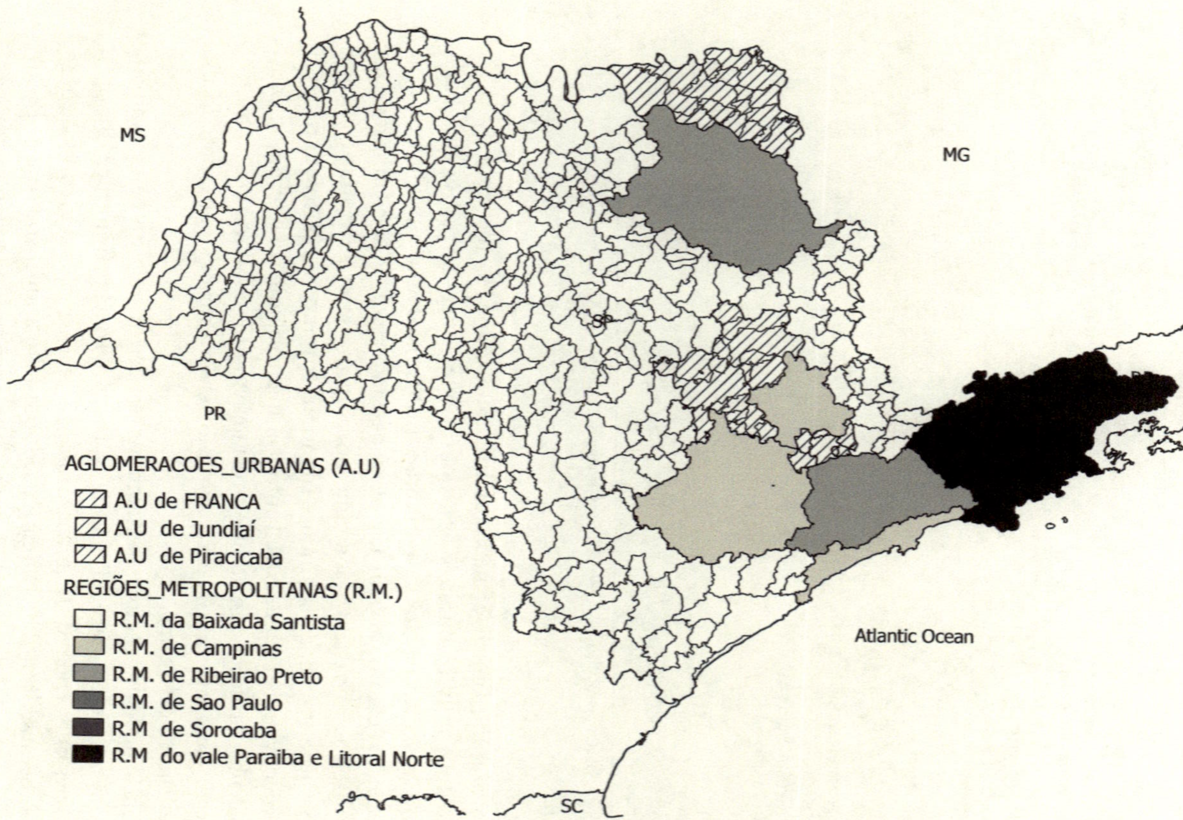

Map 2.1. Metropolitan Regions (RM) and Urban Clusters (AU), State of São Paulo

SOURCE: IBGE, Bases Cartográficas; IGC, Data Geo.

this area, as opposed to direct integration with the broader international market.

Thus Brazilian industry in the post-1990 period declined in many sectors after the opening up of the national market to foreign imports, after which most Brazilian manufacturers could not compete in the international market. At the same time there was a very significant decentralization of industry both nationally and within the state of São Paulo, which reduced the importance of both the capital and the RMSP. New industries were established in the interior of the state, and many smaller cities became important manufacturing centers. There was only one manufacturing sector in São Paulo and in Brazil as a whole that experienced high rates of productivity and could compete in the international market, and that was the state's airplane industry. But even traditional clothing and food industries saw a relative decline, as did most capital goods production as well.

If the liberal reforms enacted in the 1990s did not aid the development of the industrial sector, they did have one positive effect on another major area of the state economy: agriculture. Agriculture in São Paulo also suffered in the crisis years of the 1980s and was subjected to severe problems with the opening of Brazil to the world market in the 1990s. But unlike industry, it would thrive to such an extent in the post-1990 period that it would transform Brazil into one of the most important agricultural exporters in the world today, comparable in all respects to such giants as the United States, the European Market, Australia, and Canada.

Chapter 3

São Paulo Agriculture

Given the evolution of industry in the period since 1950, one would expect a similar history of rise and relative decline in agriculture. Yet this is not what happened, and the history of agriculture in the state of São Paulo provides an excellent guide to the changes that occurred in Brazilian agriculture more generally. To the surprise of many, it was not industry that aggressively entered the world market as a major competitor after 1990, but rather Brazilian agriculture, the supposed handmaiden of the industrial sector, that would become a world-class competitor. It was Brazilian agriculture that most benefited from the rise of China in the late twentieth century, with Brazil becoming one of China's main suppliers, along with dominating agricultural exports to the petroleum states of the Middle East. By the end of the second decade of the twenty-first century, Brazil had become one of the leading agricultural producers and exporters in the world.

Why this surprising result occurred had a great deal to do with the major investments that the state made in agriculture in the period from the 1960s to the early 1990s. Massive credit, significant mechanization, and crucial research intro tropical agriculture had all been supported by the government. Frontier lands were settled and essential paved highways constructed. New crops were being cultivated and the Cerrado region was opened to agricultural exploitation. With all the government support, agriculture could still be profitable despite the high cost of protected inputs, which had to be purchased domestically. But when the national market was opened to world competition, commercial agriculture was already highly developed and was quickly reaching crop yields comparable to those in the leading world exporters. While government support declined significantly after the late 1980s, private capital became relatively abundant, the costs of machinery and other imported inputs dropped dramatically, and there was a worldwide commodity boom as China entered the world market in a major way and its demands generated high prices for basic agricultural products. Thus despite all the infrastructural problems related to transport, Brazilian agriculture was able to respond to rising international prices and exploit already existing value chains in international markets to rapidly fulfill rising world demand for pastoral and agricultural products. Once established as a major producer, it would be able to seek markets worldwide in almost all the products that formerly had been sold into the national market and yet still was able to effectively and abundantly supply that national market with all its basic needs at ever lower prices.

In all of this development, São Paulo was a leading state in agricultural production and modernization, just as it had been in industrial growth. Until the end of the second decade of the twenty-first century São Paulo remained the preeminent agricultural state of Brazil. It was here that the coffee economy came to full development, and it was coffee that dominated Brazilian exports until late in the twentieth century. Although coffee growing has declined in the state in the past half century, São Paulo still dominates the production of this permanent crop, as well as oranges, and has expanded into such seasonal crops as sugarcane, corn, and soybeans as well. It has become the world's largest sugarcane producer and the leading maker of refined sugar and ethanol, with the creation of the most modern refining industry in the world. It was in the post-1950 period that the state became the world's largest producer and exporter of orange juice as well as one of the primary states in the production and export of broiler chickens (chickens raised for meat production), while also maintaining a significant cattle industry.

Yet despite the continued importance of its agriculture, São Paulo has one of the lowest percentages of rural population in the nation due to the extraordinary efficiency of its highly mechanized agricultural production. As early as 1960 only 37% of the state's population was rural, well below the 53% national average in that year. This population has consistently declined in both absolute and relative terms from 1960 onward and has currently reached one of the lowest rates in Brazil. By the census of 2010 only 4% of the state's population was rural, compared to the national average of 16%. Not only has the total rural population declined, but it has become more

TABLE 3.1

São Paulo: Size and Share of Rural Population and Sex Ratio of Population by Residence, 1970–2010

Census Year	Rural Population	% Total Population	Urban	Rural
1960	4,779,429	37%	97.0	111.2
1970	3,493,173	20%	98.3	112.9
1980	2,845,178	11%	98.5	112.5
1991	2,274,064	7%	96.7	112.1
2000	2,449,434	7%	95.1	109.8
2010	1,675,429	4%	93.9	119.0

SOURCE: IBGE, SIDRA, table 200; for 1960, IBGE, Censo Demográfico 1960, Série Regional, volume 1, tomo XIII, table 2.

dominated by males. In both the state and the nation as a whole, men persistently outnumbered women in the rural area, and women are more numerous than men in the urban centers of the state in all census years (see Table 3.1). This reflects the attraction of the urban labor market for women, with its abundance of opportunities for unskilled labor and domestic service.

São Paulo also had the highest literacy rate of any state in 1950.[1] Of course, the urban literacy rate was much higher than the rural one, but even this slowly changed over time, and by the census of 1991, 77% of the rural population five years of age and older were literate, whereas for the country as a whole the rural literacy rate was only 54%.[2] By the agricultural census of 2017, only 3% of the state's farm owners or managers were illiterate (compared to a national average of 23% of such persons). This high literacy rate and the rather technical nature of sugar farming may explain the unusually high rates of farm owners and managers of the state who had a technical education. A surprising 23% of the 184,798 farm owners or managers in the state had a higher level of education (technical secondary, university, or technical college), compared to 7% of farm owners and managers nationwide.[3] The larger the farm size in hectares, the higher the percentage of well-educated owners and managers. Thus over half of those who ran farms of 100 hectares or above in São Paulo held these advanced degrees. Even some 20% of the owners and managers of small farms (from 0.5 to 20 hectares) were highly educated as well, while the proportion went above a third for farms between 20 and 100 hectares.[4]

Until recently São Paulo was the leader nationally in terms of the total value of agricultural production, as it was in the total value of all Brazilian exports. But there have been profound changes in the recent agricultural development of the state. Coffee is no longer dominant in the mix of the state's agricultural production, and its traditional leadership in national coffee production has eroded as the coffee frontier has moved well beyond the state borders. Coffee was being replaced in importance by a host of other products before the end of the twentieth century, but above all by sugarcane. In the past forty years São Paulo has emerged as a world leader in the production of sugarcane, the milling of sugar, and the production of sugar-based ethanol. It is in this period that it also became the world's leading exporter of orange juice, and in several other products it is Brazil's premier producer. Despite the shocks caused by the loss of price supports, reductions in government-subsidized credit, and the end of protected markets in the 1980s and 1990s, São Paulo agriculture has been able to recuperate and grow quite impressively after 2000.[5] The shocks did affect local agriculture, which declined in the late 1980s to the point where it accounted for only 3.5% of the state's GDP, but already by 2002 that figure was back up to 7.8%.[6]

It was in the 1970s and early 1980s that São Paulo revamped and modernized its sugar milling industry and brought it up to world standards.[7] Ethanol became a major byproduct of sugarcane milling with the major support of the government, and Brazil became a world leader in production and consumption of this biofuel. Because of massive private and state investment, São Paulo has retained its dominant position as a producer of sugarcane, even though cane is produced in all states. As of the harvest of 2019/2020, the state alone accounted for 53% of all Brazilian production. São Paulo's dominant position is evident in the fact that the state of Goiás, the second-most-important grower of cane, produced only 78 million tons, compared to the 341 million tons produced by São Paulo.[8] The state is also the premier producer of both sugar and ethanol, and this activity has continued to grow in the twenty-first century. Most of the major mills are in São Paulo, and by the harvest of 2015/2106 São Paulo was grinding about two-thirds of the sugar produced nationally; it has remained at that level for the past five harvests.[9] It is also estimated that its fifteen largest *usinas* (sugar mills) accounted for 35% of national ethanol production in 2010.[10]

In most years sugar and sugar-derived ethanol are the state's most valuable exports. In the year 2016, for example, they were São Paulo's leading export products, followed by airplanes. In that year São Paulo exported US $5.1 billion worth of sugar, and if derivatives of sugarcane are added, the figure was US $7.5 billion, or 17% of total state exports.[11] Overall, the value of agricultural exports represented 35% of the state's total exports from 2010 to 2019.[12] At that point the total value of sugarcane product exports was close to the value of soybean exports from Mato Grosso. But

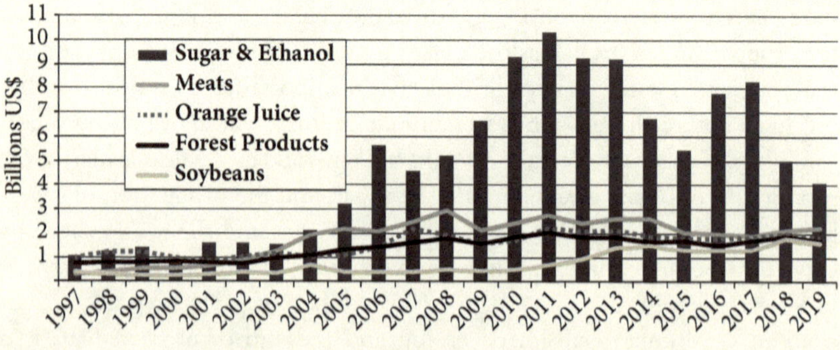

Figure 3.1. Principal Agricultural Exports of the State of São Paulo, 1997–2019

SOURCE: MAPA, http://indicadores.agricultura.gov.br/agrostat/index.htm, accessed February 9, 2020.

the sugar complex of São Paulo peaked in 2012–2013 and has since declined in the last few years. At the same time the soybeans, soybean cake, and soybean oil produced by Mato Grosso have dramatically increased in volume and value (see Figure 3.1). Thus by 2018 Mato Grosso's agricultural exports were almost equal to those of São Paulo, and in 2019 that state surpassed São Paulo in the value of its agricultural exports for the first time (see Table 3.2)

Although the state of São Paulo had once been a major center of producer cooperatives, there was a decline of these associations in the crisis years of the 1990s. The 136 agricultural cooperatives operating in the state in 1992 had 164,000 farmer members and were present in 242 municipalities, but the collapse of two key central associations (Cotia-CC and CC-Sul-Brasil) in the period of market liberalization led to a major reorganization and reduction of the system to 127 co-ops and half the numbers of members. These surviving co-ops are now more economically secure, and some, like those in milk, have become major industrial producers as well.[13] Though such milk co-ops were important in both São Paulo and Rio Grande do Sul, they are nowhere as dominant in milk production as they are in the United States, where 83% of the milk produced is from cooperatives, compared to between 20% and 40% in Brazil.[14] As of the 2006 agricultural census, the state's farmers were about average nationally in terms of their membership in such cooperatives or producer syndicates, with some 29% of the farms and 48% of the farmland included in such

TABLE 3.2

Value of Principal Agricultural Products Exported from São Paulo and Mato Grosso, 2019

SÃO PAULO			MATO GROSSO		
Products	Value in US$	% of Total Value	Products	Value in US$	% of Total Value
Sugar, Alcohol, Ethanol, etc.	4,068,752,409	26.9%	Soybeans & Derivatives	8,998,329,271	54.0%
Beef	1,912,622,673	12.6%	Corn	4,115,243,906	24.7%
Oranges & Orange Juices	1,781,234,890	11.8%	Cotton	1,598,596,043	9.6%
Soybeans & Derivatives	1,610,764,668	10.6%	Beef	1,447,530,868	8.7%
Paper & Cellulose	1,516,280,309	10.0%	Wood	142,073,021	0.9%
Coffee (Green & Roasted)	395,981,063	2.6%	Chicken Meat	93,403,104	0.9%
Chicken Meat	290,931,795	1.9%	Other Root Crops	71,279,735	0.6%
Other	3,555,430,533		Other	203,824,011	
Total Value of All Agricultural Exports	15,131,998,340	76.5%	Total Value of All Exports	16,670,279,959	99.2%

Source: MAPA, Agricultural Exports by Product and UF, http://indicadores.agricultura.gov.br/agrostat/index.htm, accessed February 9, 2020.

institutions. This was well below the association rates in Rio Grande do Sul, which had 68% of its farms and 72% of its farmland in co-ops and syndicates. But it was above Mato Grosso, which had a higher percentage of farms in such associations than São Paulo, but those farms only accounted for 30% of the farmland.[15] By the agricultural census of 2017, however, the state cooperatives and producer associations had increased significantly. Although co-ops now included only 24% of all farmers, another 52% of farmers were in new-style syndicates or producer associations. Moreover, the smaller the size of the holding, the higher the participation rate. Thus 87% of São Paulo farmers holding less than 5 hectares were in co-ops and associations.[16]

In the last quarter of the twentieth century large sugar estates came to dominate state agriculture, replacing in importance the formerly dominant large coffee fazendas.[17] Thus despite a continuing expansion of agriculture, the basic structure of land ownership in the rural area has changed little since the 1960s, when coffee was still a significant state crop. In the period 1960 to 2017 there was a decline in both the number of farms (a decline of 41%) and in total lands (a decline of 14%) There were also changes in the share of the smallest and largest properties. Farms of less than 100 hectares declined from owning 28% of the agricultural lands to 20% of all rural lands, and farms of over 1,000 hectares increased their share from 31% to 45% of all lands in the period from 1960 to 2017, which explains the major increase in the Gini index of inequality (see Table 3.3). Overall, however, the structure of landholding in the state looks rather more like the southern state of Rio Grande do Sul than the Center-West state of Mato Grosso.

There were also continuing changes in the crop and animal mix in the state's agriculture production since the 1980s. By the second decade of the twenty-first century the major agricultural products of the state in terms of value were animals, animal products, soybeans, oranges and orange juice, corn, and sugar. At the same time there had been a major decline of coffee production (see Table 3.4). Already by 1990 Minas Gerais had passed São Paulo as the nation's biggest coffee producer, accounting for a third of the crop in that year, compared to just a quarter coming from São Paulo. By the second decade of the twenty-first century São Paulo was down to 10% of the national crop and Minas Gerais alone now accounted for over half of national production. Whereas São Paulo planted over 500,000 hectares in coffee trees in 1990, twenty-five years later its coffee trees were planted on just 200,000 hectares.[18]

In contrast, there was massive growth in the production of chickens and eggs, which grew steadily at 3.2% per annum from 1974 to 2018. Another

TABLE 3.3
Distribution of Farms by Size of Land Holding, São Paulo, 1960, 2006, and 2017

1960			2006			2017	
Size	Units	Area (ha)	Size	Units	Area (ha)	Units	Area (ha)
0.1–1 ha	3,159	2,147	0.1–1 ha	11,981	4,205	8,690	3,056
1–5 ha	82,842	299,772	1–5 ha	40,782	126,919	34,316	107,156
5–10 ha	59,759	461,376	5–10 ha	31,562	242,783	27,511	210,417
10–20 ha	53,332	775,224	10–20 ha	46,547	689,651	41,037	602,690
20–50 ha	59,900	1,925,596	20–50 ha	46,332	1,473,605	36,186	1,144,754
50–100 ha	25,789	1,854,565	50–100 ha	20,688	1,467,925	16,374	1,162,843
100–200 ha	15,595	2,191,622	100–200 ha	13,036	1,834,340	10,849	1,522,201
200–500 ha	10,985	3,397,470	200–500 ha	9,583	2,965,789	8,044	2,477,639
500–1000 ha	3,547	2,500,335	500–1000 ha	2,846	1,975,819	2,674	1,868,908
1000–2000 ha	1,584	2,164,387	1000–2500 ha	1,470	2,235,513	1,342	2,027,440
2000+ ha	902	3,731,454	2500+	623	3,938,399	825	5,385,043
Total	**317,394**	**19,303,948**	**Total**	**225,450**	**16,954,948**	**187,848**	**16,512,147**
Gini Index (1)	0.787		Gini Index	0.799		0.826	

SOURCE: Censo Agricola 1960, Série Regional, volume 2, tomo XIV, parte 1, table 1; IBGE, SIDRA, table 837 (2006); IBGE, SIDRA, table 6882 (2017).

NOTE: (1) The 1960 census uses a different maximum number for the largest farms from that used in both 2006 and 2017, but this has no significant effect on the Gini index.

crop that has grown exponentially is bananas, which went from the mid-30,000 tons to an average of over 1 million tons in the same period, with an extraordinary average annual growth of 8%. The state's production of both soybeans and the associated crop of corn has also grown steadily since the 1970s, although not experiencing as dramatic a growth as in the leading states of Mato Grosso and Rio Grande do Sul. Finally, oranges have replaced coffee as the most important of the permanent crops (see Table 3.4).

Although oranges have been grown in São Paulo since colonial times, it is only recently that the state has become a world leader in orange juice production. Oranges until 1950 were locally consumed as whole fresh fruit. Fresh oranges were first exported to Argentina after 1920 and to Europe after 1930, though most of the crop was consumed domestically.[19] Until 1957 Rio de Janeiro was the leading producer in the nation, but in that year São Paulo passed it in total production and has increased its share every decade thereafter.[20] By 1972 São Paulo was growing over half the country's oranges, and by 1983 this share rose to 80%.

In 1962 São Paulo began to process whole oranges into juice, producing 203,000 tons of concentrated orange juice. In that year the first modern orange juice processor, the Companhia Mineira de Conservas, was established in the São Paulo municipality of Bebedouro.[21] This company eventually became part of Frutesp, a government company, and was later bought out by

TABLE 3.4

Growth in Volume of Major Agricultural Products, State of São Paulo, 1974–2018

Product	1974	1984	1994	2004	2014	2018	Annual Growth Rate
Sugarcane (metric tons)	39,472,166	117,209,246	174,100,000	239,527,890	401,332,100	433,059,785	5.6%
Chickens (birds)	61,592,315	94,847,599	105,120,154	157,401,748	209,483,328	204,183,349	2.8%
Oranges (metric tons)	19,250,000	52,518,026	69,025,000	14,717,790	12,290,567	12,889,878	-0.9%
Cattle (head)	10,192,202	11,487,510	12,973,841	13,765,873	10,148,423	10,771,635	0.1%
Corn (metric tons)	2,628,000	2,866,742	3,199,200	4,647,240	3,983,895	4,488,539	1.2%
Soybeans (metric tons)	522,000	870,703	1,230,900	1,854,230	1,709,229	3,410,297	4.4%
Cows' Milk (1000 liters)	1,241,478	1,816,721	2,005,189	1,739,397	1,736,144	1,640,054	0.6%
Bananas (metric tons)	35,400	46,900	54,550	1,060,520	1,056,387	1,061,410	8.0%
Eggs (1000 dozens)	281,935	574,869	685,710	805,033	962,485	1,137,630	3.2%
Coffee (metric tons)	1,160,000	930,600	409,200	258,370	289,257	342,760	-2.7%

SOURCE: For permanent and seasonal crops: IBGE, SIDRA, tables 1612 and 1613. For animals and animal products: IBGE, SIDRA, tables 74 and 3939.

Dreyfus. A year later a German company in alliance with a local German immigrant grower set up Citrosuco, which would become both the nation's and the world's largest producer of all kinds of orange juice by the end of the century. In 1967 Brazilians established Sucocítrico Cutrale, which would become Brazil's second-largest producer. The periodic freezes in Florida, especially those in the late 1970s and early 1980s, reduced US output of juice significantly and gave Brazil an opportunity to become a major international market participant. Having achieved this foothold, Brazil quickly outpaced US production. By 1975 Brazil controlled over half the world exports of orange juice, compared to the US share of only 17%, and even in total production of oranges it surpassed the United States as of the 1981/1982 harvest.[22]

The orange processors are distinct from the orchard owners. This value chain's vertical organization involves the processing companies providing credit to the farmers, the shipping of juices in special tanker trucks and specially equipped oceangoing vessels, and the management of international sales and marketing.[23] Growers are responsible for the production and delivery of the fruit to juice factories or packing houses, though they are given advance payments on their contracts by factories and packers.[24] Although considered to be highly efficient, this processing industry is highly concentrated. By the late 1980s there were over a thousand juice processers operating in the state, but only four companies accounted for three quarters of juice production: Citrosuco Paulista (with 28% of production in 1987), Sucocítrico Cutrale (with 25% of orange juice), Cargill Agrícola S.A. (15%), and the producer co-op Coopercitrus Industrial Frutesp (7%). Even though there are currently 1,061 juice processing plants in São Paulo, these four firms control 94% of them.[25] Recently this concentration increased, as several of these firms have become multinationals. In 2012 Citrosuco bought out Citrovita, leaving just three large processors of juice, with Citrosuco now accounting for 40% of all juice exports.[26] In turn, in the 1990s these major companies entered the US market by purchasing processing plants in Florida in order to get around US customs barriers. Cutrale bought Florida processing plants and became the primary supplier for the Minute Maid brand of Coca-Cola; Citrosuco, with its purchase of major Florida plants, became the chief supplier of the Tropicana brand of Pepsi-Cola.[27]

These multinational companies with their international connections and highly capitalized plants and pipelines are in sharp contrast to the Paulista sugar millers, who are also typically the growers of the cane they mill. The high level of industrial concentration and distinct separation between orange growers and juice processors has created a long-term tension between these two groups. This tension has led to considerable legal conflict, state

TABLE 3.5
Distribution of Orange Producers in São Paulo by Number of Trees, 2009

Trees (1000s)	Growers	% Growers	% Trees
< 10	9,603	76.1%	13.4%
10–19	1,408	11.2%	8.0%
20–29	518	4.1%	5.3%
30–49	442	3.5%	7.0%
50–99	372	2.9%	10.8%
100–199	164	1.3%	9.0%
200–399	69	0.5%	7.4%
400+	51	0.4%	39.3%
Total	**12,627**	100.0%	100.0%

SOURCE: Adapted from Neves and Trombin (2012), 63, table 14.

action, and local organization as growers try to balance their asymmetric relations with processors.[28]

In the crop year 2009/2010 the state had some 180.6 million orange trees, of which 9% were non-producing newly planted ones (up to two years of age), with production averaging around two boxes per tree.[29] Of the 12,627 farmers producing oranges, 76% of them had orange groves with fewer than 10,000 trees, but this group of smaller farmers accounted for only 13% of the total number of trees. The fifty-one giant orchard owners, those with over 400,000 trees, were less than 1% of the farmers, but they had 39% of the trees (see Table 3.5).[30] This meant that despite the large ratio of small farmers, the distribution resulted in a Gini index of inequality of .77, which was close to the norm for most crops farmed in São Paulo.

It is estimated that orange trees can produce fruit over a twenty-year period, but that productive period is a bit higher in São Paulo than internationally. Since 2000, however, there has been a shift in regions of production as producers have migrated to the southern portions of the state. This migration was due to both push and pull factors—the increasing cost of land due to expansion of sugar cultivation in the older zones, better climatic condition in the new areas, and also the search for growing areas free from greening disease, which had killed a significant number of trees. Three other tree diseases—citrus canker, citrus variegated chlorosis, and citrus sudden death—destroyed some 39 million trees in the traditional areas in the first decade of the twenty-first century. This was just another in a series of major plagues that have affected orange production.[31] Exports stopped after a plague in 1937, and another one struck in 1957 and destroyed 300 million trees.[32] These plagues explain the fact that orange producers are the second- largest users of insecticides in Brazil after cotton growers, but they were only twelfth in fertilizer usage.[33]

By 1990 São Paulo still accounted for 83% of the oranges grown in Brazil, which resulted in an output of 72 million tons of fruit gathered from 723,000 hectares of groves. Although production dropped to 12 million tons on just 413,000 hectares in the next quarter of a century, São Paulo was still the primary producing state and accounted for almost three-quarters of national production.[34] Recently production has increased and the current estimate for the Brazilian harvest year of 2020/2021 is for a production of 15.9 million tons of oranges.[35] Brazil is the world's largest producer of oranges (accounting for 33% of world production) and the world's biggest exporter of orange juice (accounting for 74% of world's exports in 2020/2021).[36] In turn, São Paulo producers accounted for 75% of oranges produced and 91% of all types, both frozen (FCOJ) and non-frozen concentrate (NFC), of the nation's orange juice exports in the harvest of 2020/2021.[37] The leading orange-producing mesoregion in 2015 was Bauru, which produced a fifth of the state's oranges. Other producing regions included Campinas, São José do Rio Preto, Ribeirão Preto, Itapetininga, and Araraquara, which together with Bauru accounted for 88% of production. This distribution can be seen in more detail when the data are broken down by municipality (see Map 3.1).

Bananas were the third-most-important permanent crop produced in the state. São Paulo by 2015 was the second-largest producer of bananas in Brazil and accounted for 15% of national production, with a production close to that of the leading state, which was Bahia. Moreover, the productivity of banana cultivation in São Paulo was greater than it was in Bahia. Whereas Bahia and São Paulo were both producing 1.1 tons of bananas per hectare in 1990, by 2015, São Paulo was getting 20.1 tons per hectare from its banana trees, while Bahia had only increased its yield to 14.1 tons per hectare.[38]

This high productivity in bananas reflected a phenomenon seen in the production of all the state's agricultural crops and animals. With no more room for agricultural expansion in the former frontier northern and western parts of the state by the middle decades of the twentieth century, Paulista agriculture could no longer rely on virgin lands to maintain high productivity. Thus all crops and livestock products underwent a major modernization in terms of mechanization, usage of fertilizers and insecticides, and the adoption of the latest tillage and harvesting practices. Whereas the state was not particularly distinguished in machine usage either in the first state agricultural census of 1905 or in the national agricultural census of 1960,[39]

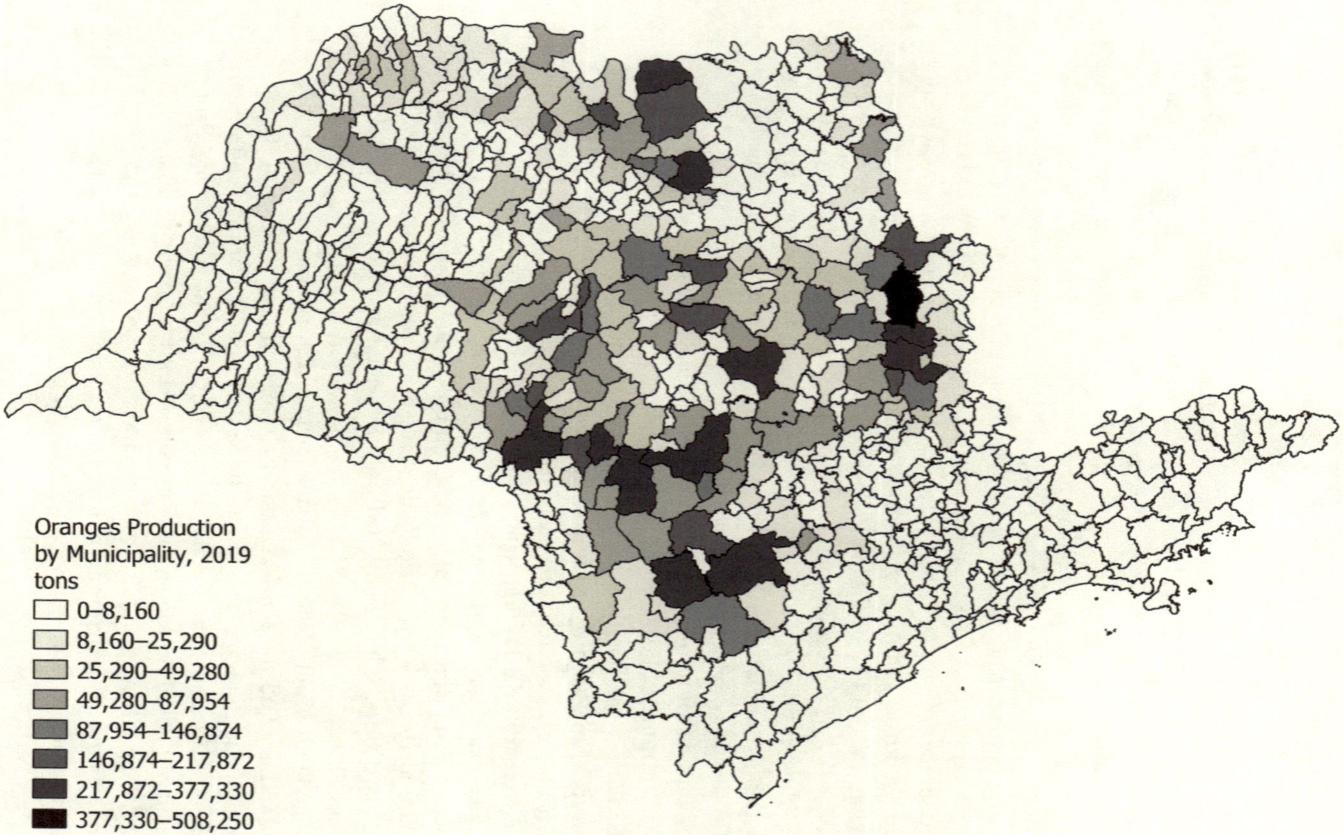

Map 3.1. Orange Production in São Paulo by Municipality, 2019

SOURCE: IBGE, Bases Cartográficas; IBGE, SIDRA, table 1613.

by 2017 it was among the most advanced, along with the southern states of Rio Grande do Sul, Paraná, and Santa Catarina, in the use of machines, fertilizers, and insecticides.[40]

Despite their traditional importance in the state, these permanent crops were absorbing an ever declining amount of land. While São Paulo still had a significant amount of land in permanent crops compared to Rio Grande do Sul and Mato Grosso, their total volume of land usage was in decline after the 1970 peak of 1.7 million hectares in these crops, going to less than half that amount (just 797,000 hectares) in 2018. Across the nation, permanent crops had declined from 7.9 million hectares to 5.8 million in the same period. The big growth in the state, as in the rest of the nation, was in the expansion of seasonally planted (temporary) crops, which in São Paulo went from using 3.6 million hectares in 1970 to using 7.9 million hectares in 2018.[41] At the same time the size of these Paulista farms differed significantly, with the 18,000 farms that planted seasonal crops averaging 59 hectares, and the 17,000 farms with permanent crops averaging just 23 hectares (see Figure 3.2).[42]

All this change in agricultural land usage by type of crop was due to the extraordinary expansion of sugarcane, which currently is the dominant product of the state in terms of value and land usage and the leasing of seasonal croplands. But this was not the case historically. Throughout the last half of the nineteenth century and most of the twentieth, the state imported the majority of its refined sugar from Pernambuco. The state did produce sugarcane, but in the 1920s plagues almost wiped out local

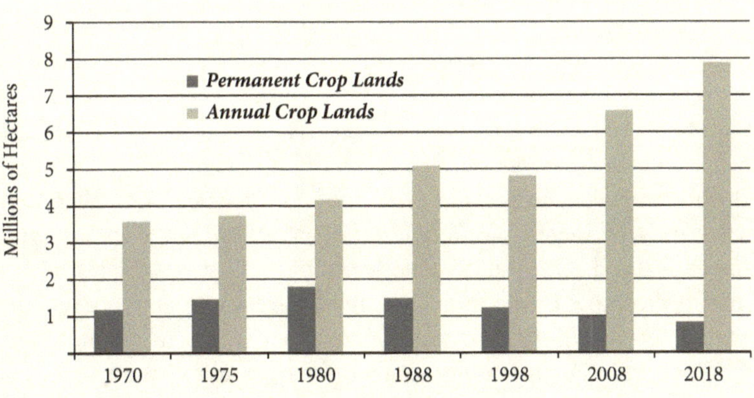

Figure 3.2. Growth of Lands Dedicated to Permanent and Temporary Crops, São Paulo, 1970–2016

SOURCE: IBGE, SIDRA, table 264; for 1988–2018, tables 1612, 1613.

plantings, and only the importation of new plague-resistant plants from Java (Indonesia) revived the industry by the end of the decade.[43] Next, the crisis in sea transport that occurred as a result of World War II led to the relative decline of Pernambuco, and São Paulo became more self-sufficient in sugar.[44] Then in the 1950s São Paulo finally exceeded Pernambuco's sugar production. Production costs were lower in São Paulo compared to Pernambuco, and the state even began exporting into the international market. This foreign market became far more open with the embargo carried out against Cuba by the United States in 1960. Brazil was given most of Cuba's quota for sugar to be imported into the United States in 1962, initially 100,000 metric tons; in 1967 this was increased to 360,000 metric tons. In turn, when Cuba created a new protected market in the socialist countries for cane sugar, those countries' local beet sugar industries declined and their sugar consumption increased. Then when Cuban harvests failed, these markets were opened up to Brazilian exports. This boom primarily affected the sugar producers of São Paulo, rather than the older and relatively inefficient Northeastern plantations. By 1976, sugar had become the single most valuable crop in São Paulo.

In this boom period the size of sugar farms grew. In 1964 small producers accounted for 60% of cane brought to the mills, but by 1970 these small farmers accounted for only 40% of the sugarcane grown. All of this growth put pressure on government control. The old Sugar and Alcohol Institute (Instituto do Açucar e do Alcool, IAA) founded by Vargas in 1933 in defense of small and medium producers had a quota system that required the mills to purchase 60% of their sugarcane from independent farmers. In the 1970s this quota system was temporarily abandoned, and under pressure from the new millers associations, the government finally abandoned the quota system altogether, which resulted in the mills progressively becoming producers as well. These mills were Brazilian-owned, often by immigrant entrepreneurs, many of whom had gotten their start in coffee.[45]

Brazilian millers and growers responded to this opening of the international market by increasing production of sugar through a whole series of technological and administrative reorganizations. First was the introduction of turbines to most of the mills, which by the harvest of 1960/1961 were averaging 100,000 to 200,000 sacks of sugar per harvest per mill. Six years later, there were an increasing number of larger units among the ninety or so mills in production at that time, and these larger processors were generating on average 200,000 to 300,000 sacks of sugar per harvest; there were even a few mills in this period that could produce over 1 million sacks per harvest.[46] A major event at this time was the founding in 1959 of the producers cooperative Copersucar (Cooperativa de Produtores de Cana-de-Açúcar, Açúcar e Álcool do Estado de São Paulo) through the amalgamation of two local sugar cooperatives.[47] Copersucar began by marketing the sugar and alcohol produced by its members. By the end of the decade, Copersucar represented 86% of the São Paulo millers and marketed over 90% of the state's sugar and alcohol production. It quickly evolved into a conglomerate, active in all aspects of the production process, from providing credit to owning distilleries.[48] It also created a research branch to promote technological change. It was Copersucar that is credited with increasing the productivity of the sugar mills by adopting the latest technology from other producing countries in a modernization program that began in 1973.[49] The initial increase in yields was due to this modernization of the mills, and only later did yield increases come from new methods of planting and harvesting sugarcane.

Finally, in 1976 the numerous local planters associations created a powerful growers association, Orplana (Organização dos Produtores de Cana do Estado de São Paulo), which created another pressure group seeking changes in the traditional policies of the IAA concerning both production and milling of sugar and alcohol. One result of all this pressure and the sugar boom of the 1970s was that the IAA provided major government credit for the modernization and consolidation of the milling industry. This, combined with the technical changes promoted by Copersucar, succeeded in creating an efficient and productive system to replace the previous archaic organization. Many mills were closed, by the end of the 1970s the smallest mills (those producing less than 18,000 metric tons of sugar) were down to just 9% of all mills in all the country, and by the end of the decade the output of the remaining mills had doubled.[50]

Expansion was so rapid that the international market could not absorb all the sugar being exported from Brazil, and prices dropped significantly. This overproduction problem, a classic one for Brazil, led to a call for government support and intervention in the industry. Fortunately for the producers of the state, the world oil shock of 1973 occurred, which led the government to establish the Proálcool program in 1975, the purpose of which was to promote sugar-derived ethanol as an alternative to gasoline. It did this by subsidizing increased plantings of sugarcane, encouraging the construction of ethanol distilleries at the *usinas*, and forcing Petrobras, the government oil monopoly, to mix increasing quantities of ethanol into imported gasoline. Until this time alcohol production had been a distant second to sugar in the output of the mills, but slowly this changed as demand for ethanol increased. The biggest impact of this program for producers was to create a whole new market for sugarcane.[51]

Although ethanol had been used in gasoline in Brazil since the 1930s and was important during World War II, this new program went even further and sought both to encourage private investment in distilling and to create a guaranteed market for this biofuel. It first required Petrobras to mix gasoline with ethanol at a rate of just under 20% of total fuel so that engines did not need to be modified. But the second world oil crisis of 1979 pushed the government to a new level of activity. Alcohol production goals were doubled, and the government encouraged the auto companies to create new ethanol engines. Biofuels were now increased to 25% in the admixture with gasoline, and massive credit enabled the construction of standalone alcohol distilleries and mills that could automatically switch between sugar and ethanol production, with the result that by 1980 alcohol production had doubled. That the long-term aims of the program succeeded is demonstrated by the figures from 2007, when there now existed in the state 414 mills processing cane, of which 248 were mixed *usinas* producing either sugar or ethanol, 151 were autonomous distillers, and 15 were *usinas* producing just sugar.[52]

But in the late 1980s world petroleum prices declined and the government abandoned its support for ethanol-only cars. In the late 1990s all prices were deregulated, and distillers were forced to control production because of the falling price of ethanol. World petroleum prices rose again after the terrorist attack on New York in 2001, the subsequent Iraq War, and the decline of Venezuelan oil production under Chávez. The increasing costs of petroleum imports led to a new government program of ethanol support. Aside from promoting increased mixture of ethanol in gasoline and in diesel fuel, it also led to the introduction in 2003 of flex fuel motors for cars, which could use any combination of ethanol or gasoline. This innovation created the modern open economy where ethanol could survive.[53] In 2005, after intense studies and discussions, the government required that a portion of diesel fuel should also be made up of biodiesel. The introduction would be in stages, reaching a minimum of 2% in three years and 5% in eight years and today is at 12%.[54] All of these programs have proceeded in fits and starts, but by 2015 some 69% of the 36 million cars in Brazil were now able to consume both products, and the expectation is that in a decade all cars will be flex fuel or run by natural gas or electricity.[55]

It was Copersucar that took greatest advantage of the first pro-alcohol program, and by the 1980s it had more than seventy *usinas* and five distilleries in the Southern region and accounted for 61% of the alcohol produced in the state and 77% of the sugar, and by the 1980s this had gathered together a significant group of foreign engineers who promoted the introduction of the latest technological inventions. This group in turn was also closely associated with Dedini S.A. Basic Industries, the leading machinery manufacturer in the town of Piracicaba, in the heart of the sugar zone. Dedini was founded in 1914 by an Italian engineer immigrant with experience in the Italian beet sugar industry. It then adopted the latest in French sugar milling technology and began producing small mills that often used reconditioned equipment. By the 1970s the company had accumulated enough experience to produce its first large mills. Dedini today produces machinery for the production of sugar, ethanol (hydrated and anhydrous), and brandy. It can construct entire sugar refineries, co-generation plants, tanks, filtration systems, and a host of other products for the industry. So advanced is its technology that it now licenses its designs for use in all types of industries.[56] But Dedini was not the only major supplier of machines. Another significant Paulista producer of machines was Zanini Renk, a Brazilian company founded in 1976, which in 1983 created a joint company with the German manufacturer Renk AG. Since the 1970s these two major companies and several smaller ones constructed approximately 200 independent distilleries and 200 co-generation mills capable of producing sugar or alcohol.[57] To maintain the state's major milling operations required a complex service and manufacturing sector. The majority of these services and the industries that build and provide replacement parts for the mills are found in the Paulista regions of Piracicaba, Ribeirão Preto, Sertãozinho, and Catanduva—a zone estimated to have some 500 industrial and service companies, of which 90% are directly involved in the sugar-alcohol industry.[58]

Along with this technological revolution and systematic government support, there was also a major structural reorganization of production into vertically integrated sections. Mills may control their own cane lands, which leads to total vertical integration. A second arrangement is that the mill enters into a long-term contract (five years or more) to rent land owned by others and use it to produce cane. Finally there is a partnership or sharecropping arrangement called *parceria*, the most common form of which the farmer prepares the land for planting, the mill plants and harvests the cane, and then the mill divides the sugar output with the landowner; in another variation on this, the *parceiro* grows the cane and the mill cuts, transports, and mills it. There is even a spot market where producers who have no mill contract sell on their own, though this is highly risky given the short life of cut cane.[59]

As production has grown, the mills, which previously had been almost exclusively nationally owned, have seen an increase in foreign ownership, and the industry as a whole has become more complex. In the first decade of the twenty-first century, major foreign companies and even foreign cooperatives entered the sugar and ethanol milling market of São Paulo. Bunge in 2006 acquired eight mills capable of turning out either sugar or ethanol. Dreyfus joined with a Brazilian company in 2009 to create Biosev with twelve mills. Royal Dutch Shell and a Brazilian company created Raizen with twenty-four mills and numerous other properties. Guarani, with seven mills, was bought by Tereos, a French beet sugar co-op in conjunction with Petrobras. Finally, Copersucar and Cargill created another milling and trading company called Alvean in 2014.[60] Copersucar itself, with its forty-seven member mills, also moved from being just a producer to becoming a transport company and a trader reaching far into the world market. Finally, the mills and cane farmers of the state also organized associations; the most important of these is Única (Associação das Usinas), founded in 1997 by 120 companies, and which today is responsible for more than 50% of ethanol output and 60% of the sugar produced in Brazil.[61]

By the end of this long process of investment and consolidation, multinational companies controlled close to a third of the industry by 2011. But national players were still important, and despite a series of crop failures and changing government support policies, the industry has continued to advance in terms of modern agricultural practices. Única on its own has invested heavily in scientific research and worker education programs and has also pushed for all producers to adopt the latest sustainability practices. Brazil's largest sugar cooperative, Copersucar, has been radically transformed into a new type of hybrid co-op/corporation. In 2008 this newly reorganized entity, called Copersucar S.A., concentrated all its capital on sugar and ethanol exports. Its União sugar brand was sold, Sara Lee bought its coffee processing plants, and it spun off its successful Copersucar Technological Center (CTC) research center (the most advanced agricultural research center for sugar in the world) as an independent entity. It increased the number of its milling companies to forty-three, and by 2014 was producing 135 million tons of sugar and 4.9 million liters of ethanol. At that point it was producing 11% of world sugar exports and proposed to reach 30% of world total exports by the end of the decade. It also bought an American corn ethanol marketing company in 2012, joined with Cargill to promote more international trading activities, and built its own pipelines and port facilities.[62]

Along with new milling systems, new technology, and new business structures, the sugar industry has revolutionized the production and cutting of cane in the past several decades. Burning of the bagasse, or remains of the plants, has declined, and no-tillage planting has become the norm. As late as the harvest of 2006/2007, only 40% of the cane planted was cut by machines. But growers agreed with the state to mechanize the harvest over time. In turn this mechanization reduced the number of workers cutting sugarcane from 260,000 to just half that number in the harvest of 2006/2007. Another major change has been the state prohibition of burning the cane stalks after harvest. In 2002 the state of São Paulo issued a decree proposing the slow decline of burning, to be replaced either by normal tilling over the stalks without plowing or by traditional plowing, and this was eventually supported by Única. By the harvest of 2008/2009 the cultivation, loading, and transport of sugarcane was 100% mechanized, and 40% of the cutting was done by machines. In fact there is a correlation between mechanization and the end of field burning, with non-burned fields requiring cane cutting by machines.[63] By 2011 it was estimated that 60% of the cane fields had moved to this new system of not burning the bagasse, and by 2015 in the state of São Paulo some 85% of the cane was harvested by machines and only some 52,000 workers were employed in the industry.[64] The one area where there has been less development compared to other Brazilian crops is in the creation of new plants and seeds for sugarcane.

All of these developments resulted in the stimulation of sugar production throughout Brazil, but above all in São Paulo. Already by 1990, São Paulo was responsible for half of the national sugar production. The amount of land planted in cane in 1990 was 1.8 million hectares, and this increased to 5.6 million hectares in the state thirty years later.[65] Brazil is considered the lowest-cost producer of sugar in the world. The cost of producing a ton of sugar in São Paulo in 2007 was US $120 per ton, while in the United States it was US $290 per ton.[66] It is also the world's largest grower of sugarcane, and in the harvest of 2020/2021 São Paulo produced 355 million tons of cane on 5.6 million hectares, which it processed into 26 million metric tons of sugar and 14.3 billion liters of ethanol.[67] In this same harvest year, São Paulo accounted for a major share of total national raw sugar exports and 93% of ethanol exports.[68]

The state today grinds over half of the sugar refined in Brazil, and produces just under half of its ethanol from this same sugarcane. In 1974 the state milled 39 million tons of sugarcane; by 2016 it was cutting 442 million tons, for an annual growth rate of 5.9%.[69] Refined sugar output went from 4 million tons to almost 24 million tons by the harvest of 2016/2017, for an annual growth rate of 4.9%. Total ethanol production also grew by 4.9% per annum, from 2.6 billion liters in 1980/1981to 13 billion liters in 2016/2017.[70] Although growth of ethanol production in the Center-West region has reduced São Paulo's share of ethanol refining, it is still the leading state, accounting for 46% of this biofuel produced in Brazil in 2020/2021.[71] In total Brazil accounted for 30% of the world's biofuels production from all sources in 2019.[72]

Aside from sugar, the fastest-growing crops in the state in this period were bananas, followed by soybeans, eggs, and corn. Oranges, while still a major product in terms of sales, have seen fairly wide swings in production from the 1980s to the present century, as did broiler chickens. Of these crops and animal products, the state was the dominant producer in Brazil of sugarcane, oranges, eggs (and of course it had the largest number of hens), and peanuts. São Paulo egg production alone accounted for a quarter of the value of national production in 2019, with its output two times greater than that of Minas Gerais, the second-leading state.[73] But the state production of broiler chickens in 2019 was only a third of the value of the output of Paraná, the leading producer.[74] It produced 94% of the peanuts grown in 2019/2020 and was second in banana production. It was also an important (though not leading) producer of soybeans (3% of national production) and corn (4%).[75]

In terms of the value of the state's agricultural production, sugar and pastoral products made up well over two-thirds of the gross value of São Paulo agricultural production in the first and second decades of the twentieth century. Second were oranges and soybeans. All pastoral products alone, including meats, eggs, and milk, now account for around 28% of the total gross value of all crops in the 2010s, while sugar averaged 38% of the total. Coffee is now less important than oranges and soybeans, averaging only 3% in this decade, while soybeans have tripled in their share to 7% of the gross value of the state's agricultural products (see Table 3.6).

Although beef ranching's share of agricultural lands in São Paulo has declined from 11.4 million hectares in 1970 to 5.4 million hectares in 2017, it still accounts for 34% of all lands in the state.[76] But this declining area had little effect on the total number of cattle being raised in the state. In 1970 cattle numbered 9.1 million head, and in 2006 there were 10.4 million, demonstrating the increasing efficiency of the pastoral industry in the state. In contrast, there was major growth in chickens (both broilers and laying hens). As in the rest of the world, it is only since the middle of twentieth century that chicken meat has become a popular and important consumption item. A

TABLE 3.6

Total Gross Value of Major Crops and Animal Products Produced in São Paulo, 2007–2020, Sorted by Importance in 2020

Product	2007	2008	2009	2010	2011	2012	2013	2014	2015	2016	2017	2018	2019	2020
Sugarcane	35%	30%	36%	35%	40%	46%	46%	42%	41%	41%	40%	36%	35%	32%
Cattle	11%	13%	13%	11%	9%	9%	10%	11%	12%	9%	10%	11%	12%	13%
Oranges	16%	17%	15%	19%	19%	9%	5%	7%	6%	8%	10%	11%	12%	12%
Chickens	12%	12%	10%	9%	9%	9%	9%	8%	8%	8%	8%	9%	10%	8%
Soybeans	2%	3%	3%	2%	2%	3%	3%	3%	4%	4%	5%	6%	6%	7%
Cows' Milk	4%	4%	4%	5%	4%	4%	5%	5%	4%	4%	5%	5%	6%	5%
Corn	4%	5%	3%	3%	3%	3%	4%	3%	3%	4%	3%	4%	4%	4%
Eggs	2%	3%	2%	2%	3%	4%	5%	5%	5%	5%	4%	3%	3%	4%
Coffee	3%	3%	2%	3%	3%	4%	2%	3%	3%	4%	3%	4%	3%	3%
Bananas	1%	2%	1%	2%	2%	2%	2%	2%	2%	3%	3%	2%	2%	2%
Tomatoes	2%	2%	2%	2%	2%	2%	4%	5%	5%	2%	2%	2%	2%	2%
Potatoes	2%	1%	2%	1%	1%	1%	1%	2%	2%	2%	1%	1%	2%	1%
Others	5%	5%	5%	5%	4%	5%	5%	5%	5%	5%	6%	3%	5%	6%
Total	100%	100%	100%	100%	100%	100%	100%	100%	100%	100%	100%	100%	100%	100%

SOURCE: For 2007–2009, "Valor bruto da produção—regional por UF—julho/2016," http://www.agricultura.gov.br/ministerio/gestao-estrategica/valor-bruto-da-producao. For 2010–2020, "Valor bruto da produção—VBP—Julho/2020—regional por UF," http://www.agricultura.gov.br/assuntos/politica-agricola/valor-bruto-da-producao-agro pecuaria-vbp.

modern segmented production organization, with new growing, feeding, and breeding practices, has reduced chicken prices everywhere since the 1950s.

In São Paulo modern broiler chicken production began in the 1940s in the region of Mogi das Cruzes. In the next decade there was the beginning of new specialized *granjas* (chicken farms) using the latest sanitary procedures, and in the 1960s came the importation of specific broiler breeds. At about this time state producers adopted the vertically integrated system developed in Santa Catarina by Sadia in 1964, which involved the packing houses signing long-term contracts with farmers and assisting them technically and with supplies and pullets.[77] As has occurred in the other major areas of meat production, there was a growing concentration of production in an ever smaller number of producers. By the late 1980s there were more than forty-five chicken slaughterhouses in the state, but just eight of them processed almost half of the chicken meat produced.[78] Between 1974 and 2015 São Paulo went from growing 29 million broiler chickens to 47 million, for an annual growth rate of 1.2%.[79] Currently the state is the fourth-largest exporter internationally of chicken meat, behind the three Southern states, and accounts for 5% of all such exports.[80]

The state is currently Brazil's leading producer in the other chicken product, eggs. It accounts for a third of national production, well ahead of any other state.[81] The modern system of industrialized production of eggs is thought to have begun in Brazil in the 1950s and was promoted in the state by the major co-op CAC (Cooperativa Agrícola de Cotia). From artisanal production of chickens and eggs on a single farm, the egg industry has now become part of the complex multi-farm system of production of broiler chickens (*galinhas de corte*) and laying hens (*poedeiras* or *galinhas de postura*), from breeding animals to producing eggs to processing chickens and eggs for sale.[82] Unlike chicken meat, for which there is a vibrant international market, eggs are almost exclusively consumed domestically.

The production of both broilers and laying hens is approximately the same, and the birds are varieties of the standard species. Usually there are two levels of hatcheries (*incubatórios*): those producing the grandparents and parents of the laying hens or broiler chickens, and those that produce the chicks themselves and raise either variety for sale to the farms when the pullets are one day old. The chicks take under a month to raise and are grown in large numbers so that they can be sold in large lots, which is especially important for the meat varieties. Before sale these one-day-old chicks are vaccinated. The meat producing chicks (*pintinhos de corte*) are bought from the hatcheries by chicken farmers and then grown in large houses until they reach slaughter weight, which is usually in five to nine weeks, after which they are delivered to the packing houses. In turn their slaughter is controlled by a few major companies. These companies have created a complex, vertically integrated value chain providing basic inputs for the producers under long-term contracts.

In contrast to the broiler chicken industry, with its vertical integration of hatcheries, farmers, and packinghouses, the egg market is an independent system where producers sell their products to local consumers or wholesalers on the spot market. The relation between hatcheries, for which São Paulo is the leading state, the producers, and the wholesalers is thus a simple purchase arrangement. In the late 1990s there were eighty to a hundred wholesalers in the greater São Paulo market, of which thirty to forty supplied the half dozen major supermarket chains. This was a reasonably competitive market. But over the subsequent years there has been a big concentration of primary producers, with one or two giant companies in each state providing most of the eggs.[83] It is estimated that the modal farm in the late 1990s was a unit with 20,000–50,000 egg-laying hens. But there were already eight major farms at this time that had over half a million egg-laying animals. The distribution of laying hens among these farms produced a very high Gini index of 0.825, showing how concentrated egg production had become by the end of the twentieth century.[84] Typical of these large producers is the Granja Mizohata, founded in 1957, which by 2005 had half a million hens producing 300,000 eggs per day.[85] This was the type of large farm that supplied interregional markets with unprocessed eggs. In 2005 it was estimated that the average egg farm in the state had 223,000 laying hens, comparable to those of Minas Gerais but far greater than the average in Paraná, which was just 79,000. The egg-producing farms are geographically concentrated in the state, with the two western mesoregions of Marília and Presidente Prudente accounting for half the eggs produced in 2015.[86]

Milk, another animal product of importance, has been produced in Brazil since colonial times, but only at the beginning of the nineteenth century were specific breeds of milk cows introduced. The first was the Turino breed, of Portuguese origin. The first Brazilian dairy was opened in the city of Rio de Janeiro in the late nineteenth century, and a few years later a larger dairy was opened in the city of São Paulo. At the beginning of the next century Holstein milk cows, originating in the Netherlands, were brought to Brazil.[87] For most of the second half of the twentieth century the government controlled the price of milk, and the industry produced milk well below international yields, with output dominated by small dairy farms. The end of price controls in 1991 and the signing of the Mercosul treaties, along with progressive elimination of tariffs throughout the decade, led to falling prices and major imports of milk and milk products. This resulted in a total reorganization of the national industry. Major imports from Argentine and Uruguay of milk products and the inefficiencies of Brazilian production made competition difficult. At the same time the stability of the newly established national currency, the real, lead to increasing national consumption of milk. As late as 1998 two-thirds of the milk was being produced by a very small number of non-specialized producers. For such small farms it was a product that could be sold on a daily basis and thus helped sustain the farm while their crops were maturing. But this lack of specialized production also had an impact on seasonal variation in production, with producers unable to satisfy markets all year long.[88]

The imbalances in the market thus led in the post-1990 period to a total reorganization of the entire chain of milk production in Brazil, from the size and nature of the dairy herds to the production of finished milk. The most basic change was the purchasing of milk in bulk, which required the dairy farms to buy refrigerated tanks to hold milk that would then be picked up by refrigerated tanker trucks. Though this process was introduced in the United States in 1939, its first occurrence in Brazil was in 1976 when the Cooperativa de Laticínios de São José dos Campos in the Valley of Paraíba used such refrigerated tanker trucks to ship its products to the processing plant. By 2002 the government required producers to have refrigeration units and mandated that all raw milk be moved by these refrigerated tank trucks.[89] This lowered the cost of production significantly. The next major innovation, also introduced in the 1990s, was the production in advanced factories of long-life (ultra-high-temperature or UHT) milk, which changed the whole geographical dynamics of the industry permitting shipping of products to distant markets. By the first decade of the twenty-first century long-life milk had replaced "C" milk as the dominant product consumed in Brazil.[90] There was also a systematic effort to increase the production of milk herds and to better organize the chain of production. It also led to a major introduction of multinationals and increasing concentration in the industry. Of the nine central milk cooperatives then in operation, the end of price supports forced out seven of them, which sold their factories to Brazilian or multinational firms. The only two cooperatives that survived were Itambé of Minas Gerais and Leite Paulista of São Paulo, and both eventually entered into partnership with private firms. Itambé was founded by the Cooperativa Central dos Produtores Rurais de Minas Gerais in 1950.[91] Currently it has 7,000 dairy farms producing milk and owns numerous factories in Minas Gerais and Goiás; in 2013 it allied with a private company (Vigor, a subsidiary of JBS), which bought half of the company. The São Paulo central co-op was founded in 1933 when several state producer co-operatives created the central Cooperativa Central de Laticínios do Estado de São Paulo, which has dominated the milk market in the state with its brand Leite Paulista until the present day. In 2000, the co-op sold part of the enterprise to the French multinational Danone, but kept the production and sale of pasteurized milk, powdered milk, long-life milk, butter, and cream.[92] But São Paulo also had private dairy companies that operated in the state beginning early in the twentieth century. Leite Vigor (established in 1917), Nestlé (1921), and Leite União (1927) were all operating before the Cooperativa Central de Laticínios do Estado de São Paulo set up its own production unit.[93]

As late as 1940 most of the dairy farms were located in the Paraiba Valley and Mogiana districts, largely due to their excellent connections to the capital. But by the second half of the century there was a major expansion throughout the state.[94] The introduction of long-life milk ended the old "dairy basins" around the big cities, and dairy activity moved westward. Although the Valley of Paraíba has maintained a prominent role in the state's dairy production, the leading zone from 1990 through the present day is the region of São José do Rio Preto, with the Paraíba Valley second, followed by Campinas, Presidente Prudente, and Ribeirão Preto.[95] The size of São Paulo's herds of milk cows has changed little since 1974. In that year the state had 1.3 million dairy cows out of 10.8 million nationally. By 2016 the state listed only 1.2 million dairy cows, now out of 19.7 million nationally. It thus dropped nationally from second place to sixth place in the size of herds.[96]

The distribution of these herds and crops across the state is quite uneven, with some of the fifteen state mesoregions dominating particular crops and products and others not significant producers (see Map 3.2). The distribution of crop- and animal-producing lands was biased toward larger holdings, and the Gini index tended to be quite high. Ribeirão Preto had by far the highest percentage of lands in farms of 2,500 hectares and above. In contrast, both Campinas and Sorocaba had more farms in the smallest and middle range than any other municipality—31% of the farms in both regions were 5 hectares or less, and they controlled over 1% of the planted area, figures far above all the other municipalities. Also, farms in the 50–200 hectare range in both areas controlled a third or more of the tilled land—the highest ratio of any of the municipalities, even though the number of farms in this group were fewer than the norm (see Table 3.7).

Six of these regions accounted for 98% of sugarcane production in 2018, with the two northern municipalities of Ribeirão Preto and São José do Rio Preto and the central region of Bauru the biggest producers, the three

Map 3.2. Mesoregions of São Paulo

SOURCE: IBGE, Bases Cartográficas.

TABLE 3.7

Distribution of Lands in Selected Regions of São Paulo, 2017

	SOROCABA		BAURU		SÃO JOSÉ DO RIO PRETO		RIBEIRÃO PRETO		CAMPINAS		PRESIDENTE PRUDENTE		ARAÇATUBA	
Hectares	Farms	Land	Farms	Land	Farms	Land	Farms	Land	Farms	Land	Farms	Land	Farms	Land
> 0 and < 0.1	1.0%	0.0%	0.7%	0.0%	0.5%	0.0%	1.2%	0.0%	0.9%	0.0%	0.3%	0.0%	0.5%	0.0%
0.1–0.2	1.2%	0.0%	0.5%	0.0%	0.4%	0.0%	0.6%	0.0%	0.9%	0.0%	0.3%	0.0%	0.3%	0.0%
0.2–0.5	2.4%	0.0%	1.1%	0.0%	0.7%	0.0%	1.6%	0.0%	1.5%	0.0%	0.4%	0.0%	0.5%	0.0%
0.5–1	2.6%	0.0%	1.0%	0.0%	0.9%	0.0%	1.3%	0.0%	2.0%	0.0%	0.4%	0.0%	1.2%	0.0%
1–2	5.6%	0.1%	1.9%	0.0%	1.8%	0.0%	4.6%	0.0%	4.6%	0.1%	1.3%	0.0%	1.6%	0.0%
2–3	7.0%	0.2%	4.9%	0.1%	4.1%	0.1%	2.8%	0.0%	8.6%	0.3%	2.4%	0.1%	2.5%	0.1%
3–4	5.4%	0.3%	2.6%	0.1%	4.8%	0.2%	3.3%	0.1%	6.1%	0.4%	3.0%	0.1%	2.9%	0.1%
4–5	6.4%	0.4%	4.6%	0.2%	6.2%	0.4%	4.1%	0.1%	6.8%	0.5%	4.3%	0.2%	4.0%	0.2%
5–10	15.6%	1.7%	12.1%	0.6%	17.7%	1.9%	12.5%	0.7%	17.3%	2.2%	13.0%	1.1%	10.7%	0.8%
10–20	17.6%	3.6%	25.4%	2.8%	22.1%	4.3%	19.0%	1.9%	17.4%	4.3%	32.1%	5.7%	34.3%	4.6%
20–50	16.8%	7.5%	17.5%	4.0%	22.4%	9.6%	19.5%	4.4%	16.9%	9.2%	22.7%	7.6%	18.8%	5.9%
50–100	7.4%	7.3%	9.3%	4.8%	8.8%	8.4%	10.7%	5.3%	7.5%	9.2%	8.1%	6.4%	9.2%	6.5%
100–200	4.9%	9.7%	7.3%	7.2%	5.0%	9.4%	8.3%	8.2%	4.7%	11.5%	5.1%	8.1%	5.7%	7.8%
200–500	3.6%	16.1%	6.7%	14.8%	2.9%	12.0%	6.3%	13.5%	3.2%	17.1%	4.2%	14.8%	4.8%	14.3%
500–1000	1.5%	14.5%	2.3%	11.5%	0.9%	8.3%	2.2%	11.0%	0.9%	11.3%	1.3%	10.7%	1.6%	11.1%
1000–2500	0.7%	15.5%	1.2%	13.1%	0.5%	9.6%	1.1%	12.4%	0.4%	10.3%	0.7%	12.3%	0.8%	11.3%
2500–10,000	0.3%	16.2%	0.8%	24.5%	0.4%	23.6%	0.7%	21.9%	0.2%	16.7%	0.4%	17.2%	0.4%	19.9%
10,000+	0.0%	6.8%	0.2%	16.3%	0.1%	12.0%	0.2%	20.6%	0.0%	6.8%	0.1%	15.6%	0.1%	17.3%
Total	100.0%	100.0%	100.0%	100.0%	100.0%	100.0%	100.0%	100.0%	100.0%	100.0%	100.0%	100.0%	100.0%	100.0%
(N)	34,373	2,434,274	11,467	1,621,801	28,601	2,102,996	15,217	2,179,125	25,602	1,485,628	21,967	1,953,561	14,084	1,430,716
Gini Index	83.1		84.2		80.8		84.6		81.1		80.3		82.5	

SOURCE: IBGE, SIDRA, table 6882.

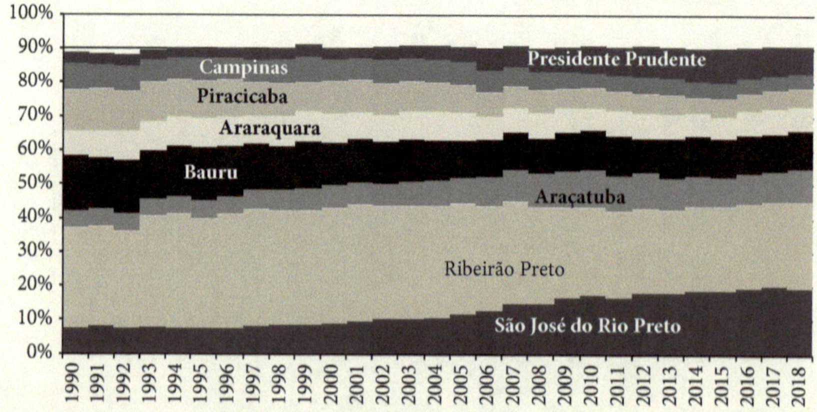

Figure 3.3. Distribution of Sugarcane Production by Mesoregion of São Paulo, 1990–2018

SOURCE: IBGE, SIDRA, table 1612.

accounting for over half of production. The growth of production in each region between 1990 and 2018 was quite dramatic (see Figure 3.3). Thus, for example, Ribeirão Preto in 1974 planted only 168,000 hectares in sugarcane, but by 2010 that had increased eightfold to 1.2 million hectares planted in sugarcane.[97] In the five years between the harvests of 2003/2004 and 2008/2009 the lands dedicated to sugar increased from 2.6 million hectares to 4.4 million hectares.[98] By 2019 cane production tended to be concentrated in a few well-defined zones of the northwestern and western part of the state (see Map 3.3).

The other major seasonal crops, soybeans and corn, were usually grown together, so their distribution is approximately the same by mesoregions of the state. The relative importance of the three major producers of these seasonal crops—Itapetininga, Assis, and Ribeirão Preto—has slowly changed over time (see Figure 3.4). By 2019 the distribution of these two crops was well defined and quite distinctive in the state's agriculture (see Map 3.4).

Corn, a key element in human foods and animal feed, was closely associated with soybeans and was often used as a rotating crop on the fields used for soybeans. Thus the two of the three leading centers of corn, Itapetininga and Assis, were also soybean-producing regions, and along with Campinas accounted for 59% of the corn planted in the state in 2018. Campinas was the outlier in that while it was not a major producer of soybeans, it was a significant producer of corn, accounting for 13% of the state's crop in 2018 (see Figure 3.5)

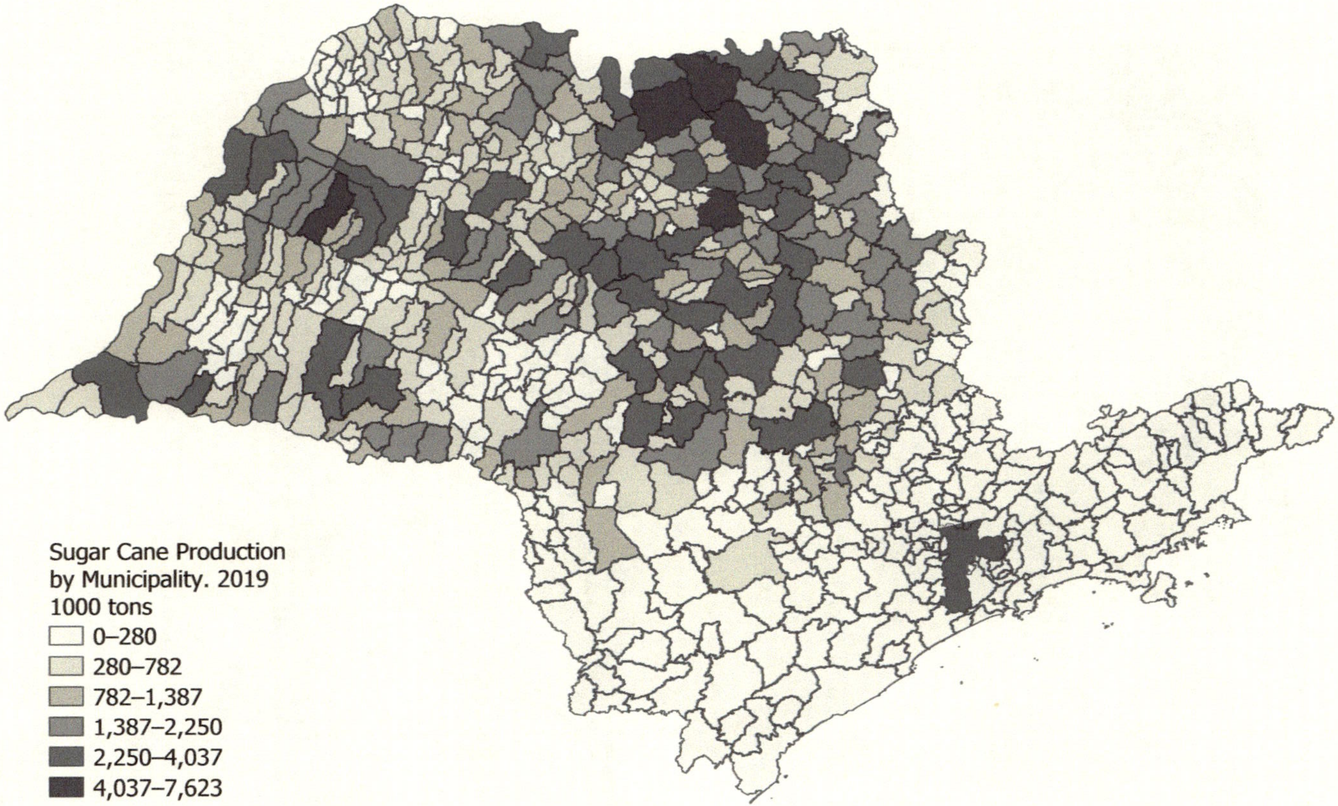

Map 3.3. Sugarcane Production in São Paulo by Municipality, 2019

SOURCE: IBGE, Bases Cartográficas; IBGE, SIDRA, table 1612.

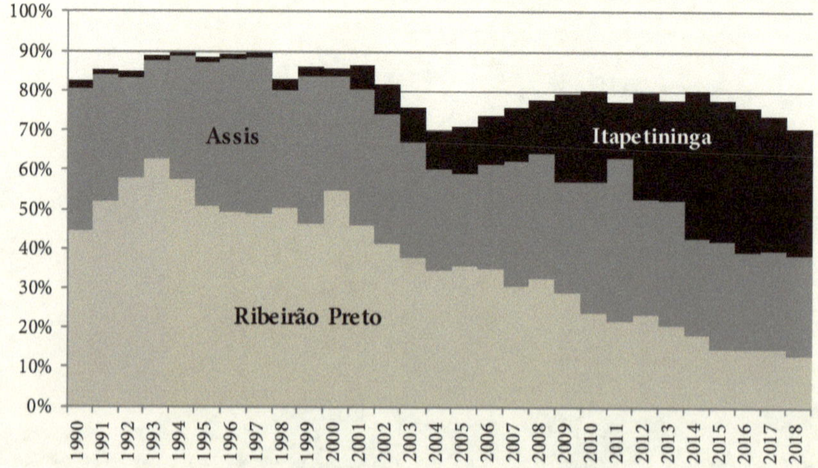

Figure 3.4. Distribution of Soybean Production by Mesoregion of São Paulo, 1990–2018

SOURCE: IBGE, SIDRA, PAM, table 1612.

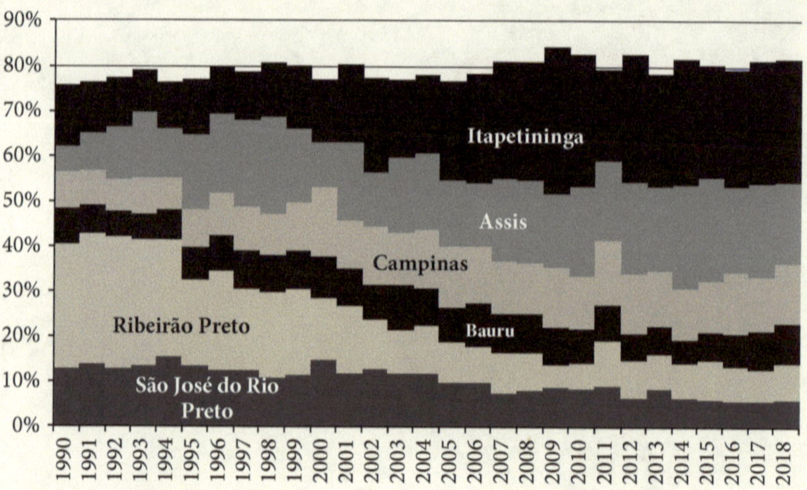

Figure 3.5. Distribution of Corn Production by Mesoregion of São Paulo, 1990–2018

SOURCE: IBGE, SIDRA, table 1612.

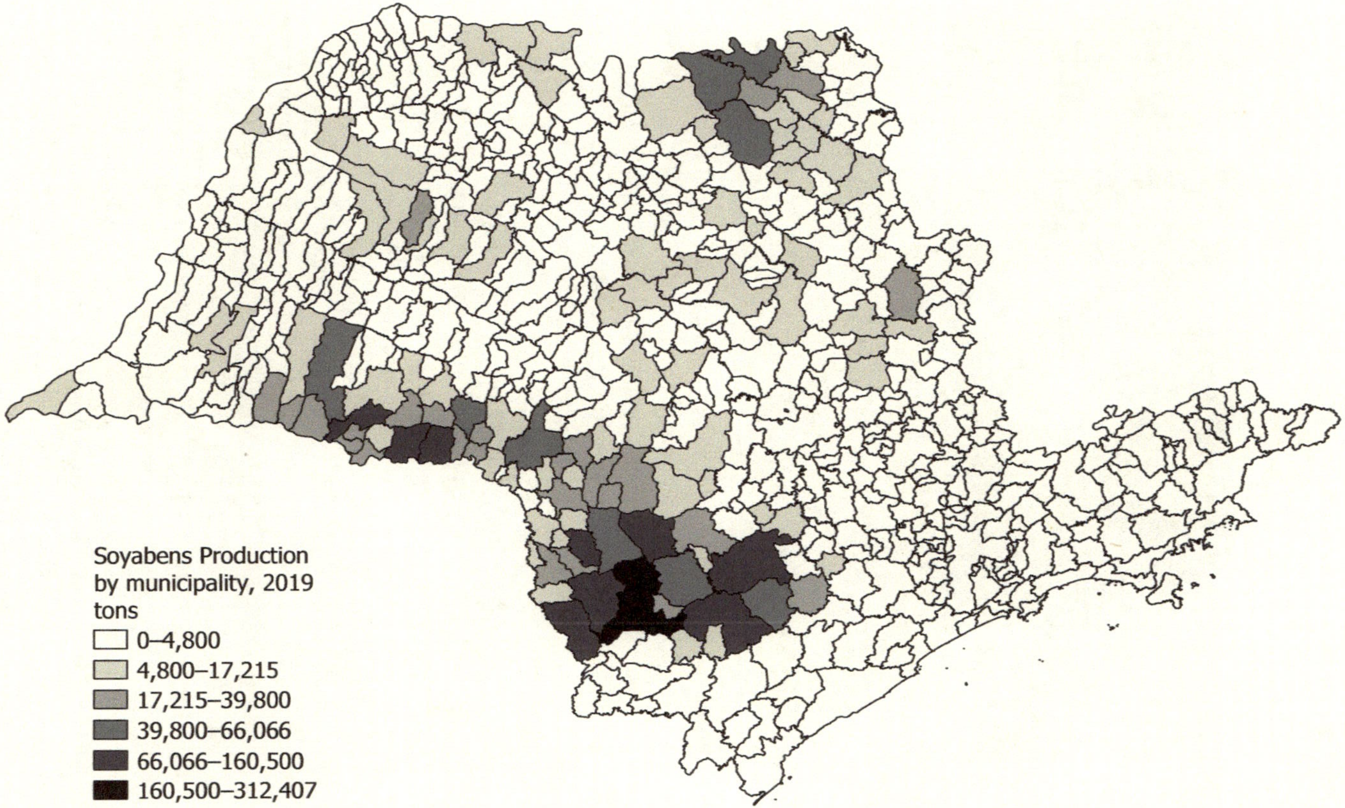

Map 3.4. Soybean Production in São Paulo by Municipality, 2019 (Tons)

SOURCE: IBGE, Bases Cartográficas; IBGE, SIDRA, table 1612.

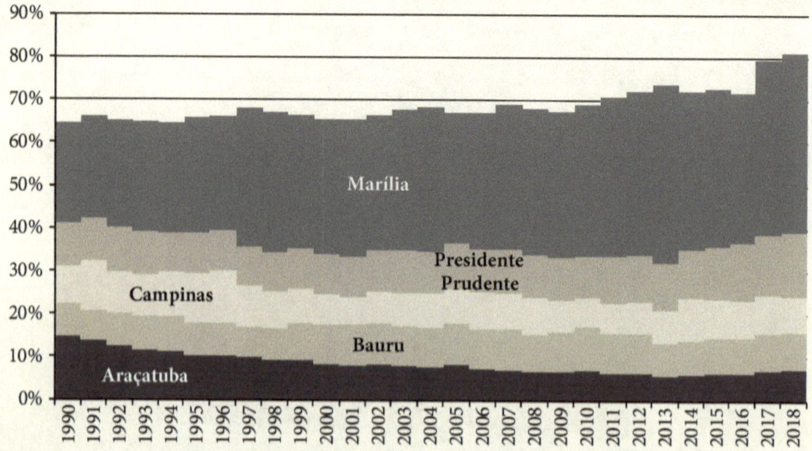

Figure 3.6. Distribution of Egg Production by Mesoregion of São Paulo, 1990–2018

SOURCE: IBGE, SIDRA, table 74.

Unusually, compared to most all other agricultural activities, cattle could be found in all fifteen mesoregions of the state. Nevertheless, the districts with the largest herds (each over a million cattle) were the four regions of Presidente Prudente, São José do Rio Preto, Bauru, and Araçatuba. Together these regions in 2017 held almost half of the herds in São Paulo (see Map 3.5)

Marília was the principal producer of eggs from 1990 to 2018, accounting for 42% of the state's egg production in 2018, followed by Presidente Prudente, the second-largest producer; Bauru was also important in egg production. The three together accounted for 65% of egg output in that year (see Figure 3.6). The Marília district also concentrated in broiler chicken production (34% of the state's total), with a secondary center in Presidente Prudente (12%). With Bauru and Campinas, these four municipalities accounted for close to two-thirds of the state's egg production (see Map 3.6).

Thus the state of São Paulo, for all the growth of its urban centers, financial institutions, factories, and a world class airplane industry, remains a vital part of Brazil's agricultural market, now comparable to the giant Center-West producer Mato Grosso in total value of agricultural production. But in the period since 1960 there has been a radical shift in major agricultural activities. Sugarcane (sugar, biofuels), oranges (and their derivatives), and chickens, eggs, and milk have replaced the old coffee economy.

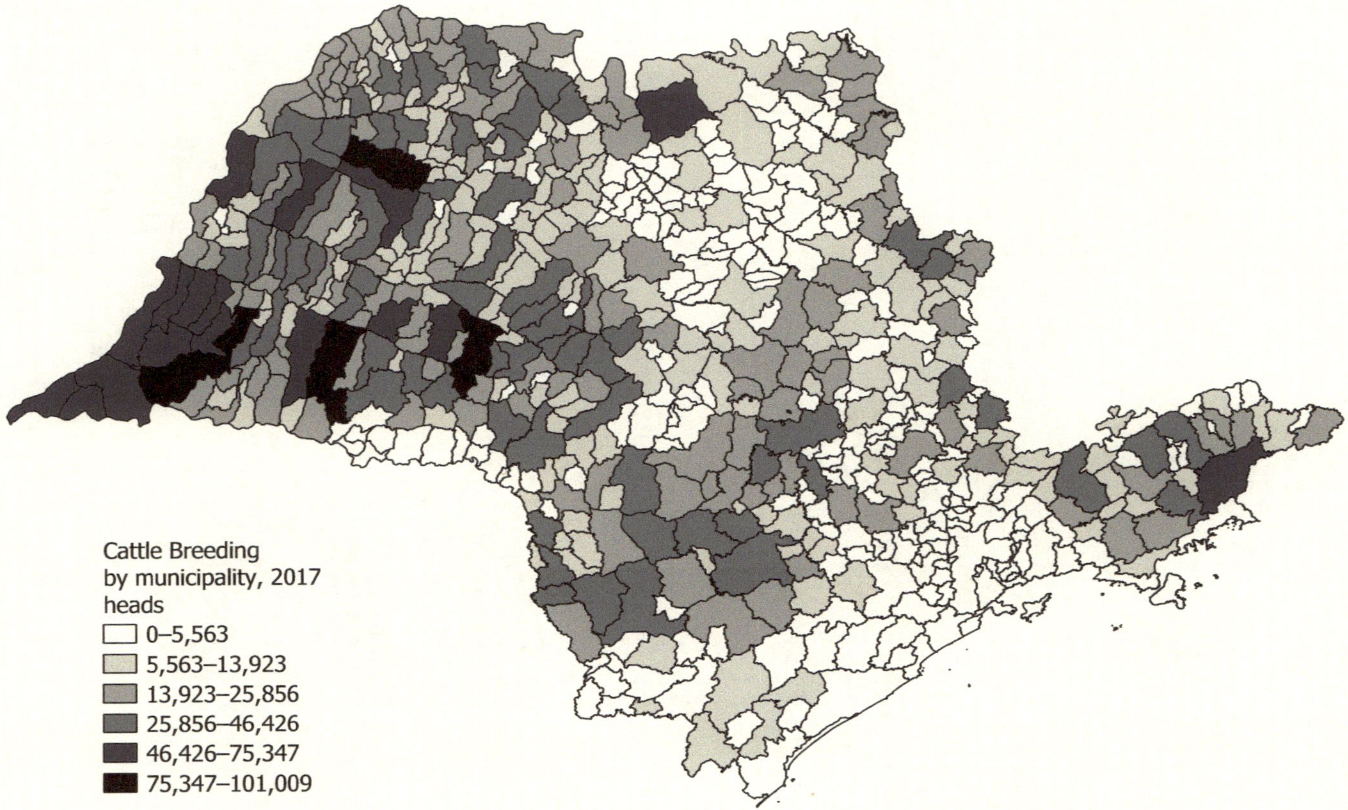

Map 3.5. Cattle Production in São Paulo by Municipality, 2019 (Head)

SOURCE: IBGE, Bases Cartográficas; IBGE, SIDRA, table 6907.

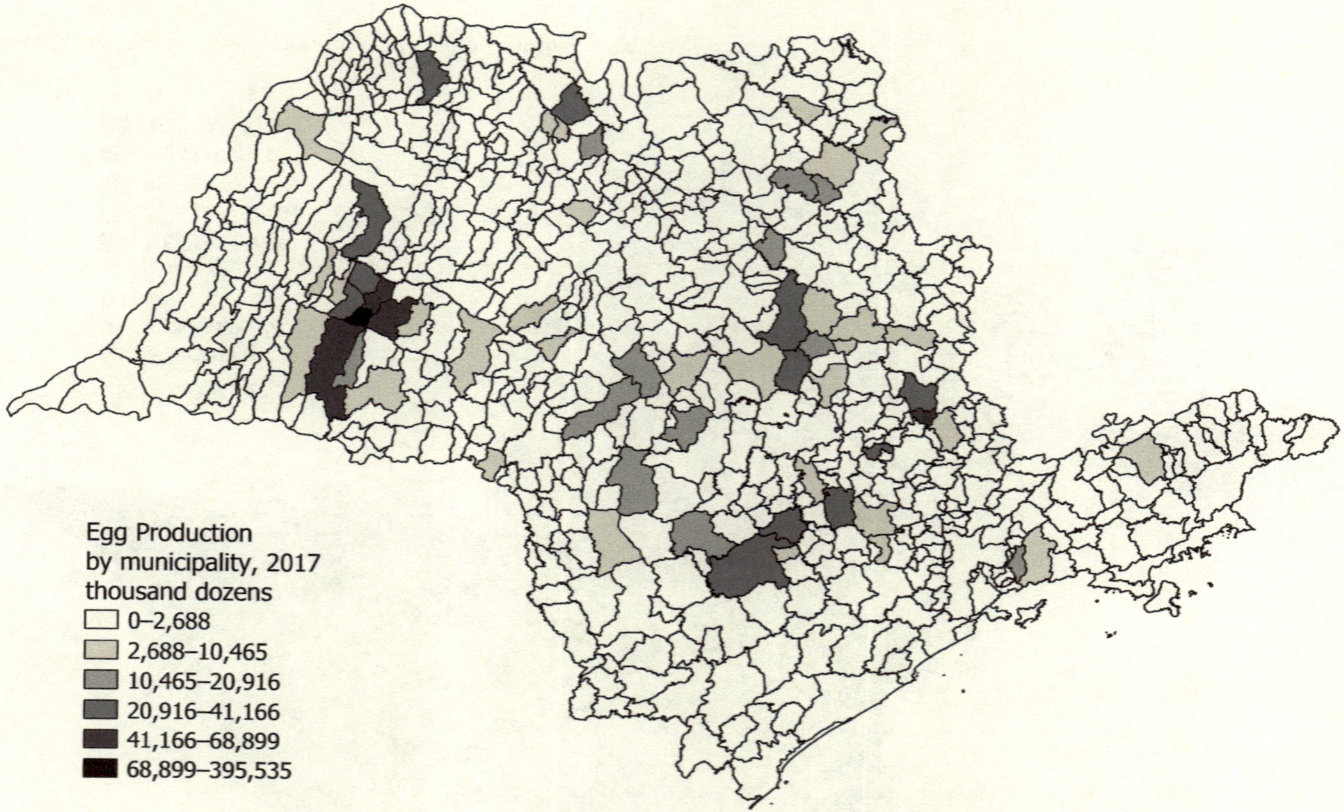

Map 3.6. Egg Production in São Paulo by Municipality, 2019 (Thousand Dozens)

SOURCE: IBGE, Bases Cartográficas; IBGE, SIDRA, table 6942,

The coffee that built the state is no longer a significant crop. It is also worth noting that the state's road, rail, and port complex still make São Paulo one of the key export areas for Brazil, with Santos being as important for soybeans and sugar exports as it was for coffee half a century ago. Finally, São Paulo, like the rest of Brazil, has emerged in the past half century as one of the world's greatest agricultural producers and world market exporters, a sharp contrast to the fate of its national and state industrial sector.

Chapter 4

Growth of a Service and Trade Economy

Along with the decline of industry and the growth of a modern internationally oriented commercial agriculture, the other basic change to the economy of the state in the late twentieth and early twenty-first centuries was the rise of a trade and service economy. Like industry, services grew out of the booming coffee economy. Just as the first stimulus for industrialization was created with coffee capital, so too did the trade and service industry expand with the arrival of European immigrants in all parts of the state. This created strong demand for services of all types, both for the productive sector and for the growing population. In turn, the opening up of the national economy in the 1990s, along with the end of inflation when the real was created, would be factors that further reinforced the growth of this sector.

As might be expected, this sector of the economy was not evenly distributed across the state. Since the capital was by far the largest metropolitan region in the state, and home to both the state government and most industries, it was inevitable that the expansion in new public and private services was mostly housed in the capital. All major cultural institutions were located here, as well as the largest merchant houses. Although still an important industrial city, the capital became essentially a city of commerce and services in the twenty-first century. As its international activities increased, the city also become the crucial center for all major financial institutions as well as headquarters for a majority of national and international companies. Nevertheless, this transformation soon affected all parts of the state. The international focus of the state's agriculture further strengthened the role of services in the state economy, as increasing productivity required increasingly sophisticated services. Even industry became ever more dependent on the service sector as it spread throughout the state. Thus by the twenty-first century this service and trade sector, populated by a well-educated labor force, dominated the state of São Paulo and its capital region, which in turn led to the relative decline of agriculture and industry as the driving force of the state's economy in terms of employment and GDP.

Although we have been able to quantify with some precision the impact of agriculture and industry on the state of São Paulo and its capital city, it is more difficult to define and measure the so-called services sector. This is not the case with trade (wholesale and retail), whose definition and statistics have been fairly coherent over time. But the category "services" comprises a range of activities, such as public administration, trade in goods, transport, financial activities, business services, and personal services, along with education and health. Moreover, classifications have changed over time due to the emergence of new activities and the transformation and disappearance of others. The IBGE, the national census bureau, has made numerous changes in this category to reflect the changes in economic activity.[1] Finally, the government has moved statistics on services out of the decennial census since the census of 1991, and now provides the data in two different annual surveys, which are not always compatible with the decennial numbers.[2]

Despite these problems, we can roughly chart the growth of services in São Paulo. Even as early as 1950 the state had an impressive level of services and trade, which made up almost half of state GDP. The volume and value of these services were less important within the state than was the case in its nearest rival, the state of Rio de Janeiro and its Federal District, where over two-thirds of the GDP was accounted for by services. Nevertheless, São Paulo already accounted for a higher proportion of the service sector nationally than did the Federal District (the city of Rio de Janeiro), which housed the federal government and its large bureaucracy, and the state of Rio de Janeiro. Even in terms of employment, the number of those working in service sector in São Paulo surpassed the total number of workers in this sector in Rio de Janeiro and the Federal District (see Table 4.1).

When broken down into discrete categories, retail trade was the most important segment of the service sector in both the nation and the state. It accounted for 36% of state employment in services. Wholesale trade, handmade garments and repair services (which include tailors, dressmakers, and custom sewers),[3] and the lodging and food sector were three other important employment segments in the state. Together these four sectors accounted

TABLE 4.1
Economic Indicators for Brazil, São Paulo, and Rio de Janeiro, 1950

	REGIONS		
Sectors	São Paulo	Rio de Janeiro (1)	Brazil
Industry	28%	23%	20%
Services	46%	69%	49%
Agriculture and Ranching	26%	8%	31%
Total	100%	100%	100%

PERCENTAGE OF NATIONAL GDP

Sectors	São Paulo	Rio de Janeiro (1)	Subtotal of the Two States
Industry	47%	21%	69%
Services	33%	27%	60%
Agriculture and Ranching	29%	5%	34%
% of National GDP	37%	21%	58%

EMPLOYMENT OF PERSONS 10 YEARS OF AGE AND OLDER

Principal Activity	São Paulo	Rio de Janeiro (1)	Brazil
Merchandise Trade	248,293	171,227	958,509
Services Provision	413,133	316,532	1,672,801
Transport, Communications	197,269	143,951	697,089
Trade and Services Subtotal	858,695	631,710	3,328,399
% Trade and Services	13%	18%	9%
Total Employed	6,691,114	3,537,360	36,557,990
Total Population	9,134,423	4,584,645	51,944,397

SOURCE: Ipeadata, Regional; IBGE, Censo Demográfico 1950, volume 1.
NOTE: (1) Includes the Federal District of Rio de Janeiro.

for 80% of state employment in the trade and services provided. In terms of sales, the most important sectors were the wholesale and retail trades. Both segments accounted for 92% of sales made in the service sector in the state.[4] By 1950, São Paulo had already surpassed Rio de Janeiro in terms of sales and employment in these sectors. There were also long-term trends developing within some specialized areas. Thus services classified as belonging to the credit market show that in the amount of loans made São Paulo and Rio de Janeiro were equal and together represented 73% of the amount of all financial loans made in Brazil.[5] But in the case of insurance and savings, Rio de Janeiro was still the national leader in 1950 (see Table 4.2).

At midcentury, transport and communications were two other important activities in the services category; in these the state employed a third of the total national workforce. Within the category of transport and communications, rail transport was the biggest employer of workers in 1950,

TABLE 4.2

Characteristics of the Service Sector: Employment and Sales in Brazil, São Paulo, and Rio de Janeiro, 1950

	TOTAL EMPLOYMENT				SALES / REVENUE / LOANS / RESERVES			
Activities	Brazil	São Paulo	São Paulo as % of Brazil	Rio de Janeiro + DF (1)	Brazil	São Paulo	São Paulo as % of Brazil	Rio de Janeiro + DF (1)
Retail Trade (Sales)	512,125	116,968	23%	84,845	63,412,248	20,289,859	32%	13,967,352
Wholesale Trade (Sales)	190,613	58,040	30%	52,629	115,391,267	45,494,976	39%	32,363,970
Real Estate / Securities	11,432	5,416	47%	3,725	1,260,719	486,840	39%	543,361
Trade Auxiliaries (Revenue) (2)	43,137	15,031	35%	12,084	2,497,093	936,137	37%	973,615
Accommodation and Food (Revenues)	150,930	41,580	28%	35,076	6,176,809	2,104,962	34%	1,940,505
Garments and Repair Services (Revenues) (3)	194,111	49,939	26%	34,727	4,788,416	1,648,438	34%	1,179,571
Personal Hygiene Services (Revenues)	43,523	12,424	29%	8,191	610,851	207,182	34%	161,989
Entertainment and Broadcast Services (Revenue)	25,509	7,158	28%	5,863	1,180,358	416,092	35%	384,876
Subtotal	1,171,380	306,556	26%	237,140	195,317,761	71,584,486	37%	51,515,239
Credit Market (Balance of Loans)	61,547	19,342	31%	17,092	77,129,154	27,357,564	35%	28,984,017
Insurance and Capitalization (Reserves)	13,223	2,536	19%	8,894	5,054,675	808,470	16%	3,471,009
Subtotal	1,171,380	306,556	26%	237,140				

SOURCE: IBGE, Censo 1950, various volumes.

NOTES: (1) Data for the state of Rio de Janeiro and the Federal District are aggregated.

(2) Trade services include brokerage of goods and insurance, agency for the purchase and sale of goods, warehouses, dispatch services, etc.

(3) Garment and repair services include arts and crafts workshops such as goldsmiths, blacksmiths, carpenters, etc.; laundries; garages; etc.

with 70,000 in São Paulo, representing 36% of all such rail workers in the nation, and twice the number identified in Rio de Janeiro, which was the second-most-important railroad state in the nation. The national railway network reached 35,000 km, of which 7,594 km were in São Paulo and only 2,653 km were in Rio de Janeiro. In 1950 there were only a thousand kilometers of electrified lines nationally, and most of these were in São Paulo. The next-most-important employer in this transport sector was the growing bus transport sector, with 18,000 employees in São Paulo, who represented 42% of this national workforce. In contrast, there was little employment in aviation, since this was still the early days of its consolidation in Brazil. Although employment in maritime navigation and cabotage (coastal trading) was important in Brazil, this sector had little significance in the state, which accounted for only 5% of national workers in this area (see Table 4.3).

As was to be expected, the capital city and its metropolitan area held a large share of the state's service workers by 1950. Although the Metropolitan Region of São Paulo was not formally created until 1973, we can determine the importance of the future RMSP.[6] In 1950 only sixteen of the thirty-seven municipalities that would later be part of the RMSP were in existence. But these sixteen contained all the future municipalities within their borders. We estimate that the metropolitan region of the capital represented 83% of the state population, 86% of its retailers, and 93% of retail sales. Metropolitan São Paulo at that time had 2.6 million residents, of which 2.2 million were in the capital. The largest of the satellite municipalities that would become part of the RMSP was Santo André, with 127,000 persons. São Bernardo and São Caetano, which would also become important automobile production centers in the decade of the 1950s, were still small urban nuclei. São Caetano had 60,000 inhabitants and São Bernardo do Campo just 29,000 (see Table 4.4).[7]

The evolution of the service industry (meaning both trade and services) in the state was one of constant growth. Already by the 1940s, São Paulo accounted for a third of the value of the national GDP in the service industry, and by 1980 it was first in in the nation. Second in importance was Rio de Janeiro, which then represented only about half of the participation of the state of São Paulo, a trend that would be even more pronounced in the twenty-first century as Rio lost most of the federal bureaucracy to Brasília. Although the intensity of industrialization through the 1980s reduced the participation of the services sector in the GDP of the state of São Paulo, there was a strong recovery beginning in the 1990s, when it became the dominant sector in the state's economy, a position that only increased in the twenty-first century (see Figure 4.1).[8]

TABLE 4.3

Transport and Communications Services in Brazil, São Paulo, and Rio de Janeiro, 1950

	Brazil	São Paulo	São Paulo as % of Brazil	Rio de Janeiro + DF (1)
Railway System				
Extension Lines in Traffic (km)	35,919	7,594	21%	2,790
Electrified Extension (km)	1,079	724	67%	209
Personnel Employed	195,811	70,375	36%	31,882
Revenue (Cr$ 1000)	4,443,809			
Navigation and Cabotage				
Applied Capital (Cr$ 1000)	3,241,366	177,260	5%	2,593,690
Personnel Employed	31,794	1,230	4%	17,851
Onboard Staff	21,152	947	4%	11,833
Salaries Paid (Cr$ 1000)	656,145	32,060	5%	496,660
Floating Material (gross tons)	780,281	34,422	4%	616,368
Revenue (Cr$ 1000)	2,187,063	129,684	6%	1,726,715
Air Navigation				
Applied Capital (Cr$ 1000)	498,636	74,520	15%	372,298
Personnel Employed	10,480	1,571	15%	7,713
Salaries Paid (Cr$ 1000)	342,618	42,446	12%	277,942
Aircraft	205	36	18%	115
Passengers Transported (thousands)	1,322	516	39%	739
Revenue (Cr$ 1000)	609,899	165,620	27%	686,760
Automobiles and Trucks				
Applied Capital (Cr$ 1000)	1,953,821	871,452	45%	520,242
Passenger Vehicles	8,719	3,420	39%	1,802
Passengers Carried (thousands)	886,472	415,865	47%	257,371
Personnel Employed	42,312	17,918	42%	12,365
Salaries Paid (Cr$ 1000)	620,038	330,407	53%	176,424
Revenue (Cr$ 1000)	2,377,370	1,030,354	43%	639,875
Urban Rail				
Extension	2,201	853	39%	659
Applied Capital (Cr$ 1000)	981,259	163,723	17%	707,325
Personnel Employed	22,753	6,273	28%	10,121
Salaries Paid (Cr$ 1000)	452,744	109,920	24%	253,596
Passenger Cars	3,202	951	30%	1,497
Passengers Transported (thousands)	1,583,653	491,470	31%	714,828
Revenue (Cr$ 1000)	651,574	226,121	35%	274,852
Communications (2)				
Applied Capital (Cr$ 1000)	2,887,529	997,335	35%	1,283,924
Personnel Employed	20,003	7,012	35%	7,489
Salaries Paid (Cr$ 1000)	381,877	116,488	31%	195,809
Revenue (Cr$ 1000)	912,697	310,472	34%	398,489
Sum of Employed Persons	**323,153**	**104,379**	**32%**	**87,421**
Sum of Revenue Figures	**11,182,412**			**915,604**

SOURCE: IBGE: Censo 1950, various volumes.

NOTES: (1) Data for the state of Rio de Janeiro and the Federal District are aggregated.

(2) Communications includes telephone, telegraph, radiotelegraph, and radiotelephone services.

TABLE 4.4
Retail Trade Activities in the State, Metropolitan Region, and Municipality of São Paulo, 1950

	Population	Establishments	Total Personnel	Sales
State Total	9,134,423	50,519	116,968	20,289,859
Metropolitan Region of São Paulo (RMSP) (1)	2,662,844	17,678	48,441	9,775,980
City of São Paulo	2,198,096	15,174	44,120	9,075,391
Other Municipalities of the RMSP	464,748	2,504	4,321	700,589
City of São Paulo % of RMSP	83%	86%	91%	93%

SOURCE: Censo 1950, Série Regional, volume XXV, tomo 3, Estado de São Paulo.
NOTE: (1) The RMSP was created in 1973. Of the thirty-seven municipalities that made up the RMSP at the time of its creation, only sixteen had been independent municipalities at the time of the 1950 census. The others were created in the 1950s (thirteen) and in the 1960s (six).

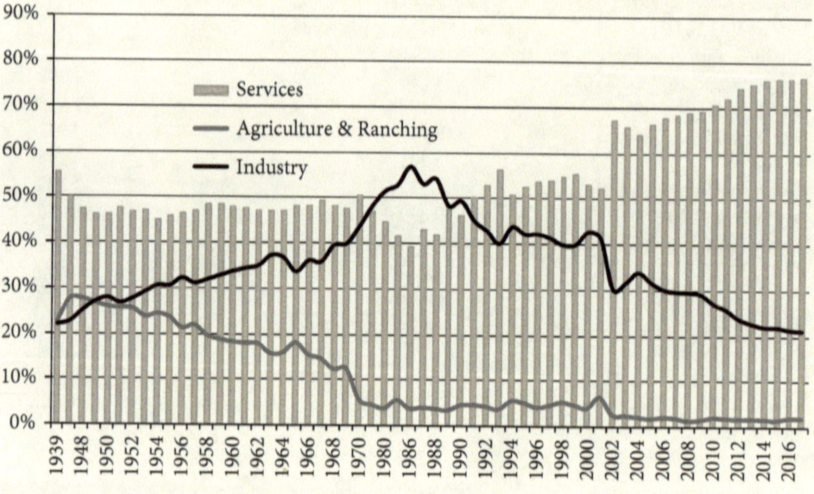

Figure 4.1. Participation of the Economic Sectors in the GDP of the State of São Paulo, 1939 to 2017

SOURCE: 1939–2009 Ipeadata, Regional; 2010–2017 SEADE.

It was in the metropolitan region of São Paulo that most of the early twentieth-century textile industry was located and in which was first established almost all the automobile industry beginning in the middle of the twentieth century.[9] This massive growth of industry gave a new dimension to the city and its metropolitan area. If in the first half of the century its population expansion was largely explained by the massive arrival of European immigrants, starting in the middle of the twentieth century it was the migrants coming from all parts of Brazil that drove this growth. In 1960 the capital, with 3.8 million inhabitants, surpassed the city of Rio de Janeiro to become the largest city in Brazil, with a population five times larger than Salvador or Porto Alegre, and the state was now the most populous in the nation. By 1991 it reached a population of 9.6 million, but then growth slowed considerably in the next three decades. On the other hand, the metropolitan region continued to expand and made up almost half of the state population from 1970 to 2020 (see Table 4.5).

It was this metropolitan market that would be the center of the trade and services sector in the state of São Paulo, just as it had been the center for industry. With the post-1960 process of industrial decentralization, the contributions of industry contained within the RMSP declined as a share of both the state industrial sector and the national figure in the last decades of the century. At the same time there was a steady growth of the tertiary sector in the capital, the metropolitan region, and the state, and it soon came to dominate the local economy. As of 1980, São Paulo's retail and wholesale activity accounted for 25% of Brazilian employment in this sector and 36% of the value of national sales. In the state there were 162,000 businesses employing 811,000 people. Wholesale firms accounted for the dominant share of sales, but it was retail activities that accounted for 80% of the employed persons. The most important segments of the retail trade were textiles, woven fabrics, and clothing (employing 119,000 workers) and food, beverages, and tobacco (employing another 113,000 people). In turn, the most important of the wholesale sector activities was the food, beverages, and tobacco segment, which employed 54,000 persons, with the fuel, food, beverage, and tobacco sectors being the leaders in sales. São Paulo had a dominant role in the nation in some of these service sectors, such as wholesale electrical supplies and non-electric machines and appliances, new and used vehicles, vehicle parts and accessories, fabrics, woven artifacts, and clothing (see Table 4.6).

The entire service sector in the state of São Paulo in 1980 accounted for 30% of employed persons and 35% of sales in Brazil. Services employed some 801,000 people in 182,000 establishments. The largest numbers of workers were employed in food services; services provided to companies, institutions, and people; and repair, maintenance, and installation services (see Table 4.7). As of 1980, workers in the wholesale and retail trades and in all the services in the state employed more people than were employed in agriculture (16 million workers compared to 1.4 million in agriculture),[10] but still less than the 2.2 million persons working in industry. In terms of value added and employment, industry still dominated the state and

TABLE 4.5

Evolution of the Population of Brazil and the State, Capital, and Metropolitan Region of São Paulo, 1950–2019

Region	1950	1960	1970	1980	1991	2000	2010	2019
				POPULATION				
Brazil	51,944,398	70,324,103	93,134,846	119,011,052	146,825,475	169,799,170	190,747,731	210,680,072
State of São Paulo	9,134,423	12,823,806	17,770,975	25,042,074	31,588,925	37,032,403	41,262,199	46,042,770
RMSP	2,653,860	4,739,406	8,139,730	12,588,725	15,444,941	17,878,703	19 683 975	21,571,866
City of São Paulo	2 198 096	3 667 899	5 924 615	8 493 226	9 646 185	10 434 252	11,253,503	12,252,023

AVERAGE ANNUAL GROWTH OF POPULATION BETWEEN CENSUSES

	1950–1960	1960–1970	1970–1980	1980–1991	1991–2000	2000–2010	2010–2019
State of São Paulo	3.5%	3.3%	3.5%	2.1%	1.8%	1.1%	1.1%
RMSP	6.0%	5.6%	4.5%	1.9%	1.6%	1.0%	0.9%
City of São Paulo	5.3%	4.9%	3.7%	1.2%	0.9%	0.8%	0.9%
RMSP Without São Paulo	7.9%	7.5%	6.3%	3.2%	2.8%	1.3%	1.0%

SOURCE: Ipeadata, Regional; IBGE, Prefeitura de São Paulo, accessed November 5, 2019.

TABLE 4.6

Retail and Wholesale Trade in the State of São Paulo and Their Relative Importance in Brazil, 1980

					SÃO PAULO AS % OF BRAZIL	
	Firms	Personnel Employed	Salaries Paid	Sales	Personnel	Sales
Retail Trade						
Food Products, Beverages, and Tobacco	51,224	112,979	2,383,600	126,066,345	12%	21%
Pharmaceutical and Dental Products	8,158	38,983	2,804,418	65,184,354	27%	30%
Fabrics, Woven Artifacts, Clothing	30,031	119,315	7,238,820	122,283,014	26%	28%
Electrical and Non-Electrical Machines and Apparatus	7,718	48,721	5,102,662	109,216,920	29%	31%
Hardware, Tools, and Metallurgical Products	10,797	65,728	5,089,532	133,059,655	31%	33%
New and Used Vehicles, Parts, and Accessories	7,813	47,701	5,620,510	198,507,977	30%	34%
Machines and Equipment for Industrial Use	1,898	17,174	3,384,904	64,138,689	29%	31%
Fuels and Lubricants	5,619	41,094	3,007,874	204,338,942	29%	34%
Paper and Cardboard	7,687	21,354	1,224,723	21,071,329	34%	35%
Goods in General, Including Food	3,862	76,113	7,046,059	218,964,436	28%	33%
Goods in General, Excluding Food	864	17,057	2,855,493	44,575,004	29%	36%
Miscellaneous Items	10,797	37,524	2,272,100	38,585,727	32%	33%
Used Articles	1,542	3,868	121,876	3,707,886	33%	42%
Retail Trade Subtotal	148,010	647,611	48,141,571	1,349,700,278	23%	31%

(continued)

TABLE 4.6
(continued)

	Firms	Personnel Employed	Salaries Paid	Sales	SÃO PAULO AS % OF BRAZIL	
					Personnel	Sales
Wholesale						
Extractive and Agricultural Products, Except Food	448	4,075	511,210	37,416,473	11%	9%
Food Products, Beverages, and Tobacco	5,380	54,214	7,756,299	507,769,757	32%	45%
Pharmaceutical and Dental Products	917	13,423	3,085,312	128,610,535	37%	47%
Fabrics, Woven Artifacts, Clothing	1,577	13,468	1,572,892	75,390,952	49%	58%
Electrical and Non-Electrical Machines and Apparatus	285	3,791	714,580	82,580,649	47%	79%
Hardware, Tools, and Metallurgical Products	2,051	27,047	5,349,839	222,227,721	47%	44%
New and Used Vehicles, Parts, and Accessories	512	8,662	1,926,527	81,794,777	51%	60%
Machines and Equipment for Industrial Use	531	8,686	2,908,970	56,034,638	52%	54%
Fuels and Lubricants	258	4,599	1,295,879	675,038,509	39%	38%
Paper and Cardboard	507	5,849	985,498	28,488,449	43%	50%
Goods in General, Including Food	79	4,075	808,262	35,444,331	24%	33%
General Merchandise, Excluding Food	45	506	58,256	1,629,963	20%	14%
Miscellaneous Items	800	7,448	1,189,528	30,616,244	54%	58%
Used Articles	1,092	8,012	610,024	20,329,841	58%	64%
Wholesale Trade Subtotal	14,482	163,855	28,773,076	1,981,372,839	37%	41%
Total Retail and Wholesale Trade	**162,492**	**811,466**	**76,914,647**	**3,331,073,117**	**25%**	**36%**

SOURCE: Recenseamento Geral 1980, volume 4, no. 1, Censo Comercial Brasil; volume 4, no. 19, Censo Comercial de São Paulo.

TABLE 4.7

Services in the State of São Paulo and Their Relative Importance in Brazil, 1980

Service Categories	Firms	Personnel Employed	Salaried Paid	Sales	SÃO PAULO AS A % OF BRAZIL Personnel	SÃO PAULO AS A % OF BRAZIL Sales
Total Services	**182,390**	**801,642**	**84,993,038**	**507,510,146**	**30%**	**35%**
Accommodation	3,987	27,293	1,816,441	10,462,028	21%	22%
Food	67,833	188,843	6,983,410	92,497,340	26%	34%
Accommodation and Food Services Subtotal	**71,820**	**216,136**	**8,799,851**	**102,959,368**	**25%**	**32%**
Repair, Maintenance, and Installation	43,910	122,767	8,129,767	43,087,185	27%	33%
Tailor-made	7,722	17,855	597,422	5,004,538	25%	31%
Repair, Maintenance, and Installation Services Subtotal	**51,632**	**140,622**	**8,727,189**	**48,091,723**	**27%**	**33%**
Personal	4,806	13,541	642,414	4,988,468	30%	36%
Personal Hygiene	15,820	28,244	701,446	6,174,842	28%	34%
Personal and Personal Hygiene Services Subtotal	**20,626**	**41,785**	**1,343,860**	**11,163,310**	**29%**	**35%**
Broadcasting and Television	256	6,374	1,372,427	12,162,285	19%	32%
Entertainment	1,792	8,842	759,617	4,725,913	27%	32%
Radio, Television, and Entertainment Services Subtotal	**2,048**	**15,216**	**2,132,044**	**16,888,198**	**23%**	**32%**
Agriculture and Livestock	677	29,739	2,717,681	7,378,827	43%	24%
Trade and Leasing of Goods and Services	3,016	21,301	4,160,109	54,160,104	31%	43%
Financial, Insurance, and Capitalization	1,283	13,629	3,114,648	35,498,055	35%	21%
Transport	3,294	28,601	4,471,097	32,653,031	36%	36%
Technical Assistance in Construction and Works	2,375	42,555	12,826,646	40,826,707	40%	44%
Cleaning and Sanitizing Buildings and Households	983	49,545	2,858,514	7,468,369	27%	28%
Provided to Companies, Entities, and People	15,852	151,672	28,366,372	98,206,636	38%	46%
Health	1,558	9,975	956,220	4,325,384	30%	33%
Miscellaneous Auxiliary Services Subtotal	**29,038**	**347,017**	**59,471,287**	**280,517,113**	**36%**	**37%**
Purchase, Sale, Subdivision, and Development	4,632	20,747	2,421,030	36,307,572	36%	39%
Administration, Rental, and Leasing of Real Estate	2,594	20,119	2,097,777	11,582,862	49%	43%
Purchase, Sale, Allotment, Incorporation Services Subtotal	**7,226**	**40,866**	**4,518,807**	**47,890,434**	**41%**	**40%**

SOURCE: Recenseamento Geral 1980, volume 5, no. 1, Censo de Serviços do Brasil; volume 5, no. 19, Censo de Serviços de São Paulo.

accounted for 47% of the state GDP, compared with 35% for services and 14% for agriculture.

The 1980 census divided the state of São Paulo into more than forty zones, including what was denoted as "Greater São Paulo." As could be expected, the Greater São Paulo region accounted for about half of the state's establishments, employed persons, and retail and wholesale sales, and also employed two-thirds of those who worked in services and took in three-quarters of the value of sales in the state's services sector. A total of 79,000 businesses were registered in Greater São Paulo, with 442,000 people employed. In services there were 98,000 establishments, with 500,000 people employed. The Campinas, Baixada Santista, and Vale do Paraíba Paulista areas were the other most representative areas in services, but with participation far below that of Greater São Paulo. Paulínia and Cubatão were also important, since they were the site of two large oil refineries and petrochemical plants. Excluding these two locations, the most important service sectors were in Santos, Campinas, São Jose do Rio Preto, and Ribeirão Preto (see Table 4.8).

Of the thirty-seven municipalities in the Greater São Paulo region, the capital city dominated the service industry, accounting for 82% of both service and commercial employment, 78% of total sales trade, and 89% of service sector sales in the area that would come to be designated the RMSP. In the capital these services now represented greater shares of the capital economy than did industry (see Table 4.9).

Within the capital, the retail and wholesale trades and services had almost equal weight in the workforce. The retail trade employed 356,000 people in 61,000 establishments; the wholesale sector had 102,000 people in 8,000 establishments. Services employed 410,000 people in 75,000 establishments. The largest of these services were listed as "miscellaneous auxiliary services," which included services rendered to entities and individuals. This large sector accounted for half of service sector workers and two-thirds of sales. Next in importance were lodging and catering services and repair, maintenance, and installation services. In commerce, the largest occupation was in food, beverages, and tobacco, and in the fabric, woven artifacts, and clothing sectors (see Table 4.10).

The 1980s and 1990s were a long period of crisis in the Brazilian economy, with rampant inflation and low growth. During this period, however, there were two internal developments that would have profound economic repercussions in the final years of the twentieth century and the first two decades of the twentieth century. The first was the opening of the economy, and the second was the end of inflation through the implementation

TABLE 4.8

Trade and Services Activities by Areas and Municipalities of the State of São Paulo, 1980

	WHOLESALE AND RETAIL COMMERCE			SERVICES		
	Firms	Personnel	Sales	Firms	Personnel	Sales
State Total	**162,492**	**811,466**	**3,331,073,117**	**182,390**	**801,642**	**507,510,146**
Greater São Paulo	78,941	442,736	1,894,035,679	97,894	500,403	386,010,228
Campinas	8,172	46,365	356,471,284	6,278	35,957	17,522,810
Baixada Santista	6,583	35,997	317,309,250	7,859	37,652	19,586,489
Vale do Paraíba Paulista	6,649	28,648	116,443,373	6,837	24,301	10,032,242
Ribeirão Preto	4,071	22,064	78,242,490	4,086	16,880	8,296,568
Bauru	2,590	14,197	46,519,500	3,244	10,367	4,055,969
São José do Rio Preto	2,420	12,290	45,218,889	2,235	7,327	2,574,085
Sorocaba	3,337	16,358	43,303,407	3,836	12,101	5,537,777
Araraquara	3,132	12,923	33,680,008	2,945	15,731	5,284,611
Alta Sorocabana de Presidente Prudente	2,860	12,028	32,630,425	2,845	8,719	2,715,530
Açucareira de Piracicaba	2,522	10,999	27,279,523	2,538	9,872	4,357,206
Jundiái	1,948	10,385	25,375,309	2,355	8,669	4,175,018
Alta Paulista	1,960	10,022	20,988,432	2,196	6,942	2,502,071
Alta Noroeste de Aracatuba	2,197	9,750	19,533,704	2,061	6,394	2,144,264
Ourinhos	1,414	5,573	19,251,015	1,344	3,141	953,227
Depressão Periférica Setentrional	2,403	9,105	18,459,023	2,141	8,569	2,502,249
Encosta Ocidental da Mantiqueira Paulista	2,103	7,206	15,687,921	1,649	4,363	1,392,868
Serra do Jaboticabal	1,876	7,285	15,169,100	1,792	5,682	1,528,342
Médio Araraquarense	1,449	5,442	15,137,240	1,270	2,948	1,200,973
Nova Alta Paulista	1,516	6,554	14,273,896	1,530	4,364	1,139,512
Jaú	1,526	5,745	13,855,279	1,542	9,203	2,868,733
Alta Sorocabana de Assis	1,304	5,099	13,024,835	1,236	3,247	970,253
Serra de Botucatu	1,795	6,445	12,921,359	1,749	6,640	2,150,571
Alta Mogiana	1,273	4,552	12,824,060	1,357	4,322	1,201,591

(continued)

TABLE 4.8

(continued)

	WHOLESALE AND RETAIL COMMERCE			SERVICES		
	Firms	Personnel	Sales	Firms	Personnel	Sales
Planalto de Franca	1,570	5,768	12,037,663	1,280	3,272	1,429,310
Campos de Itapetininga	1,956	7,100	11,906,385	1,938	5,059	1,184,592
Rio Claro	1,361	4,903	11,461,206	1,221	3,912	1,369,180
Barretos	909	3,933	10,492,845	1,022	2,653	932,675
Bragança Paulista	1,619	5,369	9,818,235	1,424	3,850	1,174,453
Alta Araraquerense de Fernandopolis	1,630	5,878	9,687,453	1,411	3,601	839,925
Estâncias Hidrominerais Paulistas	1,375	4,649	8,282,981	1,279	4,466	1,515,618
Other Zones (1)	7,620	26,089	49,751,348	7,974	21,035	6,350,706
PRINCIPAL CITIES (EXCEPTING GREATER SÃO PAULO)						
Paulínia	110	759	225,666,433	106	782	269,995
Cubatão	308	1,645	171,058,330	498	4,486	2,269,020
Santos	3,562	23,062	127,445,505	4,161	22,416	13,536,942
Campinas	3,964	27,517	92,876,743	4,035	21,160	11,419,439
São Jose dos Campos	1,492	8,776	77,634,294	1,578	7,501	4,124,390
Ribeirão Preto	2,609	17,307	68,746,539	2,615	10,670	6,436,774
São José do Rio Preto	1,614	9,700	37,506,443	1,484	5,781	2,133,447
Bauru	1,162	8,280	34,697,200	1,505	5,758	2,385,380
Sorocaba	1,582	9,452	22,678,543	1,988	6,057	3,145,452
Piracicaba	1,602	8,069	21,755,313	1,629	6,127	3,372,479
Presidente Prudente	1,028	5,863	21,412,898	1,016	4,022	1,526,201
Jundiaí	1,304	7,985	19,921,984	1,567	6,156	3,010,688

SOURCE: Recenseamento Geral de 1980, volume 4, no. 1 and no. 19; volume 5, no. 4 and no. 19.

NOTE: (1) Includes Alta Araraquarense de Votuporanga, Tatuí, Alta Noroeste de Penapolis, Paranapiacaba, Serra de Batatais, Baixada da Ribeira, Costa Norte Paulista, Divisor Turvo Grande, Divisor São José do Dourado Tiete, Médio São Jose dos Dourados, Alto Paraíba, Apiai.

TABLE 4.9

Commerce and Services Activities in the Metropolitan Region of São Paulo, 1980

	WHOLESALE AND RETAIL COMMERCE				SERVICES			
	Firms	Personnel	Salaried	Sales	Firms	Personnel	Salaried	Sales
Greater São Paulo	78,941	442,736	51,170,590	1,894,035,679	97,894	500,403	67,600,828	386,010,228
São Paulo City	60,861	355,956	43,434,162	1,478,526,804	75,366	410,373	59,591,598	342,787,496
Aruja	105	290	12,729	760,398	127	420	24,679	187,955
Barueri	314	1,702	215,851	45,711,072	410	1,441	107,329	910,503
Biritiba Mirim	50	162	4,814	180,044	51	115	1,867	22,867
Caieiras	106	314	16,050	696,418	104	334	10,648	97,848
Cajamar	74	243	10,712	402,122	104	202	3,075	61,110
Carapicuiba	547	1,706	58,213	2,064,068	754	1,553	24,042	390,623
Cotia	219	1,003	63,835	2,253,654	282	962	52,097	461,948
Diadema	787	3,952	416,483	19,972,524	1,031	2,669	127,363	1,133,934
Embu	303	1,020	69,383	1,784,535	475	10,404	710,751	1,878,139
Embu-Guaçu	85	249	8,497	453,030	117	228	3,744	7,279
Ferraz de Vasconcelos	207	538	12,704	431,813	211	388	6,640	85,367
Francisco Morato	85	219	5,374	296,657	121	206	3,418	76,721
Franco da Rocha	208	583	22,164	965,469	219	522	15,407	190,019
Guararema	76	164	4,633	275,887	46	107	3,654	43,923
Guarulhos	2,402	11,277	982,466	70,677,608	2,660	8,631	622,073	6,262,752
Itapeceirca da Serra	184	881	64,686	3,308,830	365	858	26,822	388,845
Itapevi	168	535	18,283	820,941	297	576	12,671	174,853

(continued)

TABLE 4.9
(continued)

	WHOLESALE AND RETAIL COMMERCE				SERVICES			
	Firms	Personnel	Salaried	Sales	Firms	Personnel	Salaried	Sales
Itaquacetetuba	170	516	19,122	907,717	236	485	5,061	117,148
Jandira	135	415	11,580	430,793	231	469	10,248	120,899
Juquitiba	83	210	5,363	483,100	64	132	3,238	33,774
Mairiporã	154	431	12,199	551,400	200	461	9,130	144,515
Maua	673	3,159	244,101	48,740,502	872	2,209	117,298	956,909
Mogi das Cruzes	1,169	5,709	421,268	12,882,381	1,431	4,789	264,897	1,558,955
Osasco	1,936	9,971	879,582	22,256,058	2,316	8,259	689,436	5,589,814
Pirapora do Bom Jesus	55	108	899	58,325	46	90	777	16,555
Poa	230	581	19,271	612,386	230	398	8,869	89,249
Ribeirão Pires	231	1,041	67,871	2,323,419	302	962	49,961	371,664
Rio Grande da Serra	38	122	2,777	144,541	100	178	4,337	50,300
Salesopolis	75	144	1,864	303,547	46	107	2,294	22,899
Santa Isabel	141	386	12,903	663,055	181	377	6,115	101,845
Santana do Parnaiba	27	125	6,009	230,035	47	91	2,112	29,070
Santo Andre	2,866	15,699	1,425,428	51,242,853	3,636	14,316	1,262,151	5,115,435
São Bernardo do Campo	2,107	12,886	1,845,600	76,238,084	2,486	15,445	1,988,906	9,740,800
São Caetano do Sul	1,290	6,458	614,721	39,671,801	1,708	7,066	701,480	3,891,361
Susano	508	1,903	110,083	4,678,337	578	1,726	100,407	561,959
Taboão da Serra	272	949	48,900	2,035,471	444	2,054	1,026,223	3,270,226

SOURCE: Recenseamento Geral de 1980, volume 4, no. 19; volume 5, no. 19.

TABLE 4.10

Trade and Services Activities in the City of São Paulo, 1980

	Firms	Personnel	Salaries	Sales
Retail Trade				
Food Products, Beverages, and Tobacco	15,788	35,689	974,403	44,902,563
Pharmaceutical and Dental Products	2,769	14,853	1,186,306	18,231,423
Fabrics, Woven Artifacts, Clothing	10,743	48,970	3,756,783	59,026,656
Electrical and Non-Electrical Machines and Apparatus	2,961	18,299	2,228,521	47,183,411
Hardware, Tools, and Metallurgical Products	4,031	24,535	2,287,724	55,027,182
New and Used Vehicles, Parts, and Accessories	2,932	18,724	2,611,231	86,668,663
Machines and Equipment for Industrial Use	787	8,454	2,168,232	34,702,942
Fuels and Lubricants	1,655	13,762	1,166,054	77,205,581
Paper and Cardboard	4,204	12,607	890,408	13,350,421
Goods in General, Including Food	829	27,207	2,971,902	68,168,612
General Merchandise, Excluding Food	406	10,091	1,920,116	30,039,130
Miscellaneous Items	4,770	18,125	1,446,224	22,071,611
Used Articles	734	1,874	67,255	2,073,907
Subtotal Retail Business	52,609	253,190	23,683,159	578,652,102
Wholesale Trade				
Extractive and Agricultural Products, Excluding Food	96	936	145,164	12,926,838
Food Products, Beverages, and Tobacco	2,329	25,767	4,138,229	289,070,912
Pharmaceutical and Dental Products	492	8,355	1,924,235	75,701,430
Fabrics, Woven Artifacts, Clothing	1,324	11,824	1,442,924	66,204,656
Electrical and Non-Electrical Machines and Apparatus	190	2,759	513,364	36,609,591
Hardware, Tools, and Metallurgical Products	1,398	20,149	4,216,723	128,526,313
New and Used Vehicles, Parts, and Accessories	330	5,953	1,362,124	59,918,509
Machines and Equipment for Industrial Use	405	7,438	2,632,095	45,026,427
Fuels and Lubricants	61	1,334	461,514	94,341,371
Paper and Cardboard	364	4,807	867,172	24,127,580
Goods in General, Including Food	32	2,287	586,594	28,803,700
General Merchandise, Excluding Food	29	341	41,756	1,186,828
Miscellaneous items	601	6,217	1,066,972	25,739,300
Used articles	601	4,599	352,124	11,691,249
Subtotal Retail Trade	8,252	102,766	19,751,003	899,874,702
Total Trade—Retail and Wholesale	**60,861**	**355,956**	**43,434,162**	**1,478,526,804**
Services				
Accommodation and Food Services	26,899	92,214	4,597,465	45,532,199
Repair, Maintenance, and Installation Services	21,303	61,426	4,807,614	24,415,646
Personal and Personal Hygiene Services	8,638	22,135	932,843	6,015,913
Radio, Television, and Entertainment Services	795	7,382	1,463,437	13,557,733
Miscellaneous Auxiliary Services	14,027	201,479	44,405,338	221,581,786
Purchase, Sale, and Real Estate Services	3,704	25,739	3,384,901	31,684,217
Total Services	**75,366**	**410,373**	**51,991,515**	**342,797,494**

SOURCE: Recenseamento Geral de 1980, volume 4, no. 19; volume 5, no. 19.

of the Real Plan. Moreover, beginning in the 1990s, in parallel with the process of opening the economy in Brazil, there was a profound transformation of the production processes worldwide. Initially stimulated by financial deregulation, followed by a worldwide trade opening, this change was also accompanied by the creation of global production chains. Then came the extraordinary technological transformations, particularly in data and communications, that in the late twentieth and early twenty-first centuries ushered in a new era in production. This involved the integration of production with the formation of complex value chains, in which industry and services were integrated. The old vertical industrial processes that Brazil had created prior to 1990 were turned into integrated production processes involving industrial units and complex service systems that interacted globally and had bases in different countries.

At the same time there occurred a universal financial globalization, with capital actively participating in this system, both in production and in the circulation of goods and services.[11] According to an UNCTAD report from 2013, some 60% of global trade "consists of trade in intermediate goods and services that are incorporated at various stages in the production process of goods and services for final consumption," in what is commonly called global value chains (GVCs).[12] This fragmentation of production incorporates a multiplicity of services previously located within the industrial production process itself, most typically in industrial activities.[13]

As expected, the process of expanding the service sector in the world economy was reflected in Brazil. This has involved the establishment of many international value chains, most particularly in agriculture but also in industry. Thus both a national service sector and one totally integrated into the international market have emerged in the state. This explains why from the beginning of the twenty-first century the value added of the service sector has been increasing, replacing industry and agriculture, which gradually reduced their share in the state and national GDP.[14] In the case of São Paulo, services increased their share of the state's GDP from 50% in the early 2000s to 60% in 2017. Agriculture had a share of around 2% and industry had a declining share, as was the case in Brazil as a whole. In terms of state GDP, the most representative segments of the services sector are trade, maintenance, and repair of motor vehicles;[15] financial, insurance, and related services activities; and professional, scientific, technical, and administrative activities (see Table 4.11).

By 2000, hotel accommodation and food services was one of the most representative sectors in terms of the number of companies and employed persons (461,000 people) in the state. Another major employer was building

TABLE 4.11

Gross Domestic Product of the State of São Paulo by Sector and Subsector, 2002–2017

	VALUES IN R$ MILLIONS			% OF STATE GDP		
	2002	2010	2017	2002	2010	2017
Gross Value of Production	**942,322**	**2,275,129**	**3,568,452**	100%	100%	100%
Agriculture and Ranching	**21,451**	**40,598**	**67,861**	**2%**	**2%**	**2%**
Agriculture, Including Support and Post-Harvest		31,373	54,703	0%	1%	2%
Livestock, Including Support for Livestock		7,478	11,652	0%	0%	0%
Forestry, Fisheries, and Aquaculture Production		1,747	1,506	0%	0%	0%
Industry	**430,250**	**996,829**	**1,342,852**	**46%**	**44%**	**38%**
Extractive Industry	1,401	4,220	21,203	0%	0%	1%
Transformation Industry	350,554	813,048	1,088,627	37%	36%	31%
Electricity and Gas, Water, Sewage, Waste Management Activities	23,694	49,813	77,898	3%	2%	2%
Construction	54,601	129,748	155,124	6%	6%	4%
Services	**490,621**	**1,237,702**	**2,157,739**	**52%**	**54%**	**60%**
Trade, Maintenance, and Repair of Motor Vehicles	63,653	215,875	402,840	7%	9%	11%
Transport, Storage, and Mail	41,055	110,219	180,412	4%	5%	5%
Accommodation and Food Services	20,045	47,596	85,901	2%	2%	2%
Information and Communications Services	47,079	120,822	178,703	5%	5%	5%
Financial, Insurance, and Related Services	83,411	210,842	345,397	9%	9%	10%
Real Estate Activities	50,691	93,586	198,643	5%	4%	6%
Professional, Scientific, and Technical, Administrative Activities	65,089	169,735	303,938	7%	7%	9%
Administration, Public Education and Public Health, Defense, Social Security	57,624	145,019	236,513	6%	6%	7%
Private Education and Private Health	32,588	66,978	138,033	3%	3%	4%
Arts, Culture, Sport and Recreation, Other Service Activities	29,385	44,512	66,036	3%	2%	2%
Domestic Services		12,520	21,324	0%	1%	1%

SOURCE: Fundação SEADE, https://www.seade.gov.br/produtos/pib-anual/, accessed December 1, 2019.

and house cleaning and other business services (412,000 people). In terms of gross revenue, the most representative were telecommunications; professional technical services; road freight; other transport (rail, waterway, and air); and audiovisual services. Some categories of services in São Paulo accounted for half of national sales in those categories. These included activities auxiliary to transportation and travel agencies; information technology activities; real estate development, purchase, and sales; professional technical services; auxiliary financial; and audiovisual services (see Table 4.12).

By the period 2007–2017, when systematic annual surveys began to be carried out in the service sector, we see that the São Paulo service companies represent about 37% of the national totals in terms of the number of firms and number of persons employed, but had a higher share of revenues, on the order of 47%. The most representative sectors were information and communication services and business services, both with São Paulo accounting for above half of the national total (see Table 4.13).

Another way to evaluate the representativeness of different service activities in the state of São Paulo is through the analysis of formal sector employment. That is defined as persons who pay into the social security system and who have a formal work card. For this purpose we will use the information provided by the government's Annual Report on Social Information (RAIS). Formal employment in this sector grew systematically until 2014, reaching 14.1 million people, then began to decline due to the economic crisis of the 2010s, losing almost 1 million formal jobs. This was due to the return of alarming fiscal imbalances in the mid-2010s after long years of relative fiscal equilibrium.

In the period from 1985 to 2018 there was an initial growth in the importance of São Paulo, stabilizing in the mid-1990s at around 20% of total formal national employment. Services experienced a steady growth trend between 1985 and 2018, going from about 55% to 75% of the state labor force. The most important sectors were of course retail business, followed by real estate, hospitality, government, and food production (see Table 4.14).

Within the state of São Paulo it is evident that companies rendering services to other companies are the most important in terms of number of employed persons, followed by services rendered to families, transport, and mail. In terms of revenues, information and communications services, business services, and transport, each accounts for more than a quarter of total services sector revenue (see Table 4.15).

Along with services there was a rapid growth in modern commercial activities, from supermarkets and shopping centers to central markets

TABLE 4.12

Participation of the State of São Paulo in the Services Sector in Brazil, 2000 (Value in R$ 1000)

	STATE OF SÃO PAULO				SÃO PAULO AS A % OF BRAZIL	
	Firms	Personnel	Salaries	Gross Sales	Personnel	Gross Sales
Accommodation and Food Services	104,487	461,534	1,962,745	7,731,030	22%	27%
Transport and Auxiliary Transport Services						
Passenger Road Transport	2,436	144,357	1,480,338	4,938,399	25%	29%
Road Transport Cargo	13,770	128,431	1,141,803	8,501,443	38%	44%
Other Transport (Rail, Water, Air)	101	38,015	1,027,126	6,623,348	43%	39%
Auxiliary Activities to Transport and Travel Agencies	6,814	86,952	1,048,219	5,729,582	41%	51%
Mail, Telecommunications, and IT						
Mail	389	35,183	219,573	2,070,672	33%	47%
Telecommunications	364	33,120	1,140,812	18,989,982	32%	36%
Computer Activities	14,923	70,590	1,307,347	6,283,744	34%	52%
Incorporation, Purchase, and Sale of Real Estate on Own Account	2,374	12,847	71,770	96,430	55%	54%
Administration, Brokerage, and Rental of Third-Party Properties	6,574	39,126	296,447	1,172,974	43%	39%
Rental of Vehicles, Machinery, and Personal and Household Objects	4,159	22,055	172,017	941,609	28%	37%
Services Mainly Provided to Companies						
Professional Technical Services	29,129	170,327	2,790,626	12,728,662	43%	57%
Selection, Agency, and Hiring of Labor	1,322	139,212	803,881	1,770,572	46%	57%
Investigation, Surveillance, and Cash Transport Services	719	121,897	1,052,888	2,360,199	35%	43%
Cleaning Services for Buildings and Homes, and Other Business Services	31,976	412,141	1,946,847	6,497,299	45%	49%
Other Activities and Services						
Financial Support Services	5,645	31,299	532,459	3,086,362	46%	56%
Sales Representatives and Trade Agents	14,366	32,406	234,366	1,443,058	31%	46%
Maintenance and Repair of Vehicles and Personal and Household Objects	21,988	67,600	326,251	1,295,551	28%	43%
Audiovisual Services	3,605	34,461	645,563	6,450,343	34%	51%
Other Recreational, Cultural, and Sport Services	5,669	35,593	206,189	865,275	41%	41%
Personal Services	6,143	38,180	176,146	535,072	32%	38%
Other Service Activities	1,035	33,892	305,032	1,193,803	27%	44%

SOURCE: IBGE, Pesquisa Anual de Serviços, Rio de Janeiro, volume 2, 2000.

TABLE 4.13

The Relative Importance of Services of São Paulo as a Share of Total in Brazil, 2007–2017

	2007	2009	2011	2013	2015	2017
Total	37%	36%	37%	39%	38%	36%
1. Services Provided to Families	38%	35%	34%	34%	35%	31%
1.1 Accommodation and Food Services	41%	36%	34%	34%	34%	31%
1.2 Cultural, Recreational, and Sports Activities	34%	29%	30%	29%	31%	28%
1.3 Personal Services	22%	32%	30%	30%	31%	29%
1.4 Continuing Education Activities	34%	34%	40%	43%	44%	38%
2. Information and Communications Services	44%	42%	47%	51%	50%	48%
3. Services Provided to Companies	37%	37%	38%	41%	40%	38%
4. Transport, Auxiliary Transport Services, and Mail	36%	32%	35%	38%	40%	36%
5. Real Estate Activities	31%	34%	35%	37%	37%	39%
6. Maintenance and Repair Services	32%	32%	33%	34%	33%	29%
7. Other Service Activities	34%	39%	42%	41%	37%	36%
			PERSONNEL EMPLOYED			
Total	37%	36%	36%	36%	35%	35%
1. Services Provided to Families	34%	32%	33%	32%	32%	31%
1.1 Accommodation and Food Services	35%	32%	34%	32%	32%	31%
1.2 Cultural, Recreational, and Sports Activities	37%	30%	33%	30%	31%	29%
1.3 Personal Services	27%	31%	29%	28%	31%	29%
1.4 Continuing Education Activities	30%	31%	30%	32%	30%	32%
2. Information and Communications Services	43%	43%	44%	45%	44%	42%
3. Services Provided to Companies	41%	39%	38%	37%	37%	37%
4. Transport, Auxiliary Transport Services, and Mail	33%	33%	33%	33%	33%	33%
5. Real Estate Activities	37%	39%	40%	34%	38%	37%
6. Maintenance and Repair Services	29%	31%	32%	32%	31%	28%
7. Other Service Activities	32%	32%	32%	34%	33%	35%
			SALES			
Total	49%	48%	48%	47%	46%	47%
1. Services Provided to Families	41%	42%	41%	36%	36%	36%
1.1 Accommodation and Food Services	40%	42%	41%	37%	36%	35%
1.2 Cultural, Recreational, and Sports Activities	47%	43%	47%	35%	36%	36%
1.3 Personal Services	39%	40%	32%	33%	36%	37%
1.4 Continuing Education Activities	39%	38%	40%	34%	40%	41%
2. Information and Communications Services	57%	54%	56%	54%	55%	55%
3. Services Provided to Companies	50%	51%	48%	49%	51%	51%
4. Transport, Auxiliary Transport Services, and Mail	43%	41%	42%	42%	38%	40%
5. Real Estate Activities	41%	42%	44%	42%	41%	41%
6. Maintenance and Repair Services	35%	33%	32%	31%	32%	33%
7. Other Service Activities	57%	53%	53%	53%	52%	57%

SOURCE: IBGE, SIDRA, tables 2715 and 2577: Pesquisa Nacional de Serviços.

TABLE 4.14

Labor Market Services Sector: Participation of the State of São Paulo in Formal Jobs in Brazil. RAIS data, 1985–2018

	1985	1990	1995	2000	2005	2010	2015	2018
	FORMAL EMPLOYMENT (RAIS)							
Total Jobs, State of São Paulo (All Sectors)	6,755,555	7,633,984	7,708,277	8,049,532	9,760,764	12,873,605	13,697,471	13,247,463
Retail Business	641,674	755,500	860,585	1,073,566	1,496,741	2,040,029	2,219,226	2,141,082
Wholesale	192,696	226,543	232,992	246,830	331,710	466,338	516,330	518,480
Credit, Insurance, and Capitalization Institutions	346,920	288,109	253,803	228,016	248,830	316,742	340,177	340,075
Administration of Real Estate, Securities, Etc.	580,302	639,373	654,441	946,847	1,163,725	1,693,932	1,918,516	1,974,155
Transport and Communications	315,578	323,413	422,280	450,126	545,780	786,777	875,909	817,138
Accommodation, Food, and Repair Services	629,816	711,795	595,486	693,464	880,401	1,182,045	1,345,630	1,351,420
Medical, Dental, and Veterinary Services	108,589	112,689	254,462	279,671	367,113	494,994	650,187	692,579
Teaching	50,272	62,491	249,024	265,678	295,344	402,518	518,624	553,826
Direct and Autonomous Public Administration	902,778	1,006,223	1,255,881	1,308,655	1,470,661	1,624,624	1,689,496	1,576,609
Total Commerce and Services Jobs in State	3,768,625	4,126,136	4,778,954	5,492,853	6,800,305	9,007,999	10,074,095	9,965,364
	PARTICIPATION OF SERVICE JOBS IN THE STATE OF SÃO PAULO IN FORMAL JOBS IN BRAZIL (RAIS)							
Total	18%	18%	20%	21%	20%	20%	21%	21%
Retail Business	30%	32%	32%	30%	30%	29%	28%	28%
Wholesale	38%	39%	37%	36%	35%	34%	32%	32%
Credit, Insurance, and Capitalization Institutions	37%	36%	36%	41%	40%	40%	39%	40%
Administration of Real Estate, Securities, Etc.	38%	38%	40%	37%	37%	37%	36%	37%
Transport and Communications	31%	31%	31%	32%	33%	34%	32%	32%
Accommodation, Food, Repair Services	30%	30%	34%	31%	30%	32%	31%	32%
Medical, Dental, and Veterinary Services	37%	29%	29%	30%	32%	34%	33%	32%
Teaching	28%	30%	29%	29%	29%	27%	26%	27%
Direct and Autonomous Public Administration	21%	21%	23%	22%	19%	18%	18%	17%
Total Jobs, State of São Paulo, Commerce and Services	29%	29%	30%	29%	28%	28%	28%	28%

SOURCE: RAIS and CAGED databases, http://bi.mte.gov.br/bgcaged/, accessed November 25, 2019.

TABLE 4.15

Sectoral Share of Employed Persons and Revenue from Services in the State of São Paulo, 2007–2017

	2007	2009	2011	2013	2015	2017
	PERSONNEL EMPLOYED					
Total	100%	100%	100%	100%	100%	100%
1. Services Provided to Families	19%	18%	19%	19%	20%	20%
1.1 Accommodation and Food Services	16%	14%	15%	15%	16%	15%
1.2 Cultural, Recreational, and Sports Activities	1%	1%	1%	1%	1%	1%
1.3 Personal Services	1%	2%	2%	2%	2%	2%
1.4 Continuing Education Activities	1%	1%	1%	2%	2%	2%
2. Information and Communications Services	9%	9%	9%	10%	10%	10%
3. Services Provided to Companies	44%	44%	44%	43%	42%	43%
4. Transport, Auxiliary Transport Services, and Mail	19%	20%	19%	19%	19%	19%
4.1 Road Transport	11%	11%	11%	12%	12%	12%
4.2 Other Transport	1%	2%	2%	1%	1%	1%
4.3 Storage and Auxiliary Transport Services	4%	5%	5%	5%	4%	5%
4.4 Courier and Other Delivery Activities	2%	2%	2%	2%	1%	1%
5. Real Estate Activities	1%	1%	2%	1%	2%	2%
6. Maintenance and Repair Services	3%	3%	3%	3%	3%	3%
7. Other Service Activities	4%	4%	4%	4%	3%	4%
	SALES					
Total	100%	100%	100%	100%	100%	100%
1. Services Provided to Families	7%	8%	9%	8%	9%	9%
1.1 Accommodation and Food Services	6%	7%	7%	7%	7%	7%
1.2 Cultural, Recreational, and Sports Activities	1%	1%	1%	1%	1%	1%
1.3 Personal Services	0%	1%	0%	1%	1%	1%
1.4 Continuing Education Activities	0%	0%	1%	1%	1%	1%
2. Information and Communications Services	36%	32%	31%	29%	27%	27%
3. Services Provided to Companies	23%	27%	26%	28%	30%	29%
4. Transport, Auxiliary Transport Services, and Mail	25%	24%	25%	26%	24%	25%
4.1 Road Transport	12%	12%	12%	13%	11%	12%
4.2 Other Transport	4%	4%	4%	4%	5%	5%
4.3 Storage and Auxiliary Transport Services	6%	6%	7%	7%	7%	6%
4.4 Courier and Other Delivery Activities	2%	2%	2%	2%	2%	2%
5. Real Estate Activities	2%	2%	2%	2%	2%	2%
6. Maintenance and Repair Services	1%	1%	1%	1%	1%	1%
7. Other Service Activities	6%	5%	6%	6%	6%	7%

Source: IBGE, SIDRA, tables 2715 and 2577: Pesquisa Nacional de Serviços.

provisioning the cities. In the second half of the twentieth century there were major changes in the trade model, in both wholesale and retail activities and organization. Retail is part of the distribution system that serves as a link between consumer and producer. Retail outlets in this period became increasingly proactive in identifying consumers' needs and defining what should be produced to meet market demands. Wholesale centers in turn arose to provide a central market for retail outlets. Large central markets offering fresh food were created to supply the main urban centers. In the retail part of trade the major change is the emergence of supermarket chains and shopping centers, which have replaced traditional small family-run retail shops in all major cities in Brazil, profoundly changing the configuration of cities and the life of urban populations.

The formal wholesale central food markets were promoted by private and public agencies in a model developed beginning in the 1970s by the National Supply System (SINAC), which provided general technical information for supplying national markets. SINAC defined and imposed standards and technical norms in —packaging standards, market information, production techniques, and organizational, productive, and commercial formats—in the absence of a structured market standard, and without a doubt achieved a transformation of the Brazilian fruit and vegetable system.

One result of this standardization was the establishment of a network of regional wholesale markets of mixed public and private capital to serve as a point of distribution between producers and wholesale distributors, providing the best balance between supply and prices. In association with the states and municipalities, twenty-one companies called supply centers (the CEASAs) were created, along with thirty-four urban wholesale markets, thirty-two rural wholesale markets, and various retail markets of varying sizes in both large and medium-sized urban centers.[16] Under this model, in 1964 a wholesale central food market was established by the state government for the city of São Paulo in Vila Leopoldina, along the Pinheiros River marginal highway. In 1997, in a debt arrangement with the state, the federal government took over this central market.[17] Today this market, CEAGESP, is the third-largest wholesale central market for perishables in the world, with products sold from 1,436 municipalities, 23 states, and 24 other countries.[18] The market receives tourists from all over the world, and it also supplies much of the country with flowers, fruits, plants, fish, vegetables, and legumes, handling 250,000 tons of these products per month.[19] CEAGESP receives 50,000 persons per day and accommodates 12,000 vehicles. There are currently plans to construct a new warehouse outside the central area of the city, using a space of 640,000 m^2, close to the University of São Paulo and the Institute for Technological Research, in order to create a technology district.[20]

In Brazil, the distribution of food products used to be carried out exclusively by small, specialized stores and by the traditional street market. The latter has never disappeared and is still a fundamental part of Brazilian urban life across the country. Street markets occur weekly in the same public spaces and are widely available in most urban neighborhoods, and are accessible to the majority of urban residents on foot. This system of public fairs makes for a more competitive market, particularly in horticultural products. In the city of São Paulo alone, there are approximately 850 street markets involving 16,305 suppliers.[21]

However, small neighborhood food stores have slowly and steadily been replaced by supermarkets. The first supermarkets appeared in Brazil only in the middle of the twentieth century.[22] The substantial increase in urban populations in the period motivated the search for more modern mechanisms for food production and distribution. The changes in government agricultural policy in the 1970s reflected the need to adequately supply the growing urban population at cheap prices to keep urban wages under control.[23] The government supported the supermarket sector, because through economies of scale these institutions reduced costs in distribution, allowed for lower food prices, and thus reduced the cost of living and inflation.[24] In the 1970s, several formats were tested in terms of size and variety of markets, including the hypermarket.[25] In the 1980s and 1990s, with the fiscal crisis, which substantially reduced public funding for agricultural production, there was a profound transformation in Brazilian agriculture that led to the integration of processing, distribution, and export techniques through what became known as value chains. In this case, the relative power of the efficient distribution channels, of which supermarkets were a part, expanded and became an additional source of financing for agricultural producers, offsetting part of the reduction in public sector funding.[26] Throughout the 1980s, supermarkets have consolidated their role as the most efficient distribution channel. In 1989, for example, there were 32,950 supermarkets, directly employing 533,000 employees, with 95,677 cash registers.[27] Since then, the system has grown exponentially.[28] At the end of 2016, the sector had more than 89,000 stores, with 225,025 cash registers, a total area of 21.7 million square meters (m^2), and sales of 338.7 billion reais, representing more than 5.4% of national GDP. São Paulo, with 32% of these supermarket sales, was the leading state in the nation, followed by Rio Grande do Sul, with 12% of national sales, and Minas Gerais, with 11%.[29] In the 1990s and the first decade of the new century there was increasing concentration of these supermarkets into ever larger chains through mergers and acquisitions using both national and foreign capital. But this concentration of vendors has slowed, and the growth of street markets and specialty shops has recently reduced these concentration levels.[30] Interestingly, the dominance of the large supermarket chains has not led to higher fresh food prices, though it has had an impact on processed food prices.[31] Moreover, it has unquestionably been a positive development for small producers.

Following global trends, the modernization of the retail sector in Brazil also saw the creation of shopping centers or malls, which contained multiple stores in one large complex with extensive parking. Although galleries of stores had been in existence since the middle of the century, the first modern mall of this type opened in 1966 in the city of São Paulo. It was the Shopping Center Iguatemi, which had a major impact on the urban neighborhood in which it was established. Financed by thousands of investors, Iguatemi opened with 25,000 square meters of gross leasable area. Iguatemi's early years were marked by the almost complete rejection of its facilities and innovative content; stores inside the mall closed and there was no financial return for investors.[32] Nevertheless, in 1971, the Shopping Center Conjunto Nacional started in Brasília, and in the mid-1970s several new malls were constructed, three in São Paulo, one in Salvador, and one in Belo Horizonte. Having overcome initial problems of acceptance, by the 1980s these shopping centers had become a basic part of the urban landscape in Brazil.[33]

The 1990s marked important changes in the configuration of the shopping centers, which began to have large leisure areas, movie chains, and extensive food courts to serve a varied audience. Shopping has become part of city life, particularly for young people, who use this safe space for multiple activities. The ease of use of shopping malls, with ample spaces, parking lots, and high levels of security, is an attraction in Brazilian cities, especially considering the growing problems of crime. Surveys have found that people uses these shopping malls in numerous ways, including accessing services, dining in restaurants, and even for simple leisure activities.[34] At the beginning of 2020, there were 577 shopping malls in Brazil with 105,592 stores and a leasable area of 16 million square meters. They employed more than 1.1 million workers and had 502 million visitors a month. In the regional distribution of shopping malls, 302 were concentrated in the Southeast, 95 in the South, and 88 in the Northeast. The state of São Paulo had 182 malls and the city of São Paulo had 54, followed by the city of Rio de Janeiro, with 39.[35]

Aside from all these structural changes, the service sector was unusual in that it had a higher ratio of workers who participated in the formal labor system—that is, they had work cards that guaranteed them government health and pension benefits. Service-sector workers accounted for 78% of all workers with formal work cards at both the national and state levels. And the Ministry of Economy's RAIS surveys show that São Paulo had an unusually high ratio of these registered workers. In the capital, 90% of the workers in the legal labor market were service and commerce workers (see Table 4.16).

While 43% of the state's service and commerce workers lived in the city, there were some exceptional occupations where the capital was dominant. These include artistic, creative, and performing activities in cinema, radio, and television; financial activities; information services; and insurance. Corporate headquarters and business management consultancy activities were also concentrated in the capital, as were office services, administrative support, and other business services. The importance of the capital's major business companies within the national economy are reflected in these numbers.

Some of the São Paulo companies in the service sector are of major national and even international importance. The journal *Valor* periodically compiles a list of the 1,000 largest Brazilian companies, with various data, including the state where the company's headquarters are located.[36] This list includes the ten largest companies in each sector of activity. What is evident is that the state of São Paulo is home to the headquarters of most companies in the majority of sectors. For example, in the medical services sector, nine of the top ten companies in the industry were headquartered in the state of São Paulo. The same was true of the pharmaceutical and cosmetics sector. In two other sectors, specialized services and sugar and alcohol, the capital's companies were among the ten largest. In fifteen of the twenty-eight sectors profiled, half or more of the top-ten headquarters were in the state. Although the information specifies only the state and not the host city, it can be assumed that for the state most of the headquarters were located in the capital or metropolitan region of São Paulo. Even those located elsewhere in the state use the city for financial services, consulting, communication, and innovation in general (see Table 4.17).

Another source for examining this question of the growth and importance of the service economy is data from the Banco Central do Brasil.[37] There is a high degree of concentration of financial services in the city of São Paulo. The capital houses the large private national and international banks, the largest exchanges in the country, the main entities representing

TABLE 4.16

Formal Employment by Commerce and Services Activity, Brazil, State of São Paulo, and City of São Paulo, 2018

	FORMAL EMPLOYEES			PERCENTAGE		
	Brazil	State	City	State as % of Brazil	City as % of State	City as % of Brazil
Public Administration, Defense, and Social Security	9,128,919	1,585,446	751,229	17%	47%	8%
Retail Business	6,597,513	1,871,726	582,621	28%	31%	9%
Services for Buildings and Landscape Activities	1,592,103	632,903	315,399	40%	50%	20%
Office Services, Administrative Support, and Other Business Services	1,412,136	582,677	309,442	41%	53%	22%
Human Health Care Activities	2,105,784	673,029	307,352	32%	46%	15%
Food	1,583,034	532,852	224,635	34%	42%	14%
Education	2,105,299	566,263	219,788	27%	39%	10%
Wholesale Trade, Except Motor Vehicles and Motorcycles	1,623,132	518,480	211,416	32%	41%	13%
Ground Transportation	1,656,783	491,939	164,291	30%	33%	10%
Surveillance, Security, and Investigation Activities	606,555	189,077	129,942	31%	69%	21%
Financial Services Activities	610,867	221,418	125,502	36%	57%	21%
Information Technology Services	369,782	162,626	95,674	44%	59%	26%
Specialized Construction Services	623,255	216,535	94,717	35%	44%	15%
Labor Selection, Agency, and Leasing	532,145	180,888	84,498	34%	47%	16%
Activities of Associative Organizations	783,091	216,507	83,332	28%	38%	11%
Trade and Repair of Motor Vehicles and Motorcycles	930,124	247,971	69,426	27%	28%	7%
Legal, Accounting, and Auditing Activities	458,223	146,573	66,404	32%	45%	14%
Storage and Auxiliary Transport Activities	416,305	165,082	50,334	40%	30%	12%
Insurance, Reinsurance, Complementary Pension, and Health Plans	162,398	72,389	38,945	45%	54%	24%
Architecture and Engineering Services	241,710	74,814	36,135	31%	48%	15%
Auxiliary Activities of Services: Financial, Insurance, Pension, and Health Plans	115,236	57,597	35,947	50%	62%	31%
Advertising and Market Research	108,510	51,889	35,045	48%	68%	32%
Sports and Recreation, Leisure Activities	237,795	76,622	31,510	32%	41%	13%
Social Assistance Services Without Accommodation	149,809	66,856	30,472	45%	46%	20%

(continued)

TABLE 4.16
(continued)

	FORMAL EMPLOYEES			PERCENTAGE		
	Brazil	State	City	State as % of Brazil	City as % of State	City as % of Brazil
Business Headquarters and Business Management Consulting Activities	102,870	45,742	29,742	44%	65%	29%
Telecommunications	196,352	55,391	24,723	28%	45%	13%
Real Estate Activities	150,607	47,912	23,674	32%	49%	16%
Activities for the Provision of Information Services	91,979	40,346	23,636	44%	59%	26%
Non-Real-Estate Rentals and Management of Non-Financial Intangible Assets	199,540	57,951	23,110	29%	40%	12%
Other Personal Services Activities	206,417	57,921	22,978	28%	40%	11%
Mail and Other Delivery Activities	160,346	48,372	22,885	30%	47%	14%
Human Health Care Activities with Social Assistance, in Residences	123,322	52,293	19,209	42%	37%	16%
Accommodation	337,296	69,776	18,255	21%	26%	5%
Other Professional, Scientific, and Technical Activities	100,693	38,434	16,224	38%	42%	16%
Air Transport	61,839	32,529	14,381	53%	44%	23%
Editing, Editing Integrated with Printing	65,594	26,130	14,195	40%	54%	22%
Repair of Computer and Communication Equipment and Personal Objects	93,244	29,449	13,242	32%	45%	14%
Travel Agencies, Tour Operators, and Reservation Services	67,431	25,268	12,731	37%	50%	19%
Radio and Television Activities	86,304	20,736	10,117	24%	49%	12%
Cinematographic Activities, Video Production, and Television Programs	27,811	11,355	7,300	41%	64%	26%
Research and Scientific Development	42,660	12,977	5,968	30%	46%	14%
Artistic, Creative, and Spectacle Activities	16,754	4,608	2,922	28%	63%	17%
Others	73,472	9,886	3,876	13%	39%	5%
Total Formal Workers in Trade and Services Activities	36,355,039	10,289,235	4,403,224	28%	43%	12%
Total Formal Workers in All Activities	46,631,115	13,247,463	4,903,449			

SOURCE: Ministério da Economia, RAIS and CAGED data sets, http://bi.mte.gov.br/bgcaged/, accessed November 25, 2019.

TABLE 4.17

Headquarters of the 10 Largest Public and Private Companies by Sector, 2018

				LARGEST FIRMS		LARGEST PRIVATE FIRMS	
Categories	Public and Private	Private	Headquarters in São Paulo	Name	Headquarters Location	Name	Headquarters Location
Specialized Services	2	8	8	Correios	Distrito Federal	Cielo	São Paulo
Medical Services		10	9	Rede D´Or	São Paulo	Rede D´Or	São Paulo
Transport and Logistics		10	6	Latam Airlines	São Paulo	Latam Airlines	São Paulo
Telecommunications	1	9	5	Telefonica	São Paulo	Telefonica	São Paulo
Retailer		10	7	Atacadão/Carrefour	São Paulo	Atacadão/Carrefour	São Paulo
Wholesale and Foreign Trade		10	5	Gavilon	São Paulo	Gavilon	São Paulo
Environmental Services		7	4	Solvi	São Paulo	Solvi	São Paulo
Education and Teaching		10	6	Kroton	Minas Gerais	Kroton	Minas Gerais
Real Estate Development		10	5	MRV	Minas Gerais	MRV	Minas Gerais
Communications and Graphics	1	8	7	Globo	Rio de Janeiro	Globo	Rio de Janeiro
Food and Drinks		10	7	JBS	São Paulo	JBS	São Paulo
Sugar and Alcohol		10	8	Copersucar	São Paulo	Copersucar	São Paulo
Chemistry and Petrochemicals		10	6	Braskem	Bahia	Braskem	Bahia
Mechanics		10	4	WEG	Santa Catarina	WEG	Santa Catarina
Oil and Gas	1	9	3	Petrobras	Rio de Janeiro	Raizen	São Paulo
Electricity	4	6	2	CPFL	São Paulo	CPFL	São Paulo
Vehicles and Parts		10	6	Fiat Chrysler	Minas Gerais	Fiat Chrysler	Minas Gerais
Paper and Cellulose		10	4	Fibria	São Paulo	Fibria	São Paulo
Material Construction and Decoration		10	5	Votorantim Cimentos	São Paulo	Votorantim Cimentos	São Paulo
Pharmaceuticals and Cosmetics		10	9	Natura	São Paulo	Natura	São Paulo
Water and Sanitation	8	2	3	Sabesp	São Paulo	BRK	São Paulo
Metallurgy and Mining		10	4	Vale	Rio Janeiro	Vale	Rio Janeiro
Textiles, Leather, and Clothing		10	2	Alpargatas	São Paulo	Alpargatas	São Paulo
Plastics and Rubber		10	2	Evora	Rio Grande do Sul	Evora	Rio Grande do Sul
Electronics		10	5	Samsung	Amazonas	Samsung	Amazonas
Tobacco		2		CTA	Rio Grande do Sul	CTA	Rio Grande do Sul
Construction and Engineering		10	4	Construtora Queiroz Galvão	Rio de Janeiro	Construtora Queiroz Galvão	Rio de Janeiro
Agriculture		10	1	Coamo	Parana	Coamo	Paraná

SOURCE: Valor 1000, https://www.valor.com.br/valor1000/2019/ranking1000maiores, accessed November 30, 2019.

the financial sector, and a significant portion of the large business groups operating in Brazil. The proximity of the market, the economic weight of the state, and the location of the main business service providers all stimulate the concentration of business in the city of São Paulo.[38]

The financial sector underwent profound changes during the military period, when the central bank was created and much of the basic legislation that still regulates the sector was enacted. In the 1960s and 1970s the creation of monetary correction allowed the consolidation of a relatively stable, broad financial and capital market despite dramatic inflation rates in the country.[39] The financial sector's adjustment to an economy without inflation and open to the world during the 1990s further promoted an increased concentration of banks in the city, to the detriment of the city of Rio de Janeiro.[40]

According to the central bank, in recent years the structure of the national financial system has undergone a marked transformation regarding the number of institutions in operation and the volume of operations performed. Between December 2008 and December 2018, the number of institutions authorized to operate by the Banco Central do Brasil decreased from 2,423 to 1,677. The banking segment, which accounts for about 90% of the system's assets, decreased from 182 to 172 authorized institutions. But what stands out is the high concentration of bank resources in a few leading banks. In 2016, for example, the five largest banks in Brazil (in terms of total assets) contained 82% of all national banking resources, a proportion much higher than the average in other emerging countries, such as China (37%), South Korea (37%), India (36%), Mexico (70%), and Singapore (42%), and even higher than the concentration in the United States, which was 43% in that year.[41]

Parallel to the concentration process, which began in the 1990s as the end of inflation affected the banking system, there was also a concentration of bank headquarters in the city of São Paulo. Although the large public commercial banks are headquartered in Brasília (Banco do Brasil and Caixa Economica Federal), the three largest private commercial banks are headquartered in São Paulo: Itau Unibanco, Bradesco, and Santander. In the case of Itau Unibanco and Santander, their headquarters are in the city of São Paulo. In the case of Bradesco, its headquarters are in the city of Osasco, in the São Paulo Metropolitan Region.[42]

The state of São Paulo contains almost a third of the existing bank branches in Brazil but accounts for over half of the balance-of-credit operations and time deposits. In addition, 96 out of 114 active commercial banks have operations in São Paulo. Much of this banking activity in the state was concentrated in the city of São Paulo, which had two-thirds of credit operations and three-quarters of registered bank deposits in the state; 49% of Brazil's credit operations and 39% of Brazil's time deposits originate in the city.[43] As for the rest of the state, using time deposits as an indicator, the cities of Campinas, Osasco, Ribeirão Preto, Barueri, and São Bernardo do Campo were significant centers. But the city of São Paulo has 32 times the amount of time deposits as the city of Campinas, the largest of these interior centers (Table 4.18).

The state of São Paulo has also become one of the most important health centers in Latin America. It has 178 specialized hospitals, 731 general hospitals, 1,245 general clinics, 1,849 specialized clinics, and 4,203 basic health units. There are 98,000 hospital beds, which represents 29% of the hospital beds in Brazil. Of these, about one-third are in the city of São Paulo. Of the total number of doctors in Brazil, 29% also work in the state of São Paulo, and the city absorbs a third of these state doctors. The city has 7.2 doctors per 1,000 inhabitants, against 5.9 in the state and 4.4 in Brazil. In terms of equipment, the city had about 10% of the X-ray, CT, MRI, and mammography equipment in Brazil. Some 15% of Brazil's Human Health Care Activities were in the city of São Paulo, and the ten largest private companies in the health field were headquartered in São Paulo. All these indicators show the importance of this sector in the city and São Paulo's position of absolute leadership in the national health industry (see Table 4.19).

The state of São Paulo also has a leading role in university education. It is unusual in having both state and federal public universities as well as major church-based and private universities. There are a total of 1.6 million undergraduate students in the state, of whom 286,000 are at public universities. Of those in public universities, 190,000 are in the state-supported universities and the rest are in federal and local municipal universities. These figures represented about half of the students registered in state universities in the country. In both Brazil and São Paulo most students are enrolled in private universities (70% in Brazil and 82% in São Paulo). In the city of São Paulo there are 668,000 undergraduate students, representing 41% of the state's total. The city has 63,000 students at public universities, of which 59,000 are at the University of São Paulo, and most of those are at its two existing campuses in the capital.

When we analyze the quality of the faculty, there is an extreme difference between public and private universities. Although private universities enroll 70% of university students, these institutions have only 32%

TABLE 4.18

Banking Operations in the State of São Paulo and Brazil, August 2019

	Agencies	Credit Operations	Savings Accounts	Time Deposits	Banks (1, 2)
Brazil	20,261	3,260,713,745,490	804,461,689,235	1,200,149,554,528	114
State of São Paulo	6,217	1,889,060,500,626	255,340,672,794	610,362,517,858	96
Metropolitan Region of São Paulo	3,126	1,681,476,358,723	140,279,466,054	502,950,702,991	
City of São Paulo (1)	2252	1,264,166,627,283	99,764,163,660	462,146,839,177	91
City of São Paulo (2)	2252	1,600,273,641,339	99,764,163,660	462,146,839,177	91
State of São Paulo as % of Brazil	31%	58%	32%	51%	84%
RMSP as % of the State of São Paulo	50%	89%	55%	82%	
City of São Paulo as % of the State (1)	36%	67%	39%	76%	95%
City of São Paulo as % of the State (2)	36%	85%	39%	76%	95%
City of São Paulo as % of Brazil (2)	11%	49%	12%	39%	80%
PRINCIPAL CITIES OF THE STATE OF SÃO PAULO					
Campinas	230	16,788,473,082	8,265,388,576	14,100,314,461	18
Osasco	88	336,107,014,056	3,740,088,622	6,800,365,629	11
Ribeirão Preto	125	17,765,997,100	4,022,717,665	6,629,773,185	16
Barueri	63	25,663,880,471	1,946,430,730	6,188,161,087	13
São Bernardo do Campo	99	20,015,413,929	5,938,533,438	5,688,074,165	10
Santos	92	6,503,383,509	5,120,873,129	5,504,845,854	8
Guarulhos	114	7,991,869,822	5,212,912,194	4,821,818,155	9
São José do Rio Preto	73	7,739,271,025	2,605,067,385	3,943,682,073	8
Santo Andre	94	5,577,307,927	5,418,877,574	3,839,692,769	8
Jundiaí	64	5,177,097,271	3,248,145,567	3,773,754,447	8
Sorocaba	84	8,162,746,272	3,348,834,102	3,333,766,730	10
Piracicaba	55	5,556,571,791	2,430,937,553	3,193,941,560	9
São José Dos Campos	88	6,843,507,136	3,644,207,728	2,989,614,732	10
São Caetano Do Sul	50	2,357,994,987	2,368,063,442	2,306,364,643	8
Mogi Das Cruzes	38	3,482,328,705	1,954,563,180	2,009,668,771	7
Americana	36	2,795,035,015	1,576,265,671	1,637,386,468	6
Bauru	44	4,426,020,058	1,765,909,213	1,484,819,500	7

SOURCE: Banco Central: Estatítica Mensal por Município, https://www.bcb.gov.br/estatisticas/estatisticabancariamunicipios.

NOTES: (1) Osasco is excluded from City of São Paulo.

(2) Osasco is included in City of São Paulo, https://www.bcb.gov.br/estatisticas/estatisticabancariamunicipios.

TABLE 4.19

Health Indicators, Brazil, State of São Paulo, and City of São Paulo, December 2009

	Brazil	State of São Paulo	City of São Paulo
Sanitation			
Water—Service by General Network	75.8	93.2	98.5
Sewer—Service by General Network	44.4	80.5	85.7
Garbage Destination—Collected	76.4	95.6	99.1
Hospital Establishments			
Health Center / Basic Health Unit	29,950	4,203	560
Specialized Clinic / Specialized Outpatient Clinic	27,874	6,762	1,849
Doctor's Office	102,289	31,445	8,004
Pharmacies: Exceptional, Medical and Popular	573	102	22
Urgent Care Hospital	365	87	14
Specialized Hospital	1,222	178	50
General Hospital	5,205	731	148
Central Public Health Laboratory (LACEN)	63	17	1
Polyclinic	4,381	1,245	216
Health Center	11,715	360	26
Diagnosis and Therapy Support Service Unit	15,780	3,111	555
Total Number of Establishments, All Categories	208,810	49,668	11,611
Total Number of Beds	343,640	98,423	29,047
Number of SUS Beds	468,785	62,474	15336
Units of Equipment in Use			
Diagnostic Imaging Equipment	88,694	24,736	7,535
Infrastructure Equipment	43,050	7,912	2,965
Optical Equipment	28,500	8,735	3,248
Graphical Equipment	30,659	9,067	2,605
Lifetime Maintenance of Equipment	366,497	115,548	46,859
Dental Equipment	257,762	74,875	21,198
Other equipment	83,842	21,858	4,816
Units of Equipment by Use Category			
Mammography	3,843	1,081	332
X-ray	57,441	17,064	5,182
Computerized Tomography	2,552	698	229
Magnetic Resonance	976	253	100
Ultrasound	23,144	5,457	1,615
Dental Team	97,970	22,880	5,009
Doctors			
Doctors Total	843,100	243,939	79,285
Doctors Who Attend SUS	600,399	160,083	46,949
Doctors per 1000 Inhabitants	4.4	5.9	7.2

SOURCE: Ministério Saúde, Cadernos de Informações de Saúde, http://tabnet.datasus.gov.br/tabdata/cadernos/cadernosmap.htm.

TABLE 4.20

University Students and Professors by Type of University

	Brazil	State of São Paulo	City of São Paulo
University Students			
Total	6,394,244	1,611,198	668,061
Public Universities	1,904,554	286,070	63,808
Federal Universities	1,231,909	52,051	5,025
State Universities	582,905	190,784	58,684
Municipal Universities	89,740	43,235	99
Private Universities	4,489,690	1,325,128	604,253
University Professors			
Total	397,893	82,801	
Public Universities	183,669	25,682	
Federal Universities	123,761	6,445	
State Universities	53,182	16,093	
Municipal Universities	6,726	3,144	
Private Universities	214,224	57,119	
University Professors with Doctorates			
Total	170,968	37,348	
Public Universities	115,719	18,716	
Federal Universities	82,493	5,006	
State Universities	31,503	12,646	
Municipal Universities	1,723	1,064	
Private Universities	55,249	18,632	

SOURCE: INEP, http://inep.gov.br/sinopses-estatisticas-da-educacao-superior, accessed January 12, 2019.

of professors with doctorates. In comparison, public universities have a far greater proportion of professors with PhDs. There is even a big difference between the public universities. While in the public state universities, 79% of the teachers hold PhDs, in the federal ones this percentage drops to 67% (see Table 4.20).

The São Paulo universities are also distinguished by their outstanding participation in research. Of a total of 205,000 science publications generated by Brazilian universities, more than half come from São Paulo-based universities, of which 90,000 were generated at the three universities maintained by the São Paulo state government, USP, UNESP, and UNICAMP (Figure 4.2). The importance of São Paulo in scientific research lies not only in its universities but also in its numerous other independent research institutes. In total, the state accounted for 111,000 of the 338,000 research papers cataloged in the Web of Science in the period 2011–2016. The largest concentrations of these research articles were in medicine and life sciences (see Figure 4.3).[44]

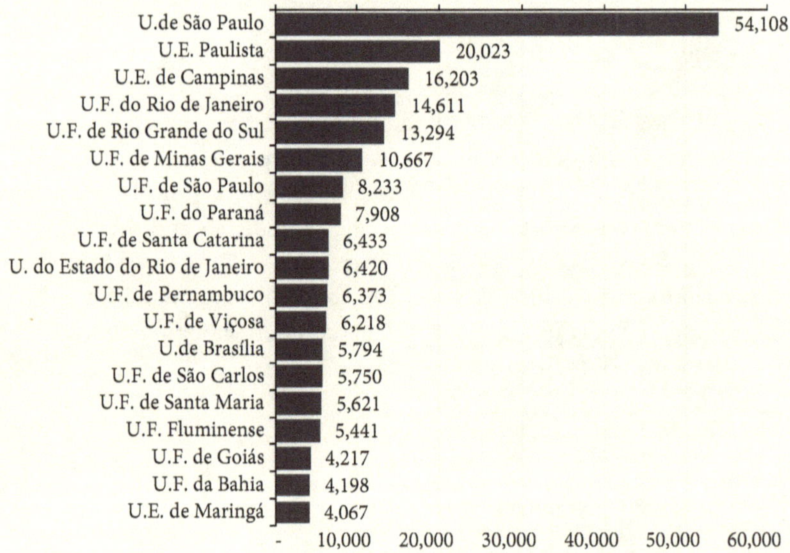

Figure 4.2. Brazilian Universities Ranked by Science Citations, 2011–2016

SOURCE: Research in Brazil, Clarivate Analytics: 42.

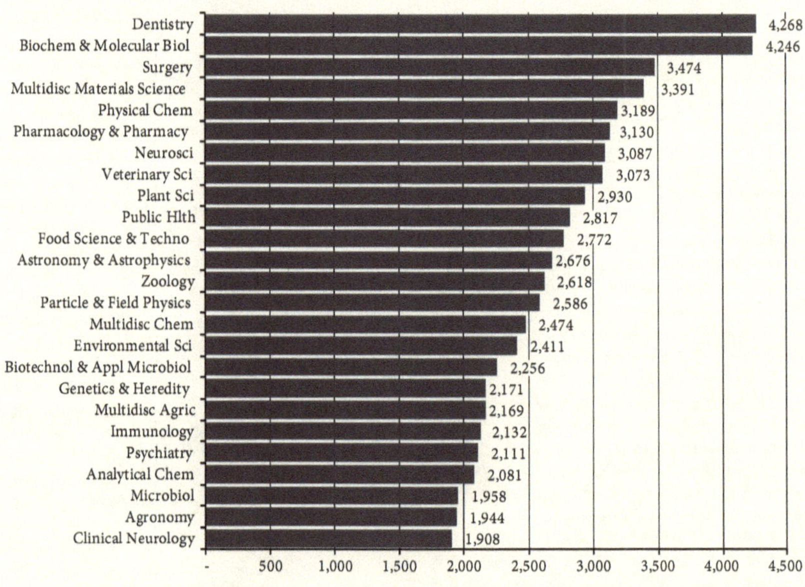

Figure 4.3. Ranking of Leading Research Disciplines, São Paulo, 2011–2016

SOURCE: Research in Brazil, Clarivate Analytics, p. 54.

The rise of a major service sector in the state in the late twentieth and early twenty-first centuries represented a fundamental change in the economy and labor force. Services have grown as the importance of industry and agriculture have declined. At the same time the capital has become a magnet for the most developed parts of this service industry and now plays a fundamental role not only nationally but internationally in finance, health, and education. Also, the size of the state's cities and the wealth of its economy have guaranteed a major expansion of commerce. The increasing specialization of commerce has made São Paulo the model for the rest of Brazil especially as its leading supermarkets and shopping centers have spread to the rest of the nation.

Chapter 5

Demographic Change in São Paulo Since 1950

São Paulo experienced major changes in its fundamental demographic makeup in the period after 1950. The state experienced historical changes in birth and death rates and became overwhelmingly urban. Rapidly declining birth and death rates along with rising life expectancy led to basic changes in the fabric of society. Post-1950 São Paulo, like the national population, experienced what has been called the demographic transition, which resulted in historically unprecedented low levels of births. Despite ever-falling death rates, these low birth rates will eventually lead to a declining population by the middle decades of the twenty-first century. Although some of these changes had their origins prior to 1950, the post-1950 changes were of a magnitude never before experienced by a Brazilian population.

The other fundamental demographic change was that of residence. This was a period of a massive shift of the state population into urban centers and the progressive decline of its rural population. In every decade the urban population grew more rapidly than the rural one, and in the 1960s the rural population of the state began to experience an actual decline in total numbers and a negative growth rate. Whereas the rural population accounted for 56% of the state in the 1940 census, it dropped steadily each decade thereafter, falling below half in 1950 and arriving at 4% of the total population in 2010. In turn, the urban population achieved its fastest rates of annual growth in the period from 1950 to 1980, with growth progressively slowing thereafter. The same pattern of urban growth held for the total

TABLE 5.1

Growth of the Population of the State of São Paulo by Residence, 1940–2010

CENSUS	NUMBERS			GROWTH RATE PER ANNUM		
Year	Total	Urban	Rural	Total	Urban	Rural
1940	7,180,316	3,168,111	4,012,205			
1950	9,134,423	4,804,211	4,330,212	2.4%	4.3%	0.8%
1960	12,974,699	8,149,979	4,824,720	3.6%	5.4%	1.1%
1970	17,958,693	14,432,244	3,526,449	3.3%	5.9%	-3.1%
1980	25,375,199		2,880,871	3.5%		-2.0%
1991	31,546,473	29,272,927	2,273,546	2.0%		-2.1%
2000	36,969,476	34,531,635	2,437,841	1.8%	1.9%	0.8%
2010	41,262,199	39,585,251	1,676,948	1.1%	1.4%	-3.7%

SOURCE: IBGE, SIDRA, table 1288; IBGE, Tendências Demográficas . . . 1940–2000, table 1.

state population too, though it would end with the state having the highest urbanization rate in the country (see Table 5.1).

The urbanization of the population progressed much faster in the state of São Paulo than in the rest of the country. While the nation as a whole was 36% urban in 1950, the population of São Paulo was already majority urban by that year. In fact, the national population did not become primarily urban (at 56%) until 1970, at which time São Paulo's urbanization rate was already 80%. Nor did this difference in urbanization change over the next several decades: by the census of 1991 the state was 93% urban compared to 75% for the rest of the nation, and by 2010, when the nation was 84% urban, the state of São Paulo was 96% urban.[1]

This more rapid urbanization was due to the earlier modernization of agriculture in the state coupled with the state's increasingly dominant role in national manufacturing. This agricultural modernization involved a massive adoption of machines and a subsequent decline in agricultural occupations. In turn, the opening up of factories and a rapidly expanding service sector in the capital city provided abundant new jobs along with better health and educational opportunities, which was a major attraction for rural migrants. The cities, and above all the capital itself, became a key attraction for the state's residents. Initially, like the rest of the nation, this urban population was highly concentrated: 52% of the national urban population resided in cities of 50,000 or more persons in 1950 (the comparable figure for São Paulo was 56%). The nation as a whole had only 32 such large cities out of 1,844 metropolitan centers in 1950, and São Paulo had the same ratio, with only 8 metropolitan centers out of 364 cities in the state having a population of 50,000 or more residents.[2] Its largest city in terms of population was

TABLE 5.2
Growth of the Municipality of São Paulo, 1900–2010

Census Year	Numbers	Annual Growth Rate
1900	239,820	
1920	579,033	4.5%
1940	1,326,261	4.2%
1950	2,198,096	5.2%
1960	3,825,351	5.7%
1970	5,978,977	4.6%
1980	8,587,665	3.7%
1991	9,626,894	1.0%
2000	10,405,867	0.9%
2010	11,253,503	0.8%

SOURCE: IBGE, SIDRA, table 1287.

the capital of the state, the municipality of São Paulo, which had grown to 2.2 million by this time, up from just 240,000 in 1900 (see Table 5.2). This city alone accounted for 48% of the state's population and was the second-largest city in the nation, behind the almost 2.4 million residents in the federal capital, Rio de Janeiro.[3] Its explosive growth beginning in the 1950s meant that it would become the nation's largest city by 1960, when its 3.8 million residents surpassed the 3.3 million residing in the city of Rio de Janeiro.[4] But this growth began to slow by the 1980s, as peripheral communities began to develop and other urban centers in the interior of the state emerged as important. This explains why, despite its massive growth, the municipality of São Paulo increasingly housed less of the state's total population. In 1980 it contained only 38% of the state's population, and by 2010 the capital of São Paulo was down to 27% of the total state population.

Before this transformation occurred, São Paulo differed little from the national population in terms of age and sex (see Figures 5.1a and 5.1b). Both had the classic pyramid structure of ages indicating high birth and death rates. They also had similar proportions of the population under 15 years of age and over the age of 60 years.[5]

But already change could be discerned. In the 1940s the state's total fertility rate was almost one child less than the national rate, a difference that persisted into the 1950s. Although there was a pause in the trend in the 1960s, the decline resumed in the 1970s, when contraceptives became readily available. It was the region of the Southeast, of which São Paulo was a major part, that led the nation toward lower fertility.[6] But by the 1980s all other regions began to follow its lead as Brazilian regional differences in birth rates slowly disappeared (see Table 5.3).

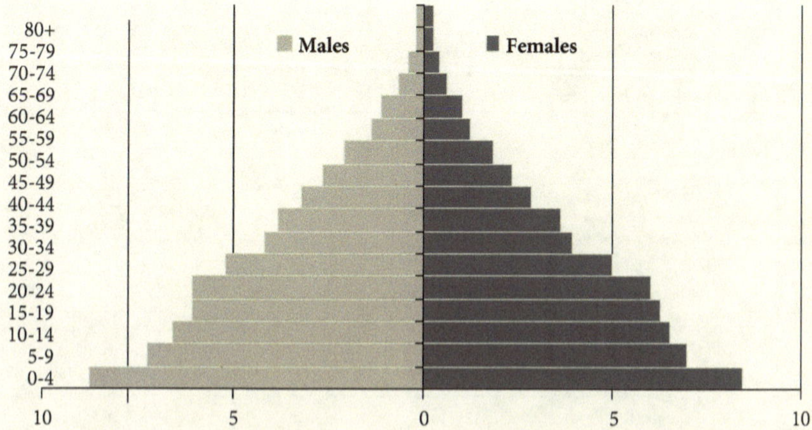

Figure 5.1a. Population Pyramid, State of São Paulo, 1950

SOURCE: IBGE, Censo Demográfico 1950, Serie Regional, volume XXXV, tomo 1: 2–3, table 1.

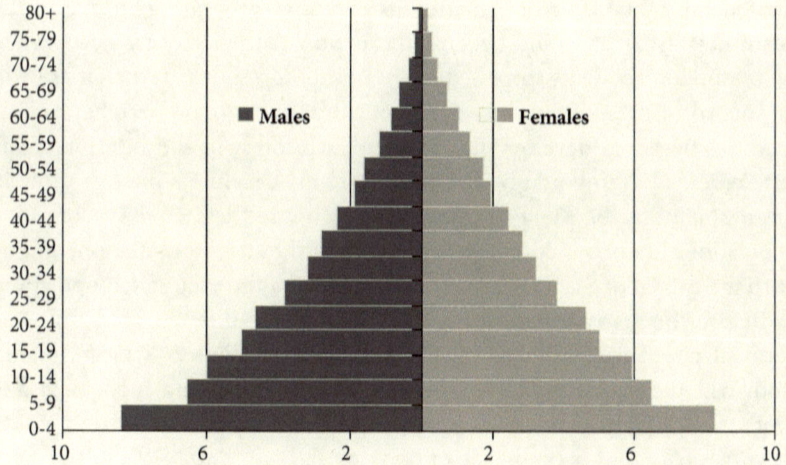

Figure 5.1b. Population Pyramid, Brazil, 1950

SOURCE: CEPAL, CEPALSTAT https://www.cepal.org/es/temas/proyecciones-demograficas/estimaciones-proyecciones-excel.

TABLE 5.3
Estimated Total Fertility Rate by Region, 1933–1983

Years	Brazil	North	Northeast	Southeast	South	Center-West
1930–35 (1933)	6.2	5.5	6.7	6.0	6.1	5.9
1940–45 (1943)	5.8	5.6	6.9	5.1	5.6	5.9
1950–55 (1953)	5.9	6.1	7.2	5.0	5.9	6.4
1960–65 (1963)	6.0	7.2	7.4	5.1	5.8	6.5
1970–75 (1973)	5.0	6.4	6.8	4.0	4.5	5.3
1980–85 (1983)	3.6	5.0	4.7	3.0	3.1	3.5

SOURCE: Frias and Oliveira (1991), 92, table 13; Horta, Carvalho, and Frias (2016), 6, table 3.

Age-specific birth rates also showed the Southeast leading the nation in declining fertility. As late as 1963 there were only modest changes from the 1953 model of age-specific fertility for the nation and the Southeastern region, but then the Southeast began to diverge significantly from national norms as older women significantly reduced their fertility. This decline became more evident in 1973, when there were major declines in fertility for all women over 20 years of age, but especially in women over 30 years of age. This was the pattern in all initial declines of fertility in the world in the nineteenth and twentieth centuries, as older women were the first to adopt fertility control. Still, by 1963 it was evident that the Southeast was on a different trajectory from the rest of the nation, which only approached the 1963 rate of the Southeastern region a decade later, by which time Southeast women's total fertility rate was already almost a child less than in the nation as a whole (see Figures 5.2a and 5.2b).

Initially it was the wealthier and more educated women who led in the decline in fertility, but by 2010 the differences had been significantly reduced, as even the poorest and least educated women followed the lead of the richest and most educated ones. Although differences persisted, the spread was less because the decline was fastest among the poorest women, with the difference going from 3.4 births in 2000 to 2.2 births in 2010 (see Figure 5.3).

It is only starting in 1980 that there are good age-specific fertility data available for the state of São Paulo. As expected, these data show the state was still advancing more rapidly in the demographic transition than the nation as a whole. São Paulo was ahead of national trends both in its cities and in its rural areas. Urban women and rural women in the state were reducing their births for all the older age cohorts (Figure 5.4a). Although the rural population was behind the urban one in this decline, it still experienced an impressive change. Comparing the pattern of births in rural areas in the state and the nation, the São Paulo rural population showed how significant this decline was among older women (see Figure 5.4b).

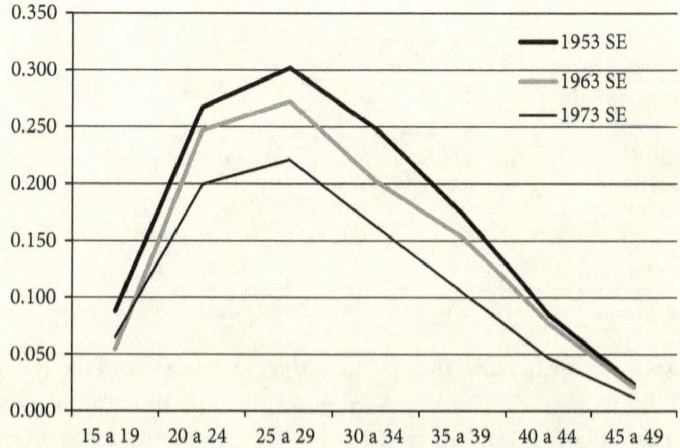

Figure 5.2a. Age-Specific Fertility Rates for Southeastern Region of Brazil, 1953–1973

SOURCE: Horta et al. (2016): 6.

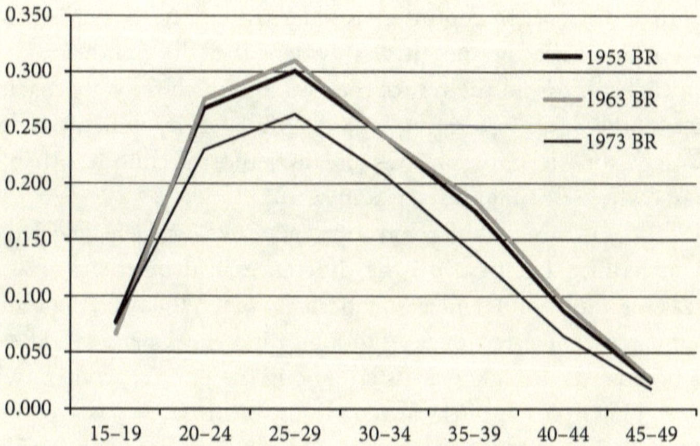

Figure 5.2b. Age-Specific Fertility Rates for Brazil, 1953–1973

SOURCE: Horta et al. (2016): 6.

One of the most sensitive indices that reflected declining fertility was the median age of the population. Given the very high pre-1960 fertility, it is no surprise that the median age of the national population was 19.2 years in 1950 and dropped even further, to 18.6 years, in the next two censuses.[7] But the increasingly rapid decline in fertility nationally slowly led to

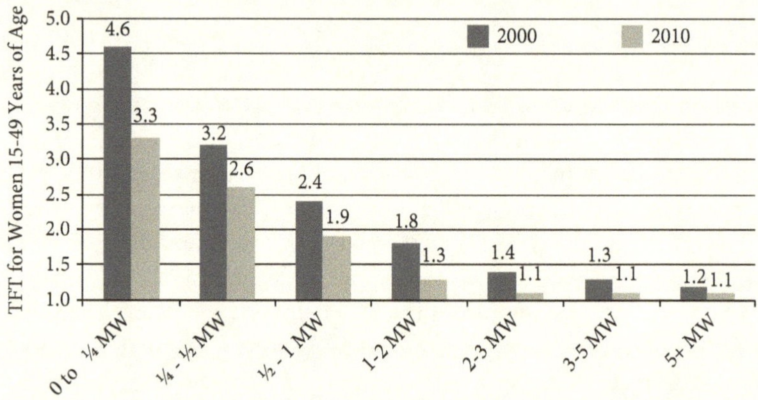

Figure 5.3. Total Fertility Rate of Brazilian Women by Income, 2000 and 2010 (in Minimum Wage categories)

SOURCE: Based on Cavenaghi and Berquó (2014): 74, table 1.

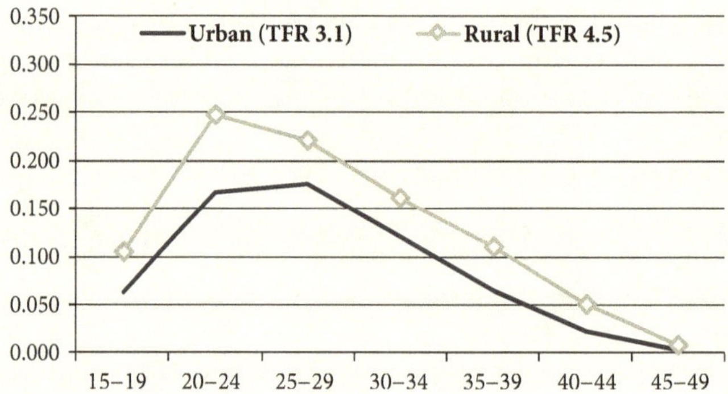

Figure 5.4a. Age-Specific Fertility Rates for Urban and Rural Populations of São Paulo, 1980

SOURCE: Oliveira (1985): 23, table 1.B.

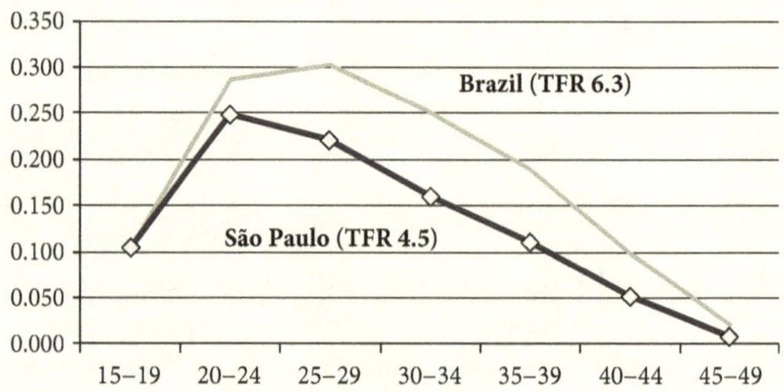

Figure 5.4b. Comparison of Age-Specific Fertility Rates of Brazilian and São Paulo Rural Populations, 1980

SOURCE: Oliveira (1985): 23, table 1.B.

a rising median age of 29 years by the census of 2010. This change was even faster in São Paulo, whose population by this date had a median age of 31.1 years. By 2020 the median age of the state population reached 35.3 years, while that of the nation was still almost two years younger, at 33.4 years.[8]

Also affecting the rising median age was declining mortality.[9] Here too the state of São Paulo was ahead of the nation. Well before the late twentieth-century decline in fertility, mortality was on a long-term downward trend. The late nineteenth century saw urban vaccination campaigns and improvements in water potability and sanitation, and these led to a slow but steady decline in mortality rates beginning early in the twentieth century. In fact, this was the case for all of Latin America, and there was an especially pronounced secular decline in mortality between 1930 and 1950 due to the introduction of antibiotics.[10] In Brazil, the crude death rate by the 1940s was in the low 20s per thousand population, and this rate dropped to just 14 deaths per thousand in the next decade and to just 6 per thousand by 1980.[11]

Infant mortality (defined as deaths of children under 1 year of age) took longer to decline. As late as 1930 the Brazilian rate was well over 200 deaths per thousand live births, which was two to three times higher than in contemporary Europe.[12] By the mid-1950s the rate was estimated to be 135 deaths per thousand, which was double the rate of Argentina and Uruguay and even above the Latin American average.[13] By 1970 the national rate was at 97.6 deaths per thousand live births—still a very high figure, and one of the worst in South America at the time.[14] It then dropped to 45 deaths by 1991, to 29 deaths by 2000, and to an estimated 11.6 deaths per thousand live births in 2020.[15]

As with fertility, São Paulo was in the lead in declining infant mortality, with rates dropping faster and further than the nation as a whole. In São Paulo the infant mortality rate dropped below 100 in the mid-1940s, while this did not occur at the national level until thirty years later (see Figure 5.5). Surprisingly, there appears to be little difference in the infant mortality rate between the capital and the rest of the state. Higher urban mortality was the norm throughout the nineteenth century in most of the world, due to crowding and increased rates of disease. But this urban penalty slowly disappeared in most societies in the twentieth century thanks to the universal adoption of sanitation and potable water, and this occurred in the state of São Paulo as well. By the late 1950s both the state and the capital finally dropped below 100 deaths per thousand live births and were at close to the same rate by the 1960s (see Figure 5.6). This decline continued for the rest of the century. By 2015 the rate of infant mortality in the state was down to 10.7 deaths per thousand live births, and in the municipalities of São Jose

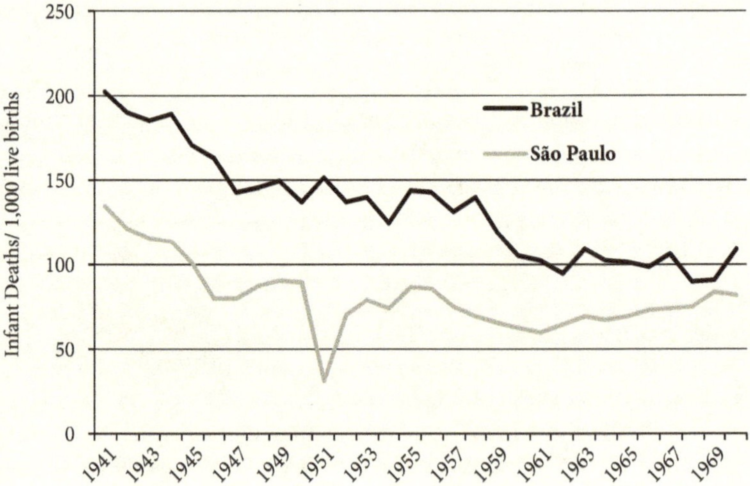

Figure 5.5. Infant Mortality Rate for Brazil and the State of São Paulo, 1941–1970

SOURCE: Yunes and Ronchezel (1974): 31, 46, tables 1 and 31.

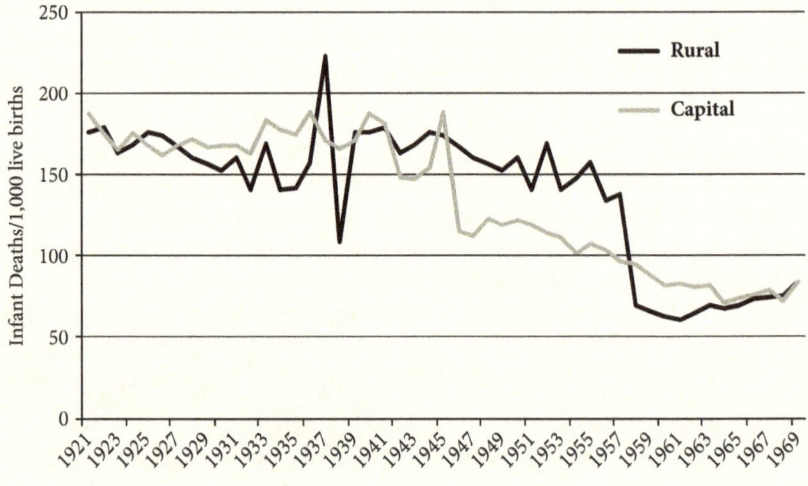

Figure 5.6. Infant Mortality Rate for Rural São Paulo and the Capital, 1921–1969

SOURCE: Yunes and Ronchezel (1974): 34–35, table 7.

de Rio Preto and Ribeirão Preto it went down to 8.4 and 8.5 respectively.[16] The estimated rate for the state in 2020 was 8.7 deaths per thousand live births, a quarter less than the national average.[17]

These major changes in infant mortality, as well as long-term trends in health provision, modern sanitation, and control of infectious diseases, had a major impact on life expectancy in the nation. By 1950 the country as a whole had a life expectancy at birth for both sexes of 51 years, that figure having risen by 2.5 years between 1940 and 1950. This improvement doubled between 1960 and 1970 for both sexes, and an impressive 9 years of life were added by the 1980s. By 2000 a total of 23 years had been added to the life expectancy of men since 1940, and 26 years for women (see Table 5.4).

In this, as with most other demographic indicators, the state of São Paulo was ahead of the nation. Life expectancy in the state of São Paulo was consistently higher for both sexes than the national average, with an exception for women in 1940. By 1960 the difference rose to 9.3 more years of life for men in the state compared to the nation as a whole, and 8.2 years more for Paulista women than for Brazilian women as a whole. But this extreme difference slowly declined as the nation caught up with the state (see Table 5.5). By 2017, when males in the state of São Paulo had a life expectancy at birth of 75.3 years, they had only 2.8 years more than the national population, with Paulista women, at 81.3 years, having just 1.7 years more than the national average.[18]

The average life expectancy figures after 1980 also reflected new and major improvements in the health of the elderly population. Whereas most of the changes in life expectancy before that period were due to improvements in the lives of the youngest elements of the population, overall survival rates were now being influenced by the decline in adult mortality. Life expectancy for those over 65 increased some 7.3 years between 1950 and 2017 for men and by 8.3 years for women (see Table 5.6).

Most of this improvement in life expectancy for all age groups was due to the decline in mortality from infectious diseases.[19] Whereas infectious diseases were the prime killers at midcentury, by the end of the twentieth century they had been replaced by the degenerative diseases of an aging population.[20] In 1901, for example, of the ten principal causes of death in the municipality of São Paulo, five were infectious diseases. By 1960 only three infectious diseases were still principal killers in the capital—pneumonia, gastroenteritis, and tuberculosis. By 2000 the only infectious disease on the list of major killers was pneumonia. In 1901 infectious diseases accounted for 46% of all deaths in the city, and by 2000 the figure was only 10%.[21]

TABLE 5.4

Average Life Expectancy at Birth in Brazil, 1940–2017

	Life Expectancy at Birth			
	Both Sexes	Men	Women	Women-Men Difference
1940	45.5	42.9	48.3	5.4
1950	48.0	45.3	50.8	5.5
1960	52.5	49.7	55.5	5.8
1970	57.6	54.6	60.8	6.2
1980	62.5	59.6	65.7	6.1
1991	66.9	63.2	70.9	7.7
2000	69.8	66.0	73.9	7.9
2010	73.9	70.2	77.6	7.4
2017	76.0	72.5	79.6	7.1

SOURCE: IBGE, *Tábua completa de mortalidade* (2018): 8, table 2. https://biblioteca.ibge.gov.br/visualizacao/livros/liv101628.pdf.

TABLE 5.5

Average Life Expectancy at Birth by Sex in the State of São Paulo, 1940–2017

Year	Both Sexes	Men	Women	Women-Men Difference
1940	45.4	44.3	46.7	2.4
1950	54.2	52.8	55.9	3.1
1960	61.2	59.0	63.7	4.6
1970	62.6	59.3	65.5	6.2
1980	66.7	63.3	70.0	6.7
1991	69.2	64.9	73.2	8.4
2000	71.6	67.0	76.1	9.0
2010	75.0	72.6	79.6	7.0
2017	78.4	75.3	81.3	6.0

SOURCE: Ferreira and Castiñeiras (1996): 35, table 1; IBGE, Projeções da População 2018; SEADE, *SP Demográfico* 19, no. 1 (2019): 3, fig. 1.

TABLE 5.6

Average Life Expectancy at Age 65 in Brazil, 1940–2017

	Both Sexes	Men	Women	Women-Men Difference
1940	10.6	9.3	11.5	2.2
1950	10.8	9.6	11.8	2.2
1960	11.4	10.1	12.5	2.4
1970	12.1	10.7	13.4	2.7
1980	13.1	12.2	14.1	1.9
1991	15.4	14.3	16.4	2.1
2000	15.8	14.2	17.2	3.0
2010	17.6	16.0	19.0	3.0
2017	18.7	16.9	20.1	3.2

SOURCE: IBGE, *Tábua completa de mortalidade* (2018): 11, table 4, https://www.ibge.gov.br/estatisticas/sociais/populacao/9126-tabuas-completas-de-mortalidade.html?t=resultados; *IBGE, Tábua completa de mortalidade para o Brasil—2017 Breve análise* (2018), https://biblioteca.ibge.gov.br/visualizacao/livros/liv101628.pdf.

With the rise of heart disease and cancer as primary causes of death at the end of the century, and with infectious diseases no longer a significant element among the major killers, the state and the nation finally fell in line with the pattern common to the advanced industrial countries of the world. This was also reflected in changes in the age of persons dying. For the country as a whole, the mean age at death was a very low 26 years in 1950–1955, reflecting both the high number of children dying and the dominance of youth in the population. But the average age at death more than doubled to 64 years in 2015–2020.[22] In 1984 those under age 15 made up an extraordinary quarter of all deaths in the country and 20% of all deaths in the state of São Paulo.[23] By 2017 such deaths represented only 3% of all persons who died in the state of São Paulo.[24]

These changes can also be seen in the state capital, where there are more precise age data. In the municipality of São Paulo in 1905 some 63% of all male deaths were of boys 10 years of age and under, and 65% of all female deaths were of girls 10 years of age and under. This was also reflected in the estimated infant mortality rate of the capital in 1900: 207 infant deaths per 1,000 live births.[25] By 2017 just 2% of all deaths occurred in infant girls and boys in the municipality of São Paulo. In 1905 the rest of the state excluding the municipality of São Paulo had 52% of all deaths occurring to children 0–2 years of age.[26] By 2017 only 2% of all deaths were in this 0–2 age cohort for the state of São Paulo as a whole.[27]

Although mortality started to decline at the end of the nineteenth century and fell more rapidly beginning in the middle decades of the twentieth century, fertility did not follow this trend until well into the second half of the century. In fact, births actually increased slightly until the mid-1960s due to declining rates of both mortality and morbidity among women. As occurred in many countries in Latin America, infertility rates for women declined and far higher numbers of women survived into their childbearing years; thus these improvements in health initially led to higher numbers of births despite declining fertility. The result of this combination was very rapid population growth in Brazil in the late twentieth century. In the 1920–1940 period population growth rates had been a relatively moderate 1.5% per annum. But in the next decade the rate of natural growth rose to 2.3% and in the 1960–1970 it was 3% per annum, a quite impressive rate.[28] The result of this growth was that the Brazilian population, which stood at 52 million in 1950, doubled to 104 million in 1974, just twenty-four years later.[29]

If that high 3% annual rate of the 1960–1970 decade had continued, the 1974 population would have doubled again to 208 million by 1983. But by the last decade of the twentieth century population growth was the lowest recorded for that century, falling to 1.3% per annum, and as of 2002 the national population had only grown to just 173 million. The reason was that fertility began to decline precipitously from the mid-1960s onward, and there was no longer any significant increase in the number of women giving birth. Thus Brazil, after a very rapid growth spurt in the middle years of the twentieth century, began to experience ever slower population growth as it finally entered the classic second phase of the demographic transition—from a high-mortality, high-fertility nation to a modern low-fertility, low-mortality society.

Although a few urban elite groups were practicing birth control before the 1960s and had lower fertility than the national average, this group exercised little influence over national trends. In 1950 the total fertility rate (the expected total number of children born to women over the course of their reproductive lifetime) was one of the highest in the world, at 6.2 children. But by the 1965–1970 period the trend suddenly began reversing, first slowly and then at an ever faster pace. The total fertility rate in Brazil declined from 4.7 in 1970–1975 to almost a full child less (3.8) in 1980–1985. It then fell even further by 2000–2005, to just 2.3 children per woman, and went below replacement value in 2005–2010, reaching 1.9. The total fertility rate has since declined again to 1.7 children for the period 2015–2020.[30] One of the most obvious consequences of this abrupt change in fertility can be seen in the rising median age of the population and the changing age distribution of the population from 1950 to 2000. By 2020 the median age nationally was 33.4, fully 14.3 years higher than the median age recorded in 1950.[31]

This decline in fertility and mortality can also be seen in the changing shape of the Brazilian population pyramid, which went from the classic pyramid at midcentury to a more jar-shaped profile with a reduced base. This is explained by the decline in fertility, which led to a decrease in the size of the younger population, and by higher survival rates among older persons. In 2000 the Brazilian age distribution looked like that of a typical post-demographic-transition society, with low fertility and low mortality. São Paulo was more advanced in this process than the country as a whole, with its 0–4 age cohort falling to just 8.6% of the total population, compared to 9.6% for the nation as a whole. In both cases the largest age cohort was no longer the 0–4 age group. By 2020 one could see the pattern for the rest of the nation converging to the pattern of the Paulista population. The national population also increased the share of its elderly population and reduced its cohort of 0–14-year-olds as its total fertility rate approached that of São Paulo. Even national mortality indices were slowly approaching those of São Paulo, which were among the best in the nation (see Table

TABLE 5.7
Population Characteristics in São Paulo and Brazil, 2000–2020

	LIFE EXPECTANCY					% OF POPULATION		
2000	Total	Males	Females	IMR (1)	TFR (2)	0–14	65+	x̄ Age (3)
Brazil	69.83	66.01	73.92	29.02	2.39	30.04	5.61	28.03
São Paulo	71.39	67.04	76.06	17.28	2.08	26.71	5.84	29.40
2010								
Brazil	73.86	70.21	77.60	17.22	1.75	24.70	7.30	29.20
São Paulo	76.10	72.60	79.55	11.98	1.67	22.40	7.70	31.08
2020								
Brazil	76.74	73.26	80.25	11.56	1.76	20.90	9.80	33.40
São Paulo	79.11	76.12	81.96	8.77	1.72	19.50	10.80	35.27

SOURCE: IBGE, Projeções da População, 2018 and 2013, https://www.ibge.gov.br/estatisticas/sociais/populacao/9109-projecao-da-populacao.html?t=resultados and https://ww2.ibge.gov.br/home/estatistica/populacao/projecao_da_populacao/2013/default_tab.shtm, accessed June 5, 2019.
NOTES: (1) IMR: infant mortality rate.
(2) TFR: total fertility rate (number of children for women ages 14–49).
(3) x̄ Age: mean age of population.

5.7). By 2020, based on the IBGE population projections of 2018, the largest age cohort in both the nation and the state was adults 35–39 years of age, and in both state and nation that group accounted for 8.2% of the total population (see Figures 5.7a and 5.7b).

The cause of this profound change in the age structure of the population was the decline in fertility, not any change in the age at first marriage, the percentage of women marrying, or the ratio of women remaining childless. The age of women marrying for the first time did not change until long after the fertility transition, nor did the number of women living in marriages or consensual unions fall, or the number of women remaining childless increase. Many of these factors, including the rate of dissolution of unions and the rate of consensual unions, did change over time, but these transformations came well after the fall in fertility. The only change that did occur was the mass adoption of contraceptives and sterilizations in the second half of the 1960s.[32] By 1986, for example, 60% of women 15 to 54 years of age living in unions in Brazil used some form of contraception (23% on the pill and 29% choosing sterilization). The rates for the state of São Paulo were 69% using contraceptives (26% on the pill, 31% choosing sterilization).[33] By 2006 some 81% of Brazilian women 15–49 years of age used some form of contraception (and only 4% of these used a non-modern form of contraception).[34] In 1992 in the metropolitan region of the São Paulo only 20% of women living in unions and aged 15–49 years did not use contraceptives, a figure lower than in the state as a whole in

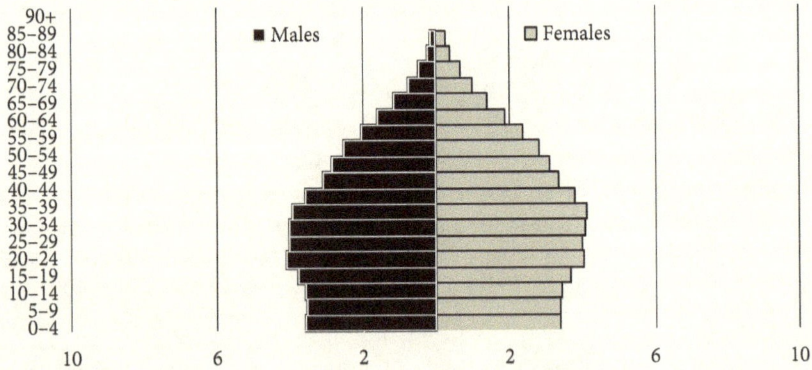

Figure 5.7a. Population Pyramid, Brazil, 2000

SOURCE: IBGE, Projeçoes 2018, https://www.ibge.gov.br/estatisticas/sociais/populacao/9109-projecao-da-populacao.html?=&t=resultados.

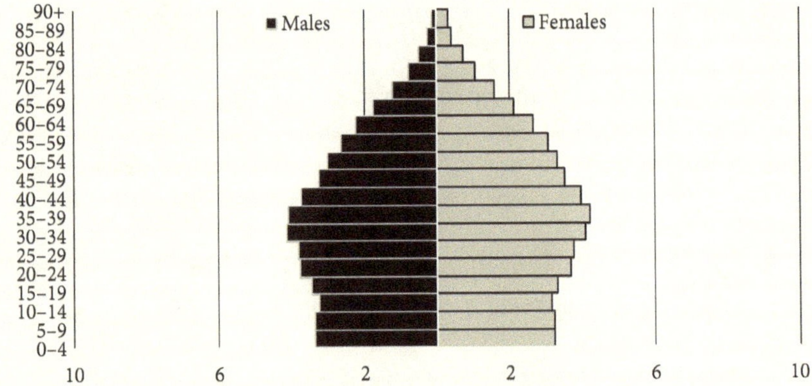

Figure 5.7b. Population Pyramid, State of São Paulo, 2000

SOURCE: IBGE, Projeçoes 2018, https://www.ibge.gov.br/estatisticas/sociais/populacao/9109-projecao-da-populacao.html?=&t=resultados.

1986. Although poorer women mostly used sterilization, 87% of them paid for this operation, and the others received it free because of health reasons.[35] Also, older women chose sterilization more often than did younger women, as did women with more children compared to those with fewer children, based on a survey of the state of São Paulo in 1991.[36]

Although older women were initially those who most enthusiastically adopted the new contraceptive procedures, no age cohort of women was exempt from the decline in fertility, as can be seen in the age-specific fertility rates for Brazil for 1960 to 2000. As occurred in most countries going through the demographic transition, initially the biggest drop in fertility occurred among older women. In fact, the relationship between age and decline in age-specific fertility rates was almost perfectly inverted, with the rate of decline highest in the older age groups and lower through the younger age groups. From 1960 to 2000, for example, the age-specific birth rate declined by 95% among women 45–49, by 89% for women 40–44 years of age, and by 80% and 71% in the next two age categories (35–39 and 30–34, respectively), by 61% in the 25–29 group, and just 13% in the 15–19 group. So dramatic has been the decline of fertility in these older age groups that the proportion of total children born to younger women has been increasing significantly: by 2000, women under 29 years of age accounted for 76% of all births, up from 62% of all births in 1950. This meant that mothers under 25 went from accounting for just over a third of all children in 1950 to half of all births in 2000 (see Figure 5.8).

Under the high-fertility regime of the 1930s the key age group of mothers was the cohort 25–29 years of age, and this group continued to be the leading one until almost the end of the century even as fertility declined.[37] In 2010 the rates were dropping so fast that the 20–24 age cohort of woman temporarily became the leading sector. But this pattern was reversed by 2020, at least for the state of São Paulo, which now saw the resurgence of the 25–29 group as the most important group of women (see Figure 5.9a and 5.9b).

As the IBGE estimates for the state of São Paulo suggest, older cohorts of women have been increasing their birth rates since 2000. This is due to

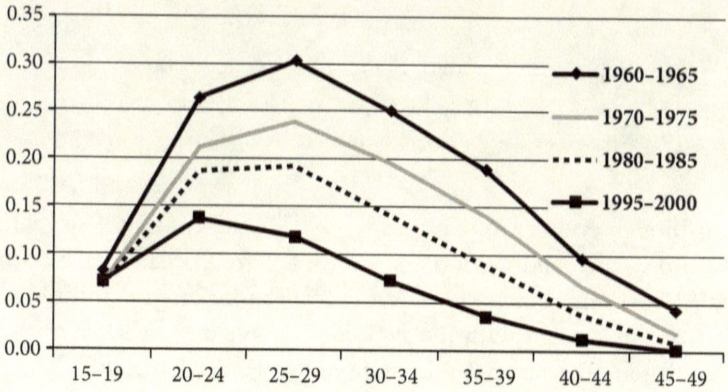

Figure 5.8. Age-Specific Fertility Rates for Women, Brazil, 1960–2000
SOURCE: CELADE, quadro A.

profound changes in women's education and in the role of women in the labor market in recent decades. As more women entered the labor market and sought advanced education, they increasingly delayed childbearing. This change in lifestyles began to show up first in the average age of women marrying. In the municipality of São Paulo the average age of women at marriage remained at roughly 23–24 years until 2000, when it rose to 26 years, and then it rose again to 31 years in 2014.[38] These changes can also be seen in the age of first marriage, which has been steadily rising. In 1991, single women nationally married for the first time at 23.7 years of age, and this was the same for single women in 1999.[39] But this changed in

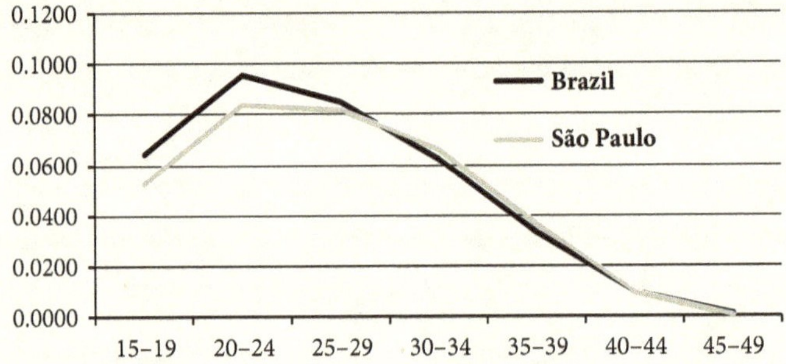

Figure 5.9a. Age-Specific Fertility Rates, Brazil and the State of São Paulo, 2010

SOURCE: IBGE, Projeçoes 2018, https://www.ibge.gov.br/estatisticas/sociais/populacao/9109-projecao-da-populacao.html?t=resultados, accessed June 5, 2019.

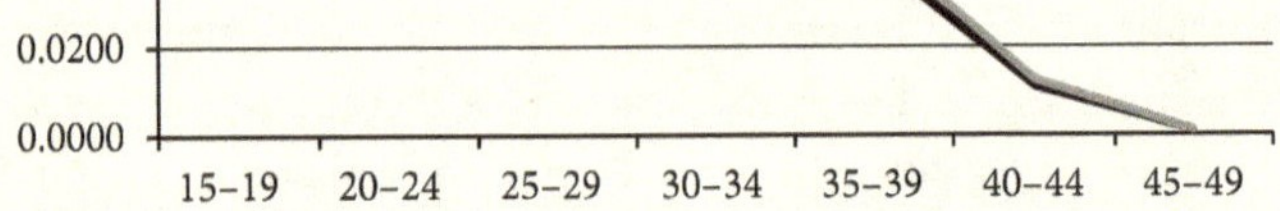

Figure 5.9b. Age-Specific Fertility Rates, Brazil and the State of São Paulo, 2020

SOURCE: IBGE, Projeçoes 2018, https://www.ibge.gov.br/estatisticas/sociais/populacao/9109-projecao-da-populacao.html?t=resultados, accessed June 5, 2019.

the new century. By 2010 the average age of single women marrying for the first time rose to 26.3 years of age, and by 2017 that rose to 27.9 years, some 4 years older than was the norm in the 1990s.[40] This was also the pattern of change in São Paulo. In 2010 single women marrying in the state of São Paulo averaged 26.2 years of age, which was also the national average that year; the average age at first marriage for women in the RMSP was 26.7 years, and for the capital city it was 27.2 years, a full year more than for the state and the nation.[41] As of 2018 the average age of women marrying for the first time in the state is 30 years.[42]

Because of delayed marriage and delayed childbearing, estimates are that by 2030 the cohort of those 25–29 years old will again become the key age group of mothers in both the state and the nation, though São Paulo will also see the 30–34 age group equal in childbearing rates to the 20- to 24-year-old mothers, a trend not yet apparent in the national data. The projected importance of the 30–34 age cohort of mothers by 2050 suggests that the more educated women are and the longer they remain in the workforce, the more they will delay marriage and childbearing.[43] This is the pattern in the advanced industrial societies, and IBGE estimates that it will also become the norm for Brazil and the state by the mid-twenty-first century. In São Paulo women in the 15-to-24 age group will be having fewer births, and there will be an increase in births in all cohorts above 30 years of age, with the peak reproductive period being 30–34 years of age. Just how different the pattern will be can be seen by comparing the age-specific fertility rates of São Paulo women in 2010 with those estimated for 2050 (see Figure 5.10).

The patterns of births, deaths, and marriages that were emerging in the state and the municipality of São Paulo were similar to what was seen in most of the state's metropolitan regions. In the 1970s the federal government created the metropolitan region of São Paulo, but the others did not come into existence until after the constitution of 1988 provided that the states should establish these groupings. By the census of 2000 those for São Paulo had been established, and since then the state and federal government have provided the basic statistics for six metropolitan regions in the state.[44] An examination of these metropolitan regions in 2017, the latest year for which there are relevant data, shows only modest differences among them (see Table 5.8). The Santos metropolitan region (Baixada Santista) and São Paulo are the metropolitan regions with the highest ratio of women, with Sorocaba the most balanced. All of them except Sorocaba have only a minimal population residing in rural areas. Campinas stands out as having the lowest infant mortality rate and the Santos region the highest, which is to be expected from a port city. Campinas as well as Ribeirão Preto have the

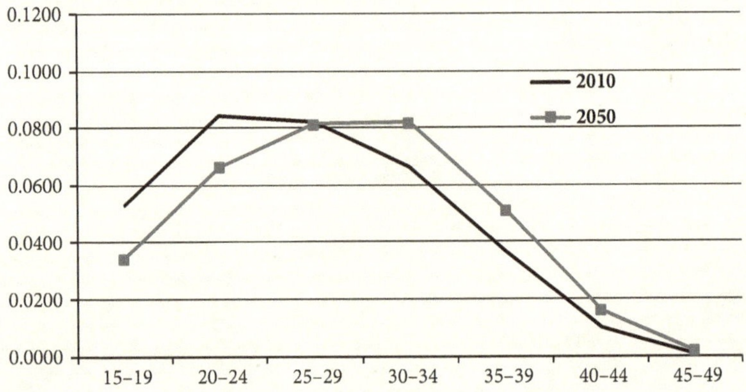

Figure 5.10. Estimated Age-Specific Fertility Rates, State of São Paulo, 2010 and 2050

SOURCE: IBGE, Projeções 2018 https://www.ibge.gov.br/estatisticas/sociais/populacao/9109-projecao-da-populacao.html?t=resultados, accessed June 5, 2019.

lowest fertility rates, and all have fertility rates below that of the metropolitan region of São Paulo. Campinas has the youngest population and Santos the oldest, but the differences are still relatively minor.

What is extraordinary about this growing uniformity of all regions in the state is that these changes in fertility and mortality occurred so rapidly. In both Brazil and most of Latin America this demographic transition occurred within roughly the same post-1960 period. This is in contrast to the demographic transition in Europe, which took far longer and began when birth rates were much lower than mid-twentieth-century Latin American figures. In fact, the Brazilian and Latin American fertility rates were the highest in the world at midcentury.[45] In the case of Brazil, with its highly stratified and partially unarticulated society, the fall initially was not uniform across all regions and classes. While all regions of the country moved in the same direction, each region began to decline from different initial levels, so the gap between regions shrank only modestly over time. Thus in 1950 and in 2016 there was still a difference between the lowest-fertility region (the Southeast) and the highest-fertility region (the North), even as fertility rates in both declined massively over this same period (see Table 5.9).

In general, fertility declined more rapidly in some states than in others, but in all save a few the total fertility rate dropped below the replacement rate of 2.1 children by 2020 (the exceptions were three small states of the North, Acre, Amazonas, and Roraima, which were at 2.2 births).[46] This

TABLE 5.8

Selected Demographic Indices of the Metropolitan Regions of São Paulo, 2017

	POPULATION								
Metropolitan Region	Total	Males	Females	Sex Ratio	% Urban	IMR (1)	GFR (2)	Index of Aging (3)	% of Live Births to Women < 18 years
São Paulo	20,717,505	9,954,154	10,763,351	92.5	98.9	10.9	52.8	65.7	5.1
Campinas	3,088,783	1,515,513	1,573,270	96.3	97.6	8.7	47.7	73.7	4.1
Vale do Paraíba e Litoral Norte	2,425,293	1,192,315	1,232,978	96.7	94.6	11.0	50.5	68.8	5.2
Sorocaba	2,018,102	999,743	1,018,359	98.2	89.9	11.2	51.7	68.1	5.3
Baixada Santista	1,781,727	853,938	927,789	92.0	99.8	14.2	50.3	75.0	6.4
Ribeirão Preto	1,625,752	799,959	825,793	96.9	97.2	10.0	45.3	77.7	5.4

SOURCE: Generated from tables at SEADE, Informações dos Municípios Paulistas, at http://www.imp.seade.gov.br/frontend/#/tabelas.

NOTES: (1) IMR: infant mortality rate, the number of deaths of infants under 1 year of age per 1000 live births.

(2) GFR: general fertility rate, calculated as (total number of births ÷ total number of women ages 14–49) ×1000.

(3) Index of aging: calculated as (population 65 years and older ÷ population ages 0–14) ×100.

TABLE 5.9
Total Fertility Rate for Brazil and Major Regions, 1940–2016

Region	1940	1950	1960	1970	1980	1991	2000	2010	2016
North	7.2	8.0	8.6	8.2	6.4	4.2	3.2	2.4	2.1
Northeast	7.2	7.5	7.4	7.5	6.2	3.7	2.7	2.0	1.9
Southeast	5.7	5.5	6.3	4.6	3.5	2.4	2.1	1.7	1.6
South	5.7	5.7	5.9	5.4	3.6	2.5	2.2	1.7	1.6
Center-West	6.4	6.9	6.7	6.4	4.5	2.7	2.2	1.8	1.7
Brazil	6.2	6.2	6.3	5.8	4.4	2.9	2.4	1.7	1.7

SOURCE: To 1991, Cerqueira and Givisiez (2015): 36, table 6. For 2000–2016, IBGE, SIDRA, table 3727.

decline began in the more advanced regions of the country and in the urban areas, and then progressively spread at an ever more rapid pace to the rural areas and from the wealthier to the poorer populations. If contraceptive practices are the key factor explaining this decline, then the spread of these practices can only be due to the better integration of the nation. Some of this integration would occur as a result of the expansion of the internal market and transport infrastructure, and another part would occur through the migration of poorer rural people to the cities and from the poorest regions of the nation to the richest ones.

This intrastate and interstate migration in São Paulo was another major factor affecting demographic structure in the state's population. Although rural-to-urban migration was a constant theme in Brazilian history, the process became far more rapid and far more dispersed throughout the nation in the second half of the twentieth century. As late as 1960 the majority of the national population still resided in rural areas. But by 1970, over half of the population was urban, and this proportion rose steadily until urban dwellers accounted for 80% of the national population in the census of 2000. It is estimated that in the twenty years from 1960 to 1980 some 27 million rural Brazilians migrated to cities, either within their state of birth or in another state.[47] Up to the 1990s, the states that had the biggest rural-to-urban migration were the southeastern ones, and above all the state of São Paulo. The reason was that agriculture modernized faster in this state and industry was more developed than elsewhere in the nation, so the state's urban centers attracted large numbers of the state's rural inhabitants as well as people from other states and regions of the nation. The peak growth of most of the state capital cities was in the twenty-year period from 1950 through 1970, when growth often reached well over 5% per annum. In the 1950s and 1960s the capital of São Paulo was growing at or above 5% per annum, and even Curitiba hit 7% growth per annum in the 1950s and almost 6% in the 1960s. Other capital cities were also growing in this period, Belo Horizonte at almost 7% per annum and Brasília at a sensational 14% per annum in the 1960s. The result was that all these cities—except Rio de Janeiro—more than doubled their populations in this twenty-year period. The pull of jobs available in the cities and in the richer zones along with educational opportunities and better social services and health facilities all were factors that helped to drive this massive late twentieth-century internal migration in Brazil. The expulsion factor was of course the increasing mechanization of agriculture and the decline of subsistence farming everywhere in Brazil as the country became a major agricultural exporter of hundreds of products aside from the traditional coffee beans. There were twenty state capitals with a population of over 1 million in their metropolitan districts by the end of the century. But all were now growing at much more reduced pace as the migration from rural to urban centers slowed down considerably in almost all the states.[48]

The state that was most affected by this internal migration was São Paulo and its capital city. Just as fertility and its natural growth rate was slowing, migration was increasing as São Paulo after 1950 became the largest industrial state as well as the premier agricultural state of the nation, offering higher salaries and more jobs than elsewhere in the country. It was international migrants who initially satisfied the increasing demand for labor in São Paulo, first with African slaves and then free Europeans and Asians after the abolition of slavery in 1888. Most of that free labor migration came in the period from the 1880s to the 1920s and had gone first to the coffee fields of São Paulo and Paraná and then to the expanding cities of the region, above all to São Paulo. By 1930 the international migrations that had brought some 4.4 million European and Asian workers to Brazil was slowing down considerably.[49]

But as this international migration slowed it was progressively replaced by interstate migrants coming from neighboring states as well as distant regions of the country. Internal migration of native-born Brazilians from the Northeast began in the late 1920s and continued unabated for the next sixty years. As early as the period 1920–1940, the state of São Paulo was receiving more internal immigrants than foreign-born ones.[50] With each decade the pace increased. Whereas a quarter of the growth of the state of São Paulo in the 1940s was accounted for by migrants coming from other states, this reached 30% of total growth in the next two decades and peaked in the 1970–1980 period, when 42% of the growth of the state population was accounted for by these migrants. Although internal migration did not stop after 1980, the flow of interstate migrants was directed more toward the new agricultural lands of the west and north, which were slowly being

TABLE 5.10
Role of Immigration in the Growth of the State of São Paulo, 1940–1991

Period	Total Growth by Period	COMPONENTS OF GROWTH		PERCENTAGE OF EACH COMPONENT		Annual Rate of Growth of State Population
		Natural (1)	Immigration	Natural	Immigration	
1940–50	1,954,107	1,469,600	484,507	75.2%	24.8%	2.4%
1950–60	3,840,276	2,691,489	1,148,787	70.1%	29.9%	3.6%
1960–70	4,797,249	3,372,211	1,425,038	70.3%	29.7%	3.2%
1970–80	7,268,764	4,185,591	3,083,173	57.6%	42.4%	3.5%
1980–91	6,505,761	5,919,097	586,664	91.0%	9.0%	2.1%

SOURCE: Perillo and Perdigão (2016): 775, table 1.
NOTE: (1) Natural growth: calculated as (births to residents) – (deaths to residents).

opened up for exploitation, or to new regional cities. Thereafter interstate migrants accounted for less than 10% of the growth rate in São Paulo (see Table 5.10). Overall the 3 million native-born migrants who arrived in the 1970s accounted for 42% of the growth of the state in that decade.

Although the Northeast is famed as the origin of the interstate immigrants to the state of São Paulo, the neighboring states of Minas Gerais and Paraná still accounted for 44% of all interstate migrants arriving in São Paulo in the 1970s, compared to 42% coming from the Northeastern region, of which Bahia was the single most important origin state (accounting for 13%). By the 1980s the Northeast and Bahia increased their share to half of the arriving migrants, with Bahia alone accounting for 16%, a figure that increased to 21% by the 1990s, when the northeasterners accounted for 53% of all immigrants.[51]

For the municipality of São Paulo the big impact of both interstate and intrastate immigration occurred in the period from 1950 to 1980. In the 1950s and 1960s immigration was more important than natural growth of the resident population in expanding the city's population. Only in the 1980s did natural growth become more important than immigration, as more immigrants left the city than arrived. The migration rate has been negative ever since. It is also estimated that the number of births in the city will be less than the number of deaths by the 2050s, meaning that the capital's population will actually decline in 2050 (see Table 5.11).

The stream of northeastern migrants was concentrated less in the capital than in the surrounding communities of the Metropolitan Region of São Paulo. From the 1970s to the 2010 northeasterners steadily increased their share of the total interstate migrants coming to the metropolitan region of

TABLE 5.11

Actual and Estimated Population Growth for the Municipality of São Paulo by Natural and Migration Components, 1950–2050

	Population	Annual Increase Between Census Years	AVERAGE ANNUAL GROWTH Natural	Migration	Growth Rate
1950	2,198,096				
1960	3,781,446	158,335	65,272	93,063	5.58
1970	5,885,475	210,403	97,046	113,357	4.52
1980	8,475,380	258,991	141,544	117,447	3.71
1991	9,610,659	103,207	165,440	-62,233	1.15
2000	10,426,384	90,636	141,049	-50,413	0.91
2010	11,245,983	81,960	114,092	-32,132	0.76
2020	*11,869,661*	*62,368*	*87,842*	*-25,474*	*0.54*
2030	*12,242,972*	*37,331*	*55,085*	*-17,754*	*0.31*
2040	*12,354,698*	*11,173*	*23,722*	*-12,549*	*0.09*
2050	*12,205,291*	*-14,941*	*-3,182*	*-11,759*	*-0.12*

SOURCE: SEADE, *SP Demográfica* 13, no. 1 (2013): 3, table 1.

the capital from 52% to 71% (see Table 5.12). But this northeastern migration has slowed considerably, and by 2010 the northeasterners were being replaced by persons migrating from within the state.[52] This decline in interstate migrations meant that by 2010, over three-quarters of the residents of both the capital and the Metropolitan Region of São Paulo were born in the state. Those residents who were born in Bahia now accounted for just 6% of the total population in both the RMSP and the capital.[53]

Although the capital grew rapidly in the 1970s, the other thirty-nine municipalities that made up the Metropolitan Region of São Paulo grew at double the rate of the capital (see Table 5.13). The large peripheral municipalities of Santo André, São Bernardo do Campo, São Caetano do Sul, and Diadema (the so-called ABCD municipalities), where industry was located and abundant jobs were available to arriving migrants, saw major growth in this period, as did the adjoining residential municipality of Osasco. Currently, the RMSP has a mixture of rich and poor municipalities. Thus São Caetano was the municipality with the highest Human Development Index in Brazil in 2010, and Francisco Morato was ranked at position 1,811 on that same indicator (see Map 5.1).

In turn, it was primarily migrants moving from the rural to urban areas within the state that accounted for the explosive growth of the interior cities of the state. These cities grew more rapidly than the capital city, and interior cities grew even more rapidly than the cities of the metropolitan region even in the peak years of migration. The biggest spurt of growth for most of

TABLE 5.12

Interstate Native-Born Immigrants (Resident Less than 10 Years) in the State of São Paulo and the Metropolitan Region of São Paulo, 1970–2010

	METROPOLITAN REGION OF SÃO PAULO			
Previous Residence	1970/80 (1)	1980/91 (1)	1990–2000 (2)	2000–2010 (2)
Total (3)	2,253,327	1,641,718	2,956,671	2,394,985
North	17,552	28,314	27,155	28,861
Northeast	1,181,358	1,085,308	2,047,168	1,704,683
Piauí	52,451	68,894	94,780	96,574
Alagoas	79,481	68,419	145,207	111,843
Ceará	52,451	68,894	235,249	190,348
Pernambuco	79,481	68,419	464,219	366,217
Bahia	387,478	355,215	777,952	663,414
Southeast (excluding São Paulo)	490,488	299,877	582,166	436,121
Minas Gerais	392,596	216,622	166,500	354,442
Sul	418,188	140,746	249,250	181,482
Paraná	379,719	111,761	197,519	134,285
Center-West	73,212	44,041	50,932	43,838

SOURCE: Cunha (2003): 229, table 8; IBGE, SIDRA, tables 617 and 631 for 2000 and 2010 for RMSP and 1981–2010 for state.

NOTES: (1) The data presented by Cunha were generated by NEPO and are not quite comparable to those given by IBGE.
(2) IBGE notes origin of persons residing in the RMSP for 10 years or less by state of birth. It does not give complete data for the 1970–1980 period for the state or 1970–1991 for the RMSP.
(3) Total excludes missing data and the Federal District (Brasília).

TABLE 5.13

Rates of Growth of the Capital and the Peripheral Municipalities That Make Up the Metropolitan Region, 1970–2000

					ANNUAL AVERAGE GROWTH RATE		
	1970	1980	1991	2000	1970/ 1980	1980/ 1991	1991/ 2000
Metropolitan Region of São Paulo	8,139,730	12,588,725	15,416,416	17,833,511	4.5%	1.9%	1.6%
Capital	5,924,615	8,493,226	9,626,894	10,406,166	3.7%	1.1%	0.9%
Periphery	2,215,115	4,095,499	5,789,522	7,427,345	6.3%	3.2%	2.8%

SOURCE: Modified from Baeninger, "Expansão" (2002), 9, table 2.

these cities occurred between 1950 and 1980, and thereafter annual average growth slowed in virtually all these other urban areas (see Table 5.14).

Since this was primarily a labor migration, with rural dwellers attracted by the occupations and higher wages available in the cities, this interstate migration to São Paulo was made up primarily of persons of working age. Thus of the 2.9 million migrants coming to the state of São Paulo in the

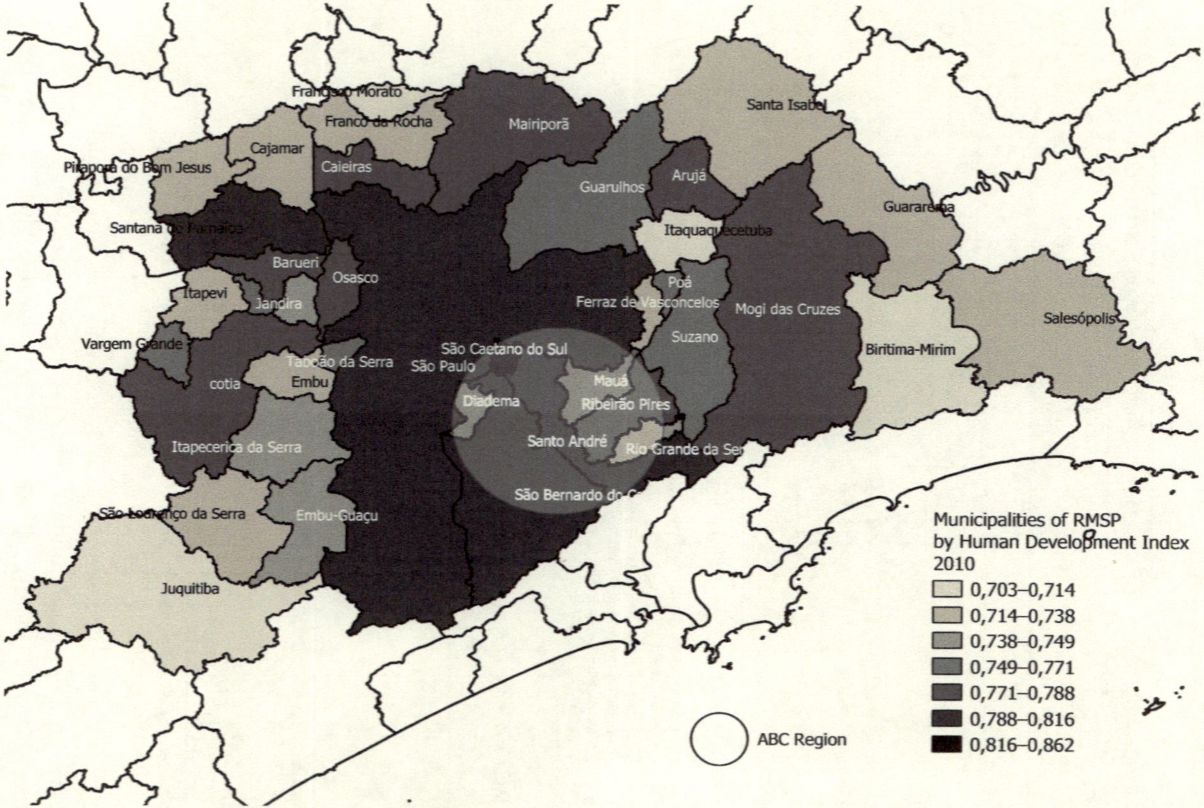

Map 5.1. Municipalities of the Metropolitan Region of São Paulo by Human Development Index, 2010

SOURCE: IBGE: Bases Cartográficas, PNUD-IDH, 2010.

TABLE 5.14

The Growth of the State, the Capital, the Metropolitan Region of São Paulo, and Major Interior Cities, 1950–2010

	POPULATION						
	1950	1960	1970	1980	1991	2000	2010
State of São Paulo	9,134,423	12,974,699	17,771,948	24,953,238	31,436,273	37,032,403	41,262,199
Municipality of São Paulo	2,198,096	3,781,446	5,924,615	8,475,380	9,610,659	10,434,252	11,253,503
Metropolitan Region of São Paulo	n.a.	n.a.	8,139,730	12,549,856	15,369,305	17,878,703	19,683,975
Major Interior Municipalities (1)							
Guarulhos	34,683	100,760	236,811	532,724	787,866	1,072,717	1,221,979
Campinas	152,547	217,219	375,864	664,566	847,595	969,396	1,080,113
São José dos Campos	44,804	76,994	148,332	287,513	442,370	539,313	629,921
Ribeirão Preto	92,160	145,267	212,879	318,544	436,682	504,923	604,682
Sorocaba	93,928	136,271	175,677	269,888	379,006	493,468	586,625
Brazil	**51,944,397**	**70,992,343**	**93,117,327**	**119,043,043**	**146,917,459**	**169,544,443**	**190,755,799**

	AVERAGE ANNUAL RATE OF GROWTH					
	1950–1960	1960–1970	1970–1980	1980–1991	1991–2000	2000–2010
State of São Paulo	3.6	3.2	3.5	2.1	1.8	1.1
Municipality of São Paulo	5.6	4.6	3.6	1.1	0.9	0.8
Metropolitan Region of São Paulo			4.4	1.9	1.7	1.0
Major Interior Municipalities (1)						
Guarulhos	11.3	8.9	8.4	3.6	3.5	1.3
Campinas	3.6	5.6	5.9	2.2	1.5	1.1
São José dos Campos	5.6	6.8	6.8	4.0	2.2	1.6
Ribeirão Preto	4.7	3.9	4.1	2.9	1.6	1.8
Sorocaba	3.8	2.6	4.4	3.1	3.0	1.7
Brazil	**3.2**	**2.8**	**2.5**	**1.9**	**1.6**	**1.2**

SOURCE: IBGE SIDRA, tables 1288, 202 and 1378; Ipeadata, Regional, "População residente—total."

NOTE: (1) Major municipalities are defined as those having over half a million residents in 2010.

1970s, 43% were in the 20–29 age group; adding in the 15–19 cohort, the total for the 15–29 age group was 57% of all migrants. Migrants over 50 years of age made up only 7% of the total (see Figure 5.11).

The urban labor market, especially in unskilled jobs, usually had more opportunities for women than men, and this explains the consistently higher ratio of women to men in the migration stream and in the capital cities. These core cities tended to attract more women than men, while the newer industrial suburbs tended to attract more men. This can be seen in the differences in sex ratios of the state of São Paulo and the capital city and its metropolitan region in the census of 2000 and 2010. The capital had a sex ratio of only 86 males to 100 females in the former year and an even lower 83 males per 100 females in 2010. Although also biased toward women, the municipalities of the RMSP outside the capital had higher ratios of males (see Table 5.15).

As the state became ever more urbanized the sex ratio of the state became more like that of the municipality of São Paulo (see Table 5.16). This was a pattern seen throughout Brazil, where the urban population in the census of 2010 had a sex ratio 93.4 males per 100 females, while the rural population had a ratio of 111.1 males per 100 females.[54]

Throughout Brazil there was a massive shift of population not only across regions but, even more importantly, from rural areas everywhere to cities, both local and in another state. These cities quickly expanded beyond their municipal boundaries. Between 1950 and 2010 the number of cities in Brazil with over 50,000 residents went from 32 to 433, and the population of these cities went from 16% to 52% of the national population. Just how advanced the state of São Paulo was in this same sixty-year period can be seen in the numbers. It had 8 such cities in 1950, and at that point those cities already contained 29% of the state population; it had 109 of them by 2010, and these now contained almost three-quarters of the state population.[55]

As the growth of the state capital cities of Brazil slowed considerably after 1980, there was new growth in their peripheries and in the newly created metropolitan centers in each state.[56] As these urban populations expanded, peripheral settlements began to emerge in nearby areas and turn into small cities, which quickly become integrated into the core urban center as transport infrastructure expanded. In 2000 the national census bureau began defining these peripheral communities and their corresponding urban core as cohesive metropolitan areas. At that time there were fifteen such metropolitan regions nationally with a population of over 1 million, and three of them were in the state of São Paulo: Campinas, Baixada Santista (Santos), and the metropolitan region of São Paulo (the largest in the

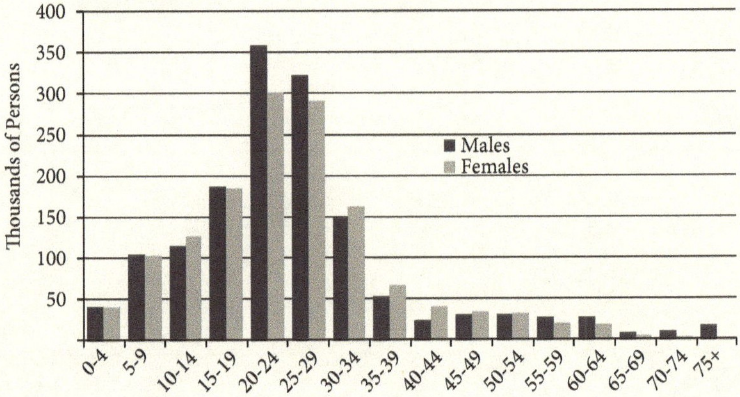

Figure 5.11. Age and Sex of Immigrants Who Remained in the State of São Paulo Between 1970 and 1980

SOURCE: Based on Cunha (1988), table 1.

TABLE 5.15
Population Resident in the State, Municipality, and Metropolitan Region of São Paulo by Sex, 2000 and 2010

	2000			2010		
	Males	Females	Sex Ratio	Males	Females	Sex Ratio
State	18,139,662	18,895,793	96.0	20,077,873	21,184,326	94.8
Municipality of SP	4,972,632	5,462,914	91.0	5,328,632	5,924,871	89.9
Metropilitan Region of São Paulo	8,629,634	9,250,363	93.3	9,433,605	10,250,370	92.0

SOURCE: IBGE, SIDRA, table 631.

nation, with over 17.8 million persons). By 2010 there were twenty metropolitan regions with populations of over 1 million. The Campinas region now had 2.8 million persons, and the São Paulo metropolitan region remained by far the largest nationally with over 19.7 million persons.[57]

Although it can be said that Brazil was on the move after 1950, that movement was not all in one direction. As typical in such migratory movements, there was both outmigration and return migration, even in this massive internal migration of native-born Brazilians from poorer to richer zones and from rural to urban residence. As the years passed there was a significant growth in return migration even to the distant poorer northeastern states from such receiving centers as São Paulo. Estimates of return migration from São Paulo from 1981 to 1991 and from 1990 to 2000 show that in both periods 56% of

TABLE 5.16

Population of the State and Municipality of São Paulo by Sex, 1950–2010

STATE OF SÃO PAULO

Census	Total	Males	Females	Sex Ratio
1950	9,134,423	4,648,606	4,485,817	103.6
1960	12,823,806	6,477,519	6,346,287	102.1
1970	17,770,975	8,929,302	8,841,673	101.0
1980	25,042,074	12,523,001	12,519,073	100.0
1991	31,588,925	15,613,989	15,974,936	97.7
2000	37,032,403	18,139,363	18,893,040	96.0
2010	41,262,199	20,077,873	21,184,326	94.8

SOURCE: IBGE, SIDRA, table 1286.

immigrants returned to their native states or regions (see Figure 5.12a and 5.12b). A survey of migrants to São Paulo from selected states in 1996–2004 also found that almost half of those who came from these states returned. In some cases, such as Piaui and Ceará, three-quarters of those who migrated returned to the state where they were born.[58]

This same pattern could be found for the metropolitan region of São Paulo. In the period 1981 to 1991 some 802,009 immigrants arrived in the RMSP from other states, and 53% returned to their state of origin in the same period. In the period 1995–2000 some 716,260 arrived, and two-thirds returned to their home state. In the two periods the intrastate migrants together numbered 306,574, but 851,024 of them left the metropolitan area for other parts of their native state, showing that outmigration from the RMSP was greater for state residents than for interstate ones.[59]

As a consequence of all these demographic changes, but above all declining fertility and increasing urbanization, there was a significant decline in the average size of households and the number of children per household. Family size dropped for all of Brazil from 5.1 persons in 1950 to 2.9 in 2015. Until the end of the 1950s there was little change, but the decline increased steadily in subsequent years, especially in 1980 and 2015, which had double the usual rate of decline in family size.[60]

As could be expected, there were different rates of decline by residence, with a significant difference between urban and rural rates. Thus, for example, in 1950 rural family size was 5.3 persons per family but 4.9 in the urban centers, with a national average of 5.1 persons.[61] In 1987 average family size was 4.0 persons, and by 1995 it was down to 3.7 persons per family nationally.[62] By 2002 the national average was 3.6 persons, although the rural average was still 4.0. By 2008 the national average had fallen to 3.3 persons

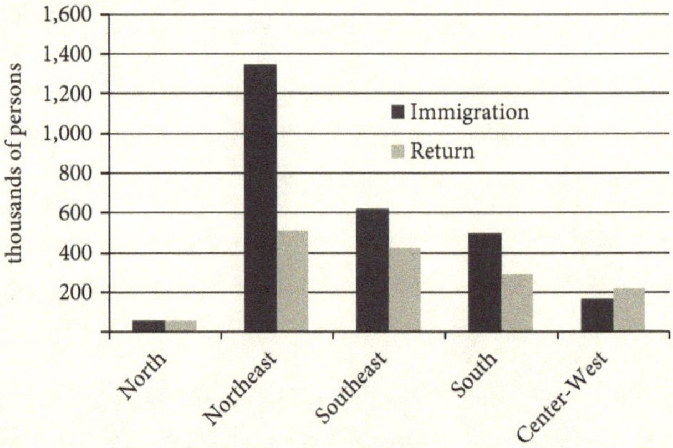

Figure 5.12a. Migration to and Return Migration from the State of São Paulo, 1981–1991

SOURCE: Based on Baeninger (2005): 87, table 1.

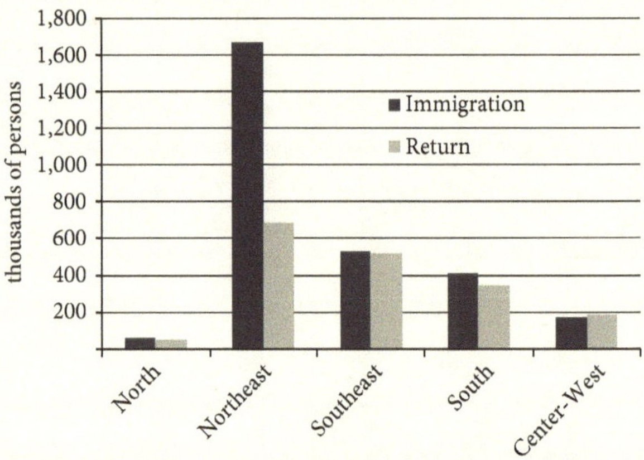

Figure 5.12b. Migration to and Return Migration from the State of São Paulo, 1990–2000

SOURCE: Based on Baeninger (2005): 87, table 1.

per family, with the urban average 3.2 and the rural average 3.6.[63] This differential urban/rural pattern could still be seen as late as the census of 2010, when the average urban family was just 2.9 persons, compared to a 3.3 average for rural families nationally.[64]

The pace of decline in average household size was also more rapid in São Paulo. By 1991 the average size of households in the municipality of São

Paulo had fallen to 3.8 persons from a high of 4.5 in 1960, and was down again to 3.5 persons by 2000.[65] In 2000 both the state and the capital were at 3.5 persons per household, and by 2010 both were down to 3.2 persons when nationally the rate was at 3.3 members per household (see Table 5.17).[66] Household size in the municipality was down to 3.1 persons, the same average as was found for the entire state in 2006, and by 2013 it was down to 3.0 persons for the RMSP and was still 3.1 persons per household for the state.[67] This average declined even further by the time of the 2015 household survey, which found the average for the state now down to 2.9 persons per household.[68]

This decline in average size of households in the state between 1960 and 2010 was experienced by every major subtype of household. Household size for married or cohabiting parents with children dropped from 5.8 to 4.1 persons in this period, as did the size for single-parent households with children, which fell from 4.5 to 3.1. Both extended families (including relatives) as well as "composite" households (made up of families plus non-relative members) experienced this decline in size as well. Only non-family households changed little in this period (see Table 5.18)

TABLE 5.17
Average Number of Residents per Household in Brazil, State of São Paulo, and Municipality of São Paulo, 1991–2015

	Brazil	São Paulo state	São Paulo municipality
1991	4.19	3.89	3.75
2000	3.76	3.54	3.46
2001	3.62	3.48	3.53
2002	3.59	3.45	3.52
2003	3.53	3.38	3.43
2004	3.51	3.37	3.40
2005	3.46	3.30	3.32
2006	3.42	3.25	3.28
2007	3.35	3.22	3.24
2008	3.28	3.15	3.13
2010	3.31	3.20	3.14
2009	3.26	3.14	3.20
2011	3.17	3.06	3.10
2012	3.12	3.00	2.98
2013	3.08	3.01	3.05
2014	3.02	2.96	2.98
2015	3.00	2.93	2.95

SOURCE: IBGE, SIDRA, table 156 for census years 1991, 2000, and 2010. Calculated from IBGE, SIDRA, table 1958, from PNAD surveys for other years.

TABLE 5.18
Average Household Size by Type of Household, State of São Paulo, 1960–2010

	Married/cohabitating couple with children	Single-parent family	Extended family, relatives only	Composite household, family and non-relatives	Non-family household
1960	5.84	4.46	6.93	7.08	2.99
1970	5.82	4.56	6.07	6.38	2.92
1980	5.31	4.28	6.41	6.33	2.84
1991	4.66	3.63	5.98	5.99	2.7
2000	4.33	3.29	5.56	5.66	2.69
2010	4.04	3.01	5.09	5.56	3.11

SOURCE: Ipums 5% sample of Brazilian censuses 1960–2010.

As many studies have shown, changes in fertility and household and family size spread from the urban and wealthiest sectors to the poorer ones during the process of transition. In 2004, for example, there was a perfect negative correlation between the number of children per household and family wealth, with the poorer households having the largest number of children (on average 4.6 in the state and 4.8 in the metropolitan region of São Paulo) and the wealthiest the lowest number of children (2.5 on average in both the state and the RMSP).[69] But over time all classes moved in the same direction, with the spread between the wealthiest and poorest classes consistently dropping.

These very rapid changes in births, deaths, and the size of families all created a new and complex society. Death in childhood was no longer a common occurrence, childbearing years were reduced, and the average number of children was less than 2. More women were becoming heads of households, and more persons were living alone; the pattern of extended-family residence was declining, replaced by older persons living alone and no longer residing with their children. All of these changes had an impact on the labor market, on the social welfare system, and on the role of women in society, work, and school. Just as demographic change greatly influenced the state population, so too did changes in attitude toward marriage and the role of women in education and the labor force influence the demographic structure of the state. The population living in São Paulo in 2020 was far different from the one that had lived in the state in 1950. It was now an overwhelmingly urban population, and one that had more in common with populations in the advanced industrial world than with its own past. Demographic change was one of the fundamental factors which accounted for this extraordinary development.

Chapter 6

Societal Changes: Households, Families, Women, and Work

The impact of demographic change, economic growth, and urbanization slowly and steadily led to basic changes in social norms in São Paulo, as it did in the nation as a whole. The meaning of marriage and the role of women were particularly affected by these changes. So massive were these changes that Paulista society in 2020 looks very different from the society that existed in 1950. Then legal marriage supported by the Church was the norm, women were less educated than men, and women's participation in the labor force was low and confined primarily to unskilled occupations. Moreover, the state supported these norms and reinforced the role of Church doctrine.

All these basic changes in societal norms about such things as the nature of the family and the role of women have multiple causal factors. These include not only the obvious ones of urbanization and industrialization, but also changes in attitudes that more or less affected most Latin American countries after World War II. The first and most obvious manifestation of this change in attitudes was the legal reforms enacted in the second half of the twentieth century. These changes included the extension of legal rights to children born outside of marriage, the legal recognition of consensual unions, and the legalization of divorce. The consequences of all these developments have also been matched by changes in attitude toward what constitutes a traditional family and what the role of women should be in society and in the labor force.

Compared to the rapid changes that were occurring in fertility, mortality, migration, and family size, change was slower to occur in household organization. As would be the case in all subsequent censuses, households still were predominantly formed by families in 1950. In the census of that year only 12% of households were headed by a woman, and two-thirds of these female heads of households were widows. For both sexes, less than 1% of heads of households were either divorced or separated (0.1% of men and 0.8% of women).[1] Clearly this was still a very traditional society in terms of stability of marriage and the low incidence of female-headed households, persons living alone, and persons divorced or separated.

Although civil marriage was established in 1891 in Brazil, divorce was made legally possible only slowly and the conditions were onerous. The Civil Code of 1916 permitted legal separation (*desquite*) only with many restrictions and limits, including the denial of remarriage. Only in 1977 was full divorce granted, but remarriage was only permitted one more time for the now officially separated partners. Finally, in the constitution of 1988 full rights to divorce and remarriage were established, and these were then incorporated into the Civil Code of 2002. As of 2007, divorce could be non-judicially arranged if no small children were involved.[2]

Equally as important as divorce has been the legal recognition of consensual unions, which only occurred in the constitution of 1988 and in the so-called Stable Union Law of 1996.[3] This guaranteed to couples in consensual unions all the traditional rights of inheritance and legal separation held by legally married couples, which included property arrangements. As important was the granting of full equal rights to children born out of wedlock (called natural children) with those legally defined as legitimate children, which only occurred in 1977 and was amplified in the constitution of 1988. This was crucial in guaranteeing all children rights to a parent's inheritance no matter what the legal standing of their parents' relationship, including if they were legally married to other partners.[4]

All these legal developments correlated with profound changes in attitudes toward traditional family life. This can be seen in the steady decline in the number of persons who were married and the rise of consensual unions and divorced or separated persons in the decennial censuses of Brazil, both for the nation as a whole and for the state of São Paulo.[5] There were clearly differences by sex, as more women tended to be married than men and more divorced or separated, although they differed little from men in terms of consensual unions. There were also some interesting variations from the norm for São Paulo. More residents of the state were married than was the case in the rest of the country, and although their rate of consensual unions grew as quickly as that of the rest of the nation, they always tended to have a lower percentage of consensual unions than the national average (see Table 6.1).

TABLE 6.1

Marital Status of All Persons 10 Years of Age and Older in Brazil and the State of São Paulo, 1960–2010

		BRAZIL						STATE OF SÃO PAULO					
Year	Sex	Single, Never Married	Married	Consensual Union	Divorced/ Separated	Widowed	Total	Single, Never Married	Married	Consensual Union	Divorced/ Separated	Widowed	Total
1960	Males	49.0	45.0	2.7	1.3	2.0	100.0	45.5	49.7	1.5	1.2	2.1	100.0
	Females	43.4	44.3	2.7	2.6	7.0	100.0	38.4	50.7	1.5	2.0	7.4	100.0
	Totals	46.2	44.6	2.7	1.9	4.5	100.0	42.0	50.2	1.5	1.6	4.7	100.0
1970	Males	50.1	43.8	3.2	1.3	1.7	100.0	47.5	47.4	1.9	1.4	1.8	100.0
	Females	44.4	42.6	3.2	2.8	6.9	100.0	40.6	47.4	2.0	2.6	7.4	100.0
	Totals	47.2	43.2	3.2	2.1	4.3	100.0	44.0	47.4	2.0	2.0	4.6	100.0
1980	Males	46.6	44.5	6.0	1.3	1.6	100.0	44.5	47.7	4.8	1.5	1.5	100.0
	Females	41.0	43.1	5.8	3.0	7.1	100.0	38.0	47.0	4.7	3.1	7.3	100.0
	Totals	43.8	43.8	5.9	2.2	4.4	100.0	41.2	47.3	4.7	2.3	4.4	100.0
1991	Males	46.1	41.4	9.0	2.1	1.4	100.0	43.2	45.5	7.5	2.4	1.4	100.0
	Females	39.4	40.3	8.7	4.9	6.8	100.0	36.3	44.1	7.3	5.0	7.3	100.0
	Totals	42.7	40.8	8.9	3.5	4.1	100.0	39.7	44.8	7.4	3.7	4.4	100.0
2000	Males	42.8	36.5	14.1	5.3	1.3	100.0	40.8	40.1	12.5	5.2	1.4	100.0
	Females	35.1	35.3	13.6	9.5	6.5	100.0	33.8	38.1	11.9	8.9	7.4	100.0
	Totals	38.9	35.9	13.8	7.4	3.9	100.0	37.2	39.1	12.2	7.1	4.5	100.0
2010	Males	38.8	33.4	18.3	7.9	1.6	100.0	37.7	37.4	15.3	7.9	1.7	100.0
	Females	31.0	32.5	17.9	11.4	7.2	100.0	30.3	35.8	14.7	11.3	8.0	100.0
	Totals	34.8	33.0	18.1	9.7	4.4	100.0	33.9	36.6	15.0	9.6	4.9	100.0

SOURCE: Ipums 5% sample of Brazilian censuses 1960–2010.

This decline in the number of legally married persons was driven by the rise in divorced and separated persons and in consensual unions. Although separated persons and those living in consensual unions always existed among the poor, the new laws had a major impact in extending this system into all classes within Brazil. It also made divorce more acceptable. Between 1984 and 2001 the number of divorces granted by the Brazilian state grew by 9% per annum.[6] There was also a growth in the number of persons legally separated. This was due to a requirement in the 1988 constitution that forced a one-to-two-year separation before a final divorce could be granted. But the ratio of divorces to separations has been steadily climbing, and final divorces made up 70% of the marriages being dissolved in the year 2002.[7] Despite the increase in persons of all ages getting divorced, the median age of women getting divorced has remained steady at 35–39 years of age.[8] Nor has the number of children affected by divorce changed dramatically, as consistently half of those filing for divorce over time have had only one child or none.[9] Finally, it appears that after dramatic rises, divorce and separation rates have become fairly stable in the past decade. In 2001, the rate of legal separation among adults 20 years of age and over was 0.9 per thousand persons, a rate that had remained steady since 1994. The rate of divorce for this same age group slowly rose through the decade of the 1990s, reaching 1.2 per thousand adults in 1999 and doubling to 2.4 per thousand adults by 2017.[10] But the length of marriage before divorce or separation changed only moderately over time: in the 1980s it was 19.5 years on average, and in 2010 it was 15.7 years.[11]

As could be expected, these rates in the state of São Paulo were somewhat higher than the national norms. The national divorce rate in 2001 was 1.2 per thousand population and the rate for São Paulo was 1.5 per thousand.[12] Yet there were actually more marriages in the state than in the nation. Between 1999 and 2008 the marriage rate increased in the state of São Paulo from 7.2 to 8.1 marriages per thousand resident population, whereas the rate for Brazil as a whole was 6.6 and 6.7 in the same period.[13] The average number of years between marriage and divorce was 10 in both the nation and the state, and the average age of women at the time of divorce was 38.6 years in both the nation and state in 2003.[14] Women divorcing with no children or with older children were the norm in the state and in its capital city in 2010, representing 53% of the divorcees in the state and 43% in the capital.[15]

The increasing importance of divorce and separation, as well as increases in unipersonal (single-person) households and in women heading a married/consensual-union household, has clearly led to changes in the sex of heads of household. In 1981 only 17% of families were headed by a woman, and the figure was only 18% as late as 1991 (which obviously did not count unipersonal households).[16] But in the last decade of the century this changed dramatically, rising to 25% of all households (family and non-family units) by 2000[17] and reaching 40% by 2015.[18] Female-headed households in the state of São Paulo were 41% of all households in 2015. The figures were even higher in the metropolitan region of the capital, which rose steadily from 31% in 2001 to 44% by 2015.[19]

The number of two-parent households have been progressively falling over time. In census after census the number of family couples with or without children has declined as unipersonal and female-headed households have increased. This is especially the case in the new century, as couples with children currently now account for less than half of all households. In 1970 dual-partner families (married or in a consensual union) represented 85% of all household/family arrangements. By 1991 it was down to 71% and by 2015 the figure was 62%. This decline nationally was matched by family arrangements in the state and metropolitan region of São Paulo, with the metropolitan region dropping fastest, to just 60% in 2015 (see Table 6.2).

Reflecting the increasing secularization of Brazilian society, there has been a decline in marriages that were only consecrated in the Church and a consequent rise in civil-only marriages. This occurred both nationally and in the state of São Paulo. Thus from 1960 to the census of 2010 the number of civil-only marriages has increased at the cost of both church-only weddings and combined church and civil ceremonies. The only significant difference between the state and the nation has been the very low rate of religious-only marriages in São Paulo. In 1960, for example, religious-only marriages were 5% of all marriages in the state, compared to 17% of all weddings in the nation. Moreover, even as church weddings declined nationally they have still not reached the low 2% found at the state level (see Table 6.3). Nevertheless, the PNAD national household survey of 2015 showed that the nation was moving toward the São Paulo model, with civil-only marriages at 30% and church-only marriages down to 5% of all married couples in the survey.[20] Thus from 1960 to 2015 people who married in church (church alone or combined with a civil ceremony) has declined from 88% of all married couples to just 75% nationally, and this was the trend in São Paulo as well, which saw such marriages decline from 88% to 74% by 2010.

What is impressive is that this change in attitude toward the Catholic Church and consensual unions can be found in both rural and urban

TABLE 6.2

Household Type in Brazil and the State and Metropolitan Region of São Paulo, 1996–2015

Region	Households (000)	Unipersonal Households	Couples Without Children	Couples with Children	Single Women with Children	Others	Total
			BRAZIL				
1996	42,645	8.0	13.1	57.5	15.8	5.7	100
2001	50,410	9.2	13.8	53.3	17.8	5.9	100
2004	56,428	10.0	14.6	51.0	18.3	6.1	100
2006	59,094	10.7	15.6	49.4	18.1	6.3	100
2015	71,253	14.6	19.9	42.3	16.3	6.9	100
			SÃO PAULO STATE				
1996	9,949	8.0	14.2	58.6	14.2	5.1	100
2001	11,568	9.0	14.3	54.5	16.4	5.7	100
2004	12,637	9.8	15.0	51.8	17.9	5.5	100
2006	13,410	11.4	15.8	49.9	17.0	5.9	100
2015	15,714	14.5	20.1	43.0	15.9	6.5	100
			METROPOLITAN REGION OF SÃO PAULO				
1996	4,768	7.9	13.6	58.2	15.0	5.4	100
2001	5,504	9.0	12.9	53.7	17.8	6.5	100
2004	6,028	9.8	13.6	50.7	19.9	6.0	100
2006	6,356	11.5	13.9	49.1	18.6	6.9	100
2015	7,412	14.9	17.8	42.3	17.7	7.3	100

SOURCE: For 1996, PNAD, Sintesis de indicadores sociais, table 4.2; for 2001–2015, see PNAD tables https://www.ibge.gov.br/estatisticas/sociais/trabalho/9221-sintese-de-indicadores-sociais.html?edicao=9222&t=downloads.

TABLE 6.3

Percentage of Married Couples Who Had Church or Civil Weddings, 1960–2010

Year	Civil Only	Religious Only	Civil and Religious	Total
		BRAZIL		
1960	13%	22%	66%	100%
1970	15%	16%	69%	100%
1980	18%	9%	72%	100%
1991	21%	7%	72%	100%
2000	23%	7%	70%	100%
2010	25%	7%	68%	100%
		SÃO PAULO STATE		
1960	12%	5%	83%	100%
1970	12%	3%	85%	100%
1980	16%	2%	82%	100%
1991	20%	2%	79%	100%
2000	23%	2%	75%	100%
2010	27%	2%	72%	100%

SOURCE: Ipums 5% sample of Brazilian censuses 1960–2010.

TABLE 6.4

Percentage of Married Women 10 Years of Age and Older Who Live with a Spouse, by Type of Marriage, for Urban and Rural Brazil and the State of São Paulo, 2010

Categories	Urban	Rural
BRAZIL		
All		
Civil and Religious	43.3	41.2
Only Civil	17.8	14.1
Only Religious	2.5	8.0
Consensual Unions	36.4	36.7
Those with Children		
Civil and Religious	44.7	42.6
Only Civil	18.0	14.1
Only Religious	2.7	8.3
Consensual Unions	34.6	35.0
SÃO PAULO STATE		
All		
Civil and Religious	50.7	49.1
Only Civil	18.9	18.0
Only Religious	1.0	1.4
Consensual Unions	29.4	31.5
Those with Children		
Civil and Religious	52.3	50.7
Only Civil	19.0	18.0
Only Religious	1.1	1.5
Consensual Unions	27.7	29.8

SOURCE: IBGE, SIDRA, table 102.

households by 2010. In that census year, women living with spouses in rural areas had types of marriages quite similar to those of urban married couples—they married almost as much in civil marriages and were as likely to be in consensual unions as their urban peers (see Table 6.4). Moreover, selecting just women who had children (34.9 million women) from all women living with spouses (40.5 million) shows that this pattern has been going on for some time. Older married women showed the same breakdowns as all married women, again with similar rates for both rural and urban women and for women with and without children. At the same time, the subset of rural married women who had children tended to be more Catholic (77%) and less Protestant (17%) than urban women.[21] Evidently the social revolution that this represents is, like fertility control, as much in the rural as in the urban areas of Brazil.

TABLE 6.5

Percentage of Married Women 10 Years of Age and Older Who Live with a Spouse, by Type of Marriage, for Brazil and the State, Capital, and Metropolitan Region of São Paulo, 2010

BRAZIL		SÃO PAULO		
Categories		State	Municipality	Metropolitan Region of São Paulo
All				
Civil and Religious	43%	51%	48%	47%
Only Civil	17%	19%	19%	20%
Only Religious	3%	1%	1%	1%
Consensual Unions	36%	29%	32%	32%
Those with Children				
Civil and Religious	44%	52%	50%	49%
Only Civil	17%	19%	19%	20%
Only Religious	4%	1%	1%	1%
Consensual Unions	35%	28%	30%	30%

SOURCE: IBGE, SIDRA, table 102.

Within the state of São Paulo and its principal city and metropolitan region a similar pattern was evident by the census of 2010. But compared to the nation, it had two-thirds fewer of religious marriages, higher rates of civil-only and civil-church ones, and considerably fewer consensual unions, and this held for both married couples without children and those who had children (see Table 6.5).

Although married and consensual-union couples are still the predominant form of family and household organization, their share of the total is slowly declining and there is a difference by sex. Among male heads of household the proportion of those who are single (around 5%) or widowed (around 3%) remained relatively constant from 1960 to 2010. But there has been a significant increase in separated and divorced males, from 1% in 1960 to over 9% by 2010. The proportion of women who have never been married has always been double or more than the rate among men. And women were seven times more likely to be widowed than men in 2010, probably due to two key factors: the longer life expectancy of women compared to men (now at over 7 years difference) and the higher remarriage rate of widowed men compared to widowed women. In all of these indicators, there appears little difference between the national figures and those for the state of São Paulo.

There has also been a fundamental change in this period in the nature of female-headed households in both Brazil and the state of São Paulo. Not only have their numbers increased dramatically, but their composition has changed in fundamental ways. In 1960 almost two-thirds of women who

TABLE 6.6

Marital Status of Heads of Household 10 Years and Older by Sex, for Brazil and the State of São Paulo, 1960–2010

	Single or Never Married	Married or in Consensual Union	Separated, Divorced, or Spouse Absent	Widowed	Total
			BRAZIL		
Men					
1960	5%	92%	1%	3%	100%
1970	5%	92%	1%	2%	100%
1980	5%	92%	1%	2%	100%
1991	4%	92%	2%	2%	100%
2000	4%	90%	5%	2%	100%
2010	6%	83%	9%	3%	100%
Women					
1960	17%	n.a	20%	63%	100%
1970	19%	n.a	23%	58%	100%
1980	22%	2%	22%	55%	100%
1991	20%	5%	30%	46%	100%
2000	12%	15%	41%	33%	100%
2010	10%	40%	29%	21%	100%
			SÃO PAULO STATE		
Men					
1960	5%	92%	1%	2%	100%
1970	5%	92%	1%	2%	100%
1980	5%	92%	1%	2%	100%
1991	5%	92%	2%	2%	100%
2000	4%	90%	4%	2%	100%
2010	6%	83%	8%	3%	100%
Women					
1960	14%	n.g.	18%	68%	100%
1970	16%	n.g.	23%	61%	100%
1980	22%	2%	23%	53%	100%
1991	21%	5%	30%	44%	100%
2000	14%	14%	38%	34%	100%
2010	11%	39%	28%	22%	100%

SOURCE: Ipums 5% sample of Brazilian censuses 1960–2010.

headed a household were widows. There were about equal numbers of single women and divorced/separated women heading households. By 2010, widows made up only a fifth or so of all such female heads of household, with women heading dual-couple houses—a category with few members in 1960—now the dominant form of female household heads, and divorced/separated women second (see Table 6.6).

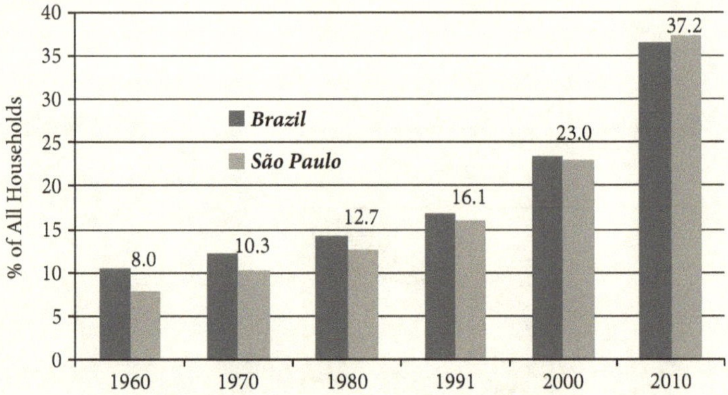

Figure 6.1. Ratio of Female Heads of Households in Brazil and the State of São Paulo, 1960–2010

SOURCE: Ipums 5% sample of Brazilian censuses 1960–2010.

Not only have the types of female-headed households changed, but their relative weight among all households has increased dramatically in both the state of São Paulo and in the nation. In census after census, São Paulo has increased its share of female-headed households more dramatically than has the nation as a whole (see Figure 6.1). Moreover, the growth of such households in the municipality of São Paulo has been more rapid than in the state, as seen in the latest PNAD surveys. Thus the proportion of such female-headed households went from 27% to 41% at the state level and from 31% to 44% in the municipality of São Paulo between 2001 and 2015 (see Figure 6.2).

In a pattern not that unusual by Latin American standards, the increasing importance of female heads of households did not in and of itself mean that males were not present. In fact, the very rapid increase of female-headed households in Brazil has been accompanied by an increasing number of such households having a male spouse as a member, especially in the present century. In 2011 some 27% of households were led by women, and 9% contained male spouses. By 2015 the figures were 41% and 34%, respectively.

This pattern of women heading dual-spouse homes seems to be a result of several factors. These include the increasing decline of economically active men within the working-age cohorts, the increasing participation of women in the labor force, the increasing educational attainment of women compared to men, and government policies.[22] Crucial has been the massive

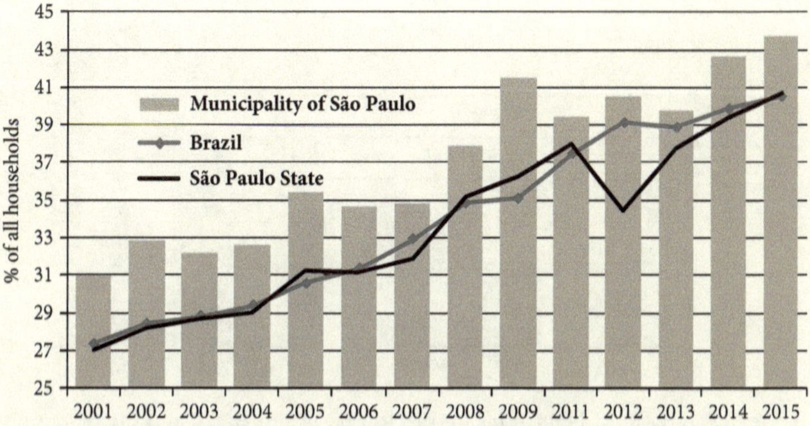

Figure 6.2. Ratio of Female Heads in All Households in Brazil and the State and Municipality of São Paulo, 2001–2015

SOURCE: IBGE, SIDRA, table 1947, based on PNAD surveys.

state income transfer programs, starting in the 1990s, which have designated women as the recipients of state income transfers for a household even when a male spouse is present.[23] What is impressive is that the type of households that were female-headed did not make any difference since all groups had approximately the same number of men assisting their female spouses in the married or consensual-union households.[24] In terms of the growth of female-headed households, the state of São Paulo followed closely the national pattern, whereas the municipality of São Paulo began at a higher rate. But all moved quickly to over a third of female-headed households having a male spouse present (see Figure 6.3). Thus, even some traditional dual-spouse family households are now headed by women as they become the primary breadwinners of the family and males become less important in this crucial role.

The other basic change among female-headed households is that they are being led by more ever-married woman than previously.[25] But despite the increase of divorces, the median age of persons getting a divorce in 2015 remained high, being 35–39 for women and 40–44 for men, a characteristic that has held steady over time.[26] Nor has the number of children affected by divorce changed much in recent years. Some 44% of the married couples getting a divorce in both 2014 and 2019 had either no children or only adult children living at home, and these rates were identical for the capital of São Paulo.[27] Finally, it appears that after

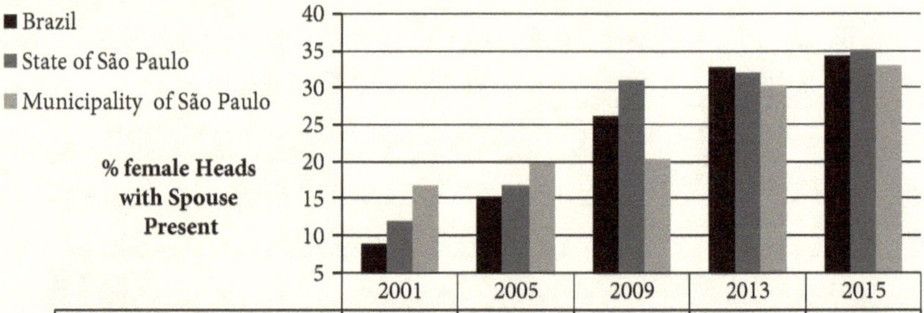

	2001	2005	2009	2013	2015
Brazil	8.8	15.3	26.2	32.6	34.3
State of São Paulo	12.1	16.7	31.0	31.8	35.0
Municipality of São Paulo	16.8	19.8	20.2	30.1	33.0

Figure 6.3. Ratio of All Female Heads of Households with Spouse Present, Selected Years, in Brazil and State and Municipality of São Paulo, 2001–2015

SOURCE: IBGE, SIDRA, table 1947.

dramatic rises, divorce and separation rates have become fairly stable in the past decade. As could be expected, these rates were much higher than the norms in the Southeastern and Southern states, where both separation and divorce rates were 1.3 per thousand adults (Southeastern states) and 1.2 per thousand adults (Southern states) in 2001.[28] As divorce became easier to obtain, legal separations slowly declined, especially after 2000. Overall, São Paulo state was only modestly lower than the national average in the proportion of persons who were separated, divorced, or widowed (see Table 6.7).

All these changes meant that single-headed households could now be found in the middle and upper classes as well as among the working classes. Female-headed households in Brazil are far more diverse in terms of income, and even color than female-headed households in North America. In the case of Brazil, as the number of female household heads increased over time their level of education and literacy actually passed that of male heads of household by 2015. The annual Brazilian household surveys showed that while initially women household heads had 0.6 years less of schooling then male household heads as late as 1992, by the time of the PNAD survey of 2016 female heads of households passed male heads of households in years of education (8.6 for women and 8.5 years for men).[29] Females heads of households thus followed the same pattern as women in general, since women have since the late twentieth century become more literate and have more years of schooling than men.

TABLE 6.7

Percentage of Population 10 Years of Age and Older Who Are Separated, Divorced, or Widowed, by Sex, for Brazil and the State of São Paulo, 1960–2010

	BRAZIL			SÃO PAULO STATE		
	Separated	Divorced	Widowed	Separated	Divorced	Widowed
	MALES			MALES		
1960	1.3	*	2.0	1.2	*	2.1
1970	1.3	*	1.7	1.4	*	1.8
1980	1.3	*	1.6	1.4	*	1.5
1991	2.0	0.2	1.4	2.2	0.3	1.4
2000**	4.7	0.6	1.3	4.3	0.9	1.4
2010**	6.7	1.2	1.6	6.2	1.7	1.7
	FEMALES			FEMALES		
1960	2.6	*	7.0	2.0	*	7.4
1970	2.8	*	6.9	2.6	*	7.4
1980	2.9	0.1	7.1	3.0	0.1	7.3
1991	4.4	0.4	6.8	4.3	0.7	7.3
2000**	8.2	1.3	6.5	7.0	1.8	7.4
2010**	9.3	2.2	7.2	8.1	3.2	8.0

SOURCE: Ipums 5% sample of Brazilian censuses 1960–2010.
NOTES: * Indicates that divorces were less than 0.1% of persons over 10 years.
** 2000 and 2010 census adds separation of consensual unions, which is included here.

Until 1980 there was a ten-year difference in the mean age of male and female heads of households. But the increasing number of divorced and separated women who are educated has progressively reduced that age difference, to eight years by 1991 and just two years in 2010. Clearly before modern divorce, the existence of widows and women who never married significantly influenced the higher average and median ages of women heads of household, while the legal changes since 1980 have reduced this difference considerably. The median age for male heads of household was 40–42 years from the 1960 census to the 1991 census, and for women it was 50–52 years in the same period. By the census of 2010 the mean age had risen to 46 years for male heads of household and had declined to 48 years for female heads of household. The median age of male heads of household has continued to rise, reaching 47 years by the time of the PNAD survey of 2015; the median age of female heads of household seems to have stabilized at 50 years.[30] Widows are a declining share of female heads of household, which explains the declining age of women heading such households. In this case, São Paulo followed the national trends, with the median age of female heads of households declining by 8 years from 1960 to 2010. As with

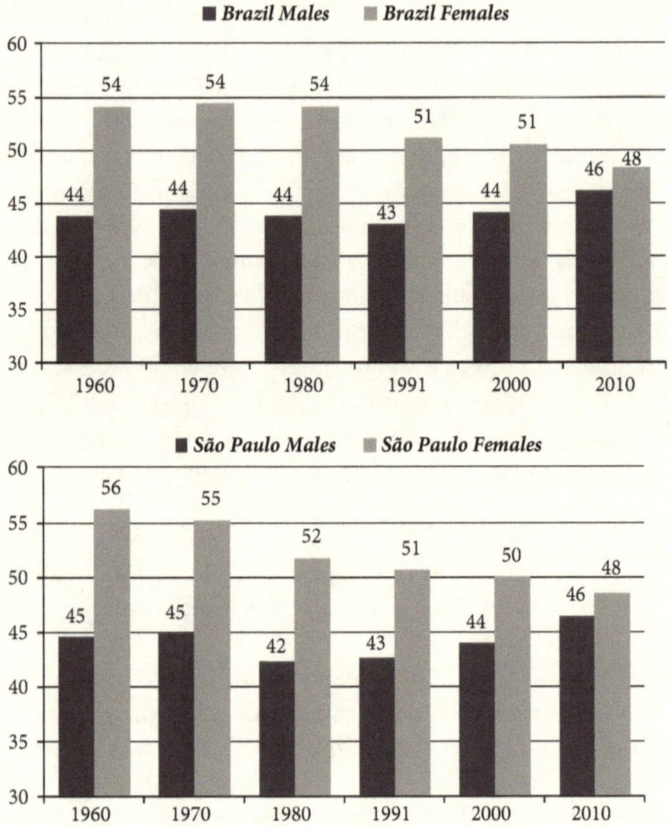

Figure 6.4. Mean Age of Heads of Households by Sex, for Brazil and the State of São Paulo, 1960–2010

SOURCE: Ipums 5% sample of Brazilian censuses 1960–2010, with persons under 10 excluded.

the national population, male heads of household remained relatively stable in terms of median age during this entire fifty-year period (see Figure 6.4).

There has been little difference in these household patterns by race and sex. In 1992 there were slightly more white males than white females as head of families (or 57% whites among male heads versus 53% among female heads), but by 2009 there was no difference whatsoever. There were, however, sharp difference in salary earned by sex of household head, with female-headed households earning on average a third less than what male household heads earned. While the median monthly salary of women employed in the formal sector was 75% of what male workers earned in 2010, the median monthly salary for all working women (in both the formal and informal sectors) in that year was 67% of the median salary for all male workers, approximately the same as in 2015, when female-headed households earned just 68% of their male counterparts.[31] In female-headed family households with children that contained no spouse, women were obviously the primary breadwinner and accounted for 88% of the family income. In dual-spouse households headed by a male, however, female income contributed under a quarter of total family income.[32] While salaries are much lower among female-heads of households, total income may be equal to or higher than that of male-headed households given that state income transfers are directed exclusively to women, as well as the higher proportion of widows and pensioners in these female-headed households.[33]

In 1960 there were significant differences between the average number of children in a household depending on the sex of the head of household, with female-headed households having fewer children. But as fertility declined everywhere there was increasing convergence between male- and female-headed households in the number of children per household, and by 2010 there was no difference, either in the nation or in the state of São Paulo (see Table 6.8)

There was, however, a major difference in the age of the children in households headed by a married couple and those headed by a single mother. Single mothers had a much lower number of young children compared to married couples and a higher number of children over 14 years of age resident in the home. In 2015, for example, some 61% of female-headed households contained children over 14 years of age, and less than a quarter had children younger than 14. Among males the proportions were reversed.

TABLE 6.8
Mean Number of Children by Sex of Head of Household for Brazil and the State of São Paulo, 1960–2010

	BRAZIL		SÃO PAULO STATE	
Year	Male	Female	Male	Female
1960	2.9	1.8	2.4	1.7
1970	2.8	1.8	2.4	1.7
1980	2.4	1.6	2.0	1.5
1991	2.2	1.6	1.8	1.4
2000	1.8	1.4	1.6	1.3
2010	1.3	1.3	1.2	1.2

SOURCE: Ipums 5% sample of Brazilian censuses 1960–2010.
NOTE: This includes households with no children.

TABLE 6.9
Type of Household with Age of Children in Selected Years 1992–2015 for Brazil and the State São Paulo

Category	1992	2002	2012	2015
BRAZIL				
Married Couple with Children Under 14 Years of Age	50.0	46.5	42.6	41.0
Married Couple with Children 14 Years of Age and Older	18.0	27.8	34.9	37.5
Married Couple with Children Both Under and Over 14 Years of Age	32.0	25.7	22.5	21.5
Total	100.0	100.0	100.0	100.0
Single Mother with Children Under 14 Years of Age	34.3	33.9	25.1	23.5
Single Mother with Children 14 Years of Age and Older	40.8	48.0	58.4	61.1
Single Mother with Children Both Under and Over 14 Years of Age	24.8	18.1	16.5	15.4
Total	100.0	100.0	100.0	100.0
SÃO PAULO STATE				
Married Couple with Children Under 14 Years of Age	50.1	45.4	41.0	39.1
Married Couple with Children 14 Years of Age and Older	20.8	32.4	38.8	40.8
Married Couple with Children Both Under and Over 14 Years of Age	29.1	22.2	20.2	20.1
Total	100.0	100.0	100.0	100.0
Single Mother with Children Under 14 Years of Age	30.9	34.3	23.2	20.1
Single Mother with Children 14 Years of Age and Older	45.0	40.8	60.1	64.6
Single Mother with Children Both Under and Over 14 Years of Age	24.1	24.8	16.6	15.3
Total	100.0	100.0	100.0	100.0

SOURCE: Generated from PNAD microdata files (using v4723).

This pattern held for both the nation and the state of São Paulo, although in São Paulo 65% of female-headed households contained children over 14 years of age in that year. Taking into consideration both female-headed households with children over 14 and those with both younger and older children, the difference was 80% in São Paulo and just 76% in the nation (see Table 6.9).

All these factors have led scholars to note that the rise of female-headed households has not created a major social problem in Brazil, as most of these households are created by divorce or widowhood and that a very significant percentage of the resident children are much older than among married couples.[34] This means that Brazil is not experiencing the so-called feminization of poverty—that is, when the increasing proportion of female-headed households automatically leads to increased poverty. Are such households more likely to be poor than dual-spouse ones? Recent analysis of Latin American household surveys suggests that the increase in such households is not in fact linked to increased poverty levels.[35] This seems to be the case in Brazil as well. However, some have argued that there may be other negative consequences, aside from poverty, for such households.[36]

Just as impressive as the growth of female-headed households has been the growth in consensual unions. Consensual unions have always been part of Latin American family organization since colonial times. But changes in the law relating to consensual unions, divorce, and the recognition of the rights of natural children in twentieth-century Brazil, as in all Latin American countries, have seen the number of consensual unions expand. Initially confined to the lowest economic classes before all the legal reforms, these unions have now become more common among the middle and upper classes.[37] In 1960 consensual unions made up some 5% of households nationally, and by 2010 the figure was 23%. The state of São Paulo had consistently fewer consensual unions than the nation, with only 3% in 1960 and 19% in 2010 (see Figure 6.5). By the PNAD survey of 2015 such consensual unions were up to 35% of all households nationally and were approaching the number of female-headed households, which was 41% of households in that year.[38]

Consensual unions are so thoroughly accepted within Brazil today that social convention now uses spousal referential terms for partners, whether a couple is married or in a consensual union. Moreover, given their patterns of seemingly settled domestic life it is often unknown if a couple is legally married (*casamento de papel passado*) or not. There has been a steady decline in the number of persons officially married. In 1990, for example, there were 7.5 marriages per 1,000 resident population aged 15 years and older, and this declined to 5.7 marriages per 1,000 adults in 2002.[39]

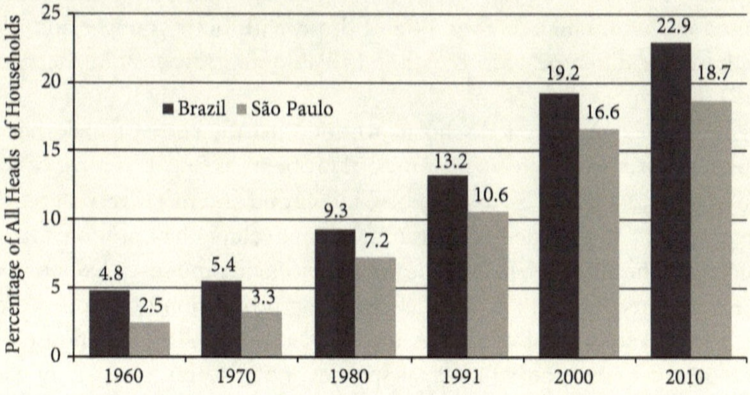

Figure 6.5. Percentage of Consensual Unions Among All Households in Brazil and the State of São Paulo, 1960–2010

SOURCE: Ipums 5% sample of Brazilian censuses 1960–2010.

TABLE 6.10
Percentage of Unipersonal Heads of Households by Sex, for Brazil and the State of São Paulo, 1960–2010

	BRAZIL		STATE OF SÃO PAULO	
	Male	Female	Male	Female
1960	3.3	17.2	2.9	17.2
1970	3.5	17.1	3.0	17.9
1980	4.2	20.8	3.5	22.3
1991	3.9	18.9	3.7	22.4
2000	5.8	19.9	5.4	20.7
2010	9.9	14.9	9.1	16.6

SOURCE: Ipums 5% sample of Brazilian censuses 1960–2010.

Another aspect of changing demographic and cultural norms is the rise of so-called unipersonal households—that is, households in which just one adult lived. Unipersonal households are still a small minority of households, but these households have now become an increasing share of all households, going from 5% in 1960 to 12% in 2010 and 15% in 2015. In all years, women were on average five times more likely to be resident in unipersonal households than men (see Table 6.10)

Over time the average age of these unipersonal householders has changed in different ways. At first there was a general decline in average age as more younger people started such households. But then it rose again in the last several decades for both men and women. These changes can be clearly seen when we compare the distribution of such households by sex between 1960 and 2010 (see Figure 6.6). Even as numbers have changed, men in unipersonal households are concentrated in the middle range of ages, while women in such households have consistently been older.

In terms of color, 60% of female single-person households were white, compared to just 47% among men. Finally, the census of 2010 shows there was relatively little difference between urban and rural areas, with the urban areas having a slightly higher ratio of such households (12.5% of all households, compared to 10.5% in the rural areas), with little difference by sex.[40] What is probably not surprising is that these unipersonal households were richer than regular family units. In the census of 2010, of all households that had an income, only 18% earned over two minimum wages. This compared to 32% of all single-person households having this income—and here there was no difference between male and female single-person households (32.7% of the males and 32.0% of the females). Moreover, 71% of women living in single-person households in São Paulo in 2010 owned their own

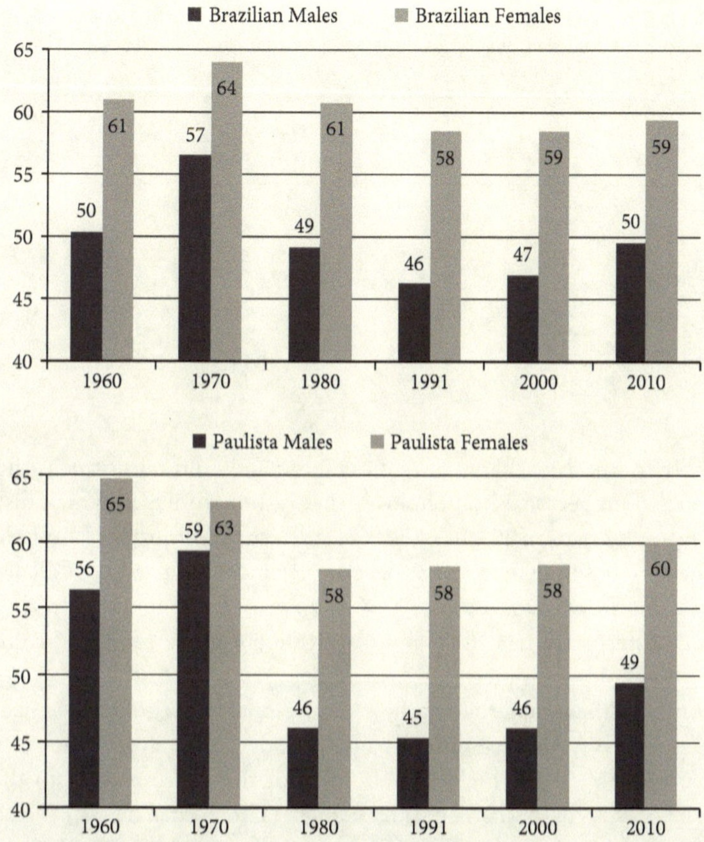

Figure 6.6. Mean Age of Unipersonal Heads of Household by Sex for Brazil and the State of São Paulo, 1960–2010

SOURCE: Ipums 5% sample of Brazilian censuses 1960–2010.

residence, compared to just 57% of men. Although in general both men and women had finished high school or attended university in the same proportions, women in São Paulo had more university degrees than men (22% of them compared to just 19% of the men). The average income of women living alone was only 85% of the average income of men in single-person households in São Paulo in 2010. In a recent study of women aged 60 and above living alone in 2010, a surprisingly high percentage of these elderly women were quite comfortable economically. Some 92% of them were classified as having a middle-class income or above, and fully a third were defined as being part of the upper class.[41]

It is evident that divorce was causing more working-age men to live alone. But widowhood was still an important factor for women living alone. This accounts for the fact that women living alone had overall incomes higher than men living alone. It has also been suggested that the decline in multigenerational households, greater life expectancy, and a better quality of life in people's later years have led to an increasing number of elderly persons living alone, even if they have family. A study of women 60 years and older living alone showed that 80% of these women had one or more children, none of whom were living with them.[42]

Along with changes in the family and in housing arrangements, there has been an important change in women's level of educational attainment. In the census of 1950, for example, for those 15 years of age and older, the literacy rate for men was 55% and for women it was only 44%. With each subsequent census women increased their literacy faster than men. In 1960 the rate was 65% for men 15 years and older and 56% for women.[43] By the census of 2000 the literacy rate for women in this age group finally equaled that of men, at 88%.[44] Subsequently women's literacy rate passed that for men in later years: as of the household survey of 2015, women over 15 years of age were 92.3% literate, compared to 91.7% of the men.[45] These trends in the literacy rate reflected the fact that differences between women and men in years of schooling increased over time.[46] In 1950, equal number of men and women attended primary and secondary schools, at a rate of 18% among persons 10 years of age and older. For those who obtained a university or other post-high-school degree, however, the spread was quite large, with 29% of the men and only 3% of the women being tertiary education graduates.[47] It was only in the census year of 1991 that women finally passed men in years of schooling.[48] By the PNAD household survey of 2015 women were listed with an average of 8.0 years of schooling compared to just 7.7 years for men.[49] In this year only 12% of men 25 years and older had completed university or other tertiary education, compared to 15% of the women.[50]

The historical educational deficit for women can be clearly seen in the illiteracy rates by age and sex for the census of 2010, where women were more literate than men in every age group except over 60, where the rates were reversed.[51] In terms of completing secondary school, women caught up to men in 1970, and by 1980 they were ahead of them. By 1991 they were ahead of males at all levels up to university, and by 2000 they had even passed men in rates of university completion. By 2010 they not only had passed men at every level but were increasing their distance. This pattern can be seen in the state of São Paulo as well, which overall had a better-educated population than the nation. Here women equaled men by 1991

TABLE 6.11

Level of Education Completed by Persons 15 Years of Age and Older by Sex for Brazil and the State of São Paulo, 1960–2010

	LESS THAN PRIMARY COMPLETED		PRIMARY COMPLETED		SECONDARY COMPLETED		UNIVERSITY COMPLETED		TOTAL	
Year	Males	Females	Males	Females	Males	Females	Males	Females	Males	Females
BRAZIL										
1960	92	94	5	5	2	0	1	0	100	100
1970	86	87	9	8	3	4	2	0	100	100
1980	73	73	17	17	7	8	3	2	100	100
1991	66	65	20	20	10	12	4	4	100	100
2000	55	52	26	26	15	18	4	4	100	100
2010	37	33	33	31	23	26	6	9	100	100
SÃO PAULO STATE										
1960	87	89	8	7	4	3	2	0	100	100
1970	80	83	12	10	6	6	2	1	100	100
1980	65	67	21	20	10	10	4	3	100	100
1991	55	57	25	24	13	14	6	5	100	100
2000	42	42	31	29	20	22	7	7	100	100
2010	27	27	33	30	29	30	10	13	100	100

SOURCE: Ipums 5% sample of Brazilian censuses 1960–2010.
NOTE: "0" refers to less than 1%.

in terms of the combined group of university and high school graduates, and then passed men by 2000 (see Table 6.11). In that year women made up 54% of the total of persons 15 years of age or more who graduated from secondary school and 59% of the total graduates of universities and other tertiary educational institutions. In contrast, they made up only 48% of all those who did not complete their primary education and 49% of those who had completed only primary school.

But women have been slower to match men in the labor force due to a series of factors. In the nineteenth and early twentieth centuries, high maternal mortality rates meant that there were more men than women in the population. Thus the sex ratio was a high 107 men to 100 women in the census of 1872 and only slowly dropped down to 99 men per 100 women by 1950, which was the first national census in which women finally surpassed men in the total population. With each subsequent census since then the number of women grew more rapidly than the number of men, so that by the census of 2010 the sex ratio was just 95 men per 100 women.[52] This secular change was due to two factors. The first was the decline of the foreign-born population, since both those brought over in the Atlantic slave trade and the European and Asian migrations had been predominantly male. By 1950 the foreign-born had declined to just 2.4% of the population.[53] The second was the steady decline in maternal mortality, which led to a longer life expectancy for women. By the middle of the twentieth century women lived on average 3.5 years more than men and were more numerous than men at all ages above 25 years—the peak working ages.

Nevertheless, women until recently were excluded from major areas of the economy and had been concentrated in domestic service and lower-skilled jobs with incomes lower than their male counterparts. They had very low labor participation rates and were primarily found in the informal economy. But the increasing decline in fertility after 1960, along with the increasing longevity of women, offered a potential demographic bonus for Brazil if women could be incorporated into the labor force. That is, their increasing participation in the labor force made up for the decline of males in the labor force, and thus kept the dependency ratio (the ratio of workers to non-workers—that is, the ratio of children and elderly persons to working-age persons) quite low.[54] At the same time cultural and political attitudes toward educating women changed, and by the last quarter of the century this led to women becoming more literate and having more years of education on average than men. Delaying childbirth allowed women both to enter the labor market and to obtain more education.

All of these factors have led to an extraordinary growth in female labor participation rates. As one economist noted, the growth "of the female demographic bonus was one of the forces responsible for advancing the quality of life of the Brazilian population between 1970 and 2010."[55] In the census of 1950 the female labor force participation rate—that is, the number of women working as a percentage of all women of working age—was only 13.6% at a time when the male participation rate was 80.8%. This female participation rate was virtually the same as in the census of 1920 (14%), and even in 1970 it had only risen to 18%. But by the census of 1991, the female participation rate increased to 33%, and for males it had declined to 72%.[56] By 2010 women had increased their participation rate to 49%.[57] In the PNAD National Household Survey of 2015, at the height of a depression, women's labor force participation rate reached 55%. These rates were not that different from those seen in the United States, where 57% of women aged 16 and above were in the labor force in the same period.[58]

The same developments of increasing female labor participation rates and declining male rates can be seen in São Paulo at the levels of the state, the Metropolitan Region of São Paulo, and the capital city. From 1991 to 2010 the female labor force participation rate within the state increased

TABLE 6.12

Economically Active Population by Sex for Those 10 Years and Older, Brazil and the State, Metropolitan Region, and Municipality of São Paulo, 1991–2010

	WOMEN			MEN		
	1991	2000	2010	1991	2000	2010
Brazil	32.9	44.1	48.9	71.5	69.6	67.1
State of São Paulo	37.8	48.0	52.5	73.5	71.7	69.3
Metropolitan Region of São Paulo	39.8	50.0	53.4	73.1	72.0	68.8
Municipality of São Paulo	42.2	51.5	54.6	73.4	72.3	69.0

SOURCE: IBGE, SIDRA, table 616.

from 38% to 52%. In the metropolitan region it was already seven percentage points higher than the national rate. Here the participation rate went from 38% to 53%, and within the capital it increased an extraordinary 13% to reach 55%. In each decade and in each region the male EAP (economically active participation) figure has systematically declined in this same period (see Table 6.12).

How high these rates might go in Brazil is suggested by data from the northern European nations, with their systematic state support for working mothers and families. Typical of these is Denmark, where the female labor force participation rate was 77% in 2016.[59] But Brazil is far more similar to the rest of the Americas, except for Canada, which has rates comparable to Denmark's. In most of the major Latin American countries the male EAP rate in the late twentieth century has been declining and the female labor participation rates have been increasing, but for women this level is still far from what can be achieved with direct state support for working mothers. Although the growth in labor force participation for women has slowed considerably since the early 1990s, it has still been positive even in the twenty-first century.[60] This increase in the rates of women entering the labor market appears in all age cohorts above 20 years. This is in sharp contrast with the experience of men in the labor force. Between the census of 1991 and that of 2010 one can clearly see an increase in women working in almost every age category; in contrast, the numbers of men working declined in every age group in this same period. The relative decline or stability of participation in youths under 20 years of age was being affected by higher school attendance rates in this same period. This pattern was the norm at the national level as well as in the capital of São Paulo, which in general had higher rates than the nation as a whole (see Table 6.13).

In Brazil, as in many advanced industrial countries, women have begun to outpace men in schooling in the current century. Using crude

TABLE 6.13

Economically Active Participation Rates by Age and Sex for Brazil and the State, Metropolitan Region, and Municipality of São Paulo, 1991–2010

BRAZIL	1991		2000		2010	
Age	Men	Women	Men	Women	Men	Women
10–14	14.3	6.6	11.9	6.7	8.5	6.2
15–19	61.9	31.8	58.4	40.6	45.8	35.0
20–24	89.3	45.7	86.9	60.9	79.9	63.3
25–29	95.3	46.1	92.3	62.4	87.3	68.9
30–34	96.4	46.6	93.4	63.1	89.3	70.1
35–39	96.3	47.2	93.1	63.6	89.7	69.7
40–44	95.1	45.0	91.8	61.2	88.8	67.9
45–49	92.1	38.8	88.2	54.6	87.0	63.9
50+	70.1	22.2	56.2	23.3	57.9	31.9
Total	71.5	32.9	69.6	44.1	67.1	48.9

STATE OF SÃO PAULO

Age	Men	Women	Men	Women	Men	Women
10–14	11.8	6.9	7.7	5.3	5.2	4.3
15–19	67.9	43.7	63.0	49.9	48.7	41.5
20–24	91.3	56.4	90.3	69.7	83.2	71.9
25–29	95.6	52.0	94.2	68.3	89.2	75.4
30–34	96.4	49.4	95.1	66.8	91.0	74.6
35–39	96.3	49.4	94.5	66.0	91.2	73.1
40–44	95.1	46.9	92.8	62.7	90.4	70.7
45–49	91.2	40.5	88.3	55.2	88.5	65.7
50+	64.9	22.0	53.3	22.5	57.7	32.0
Total	73.5	37.8	71.7	48.0	69.3	52.5

MUNICIPALITY OF SÃO PAULO

Age	Men	Women	Men	Women	Men	Women
10–14	8.3	5.2	6.1	4.5	5.2	4.7
15–19	62.2	43.0	60.0	50.4	43.4	39.5
20–24	89.7	63.3	89.6	74.6	80.8	72.3
25–29	94.9	60.1	93.9	73.8	87.7	76.8
30–34	96.0	55.9	95.0	71.5	89.5	76.1
35–39	96.3	54.3	94.6	69.7	89.6	74.7
40–44	95.4	51.8	93.2	67.1	88.9	72.7
45–49	92.1	45.6	90.0	59.6	87.5	68.9
50+	65.4	25.8	54.9	25.1	60.3	35.7
Total	73.4	42.2	72.3	51.5	69.0	54.6

Source: IBGE, SIDRA, table 616.

TABLE 6.14

Ratio of Children in Each Age Group Attending School by Sex, 2000 and 2010

	2000			2010		
Age	Total	Men	Women	Total	Men	Women
4–5	51.4	50.7	52.1	80.1	79.8	80.4
6–14	93.1	92.7	93.5	96.7	96.5	96.9
15–17	77.7	77.6	77.8	83.3	83.2	83.4
18–24	32.7	32.4	32.9	30.6	29.4	31.9
25+	5.1	4.3	5.7	7.4	6.6	8.0

SOURCE: For data up to age 17 years, IBGE, *Estatísticas de Gênero*, 2014, fig. 23; table generated from IBGE, https://www.ibge.gov.br/apps/snig/v1/?loc=0.

participation rates (defined as the number of persons attending school as a percentage of their age cohort), an analysis of the data shows that women are now outdistancing men in post-secondary education (see Table 6.14). More men than women worked and studied (20% to 14%). Men also did poorly compared to women in terms of high school and university dropout rates and enrollment. Some 41% of the males and 32% of the females in the age group 18–24 years dropped out of school in 2010—a rather high rate by European standards. At the same time, 15% of the women and only 11% of the men in this age group were attending universities or other institutions of higher learning.[61] Although labor force participation rates for men and women as late as 2010 were far from parity, recent projections suggest that if women continue to increase their level of education at the same rate as in the past, their labor participation will reach 80% in the high-participation age groups by the 2040s.[62]

Given its wealth and more developed institutional structure, the state of São Paulo was a leader in these educational trends for women and men. The census of 2010 showed some interesting variations from national norms. While nationally only 49% of males 25 years of age and older had completed at least primary school, some 52% of females had done so. Also, in the state of São Paulo and the São Paulo Metropolitan Region more women were graduates of university or other tertiary education institutions than were men. But in the capital city men were roughly equal to women on this measure—though in both cases their rates of completion were far higher than in Brazil, the state, and the metropolitan region (see Table 6.15).

The increasing level of education among women has been a significant influence in the type of work available to them. From the extremely low participation rates in the twentieth century, when women primarily worked as agricultural laborers or domestic servants, women have

TABLE 6.15

Level of Education Completed in Brazil and the State, Metropolitan Region, and Municipality of São Paulo for Those 25 Years of Age and Older, 2010

	BRAZIL		STATE OF SÃO PAULO		METROPOLITAN REGION OF SÃO PAULO		MUNICIPALITY OF SÃO PAULO	
Level Completed	Males	Females	Males	Females	Males	Females	Males	Females
No Education or Incomplete Primary	50.9	48.0	40.8	41.5	36.8	38.1	34.4	36.0
Primary Complete and Middle School Incomplete	15.0	14.4	16.8	15.9	17.2	16.5	16.7	16.2
Middle School Complete and Tertiary Education Incomplete	24.1	25.1	28.0	26.8	29.2	28.1	27.9	27.1
Tertiary Education Complete	10.0	12.5	14.4	15.9	16.9	17.3	21.0	20.6
Total	100.0	100.0	100.0	100.0	100.0	100.0	100.0	100.0

SOURCE: IBGE, SIDRA, table 3547.

slowly and steadily increased their participation in industry as well as the professions. This rate has even increased in the industrial sector, from 22.5% of all workers in 1995 to 25.8% of all workers by 2015. They are also several industries in which women are even better represented than this average. Thus women currently make up over a third of workers in the fields of electricity and communications, paper and publishing, and food and drinks industries.[63] The ratio of domestic workers among women has also significantly declined as they shifted into all the other sectors of the economy. Given current trends, all indicators suggest that in the future many prestigious fields will be dominated by women, much as has been occurring in all the advanced industrial societies. Women have slowly come to be the majority of students in professional fields in Brazil, some of which are considered high-status ones in Brazil. Although 44% of the doctors who graduated in 2010 were women, women make up 54% of all medical students matriculated in that year. While 46% of the lawyers who graduated in 2010 were women, women now made up 52% of all law students matriculated. Women of course have dominated in education and nursing, which are not considered high-prestige occupations, both currently and in the past. But they also have begun to penetrate engineering in Brazil. Only 20% of engineers graduating in 2010 were women, but women made up 28% of students matriculated in engineering in 2010.[64]

These positive trends in education are also reflected in the distribution of educational attainment in the workforce. Nationwide 56% of working males and 68% of working females had completed primary school or more. Some 17% of working females had a university-type degree compared to only 10% of working males. The São Paulo workforce had higher educational levels than the nation both at the state level, in the city of São Paulo, and in its metropolitan area. Here the sex differences are not as extreme as in the nation, with 72% of the capital's male workers having completed primary school or above, compared to 77% of the females. Yet even in all the three areas of São Paulo, women in the workforce had consistently higher numbers of university graduates in the workforce than men (see Table 6.16).

The impact of education has been impressive for women. Thus despite the still moderate levels of female employment, women who completed high school (middle complete) or university (tertiary complete) did better than men at the national, the São Paulo state, capital and MRSP areas, whereas men tended to be overrepresented among those workers who were less well educated (those who did not complete middle school) (see Table 6.17).

The industries in which the better-educated workers found jobs were approximately the same for both sexes in 2015. The public sector and service industries, which included health, education, and social services, were major occupations for women with high participation rates. Those women

TABLE 6.16

Educational Level of Persons 10 Years of Age and Older Employed in Brazil and the State, Metropolitan Region, and Municipality of São Paulo, 2010 (Percentage of Total)

	BRAZIL		STATE OF SÃO PAULO		METROPOLITAN REGION OF SÃO PAULO		MUNICIPALITY OF SÃO PAULO	
Level Completed	Men	Women	Men	Women	Men	Women	Men	Women
No Education or Incomplete Primary	43	32	30	26	30	24	28	23
Primary Complete and Middle School Incomplete	18	17	19	18	19	17	19	17
Middle Complete and Tertiary Education Incomplete	28	34	35	36	34	36	33	34
Tertiary Education Complete	10	17	17	21	17	22	21	26
Total	100	100	100	100	100	100	100	100

SOURCE: IBGE, SIDRA, table 3581.

TABLE 6.17

Percentage of Men and Women 10 Years of Age and Older and Employed, by Level of Education in Brazil and the State, Metropolitan Region, and Municipality of São Paulo, 2010

	BRAZIL		STATE OF SÃO PAULO		METROPOLITAN REGION OF SÃO PAULO		MUNICIPALITY OF SÃO PAULO	
Level Completed	Men	Women	Men	Women	Men	Women	Men	Women
No Education or Incomplete Primary	65	35	62	38	60	40	58	42
Primary Complete and Middle School Incomplete	60	40	59	41	57	43	56	44
Middle Complete and Tertiary Education Incomplete	53	47	55	45	54	46	52	48
Tertiary Education Complete	44	56	47	53	48	52	48	52

SOURCE: IBGE, SIDRA, table 3581.

who completed primary school or who had a high school degree tended to be more evenly distributed among occupations. But those without education were concentrated in agriculture in the case of both sexes. Overall, the patterns of industrial concentration were relatively similar for men and women, suggesting that education was the key variable determining the industry in which one was employed (see Table 6.18). Moreover, for employed person 25 years of age or older, 6.2% of the males were in administration or heads of companies, compared to 4.7% of the women—which was just a quarter less than the male rate.[65]

Another profound change is that women are now equal to men in terms of being part of the formal labor force. Since the beginning of the twenty-first century the proportion of working women who held a signed work card was close to that of working men. This work booklet (*carteira de trabalho assinada*) indicated that a person was contributing to social security and had standard worker rights and benefits.[66] These workers were under the standard labor code (Consolidação das Leis do Trabalho).[67] Public officials also could belong to a separate Statutory Regime (Estatutário), where there is no signed work permit and retirement is through the civil service pension schemes, which may be from the federal, state, or municipal government, depending on where a person was employed. In 2001 55% of employed men and 54% of employed women were in the formal sector and had such working papers. By 2015 this had increased to 65% for employed men and 62% for employed women.[68]

TABLE 6.18

Percentage of Employed Population by Sector by Sex and Level of Education, Brazil, 2015

	NO EDUCATION OR INCOMPLETE PRIMARY		PRIMARY COMPLETE AND HIGH SCHOOL INCOMPLETE		HIGH SCHOOL COMPLETE AND UNIVERSITY INCOMPLETE		UNIVERSITY COMPLETE		TOTAL	
Industry	Men	Women	Men	Women	Men	Women	Men	Women	Men	Women
Total	36	26	18	14	35	40	12	20	100	100
Agriculture	72	72	14	13	12	12	2	2	100	99
Industry	25	28	19	18	46	42	10	12	100	100
Construction	51	16	23	14	23	40	3	29	100	100
Commerce	28	17	22	17	43	56	8	10	100	100
Housing and Food	32	31	24	23	38	40	5	5	100	100
Transport and Warehousing	30	7	21	13	42	57	7	23	100	100
Public Administration	14	8	10	7	48	43	29	42	101	100
Education, Health, and Social Services	6	6	5	5	38	40	51	50	100	101
Other Services	18	31	13	18	42	37	27	14	100	100
Poorly Defined Occupations	57	19	20	34	19	21	3	25	100	100

SOURCE: IBGE, Sintese deIndicadores_Sociais_2016, table 5.9; https://www.ibge.gov.br/estatisticas/sociais/populacao/9221-sintese-de-indicadores-sociais.html?edicao=9222&t=downloads.

NOTE: Totals do not always add to 100 because of rounding.

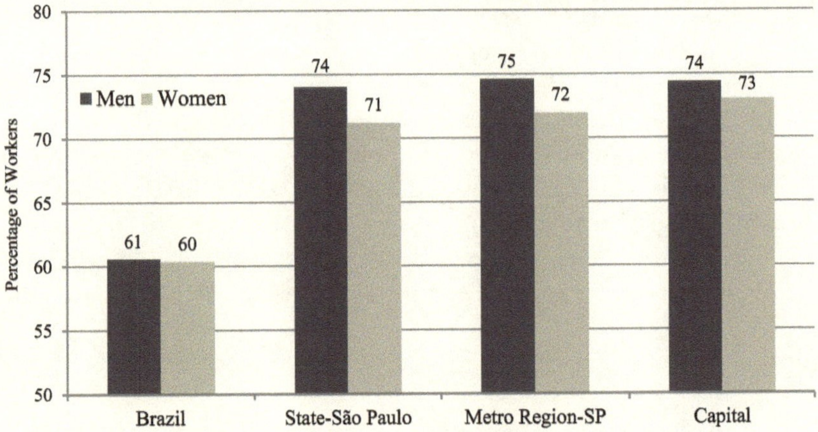

Figure 6.7. Percentage of Workers Contributing to Social Security by Sex for Brazil and the State, Metropolitan Region, and Municipality of São Paulo, 2010

SOURCE: IBGE, SIDRA, table 3581.

This equal participation of men and women in the formal labor market holds across all ethnic and racial groups as well. Although women earn less than men at all levels of education and in all types of occupation, and are often less numerous than men in given occupations, in this one area there is surprising equality between men and women in the labor market, no matter what the geographic area (see Figure 6.7).

The wage differential between women and men has narrowed over time. Women's wages have increased faster than the wages of male workers, thus reducing the distance between the two. In 2004 women's average salary was 70% of men's average salary; by 2015 it was 76% (see Figure 6.8). But at the same time the number of hours per week worked by women was just 34.9 in 2015, compared to an average of 40.8 hours for men. In contrast, women spent 20.5 hours per week on domestic chores, compared to half that amount for men.[69] Even in high-status professions average male salaries are always higher than female salaries, despite the fact that many of these professions have at least half or more employees who are women (see Table 6.19).

Finally, in terms of their structural position within the labor market, women are quite close to men in in most categories. They do better in public administration, largely on account of their domination of primary and secondary teaching, though they are well represented in the universities.

They are equal to men in participating in the legally recognized labor market and paying into social security, but they do unpaid labor at double the rate men do (see Table 6.20).

But, as noted, the wage differential, though narrowing, still shows up in almost all occupations. Thus in 2010, women's wages, even when women are working for the government or the military, were usually a quarter less than male wages (see Figure 6.9).

When the data are broken down by age groups, it is evident that younger female workers are more likely to have a salary closer to that of their male

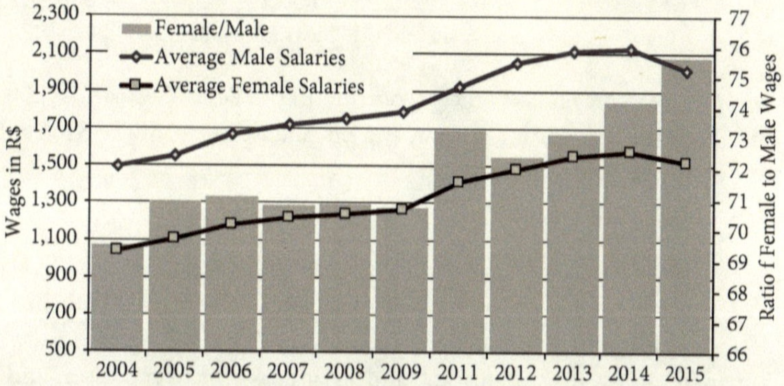

Figure 6.8. Average Wage by Sex of Persons 16 Years and Older in Brazil, 2004–2015

SOURCE: IBGE, Síntese de Indicadores Sociais, 2016, table 5.10, https://www.ibge.gov.br/estatisticas-novoportal/multidominio/genero/9221-sintese-de-indicadores-sociais.html?&t=resultados.

TABLE 6.19

Comparative Salaries of Men and Women and Ratio of Women in Professions in Brazil, 2010

Fields	Women's Salaries as Ratio of Male Salaries (%)	% of Women Workers
Education	72	83
Humanities and Arts	79	74
Social Sciences, Business, and Law	66	49
Sciences, Math, and Computing	65	47
Engineering, Production, and Construction	66	22
Agriculture and Veterinary Medicine	63	27
Health and Social Welfare	56	68
Services	53	55

SOURCE: IBGE, *Estatísticas de Gênero*, 2014, 107, table 17.

TABLE 6.20

Ratio of Workers in Various Categories of Work by Sex, for Brazil and the State, Metropolitan Region, and Municipality of São Paulo, 2010

	BRAZIL		STATE OF SÃO PAULO		METROPOLITAN REGION OF SÃO PAULO		MUNICIPALITY OF SÃO PAULO	
Type of Work	Men	Women	Men	Women	Men	Women	Men	Women
Employed	68.1	74.5	75.2	81.4	75.7	81.8	74.1	81.1
Employed with Signed Work Booklet	46.1	48.0	79.7	70.6	80.1	71.3	79.7	72.8
Employed in Military or Public Administration	4.1	7.8	3.4	5.7	3.1	5.5	3.2	5.1
Employed Without Signed Work Booklet	17.9	18.8	16.8	23.7	16.8	23.2	17.1	22.1
Non-Remunerated Work	1.1	2.4	0.6	1.6	0.6	1.6	0.7	1.7
Works for Their Own Consumption	3.9	2.7	0.4	0.5	0.1	0.1	0.1	0.1
Employer	2.3	2.2	2.7	1.7	2.6	1.6	3.1	1.8
Works on Own Account	24.5	18.2	21.0	14.7	20.9	14.9	22.0	15.4
Total	100	100	100	100	100	100	100	100

SOURCE: IBGE, SIDRA, table 3461.

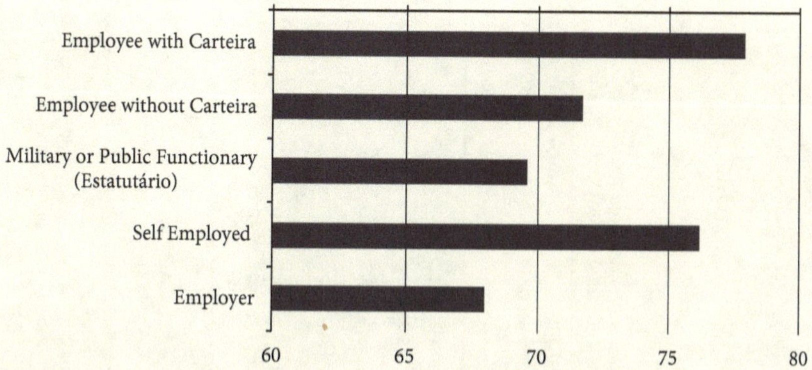

Figure 6.9. Ratio of Female to Male Monthly Salaries by Category of Workers, Brazil, 2010

SOURCE: IBGE, *Estatísticas de Gênero*, 2014, 135, table 35.

cohorts. For the employed age cohort 16–24 in the year 2010, women made 88% of the wages of men; for the 25–39 cohort, it dropped to 78%; for the 40–59 cohort, it declined further to 69%; then it drops to 60% for women who are 60 years of age and older.[70] This would suggest that the increasing educational level of women is finally having an impact on wages, and if this trend continues, wages should begin to reach parity in the future.

As one leading scholar concluded, all these changes have produced a mix of trends. On the one hand, there is "the massive and steady increase of female participation in the labor market . . . and on the other hand is the prevalence of high unemployment rates among women and the lower quality of female jobs; on the one hand, there is access to prestige careers and jobs, and to management and board positions, and on the other hand, the prevalence of female presence in precarious and informal activities."[71]

But even in these precarious positions there been some very important recent changes. One such traditional occupation that still absorbed 14% of economically active women in 2015 is domestic service. The post-1988 civil and labor codes have given domestic workers far more rights and have incorporated many more such workers into the formal sector. Thus domestic servants with signed working papers went from 25% of all women domestics in 2001 to 30% percent in 2016. Moreover, given these changes, live-in workers are now the exception rather than the norm, and modern apartment construction in Brazil no longer provides a living space for domestic servants. All these changes began in 1972 with the first law that recognized basic rights for domestic workers (including vacation time, contributions to social security, and access to public health).[72] Then came a far more detailed law in 2015 that more precisely defined formal domestic service as being more than two days per week (someone working two days or less was a day worker), required a legal formal labor contract between workers and their employers, provided vacation time, conferred the right to organize, and prescribed very specific regulations regarding daily hours and payment for overtime.[73] This law took on even more significance with the passage in the 1990s of the anti-slavery laws, which defined very specific working conditions for all workers.[74] Finally, the existence of a complete set of autonomous labor courts guarantees that cases against employers can easily be undertaken by domestic workers.

Although conditions have improved, domestic service is still a low-paying and low-status occupation that is dominated by women. But the proportion of female labor force participants working in domestic service has been systematically declining in recent years. In 1950 some 27% of the women employed worked as domestic servants, and they were the second-largest category of workers after agricultural laborers.[75] By 2001 domestic service absorbed only 22% of all women in the labor force, and by 2015 the ratio was down to 16% of all economically active women (see Table 6.21). But for all the changes, domestic service still remains an overwhelmingly female occupation, with women making up 92% of all domestic servants in 2015, a ratio that had changed little since 2001.[76] Moreover, domestic servants in 2015 were still the lowest-paid category among women workers, earning half of the monthly salary average of all working women, less than half of what salaried employed women make, and even 37% less than the next-worst-paid workers, self-employed women.[77]

By all indicators women receive less income from the same work as men, even if they have the same level of education. Women, for example, were earning consistently lower median salaries at every level of completed education than men from 2001 until 2015, and that holds for the nation and for the state, city, and metropolitan region of São Paulo (see Table 6.22).

The revolution that began with the equalization of education, the introduction of the contraceptive pill, changing laws favorable to women, and the subsequent massive decline in fertility all had a liberating effect on women in Brazilian society. The past half century has been one of profound changes for families in general and women in particular. Over the course of this period families have become far more diverse. Consensual unions, once confined to the poorer classes, can now be found among all economic groups in Brazil. The proportion of households headed by men has steadily declined, with a consequent increase in female-headed households. In turn,

TABLE 6.21

Percentage of Women in Sectors of the Labor Force, Workers 10 Years of Age and Older, for Brazil and the State of São Paulo, 2001–2015

Year	Salaried Employee	Domestic Servant	Employer	Self-Employed
BRAZIL				
2001	56.4	21.6	2.8	19.2
2002	56.6	21.0	3.1	19.3
2003	56.9	20.8	2.9	19.3
2004	57.5	20.4	2.9	19.2
2005	57.3	20.3	3.1	19.3
2006	58.1	19.7	3.2	18.9
2007	59.1	19.3	2.7	18.9
2008	60.4	18.3	3.2	18.0
2009	59.4	19.5	2.9	18.1
2011	62.9	17.6	2.4	17.1
2012	63.9	16.4	2.7	16.9
2013	64.4	16.3	2.7	16.6
2014	64.2	15.6	2.6	17.6
2015	63.0	15.7	2.6	18.8
STATE OF SÃO PAULO				
2001	62.0	20.6	3.0	14.5
2002	62.1	19.6	3.3	15.0
2003	62.4	19.8	3.2	14.6
2004	63.9	19.4	2.9	13.9
2005	61.8	19.6	3.6	15.1
2006	62.7	19.3	3.6	14.3
2007	64.7	17.4	2.9	15.0
2008	65.1	17.4	3.5	14.0
2009	64.0	18.4	2.8	14.8
2011	68.3	16.1	2.2	13.3
2012	69.7	14.7	2.8	12.7
2013	68.6	15.9	2.7	12.8
2014	69.0	14.7	2.5	13.7
2015	68.3	14.4	2.4	14.8

SOURCE: IBGE, SIDRA, table 1907.

these female-headed households have changed in terms of their composition, now encompassing more children, more educated women, and more younger women—a result of the increase in divorce and separation.

Women as a whole have also experienced profound changes in this period in relation to education and their participation in the workforce. The traditional deficit that women had in years of education and school attendance at all education levels prior to 1950 has been replaced by an increasingly large male deficit as women have entered high schools and universities

TABLE 6.22

Median Income in Reais of Workers in the Formal Labor Market by Sex for Brazil and the State, Metropolitan Region, and Municipality of São Paulo, 2010

	BRAZIL		STATE OF SÃO PAULO		METROPOLITAN REGION OF SÃO PAULO		MUNICIPALITY OF SÃO PAULO	
Level of Education	Men	Women	Men	Women	Men	Women	Men	Women
No Education or Primary Incomplete	510	500	800	530	800	600	815	600
Primary Complete and Secondary Incomplete	750	510	900	600	900	700	1000	700
Secondary Complete and Some University	1000	650	1100	800	1100	800	1200	850
University Complete	3000	1800	3000	2000	3500	2100	4000	2500
Number of Workers	49,823,312	36,530,527	11,283,702	8,717,568	5,191,254	4,288,147	2,966,588	2,583,199

SOURCE: IBGE, SIDRA, table 3577.

in ever larger numbers and now are more numerous than males at all educational levels, including at the most elite professional schools.

Women have also entered the labor market as never before. Although still not at the male level of participation, they have dramatically increased their participation at all ages. They have now entered the elite professions and have even become managers and administrators in impressive numbers. Although their pay is still less than men's, the gap has been slowly closing over time, and this wage differential should disappear in the next several decades if these trends continue. Within the labor market they are now as much in the formal labor market as men. Although they are still more likely to be unemployed than men—last hired being the first fired—their indicators of employment and unemployment closely correlate with men's, and both are highly correlated with changes in the economy. All of these profound labor market changes for women have been made possible by the revolution in fertility that occurred in this period, giving women more time to enter and remain in the labor force.

The rise of women's support groups, NGOs dedicated to women's issues, and a more sympathetic government have together profoundly changed national laws in favor of women since the 1980s, raised consciousness about the rights of women within Brazilian society, made it easier for women to control their own lives, and brought them into the labor market as never before in Brazilian history. But for all the gains for women in general, not all women have experienced the same rates of participation and success. Here as in so many other areas of Brazilian life, there are differences based on race and class.

Chapter 7

Societal Changes: Stratification, Color, and Social Mobility

Brazil is one of the most unequal societies in the world. This statement is even more emphatic when we consider just the industrial countries. None of these countries presents indicators of inequality similar to Brazil's. In 2014 the top 10% of the Brazilian population controlled 44% of income and the bottom half accounted for just 16%.[1] How severe this distortion is can be seen from comparable data for Canada in 2014. There the top 10% of the population accounted for only a quarter of the national income and the poorest half for 27%. In a typical Scandinavian country like Sweden in 2014, the richest decile controlled just 20% of the national income and the poorest half accounted for a third.[2] Brazil had an estimated Gini index of inequality of .514, calculated from the annual household surveys (PNAD, Pesquisa Nacional por Amostra de Domicílios).[3] Compare this to Sweden, which had a Gini index less than half that, at .252. In this Brazil was like most Latin American countries, with a Gini index in the .50s, which compared to indices in the upper .20s to lower .40s for most advanced industrial countries (see Figure 7.1).[4]

Although the Gini index for Brazil is not as extreme as in Haiti or Colombia, other measures suggest that inequality in Brazil is even more pronounced than this GINI index would suggest. When data from income tax returns are used, which more accurately capture income derived from rents, interest, and dividends as well as salaries,[5] Brazil is even more skewed toward the top earners than almost any other country. When we compare

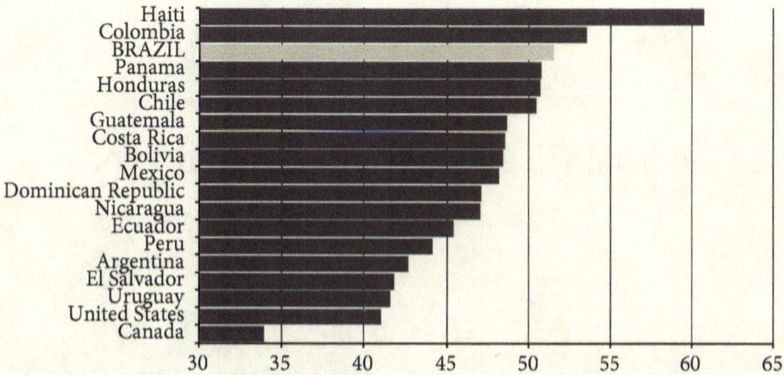

Figure 7.1. World Bank Estimates of Gini Index of Inequality for Western Hemisphere Countries Circa 2014

SOURCE: https://data.worldbank.org/indicator/SI.POV.GINI?year_high_desc=false, data updated January 30, 2019. The data for the USA and Canada are for 2013.

the pre-tax total income of the top 1% of income earners and their share of national wealth, Brazil, even as late as 2010, stands out as the country with the most extreme inequality in the modern world. In Brazil the top 1% of earners controlled 28% of the wealth. In Denmark the same group held just 6% (see Figure 7.2).

Even when government income transfers such as pensions and conditional cash transfer programs are included, this finding of stable and extremely high inequality is found. The best data on combined salaries and government transfers, as well as a host of economic and social indicators, come from the National Household Surveys. These are among the largest such surveys undertaken in the world and have been carried out on a systematic basis for the past forty years. Based on salary data from these national household surveys and income from tax returns, the Gini index for adults between 2006 and 2012 was around .70, an extraordinary high rate and well above the salary-alone rate, which was in the lower .50s in the same period.[6] And the share of total salary and income going to the top 1% remained stable at a quarter of the total income from 2006–2013.[7]

It would appear that this high level of inequality is not new. Inequality levels have been relatively stable for Brazil since at least the1930s, in contrast to other countries where reforms or economic crises have led to some significant fluctuations.[8] This can be seen in a comparison of Brazil with Sweden and the United States in three quite different time periods. In the 1930s, 1970s, and 2010s, Brazil's top 1% of wealth holders controlled almost an

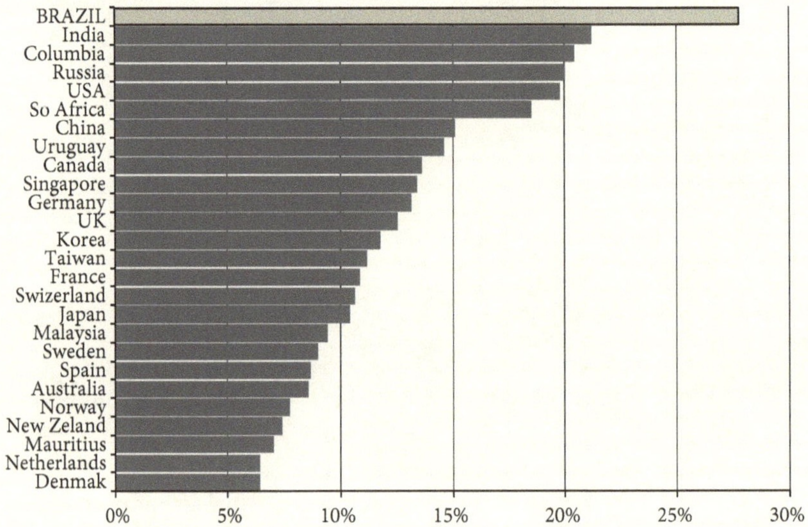

Figure 7.2. Share of Pre-Tax Income for Richest 1% for Selected Countries, 2010

SOURCE: World Inequality Database, http://wid.world/data/.

identical quarter of total national income and capital. Sweden and the United States, in contrast, saw rates change over time, going from high rates in the pre–World War II period to quite low rates in the post-war period, due to massive changes in the education of their populations and the introduction of the modern welfare state with high taxes and state redistribution of income. As Piketty and others have shown,[9] the most recent period has seen a rise in these shares from their lows in the 1970s, but even the United States has not reached the level of Brazil in the current period (see Table 7.1). While the first two decades of the current century saw the bottom half of the population grow the fastest and increase their share of total wealth to 13.9%, the top 1% also increased their share to 28.3% of wealth from all sources of income.[10]

It is not easy to understand the cause of this extraordinary disparity between Brazil and other countries of its size, type of organization, and even historical evolution. Since the 1970s there has been an intense debate in the country about the cause for this concentration of wealth. Why has it been that despite major industrialization and the modernization of the economy, there has been little improvement in the distribution of income and resources among the Brazilian population, who now are much more educated than ever before in their history?[11]

TABLE 7.1
Average Fraction of Income and Capital Gains of the Richest 1% of Persons, 1930–2015

	PERIOD		
Country	1930–1935	1970–1975	2010–2015
Brazil	24.3	24.6	23.2
USA	16.9	9.2	20.7
Sweden	12.3	5.8	8.8

SOURCE: Souza (2016), 249, table 5.

One factor is land ownership. Until the beginning of the nineteenth century, land was given out only in large parcels, and its possession represented a clear indication of power. In these large landholdings there was an enormous disparity between their size and their actual economic utilization. Slaves were also the primary workers. At the margin of this universe of great estates formed a world of small subsistence farmers, many of whom were squatters or held only precarious title to the land. These subsistence farmers represented the majority of the population. In the late nineteenth century, with abolition of slavery and the abandonment of the plantations by the ex-slaves, European immigrants were introduced as their replacement labor force, and this led to an alteration in the rules of access to land. The colonial *sesmaria* forms of extensive land grants would be replaced by a modern land market. But the Land Law of 1850, which regulated this new form of access to land, made it difficult for immigrants to purchase property.[12] These immigrants were brought in to serve as salaried workers in the existing commercial agriculture, especially in coffee, and not to become small independent farmers. There was never in Brazil, except with the southern agricultural colonies, a generalized distribution of land to small landowners who could effectively exploit the land, as would occur in the western United States. Nor was there ever a violent revolution, a systematic land reform, or any other abrupt break in the power of the elite that could have altered the structure of land ownership.

Even when the occupation of land was extended in the twentieth century and commercial agriculture expanded and became generalized throughout Brazil, the agrarian structure remained one of the most concentrated in the world. The technological revolution in Brazilian commercial agriculture, which has become one of the most productive in the world in the last twenty years, involved only a minority of the some five million rural properties in Brazil. This means that there is a dynamic minority of highly productive, capitalized and globalized agricultural producers, and a majority of farmers who are engaged in subsistence or minimal agricultural production, who now and in the future depend on public subsidies through income transfers to remain in the rural world.[13] As measured by the Gini index, land distribution remains virtually unchanged since the first agricultural census in 1920.[14]

With the abolition of slavery in 1888, most of the former slaves were incorporated into the labor market as wage workers or turned toward subsistence agriculture. But initially the skilled occupations and the major commercial activities, especially in agriculture, went to the European immigrants who arrived in massive numbers in the last two decades of the nineteenth century. The Afro-Brazilians from the slave era remained at the lowest levels of the free labor market in the post-slavery era for most of the first half of the twentieth century. Even the industrial process, which was firmly implanted by the 1930s, depended initially for a greater part of its labor force on European immigrant workers and their descendants, and only later on were native rural workers attracted to the urban centers.[15] Much of this history helps to explain the variations in opportunities by color as well as class within Brazil.

It was not until the middle of the twentieth century that the Brazilian government finally committed itself to public education for all its citizens, long after this had become the norm in most other Latin American countries. This policy explains in large part the extraordinarily high levels of illiteracy that existed in the country until recently. Even by the low standards of Latin America in 1950, Brazil had one of the least educated of populations on a par with the Central American countries. This was due to the low level of investments in education under the Empire and Old Republic (see Figure 7.3).

Nor would there be much change in the next three decades. Comparing student attendance by age cohort across all the Latin American Countries, it was evident that the pace of change was slow, leaving Brazil still ranked with the poorest countries in the hemisphere from 1960 to 1980 in the ratio of students aged 6 to 11 years attending school. Thus despite major investments and significant increase of attendance of primary grade students, all the low performing countries, which includes Brazil, remained in their same place from 1960 to 1980 except for Bolivia which had lower rates than Brazil in 1960 and was ahead of Brazil by 1980.[16]

With states responsible for primary and secondary education, it is no wonder that the richest state of the union, São Paulo, had among the best educational rates in Brazil. Almost two-thirds of the men and just over

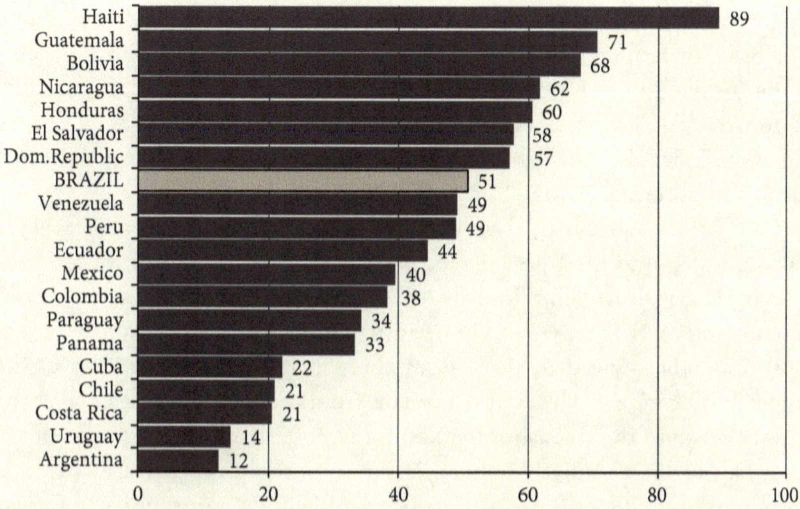

Figure 7.3. Illiteracy by Latin American Country, 1950 (percentage of population)

SOURCE: CEPAL, Anuario Estadistica de America Latina, 1980, 97, table 33.

half of the women were listed as literate in São Paulo in the 1950 census, whereas national literacy rates were well below these figures.[17] Within the state the capital city of São Paulo looked more like neighboring Argentina than like the rest of Brazil. Once outside the urban areas, however, even in this state literacy rates were like the national figures (see Table 7.2).

But the expansion of primary and secondary education in the state after 1950 was quite rapid. Between 1958 and 1986, for example, matriculation rates for first grade went from 1.5 million to 5 million students.[18] In turn, literacy rates also increased dramatically, and by 1980 84% of the male population in the state was literate, as was 80% of the female population. At this point there was little difference in literacy rates by sex for the youngest generations, and only for those older than 30 years of age were women less literate than men, a reflection of older trends.

Paradoxically, the opening up of the public educational system to the entire population would eventually lead to even greater inequalities. From the 1970s on the government undertook a policy of universalization of basic education, which finally reached its goal of complete coverage by the last decade of the twentieth century. But this universalization did not signify equality of opportunity, since "massification" of primary and secondary education occurred at the cost of quality. This has created a bifurcated

TABLE 7.2
Literacy of Population 5 Years of Age and Older by Sex and Residence in the State of São Paulo, 1950

	Literate	Illiterate	Total	% Literate
	STATE OF SÃO PAULO			
Men	2,563,437	1,406,250	3,969,687	65%
Women	2,063,892	1,763,278	3,827,170	54%
Total	4,627,329	3,169,528	7,796,857	59%
	CAPITAL OF SÃO PAULO			
Men	754,846	126,507	881,353	86%
Women	705,333	214,096	919,429	77%
Subtotal	1,460,179	340,603	1,800,782	81%
	ALL CITIES			
Men	1,614,767	344,794	1,959,561	82%
Women	1,475,543	571,702	2,047,245	72%
Subtotal	3,090,310	916,496	4,006,806	77%
	VILLAGES			
Men	76,901	31,395	108,296	71%
Women	59,251	45,093	104,344	57%
Subtotal	136,152	76,488	212,640	64%
	RURAL			
Men	871,769	1,030,061	1,901,830	46%
Women	529,098	1,146,483	1,675,581	32%
Subtotal	1,400,867	2,176,544	3,577,411	39%

SOURCE: Recensamento Geral de 1950, Série Regional, volume XXV, tomo 1: 188, 192, table 46.

system in which the poor go to lower-quality public primary and secondary schools and the rich send their children to high-quality private primary and secondary schools. In turn, these better-educated private school graduates gain a disproportionate share of entrance, via difficult entrance exams, into the free public universities, which are the best schools in the country. But the vast majority of graduates of the public schools do not obtain an education sufficient for them to pass the public university entrance exams, and many end up paying for an inferior university education in poorly organized for-profit private institutions. Although there are some high-quality private institutes and university faculties, they only take students who could pass the entrance examinations for the public universities. The majority of private university graduates find themselves ill prepared for the labor market, in contrast to those who go to the free public universities and special institutes.

Thus the Brazilian education system, as it is now constituted, although it undeniably promotes social mobility, has done little to reduce the concentration of wealth. There are now quite distinct trajectories for the rich and the poor: the former receive an education comparable to first-world standards, and the latter, despite their universal access to primary education, are marginalized by the quality of the teaching they receive. So poor is the quality of primary public education that many students who have attended the primary grades are still defined as functionally illiterate.[19]

The process of induced industrialization, which occurred from the 1950s onward, profoundly altered the productive structure of the country, modernizing the economy and provoking a dramatic movement of the population to the urban centers. Today all parts of the nation are integrated into a market economy, which without doubt was furthered by industrialization and the expansion of the modern labor market. For the population as a whole income has risen dramatically. There has also been a major expansion in the service sector and greater specialization in the labor force with many new positions opening up in industrial labor. This has resulted in significant generational mobility, with children increasing their occupational status and income compared to their parents. But despite all these changes, the structure of wealth concentration, which marks the country as one of the most unequal in the world, has only modestly changed until the first few decades of the twenty-first century.

The crisis of the 1980s, marked by low growth and high inflation, did not reduce these distortions in income. Absolute income per capita grew little in this period, and there was no redistributive process. Inflation, in fact, was a perverse process that caused deterioration in all incomes, but above all in those of workers who had no effective mechanism in place to protect them from inflation. In contrast, the wealthy and high-salaried workers could rely on indexing to protect their earnings. Thus recession and high inflation had profoundly negative effects on the evolution of the absolute level of income and its distribution.

The Plan Real of 1994 controlled the inflation that had plagued the country for decades. This inflation had often reached levels that could be considered hyperinflation, and it had a particularly negative influence on worker wages.[20] The stability created by the Plan Real provided a breathing space for the poorest segments of the population. The end of inflation represented an end to the "inflation tax" that had consumed their income, and permitted a major increase in demand for food and goods, particularly among the poorer segments of society. Another major change has been the creation of a very extensive program of government income transfers to the poor. Beginning in the late 1990s, government succeeded in expanding social policies through an intensification of conditional cash transfer programs and a significant increase in the minimum wage. The most important of these cash transfer programs was the Bolsa Família, a consolidation of several existing programs. There were also numerous other income-support programs—some preexisting, others established in the period, and several relaunched with a new name and configuration. In addition to these programs, the gradual increase in the minimum wage was significant, with the wage growing over two and a half times in real terms from July 1994 (the date of the debut of the Real Plan) until August 2017. Most of these programs had a positive effect in providing basic services and financial support for the poor and indigent population. These policies, along with an expanding economy, brought millions of workers into the formal economy and thus increased the number of persons participating in social security. They succeeded in massively reducing poverty in Brazil and expanding the middle class, and led to a modest decline in inequality.

The recent growth of the economy and the beginning of systematic government income transfers since the late 1990s have seen the shares of income and wealth going to the bottom 50% of the population increase faster than those going to the top 10%. This in turn explains the progressive reduction of the Gini index in the two most recent decades. From the 1950s to 2001 the Gini index for income and salaries fluctuated around .60, with no secular trend evident. But in the first and second decades of the new century there has been a slow but very steady decline, leading to a Gini index in the low .50s by the mid-2010s (see Figure 7.4).[21] Whether this decline will continue is still not clear since we do not yet know the consequences of the profound political and economic crisis that began in the mid-2010s, which caused a sharp drop in GDP and reduced future growth prospects.

The recent poor performance of the Brazilian economy compromises the continuity of improvements in the living conditions of the population and in the reduction of inequalities. This has led to a dramatic retraction of the resources allocated to the main social programs, with an increasingly negative impact on inequality. In addition, a sharp decline in the investment rate, which hovered around 15% of GDP in 2016 and 2017, jeopardizes the future performance of the Brazilian economy. According to data from the World Bank, income per capita in Brazil in 2019 had fallen 27% in relation to pre capita income in 2013.[22]

Thus the recent reduction of inequality seen in the past three decades has now slowed or even reversed. Moreover, Brazil still suffers inequality

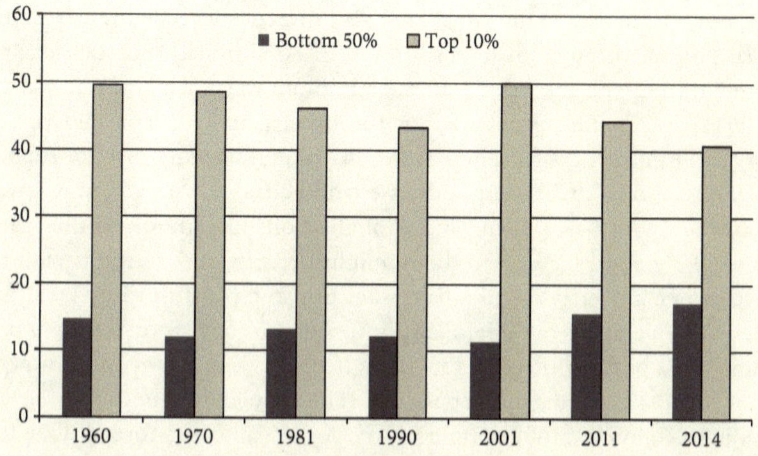

Figure 7.4. Changing Shares of Income of Bottom 50% and Top 10% per Capita in Brazil, 1960–2014

SOURCE: World Income Inequality Database, Version 3.4, using mostly ECLA numbers.

not only in income but also in terms of residence. Like many countries, Brazil experienced strong regional disparities, and although common even in advanced industrial societies, they were especially pronounced in this continental country. Some economists argued that Brazil, even as late as the 1980s, was really two distinct countries, which they called Belíndia.[23] That is, the population inhabiting the Northern and Western states had economic and social indices equivalent to India, while the population in the Southeastern and South regions had a standard of living comparable to Belgium. Even as most social and demographic indices indicate a closing of regional differences in Brazil, economic indicators show far less homogenization.

If there was a Belgium in Brazil in the 1980s, it was the Southeastern region that led in terms of household income and accounted for over half of the national GDP (56%), even though it had just 42% of the national population. Within the Southeastern Region, it is the state of São Paulo that stands out from the rest of the nation as the state with the highest per capita income and the highest GDP of any state in the union. From the early twentieth century until today, São Paulo has been the richest state in Brazil. In 2010 São Paulo had only 22% of the national population but accounted for 37% of the national GDP (see Table 7.3 and Map 7.1).

TABLE 7.3
Index of Per Capita GDP by State in Brazil, 2006–2013 (Brazil = 100)

State	2006	2008	2009	2010	2011	2012	2013
São Paulo	154	153	156	153	151	149	148
Rio de Janeiro	139	135	133	141	143	146	145
Tocantins	57	64	66	119	58	59	124
Santa Catarina	123	127	125	122	122	121	122
Espírito Santo	120	127	114	116	128	128	115
Paraná	104	106	105	106	107	108	114
Rio Grande do Sul	113	115	117	110	108	107	112
Mato Grosso	97	112	111	93	101	105	106
Mato Grosso do Sul	84	89	90	96	99	101	101
Minas Gerais	87	89	85	88	89	90	89
Goiás	79	81	85	87	88	91	89
Amazonas	93	88	62	85	87	80	83
Roraima	72	74	77	73	70	67	70
Rondônia	66	75	78	72	75	73	68
Amapá	67	69	68	60	60	64	66
Sergipe	60	61	57	63	61	63	61
Pernambuco	51	50	53	54	55	58	58
Rio Grande do Norte	53	51	52	56	56	58	58
Pará	49	50	46	54	57	56	57
Acre	55	62	29	57	54	55	56
Bahia	55	52	55	53	51	51	51
Ceará	44	44	45	47	47	46	47
Paraíba	43	43	44	48	43	45	45
Alagoas	41	39	39	42	44	45	43
Maranhão	36	38	36	35	35	37	38
Piauí	33	34	35	36	37	37	37

SOURCE: IBGE, SIDRA, table 1194.

A study of wages also shows that the state has a much larger share of higher income earners than the nation as a whole, and within the state the municipality of São Paulo is the city with the highest percentage of top wage earners. But the PNAD survey data also suggest that the reduction of poverty in other states of the union has proceeded faster than in São Paulo. Whereas the state and its largest metropolitan region in 1992 had the lowest poverty rate (27%) in their respective categories, by 2014 there were eight states with lower poverty rates than São Paulo's 7.9% poverty rate, including not only the usual Southern ones of Paraná and Santa Catarina (the lowest at 4.3%) but all the states of the Center-West, and the Southeastern states of Minas Gerais and Espírito Santo. Even the metropolitan region of São Paulo, with a rate of 9.1%, moved from having the lowest rate to being behind the metropolitan regions of Curitiba (which was the lowest at 4.8%) and Belo Horizonte (see Figure 7.5).[24]

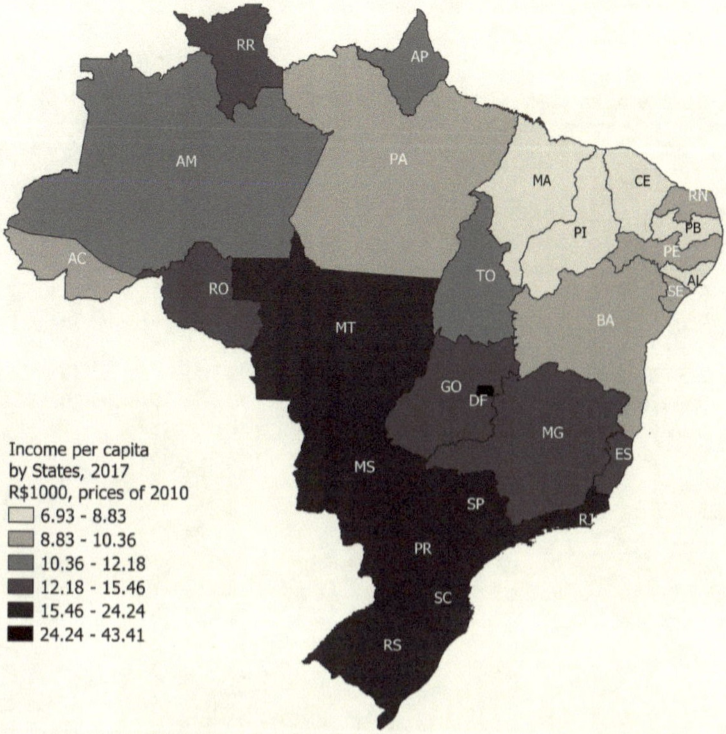

Map 7.1. Income per Capita by State, 2017

SOURCE: IBGE, Bases Cartográficas; Ipeadata.

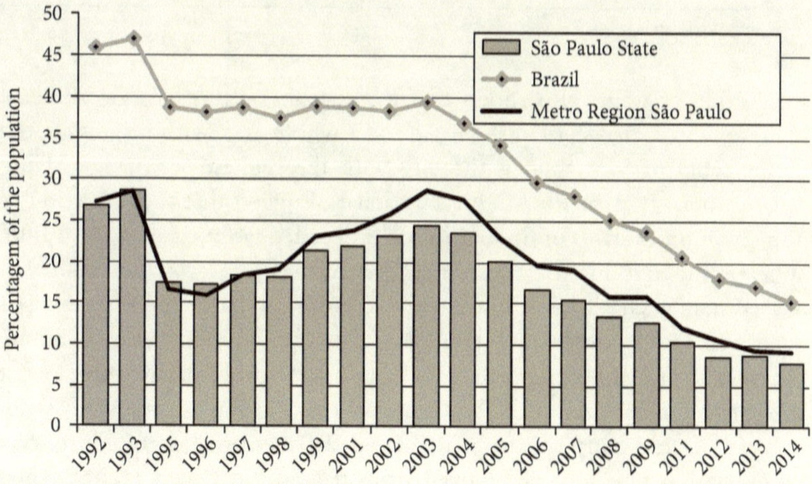

Figure 7.5. Percentage of the Population Living in Poverty in Brazil and the State and the Metropolitan Region of São Paulo, 1992–2014

SOURCE: IETS/OPE Sociais, based on PNAD, https://www.iets.org.br/spip.php?article406.

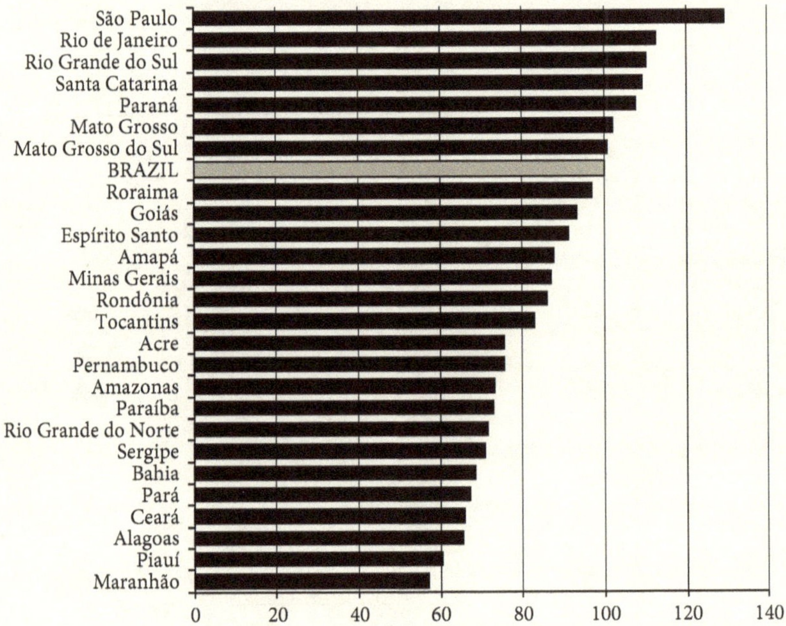

Figure 7.6. Index of Average Effective Wages Received by Workers Age 10 Years and Older by State, 2018

SOURCE: IBGE, SIDRA, table 5431 (average for the year).

This relatively slow decline of poverty in São Paulo compared to other states did not change the relative position of the state in terms of average effective wages. As late as 2018 the state still had by far the highest effective wages in the nation (see Figure 7.6).

In the period since the middle of the twentieth century, the state of São Paulo has undergone major transformations in its occupational structure. Agriculture has dramatically declined and the wholesale and retail trades have increased their share of the workforce. All the service occupations have increased, and there has been major growth in education and social services. All this reflects the growth of a primarily urban society and the modernization of agriculture, which has been producing more with fewer workers (see Table 7.4).

When examined by occupations, the role of the expanding service sector is even more clearly defined in the fifty-year period from 1960 to 2010. Service and sales workers almost tripled, liberal professionals doubled, and technicians and associated professionals have increased by a factor of four. Rural workers have declined from almost a third of all workers in 1960 to just 3%

TABLE 7.4
Changing Size of Workforce by Industry in the State of São Paulo, 1960–2010

Industry	1960	1970	1980	1991	2000	2010
	YEAR					
Agriculture, Fishing, and Forestry	33.3	22.0	12.1	10.4	8.2	8.6
Mining	0.3	0.3	0.2	0.4	0.1	0.2
Manufacturing	18.5	23.5	29.8	24.4	19.0	18.4
Electricity, Gas, and Water	0.9	1.2	0.9	0.7	0.5	0.9
Construction	4.8	7.6	7.8	7.3	7.5	7.6
Wholesale and Retail Trade	12.0	13.7	12.1	12.9	15.3	17.6
Hotels and Restaurants	1.6	0.3	2.5	3.6	5.3	3.9
Transportation and Communications	6.5	5.7	5.3	5.5	5.9	6.5
Financial Services and Insurance	1.4	2.3	3.1	2.7	2.1	1.7
Public Administration and Defense	3.4	4.3	3.7	4.0	4.5	5.0
Real Estate and Business Services	2.0	1.9	5.1	6.1	7.1	8.4
Education	2.3	3.1	3.5	4.4	5.1	5.4
Health and Social Work	1.5	1.8	2.6	3.1	4.7	4.6
Other Services	6.0	2.5	4.6	7.5	6.5	3.5
Private Household Services	5.6	10.0	6.7	6.8	8.3	7.9
Total	100.0	100.0	100.0	100.0	100.0	100.0

SOURCE: Ipums 5% sample of Brazilian censuses 1960–2010.

TABLE 7.5
Relative Importance of Occupations in the State of São Paulo, 1960–2010

Industry	1960	1970	1980	1991	2000	2010
	YEAR					
Legislators, Senior Officials, and Managers	4.5	6.7	6.8	8.4	5.3	4.1
Professionals	4.9	5.2	7.1	8.4	7.2	10.0
Technicians and Associate Professionals	1.7	3.4	4.6	4.3	8.7	6.7
Clerks	6.4	7.4	12.0	10.8	10.4	7.8
Service Workers and Shop and Market Sales	6.6	9.6	6.8	9.0	24.6	17.0
Skilled Agricultural and Fishery Workers	32.2	21.2	11.7	9.9	7.4	3.1
Crafts and Related Trades Workers	21.4	21.5	22.2	20.8	17.1	12.6
Plant and Machine Operators and Assemblers	5.3	7.1	10.3	8.6	11.2	10.0
Unskilled Occupations	10.5	11.7	13.5	13.3	7.5	20.4
Armed Forces	0.6	1.0	0.6	0.5	0.5	0.3
Other Occupations, Unspecified	5.9	5.2	4.4	6.0	0.0	7.9
Total	100.0	100.0	100.0	100.0	100.0	100.0

SOURCE: Ipums 5% sample of Brazilian censuses 1960–2010.

of all workers in the state in 2010, and craft workers have also declined as machine operators doubled their participation in the workforce (see Table 7.5).

Within the state it was the municipality and the metropolitan region of São Paulo that had the highest proportion of high-status professionals in the workforce in 2018. Some 37% of the municipality's workforce consisted

TABLE 7.6
Distribution of Occupations in Brazil and the State, Metropolitan Region, and Municipality of São Paulo, 2018 (1)

Occupation	Brazil	State of São Paulo	Metropolitan Region of São Paulo	Municipality of São Paulo
Directors and Administrators	4.5	6.3	8.0	9.1
Scientists and Intellectuals	11.0	13.0	15.4	17.8
Technicians and Midlevel Professionals	7.6	8.8	9.7	10.1
Administrative Support Workers	8.2	9.4	10.0	9.6
Service Workers and Sellers in Commerce and Markets	22.9	22.8	22.8	22.8
Skilled Workers in Agriculture, Forestry, and Fishing and Hunting	6.1	1.7	0.3	0.2
Skilled Workers, Construction Workers, Mechanical, and Other Craftspeople	13.3	13.8	12.6	10.8
Industrial Plant and Machine Operators and Assemblers	8.4	8.7	7.9	7.4
Unskilled Occupations	17.2	15.2	12.9	11.8
Members of the Armed Forces, Police, and Firefighting Services	0.9	0.4	0.4	0.3
Total	100.0	100.0	100.0	100.0

SOURCE: IBGE, SIDRA, table 5435.
NOTE: (1) This is the average of the year.

of midlevel and highly skilled technicians or above, compared to 28% of this group in the state and only 23% nationally, which explains the high average wage levels in the state compared to all other states in the union (see Table 7.6).

Although São Paulo initially showed a major distinction between its rural and urban populations in terms of basic social and economic indicators, with the rural area far behind the urban sector, this difference progressively declined. The growth of a machine-based modern agriculture in the rural areas of the state has led to both a decline in the number of rural workers and an increase in the income of those who remained. Thus wage differentials for rural salaries in the state went from 51% of urban salaries in 2001 to 68% in 2015.[25] Pension and public services were made widely available to all rural residents. Among the many policies that were enacted, the most revolutionary was the federal government's decision in 1991 to provide a basic retirement (of one minimum wage) to all rural workers—a revolutionary concept in Latin American social security and one that virtually eliminated abject poverty in the rural areas. In the constitution of 1988 the right to a pension was granted to all rural persons of retirement age, whether or not they had contributed to a pension plan.[26]

If differences by sex and residence have slowly declined, the general unjust distribution of income by class remains significant despite recent modest changes. This is the single most intractable problem Brazil faces. Poverty and illiteracy are declining through more intensive state social policies, but wealth distribution has changed only moderately over time.[27] The slow recent decline of inequality has been due to the increasing share of income taken by the bottom half of Brazilian households. From 1992 to 2012 their share of total wages rose from 12.5% to 16.7% of total wage income. Though this percentage is low by world standards, it has had a major impact on distribution of income. The share of the top 10% dropped in this period from 47.7% to 41.5%, that of the top 5% dropped from 34% to 29.5% and even the top 1% saw their share decline in this period by 1.5%. This has led to a progressive decline in the Gini index from .60 in 1992 to .52 in 2012, due to rising employment, better wages and government income transfers.[28]

The massive shift of population from rural to urban areas, the creation of a major industrial and service sector, and the significant increase in years of schooling have led to Brazil experiencing high levels of social mobility since the middle of the twentieth century. The economically active population went from 17 million in 1950 to 30 million in 1970 and to 44 million in 1980.[29] Non-manual laborers went from 2.5 million persons in 1960 to 8.2 million twenty years later, while the number of workers in the service sector went from 4.5 million to 8.1 million in the period from 1979 to 1989. These were the decades of the massive expansion of national industry and the corresponding growth of the urban population. All of these rapid changes can be seen in the decline of workers in the primary sector (agriculture and mining), which went from 61% of the labor force in 1950 to 31% by 1980, while the secondary sector (industry) increased its share from 17% to 29% and the tertiary (service) sector went from 22% to 40% in the same period.[30] Services were the most rapidly growing sector, although not all of these service occupations were skilled ones. It is estimated, for example, that domestic servants went from 680,000 to 1.8 million between 1950 and 1970, and another significant segment of workers were in the informal economy.[31] Nevertheless, overall there seems to have been a significant expansion of high-skilled jobs both in the secondary and tertiary sectors throughout the last half of the twentieth century and into the first decades of the twenty-first. Thus just in the period from 2002 to 2014 there was an expansion of 19.6 million urban jobs, compared to a loss of 1.6 million rural ones in the same period. Of these urban jobs, some 4.5 million were in occupations defined as upper-class or upper-middle-class.[32]

Because all these new occupational opportunities opened quickly, Brazil experienced what has been defined as structural mobility, which means that there was more upward than downward mobility in the boom years of rapid industrial growth. Instead of the more traditional circular pattern of an advanced industrial society where there is as much upward as downward mobility, in this case more persons exceeded the socioeconomic position of their parents than fell below that position.[33] It has been estimated by one study that by the 1970s Brazilian social mobility was predominantly structural (57% of the change between fathers' and sons' occupations was structural and 47% was circular).[34] More recent studies using more refined occupational groupings found that structural mobility went from 61% in 1973 to 67% in 1988 and was still at 66% in 1996, these three years being ones when the PNAD survey provided questions on parents' and children's occupations. Immobility—that is, the failure to move beyond one's parents' occupation—declined from 39% to 33% in this period.[35] A more complete analysis by sex, which was added in the PNAD survey of 2008, showed that upward mobility for men went from 55.3% in 1973 to 67.3% in 2008, and for women it went from 57.5% to 75.4% in 2008.[36]

But for all the mobility, most authors agree that much of this structural mobility came primarily at the bottom portion of the occupational structure—that is, the bulk of the change was manual rural workers moving to manual urban work—whereas most of the mobility in elite occupations still tended to be circular. Thus in the years between 1973 and 1996 some 24% to 25% of rural workers ended up in urban unskilled manual labor, and another 17% to 19% ended up in urban skilled manual labor. This is also reflected in the surveys of mobility to 2008, which show for rural men a steady decline in sons following their fathers into agricultural labor, going from 36.7% in 1973 to 13.7% in 2008.[37] The increasing stability of the relatively small rural population in recent years suggests that this pattern of upward mobility through urban migration will be declining in the future as the rural population slows its urban migration and education and job quality increase in the rural area.

All recent studies stress the relative immobility in the upper levels of occupational categories as the elite use the educational, tax, and pension systems to their advantage to pass on their wealth and prevent downward mobility of their children.[38] But at the same time the increasing level of education for all workers over time has meant that the excessive bonus for education that existed earlier, when the average was 3.4 years of schooling (1973), has declined as the average years of schooling rose to 8.4 (2014). This decline in the bonus for education has had an important impact in reducing inequality, as shown by the Gini index, which dropped from the low .60s to the low .50s. In every level of occupation, from the highest to the lowest, there has been an increase in the years of schooling, with rural workers and skilled and unskilled urban workers doubling their years of schooling in the period from 1973 to 2014.[39]

Given the steady expansion of education in the post-1950 period, the age of entry into the labor market keeps rising. It is estimated from the PNAD surveys that persons entering the labor market in the 1920s and 1930s averaged 14 years of age, and this age rose steadily until it reached 17 years by the 1960s as more and more persons continued to complete their primary education and even their secondary education.[40] Thus using the 17-year age of entry into the labor market, we can assess the maturing of social mobility in the PNAD survey of 2014, which is the latest to ask questions about occupational and educational differences between children and parents. This survey also broke down children's occupation by age for some 55 million persons, thus permitting researchers to see how mobility has been changing over time. The group who were 45 to 65 years of age in 2014 entered the labor market in the late 1960s to the late 1980s, while the group aged 25 to 44 years entered the labor market between the late 1980s and 2006.

What is evident from this 2014 survey is that the older group had more upward mobility into the highest occupational levels, that is, Stratum A (defined as administrators, executives, and liberal professionals) and Stratum B (skilled technical workers), than did the younger age group, even though the total number of positions was smaller in the earlier period. There was also a big change in origin, with 50% of those interviewed among the older group having fathers who were farm workers (Stratum F), while among the younger workers only 36% had fathers who came from this rural background. This clearly shows that in the more recent period the slowing of outmigration from the rural areas and the increasing number of workers born in urban areas means that ever fewer workers are coming from a rural background. It also shows that for the elite positions immobility is increasing in the more recent period as fewer recruits are entering from the lowest two occupational strata and a higher ratio are remaining in their fathers' high-status position. Looking at the absolute differences between the younger and older cohorts, it is evident that the older cohort, who entered the labor force in the 1960s and 1970s, had much higher rates of mobility. They were far more likely to reach the upper strata, they were in most cases more likely to be in a different stratum than their fathers, and a much higher ratio of them moved up from the lowest strata of rural and non-manual urban occupations. Overall, half of the persons were upwardly mobile, but among the older contingent, only 15% were downwardly mobile, compared to 18% among the younger workers. All of this would seem to suggest that the structural mobility is slowly being replaced by the traditional circular form of mobility.[41] Thus, relative stability of stratification and increased social mobility are the dual patterns that emerge from this study of Brazilian society in the post-1950 period. The elite still retain a very large share of national wealth, but there has been massive socioeconomic change at the middle and lowest economic levels, leading to the emergence of a large middle class and a stable working class, a pattern that can be found in other rapidly growing Latin American countries.[42]

Like gender, class, and residence, color has been one of the major factors defining the Brazilian population, and it has been so since the introduction of African slavery in the sixteenth century. For all the mobility of African and Afro-Brazilians that occurred before and after the abolition of slavery in 1888, color still remains an important, if not always precise, marker of class and status in Brazil. To confuse things even more, Brazil went from being a primarily non-white society in 1872 to a primarily white society in 1900 after the massive immigration of some 5 million European and Asian immigrants. It remained a predominantly white nation until 2010, when it once more became a primarily non-white society, and it will continue to be primarily a non-white society for the foreseeable future. The census of 1940 was the peak year for whites and the nadir for Browns (called *pardos* in Brazil). Since that time there has been a steady rise of Browns and a relative decline of whites, with no significant differences in fertility accounting for these changes. Of course, increasing racial intermarriage would have an impact on the growth of the Brown population. But it also appears that changing attitudes toward color and the generalized acceptance of Brown as the normal color for Brazilians, combined with both a rising Afro-Brazilian consciousness and the recent movement for affirmative action for non-whites, have led to this profound change of color self-identity. The only group recently affected by migration are Asians, who rose to 1.1% of the population in 2010 due to the arrival of Korean, Chinese, and other Asian immigrants along with the original Japanese migrants.[43]

Does color matter as much as class in defining a person's place in Brazilian society? This is one of the most debated questions in contemporary Brazilian social sciences. To begin with, it is clear that the three-color distinction of Blacks (*preta*), Browns (*parda*), and whites (*branca*), which is the norm in Brazilian society, allows for a more integrated system than a simple Black/White division. Under this three-color scheme, defining a person's color is far more ambiguous than in a dual-color one. While discrimination against Blacks is more clear-cut, discrimination against Browns—the largest color class in Brazil today—is far less precise. This is because defining who is Brown does not involve simply skin color or so-called African features, but may also include a host of class and educational characteristics. In fact there is even confusion among Brazilians as to their actual color definition.[44]

There is much debate in the literature as to whether racial discrimination ever existed, or existed only in the slavery period and will disappear in the modern industrial society, or is a reflection of the accumulated inheritance of poverty and earlier racist positions that affects subsequent generations, or is still functioning within Brazilian society today as a form of guaranteeing white elite positions.[45] It is worth noting that ex-slaves entered the free market economy with few financial resources and a limited number of skills and thus tended to form the poorest element of the post-emancipation society. The usual discrimination against the poor in general, who were mostly unskilled, illiterate rural workers with limited access to government services, also meant that Blacks and Browns started from a lower economic level than most whites during the early part of the twentieth century. This meant that mobility was slower and took more generations than it did for literate white foreign-born workers, for example.

In analyzing this question for the population of the state of São Paulo we will examine intermarriage, family organization, education, and income by color, in order to determine the levels and intensity of this discrimination over time. The earlier quantitative materials available on race show much higher rates of disadvantage in income, education, and health of non-whites due to their greater isolation in rural areas and their concentration in the poorest states of the federation. Given the control over health and education by state governments, this in turn meant that the richer and whiter Southeastern and Southern states provided their citizens with greater benefits than were available in the poorer Northeastern states where the non-white population was concentrated. In 1950, for example, the largest Northeastern state, Bahia, had a non-white population of 70% compared to São Paulo, the largest state in the Southeastern region, which had only 11% of its residents listed as non-white. As late as 1991, even despite the mass migration from the Northeast to the Southern regions, the North and Northeast were still 77% and 73% non-white, compared to the South and Southeastern regions, which were 37% and 17% non-white, respectively.[46] By 2001 the non-white population in the state was still only 28%, but it had increased to 35% in the metropolitan area of São Paulo, and by 2015 the combined Black and Brown population had grown to 37% of the total population of the state and 40% of the metropolitan region of São Paulo.[47]

With the massive migrations out of the North and Northeast toward the Southern regions and the creation of an ever more universal system of education and health, things began to slowly change. Blacks and Browns had been less literate and had fewer years of education, lower income, and poorer health than whites or Asians at midcentury, but this gap between whites and non-whites has slowly begun to decline in the following decades. This decline can best be seen in terms of health and fertility. Although vital statistics by race were not systematically collected by the national government until the late 1990s,[48] there are some regional-level data and national estimates that do provide some approximate idea of basic differences. In general the heavily non-white region of the Northeast was systematically worse off in all health indices, from infant mortality to life expectancy and from diseases to health outcomes, than were the population of the mostly white Southern region.[49] But of course this introduces an ecological bias, since it is difficult to separate out poverty from color in these data. Some data from the state of São Paulo show that the combined category of Blacks and Browns had a 40% higher rate of infant mortality than whites even as late as 1993.[50] A national estimate shows that while whites and non-whites have all experienced rising average life expectancy since the 1950s, there have been only modest changes in the difference between white and non-white rates since then. Although the difference has fluctuated by census year, it was still a minimum of six years' difference between 1950 and 2000.[51]

Many of the above are estimates, but once systematically collected data became available for the current century we still see mortality differences by color. One early study was based on some 169,000 deaths of whites and Blacks (with Browns excluded) in the state of São Paulo in 1999. Among women, Blacks suffered over six times the rate of maternal mortality than did white women. As expected, men suffered much higher rates of violent deaths than women, but in terms of color, Black men had twice the rate of such deaths than white men, though the difference among women was far less dramatic. For all other causes of death, there was no trend, in that sometimes whites had much higher rates than Blacks for both men and women, as in the case of cancer, for example, but the reverse occurred for cardiovascular and infectious diseases. With other diseases there was basically no difference in color terms, with sex being the more important determinant of mortality differences (see Table 7.7).

This same pattern emerged in a more complete study of deaths in the state of São Paulo from 1999 to 2001. Blacks and Browns (the latter group

TABLE 7.7

Rates of Mortality by Cause for Whites and Blacks in the State of São Paulo, 1999 (per 1,000 Population)

	WOMEN		MEN	
Cause of Death	Whites	Blacks	Whites	Blacks
Infectious and Parasitic Diseases	19.3	31.0	36.3	67.3
Cancer	81.7	74.8	108.6	87.0
Lymphoma and Leukemia	2.1	1.4	2.3	2.2
Diabetes, Thyroid Diseases	29.8	39.7	25.9	30.8
Mental and Behavioral Disorders	1.9	3.3	6.4	19.6
Neurological Diseases	7.4	5.4	9.8	11.4
Cardiovascular Diseases	174.5	199.6	212.9	244.5
Pulmonary Diseases	56.3	43.8	77.4	72.5
Gastrointestinal Diseases	20.9	21.9	46.4	44.4
Genito-Urinary Diseases	8.8	9.8	10.7	11.0
Maternal Mortality	37.9	245.5		
Congenital Malformations	5.5	2.3	7.0	3.5
External Causes (Accidents and Violence)	23.3	30.4	136.2	274.4
Total Number	64,512	4,085	93,000	6,921

SOURCE: Seade(2005) (2005), 988.
NOTE: *Pardos* are not included.

now included) suffered much higher rates of infectious diseases, maternal mortality, diabetes, and violent deaths, but it was whites who were more likely than either of the other two to die of cancer, lung diseases, and most other major forms of death.[52] On the other hand, a study of strokes and other cardiovascular disease deaths in Brazil in 2010 found that such mortality rates adjusted for age showed major differences by color that differed from the São Paulo study. Among men, whites had a median 44.4 deaths per 1,000 population for heart disease, while for Browns it was 48.2 deaths and for Blacks 63.3 deaths per 1,000 population; with women, the rates for whites were 29 deaths per 1,000 population, 33.7 for Brown women, and highest for Black women at 51. As the study concluded, "The burden of stroke mortality is higher among blacks compared to brown and white."[53]

But it should be noted that region plays a major role in influencing racial differences in mortality. Thus a recent detailed study of some 34,000 infant deaths shows that, except for Asians, there is virtually no difference by race for the rate of infant mortality in the three states of the Southern region, in contrast to the sharp Black/white differences in the Northeast and even in the Southeast and Center-West (see Table 7.8). Finally in this same study, post-neonatal deaths were highest among whites and Blacks in the North

TABLE 7.8
Infant Mortality by Region, 2009/2010 (1)

Region	White	Black	Asian	Brown	Total
North	29.9	52.5	28.0	18.8	21.5
Northeast	26.5	50.1	8.8	17.8	19.7
Southeast	13.3	24.1	8.1	13.6	13.6
South	11.5	11.4	6.8	11.9	11.6
Center-West	16.7	43.2	6.3	14.4	16.2
BRAZIL	15.2	29.1	9.7	16.6	16.3

SOURCE: Caldas et al. (2017), 6, table 3.
NOTE: (1) August to July. The infant mortality rate is the number of infant deaths (up to age 1 year) divided by the total of live births in that year.

and Northeast compared to all other groups, but the same for all groups in the other regions.

Almost all studies thus find some health differences by race, but much influenced by residence and sex. All such studies also indicate that the differences between the groups are slowly declining as all states converge toward a common national pattern. Much of this decline has occurred since the late 1990s and especially in the twenty-first century with the expansion of SUS, the national health system. As the latest National Health Survey (2013) shows, there is relatively little difference between whites and non-whites in basic access to health care, medical examinations, and utility of health services.[54]

If things have improved in terms of the narrowing of health disparities by race, racial differences in income have changed only modestly over time. Average monthly income nationally has increased for both whites and non-whites, but the gap between the two groups has narrowed very slowly, with combined Black and Brown wages going from 51% of white wages to 60% of such wages in 2011.[55] Although wages are higher in São Paulo than in the rest of the country, even here the wages of Blacks and Browns are consistently below white wages. What is surprising is the almost constant lower level of average Brown salaries compared to Black wages.

Even more differences emerge in median monthly income when we consider sex and color. Women in general in the state of São Paulo earned 36% less than the median white male wage. For white women the difference was only 20%, but for Black and Brown women it was double, or 40% less than the average white male salary in the state. When compared within each sex, very significant differences emerged in most regions between whites and non-whites. An unusual finding of this census survey is that Asian men and women, though doing less well than their

TABLE 7.9

Ratio of Black and Brown Median Income to White Median Income, by Sex for Persons 10 Years and Older with Income, for Brazil and the State, Metropolitan Region, and Municipality of São Paulo, 2010

	MEN				WOMEN			
Region	White	Black	Brown	Asian	White	Black	Brown	Asian
Brazil	100	60	60	90	100	76	76	84
State of São Paulo	100	77	73	136	100	75	75	128
Municipality of São Paulo	100	60	57	133	100	70	65	150
Metropolitan Region of São Paulo	100	75	69	167	100	70	60	149

SOURCE: IBGE, SIDRA, table 1381.

white counterparts at the national level, outperform whites of both sexes at the levels of the state, metropolitan region, and capital in São Paulo (see Table 7.9).

Brazil's population of color was also far more likely to be in the lower half of the income deciles than non-whites. Some 51% of whites were to be found in the top 30% of income earners, whereas only 27% of Black and Brown income earners were found in this elite position. This strong inequality was evident in the occupational distribution as well as in wages.[56] In the PNAD survey of 2015 some 6% of the whites were in domestic service both nationally and in São Paulo, compared to between 10% and 12% of Blacks and Browns in this occupation. Blacks and Browns made up the same share of whites as employees in the state of São Paulo, but were far less likely to be employers in São Paulo than in Brazil in general (see Table 7.10).

Even when the population of color had the same occupations as whites, their average income was consistently lower than the whites'. Thus in 2003 Black and Brown workers in the formal sector earned a third less on average than white workers, and those in the informal sector earned just under half of a white informal worker's salary. By 2004 when 54% of the whites were in the formal sector (with working papers and receiving at least a minimum monthly wage), only 37% of the Black and Brown workers were in that sector. By 2017, 66% for whites and 53% of Blacks and Browns combined were now in the formal sector.[57]

Examining these groups' roles within each major sector of the economy, it is evident that Browns were overrepresented in agriculture and in domestic service. Both Blacks and Browns were underrepresented in public administration, education, and health, areas where whites were overrepresented. What is impressive is that Browns together with Blacks made up

TABLE 7.10
Structure of the Labor Market by Color for Brazil and the State of São Paulo, 2015

	Employee	Domestic Worker	Self-Employed	Employer	Miscellaneous	Total
BRAZIL						
SHARE OF POSITION BY COLOR						
White	67.3	5.7	20.3	5.5	1.2	100
Black	64.8	11.5	20.8	1.9	1.0	100
Brown	63.7	9.2	23.0	2.6	1.5	100
Total	65.5	7.7	21.5	3.9	1.3	100
SHARE BY COLOR WITHIN EACH POSITION						
White	49.4	35.3	45.5	67.6	42.9	48.1
Black	9.8	14.8	9.6	4.7	7.9	10.0
Brown	40.7	49.8	44.8	27.8	49.2	41.9
Total	100.0	100.0	100.0	100.0	100.0	100.0
STATE OF SÃO PAULO						
	Employee	Domestic Worker	Self-Employed	Employer	Miscellaneous	Total
SHARE OF POSITION BY COLOR						
White	69.7	5.5	18.7	5.2	0.8	100
Black	69.7	10.8	16.7	1.8	1.0	100
Brown	69.5	9.6	18.5	1.8	0.6	100
Total	69.6	7.2	18.5	3.9	0.8	100
SHARE BY COLOR WITHIN EACH POSITION						
White	61.9	47.8	62.6	82.3	66.6	66.6
Black	7.8	11.7	7.1	3.6	10.0	10.0
Brown	30.3	40.5	30.4	14.1	23.4	23.4
Total	100.0	100.0	100.0	100.0	100.0	100.0

SOURCE: Elaborated from microdata from PNAD 2015.

two-thirds of agricultural and domestic workers and half or more in all other fields except Education, health, and industries. In São Paulo they were over half of the construction and domestic workers, even though they were only 39% of all workers, and were above their total workforce participation in agriculture and transport and well below their total participation level in industry, commerce, public administration, and education. Except for transport and communications, their weights in each of these areas were the same in the state as in the nation (see Table 7.11).

Clearly, then, well over a century after emancipation, the African-descended population of Brazil remains overwhelmingly poor and

TABLE 7.11

Distribution of Workers in the Major Sectors of the Economy for Brazil and the State of São Paulo by Color, 2015

	Agriculture	Transformative Industries*	Construction	Commerce	Food and Lodging	Transport and Communications	Public Administration	Education, Health, and Social Services	Domestic Services	Miscellaneous	Total
BRAZIL											
SHARE OF SECTOR BY COLOR											
White	10.4	14.6	7.1	19.0	4.7	5.7	5.5	12.6	5.2	15.4	100.0
Black	12.6	11.1	12.2	16.5	5.5	5.3	4.7	9.2	10.1	12.9	100.0
Brown	17.7	11.6	10.6	18.1	5.2	5.3	4.5	8.7	7.7	10.5	100.0
Total	13.9	12.9	9.1	18.3	5.0	5.5	5.0	10.5	6.8	13.0	100.0
SHARE OF COLOR WITHIN SECTOR											
White	34.3	51.5	35.2	47.2	42.7	47.2	50.3	54.6	34.6	54.1	45.6
Black	9.0	8.5	13.3	8.9	10.9	9.6	9.3	8.8	14.8	9.9	10.0
Brown	56.7	39.9	51.5	43.9	46.3	43.2	40.4	36.6	50.6	36.0	44.4
Total	100.0	100.0	100.0	100.0	100.0	100.0	100.0	100.0	100.0	100.0	100.0
STATE OF SÃO PAULO											
SHARE OF SECTOR BY COLOR											
White	2.8	17.4	6.6	18.9	5.2	6.6	4.3	13.4	5.3	19.5	100.0
Black	3.2	15.8	11.6	16.7	5.7	6.4	4.2	9.4	9.7	17.4	100.0
Brown	3.8	17.9	11.2	18.0	6.6	7.1	2.9	7.9	9.0	15.7	100.0
Total	3.2	17.4	8.4	18.4	5.7	6.7	3.9	11.3	6.8	18.1	100.0
SHARE OF COLOR WITHIN SECTOR											
White	54.5	60.7	47.9	62.4	55.6	59.7	67.7	71.8	47.7	65.4	60.9
Black	8.1	7.2	10.9	7.2	8.0	7.6	8.8	6.6	11.3	7.6	8.0
Brown	37.4	32.0	41.2	30.4	36.4	32.7	23.5	21.6	41.0	26.9	31.2
Total	100.0	100.0	100.0	100.0	100.0	100.0	100.0	100.0	100.0	100.0	100.0

SOURCE: Elaborated from microdata from PNAD 2015.

NOTE: * This includes the two categories of "industries of transformation" and "other industrial activities" (the latter is usually 1% or less).

underrepresented in the higher-level occupations and among the wealthiest classes. Nevertheless, there has been a major movement out of indigence and poverty in the last quarter century, which has benefited the non-white population in terms of access to new occupations and better income. But whereas all groups have benefited, the gap between non-whites and whites has changed only modestly over this period.

In contrast, health and education have improved for non-whites nationally. The differences in health between whites and non-whites have narrowed considerably and the gap in average years of education has been slowly narrowing. So rapid has been this decline in educational differences that it can be expected that whites and non-whites will soon achieve parity in educational achievement. This can be seen in the school enrollment figures for 2003, which show little difference by color of almost all age groups. Only in the older groups was there a meaningful difference, and here the spread was not that extreme. Thus for 15-to-17-year-olds (high school students) and 20-to-24-year-olds (those enrolled in post-secondary schools) there was a 7% spread between Black/Brown and white enrollments.[58] While years of schooling are now becoming normalized for all groups, the increasing divide between public and private primary and secondary education in terms of quality has become a major blockage as the rich have dominated private primary and secondary education and the poor have been left with a public primary and secondary education of poor quality. In regard to tertiary education, the rich dominate the far more advanced public universities and the poor are relegated to mostly unqualified private faculties. Thus education, which was the prime motor for mobility until the 1980s and 1990s, has now created new blockages just as all whites and non-whites are achieving similar numbers of years of schooling.

Almost all the studies of income and race, however, still show significant differences up to today, some of which may be due to this new blockage in education. A much-cited IPEA study shows that the discrimination still exists, but suggests that it is far worse in terms of gender differences than in terms of race: average white salaries are around 11% to 12% more than Black salaries, but male salaries in general were two-thirds to more than half as much as female wages, though the difference is declining fast (see Figure 7.7).[59]

These results for Blacks and Browns as well as men and women raise the question of what explains this continuing difference. Is it due to active discrimination by employers, leading to a segmentation of the market with women and non-whites concentrated in low-paying jobs? Is the segmentation only by type of industry, or is it spatial, by region or state? Or is it

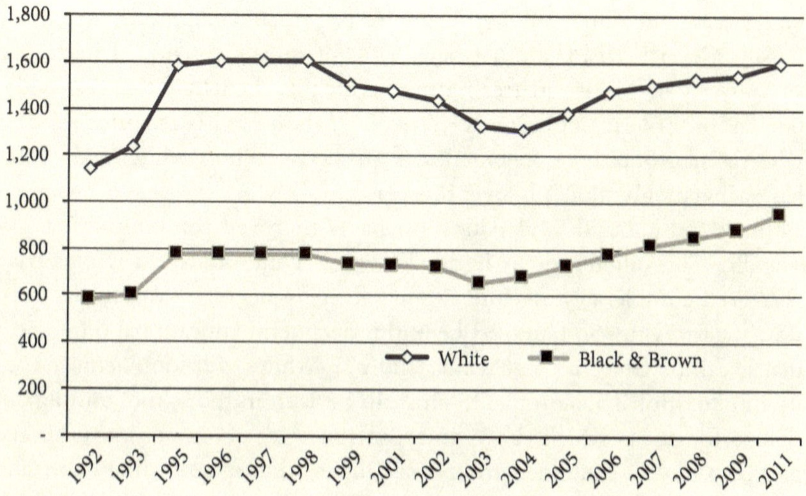

Figure 7.7. Average Monthly Income of Persons 10 Years of Age and Older by Race, 1992–2011

SOURCE: IBGE, SIDRA, table 1173.

due to the relative weight of formal and informal markets, or to different individual characteristics for women and Blacks compared to white males? As Ricardo Paes de Barros and his coauthors noted:

> The market generates inequality both when it remunerates differently men and women or whites and blacks of the same productivity, as when there are differences of remuneration between perfect substitute workers in production occupying positions in different segments of the labor market. In the first case, we say that the differentials result from discrimination in the labor market and, second, from its segmentation.[60]

This is the fundamental question in the literature and has been answered in several different ways. Several studies show that although the percentage of women who are employed is less than that for men, for those who are economically active there is little difference in employment and unemployment rates. But in general, a women's work week is five hours less than that of men, which can explain some of the wage differences. However, several authors have stressed that there is segmentation in the market, with a very high ratio of women working in female-dominated industries (such as teaching or domestic service), in which males are less concentrated, which explains their wage differences. But even controlling for education and segmentation of the market, women still receive lower salaries than men. Recently it has been argued that the big difference is intra-occupational status, with men consistently having higher status and thus more income than women within a given occupation, is possibly due to their earlier positioning in the labor market compared to later-arriving women.[61] All studies do show that the higher the educational level of the workers, the less wage discrimination occurs. All of this suggests the future continuation of the decline of discrimination by sex as women increase their levels of education over men.[62]

But if this wage discrimination is declining for white women, what is the situation for non-whites versus whites? Even when Blacks achieved higher occupational status, their income is less than whites; in fact, for directors and administrators of enterprises in São Paulo in 2002, the median income of Blacks was half that of whites. Moving down the occupational hierarchy, however, monthly wage workers with registered work permits showed only a modest difference in salary between whites and Blacks and Browns of both sexes and between white men and white women. At the bottom of the income scale there is equality by color and sex (see Figure 7.8). Using average salaries, Black men actually do better than white women among managers and directors in the state of São Paulo as well as in the state of Bahia. Finally, the higher the educational level, the lower the wage differences between all four categories, though white males still do the best. But

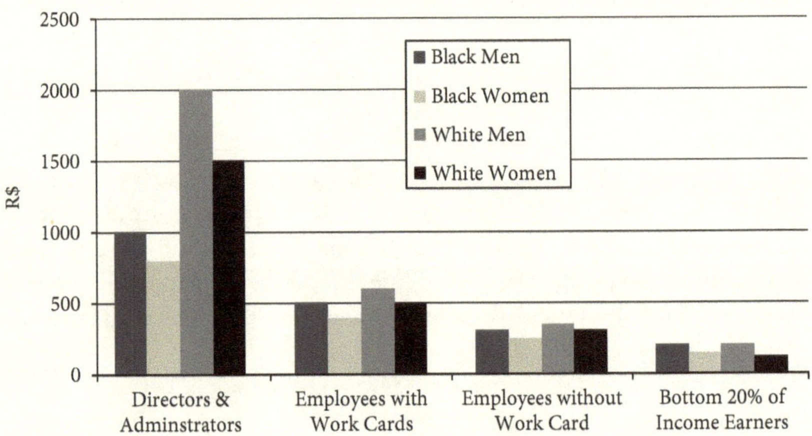

Figure 7.8. Median Income by Color, Sex, and Status of Work, State of São Paulo, 2002

SOURCE: Cacciamali and Hirata (2005), 775, table.

in conclusion the authors of this comparative 2002 study still find that "discrimination [racial and sexual] is to a greater or lesser extent present in the Brazilian labor market," no matter what the structure of the market or the racial composition of the workforce.[63]

Because of education's crucial role in mobility and in income, the role of discrimination in education has become a major area of recent research. As numerous studies have emphasized, wages and mobility are intimately linked to levels of education. So the question is how well or poorly Blacks and Browns do compared with whites in entering centers of advanced studies. The differences between sexes in terms of education have changed more rapidly than differences between whites and non-whites. Whereas women reached equality of school attendance by the 1980s, it is only now, at the end of the second decade of the twenty-first century, that non-whites and whites are approaching equality in school matriculations. This in turn has led to a slow but steady decline in the spread between white and non-white literacy rates. But given the late development of equal educational participation at the primary level, it will take more time before literacy rates will be the same in white and non-white populations. In 2004 the literacy rate for the São Paulo population 15 years of age and older was 95% for whites and 92% for non-whites, both of those rates being higher than the national ones (93% and 84%, respectively). The gap has been slowly closing because literacy has increased faster for Blacks/Browns than for whites: the difference between the two groups declined from 3.4% in 2004 to just 2.2% in 2015 (see Figure 7.9).

These changes can also be seen in the number of those who are functionally illiterate—persons who have had some schooling but still cannot properly read and write. In the PNAD survey of 2004, for example, some 67% of non-white adults were functionally illiterate, while only half of whites were considered this disadvantaged. By 2015 some 49% of Black and Brown adults (those 25 years of age and older) were functionally illiterate compared to 35% of the whites. Though non-whites are still disadvantaged, the slowly declining gap between whites and non-whites should continue over time since Blacks and Browns are increasing their literacy rates more rapidly than whites.[64]

In the same period the gap in average years of schooling between Blacks/Browns and whites has declined from 2.1 years (below the white average of 7.0 years of schooling) in 2001 to just 1.8 years (below the average 8.8 years of schooling for whites) in 2015.[65] This gap between whites and non-whites is the norm for all regions of Brazil. But as with all other educational indicators, the spread in years of schooling between whites and non-whites

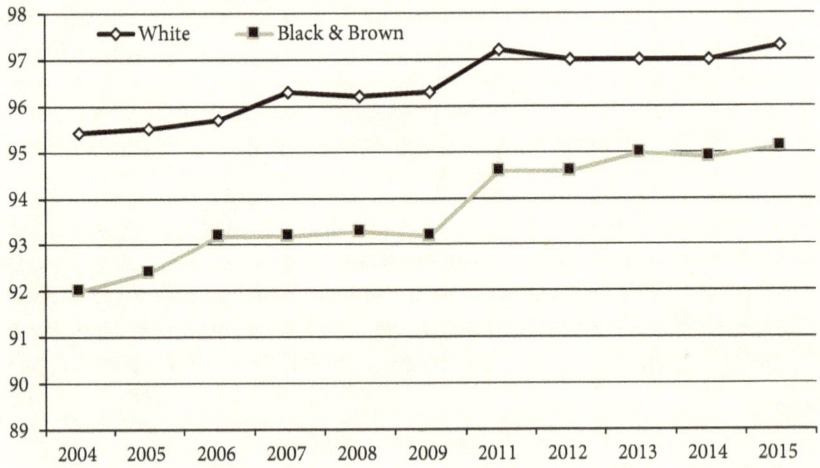

Figure 7.9. Literacy Among Adults 15 Years and Older by Race in State of São Paulo, 2004–2015 (Percentage)

SOURCE: IBGE, SIDRA, table 1188.

has declined considerably recently as far more persons obtain an advanced secondary education. High school graduates among whites increased by 0.4% per annum between 2009 and 2015 and accounted for 29.4% of all adult whites in this period, but Blacks and Browns increased their numbers by 2.9% per annum in the same period, which meant that 27.4% of them were high school graduates in 2015. Thus the gap was reduced by half, with Blacks and Browns now at 93% of the white graduation rate. Moreover, the Southeastern region moved from having one of the larger gaps between whites and non-whites (at 86% of the white graduation rate in 2009) to 98% of the white rate in 2005, a change not experienced in the Southern region, which remained the worst of all the regions in 2015 in terms of the difference between whites and Brown/Black rates of graduation, despite being one of the richest regions in the country.[66]

But there are still differences by sex and color. While all women have done better than all men in educational attainment, non-white women are still well behind the levels achieved by white women and are even below those achieved by white men. This can be seen in the evolution of years of schooling. By the late 1980s in the PNAD surveys, women were consistently better-educated than men of their color, and this has continued until today. Although all groups of men and women increased their educational levels by 2015, it is Blacks who have increased the fastest, going from

2.5 years' difference between Black men compared to white men and a full 3.0 years' difference between Black women and White women in 1989 to just 0.9 and 0.8 years' difference, respectively, in 2015. In contrast, Browns have only moderately changed their position from the earlier period.[67] But the overall differences between whites and non-whites in educational attainment have continued to decline systematically. By 2019, data on years of schooling for persons 18–29 years of age showed that Blacks and Browns had reduced their difference from whites, with the gap now at 1.2 years (12.3 years for whites and 11.1 years for *pardos* and *pretos*). At the same time there was an increasing difference between men and women, with women reaching 11.9 years of schooling for this age group and men just 11.2 years.[68]

As all studies show, there has been a significant increase in the educational level of the population between 1960 and 2010. This is true nationally as well as in the state of São Paulo. Both sexes and all races have greatly increased their educational level, especially after the universalization of primary education in Brazil by the 1990s. But it is evident that women have done better than men in schooling and that Blacks and Browns are still below white educational attainment at all levels. The major change for whites and non-whites for both sexes is that the gap has narrowed considerably among men and women since 1960. For those completing secondary school or higher, the Brown/white gap among men dropped from 7% to nearly half of that rate by 2010. In the case of women, the direction of the gap was actually reversed: 37% of the Brown women and 37% of Black women completed a high school education or better in 2010 compared to only 35% of white women (see Table 7.12).

Most of the other educational indicators analyzed, such as age of enrolled students by grades and retention rates, also show that the racial gap has been closing. Thus for enrolled students 15–17 years of age who were older than their respective class's age group—a clear sign of dysfunctional education—there was initially a much higher gap between whites and Blacks/Browns. As late as 2004 fully half of the Brown and Black students were overage, compared to just over a quarter of the whites. By 2015 the rate was down to 19% for whites and to 31% for non-white students.[69]

Two distinct patterns emerge when we compare completion rates by level of schooling for color and sex in 2015. Women consistently do better than men for all race groups. At the same time, Blacks and Browns still are the least educated. Whites who had no education or an incomplete primary one accounted for 35% of all white persons over 25 years of age; for Blacks the figure was 47%, and for Browns it was 50%. In contrast,

TABLE 7.12

Years of Schooling for Persons 25 Years of Age and Older by Sex and Race for the State of São Paulo, 1960 and 2010

	1960			2010		
Males	White	Black	Brown	White	Black	Brown
No Schooling	22.6	41.8	42.0	0.9	2.4	2.2
Some Primary Completed	30.1	34.3	36.6	20.3	32.9	31.7
Primary (4 Years) Completed	32.6	22.1	19.0	11.7	13.2	13.3
Primary (6 Years) Completed	7.3	1.3	1.7	16.7	20.3	20.6
Lower Secondary General Completed	1.0	0.1	0.2	4.5	5.1	5.5
Secondary, General Track Completed	3.7	0.3	0.4	18.2	16.7	16.7
Some College Completed	0.7	0.0	0.1	6.2	3.4	3.3
University Completed	2.2	0.1	0.1	21.4	6.0	6.7
Total	100.0	100.0	100.0	100.0	100.0	100.0
Females	White	Black	Brown	White	Black	Brown
No Schooling	32.4	53.7	54.2	0.9	2.5	2.3
Some Primary Completed	24.6	25.8	26.7	21.9	33.1	32.6
Primary (4 Years) Completed	31.0	19.3	17.2	15.2	12.5	13.9
Primary (6 Years) Completed	6.9	0.8	1.3	13.8	15.5	16.0
Lower Secondary General Completed	0.8	0.1	0.1	3.5	4.4	4.3
Secondary, General Track Completed	3.6	0.2	0.3	17.2	16.9	17.0
Some College Completed	0.2	0.0	0.0	4.3	4.2	3.4
University Completed	0.4	0.0	0.0	23.2	10.9	10.5
Total	100.0	100.0	100.0	100.0	100.0	100.0

SOURCE: Public use sample censuses 1960, 2010, Ipums.

the impact of increasing educational opportunities is seen in middle school graduates, whose numbers are basically equal regardless of sex and color. But this equalization has yet to appear among university graduates. Among these tertiary-level graduates, not only do women outpace men, but there is still a very significant difference between white males and females and non-white males and females, as can be seen in the PNAD survey of 2015. As in all other census and PNAD surveys, it is clear that São Paulo was more advanced than the rest of the nation for both sexes and all colors (see Table 7.13).

What of marriage and cohabitation and race? Do these reflect discrimination based on skin color? How endogamous are cohabiting partners in terms of color? To begin with, it is important to recognize that there has been a significant change in cohabitation patterns among all classes and racial groups. This of course is the decline in formal marriage and the growth in consensual unions. Although consensual unions were traditionally a lower-class institutional arrangement, and were thus most prevalent among

TABLE 7.13

Level of Education for Persons 25 Years of Age and Older, Brazil and the State of São Paulo, 2015 (Percentage of Total)

Level	MALES White	MALES Black	MALES Brown	FEMALES White	FEMALES Black	FEMALES Brown
BRAZIL						
No Education	7.2	14.6	15.1	7.6	14.3	13.7
Primary Incomplete	28.7	34.3	36.5	27.2	31.2	33.8
Primary Complete	10.1	10.3	10.1	9.0	9.8	9.4
High School Incomplete	3.6	5.3	4.8	3.2	4.7	4.6
High School Complete	27.3	26.7	24.3	27.6	27.9	25.9
Tertiary Incomplete	5.0	3.0	2.8	4.3	3.6	3.3
Tertiary Complete	18.1	5.8	6.4	21.2	8.5	9.2
Total	100.0	100.0	100.0	100.0	100.0	100.0
STATE OF SÃO PAULO						
No Education	4.4	8.2	7.6	5.4	9.6	10.0
Primary Incomplete	23.0	28.1	32.9	24.2	28.8	30.7
Primary Complete	9.9	11.4	12.4	9.4	12.9	11.8
High School Incomplete	3.5	5.2	5.3	2.8	4.1	4.8
High School Complete	30.9	34.7	31.0	29.9	31.5	30.9
Tertiary Incomplete	5.5	3.5	3.5	4.0	3.4	2.7
Tertiary Complete	22.8	8.9	7.3	24.2	9.6	9.0
Total	100.0	100.0	100.0	100.0	100.0	100.0

SOURCE: Microdata from PNAD 2015.

Blacks and Browns, the changes in legal status of women living in consensual unions and the guarantee of the rights of their children (discussed in Chapter 6) has led to an increase in consensual unions among all groups, including whites.

As can be seen in an analysis of married persons by sex and color in the state of São Paulo, the proportion of women living with men in consensual unions has been growing steadily beginning in the mid-twentieth century and has increased in a secular pattern for all groups. There is a basic difference by color, but little difference within color groups by sex. White women in consensual unions have gone from 2% in 1960 to 25% of all white women living with men in 2010, a figure identical to white men. Among Black men and women the ratio of consensual unions has gone from 8% to 40% for both sexes between 1960 and 1980. Only among Browns have there been significant differences by sex, at least initially. Brown males in consensual unions went from 6% of all men living with women in 1960 to 38% in 2010, whereas Brown women began from 9%

in 1960 and reached 38% (the same as the male rate) in 2010. This change has gone farthest and fastest for Brown and Black persons, but consensual unions are now becoming a very significant form of cohabitation for all groups (see Table 7.14).

Equally, there has been a decline in endogamous relations based on color. That is, whites marrying whites went from over 90% for husbands and wives in 1960 to around 80% for both in 1991.[70] Overall, for all groups of Blacks, Browns, and Whites, racial endogamy went from 88% of marriages in 1960 to 80% in 1980 and down to 69% in 2000. While this is far from total equality for all groups, the decline in endogamous relationships suggest that the pattern is coming closer to what would occur if no class or color prejudice existed. One estimate based on shares of population suggests that endogamy rates would have been 51% in 1960, 48% in 1980, and

TABLE 7.14
Type of Union by Color and Sex for the State of São Paulo, 1960–2010

	IN CONSENSUAL UNION		MARRIED	
Race	Men	Women	Men	Women
		1960		
White	2.3	2.2	97.7	97.8
Black	7.5	8.4	92.5	91.6
Brown	5.6	9.0	94.4	91.0
		1980		
White	7.3	7.2	92.7	92.8
Black	17.6	18.9	82.4	81.1
Brown	15.0	16.0	85.0	84.0
		1991		
White	11.8	12.0	88.2	88.0
Black	23.6	24.4	76.4	75.6
Brown	21.9	22.5	78.1	77.5
		2000		
White	20.0	20.2	80.0	79.8
Black	35.4	35.3	64.6	64.7
Brown	33.9	35.2	66.1	64.8
		2010		
White	24.8	24.9	75.2	75.1
Black	39.8	40.0	60.2	60.0
Brown	37.7	38.4	62.3	61.6

SOURCE: Ipums 5% sample of Brazilian censuses 1960–2010.

45% in 2000 if no preferences by color existed.[71] Of these self-identified color groups, census data from 1991 show whites and Browns mostly living with partners within their racial groups, while Blacks of both sexes married most exogamously both nationally and in the state of São Paulo. While Browns and especially Blacks married out even more in 2000, there was little change in white endogamy rates. The rates of racial endogamy in 2000 for the state as a whole were virtually the same for both the municipality of São Paulo and its metropolitan regions (see Figure 7.10).

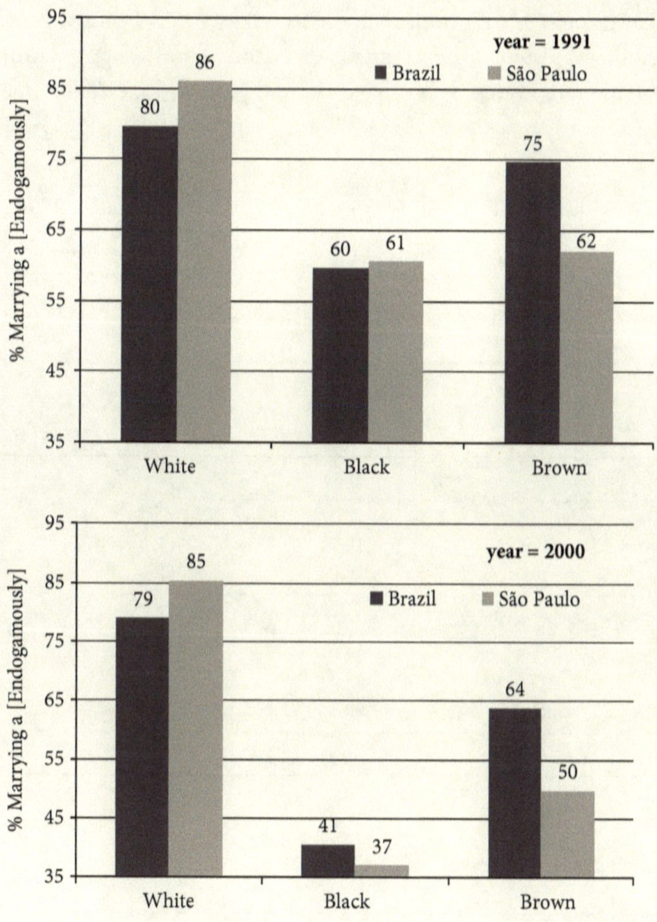

Figure 7.10. Racial Endogamy of Couples for Brazil and State of São Paulo, 1991 and 2000

SOURCE: IBGE, SIDRA, tables 273 and 2642.

Given these changing long-term patterns, it was evident, as an analysis of the PNAD surveys of 1987 and 1998, showed, that the younger the married couple, the higher the rate of exogamous marriages, and this was similar for all color groups.[72] Moreover, given the increasing advantage of women at all levels of education, the overall spread between husband's and wife's educational attainment in these exogamous marriages has declined by half from 1960 to 2000. In the case of Blacks marrying each other, educational levels between male and female partners are now equal, and there is only a modest difference in educational level between partners in white/Black and white/Brown marriages.[73] As another study of education and interracial marriages concluded: "In 1960, 1 in every 10 marriages was between persons of different color groups; in 1980 this number increased in 1 in every 5 marriages; in 2000 to 1 in every 3 marriages."[74]

Another area where discrimination plays a role is in housing and residence. A methodology has been developed in the United States to measure racial segregation in housing. The two most-used methods are the index of dissimilarity (which measures racial concentration by showing what percentage of one racial group would have to leave an area for equality to be achieved with a second group—say, for the numbers of whites to be equal to Blacks and Browns in terms of their share of population) and the index of isolation (which shows how much exposure one group has to another, with a higher percentage of isolation indicating a lower degree of contact). A recent detailed study of all the major metropolitan centers of Brazil found that the index of dissimilarity was quite low in Brazil compared to the United States. Thus in 1980 New York City had a dissimilarity index of 75, with São Paulo at 37; Washington, DC, was at 79, and Brasília was at 39; Chicago was at 92 and Salvador at 48. It also found that "white residential exposure to non-whites in Brazil is clearly greater than in US cities of comparable racial composition."[75] Another study did find increasing discrimination in housing at the upper levels of the income brackets in Brazil.[76] But again, racial segregation in housing, like racial differences in income, was only mild to moderate in Brazil, compared to the extreme levels of housing segregation in the United States.

Another question to ask is whether race influences chances of social mobility. From the most recent studies of mobility in Brazil it appears that upward mobility is determined primarily by economic and social conditions and not by color, but that in patterns of downward mobility race begins to have far more of an impact than income.[77] Brazil underwent a great deal of structural mobility in the middle decades of the twentieth century, which resulted in a great deal of social mobility at the top of the occupational ladder. Some 80% of administrators, owners, and professionals come from other classes.[78] At the bottom of the occupational structure, as late as the 1990s over half of urban manual workers had a rural origin as manual workers. The question is how non-whites experienced this mobility from the 1970s to the 2000s.

A recent group of studies based on detailed questions about parent and child occupations in the periodic National Household Surveys have provided economists and sociologists with a wealth of data to analyze this question of social mobility by race.[79] Does race affect the rates at which children stay in the same occupational status as their parents, or move to a higher or lower occupational and income level than their fathers? In the latest such survey, carried out in 2014 and recently made available, the IBGE provided panel data on older and younger persons and their occupational positions compared to their fathers, broken down by race. The key finding in this PNAD survey was that white elite fathers had 59% of their children ending up in the same status as they were, while for a combined Black/Brown category of elite fathers, only 40% had children that reached their parents' status. This same variance occurred for upper-middle-class fathers by race, where the comparable rates were 42% and 22%.[80] This same survey also broke down the sons and daughters into two age groups, those 25–44 years of age and those 45–65. The older cohort thus includes a generation that came of working age between the late 1970s and early 1990s, a period of major structural change. The results are approximately the same for both age groups of offspring, thus suggesting that little has changed over time in the pattern of social mobility by race.

But as several others have suggested, these data do not take into account education, income, share of the population, residence, and other variables that could mitigate the impact of race. One study selected just São Paulo using the 1996 PNAD data set and eliminated all migrants. But it too used the model of absolute differences, and the results obtained suggest that race was influential. However, this study also showed a much more extreme difference in mobility by race for women compared to men than that evident from the 2014 mobility data set from the PNAD surveys.[81] To fully analyze the impact of race, it is essential to include all the variables and to assess the relative importance of each color group within each original occupational stratum, which can influence the findings.[82] Several recent detailed studies based on the same data sets from the household surveys, but using far more causal variables than sex and race, found that upward mobility was the same for whites and non-whites when all the relevant variables were included, but that a racial difference emerged in downward mobility, with fathers of color unable to maintain their sons in equal or better positions as much as white fathers were able to do. As the author of one of the key studies noted: "Racial inequality affects the chances of mobility only for individuals within the highest classes. White, Brown, and Black men with origins in the lower classes have similar chances of social mobility." The authors of several of these more recent studies see some race prejudice functioning in Brazilian society, but it is not as powerful as other factors such as income and education in determining a person's life chances and opportunities.[83] It would thus appear from the latest and more sophisticated surveys that racial prejudice is one of several factors influencing mobility but is less important than income, education and a host of other factors. It would also appear that color becomes more important at the very elite positions, at the same time as it has less of an influence in social mobility for all other classes and groups.

Without question Brazil today still remains a highly stratified society by world standards, though not as much as in 1950. In the past seventy years the control of inflation, the elimination of illiteracy, the growth of industry, and the modernization of agriculture, along with massive government income transfers to the poor, have reduced the extreme inequality that existed in the middle of the twentieth century. There has also been a major effort to eliminate the social and health disparities that existed among regions, between men and women, and between those of different races and origins. This has led to a reduction in the disparities in health, education, and well-being that existed before, if not totally eliminating them. But in income there has been less reduction than in these other indices. Paradoxically, the massive expansion of education initially had a major impact on reducing inequality by eliminating illiteracy, but the subsequent decline of quality in public education and the rise of a profit-driven low-quality tertiary educational system has created new impediment to reducing inequality. At the same time, the relative stagnation of the economy during the past decade has meant that some of the gains of earlier periods have been lost and trends toward declining inequality have slowed if not stopped.

Within Brazil, the state of São Paulo and especially its capital city stand out as unusually prosperous areas. Here industry and modern agriculture were most fully developed, and São Paulo's citizens often led the nation in all basic social and welfare indices. Here the highest salaries can be found, and the workforce is more weighted toward high-status and highly educated occupations. Here too reductions in inequality have often come before they appeared in the rest of the nation. The state's interior cities and rural areas now have a standard of living not that different from the standard of living in the capital city. Like the nation, it too has experienced a large increase in the size of the middle class. Yet on many indicators it is as stratified as the rest of the nation and still exhibits high levels of economic inequality.

Chapter 8

São Paulo, from an Industrial City to a City of Services

Today the city of São Paulo, with its 11.9 million inhabitants, is the largest city in the Western Hemisphere and one of the ten largest cities in the world. Yet its beginnings were quite humble. The city began as a Jesuit mission in 1550 on the Teitê River, in an area well populated with Indians, on a high ridge overlooking a vast open plain with limited vegetation. In order for the Jesuits to carry out the conversion and protection of the Indian subjects, the village was established far from the small settlements the Portuguese had established on the coast. Thus for most of its early development this capital of the province remained practically on the margins of the main productive and commercial currents of the colonial world. Far from the coast on a plateau behind the Serra do Mar Mountains and with a modest local agriculture, it was relatively isolated from the rest of the colony. The survival of the village depended essentially on the activities of backwoodsmen (*sertanistas*) who used the village as a base to explore the interior regions of South America, and did so without respect for the still poorly defined boundaries between Portuguese and Spanish settlements. The search for precious metals and the capture of indigenous people were the goals of these so-called *bandeirantes*—metals were their primary goal, and subjugated Indians supported their material survival. Agriculture was still quite limited even on the coast, and the captaincy (province) as a whole was only a very minor participant in the booming Brazilian sugar industry of the sixteenth and seventeenth centuries.

With the relative decline of the Brazilian sugar industry in the eighteenth century due to the rise of West Indian production, one of the alternatives was to resume the search for precious metals, which had initially been unsuccessful in the first phase of colonization. The crown sought to encourage the inhabitants of São Paulo to use their knowledge of the Brazilian interior to intensify their search for metals. In the final years of the seventeenth century the *bandeirantes* found gold in the then-unoccupied territory that now belongs to the state of Minas Gerais. The gold rush in the Minas Gerais region promoted an immense flow of people to these new mineral deposits from all parts of Brazil and Portugal in search of wealth, a phenomenon similar to what happened with gold exploration in other parts of the world. The concentration of exploratory activities in an inhospitable location, hundreds of kilometers from the coast, required the formation of a wide and complex supply network of varied goods and foodstuffs to this region from the colony and from abroad. It was this new mining economy that promoted the growth of the city and the region in the eighteenth century and slowly incorporated this marginal area into the colonial economy.

By the late eighteenth and early nineteenth centuries it was sugar plantations that, along with food-producing farms, guaranteed the ever-increasing importance of the region in the colonial economy. An important sugar-producing nucleus emerged in the interior of the captaincy, in the region called the "sugar quadrilateral," involving the municipalities of Piracicaba, Itu, Campinas, and Mogi Guaçu. The soil around the city of São Paulo never lent itself to export commercial agricultural production. Nevertheless, its central location on the route from the plateau to the coast meant that the city played an important role not only as the administrative center of the captaincy, but also as a growing commercial, financial, and logistical hub for the movement of sugar from the interior to the coast. The city's privileged location gave it a fundamental role that allowed it to accompany the growing strength of the São Paulo economy.[1]

But it was coffee that turned the city and province of São Paulo into a leading sector of Brazil.[2] Gradually coffee plantations penetrated the interior plateau of São Paulo, but it was only with the opening of the railroads that coffee production could expand to the western part of the state of São Paulo. The first railway to be implemented in the area was the São Paulo Railway, connecting the western coffee-producing region around Jundiaí to the port of Santos, passing through the city of São Paulo. Other railways would be gradually constructed in the province of São Paulo, either connecting with the São Paulo Railway in Jundiaí or with hubs in the city of

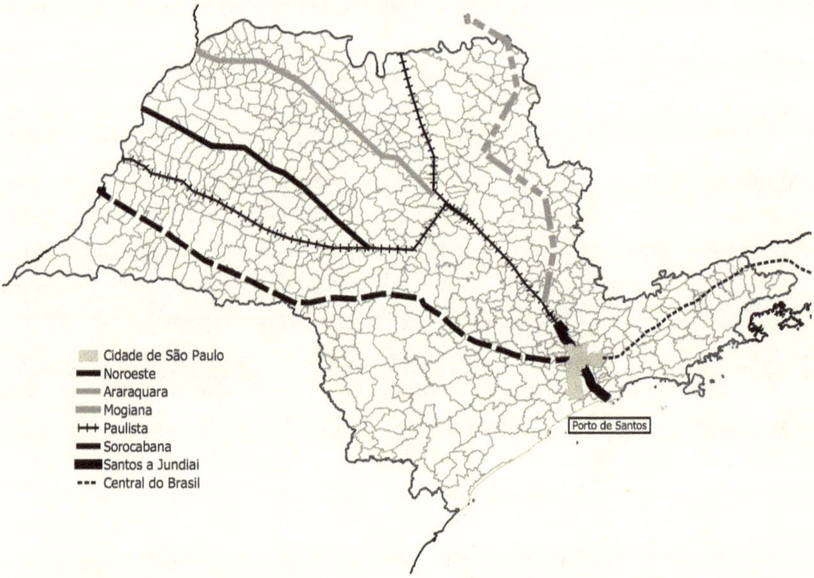

Map 8.1. São Paulo Railways, 1960

SOURCE: IBGE, Bases Cartográficas.

São Paulo, as until the 1930s this railway remained the only alternative to descend from the Serra do Mar towards the port of Santos.

The growth of coffee, the replacement of slave labor with free wage labor, and the massive immigration of foreign workers all had their impact on the capital. Especially after the republican revolt of 1889, the coffee elite consolidated its political and economic power in the state and nationally. In addition, the capital generated by coffee was soon invested in manufactures, financial activities, public services such as railroads, and a multiplicity of other economic activities. The result was that the city of São Paulo would become the leading industrial city in the nation by the middle of the twentieth century (see Map 8.1).

As a result of its economic and political expansion, the city of São Paulo would grow rapidly in the late nineteenth and early twentieth centuries. In the 1872 census, the capital had just over 30,000 inhabitants, and it was much smaller than Rio de Janeiro (with 274,000 inhabitants) and such other provincial capitals as Salvador (129,000), Recife (116,000), Belém, Porto Alegre, and even Cuiabá. But by 1900 the city had grown to 240,000 inhabitants and was now the second-most-populated metropolis in the nation, surpassed only by the city of Rio de Janeiro, which was the national capital. In 1920, the population of São Paulo (579,000 people) was still less than half of the population of Rio de Janeiro, and by 1950 the city of São Paulo had over 2 million inhabitants, though it was still smaller in population than Rio de Janeiro. But in the period after 1950 its population exploded and would almost double in each decade, finally reaching 11.2 million persons in 2010. In this sixty-year period the city would become more like the rest of Brazil in color, and different from all the others in both having a major industrial component for about half this period and then becoming a world-class center for services and the largest metropolis in Latin America and the hemisphere.

The early growth of the city was largely due to European immigration, which explains the initially high representation of whites in the city despite centuries of African slavery. From the 1880s onward immigrants arrived in the city from all areas of Europe, with Italians being the most important group, followed by Spaniards and Portuguese. Japanese migrants to Brazil, who began arriving in 1908 and came overwhelmingly to the state, remained primarily rural or settled in secondary cities such as Mogi das Cruzes and Marília, which had a significant minority of Japanese immigrants.[3] But gradually, with the rural exodus of workers from farming, the Japanese and their descendants moved to the capital and transformed the Bairro da Liberdade into a typically Japanese urban area.[4] The city of São Paulo thus became the metropolis with the largest number of persons of Japanese origin outside Japan.[5] Other groups of immigrants also made the city their home. There was an intense Middle Eastern migration from the Ottoman Empire to the state and the city of São Paulo. Even though the city contained only 24% of the state's population, it had 48% of all foreign-born individuals residing in the state. This explains the emergence of ethnic barrios or neighborhoods, such as Liberade and the Jewish neighborhood in Bom Retiro. The city was evolving in a typical North American urban style of a metropolis with ethnic barrios. It was also becoming more diverse in terms of its religious identity. It had an ever larger share of non-Catholics and atheists than the state or the nation. Most Buddhists and most of the Jews in Brazil resided in the capital, and it would become a core city for the rise of Pentecostal churches.

As early as the 1920s there also began an intense internal migration of native-born individuals, which in the last quarter of the century included ever larger numbers of migrants from the Northeastern region. This led to an increase of the non-white population in the city. The heavy concentration of the foreign-born also slowly declined. By 1950 some 86%

of the population of the city of São Paulo was native-born. The city also differed in other ways even as early as 1950. It had a higher rate of literate men and women than the state and national population, and it contained a disproportionate number of persons who had completed secondary and tertiary education. It also had more women than men, a bias typical of most nineteenth- and twentieth-century cities given the high demand for domestic service in the urban areas. The sex ratio of the city was 98 men per 100 women, while the state as a whole—which was mostly rural in this period—had a rate of 104 men per 100 women. In terms of whites and Blacks, the city was now typical of the rest of the state, but it still had a much lower rate of Asians and Browns than the state as a whole. It had approximately the same ratio of single and married persons in the adult population as in the state, but already over half the divorced (*desquitado*) population of the state resided in the city (see Table 8.1).

By the mid-twentieth century the capital was defined as an industrial city, though it was still primarily light industry, dominated by textiles, clothing, and food processing industries. In 1950 the largest portion of the city's economically active population was concentrated in the manufacturing sector. Manufacturing was the single largest employer of men and even had a significant proportion of women. However, probably the majority of women in the capital worked in domestic service. A miscellany of services absorbed the rest of the economically active population, though it is difficult to tease apart the large category that the census listed as "domestic activities and public education" (see Table 8.2).

What would become the metropolitan area of this expanding city was still mostly farmland in 1950. At midcentury some seventeen of the thirty-nine cities that are currently part of the São Paulo Metropolitan Region (RMSP) already existed. They were still very small towns and the majority of them were predominantly agricultural communities. However, three municipalities already stood out. These were Santo André, São Bernardo do Campo, and São Caetano do Sul, the so called ABC district.[6] These cities were situated along the Santos-to-Jundiaí railroad,[7] and along the newly built road known as the Via Anchieta, which connected the city of São Paulo to the port of Santos. These three communities already accounted for almost half of the population of these metropolitan regional communities outside the capital and for some 80% of industrial employees and 88% of the value of industrial production. Although they held only 8% of the entire RMSP population (which includes the capital), they accounted for 13% of the employed persons in industry and 16% of the value of industrial production of this region. Their importance would grow with the

TABLE 8.1

Demography of the State and Municipality of São Paulo, 1950

	State	Capital City	Capital as a % of State
POPULATION			
Total	**9,134,423**	**2,198,096**	**24%**
Men	4,648,606	1,085,965	23%
Women	4,485,817	1,112,131	25%
POPULATION BY KNOWN COLOR/ETHNICITY (1)			
Total	**9,120,420**	**2,195,773**	**24%**
Whites	7,823,111	1,929,410	25%
Blacks	727,789	169,564	23%
Asians	276,851	41,457	15%
Browns	292,669	55,342	19%
POPULATION BY CIVIL STATUS (15 YEARS OR OLDER)			
Total	**5,713,089**	**1,556,766**	**27%**
Single	2,006,637	566,434	28%
Married	3,348,850	881,911	26%
Separated (*desquitado*)	11,392	6,346	56%
Widowed	346,210	102,075	29%
POPULATION BY NATIONALITY			
Native-Born	**8,440,768**	**1,881,362**	**22%**
Naturalized	68,888	16,159	23%
Foreign-Born	627,433	300,430	48%
POPULATION BY LEVEL OF EDUCATION (PERSONS 5 YEARS OR OLDER)			
Total	**2,148,152**	**1,017,422**	**47%**
Elementary School	1,793,538	810,212	45%
Middle School	309,085	179,430	58%
Tertiary Education	45,529	27,780	61%
LITERACY (PERSONS 5 YEARS OR OLDER)			
Total	**7,795,857**	**1,952,194**	**25%**
Literate	4,627,329	1,550,731	34%
Illiterate	3,168,528	401,463	13%
Men	1,405,250	153,692	11%
Women	1,763,278	247,771	14%
POPULATION BY RELIGION			
Roman Catholics	8,284,465	1,937,175	23%
Protestants	317,904	101,132	32%
Spiritists	242,966	71,638	29%
Buddhists	128,014	11,551	9%
Jews	26,443	22,808	86%
Orthodox Catholics	25,543	18,567	73%
Others	39,439	12,471	32%
No religion	42,668	17,762	42%

SOURCE: Censo 1950, Séries Regionais, volume XXV, tomos 1–3.

NOTE: (1) All totals in the panels exclude unknowns.

TABLE 8.2
Population by Activity, City of São Paulo, 1950

Activities	Men	Women	Total
Total	861,483	893,344	1,754,827
Agriculture, Livestock, and Forestry	14,753	889	15,642
Extractive Industries	4,180	95	4,275
Transformation Industries	319,500	100,571	420,071
Trade in Goods	107,741	14,688	122,429
Real Estate, Securities, Other (1)	21,923	3,276	25,199
Services Provision	95,970	97,417	193,387
Transport, Communications, and Armaments	56,118	3,158	59,276
Liberal Professions	11,680	2,531	14,211
Services, Social Activities	24,288	23,677	47,965
Public Administration, Justice, Public Education	19,720	6,275	25,995
National Defense, Public Security	18,292	657	18,949
Domestic Activities, School Activities	91,875	613,823	705,698
Unemployed or Other Unspecified	73,894	25,791	99,685

SOURCE: Censo 1950, Séries Regionais, volume XXV, tomos 1–3.
NOTE: (1) Trade in real estate, securities, credit, insurance, capitalization.

installation of a petrochemical complex in Santo André and the establishment in the 1950s and 1960s of a major automotive industrial park in these cities.

Most of these municipalities were really villages (*vilas*).[8] Even some of the districts within the capital itself were classified as villages. As for the various municipalities outside the capital, only Santo André, São Caetano, Mogi das Cruzes, Guarulhos, and São Bernardo had a significant urban area. Guarulhos then had a total population of 34,000, of which 16,000 were in the urban nucleus. In the other towns, the urban core was still very small. Only Mogi das Cruzes and the ABC communities served as a major distribution center outside the capital and thus had people working in commerce.

The industrial leadership in the capital encouraged foreign auto companies to set up their factories in the city and metropolitan area of São Paulo in the decade of the 1950s and 1960s. Practically the entire Brazilian automobile industry was concentrated within approximately 20 kilometers from the capital center in the early 1960s. By 1980 there were 24,000 industrial establishments in the capital alone, employing 920,000 people, or three times the size of the capital's industrial workforce in 1950. Even the municipalities outside the capital doubled their industrial workforce to over half a million workers in this period (see Table 8.3 and Map 8.2).

TABLE 8.3
Comparisons of Economic Activities in the City and Metropolitan Region of São Paulo Between 1950 and 1980

	1950		1980	
	RMSP	City	RMSP	City
Population	2,662,786	2,198,096	12,119,133	8,112,464
Establishments	8,740	7,374	33,369	24,842
Personnel Employed	356,911	299,213	1,463,766	920,481
Total Salaries	5,367,329	4,525,331	272,900,964	154,447,038
Value of Production (1)	34,954,162	28,565,661	2,963,594,590	1,519,185,554

SOURCE: Censo 1950, Séries Regionais, volume XXV, tomos 1–3; Recenseamento Geral 1980, vol. 3, tomo 2.

NOTE: (1) Value of production in current Cr$.

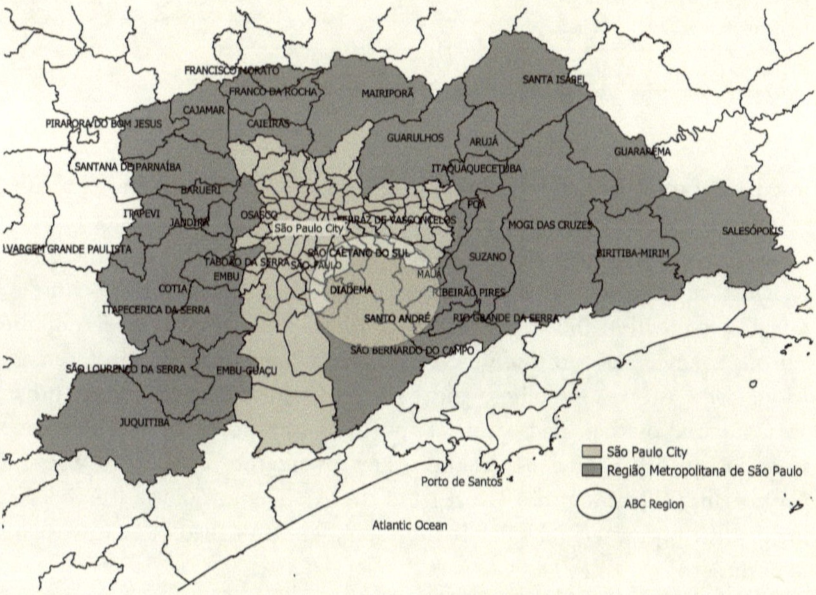

Map 8.2. Metropolitan Region of São Paulo

The increase in overall employment in the region in these thirty years was extraordinary, with the total number of employed persons growing more than eight times compared with 1950. Of the 5.3 million employed persons in the state, 1.7 million were in the city of São Paulo. In the capital, more than half of the employed population worked in the industrial sector. Using the national census and a self-identified survey of a person's occupation provides a useful guide to economic activities in 1980. This

TABLE 8.4
Population 10 Years of Age and Older, by Sector of Activity, 1980

	RMSP	City of São Paulo
Agricultural Activities	163,883	8,284
Industry	1,990,963	1,271,116
Construction Industry	372,174	242,061
Other Industrial Activities	62,266	43,182
Trade in Goods	615,866	457,424
Transport and Communication	271,142	194,307
Services Provision	1,104,618	843,939
Social Activities	376,373	285,663
Public Administration	172,416	126,121
Other Activities	297,618	239,085
Total Economically Active	**5,427,319**	**3,711,182**
Looking for Work	11,823	69,408
Out of the Labor Market	1,124,533	761,243

SOURCE: Census of 1980

data indicates that there were 3.7 million economically active people in the capital. Of these, one-third declared that they worked in manufacturing (see Table 8.4).[9]

The major industries in the capital employing these industrial workers were factories in metallurgy, machine tools, electrical materials, and communications and transport materials. These four segments represented more than 40% of both the value of industrial transformation and the number of employed persons. More traditional activities such as textiles, clothing, footwear, food products, and beverages accounted for 20% of the value of industrial transformation and a quarter of the persons employed in the capital's industry (see Table 8.5).

These data on employment show that the city of São Paulo in 1980 was still an essentially industrial city. But this was the high point in the city's role as an industrial leader within the nation. Already over half a million industrial workers were employed in the surrounding towns of the metropolitan region, and 49% of the value of industrial production was occurring there. The intense diffusion of industry that would occur in the following years, both toward other cities in the metropolitan region and toward the interior of the state of São Paulo, would systematically reduce the importance of industry within the Capital. Industrial nuclei were formed in such interior regions as Campinas, São José dos Campos, and Sorocaba, among others. By the 2010 census, the segment of "workers in the production of industrial goods and services" totaled only 904,000 workers in the city of São Paulo, significantly down from the number in 1980, and these workers

TABLE 8.5

Industrial Indicators by Sector for the City of São Paulo, 1980

	Firms	Personnel Employed	Total Salaries	Value of Industrial Production	IVA
Metropolitan Region of São Paulo	33,369	1,463,766	272,900,964	2,963,594,590	1,322,721,474
City of São Paulo	24,842	920,481	154,447,038	1,519,185,554	731,835,394
CITY OF SÃO PAULO, 1980 INDUSTRY SORTED BY SIZE OF LABOR FORCE					
Metallurgy	3,152	135,824	22,698,011	213,083,569	96,451,817
Mechanics	2,332	109,068	28,665,826	161,346,220	88,437,210
Clothing and Footwear	4,402	104,661	9,292,724	102,085,671	42,874,773
Electrical and Communications Equipment	1,292	91,785	16,446,389	166,898,124	86,051,210
Textile	1,425	74,250	10,573,495	138,133,058	57,801,400
Food Products	2,845	53,717	5,776,380	112,460,846	41,252,032
Transport Equipment	593	51,136	9,833,555	88,952,501	42,118,330
Plastic Materials	1,094	46,249	6,398,359	70,502,133	34,621,032
Editorial and Graphic	1,715	45,645	9,877,716	62,176,088	41,194,941
Others	1,135	37,525	5,022,082	51,915,696	33,330,839
Paper and Cardboard	492	29,155	4,886,471	56,844,855	24,043,117
Non-Metallic Minerals	1,026	26,862	4,157,300	37,446,479	20,898,439
Furniture	1,200	22,940	2,912,202	22,321,346	11,070,409
Chemistry	502	18,657	3,874,780	91,990,703	36,404,942
Rubber	253	14,327	2,349,572	32,395,834	12,355,397
Pharmaceutical and Medicinal Products	124	10,587	2,103,623	35,895,119	22,222,769
Wood	470	8,755	1,247,238	8,524,263	3,753,237
Perfumery Products	172	8,274	1,440,641	31,835,777	14,656,541
Drinks	30	3,177	729,588	8,835,766	4,446,232
Hides and Skins and Their Products	108	3,096	269,731	1,973,908	1,003,998
Support Utilities and Service to Industries	453	23,375	5,307,923	14,341,140	10,590,594
Administrative Assistants	2,461	50,747	23,665,903		

SOURCE: Recenseamento Geral 1980, volume 3, tomo 2, parte 1, no. 19: 2–3.

now represented only 16% of the persons employed in the capital in that year and just 20% of all workers in the RMSP.[10]

All this early industrial growth led to an expansion of the local labor market, which in turn became a magnet for rural workers being displaced by the modernization of agriculture. There now began a massive internal migration, both from the countryside toward the cities and from one region to another. All states and regions participated in this migration, with the Northeast sending masses of emigrants to the South and especially to the metropolitan region of São Paulo. The capital, now the largest city in Brazil, also was expanding rapidly in all areas of the economy, and thus provided lots of low-skilled manual jobs in construction as well as semi-skilled and skilled jobs in manufacturing and services. This internal migration profoundly altered the urban landscape and the population of the city of São Paulo and its neighboring municipalities of the RMSP. As of 1980, 8.5 million people resided in the capital, which represented one-third of the population of the state of São Paulo. The Metropolitan Region of São Paulo contained half the population of the state, then the most populous state in Brazil, and a significant 11% of the Brazilian population.

The massive immigration to the city led to rates of growth of between 4.5% and 6% per annum for the city, and even higher rates for the metropolitan region. This stream of migrants would change many of the social characteristics of the city. The migration was heavily female, which resulted in an increasing dominance of women in the resident population of the capital. The migration streams from the North had only about 70 or so males per 100 females, and those from the Northeast and the Center-West states averaged around 80 men per 100 women. By 1980 the sex ratio of the city was 95.6; in 1991 it was 93.1, and dropped further to 89.9 men per 100 women by 2010.[11]

The growth in population in the capital and metropolitan region resulted in a disorderly process of urbanization, with consequences that persist to the present day. These migrants initially went to the capital, but increasingly they moved to the other municipalities of the metropolitan region. Already growth after 1980 was systematically greater in the municipalities of the Metropolitan Region than in the capital itself, a pattern that continued on into the twenty-first century. The capital's growth rate of 5.3% per annum in the 1950s dropped to just 1.2% per annum by the 1980s and below 1% in the next three decades. In contrast, the metropolitan regional cities were already growing more rapidly than the capital in the 1950s and grew at much higher rates throughout the next decades. Given these differing growth rates, the importance of the capital within the metropolitan region has declined. Whereas the city represented 83% of the metropolitan region population in 1950, it would eventually drop to just 57% of the RMSP by 2010.

From 1950 to the 1980s many of these original RMSP towns were divided up into new municipalities as their populations increased. Some of these villages had become major cities by the census of 1991. Thus Guarulhos became the third-largest city in the state, with 786,000 inhabitants, and San Andre was fourth with 615,000; Osasco and São Bernardo, both with over half a million people, were fifth and sixth in size, and seventh was São José dos Campos with 422,000.[12] While some of these municipalities of the RMSP became important industrial or economic hubs like Mauá, others have become "dormitory cities" linked to the capital, such as Carapicuíba, Ferraz de Vasconcelos, and Francisco Morato.[13]

In this long period of accelerated growth of the city and its surrounding municipalities, local governments could not develop urban infrastructure as quickly as needed, nor did they build adequate housing in quantities sufficient to receive this enormous migration. In contrast to Rio de Janeiro with its limited space, the open lands in the metropolitan region at first discouraged the development of significant favelas—illegal land occupations with self-built homes—and this lasted until the 1970s.[14] In São Paulo, for a long time home ownership in these peripheral municipalities was possible, though these illegal favelas slowly appeared in many of the peripheral towns lacking urban infrastructure.[15]

Today favelas are a basic part of the metropolitan and urban structure. There is still disagreement about their size and importance, which depend on the indicators that are used. In 1973 and 1975, for example, two surveys were carried out by the city of São Paulo that identified a favela population of between 72,000 and 117,000 people, numbers that are not very significant in relation to the population of the capital in those two years.[16] In 1980, for the first time, IBGE introduced this variable in the demographic census. Favelas were identified in twenty-nine cities in the state of São Paulo, totaling 133,000 households and 634,000 people. Of these twenty-nine cities, eight were part of the São Paulo Metropolitan Region, with significant numbers in São Bernardo do Campo (45,000 residents), Guarulhos (26,000 residents), Diadema (24,000 residents), Osasco (19,000 residents), and Santo André (15,000 residents). In the city of São Paulo there were 438 favelas, with 71,259 households and 335,344 people, which represented 4% of the population.[17] Since then, favelas have expanded and transformed themselves throughout the city and in the metropolitan region, in terms of their urban aspects, their infrastructure, and the composition of their residents (see Map 8.3).[18]

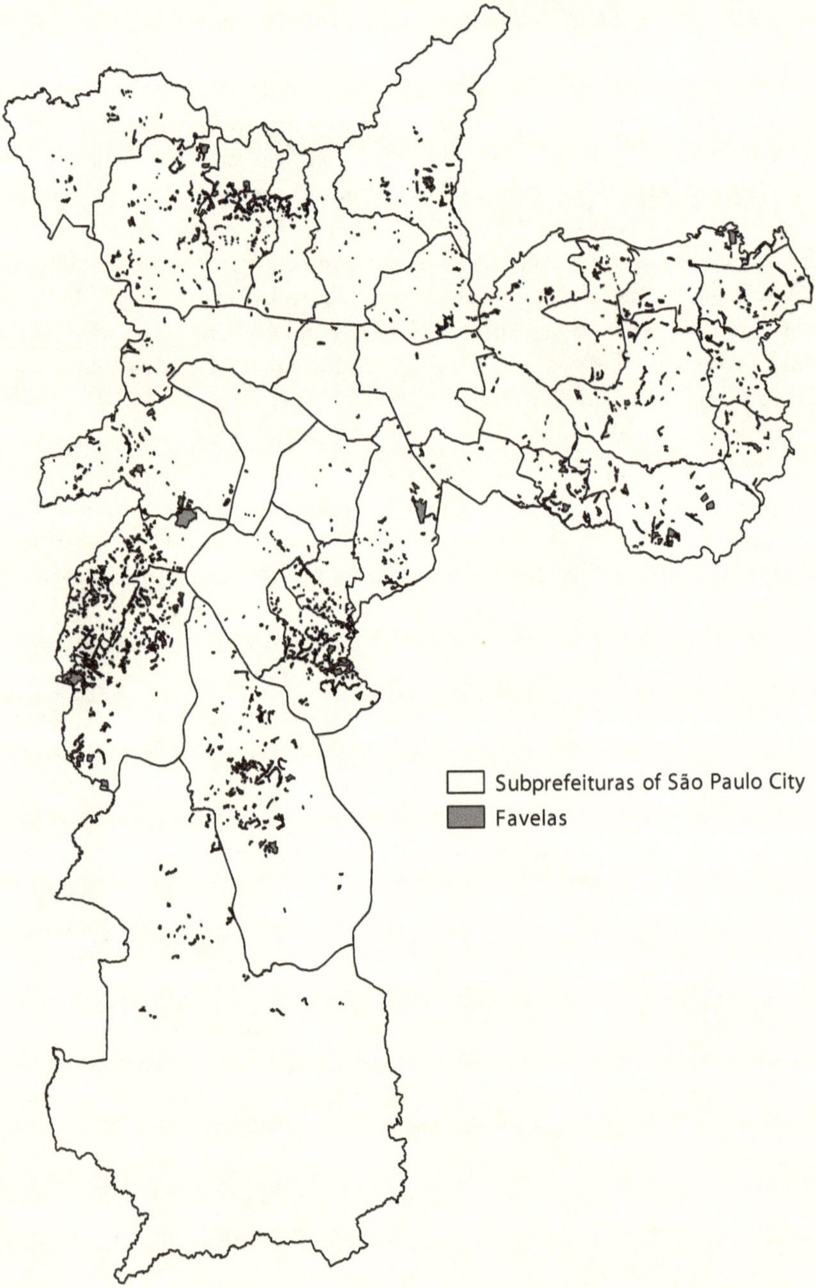

Map 8.3. Distribution of Favelas, Municipality of São Paulo, 2017

SOURCE: Geosampa, Prefeitura de São Paulo.

Since the middle of the last century, government policies toward favelas have alternated between eradication and urbanization. The latter approach accepts their existence and gives them a minimum of infrastructure. This includes widening their access roads, eliminating areas where the risk of collapsing housing is high, installing basic services such as education and health, and offering sanitation services (one of the most important needs for many of the favelas in the region).[19] There are examples of great success in the urbanization of favelas, such as the favelas of Paraisópolis, Heliópolis, Nova Jaguaré, and at a minimum almost all favelas now have potable water.[20] On the other hand, when favelas are bulldozed and alternative housing is supplied, the government often ended up creating real ghettos in several cities in Brazil. This is because they mostly offer alternative housing in large residential complexes in peripheral areas, without adequate infrastructure and transport and far from the centers that generate employment. This occurred mainly in in the 1970s and 1980s, when housing and sanitation policy was dictated by the National Housing Bank. The case of Cidade Tiradentes in São Paulo is emblematic of these failed public housing programs.[21]

The demographic structure of the city was also influenced by its economy. Given the great migration to the city in the middle decades of the century, the city's population was younger and contained more working-age adults than most of the country by the 1980s, as can be seen in the capital's population pyramid for 1980. Also, the higher ratio of women migrating to the city is reflected in the steady decline of the proportion of males in the capital, from 96.5 males per 100 females in 1970 to just 89.9 males per 100 females by 2010. An impressive 56.4% of women in the metropolitan district were economically active in 2017, compared to a rate of 70% for men, and the rates for both sexes were considerably higher than in any other metropolitan region except for Brasília.[22] In turn, the steadily declining birth rates in the capital are reflected in the jar-like structure of the population pyramids for 2000 and 2010, which show a big drop in the youngest age groups as a proportion of the total population. Whereas the population under 15 years of age represented 32% of the total in 1970, it steadily declined to just 21% of the total in 2010 (see Figure 8.1).

There were also significant changes in the color and ethnicity of the capital population as a result of this massive migration. The city became darker in color and less Catholic with each census. Although the white population grew in this period, its share of the city's population declined from 88% in 1950 to just 61% in 2010, while Blacks and Browns went from 10% to 37% in the same period. The cities of the metropolitan region,

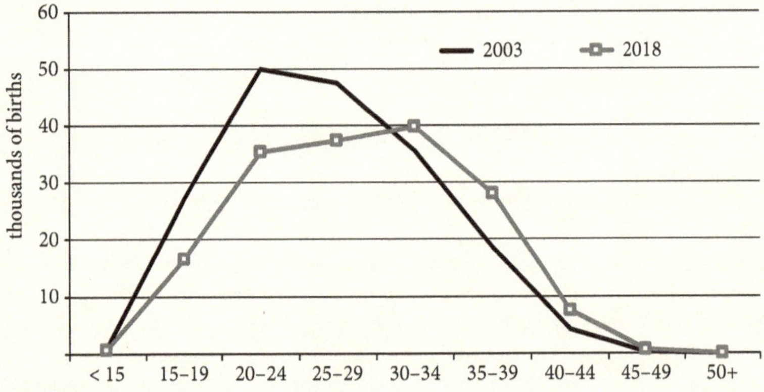

Figure 8.1. Total Births by Age of Mother, Municipality of São Paulo, 2003 and 2018

SOURCE: IBGE, SIDRA, table 2609.

which had 4.8 million persons when the capital is excluded, had even fewer whites than the capital, with whites being just 56% of their population. Even more impressive is the decline in the number of Roman Catholics, both in absolute terms and in their relative position in the population of the capital. In 1950 some 88% of capital residents self-defined as Catholics; by 2010 that figure was only 58%. In fact, the Catholic Church lost over half a million adherents between 2000 and 2010. In these aspects the metropolitan region was even less Roman Catholic and more Protestant than the capital, being just 52% Catholic in 2010. Protestants were 22% of the capital population in that year, and 26% in the other cities of the metropolitan area (see Table 8.6).

Moreover, the Protestant churches that were expanding in the capital and in the metropolitan region were not the old mainline Protestant denominations such as Presbyterians, Methodists, and Baptists, but Pentecostal evangelicals. The rise of the evangelical churches explains this growth of the Protestant movement in São Paulo. Although Brazil remains the largest Roman Catholic country in the world in the twenty-first century, it also has the largest Pentecostal population in the world, and is the fourth-largest Protestant country.[23] This makes it second only to the United States as the largest Christian country in the world.[24]

The traditional Protestant religions arrived in the nineteenth century, but Pentecostal Protestantism did not start in Brazil until the twentieth century. Nevertheless, the Pentecostals grew so fast that by 2010 they

TABLE 8.6

Demographic Indicators for the City and Metropolitan Region of São Paulo, 1950–2010

	1950	1980	2000	2010
		MUNICIPALITY OF SÃO PAULO		
Population Resident				
Total	2,198,096	8,493,226	10,435,546	11,253,503
Men	1,085,965	4,150,555	4,972,632	5,328,632
Women	1,112,131	4,342,671	5,462,914	5,924,871
Color and Ethnicity				
Total	2,198,096	8,493,217	10,435,546	11,253,503
Whites	1,929,410	6,129,733	6,988,908	6,823,004
Blacks	169,564	400,970	527,191	717,215
Asians	41,457	23,690	208,677	250,146
Browns	55,342	1,688,883	2,606,124	3,447,290
Religion				
Roman Catholics	1,937,175	7,203,904	7,107,261	6,549,775
Protestants	101,132	591,305	1,663,131	2,487,810
Spiritist	71,638	175,096	286,600	531,822
Buddhists	11,551	79,754	67,591	75,075
Jews	22,808	41,308	37,500	43,610
Others	31,038	132,375	336,989	509,403
No Religion	17,762	213,988	936,474	1,056,008
		METROPOLITAN REGION OF SÃO PAULO EXCLUDING CAPITAL (RMSP)		
Population Resident				
Total			7,444,451	8,430,472
Men			3,657,002	4,104,973
Women			3,787,449	4,325,499
Color and Ethnicity				
Total			7,271,034	8,398,599
Whites			4,725,964	4,726,948
Blacks			345,418	527,741
Asians			86,443	111,755
Browns			2,217,855	3,048,003
Religion				
Roman Catholics			4,880,928	4,570,197
Protestants			1,471,809	2,369,120
Spiritist			113,073	224,997
Buddhists			30,580	32,018
Jews			2,049	2,359
Others			232,858	372,484
No Religion			713,154	859,297

SOURCE: Censos Demográficos 1950 and 1980; IBGE, SIDRA, tables 136, 2093, and 2094.

accounted for 60% of Protestants nationally.[25] What is impressive about all these developments is that these new Pentecostal churches are essentially based in Brazil. Although many had their origin in foreign missionaries coming to Brazil or have some international connections, they are now fully staffed by Brazilian ministers. These churches have spread throughout Brazil and range from small storefront establishments to megachurches.

The Pentecostal churches that were the most important in the state of São Paulo were the Assembly of God and the Christian Congregation of Brazil. The latter was overwhelmingly a local Paulista church, with 52% of its adherents within the state. Other churches that were overrepresented in the state (with more than a quarter of their national membership living in the state) were the Brazil for Christ Church, the Evangelical Community Church, and the Evangelical Undetermined Renewal. In the capital and the metropolitan area the two largest Pentecostal churches in Brazil, the Assembly of God and the Christian Congregation of Brazil, were the most important of the Pentecostal movements. In this case there was little difference between the capital and the surrounding municipalities, as all the major churches were found almost equally in the capital and the cities of the metropolitan regions (see Table 8.7).

These churches showed some differentiation by sex, color, and residence of their followers. Pentecostals were clearly more an urban rather than rural phenomenon, as the rural areas of the state consistently remained more

TABLE 8.7

Major Pentecostal Churches in the Capital and Metropolitan Region, 2010

	Capital	RMSP Less Capital	RMSP
Total Pentecostal Evangelical Protestants (1)	**1,423,743**	**1,444,106**	**2,867,849**
Igreja Assembléia de Deus	533,362	545,794	1,079,156
Igreja Congregação Cristã do Brasil	199,565	269,382	468,947
Igreja Universal do Reino de Deus	126,228	101,313	227,541
Igreja Evangelho Quadrangular	58,013	45,821	103,834
Igreja Deus é Amor	36,580	46,800	83,380
Igreja o Brasil para Cristo	16,723	21,525	38,248
Comunidade Evangélica	16,276	16,770	33,046
Igreja Casa da Benção	4,126	6,723	10,849
Igreja Maranata	2,171	2,184	4,355
Other Pentecostals	429,598	384,392	813,990
Evangelical Unknown (2)	797,853	690,848	1,488,701

SOURCE: IBGE, SIDRA, table 137.

NOTES: (1) This total includes smaller churches with fewer than 4,000 members.
(2) Unknown Evangelicals not included in total Pentecostal.

TABLE 8.8
Adherents by Color for Major Religious Groups, Capital and Metropolitan Region of São Paulo, 2010

	White	Black	Brown	Other (1)
CAPITAL				
Total All Respondents	61%	6%	31%	2%
Roman Catholic	63%	6%	30%	2%
Traditional Protestants	64%	6%	28%	2%
Evangelical Pentecostals	51%	8%	40%	1%
Other Christian Religions	61%	7%	29%	3%
Spiritist	77%	6%	15%	2%
Umbanda and Candomblé	61%	13%	25%	1%
Oriental Religions	26%	3%	12%	59%
No Religion	54%	8%	35%	3%
METROPOLITAN REGIONS OF SÃO PAULO				
Total All Respondents	59%	6%	33%	2%
Roman Catholic	61%	5%	32%	2%
Traditional Protestants	62%	6%	30%	2%
Evangelical Pentecostals	50%	8%	41%	1%
Other Christian Religions	60%	6%	31%	2%
Spiritist	76%	6%	16%	2%
Umbanda and Candomblé	60%	13%	26%	1%
Oriental Religions	31%	4%	16%	49%
No Religion	52%	8%	38%	2%

SOURCE: IBGE, SIDRA, table 2094.
NOTE: (1) Indians and Asians.

Roman Catholic than the cities. The urban population, both in Brazil as a whole and in the state of São Paulo, was consistently less Roman Catholic than the national average. At the same time there was an increasing imbalance in the sexes, with men remaining more loyal to Roman Catholicism and women being far more committed to these new Protestant movements. This can probably be explained by the role of the new churches in combating alcoholism and promoting family stability, a theme of direct interest to women.[26] No matter the size or origin of the Pentecostal churches in the capital or in the metropolitan region, women dominated. The sex ratio for Pentecostal churches both in the districts outside the capital and in the capital itself was an extraordinary 78 men per 100 women in the RMSP cities and 77 men per 100 women in the capital. Not only were the Pentecostal churches heavily female, but they were more non-white than all other religions, including, surprisingly, the Afro-Brazilian religions Umbanda and Candomblé (see Table 8.8).

Given the pace of growth of these Protestant denominations, it is estimated that Catholics will fall below 50% of the Brazilian population by

2030 and a decade later Pentecostals will be equal in number to Catholics.[27] This growth of Pentecostal Christians is due to their theology and church structure. In theological terms Pentecostalism's concern with this life rather than the afterlife, its acceptance of individual salvation, and its sense of equality and community make it a perfect fit for migrants to the city in need of structure, community, and identity. Of the Pentecostal Churches founded in the second half of the twentieth century, some have even adopted Afro-Brazilian church practices such as exorcism, and others have become more secular and more hierarchical in what has been called a neo-Pentecostal movement.[28] However, the overwhelming majority of Pentecostal churches have little hierarchical structure and are the most open of the major religions in Brazil. All comers are admitted, and evangelism is encouraged. The clergy are all Brazilians, whatever hierarchy exists is local or at most regional, and their priesthood is open to all. New pastors need feel only the call of God, with no need for formal religious training, and thus many Pentecostal pastors come from the popular classes.[29] Their funding is local as is their language and even their music. Thus the proliferation of pastors and new churches is an ongoing development. All urban favelas in all the major cities are filled with Pentecostal churches, and they are also to be found in large numbers in Brazil's other centers of poverty, the state prisons, where they are the dominant group among the prisoners.[30]

The power and importance of the Pentecostal churches is felt not only at the level of the favela or the prison, but also more and more in politics. Evangelicals from both the traditional churches and the Pentecostal movement have become an enormous force in national politics. The leading church behind this was the Brazilian-originated Pentecostal IURD church, which was soon followed by the Assembleia de Deus churches in formally promoting their own candidates.[31] Churches began running their own candidates in the post-military elections of the late 1980s, and today the so-called Evangelical Caucus (Bancada Evangélica), which includes both individual church members running for election and candidates formally supported by their churches, increased their share to one hundred and five deputies and seventeen senators by 2021.[32]

Along with all these social and religious changes, there has been a major change in the economy in recent decades. The capital and its allied cities have progressively moved away from an industrial economy and toward one dominated by services and trade, which demand higher levels of human capital. Because of the government's industrial deconcentration policies, state tax wars, the high costs of land, and powerful local unions in the metropolitan regions, industry has moved out of the capital and its metropolitan region, and in turn the capital has become the national leader in services. This began in the 1980s and has continued ever since, especially as the whole country urbanized, and this has led to the rise of a new group of large non-capital secondary cities throughout Brazil. All these changes are reflected in the distribution of jobs in the capital, the RMSP, and the state in 2018. Over half of the jobs in the capital and the RMSP are now in services, and even in the state those employed in services are the largest category of workers. Industry is less than a quarter of employment in all areas (see Table 8.9).

The development and formalization of the service sector have given the Municipality of São Paulo and its metropolitan region national leadership

TABLE 8.9

Economic Activities and Formal Employment in the Capital, Metropolitan Region, and State of São Paulo, 2018

	ESTABLISHMENTS					
Sectors	CAPITAL		METROPOLITAN REGION		STATE	
Industry	Number	%	Number	%	Number	%
Transformation Industry	25,561	9%	41,693	10%	97,659	10%
Construction Industry	12,387	4%	18,604	4%	42,737	4%
Public Utilities	539	0%	862	0%	2,657	0%
Trade	103,629	35%	157,576	37%	375,637	38%
Services	149,811	51%	206,801	48%	422,913	42%
Public Administration	202	0%	358	0%	1,975	0%
Agriculture	739	0%	2,183	1%	56,927	6%
Total	292,925	100%	428,223	100%	1,001,422	100%

	WORKERS					
Sectors	CAPITAL		METROPOLITAN REGION		STATE	
Industry	Number	%	Number	%	Number	%
Transformation Industry	390,123	8%	881,844	12%	2,318,161	17%
Construction Industry	216,257	4%	296,437	4%	515,190	4%
Public Utilities	29,210	1%	54,591	1%	108,470	1%
Trade	872,634	18%	1,344,713	19%	2,659,562	20%
Services	2,639,371	54%	3,620,965	51%	5,729,193	43%
Public Administration	749,008	15%	933,560	13%	1,576,609	12%
Agriculture	5,357	0%	14,375	0%	323,537	2%
Total	4,903,449	100%	7,151,001	100%	13,247,463	100%

SOURCE: Ministério Economia, http://bi.mte.gov.br/bgcaged/caged_rais_vinculo_id/caged_rais_vinculo_basico_tab.php.

in this new and growing economic sector. The capital strengthened its strategic role in the state and country's economy by developing a significant part of the most complex and sophisticated services used both nationally and internationally. This was one of the main reasons the city could be categorized as a world metropolis in many ways equivalent to London, New York, or Tokyo.[33]

The city's service sector was of course quite important within the state as well as nationally. Half of the state's jobs in credit institutions, insurance, capitalization, commerce, and real estate management were found in the capital. Over 40% of the state's employees in wholesale trade, housing, food, repair and maintenance services, medical and dental and veterinary services, and public administration were in the city. The city of São Paulo thus provided a significant share of the services within the state, centralizing many service functions in the capital. But while the city maintained its premier status, the growth of significant cities throughout the state meant that its share of various services within the state was declining as other cities also expanded into the service sector (see Table 8.10).

Using data on the formal labor sector provides another, more detailed classification of activities in the city of São Paulo. These data show significant growth both in firms that provided formal jobs, which went from 175,000 to 257,000 companies between 2002 and 2018, and in the number of their employees, which grew from 2.7 million to 4.3 million in the same period. In 2002, 2010, and 2018, service activities including commerce accounted for more than 80% of firms and formal jobs, demonstrating the fundamental importance of services in the capital's economy. In terms of formal employment, the major activities were in services provided primarily to companies, public administration, defense, and social security. While there was a drop in total formal government employment in the city of São Paulo, services provided mainly to companies multiplied threefold between 2002 and 2018.[34] Surprisingly, the size of firms remained constant over this period. Thus the average number of formal jobs per establishment in this service sector remained relatively stable, around 17 formal jobs per firm. Excluding the public administration sector, which presents a different configuration than other activities, the average per establishment changed only modestly, going from 10 persons per company in 2002 to 14 persons per company in 2010 and 2018 (see Table 8.11).

This labor force reflects the importance in the city of such sectors as banking and finance. By any indicator (number of employees, branches, total assets, equity, credit operations, and management of third-party resources),

TABLE 8.10

Labor Market: Formal Jobs in the Services Sector, City of São Paulo, 1985–2018

	1985	1990	1995	2000	2005	2010	2015	2018
	FORMAL LABOR EMPLOYMENT ACCORDING TO RAIS							
Total City of São Paulo Jobs (All Sectors)	3,193,449	3,502,570	3,354,150	3,212,039	3,684,599	4,873,339	5,126,131	4,903,449
Stock and Other Financial Markets and Real Estate	305,499	322,057	365,416	416,878	556,121	890,017	1,011,263	1,050,848
Direct and Autonomous Public Administration	634,591	690,292	778,443	822,730	850,854	883,326	849,732	749,008
Retail Business	272,566	302,349	337,128	374,885	490,999	659,345	682,129	661,218
Food, Lodging, and Repair Facilities	279,276	318,478	261,275	255,083	333,829	476,106	567,444	571,065
Medical, Dental, and Veterinary Services	55,241	46,667	111,513	105,856	162,162	216,156	299,855	318,810
Transport and Communications	172,804	168,569	200,416	197,529	209,658	302,786	323,337	288,739
Teaching	27,297	31,523	106,025	112,381	115,651	151,091	200,523	217,135
Wholesale	108,978	124,267	121,525	125,505	150,835	212,407	210,701	211,416
Banking	191,636	158,645	144,000	134,810	146,125	189,019	200,430	192,774
Total Jobs City of São Paulo, Commerce and Services	2,047,888	2,162,847	2,425,741	2,545,657	3,016,234	3,980,253	4,345,414	4,261,013

SOURCE: Based on the RAIS and CAGED databases, Ministério da Economia, http://bi.mte.gov.br/bgcaged/, accessed November 25, 2019.

TABLE 8.11

Numbers of Formal Jobs and Firms by Sectors of Commerce and Services, City of São Paulo, 2002, 2010, and 2018

	2002	2010	2018	2002	2010	2018
	NUMBER OF FIRMS			FORMAL EMPLOYEES		
Services Mainly Provided to Companies	20,058	26,587	31,924	287,973	724,987	874,617
Public Administration, Defense, and Social Security	289	202	209	912,913	885,919	751,229
Retail and Repair of Personal and Household Objects	55,654	73,481	74,437	344,318	560,316	572,558
Health and Social Services	11,995	14,593	17,329	154,587	245,574	358,818
Accommodation and Food	13,044	19,174	24,644	118,640	201,260	242,890
Education	4,192	5,897	8,349	109,308	151,091	217,135
Wholesale Trade and Commercial Representatives and Trade Agents	13,371	16,603	16,400	125,798	212,407	211,416
Real Estate Activities	18,687	21,538	25,060	104,762	153,220	189,181
Ground Transportation	3,900	4,962	6,250	115,022	140,235	164,692
Computer Activities and Related Services	2,299	4,434	5,610	34,545	84,978	122,250
Financial Intermediation	2,643	3,443	3,256	103,715	132,807	119,970
Trade and Repair of Motor Vehicles and Motorcycles	10,413	13,682	12,792	67,187	99,029	88,660
Associative Activities	4,989	5,662	5,829	69,507	120,284	83,332
Attached and Auxiliary Activities of Transport and Travel Agencies	4,179	6,215	6,995	33,618	67,170	61,673
Recreational, Cultural, and Sports Activities	2,793	3,741	4,744	37,322	48,686	58,083
Mail and Telecommunications	785	1,719	1,802	41,788	68,494	47,608
Insurance and Pension Plans	453	391	380	20,987	30,296	38,945
Auxiliary Activities of Financial Intermediation, Insurance, and Pension Plans	1,577	2,448	3,357	12,765	25,916	33,859
Social Services	3,252	4,276	5,055	16,737	22,880	22,978
Rental of Vehicles, Machines, Equipment, and Personal and Household Objects	833	2,087	2,142	6,919	19,770	20,711
Urban and Sewer Cleaning and Related Activities	97	185	271	11,990	16,184	14,991
Air Transport	122	130	102	15,077	26,758	14,381
Research and Development	57	112	121	2,816	2,730	5,968
International Organizations and Other Extraterritorial Institutions	41	57	67	248	464	640
Water Transportation	22	18	9	445	129	385
Domestic Services	164	129	38	194	216	70
Total Establishments in Services	175,909	231,766	257,172	2,749,181	4,041,800	4,317,040
Total Establishments in all Activities with Formal Jobs	208,779	270,123	292,925	3,360,921	4,873,339	4,903,449
Participation of Trade and Services in Formal Jobs	84%	86%	88%	82%	83%	88%

SOURCE: Based on the RAIS and CAGED databases, Ministério da Economia, http://bi.mte.gov.br/bgcaged/, accessed November 25, 2019.

the five largest commercial banks account for two-thirds of the national market. The capital itself has three of the six largest branch networks in the country and the three largest national banking groups, Bradesco, Itaú, and Unibanco. Except for HSBC, which maintained its headquarters in Curitiba, all major private banks, national and foreign, have headquarters and main operations centered in the capital city of São Paulo.[35] Considering all public and private banks and entities, São Paulo accounts for between 80% and 90% of branches, jobs offered, deposits, assets, and loans.

Also in São Paulo are located the main entities representing the financial market and services to that sector, including Febraban (Brazilian Federation of Banking Associations), Andima (National Association of Financial Market Institutions), CETIP (Chamber of Custody and Settlement), ABBI (Brazilian Association of International Banks), and ABBC (Brazilian Association of Banks). This concentration process also occurred with the stock exchanges and the commodities and futures exchanges. As of 1964, with the new capital market legislation, the Rio de Janeiro stock exchange (BVRJ) and the São Paulo stock exchange (BVSP) were reorganized, and numerous regional exchanges emerged. Brokerage firms grew significantly, in part because of the increasing quantity of stock transactions, but mainly due to the dynamic public debt market.

For many years, the São Paulo and Rio de Janeiro stock exchanges divided the market. But during the 1990s, the Rio de Janeiro exchange lost importance in secondary stock market transactions, with the São Paulo exchange accounting for 95% of such transactions in the second half of the 1990s. This situation justified the signing of an exchange integration agreement, keeping the São Paulo stock exchange as the exclusive center of transactions for the secondary stock market. This concentration of operations made BVSP the largest trading center for shares in Latin America.[36] Something similar happened in the futures market. In 1985, the Bolsa Mercantil & de Futuros (BM&F) was created, with operations essentially in the financial market. In 1991 this was combined with the traditional São Paulo stock exchange, which has existed since the beginning of the twentieth century. Since its foundation, BM&F has become the fundamental market for companies and institutional investors, as it is allowed to carry out transactions involving derivatives, particularly with currencies and interest rates. In 1997, by an operational agreement, the Brazilian Futures Exchange, headquartered in Rio de Janeiro, joined BM&F, concentrating all transactions with commodities and derivatives in the latter institution. The growth of this market was exceptional, and today BM&F is the largest futures and options exchange in Latin America.[37]

The concentration process also took place in other areas of the financial market. The capital of São Paulo was the location of the main Brazilian insurance companies, with four of the five largest insurance companies in the country based there. Regardless of the location of their production units, several large business groups maintain some fundamental areas of business management (financial, commercial, technological, etc.) in the city of São Paulo, due to its importance as a market, as a business center, and as the hub for business service providers. Large law firms, accounting and auditing companies, human resources advisory companies, advertising and marketing agencies, and companies related to corporate communication and information technology, among others, tend to be located in the city of São Paulo. Of the twenty largest advertising companies in the country, for example, only the nineteenth-largest is located outside São Paulo. Of the fifty largest companies in the IT sector, thirty are located in the capital of São Paulo and seven others in its surrounding municipalities. Nine of the ten largest magazine publishers are in the capital, as are three of the top five newspapers and seven of the ten largest book publishers.[38] Most large international auditing and consulting companies operate in São Paulo.[39] The capital also hosts many services related to national and international travel and attracts a high percentage of business travelers.[40] For this reason there was a major expansion in the hotel business.[41]

Along with banking, the city of São Paulo is also the most important center for health services in the country. The city is home to an important health technology center, with a nationally and internationally renowned hospital and medical complex, which has a major impact on the local economy. Public clinics and hospitals in the city are responsible for the largest number of low-, medium-, and high-complexity outpatient procedures in the country, as well as the largest number of SUS (national health service) hospitalizations.[42] According to the National Agency of Supplementary Health (ANS), there are seventy Brazilian hospitals with accreditation granted by ONA, CBA, IQG, and DNV. Of these, thirty-five are located in the state of São Paulo, thirty-one in the Metropolitan Region of São Paulo, and twenty-four in the city of São Paulo. This shows the importance of the city in high-quality health care, for which it is the main center in Brazil and one of the most important in Latin America. In fact, in an evaluation of the fifty-eight best hospitals in Latin America, sixteen were Brazilian, and of those ten are located in the city of São Paulo.[43]

In this new service economy women did extremely well. A breakdown of formal workers by sex and by major category of employment shows that women dominated the medical and health professions and were more than

TABLE 8.12

Distribution of Workers in the Formal Sector of the Capital by Sex in 2018

Municipality of São Paulo	Total	Men	Women	% women
Administrative, Technical, Professional	1,050,848	611,826	439,022	42%
Public Administration	749,008	318,013	430,995	58%
Hotels, Accommodations and Tourism Etc.	571,065	256,763	314,302	55%
Retail Business	661,218	351,650	309,568	47%
Veterinarians, Dentists, and Doctors	318,810	84,001	234,809	74%
Financial Institutions	192,774	88,760	104,014	54%
Wholesale	211,416	126,110	85,306	40%
Transport and Communications	288,739	222,295	66,444	23%
Textile Industry	69,341	25,463	43,878	63%
Food and Drinks	71,504	34,266	37,238	52%
Chemical Industry	66,235	40,030	26,205	40%
Construction	216,257	190,774	25,483	12%
Paper and Graphics	36,506	21,985	14,521	40%
Mechanical Industry	35,055	26,978	8,077	23%
Metallurgical industry	36,215	29,709	6,506	18%
Public Utility Service	29,210	23,581	5,629	19%
Electric and Communications	15,364	10,317	5,047	33%
Transport Material	19,205	15,992	3,213	17%
Agriculture	5,357	3,820	1,537	29%
Non-Metallic Mineral Products	6,466	4,969	1,497	23%
Mineral Extraction	1,489	1,129	360	24%
Footwear Industry	693	453	240	35%
Total	4,903,449	2,583,222	2,320,227	47%

SOURCE: Using IBGE Subsector Divisions, found at http://bi.mte.gov.br/bgcaged/.

half the workers in public administration, banking, hotel and lodgings, and food and drinks. In short, they were well represented in the service sectors that were the largest employers in the capital (see Table 8.12).

Examining the labor market in a more refined way also shows the growing quality and importance of the service industry in the capital. Thus the city and the metropolitan region had twice the share of company directors and managers than was the norm in the rest of the country, as well as a very much higher share of scientists and intellectual professionals. It even had more midlevel managers in proportion to the total labor force than was the norm in Brazil (see Table 8.13).

This shift to a primarily services-oriented city is also reflected in educational levels in the capital. While the population of the capital differed little from the country as a whole in the proportion of those who had completed a primary education or a secondary degree, a major difference was that fewer persons with little or no education were located in the capital. Also the capital had a far higher number of tertiary education graduates than was

TABLE 8.13

Persons 14 Years of Age and Older, Employed in the Week of Reference, by Employment Status and Social Security Contributor for Brazil, the Metropolitan Region of São Paulo, and the Capital, 3rd Trimester 2019

Level of Skill	Brazil	RMSP	Capital
Directors and Managers	4.5%	7.6%	8.7%
Scientists and Intellectuals	11.2%	16.0%	18.9%
Midlevel Technicians and Professionals	7.8%	9.8%	10.1%
Administrative Support Workers	8.2%	9.8%	9.3%
Service workers, Tradespeople, and Markets	22.8%	22.3%	22.6%
Skilled Workers in Agriculture, Forestry, Hunting, and Fishing	6.0%	0.3%	0.1%
Skilled Workers, Construction Workers, and Artisans, Mechanical and Other Crafts	13.2%	12.0%	10.0%
Plant and Machine Operators and Assemblers	8.4%	8.5%	7.2%
Elementary Occupations	17.0%	13.2%	12.7%
Members of the Armed Forces, Police and Military Firefighters	0.9%	0.5%	0.4%
Total	100.0%	100.0%	100.0%
Number of Workers (in Thousands)	**93,801**	**10,858**	**6,322**

SOURCE: IBGE, SIDRA, table 5435.

the norm in the nation (see Table 8.14). This well reflected the increasing importance of professionals and well educated workers in the expanding service economy of the capital in this period.

In this respect woman appear to be better prepared for working in the service industry by having a higher level of education than men: 44% of the women in the formal labor force had at least some university or other tertiary education, compared to only 30% of the men (see Table 8.15).

The high levels of women with advanced education in the capital is also reflected in changing patterns of the age of mothers giving birth. As more women get advanced education and enter the professions, they are more likely to delay births and marriages. While in the earlier years of the demographic transition it was older women whose birth rate dropped most significantly (which meant that more births were to younger women), recently women in the capital are, as in advanced countries, delaying childbirth to complete their education and to enter the labor force. In the period from 2003 to 2018 the cohort with the highest number of births shifted from 20–24-year-olds to 30–34-year-olds (see Figure 8.2). Yet for the nation as a whole in 2018, the peak age in terms of total number of births continued to be 20–24 years, which is what it had been for mothers in São Paulo some fifteen years earlier.

TABLE 8.14

Level of Education for Persons 10 Years of Age and Older by Sex, Brazil and the Capital of São Paulo, 2010

Brazil	Total	Men	Women
No Education or Fundamental Incomplete	38.6%	43.3%	32.2%
Fundamental Complete and Middle School Incomplete	17.9%	18.5%	17.0%
Middle School Complete and Higher Education incomplete	30.8%	28.4%	34.1%
High Education Completed	12.7%	9.8%	16.8%
Total Educational Level Known	100.0%	100.0%	100.0%
(N)	85,974,841	49,618,496	36,356,345
Capital of São Paulo			
No Education or Fundamental Incomplete	25.9%	28.1%	23.5%
Fundamental Complete and Middle Incomplete	17.7%	18.5%	16.8%
Middle School Complete and Higher Education Incomplete	33.2%	32.5%	34.0%
Higher Education Completed	23.1%	20.9%	25.7%
Total Educational Level Known	100.0%	100.0%	100.0%
(N)	5,497,275	2,938,423	2,558,852

SOURCE: IBGE, SIDRA, table 3577.

TABLE 8.15

Level of Education of Workers in the Formal Sector by Sex in the Capital, 2018

Level of Education	Men	Women
Illiterate	4,906	1,660
Up to Fifth Incomplete	45,767	15,831
Fifth Completed Elementary	52,153	24,074
Sixth to Ninth Elementary	106,238	52,539
Elementary Completed	220,063	121,986
Secondary Incomplete	153,464	87,256
Secondary Completed	1,214,894	987,954
Tertiary Incomplete	101,084	111,191
Tertiary Complete	658,858	894,190
Master's	16,878	15,863
Doctorate	8,917	7,683
Total	2,583,222	2,320,227

SOURCE: http://bi.mte.gov.br/bgcaged/.

Along with social and economic changes, the growth of São Paulo into a world metropolis has led to a reconfiguration of the city's spatial organization, a process that has not yet ended. Due to the size and importance of industry in the capital, wide areas were dedicated to industrial activities, and while the process of converting these for alternative uses better suited to a

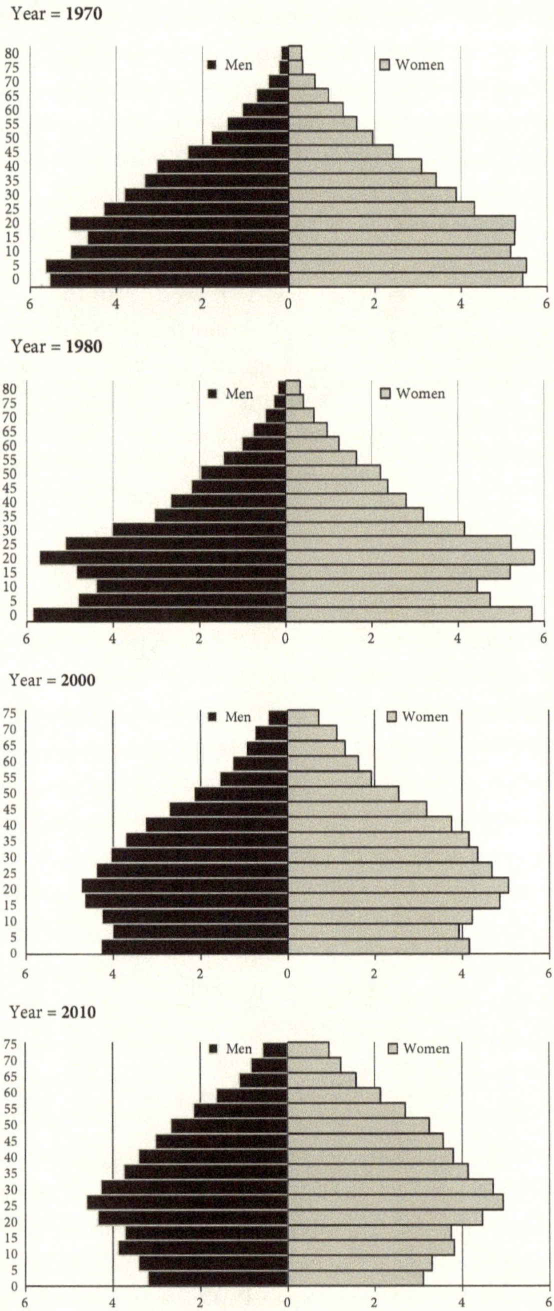

Figure 8.2. Population Pyramids, Municipality of São Paulo, 1970-2010

SOURCE: IBGE, SIDRA, table 200.

services-oriented economy has been taking place since the 1980s, many of these old factory areas have not yet been adequately reconfigured. This did not affect the capital so much since it quickly became the financial, commercial, and financial center not only of the metropolitan region and the state but also of the nation. The municipalities of the metropolitan region, however, were not so fortunate in their transition, as they were generally less able to integrate their former industrial zones into places adopted to modern services.

But even within the limits of the city there have been major changes in population density, living arrangements, and the organization of key subdistricts and their respective economies. In the central area and adjacent districts there has been both growth and decline. Thus despite their excellent infrastructure, the neighborhoods that surrounded the historic center have declined, suffering a long period of stagnation and disinterest on the part of the real estate market. The opposite occurred in the expanded center—the region between the Pinheiros and Tietê Rivers (see Map 8.4). This expanded center is undergoing an intense process of transformation, with single-family houses replaced by vertical residential or office buildings. Many of the older as well as the new services are concentrated in this area of intense urban transformation. This replacement process often results in a reduction in the density of occupation of these areas due to the construction of high rise buildings.[44] In contrast, the remaining forty-three peripheral districts have become more densely populated, even though they lack adequate infrastructure and public services (see Table 8.16).

One of the most problematic issues in the city of São Paulo is physical mobility. The city has a low density, and its population is spread over areas unequally provided with occupational opportunities, requiring long travel between areas of population concentration and the concentration of jobs. This situation puts great pressure on the public transport system. Unfortunately, the modern high-capacity rail system is modest for the requirements of a city like São Paulo. There are three alternative and integrated systems. There is the system of metropolitan trains, which was built from the traditional railway system implanted in São Paulo to move coffee to the coast. This system was gradually converted into a modern suburban metropolitan train system, which currently has adequate facilities. This system is 270 km in length, with 94 stations, and serves 23 municipalities. It transports about 3 million passengers per day. The city also has a metro system, which exclusively serves the area of the city of São Paulo. Unfortunately, this network is rather limited given the needs of the city. Today the metro system has only 101 km of track and 89 stations, and transports more than 5 million

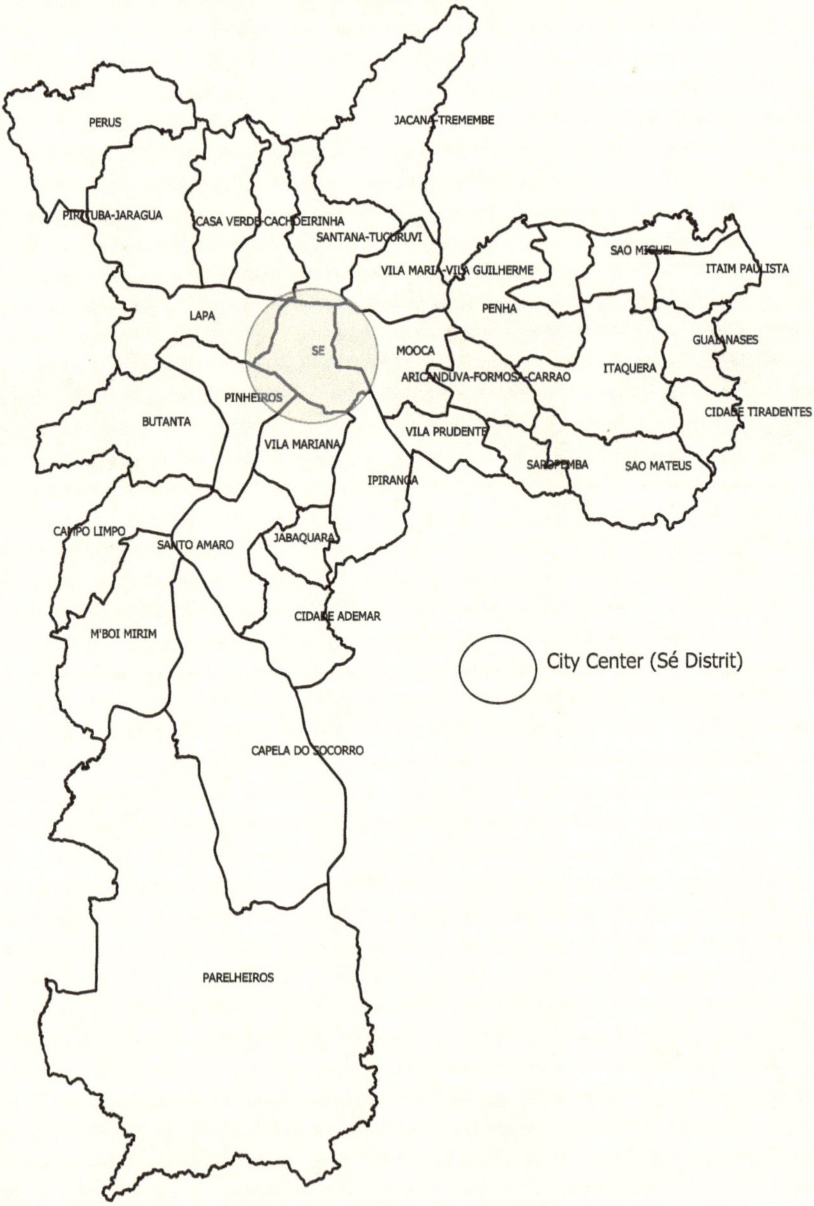

Map 8.4. Districts (Subprefeituras) of the Capital

SOURCE: Geosampa, Prefeitura de São Paulo.

TABLE 8.16

Population of the Capital and the Municipalities of the Metropolitan Region of São Paulo, 2018

	Area (km²)	Population 2018	Density (persons/ km²)	Annual Growth Rate (2010–2018)(1)	PIB 2016 (R$ 1000)	Distance from São Paulo
Metropolitan Region of São Paulo	7,947	21,571,281	2,714	1.2	1,107,867,636	
City of São Paulo	**1,521**	**12,176,866**	**8,005**	**1.0**	**687,035,889**	
Arujá	96	88,455	920	2.1	4,730,400	45
Biritiba-Mirim	317	32,251	102	1.5	738,495	79
Ferraz de Vasconcelos	30	191,993	6,494	1.7	2,859,009	45
Guararema	271	29,451	109	1.7	1,427,047	79
Guarulhos	319	1,365,899	4,286	1.4	53,974,919	16
Itaquaquecetuba	83	366,519	4,436	1.6	6,507,690	36
Mogi das Cruzes	713	440,769	619	1.6	14,426,294	57
Poá	17	116,530	6,750	1.2	4,343,585	42
Salesópolis	425	17,022	40	1.1	196,020	101
Santa Isabel	363	56,792	156	1.5	1,238,723	61
Suzano	206	294,638	1,429	1.5	9,468,888	44
Subtotal Eastern Region	2,840	3,000,319	1,057	1.5	99,911,072	
Caieiras	98	100,129	1,025	1.8	2,706,457	38
Cajamar	131	75,638	576	2.1	13,020,610	41
Francisco Morato	49	174,008	3,551	1.5	1,372,211	48
Franco da Rocha	133	152,433	1,148	1.9	2,460,082	47
Mairiporã	321	98,374	307	2.5	1,639,191	37
Subtotal Northern Region	732	600,582	821	1.9	21,198,551	
Barueri	66	271,306	4,129	1.5	47,088,302	30
Carapicuíba	35	398,611	11,539	1.0	5,214,113	26
Itapevi	83	234,352	2,835	2.0	12,147,662	40
Jandira	17	123,481	7,077	1.7	3,419,632	34
Osasco	65	696,850	10,728	0.6	74,402,691	22
Pirapora do Bom Jesus	108	18,604	171	2.1	268,354	55
Santana de Parnaíba	180	136,517	759	2.9	8,485,338	40
Subtotal Western Region	554	1,879,721	3,395	1.2	151,026,091	
Diadema	31	420,934	13,697	1.1	13,229,745	21
Mauá	62	468,148	7,562	1.5	13,963,846	27
Ribeirão Pires	99	122,607	1,238	1.0	3,021,839	55
Rio Grande da Serra	36	50,241	1,382	1.7	578,087	50
Santo André	176	716,109	4,074	0.7	25,837,046	24
São Bernardo do Campo	410	833,240	2,035	1.1	42,131,380	19
São Caetano do Sul	15	160,275	10,454	0.9	13,286,711	14
Subtotal Southeast Region	829	2,771,554	3,344	1.0	112,048,654	
Cotia	324	244,694	755	2.5	10,991,458	31
Embu das Artes	70	270,843	3,847	1.5	10,004,647	27
Embu-Guaçu	156	68,856	442	1.2	1,063,716	49
Itapecerica da Serra	151	173,672	1,152	1.6	3,853,304	34
Juquitiba	522	31,235	60	1.1	442,469	72
São Lourenço da Serra	186	15,667	84	1.4	196,331	54
Taboão da Serra	20	285,570	14,007	2.0	8,350,023	30
Vargem Grande Paulista	42	51,702	1,217	2.3	1,745,432	44
Subtotal Southwest Region	1,472	1,142,239	776	1.8	36,647,378	

SOURCE: https://emplasa.sp.gov.br/RMSP, accessed January 20, 2010.

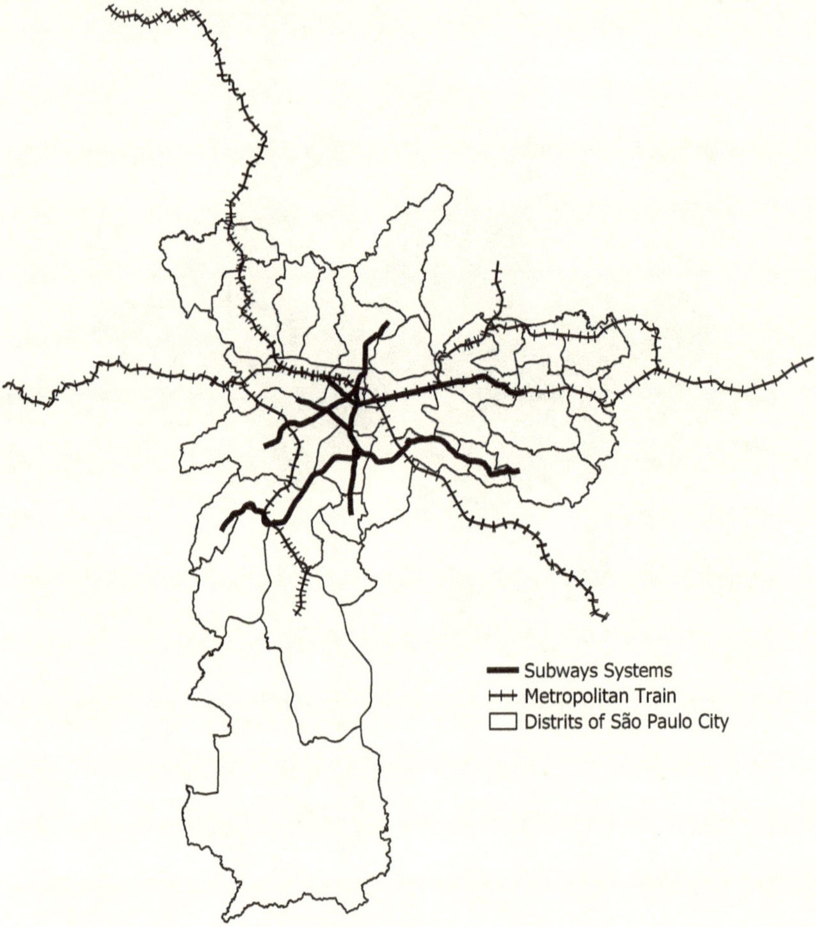

Map 8.5. Metropolitan Train, Bus, and Subway Systems, Municipality of São Paulo, 2017

SOURCE: Geosampa, Prefeitura de São Paulo.

passengers daily (see Map 8.5). Despite its limited size, the metro is one of the most efficient systems in terms of passengers transported per km of track. In addition, it is modern and of excellent quality. The third system is the extensive urban bus network that serves the city, which offers lower quality of services, as it operates on congested roads, which limit the speed of the system. This system uses approximately 15,000 buses and carries approximately 8 million passengers per day. The city has established 500 km

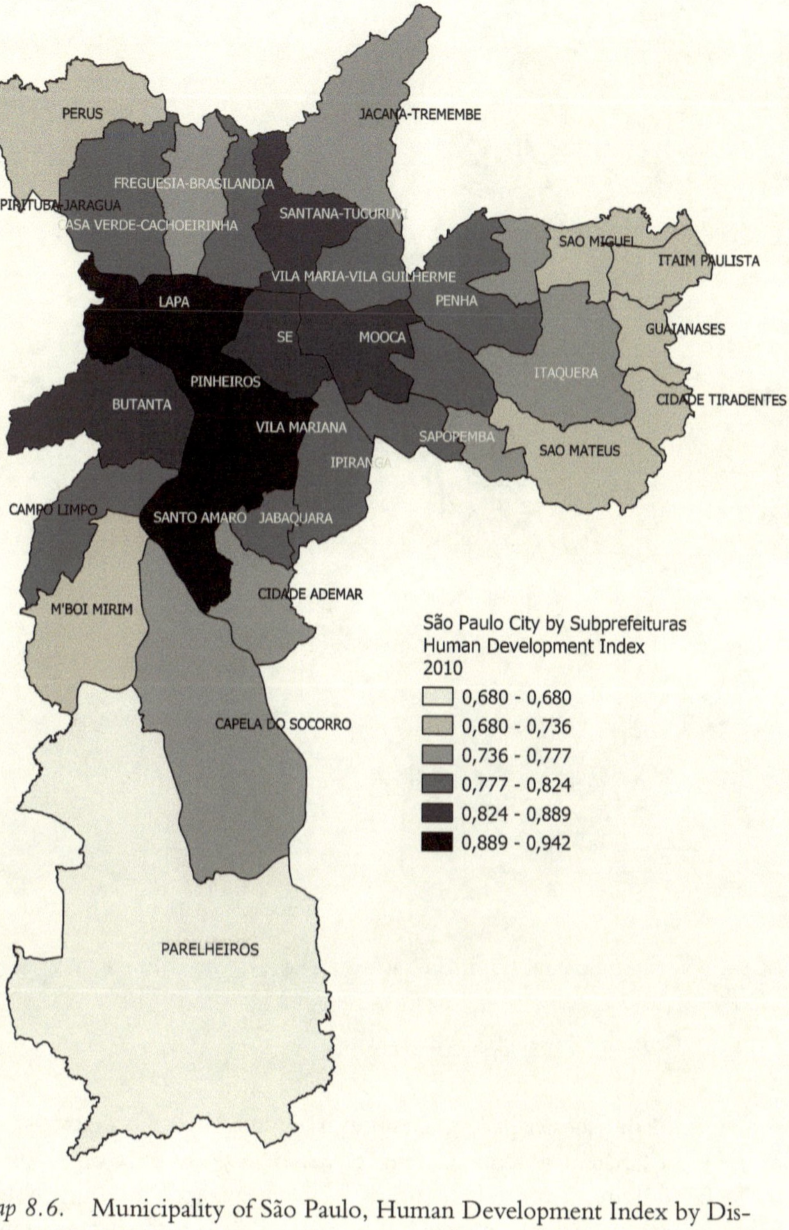

Map 8.6. Municipality of São Paulo, Human Development Index by District (Subprefeitura), 2010

SOURCE: Prefeitura de São Paulo, Geosampa, Informes Urbanos no. 29, November 2017.

of exclusive bus lanes with stations on major highways, and 132 kilometers of bus lanes which use regular bus stops on the side of the road.[45]

Like any city, the capital's different income groups reside in different districts of the city. Using the minimum wages standard (MW) per household of the population of the city of São Paulo in 2010, this division is evident. A quarter of the families received up to 2 MW, 36% received from 2 to 5 MW, 21% between 5 and 10 MW and 18% more than 10 MW. The distribution of these families within the city was quite unequal. Areas such as Pinheiros, Vila Mariana, Santo Amaro, and Lapa had more than two-thirds of households with an average household income greater than 10 MW; on the other hand, peripheral areas such as Cidade Tiradentes, Parelheiros, Guaianases, Itaim Paulista, M'Boi Mirim, and Perus had less than a fifth of households in this income range. In the latter regions, about 40% of households declared household income of up to 2 MW. These residential differences largely coincide with differences in UN's Human Development Index, which combines education, health, income, and other data to create an index of quality of life (lower numbers reflect lower classes, higher numbers reflect more elite groups). These data are shown for the subprefectures in the capital as of 2010 in Map 8.6. In 2017 the city of São Paulo listed 1,709 favelas or slums, comprising 391,000 households. Using the average number of people per household in the favelas in São Paulo in 2008, we can estimate that there were 1.6 million people living in these favelas in 2017, which would represent 14% of the city's population.

As the industrial growth of the capital slowed, its dynamic economy was moving with ever greater speed into service industries. With its traditional landed and industrial wealth, the capital soon became the nation's financial center, housing the leading banks and insurance companies and the most important stocks and futures markets. It was also the capital and its metropolitan region that had the best national universities and the leading hospitals and medical schools. The growth of tertiary education produced a large number of professionals of both sexes who filled the companies that the services industry and commerce supported. The city also was the earliest to revolutionize commercial activity, from establishing a major wholesale perishable food market, one of the largest in the world, to opening the biggest supermarkets and the first shopping centers and malls. All these superlatives did not prevent the city from having a serious housing and transportation problem, nor was it able to avoid the favelas which affected all the other cities of the nation. Despite having reasonably efficient state and city governments by Brazilian standards, it was still not able to keep pace with the extraordinary growth the metropolitan region and its capital experienced in this period. Whether any major city in the world could have done better when growth was at 5% per annum is another question. But at the end of the day the capital and the RMSP are today the single most important urban region in the nation, with a dynamism that has continued to distinguish Paulista development since the colonial period.

Conclusion

After almost four centuries of growth, the state of São Paulo has emerged as one of the most dynamic zones in Latin America. With an economy roughly the size of Portugal's or Finland's, it would be approximately the fifth-largest economy of Latin America if it was an independent country. Its dominant position within the nation emerged in the past two centuries as it became both the leading agricultural and industrial state of the union. In these three volumes on the Social and Economic History of the State since 1750,[1] we have explored the history and causal factors that led to this extraordinary growth of the state. First there was the association of the province with the dynamic mining economy of Minas Gerais, then the spread of coffee from Rio de Janeiro into the ever more fertile regions of the Paulista plains. The impact of African, European, Asian, and Brazilian migrations also provided a dynamism to the local population and its economy that allowed the state to develop a vibrant market economy.

While all the basic components were already in place by 1950, it was only in the last seventy years that all these factors finally produced the powerhouse that is the state today. The implantation of the auto industry in the state in the 1950s and 1960s created a basic heavy industry, which when added to the state's extensive light industry created an extraordinary industrial sector that dominated the national scene. It even developed a modern airplane industry unique in Latin America. Along with its increasing industrialization, there has been a massive change in the agricultural sector. The state's agriculture mechanized and modernized in this period, and developed a host of new products for national and international consumption, from sugar and ethanol to oranges and chickens, while still maintaining its leadership in coffee. Until the 2010s São Paulo remained the largest agricultural and industrial state in the nation. It was this wealth in industry and agriculture that permitted the state to emerge as the nation's leading center for services and commerce in the past several decades. Finally, even as industry has seen a relative decline, São Paulo has become the leading banking and financial state of the union.

It was this economic wealth that permitted the state government to invest in education, health, and social services to finally provide the population with the resources to experience major development in terms of schooling, health, and life expectancy. At the beginning of this period a major share of the state's population was illiterate, and average life expectancy was low by world standards. Today the population of São Paulo has indices of education and health close to the standards of most advanced countries of the world. Finally, the development of urban centers throughout the state has promoted the growth of a middle class in the state. For all this increase in education and the growth of a middle class, however, the income distribution has improved only modestly, and housing has remained a constant problem for the state government, as the continued existence of the favelas has shown.

Even more dramatic has been the change in basic social institutions. In the mid-twentieth century the state was still a traditional society in terms of marriage, the family, and religion. Seventy years later it has changed profoundly. Marriage is on the decline, consensual unions have increased, divorce is common, and the Catholic Church is heading toward minority status due to the rise of Pentecostal churches and an increasingly nonreligious population. For the first time in Brazilian history fertility has dramatically declined to close to or below replacement level as women have become even better educated then men and have moved massively into the labor market. In turn, the rise of divorce and consensual unions has profoundly changed such basic institutions as the family and household. Multigenerational family households have declined as unipersonal homes have increased. Although all these changes occurred throughout Brazil during these past seven decades, it was São Paulo and the other leading states of the Southeast and Southern regions which led this movement.

But for all its importance and dominant role in the society, the state of São Paulo is no longer as independent an actor as it was in the period from 1889 to 1930. Its fate is now determined as much in Brasília as it is in the municipality of São Paulo, This is especially the case as more and more of the other regions of the nation reach levels of education, income, and health similar to those of the Paulistas. The dynamism is still there and the leadership of its elite in the economic sphere is fully recognized, but it no longer exercises the political power it held in the past. Even its leadership in social trends is slowly declining as the nation adopts the same attitudes toward births and marriages. The old Belíndia bifurcation of the country is slowly disappearing as formerly poorer regions like the Center-West and the North increase their wealth and well-being to levels comparable to those of São Paulo. Thus the state no longer stands out as dramatically as it did in earlier decades, which is a long-term positive development. But it also means that in the future the country will become ever more like the state, and São Paulo will be just the strongest among equals.

NOTES

Chapter 1

1. See Sérgio Silva, *Expansão cafeeira e origens da indústria no Brasil* (São Paulo: Alfa-Omega, 1995); Joseph Love, *São Paulo in the Brazilian Federation, 1889–1937* (Stanford, CA: Stanford University Press, 1980); William R. Summerhill, *Order Against Progress: Government, Foreign Investment, and Railroads in Brazil, 1854–1913* (Stanford, CA: Stanford University Press, 2003); Flávio A. M. de Saes, *A grande empresa de serviços públicos* (São Paulo: Hucitec, 1986); Renato Monseff Perissinotto, *Estado e Capital Cafeeiro em São Paulo (1889–1930)* (São Paulo: Fapesp, 1999); Richard Graham, *Britain and the Onset of Modernization in Brazil 1850–1914* (Cambridge: Cambridge University Press, 1968).

2. Warren Dean, *The Industrialization of São Paulo, 1880–1945* (Austin: University of Texas Press, 1969).

3. Wilson Cano, *Raízes da concentração industrial em São Paulo* (São Paulo: Difel, 1977); Fernando Henrique Cardoso, "Condições sociais da industrialização: o caso de São Paulo," *Revista Brasiliense* 28 (March/April 1960): 31–46; Wilson Suzigan, *Indústria Brasileira. Origens e Desenvolvimento* (São Paulo: Brasiliense, 1986).

4. Ford, General Motors, Volkswagen, Mercedes-Benz, Scania, and Toyota were some of the manufacturers of trucks, cars, and buses established in São Paulo during that period.

5. IBGE, Estatísticas do Século XX, 2003, table "pop_S2T04."

6. IBGE, Censo 2010, table 1.4: "População nos Censos Demográficos, segundo Grandes Regiões e as Unidades da Federação," accessed May 25 2019, at https://censo2010.ibge.gov.br/sinopse/index.php?dados=4&uf=00.

7. José Francisco de Camargo, *Crescimento da População no Estado de São Paulo e seus Aspectos Econômicos*, 2 vols., Ensaios Econômicos no. 14 (São Paulo: IPE/USP, 1981).

8. On São Paulo industry in the mid-twentieth century, see Wilson Cano, *Raízes da concentração industrial em São Paulo* (São Paulo: Difel, 1977); Wilson Cano, *Desequilíbrios regionais e concentração industrial no Brasil, 1930–1995* (Campinas: Universidade Estadual de Campinas Instituto de Economia, 1998); Heitor Ferreira Lima, Morvan Dias de Figueiredo, Pereira Ignacio, Irmãos Jafet, Conde Matarazzo, Coronel Rodovalho, Roberto Simonsen, and Jorge

Street, *Evolução industrial de São Paulo: esboço histórico* (São Paulo: Martins, 1954); Henrique Rattner, *Industrialização e concentração econômica em São Paulo* (Rio de Janeiro: Fundação Getúlio Vargas, 1972).

9. Persons age 10 years and over, according to their main economic activity and their occupational position; 1950 census.

10. To compute numbers for Rio de Janeiro, we add the state of Rio de Janeiro and the Federal District, which today are defined as the state of Rio de Janeiro. When the national capital was transferred to Brasília, the former Federal District became the state of Guanabara. In 1975, the states of Guanabara and Rio de Janeiro merged, forming the current state of Rio de Janeiro.

11. There is a divergence between the figures presented for workers in the industry, age 10 years and over, which appear in the demographic census, and the data for industry workers, which appear in the industrial census, due to different criteria for selection. IBGE, Censo Demográfico, Série Nacional, volume I: XXII.

12. The "Metropolitan Mesoregion of São Paulo" should not be confused with the current "Metropolitan Region of São Paulo." The latter was created by Federal Complementary Law no. 14 of 1973, and then reorganized through State Complementary Law no. 1,139 in 2011. It currently comprises thirty-nine different municipalities and has a Development Council of a normative and deliberative nature. The "Metropolitan Mesoregion of São Paulo," used here, was the one adopted by IBGE. This mesoregion had forty-five municipalities, and contained all the municipalities of the current Metropolitan Region of São Paulo, in addition to six municipalities of the Baixada Santista.

13. The 1950 population census uses a classification of urban, suburban, and rural households. In the census methodology, urban and suburban areas are defined as the areas corresponding to cities (municipal headquarters) and towns (district headquarters). The rural area is defined as being outside the limits of cities and towns.

Chapter 2

1. On these debates, see Alexandre Macchione Saes, "A historiografia da industrialização brasileira," *Anais do 3º Seminário Nacional de História da Historiografia* (Ouro Preto, 2009).

2. Aníbal Vilella and Wilson Suzigan, *Política do governo e crescimento da economia brasileira, 1889–1945* (Rio de Janeiro: IPEA/INPES, 1973), 70.

3. Furtado emphasized the Great Depression as the key moment of the industrialization process, while Caio Prado gave great importance to World War I in this process. Celso Furtado, *Formação econômica do Brasil* (Rio de Janeiro: Paz e Terra, 1959), chaps. XXX–XXXII; Caio Prado Jr., *História econômica do Brasil* (São Paulo: Brasiliense, 1945), 266–267.

4. Warren Dean, *The Industrialization of São Paulo, 1880–1945* (Austin: University of Texas Press, 1969); Carlos Manuel Peláez, "A balança comercial, a grande depressão e a industrialização brasileira," *Revista Brasileira de Economia* 2, no. 1 (1968); Albert Fishlow, "Origens e consequências da substituição de importações no Brasil," *Estudos Econômicos* 2, no. 6 (1972): 7–75; Flávio Rabelo Versiani and Maria Teresa R. O. Versiani, "A industralização antes de 1930: Uma contribuição," *Estudos Econômicos* 5, no. 1 (1975): 37–63; Wilson Suzigan, *Indústria Brasileira. Origens e Desenvolvimento* (São Paulo: Brasiliense, 1986).

5. The importance of introducing wage labor, replacing the limited consumption that occurred under the slave labor regime, was highlighted by Fernando Henrique Cardoso, "Condições sociais da industrialização: o caso de São Paulo," *Revista Brasiliense* no. 28 (1960): 31–46.

6. These were the factors stressed by Roberto Simonsen, *Evolução industrial do Brasil e outros estudos* (São Paulo: Companhia Editora Nacional, 1939), 12. For an alternative position, see Carlos Manuel Pelaéz, "As consequências econômicas da ortodoxia monetária, cambial e fiscal no Brasil entre 1889–1945," *Revista Brasileira de Economia* 25, no. 3 (1971): 5–82.

7. Wilson Cano, *Raízes da concentração industrial em São Paulo* (Rio de Janeiro: DIFEL, 1977), 74–75; Anne G. Hanley, *Native Capital: Financial Institutions and Economic Development in São Paulo, Brazil, 1850–1920* (Stanford: Stanford University Press, 2005), chap. 4.

8. Stanley J. Stein, *The Brazilian Cotton Manufacture: Textile Enterprise in an Underdeveloped Area, 1850–1950* (Cambridge, MA: Harvard University Press, 1957); Suzigan, *Indústria Brasileira.*

9. IBGE, *Estatísticas retrospectivas*, volume 2, tomo 3: 26.

10. Paulo R. Pestana, "A indústria do vidro," *BDIC* 1928, no. 9 and no. 10: 199–202. Although the data represent only the capital of São Paulo, it seems that there were no other factories within the state.

11. Given the varied origin of capital in companies, and the frequency of domestic and foreign capital in the same company, it is difficult to determine whether the company was controlled by foreign capital. It is usually assumed that the company is foreign if it is predominantly controlled by foreign capital and/or if management is foreign.

12. *Recenseamento de 1920*, volume 5, parte 1a: XI.

13. The census shows that at the thirty-one textile factories in São Paulo in 1912, women constituted 72% of the approximately 9,500 workers; children of both sexes under 12 were 4% of the workers, and children under 16 accounted for 31% of the total. Joel Wolfe, *Working Women, Working Men: São Paulo and the Rise of Brazil's Industrial Working Class, 1900–1955* (Durham: Duke University Press, 1993), 8, table 1.1.

14. *Anuário Estatístico do Brasil, 1952*, 207.

15. Ipeadata, Regional, http://www.ipeadata.gov.br/Default.aspx; PIB Estadual preços básicos.

16. Ipeadata, Regional, accessed at http://www.ipeadata.gov.br/Default.aspx; PIB Estadual preços básicos.

17. Censo Demográfico de 1950, Série Nacional, volume III, tomo 1: 38.

18. The census of 1950 divided industry into three broad segments: extractive industry, manufacturing industry, and civil construction and public utilities. Within the state of São Paulo manufacturing predominated, with 92% of the total value of industrial production. The construction industry accounted for only 5% of this value, and the extractive industry was insignificant in the state.

19. On the government of Vargas, see Boris Fausto, *A Revolução de 1930: Historiografia e História* (São Paulo: Editora Brasiliense, 1970); Lira Neto, ed., *Getúlio Vargas*, 3 vols. (São Paulo: Companhia das Letras, 2006–2014); Sonia Draibe, *Rumos e Metamorfoses. Estado e Industrialização no Brasil: 1930–1960* (Rio de Janeiro: Paz e Terra, 1985); Pedro Paulo Zaluth Bastos and Pedro Cesar Dutra Fonseca, *A Era Vargas: Desenvolvimento, Economia e Sociedade* (São Paulo: Editora da UNESP, 2012); Maria Victoria de Mesquita Benevides, *O governo Kubitschek. Desenvolvimento Econômico e Estabilidade Política* (Rio de Janeiro: n.p., 1977).

20. Carlos Lessa, *Quinze anos de política econômica* (São Paulo: Brasiliense/UNICAMP, 1975), 14.

21. On this topics, see Carlos Manuel Peláez and Wilson Suzigan, *História Monetária do Brasil* (Brasília: Universidade de Brasília, 1981), 267–258; L. Orenstein and A. C. Sochaczewski, "Democracia com Desenvolvimento: 1956–1961," in Marcelo de Paiva Abreu, ed., *A ordem do Progresso* (Rio de Janeiro: Editora Campus, 1992), 171–212.

22. On the role of the military as a "moderating power" in this period, see Benevides, *O governo Kubitschek. Desenvolvimento Econômico e Estabilidade Política*, 170–171.

23. In 1961, Brazilian crude oil production reached 95 barrels per day and refined oil production reached 308 barrels per day. Electricity generation capacity increased from 3.5 million kW to 4.77 million kW.

24. Between 1956 and 1961 the federal highway system went from 20,000 kilometers to 35,000 kilometers, and paved federal highways went from 2,800 kilometers to 9,600 kilometers. IBGE, *Anuário Estatísticos do Brasil, 1957*, 147; IBGE, *Anuário Estatístico do Brasil, 1962*, 111.

25. For a useful review of this government automobile policy and its evolution, see Joel Wolfe, *Autos and Progress: The Brazilian Search for Modernity* (New York: Oxford University Press, 2010), chap. 5.

26. Luiz Bias Bahia and Edson Paulo Domingues, *Estrutura de inovações na indústria automobilística brasileira* (Brasília: IPEA, 2010), TD no. 1472, p. 9.

27. The relocation of the capital to the central region of the country was a goal of the government since the first republican constitution of 1891. However, it was only in Juscelino's administration that the decision to build Brasília was made. Construction began in 1956, and in 1960 the federal capital was moved from Rio de Janeiro to Brasília, although the transfer of the central administration was not completed until 1970. The construction of Brasília was widely criticized at the time because of its high cost.

28. Ana Cláudia Caputo and Hildete Pereira de Melo, "A industrialização brasileira nos anos de 1950: Uma análise da Instrução 111 da Sumoc," *Estudos Econômicos* 39, no. 3 (2009): 513–538.

29. Rosane de Almeida Maia, "Estado e industrialização no Brasil: estudo dos incentivos ao setor privado nos quadros do Programa de Metas do Governo Kubitschek," MA thesis, FEA-USP, São Paulo, 1986.

30. The Law of Usury (decree no. 22,626) was promulgated on April 7, 1933. The government bond market would not be established until the late 1960s, with the introduction of monetary correction, which would preserve the real value of long-term securities.

31. In October 1958, an attempt was made to implement the Monetary Stabilization Program (PEM), whose targets were strictly monetary and fiscal. However, the program faced strong opposition. The lack of objective conditions for its implementation led to the resignation of the minister of finance, who was replaced by the president of Banco do Brasil, as was the custom at the time.

32. Relatório SUMOC, in Carlos Lessa, *Quinze anos de política econômica* (São Paulo: Brasiliense/UNICAMP, 1975), 34–37.

33. Wolfe, *Autos and Progress*, 120–121; Flávio Limoncic, "The Brazilian Automotive Industry in International Context: From European to American Crisis," paper presented in the New Perspectives on Latin American and US Noon Lectures Series, University of Michigan, January 2009. On the evolution of the industry, including an analysis of the car models produced in Brazil, see Ramon de Lima Brandão, "O automóvel no Brasil entre 1955 e 1961: a invenção de novos imaginários na era JK," MA thesis, Universidade Federal de Juiz de Fora, 2011.

34. To benefit from the incentives offered, projects had to be approved by the GEIA (Executive Group of the Automotive Industry) and were required to include a vehicle engine production factory as well as an assembly plant, as well as use a given percentage of domestically produced parts for the cars. Marcos Lopez Rego and José E. M. Faillace Jr., "O projeto de implantação da indústria automotiva no Brasil: por uma abordagem sob a ótica da Teoria dos Stakeholders," *O&S—Salvador* 24, no. 81 (2017): 230.

35. The GEIA vigorously supported the development of a horizontally structured industry with complete subcontracting resources. Flávio Limoncic,

"A civilização do automóvel: a instalação da indústria automobilística no Brasil e a via brasileira para uma improvável modernidade fordista, 1956–1961," MA thesis, UFRJ, 1997, 96, 98–99.

36. In 1963 the famous Rodovia Rio–Bahia was inaugurated, with 1,621 paved kilometers. See http://memoria.bn.br/DocReader/Hotpage/HotpageBN.aspx?bib=348970_06&pagfis=8410&url=http://memoria.bn.br/docreader. The Rio–Bahia would be fundamental for the integration of the national market, and it also served as the main route for migrants from the northeast traveling to the south of the country (the so-called *pau-de-arara*, or migrants arriving in trucks). Marco Antonio Villa, *Quando eu vim-me embora: História da migração nordestina para São Paulo* (São Paulo: Leya, 2017).

37. Antonio Carlos Accorsi, "Estado e grupos econômicos: a política de expansão rodoviária no Brasil a partir de 1930," MA thesis, EAESP/FGV, 1996; Dilma Andrade de Paula, "Estado, sociedade e hegemonia do rodoviarismo no Brasil," *Revista Brasileira de História da Ciência* (Rio de Janeiro) 3, no. 2 (2010): 142–156; José Barat, "O setor transporte na economia brasileira," *Revista de Administração Pública* (Rio de Janeiro) 2, no. 4 (1968): 117–166.

38. On the origins and development of the Fábrica Nacional de Motores, see Wolfe, *Autos and Progress*, 107, 121; "Autos (FNM)," FGV CPDOC, http://www.fgv.br/CPDOC/ACERVO/dicionarios/verbete-tematico/fabrica-nacional-de-motores-fnm, accessed August 23, 2019; Eduardo Nazareth Paiva, "Fábrica Nacional de Motores (FNM): Historiando e considerando a ideia de um contra-laboratório na indústria automotiva brasileira," paper presented at ANPUH—XXIII Simpósio Nacional de História, Londrina, 2005, at https://anpuh.org.br/uploads/anais-simposios/pdf/2019-01/1548206371_9f108591a8d1659248649711aac58ad2.pdf, accessed August 23, 2019.

39. Vemag began in 1945 as a distributor of Studebaker cars. The motto of Vemag was "Brazilians produce cars for Brazil." The phrase was a bit ironic since on November 19, 1956, the company began producing the DKW-Vemag Universal van, which was a copy of the model made by Auto-Union in Germany. Glaucia Garcia, "A história da fábrica da DKW Vemag," *São Paulo Antiga*, http://www.saopauloantiga.com.br/vemag-uma-fabrica-que-agoniza-no-tempo/, accessed August 24, 2019.

40. For the history of Simca do Brasil, see https://falandodegestao.com/2012/06/18/a-historia-da-simca-do-brasil/, accessed August 23, 2019.

41. Mercedes-Benz do Brasil and Simca do Brasil both had Brazilian capital. WOB, FNM, and Scania-Vabis had both Brazilian and foreign investors. Wolfe, *Autos and Progress*, 141.

42. Clube do Fordinho, at http://www.clubedofordinho.com.br/si/site/0058/p/Hist%C3%B3rico%20da%20Ford%20Brasil, accessed August 24, 2019.

43. GM Notícias, https://media.gm.com/media/br/pt/chevrolet/news.detail.html/content/Pages/news/br/pt/2015/jan/0126-1925.html, accessed August 24, 2019.

44. Imprensa Volkswagen, http://vwbr.com.br/ImprensaVW/page/Historia.aspx, accessed August 24, 2019.

45. Toyota do Brasil, https://www.toyota.com.br/mundo-toyota/sobre-a-toyota/, accessed August 24, 2019.

46. Merce-denco, http://merce-denco.blogspot.com/2012/10/l-312-o-caminhao-que-deu-inicio-saga-da.html, accessed August 24, 2019.

47. See Pasquale Petrone, "A cidade de São Paulo no século XX," *Revista de História* 10, nos. 21–22 (1955): 127–170.

48. Joaquim Miguel Couto, "Entre estatais e transnacionais: o polo industrial de Cubatão," PhD thesis, Campinas, UNICAMP, 2003, 47–49.

49. A critique of this new syndicalism that challenges its rejection of earlier populist labor movements in the ABC districts is found in John D. French, *The Brazilian Workers' ABC: Class Conflict and Alliances in Modern São Paulo* (Chapel Hill: University of North Carolina Press, 1992)

50. Labor legislation stipulated stability after ten years of work in a job. This norm, while on the one hand conferring greater stability on employment, made the labor relationship rigid, hampering the progress of capitalist relations in urban areas. The stability mechanism was replaced by the Fundo de Garantia por Tempo de Serviço (FGTS), which had a monthly allowance deposited in the name of the worker and which constituted an important institutional fund for financing housing and sanitation.

51. See Herbert S. Klein and Francisco Vidal Luna, *Brazil: The Military Regimes of Latin America in the Cold War* (New Haven: Yale University Press, 2017), chaps. 3 and 4.

52. Marcelo Badaró Mattos, *Trabalhadores e sindicatos no Brasil* (São Paulo: Editora Expressão Popular, 2009), 101–102. Even in this period of violent repression two historic strikes occurred, one in Contagem (Minas Gerais) and the other in Osasco (São Paulo), both in 1968, both strongly repressed with violence by the police forces. An overview of the trade union movement in São Paulo can be seen in Alessandro Moura, "Movimento Operário e sindicalismo em Osasco, São Paulo e ABC Paulista: Rupturas e descontinuidades," PhD thesis, UNVESP, Marília, 2015.

53. The resurgence of this new syndicalism had major repercussions in the ABC region and in the so-called opposition movement. The Sindicato dos Metalurgicos of São Paulo had strong support from segments of the Catholic Church. Iram Jácome Rodrigues, "Igreja e movimento operário nas origens do novo sindicalismo no Brasil (1964–1978)," *História, Questões & Debates* (Curitiba) 29 (1998): 25–58. Because of its more combative origins, the new syndicalism was also known as "authentic syndicalism."

54. Under the direction of the São Bernardo and Diadema Metalworkers' Union, headed by Luiz Inácio Lula da Silva, the workers decided not to participate in the annual wage negotiations, denouncing the negotiations as a farce, since wage law limited readjustments. After determining the rate of

adjustment, the workers of some companies, starting with Scania, decided to stop the machines and remain in the factory. This form of protest spread to other factories in the ABC region and other cities in São Paulo, representing a milestone in the new trade unionism. https://cnmcut.org.br/noticias/abc-de-luta-historia-do-sindicato-agora-em-nova-roupagem-fa08

55. This act was a defining moment in the struggle for redemocratization, with the participation of representatives of civil society and the consolidation of Lula's position as one of the main national leaders.

56. On the influence of the Catholic Church on the formation of the PT, see Adriano Henriques Machado, "A influência dos setores católicos na formação do Partido dos Trabalhadores: da relação com os movimentos sociais à ideia de formar um novo partido," *ANPUH–XXV Simpósio Nacional de História, 2009* (Fortaleza), http://anais.anpuh.org/wp-ontent/uploads/mp/pdf/ANPUH.S25.0956.pdf, accessed November 11, 2017.

57. Roberto Antonio Iannone, "A evolução do setor elétrico paulista," PhD thesis, FFLCHUSP, 2006.

58. Iannone, "A evolução do setor elétrico paulista," 29. It should be recalled that the Brazilian electrical system was then not interconnected, as it is today. Thus, the demand for electric energy had to be met by regional production. The government of the state of São Paulo played a fundamental role in meeting demand through massive public investment.

59. In 1925, the city of São Paulo experienced electricity rationing. Due to this 1925 energy crisis, São Paulo Light began the construction of the largest hydroelectric dam in the country, the Cubatão Plant. Joaquim Miguel Couto, "Entre estatais e transnacionais: o polo industrial de Cubatão," PhD thesis, UNICAMP, 2003, 41.

60. The Canadian company had been looking for new sources of energy since 1911, and in 1923, its engineer Asa Billings designed the Serra do Cubatão hydroelectric project, which was considered an unprecedented work in the country's engineering history. Couto, "Entre estatais e transnacionais: o polo industrial de Cubatão," 41; Antonio Augusto da Costa Faria, "A Light e a utilização dos recursos hidrícos da Bacia do Tietê para a geração de energia elétrica," http://arquivos.ambiente.sp.gov.br/cea/2011/12/AntonioAugusto.pdf.

61. Iannone, "A evolução do setor elétrico paulista," 79.

62. Centrais Elétricas de São Paulo S.A. (CESP) was created through the merger of five state companies, Paranapanema Power Plants (USELPA), Rio Pardo Hydroelectric Company (CHERP), Urubupungá SA (CELUSA), Paraibuna Improvements Company (COMEPA), and Bandeirante de Eletricidade SA (BELSA), and six other companies that were formally private but already controlled by state companies. They were S.A. Rio Claro Power Plant (SACERC) and its associates Mogi Mirim S.A. Light and Power Company, Jacutinga S.A. Light and Power Company, and Mogi Guaçu S.A. Improvement

Company, all controlled by CHERP, in addition to the Light and Power Company of Mogi Guaçu S.A. Tietê S. and Companhia Luz e Força de Tatuí, both controlled by BELSA. See http://www.cesp.com.br/portalCesp/portal.nsf/V03.02/Empresa_Historia?OpenDocument

63. Iannone, "A evolução do setor elétrico paulista," 58.

64. Couto, "Entre estatais e transnacionais: o polo industrial de Cubatão," 59. According to the author, the construction of the Santos–São Paulo Pipeline was included among the projects contained in the 1948 SALTE Plan. The construction and operation of the pipeline were awarded to the Santos-Jundiaí Railway. Such concession was justified because Santos-Jundiaí already carried 80% of the volume of liquid fuels received by the Port of Santos.

65. Couto, "Entre estatais e transnacionais: o polo industrial de Cubatão," 59.

66. Couto, "Entre estatais e transnacionais: o polo industrial de Cubatão," 78.

67. Petrobrás, http://www.petrobras.com.br/fatos-e-dados/refinaria-presidente-bernardes-completa-60-anos-de-atividades-em-cubatao.htm, accessed August 29, 2019.

68. Couto, "Entre estatais e transnacionais: o polo industrial de Cubatão," 113.

69. "It was intended to reach the production of 2.4 million tons / year of rolled products in 1960, with an increase of 1.4 million tons / year over the production of 1954." Maria Lucia Amarante de Andrade and Luiz Maurício da Silva Cunha, "O setor siderúrgico." BNDES, 22, https://web.bndes.gov.br/bib/jspui/bitstream/1408/13314/1/BNDES%2050%20Anos%20-%20Hist%C3%B3rias%20Setoriais_O%20Setor%20Siderurgico_P.pdf. See also Martinho Prado Uchoa, "A história da Cosipa," http://www.novomilenio.inf.br/cubatao/ch027.htm, accessed August 30, 2019.

70. Amarante de Andrade and da Silva Cunha, "O setor siderúrgico," 22.

71. Couto, "Entre estatais e transnacionais: o polo industrial de Cubatão," 118.

72. On Campinas, see Ulisses Cidade Semeghini, "Campinas (1860 a 1980): agricultura, industrialização e urbanização," MA thesis, UNICAMP, 1988; Ulisses Cidade Semeghini, "A região administrativa de Campinas," Fundação Seade, *São Paulo no Limiar do Século XX* (São Paulo) 8 (1992): 15–70. On Sorocaba, see Gustavo Zimmermann, "A região administrativa de Sorocaba," Fundação Seade, *São Paulo no Limiar do Século XX* (São Paulo) 8 (1992): 147–180; Andressa Celli, "Evolução urbana de Sorocaba," MA thesis, FAUUSP, São Paulo, 2012.

73. André Lara Resende, "Estabilização e reforma," in Marcelo de Paiva Abreu, ed., *A ordem do Progresso* (Rio de Janeiro: Editora Campus, 1992), 213–232; Mario Henrique Simonsen and Roberto Campos, *A nova economia brasileira* (Rio de Janeiro: José Olympio, 1979); Albert Fishlow, "Algumas

reflexões sobre a política brasileira após 1964," *Estudos Cebrap* 6 (1974); Mario Henrique Simonsen, *Inflação, gradualismo x tratamento de choque* (Rio de Janeiro: Apec, 1970); Paul Singer, *A crise do "Milagre"* (Rio de Janeiro: Paz e Terra, 1977); Antonio Delfim Netto, "Análise do comportamento recente da economia brasileira: diagnóstico," São Paulo, mimeo, 1967.

74. Ipeadata; IBGE/SCN: PIB, variação real anual e PIB da indústria de transformação, valor agregado, valor real anual.

75. The II PND projected an accumulated growth of 61% in GDP and 76% in industrial GDP between 1974 and 1979. Effective growth was on the order of 45% in the period—high, but with irregular behavior. See II Plano Nacional de Desenvolvimento (1975–1979), quadro 1, http://www.planalto.gov.br/ccivil_03/leis/1970-1979/anexo/ANL6151-74.PDF

76. On the Geisel period, see Antonio Barros de Castro and Francisco Eduardo Pires de Souza, *A economia brasileira em marcha forçada* (Rio de Janeiro: Paz e Terra, 1985), 295–322; Rogério Werneck, *Empresas estatais e política macroeconômica* (Rio de Janeiro: Campus, 1987); Pedro Cezar Dutra Fonseca and Sergio Marley Modesto Monteiro, "O estado e suas razões: o II PND," *Revista de Economia Política* 28, no. 1 (2007): 28–46; João P. dos Reis Velloso, "A fantasia política: a nova alternativa de interpretação do II PND," *Revista de Economia Política* 18, no. 2 (1998): 133–144; Carlos Lessa, "Estratégia de desenvolvimento, 1974–79: sonhos e fracasso," tese de professor titular, UFRJ, Rio de Janeiro, 1978; Vanessa Boarati, "A discussão entre os economistas na década de 1970 sobre a estratégia de desenvolvimento econômico II PND: motivações, custos e resultados," MA thesis, FEAUSP, São Paulo, 2003.

77. While there was an interest in reducing existing disparities and creating new development centers, the II PND recognized the importance of the Center-South. II PND, 16–17. Also see Carlos Lessa, *Estratégia de desenvolvimento, 1974–79: sonhos e fracasso* (Campinas: UNICAMP, 1998), chap. 2. The II PND also aimed to develop large areas still poorly colonized, such as the Amazon and the Center-West, as well as boosting social development in the Northeast. II PND, 15.

78. "The factory was inaugurated with the model 147. Since its inauguration in the country, Fiat revolutionized the Brazilian automobile market: it established the basic technologies and processes, which until then were only available in the most advanced countries." *A Fiat Automóveis inicia sua história em nosso País*, https://1library.org/document/zk606key-fiat-autom%C3%B3veis-inicia-sua-hist%C3%B3ria-em-nosso-pa%C3%ADs.html

79. The Manaus Free Trade Zone was created by Decree-Law 288 of 1967 as a free trade area. The center has approximately five hundred approved projects, spread over several sectors of activity. See Marcio Holland, ed., *Zona franca de Manaus, impactos, efetividade e oportunidades* (São Paulo: FGV EESP), https://eesp.fgv.br/sites/eesp.fgv.br/files/estudos_fgv_zonafranca_manaus_abril_2019v2.pdf, accessed September 23, 2019.

80. In São Bernardo do Campo, half of the MVA was generated by the transportation material sector, and an additional 22% by the metallurgical and mechanical sectors. Censo Industrial 1980, volume 1, tomo 2, no. 19: 176–177; Petrobras, http://www.petrobras.com.br/pt/nossas-atividades/principais-operacoes/refinarias/refinaria-capuava-recap.htm, accessed September 23, 2019.

81. Which had a significant metallurgical, mechanical and chemical sector, with this last sector based on the production of the Capuava petrochemical complex.

82. In Guarulhos the most representative segments were metallurgical, mechanical, and electrical materials and communications. Censo Industrial 1980, volume 1, tomo 2, no. 19: 166–167.

83. Regis Bonelli and Armando Castelar Pinheiro, "Abertura e crescimento econômico no Brasil," in Octavio de Barros and Fabio Giambiagi, eds., *Globalizado* (Rio de Janeiro: Campus, 2008), 89–124; José L. Rossi Jr. and Pedro C. Ferreira, *Evolução da produtividade industrial brasileira e a abertura comercial*, discussion paper no. 651, IPEA, Rio de Janeiro, 1999; André Averbug, "Abertura e integração comercial brasileira na década de 90," in Fabio Giambiagi and Maurício Mesquita Moreira, eds., *A economia brasileira nos anos 90* (Rio de Janeiro: BNDES, 1999): 43–84; Marcio de Oliveira Júnior, "A liberação comercial brasileira e os coeficientes de importação—1990/95," discussion paper no. 703, IPEA, Rio de Janeiro, 2000; Lia Valls Pereira, "Brazil Trade Liberalization Program," http://citeseerx.ist.psu.edu/viewdoc/download;jsessionid=B99D9D94B14472D8DA1E4359282B2C0D?doi=10.1.1.596.5279&rep=rep1&type=pdf accessed October 7, 2019.

84. On Mercosul, see Sérgio Abreu and Lima Florêncio, "Trajetória do Mercosul e mudança de paradigmas e de posições da política externa brasileira: começo virtuoso e crise recente—possíveis interpretações," discussion paper no. 2125, IPEA, Rio de Janeiro. 2015; Ernesto Henrique Fraga Araújo, *O Mercosul: negociações extra-regionais* (Brasília: Fundação Alexandre de Gusmão, 2007).

85. Although the discussion on foreign debt began in the late 1980s, it was not concluded until 1994, following the model of the Brady Plan, also adopted by other countries. Banco Central do Brasil, "Dívida externa brasiliera," 2003, https://www.bcb.gov.br/content/publicacoes/Documents/outras_pub_alfa/D%C3%ADvida_Externa_Brasileira_-_Segunda_Edi%C3%A7%C3%A3o_Revisada_Ampliada.pdf, accessed October 7, 2019.

86. The extensive bibliograpy on the subject includes João Sayad, "Planos cruzado e real: acertos e desacertos," Dimac Seminaro, IPEA, Rio de Janeiro, September 30, 2000; Luiz Filgueiras, *História do Plano Real* (São Paulo: Boitempo, 2000); Aloízio Mercadante, ed., *O Brasil pós-real: a política econômica em debate* (Campinas: UNICAMP, 1997); Maria da Conceição Tavares, *Destruição não-criadora* (Rio de Janeiro: Record, 1990); Gustavo H. B. Franco, *O Plano*

Real e outros ensaios (Rio de Janeiro: Francisco Alves, 1995); Gustavo H. B. Franco, *O desafio Brasileiro: ensaios sobre desenvolvimento, globalização e moeda* (São Paulo: Editora 34, 1999); Francisco Vidal Luna and Herbert S. Klein, *The Economic and Social History of Brazil Since 1889* (Cambridge: Cambridge University Press, 2014), chap. 4.

87. Licínio Velasco Jr., *Privatização: mitos e falsas percepções* (Rio de Janeiro: BNDES, 1999); Armando Castelar Pinheiro, "A experiência brasileira de privatização: o que vem a seguir," discussion paper no. 87, 2002, IPEA, Rio de Janeiro; Armando Castelar Pinheiro and Kiichiro Fukasaku, *A privatização no Brasil: o caso dos serviços de utilidade pública* (Rio de Janeiro: BNDES, 2000); Francisco Anuitti-Neto et al., "Os efeitos da privatização sobre o desempenho econômico e financeiro das empresas privatizadas," *Revista Brasileira de Economia* 59, no. 2 (2005): 151–175.

88. There was intense debate about the opening process and its consequences. Gustavo Franco, one of the main characters in the implementation of the Real Plan, was his main defender. Among the main critics were several scholars linked to UNICAMP. See Gustavo Franco, *O Plano Real e outros ensaios* (Rio de Janeiro: Francisco Alves, 1995); Gustavo Franco, "A inserção externa e o desenvolvimento," *Revista de Economia Política* 18, no. 3 (1998): 121–147; Maria da Conceição Tavares, *Destruição não criadora* (Rio de Janeiro: Record, 1999); Luciano G. Coutinho and Luiz Gonzaga Mello Belluzo, "Desenvolvimento e estabilização sob finanças globalizadas," *Economia e Sociedade* (Campinas) 7 (1996): 129–154.

89. The fiscal policy proposal from 2006 rejected the neoliberal model and reemphasized the role of the state in favor of growth. F. L. Lopreano, "Aspectos a atuação estatal de FHC a Dilma," discussion paper no. 2039, IPEA, Brasília, February 2015, 18.

90. R. L. F. Werneck, "Alternância política, redistribuição e crescimento, 2003–2010," In M. P. Abreu, ed., *A ordem do progresso. Dois séculos de política econômica no Brasil*, rev. ed. (Rio de Janeiro: Elsevier, 2014), 357–397.

91. Launched in 2009, the program aimed to build one million homes, with four hundred thousand of them designated for families with incomes below a specific amount (which was three times the minimum wage). The program required a major contribution of public subsidies. Raquel Rolnik et al., "O Programa Minha Casa Minha Vida nas regiões metropolitanas de São Paulo e Campinas: aspectos socioespaciais e segregação," *Cadernas Metropitanos* 17, no. 33 (2015): 127–154; Maria Rita Loureiro, Vinicius Macário, and Pedro Guerra, "Democracia, arenas decisórias e políticas públicas: o Programa Minha Casa Minha Vida," discussion paper no. 1886, IPEA, Brasília, 2013.

92. http://www.brasil-economia-governo.org.br/2013/10/23/o-que-e-o-plano-brasil-maior/

93. Banco Central do Brasil, *Relatório de Inflação* 13, no. 3 (2011).

94. About targeted credit, see Eduardo Lundberg, "Bancos oficiais e crédito direcionado–o que diferencia o mercado de crédito brasileiro?," no. 258, Central Bank of Brazil, Research Department, Brasília, 2011.

95. For a critique of this policy which promoted already competitive Brazilian companies rather than modifying the productive structure of industry and encouraging higher spending on R&D, see Monsueto Almeida, "O novo estado desenvolvimentista e o governo Lula," *Revista Economia & Tecnologia* 7 (2011): 68–89. On this theme also see Mansueto Almeida, Renato Lima-de-Oliveira, and Ben Ross Schneider, "Política industrial e empresas estatais no Brasil: BNDES e Petrobras," discussion paper no. 2013, IPEA, 2014, 323–327.

96. BNDES is responsible for more than 20% of the balance of credit operations in Brazil. BNDES active operations had exceptional growth, from 6% of GDP in 2007 to 12% in 2014. This expansion was realized with public resources obtained by issuing national treasury debt.

97. The study shows the perverse effect of the cumulative increase in real labor costs, exchange rate mismatch, and low labor productivity growth in Brazil. *Nota Econômica* (CNI) 1, no. 1 (2015), http://arquivos.portaldaindustria.com.br/app/conteudo_24/2015/02/20/526/Notaeconomica01-Competitividade.pdf. The same study shows that it evaluates the unit cost of labor in real dollars, which is a function of labor productivity, wages, and exchange rate. Between 2002 and 2012 Brazil presented an annual growth of 9%, against -1.4% in Germany, -3% in Korea, and -5.2% in the United States. This represents a loss of competitiveness for industrial production. Also see Elizabeth Croffot, Eric Hayek and Michael Paterra, "Charting International Labor Comparisons," The Conference Board, 2014, https://www.conference-board.org/publications/publicationdetail.cfm?publicationid=2715, accessed December 1, 2019.

98. "Participação da indústria manufatureira no PIB calculada a preços correntes," available at http://www.ipeadata.gov.br, accessed August 23, 2020.

99. Available at http://www.ipeadata.gov.br/, accessed August 23, 2020.

100. On the fiscal war, see André Eduardo S. Fernandes and Nélio Lacerda Wanderlei, "A questão da guerra fiscal: uma breve resenha," *Revista de Informação Legislativa* (Brasília) 37, no. 148 (2000): 5–20; Danilo Jorge Vieira, "Um estudo sobre a guerra fiscal no Brasil," PhD thesis, Campinas, UNICAMP, 2012; José Roberto F. Affonso et al., "Guerra fiscal do ICMS: organizar o desembarque," *Revista de Direito Internacional Econômico Tributário* (Brasília) 12, no. 1 (2017): 416–443; José Roberto F. Affonso, Melina Rocha Lukic, and Kleber Pachco de Castro, "ICMS: crise federativa e obsolescência," *Revista Direito GV* 14, no. 3 (2018); Paulo Araújo Pontes, "Três ensaios sobre a guerra fiscal e incentivos estaduais para a industrialização," PhD thesis, São Paulo, FGV-SP, 2011.

101. Law 5,172 of 1996, approved the Código Tributário Nacional. The Constitutional Supplementary Law of 1975 created the Conselho de Política Fazendária (Confaz).

102. In general, there is an exemption for basic food products, and higher tariffs for products such as fuels.

103. Let's suppose that a car produced in another state is "exported" to São Paulo. In this state the car will be sold with 18% tax. But as it was the subject of an interstate transaction, it was originally taxed at 12%, a tax that will be credited to the final transaction because it is a value-added tax. That is, when selling the car to the final consumer there will be a final tax of 18%, but as 12% was collected in the seller state, only 6% will be collected in São Paulo. If there were no fiscal war, part of the tax would be collected at the source (12%) and part at the destination (6%), and price competition would be tax neutral. But the state that attracted the industry to its territory, which was supposed to receive 12% of the car's value for the interstate transaction, gives the manufacturer an economic advantage to offset the tax it should pay. Either it gives many years for the tax to be collected without charge or it finances the construction of the factory with subsidized interest to offset the future flow of ICMS.

104. These fiscal wars, in promoting local production, sometimes have had negative effects on the local economy or the gains have been negligible. Artur Tranzola Santos, "Abertura comercial na década de 1990 e os impactos na indústria automobilística," *Fronteira* (Belo Horizonte) 8, no. 16 (2009): 107–129.

105. Fiscal incentives did not alone contribute to the regional deconcentration of industrial activity, which was influenced by other constraints. Also, states that had a less diversified and less complex production structure faced great difficulties in attracting companies that produced more complex and technological goods. Soraia Aparecida Cardozo. "Guerra fiscal no Brasil e as alterações das estruturas produtivas estaduais desde os anos 1990," PhD thesis, UNICAMP, 2010, 199–200. In 2007, a Parliamentary Inquiry Commission was created in the Legislative Assembly of the state of São Paulo in which fiscal war mechanisms and losses for the state of São Paulo were discussed. Assembléia Legislativa do Estado de São Paulo, "Relatório CPI da guerra fiscal," March 2007, https://www.al.sp.gov.br/StaticFile/documentacao/cpi_guerra_fiscal_relatorio_final.htm, accessed August 24, 2020.

106. An illustrative example is the case of the Ford factory in Bahia. See Otávio Soares Dulci, "Guerra fiscal, desenvolvimento desigual e relações federativas no Brasil," *Revista de Sociologia e Política* no. 18 (2002): 95–107; Angela Franco, "Em tempos globais, um 'novo' local: a Ford da Bahia," *Caderno CRH* (Salvador) 22, no. 56 (2009): 359–380; Glauco Arbix, "Políticas do desperdício e assimetria entre público e privado na indústria automobilística," *RBCSi* 17, no. 48 (2002); Polo Industrial de Camaçari, *Plano Diretor* (Salvador:

Secretaria da Indústria, Comércio e Mineração do Estado da Bahia, 2013). In 2021 Ford decided to leave Brazil, closing all of its factories in the country.

107. Of the amount collected in the state, a 25% share is passed on to the state's municipalities, largely based on their share of the state's value of industrial production.

108. José Luiz Rossi Jr. and Pedro C. Ferreira, "Evolução da produtividade industrial brasileira e abertura comercial," discussion paper no. 651, IPEA, Rio de Janeiro, June 1999; Regis Bonelli and Renato Fonseca, "Ganhos de produtividade e de eficiência novos resultados para a economia brasileira." *Pesquisa e Planejamento Econômico* (Rio de Janeiro) 28, no. 2 (1998): 273–314; Danielle Barbosa Lopes da Silva, "O impacto da abertura comercial sobre a produtividade da indústria brasileira," MA thesis, FGV, 2004; Enéas Gonçalves de Carvalho, "Globalização e estratégias competitivas na indústria automobilística: uma abordagem a partir das principais montadoras instaladas no Brasil," *Gestão & Produção* 12, no. 1 (2005): 121–133; Artur Tranzola Santos, "Abertura comercial na década de 1990 e os impactos na indústria automobilística," *Fronteira* (Belo Horizonte) 8, no. 16 (2009): 107–129.

109. Rubens Ricupero, "Global Trends and Prospects," in UNCTAD, *Trade and Development Report, 2003: Capital Accumulation, Growth and Structural Change* (Geneva: UNCTAD, 2003): X. Also see Rubens Ricupero, "Desindustrialização precoce: futuro ou presente do Brasil," *Le Monde Diplomatique* 80 (March 6, 2014), https://diplomatique.org.br/desindustrializacao-precoce-futuro-ou-presente-do-brasil/, accessed October 12, 2019.

110. Garcia, "Uma análise das mudanças," 111–113; Ricupero, "Global Trends and Prospects"; Ricupero, "Desindustrialização precoce."

111. Ricupero, "Desindustrialização precoce."

112. Robert Rowthorn and Ramana Ramaswamy, "Growth, Trade, and Deinstrialization," *IMF Staff Papers* 46, no. 1 (March 1999), https://www.imf.org/external/Pubs/FT/staffp/1999/03-99/pdf/rowthorn.pdf, accessed October 14, 2019.

113. José Gabriel Palma, "Quatro fontes de desindustrialização e um novo conceito de doença holandesa," in *Conferência de industrialização, desindustrialização e desenvolvimento* (São Paulo: Centro Cultural da Fiesp, 2005), 2–3, https://macrododesenvolvimento.files.wordpress.com/2013/06/520-20quatro20fontes20_2_.pdf, accessed October 13, 2019.

114. Wilson Cano, "A desindustrialização no Brasil," *Economia e Sociedade* (Campinas) 21, special number (December 2012): 831–851; Regis Bonelli and Samuel de Abreu Pessoa, "Desindustrialização no Brasil: um resumo da evidência," discussion paper no. 7, FGV/IBRE, Rio de Janeiro, March 2010; André Nassif, "Há evidências de desindustrialização no Brasil?," *Revista de Economia Política* 28, no. 1 (2008): 72–96; Octávio de Barros and Robson Rodrigues Pereira, "Desmistificando a tese da desindustrialização: reestruturação

da indústria brasileira em uma época de transformações globais," in Octávio de Barros and Fabio Giambiagi, eds., *Brasil globalizado: o Brasil em um mundo surpreendente* (Rio de Janeiro: Campus, 2008): 299–330; Paulo César Morceiro, *Desindustrialização na economia brasileira no período 2000–2011, abordagens e indicadores* (São Paulo: Cultura Acadêmica, 2012); Paulo César Morceiro, "A indústria brasileira no limiar do século XXI: uma análise da sua evolução estrutural, comercial e tecnológica," PhD thesis, FEA-USP, 2018; Luiz Carlos Bresser Pereira, *A construção política do Brasil: sociedade, economia e estado desde a independência* (São Paulo: Editora 34, 2014).

115. Paulo César Morceiro and Joaquim José Martins Guilhoto, *Desindustrialização setorial e estagnação de longo prazo na manufatura brasileira* (São Paulo: Nereus, 2019): 8–9.

116. Using deindustrialization of the "world without China" as normal deindustrialization due to factors affecting all countries, like globalization, Brazilian deindustrialization is very abnormal, since the share of Value Added of Manufacturing in the GDP of the "world without China" at constant prices fell by only 1% and that of Brazil decreased by 42% between 1980 and 2015. See Morceiro and Guilhoto, *Desindustrialização setorial e estagnação*, 11.

117. N. Haraguchi, "Patterns of Structural Change and Manufacturing Development," in J. Weiss and M. Tribe, eds., *Routledge Handbook of Industry and Development* (Abingdon: Routledge, 2016), 38–64.

118. On incentives, see Geciane S. Porto and Caroline V. Memória, "Incentivos para inovação tecnologia: um estudo da política pública de renúncia fiscal no Brasil," *Revista de Administração Pública* (Rio de Janeiro) 53, no. 3 (2019): 520–541; João Alberto de Negri and Mauro Borges Lemos, *Avaliação das Políticas de Incentivos à P&D e inovação Tecnológica no Brasil,* Nota Técnica (Brasília: IPEA, 2009).

119. Lenita Maria Turchi and José Mauro de Morais, eds., *Políticas de apoio à inovação tecnológica no Brasil* (Brasília: IPEA, 2017), 9–10. On this theme also see Pedro Cavalcante, ed., *Inovação e política públicas, superando o mito da ideia.* (Brasília: IPEA, 2019); Priscila Koeller, Renato B. Viotti, and André Rauen, "Dispêndios do governo federal em C&T e P&D: esforços e perspectivas recentes," *Radar* 48 (December 2016): 13–18; Fernanda de Negri, *Novos caminhos para a Inovação no Brasil.* (Brasília: IPEA, 2018).

120. See Ministério de Ciência, Inovações e Comunicações, *Plano de ciência, tecnologia e inovação para petróleo & gás natural*, Brasília, 2018; Fabiano M. Pompermayer, Fernanda de Negri, and Luiz R. Cavalcante, *Innovação tecnológica no setor eletríco brasileiro. Uma avaliação do programa de P&D regulado pela ANEEL* (Brasília: IPEA, 2011); Raquel F. de Almeida, "Políticas de conteúdo local e setor para-petroléo: uma anlálise comparativa Brasil e Noruega," MA thesis, Rio de Janeiro, COPPE/UFRJ, 2015; Marcos F. C. Lima and Marconi Aurélio da Silva, "Inovação em Petróleo e gás no Brasil: a parceria Cenpes-Petrobrás e Coppe-UFRJ," *Revista Sociedade e Estado* 27, no. 1 (2012); Koeller,

Viotti, and Rauen, "Dispêndios do governo federal em C&T e P&D"; *The 2016 Global R&D Funding Forecast*, supplement to *R&D Magazine*, winter 2016.

121. Ricardo Renzo Brentani and Carlos Henrique de Brito Cruz, eds., *Indicadores de ciência tecnologia e inovação em São Paulo 2010* (São Paulo: Fapesp, 2011), volume 1, chap. 4, 4–12.

122. A recent World Bank study, which analyzed the difficulties and advantages for doing business in 190 countries, placed Brazil in 124th place. World Bank Group, *Doing Business 2020: Comparing Business Regulation in 190 Economies* (Washington, DC: World Bank, 2020); World Bank Group, *Doing Business 2020: Brasil* (Washington, DC: World Bank Group, 2020). Brazil is far behind other BRICS, such as Korea (in 5th place), India (63rd), and South Africa (84th), as well as Latin American countries such as Mexico (60th place) and Chile (59th), and is similar to Argentina (126th place).

123. Naercio Menezes Filho, Bruno Komatsu, Andrea Lucchesi, and Marcelo Ferrario, "Políticas de inovação no Brasil," policy paper no. 11, Insper, São Paulo, August 2014.

124. On PINTEC, see Luiz Ricardo Cavalcante and Fernanda Negri, "Trajetória recente dos indicadores de inovação no Brasil," discussion paper no. 1659, IPEA, Brasília, 2011; Camila B. Mourad, "Ralação entre as atividades internas e externas no desempenho em inovação das empresas do setor industrial brasileiro: constatações baseadas em uma dácada de PINTE/IBGE," PhD thesis, Universidade de São Paulo, 2017; Fernanda de Negri and Luiz R. Cavalcante, *Análise dos dados da PINTEC 2011*, Nota Técnica no. 15 (Brasília: IPEA, 2013); Tatielle M. Longhini et al., "Investimentos em inovação e sua influência na receita líquida de vendas. Uma análise com base dos dados do PINTEC," *BBR Brazilian Business Review* 15, no. 1 (2018): 1–16; Ullisses Kazumi Shimizu, "A influência da inovação no desempenho das firmas no Brasil," PhD thesis, Universidade Presbiteriana Mackenzie, 2013.

125. Brentani and Cruz, *Indicadores de ciência tecnologia e inovação*, chap. 4, 22–24.

126. Embraer, https://historicalcenter.embraer.com/br/pt/historia, accessed October 27, 2019.

127. See Sérgio B. V. Gomes, "A indústria aeronáutica no Brasil. Evolução recente e perspectivas," BNDES, https://web.bndes.gov.br/bib/jspui/bitstream/1408/919/1/A%20ind%C3%BAstria%20aeron%C3%A1utica%20no%20Brasil_P-final_BD.pdf, accessed October 27, 2019; BNDES, "Aeroespaço e defesa," BNDES-Setorial, 2010–2018, https://www.bndes.gov.br/wps/wcm/connect/site/648bf519-e15e-41a0-a599-a7cb4827be8a/BNDES_Setorial__A%26D_completo.pdf?MOD=AJPERES&CVID=mHlAmTY, accessed October 27, 2019; Sérgio B. V. Gomes, João A. Barcellos, and Nelson Tucci, "Embraer e Boing vis-à-vis Airbus e Bombardier: Quais as Implicações para o Brasil?," *Aesroespecial e Defesa/BNDES Setorial* 47: 61–122 (2018); Maria R. E. Martinez, "A globalização

da indústria aeronáutica: o caso da Embraer," PhD thesis, Universidade de Brasília, 2007; Flavio Riva Gargiulo, "Indústria de construção aeronáutica, o caso da Embraer: história e avaliação," MA thesis, FGV, 2008; Luiz Guilherme de Oliveira, "A cadeia de produção aeronaútica no Brasil: Uma análise sobre os fornecedores da Embraer," MA thesis, UNICAMP, 2005; Vanessa de Lima Ferreira, "Estratégia na relação com os fornecedores na indústria aeronáutica brasileira. O caso Embraer," MA thesis, Escola Politécnica da USP, 2010.

Chapter 3

1. The literacy rate was 59.4% for the total population for São Paulo and 58.6% for Rio Grande do Sul. IBGE, Recenseamento Geral de 1950, Série Nacional, volume 1, Censo Demográfico, p. 90, table 47.

2. Censo Demográfico de 1991, "População residente de 5 anos ou mais por situação (urbana e rural), segundo a alfabetização," http://www.ibge.gov.br/home/estatistica/populacao/censodem/tab203.shtm.

3. IBGE, SIDRA, table 6755.

4. IBGE, SIDRA, Agro, table 801.

5. César Roberto Leite da Silva and Sérgio Antonio dos Santos, "Política agrícola e eficiência econômica: o caso da agricultura paulista," *Pesquisa & Debate: Revista do Programa de Estudos Pós-Graduados em Economia Política* 12, no. 2 (2001): 66–82.

6. José Sidnei Gonçalves, "Dinâmica da agropecuária paulista no contexto das transformações de sua agricultura," *Informações Econômicas SP* 35, no. 12 (2005): 67.

7. On the modernization of the *usinas* in this period, see Marili Arruda Mariotoni, "O desenvolvimento tecnológico do setor sucroalcooleiro no estado de São Paulo (1975–1985)," MA thesis, Universidade Estadual de Campinas, 2004.

8. CONAB, "Produtos da indústria sucroalcooleira comparativo de área, produtividade e produção safras 2018/19 e 2019/20," https://www.conab.gov.br/info-agro/safras/cana, accessed February 10, 2020.

9. Observatório da Cana, "Histórico de produção e moagem | por safra," http://www.unicadata.com.br/historico-de-producao-e-moagem.php?idMn=32&tipoHistorico=4.

10. Ricardo Castillo, "Região competitiva e circuito espacial produtivo: a expansão do setor sucro-alcooleiro (complexo cana-de-açúcar) no território brasileiro," 2009, 1, 7, http://www.observatoriogeograficoamericalatina.org.mx/egal12/Geografiasocioeconomica/Geografiaespacial/60.pdf.

11. MDIC, "Exportação Brasileira, São Paulo, Principais Productos, 2016," http://www.mdic.gov.br/comercio-exterior/estatisticas-de-comercio-exterior/balanca-comercial-brasileira-unidades-da-federacao.

12. MDIC and MAPA data, http://indicadores.agricultura.gov.br/agrostat/index.htm and http://www.mdic.gov.br/index.php/comercio-exterior/estatisticas-de-comercio-exterior/series-historicas, accessed February 9, 2020.

13. Sigismundo Bialoskorski Neto and Waldemar Ferreira Júnior, "Evolução e organização das cooperativas agropecuárias paulistas na década de 90," paper presented at the XLII Congresso da Sociedade Brasileira de Economia e Sociologia Rural, 2004.

14. Fabio Ribas Chaddad, "Cooperativas no agronegócio do leite: mudanças organizacionais e estratégicas em resposta à globalização," *Organizações Rurais & Agroindustriais* 9, no. 1 (2011): 70.

15. IBGE, Sidra, Agro, table 840.

16. IBGE, Sidra, table 6846.

17. On the decline of coffee production in the state, see Vera Lúcia F. dos Santos Francisco, Celso Luis Rodrigues Vegro, José Alberto Ângelo, and Carlos Nabil Ghobril, "Estrutura produtiva da cafeicultura paulista," *Informações Econômicas SP* 39, no. 8 (2009): 42–48. On the transition from sugar to coffee, see Thiago Franco Oliveira de Carvalho, "Modernização agrícola e a região da alta mogiana paulista análise da expansão da produção de cana-deaçúcar em uma tradicional região cafeeira," MA thesis, Universidade Estadual Paulista Júlio de Mesquita Filho, Rio Claro, 2014.

18. IBGE, Sidra, PAM, table 1613.

19. Sarah Silveira Diniz, Marcia Regina Gabardo da Câmara, Marcelo Ortega Massambani, João Amilcar Rodrigues Anhesini, and Umberto Antonio Sesso Filho, "Analise espacial da produtividade da Laranja dos municípios do estado de São Paulo: 2002 a 2010," paper presented at the 50 Congresso da SOBER, 2012, 2.

20. Luis Fernando Paulillo, ed., *Agroindústria e citricultura no Brasil: diferenças e dominâncias* (Rio de Janeiro: Editora E-papers, 2006), 75.

21. One of the fruit packing houses in Bebedouro is sometimes cited as being the first producer of juice as early as the 1950s, but the first modern plant is recognized as the Mineiro one in 1962.

22. The standard survey of the modern history of the industry is Ronaldo Sued, *O desenvolvimento da agroindústria da laranja no Brasil: o impacto das geadas na Flórida e na política econômica governamental* (Rio de Janeiro: Fundação Getúlio Vargas, 1993), esp. chaps. 1 and 2.

23. Marcos Fava Neves and Vinícius Gustavo Trombin, eds., *The Orange Juice Business: A Brazilian Perspective* (Wageningen: Springer Science & Business Media, 2012).

24. Neves and Trombin, *The Orange Juice Business*, 81, 85.

25. Together the four big firms in 2010 owned 1,004 of them: Citrosuco (312), Cutrale (290), Dreyfus (214), and Citrovita (188). Neves and Trombin, *The Orange Juice Business*, 19, 54.

26 https://www.citrosuco.com.br/a-citrosuco/

27. Fabio Chaddad, *The Economics and Organization of Brazilian Agriculture* (London: Academic Press, 2015), 106.

28. Luiz Fernando Paulillo and Luiz Manoel de Moraes Camargo Almeida, "A coordenação agroindustrial citricola brasileira e os novos recursos de poder: dos politicos aos juridicos," *Organizações Rurais & Agroindustriais* 11, no. 1 (2009): 11–27; Adelson Martins Figueiredo, Hildo Meireles de Souza Filho, and Luiz Fernando de Oriani Paullilo, "Análise das margens e transmissão de preços no sistema agroindustrial do suco de laranja no Brasil," *Revista de Economia e Sociologia Rural* 51, no. 2 (2013): 331–350; Haroldo José Torres da Silva, "Estudo da viabilidade econômico-financeira da indústria de citros: impactos da criação de um conselho setorial," PhD thesis., Escola Superior de Agricultura Luiz de Queiroz, 2016.

29. Neves and Trombin, *The Orange Juice Business*, 58.

30. These figures include all of the state of São Paulo and a small adjacent section of the state of Minas Gerais that also produces oranges and is known as the Triângulo Mineiro district.

31. Diniz et al., "Análise espacial da produtividade da Laranja," 3–4; Marcos Fava Neves and Vinícius Gustavo Trombin, "Mapping and Quantification of the Brazilian Citrus Chain," *Fruit Processing*, March/April 2012, 56.

32. See IBGE, SIDRA, PAM, table 1613; Neves and Trombin, *The Orange Juice Business*, 55.

33. Neves and Trombin, "Mapping and Quantification of the Brazilian Citrus Chain," 53.

34. IBGE, SIDRA, PAM, table 1613.

35. USDA Foreign Agricultural Service, "Citrus Semi-Annual Brazil," June 17, 2021, 1.

36. USDA Foreign Agricultural Service, "Citrus: World Markets and Trade," July 2021, 8, 10.

37. USDA Foreign Agricultural Service, "Citrus Semi-Annual Brazil," June 17, 2021, 2, 9.

38. IBGE, SIDRA, PAM, table 1613.

39. See Francisco Vidal Luna, Herbert S. Klein, and William Summerhill, "The Characteristics of Coffee Production and Agriculture in the State of São Paulo in 1905," *Agricultural History* 90, no. 1 (2016): 22–50; IBGE, Censo Agro de 2006, volume 2, parte 2: 25–26, tables 21–22.

40. IBGE, SIDRA (Censo Agro 2017), tables 6845, 5846, and 6847.

41. IBGE, SIDRA, table 264 for data from 1970 to 2006 and tables 1612 and 1613 for 2018 data.

42. IBGE, SIDRA, table 1112.

43. For a general survey of the developments of the Paulista sugar industry to the 1970s, see Mariotoni, "O desenvolvimento tecnológico do setor sucroalcooleiro no estado de São Paulo," chap. 1.

44. On the impact of the world war on cabotage shipping and its influence in shifting sugar production to the Southeast, see Tamás Szmrecsányi and Eduardo Pestana Moreira, "O desenvolvimento da agroindústria canavieira do Brasil desde a Segunda Guerra Mundial," *Estudos Avançados* 5, no. 11 (1991): 57–79.

45. Barbara Nunberg, "Structural Change and State Policy: The Politics of Sugar in Brazil Since 1964," *Latin American Research Review* 21, no. 2 (1986): 56–57.

46. Mariotoni, "O desenvolvimento tecnologico do setor sucroalcooleiro no estado de São Paulo," 31.

47. Marcos Fava Neves, Allan W. Grayb, and Brian A. Bourquard, "Copersucar: A World Leader in Sugar and Ethanol," *International Food and Agribusiness Management Review* 19, no. 2 (2016): 209.

48. Nunberg, "Structural Change and State Policy," 63–64.

49. On the role of Copersucar in modernizing the mills, see Mariotoni, "O desenvolvimento tecnologico do setor sucroalcooleiro no estado de São Paulo."

50. Nunberg, "Structural Change and State Policy," 70–71 and table 7.

51. Mariotoni, "O desenvolvimento tecnologico do setor sucroalcooleiro no estado de São Paulo," 33–35.

52. Castillo, "Região competitiva e circuito espacial produtivo," 3.

53. Anil Hira and Luiz Guilherme de Oliveira, "No Substitute for Oil? How Brazil Developed Its Ethanol Industry," *Energy Policy* 37 (2009): 2451–2454; Antonio Carlos Augusto da Costa, Nei Pereira Jr., and Donato Alexandre Gomes Aranda, "The Situation of Biofuels in Brazil: New Generation Technologies," *Renewable and Sustainable Energy Reviews* 14 (2010): 3044.

54. On these experiements, see Lauro Mattei, "Programa Nacional para Produção e Uso do Biodiesel no Brasil (PNPB): trajetória, situação atual e desafios," *BNB* [Banco Nordeste do Brasil] *Documentos Técnicos Científicos* 41, no. 4 (2010): 731–740; Fernando Ferrari Filho, "Análise de um motor do ciclo diesel operando no modo bicombustível: diesel / etanol," MA thesis, PUC, Rio de Janeiro, 2011. Most of the biodiesel is now made from soybean oil; see Neyda de la Caridad Om Tapanes, Donato Alexandre Gomes Aranda, Rodolfo Salazar Perez, and Yordanka Reyes Cruz. "Biodiesel no Brasil: matérias primas e tecnologias de produção." *Acta Scientiae et Technicae* 1, no. 1 (2013): 120 https://www.researchgate.net/profile/Neyda-Tapanes/publication/281164918_Biodiesel_no_Brasil_materias_primas_e_tecnologias_de_producao/links/57f5a0d708ae91deaa5c83b8/Biodiesel-no-Brasil-materias-primas-e-tecnologias-de-producao.pdf.

55. UNICA, "Frota brasileira de autoveículos leves . . . 2007–2015," http://www.unicadata.com.br/listagem.php?idMn=55, accessed July 8, 2017. On the environmental impact of these pro-ethanol programs, see José

Goldemberg, Suani Teixeira Coelho, and Patricia Guardabassi, "The Sustainability of Ethanol Production from Sugarcane," *Energy Policy* 36 (2008): 2086–2097.

56. Mariotoni, "O desenvolvimento tecnologico do setor sucroalcooleiro no estado de São Paulo," chap. 3; Lara Bartocci Liboni, Luciana Oranges Cezarino, Michelle Castro Carrijo, and Rudinei Toneto Jr., "The Equipment Supply Industry to Sugar Mills, Ethanol and Energy in Brazil: An Analysis Based in Leading Companies and Key-Organizations of Sector and of LPA of Sertãozinho," *Independent Journal of Management & Production* 6, no. 4 (2015): 1070–1096.

57. Liboni et al., "The Equipment Supply Industry to Sugar Mills, Ethanol and Energy in Brazil."

58. Castillo, "Região competitiva e circuito espacial produtivo," 1, 7.

59. On the links created in this complex system, see Marco Antonio Conejero, Eduardo José Sia, Mairun Junqueira Alves Pinto, Ricardo Kouiti Santos Iguchi, and Rafael Oliveira do Amaral, "Arranjos contratuais complexos na transação de cana à usina de áçucar e alcool: um estudo de caso no centro-sul do brasil," paper presented at XXXII Encontro da ANPAS, 2008 (Rio de Janeiro), 5, http://www.anpad.org.br/admin/pdf/GCT-D2072.pdf, accessed February 7, 2017.

60. Ben McKay, Sérgio Sauer, Ben Richardson, and Roman Herre, "The Politics of Sugarcane Flexing in Brazil and Beyond," Transnational Institute Agrarian Justice Program, Think Piece Series on Flex Crops & Commodities, no. 4, September 2014, 6, table 2, http://repub.eur.nl/pub/77677/Metis_202533.pdf, accessed February 7, 2017.

61. Taís Mahalem do Amaral, Marcos Fava Neves, and Márcia A. Dias de Moraes, "Cadeias produtivas do açúcar do estado de São Paulo e da França: comparação dos sistemas produtivos, organização, estratégias e ambiente institucional," *Agricultura São Paulo* 50, no. 2 (2003): 70–71. Also see UNICA, "Histórico e missão," http://www.unica.com.br/unica/?idioma=1.

62. Chaddad, *The Economics and Organization of Brazilian Agriculture*, chap. 4.

63. Márcia Azanha Ferraz Dias de Moraes, "O mercado de trabalho da agroindústria canavieira: desafios e oportunidades," *Economia Aplicada* (Ribeirão Preto) 11, no. 4 (2007): 607–611.

64. Helena Ribeiro and Thomas Ribeiro de Aquino Ficarelli, "Queimadas nos canaviais e perspectivas dos cortadores de cana-de-açúcar em Macatuba, São Paulo," *Saúde Social* (São Paulo) 19, no. 1 (2010): 48–51; John Wilkinson, *O setor sucroalcooleiro brasileiro na atual conjuntura nacional e internacional* (Rio de Janeiro: ActionAid, 2015), 11.

65. USDA, "Sugar Annual Brazil," Report BR2020-0012, April 14, 2020; IBGE, SIDRA, table 1612.

66. Rosangela Aparecida Soares Fernandes and Cristiane Márcia dos Santos, "Competitividade das exportações sucroalcooleiras no Estado de São

Paulo," *Anais do 4° ECAECO [Encontro Científico de Administração, Economia e Contabilidade]* 1, no. 1 (2011): 4; Beate Zimmermann and Jurgen Zeddies, "International Competitiveness of Sugar Production," paper presented at the 13th International Farm Management Congress, Wageningen, The Netherlands, July 7–12, 2002, 5, http://econpapers.repec.org/paper/agsifma02/.

67. CONAB, "Boletim de cana-de-açúcar, tabela de levantamento, 20/08/20," https://www.conab.gov.br/info-agro/safras; USDA, "Sugar Annual Brazil," April 15, 2021. When the data conflict, we use the CONAB data.

68. UNICA, "Exportação anual de etanol pelo brasil por estado de origem," http://www.unicadata.com.br/listagem.php?idMn=43, accessed August 22, 2020.

69. IBGE, SIDRA, table 1612.

70. UNICA, various production tables accessed June 4, 2017, for the period 1980/81 to 2016/17 by state at http://www.unicadata.com.br/historico-de-producao-e-moagem.php?idMn=32&tipoHistorico=4.

71. CONAB, "Boletim de cana-de-açúcar, tabela de levantamento, 20/08/20."

72. US Department of Energy, Alternative Fuels Data Center, "Global Ethanol Production by Country or Region," https://afdc.energy.gov/data/10331.

73. For 2019, see CONAB, "VPB valor produção bruto," July 2020, https://www.gov.br/agricultura/pt-br/assuntos/politica-agricola/valor-bruto-da-producao-agropecuaria-vbp; for the period 1974–2018, see IBGE, SIDRA, PPM, table 74.

74. CONAB, "VPB valor produção bruto," July 2020.

75. CONAB, "Boletim grãos agosto 2020—resumo, tabela de levantamento," https://www.conab.gov.br/info-agro/safras/graos. For the analysis of peanut production in São Paulo, see Renata Martins, "Produção de amendoim e expansão da cana-de-açúcar na Alta Paulista, 1996–2010," *Informações Econômicas SP* 41, no. 6 (2011): 5–16.

76. IBGE, SIDRA, table 6754.

77. Antonio Carlos Lima Nogueira and Decio Zylbersztajn, "Coexistência de arranjos institucionais na avicultura de corte do estado de São Paulo," USP–Faculdade de Economia, Administração e Contabilidade, Departasmento de Administração, working paper no. 03/022, 2003, 7; Luiz Antonio Rossi de Freitas and Oscar Bertoglio, "A evolução da avicultura de corte brasileira após 1980," *Economia e Desenvolvimento* 13 (2001): 102.

78. P. V. Marques, "Contribuição ao estudo da organização agroindustrial: o caso da indústria de frango de corte no estado de São Paulo," *Scientia Agricola* 51, no. 1 (1994): 12, table 2.

79. IBGE, SIDRA, tables 281, 3939.

80. ABPA [Associação Brasileira de Proteína Animal], *Relatório Anual 2020*, 39.

81. ABPA, *Relatório Anual 2020*, 129. Espírito Santo is second in production but accounts for only 10% of national production.

82. Sérgio Kenji Kakimoto, "Fatores críticos da competitividade da cadeia produtiva do ovo no estado de São Paulo," MA thesis, Universidade Federal de São Carlos, 2011, 46.

83. Sonia Santana Martins, "Cadeias produtivas do frango e do ovo: avanços tecnológicos e sua apropriação," PhD thesis, Fundação Getulio Varas, São Paulo, 1996, chap. 2.

84. Sonia Santana Martins, Ana Lúcia Lemos, Antônio de Pádua Deodato, Erica Salgado Politi, and Nilce M. S. Queiroz, "Cadeia produtiva do ovo no estado de São Paulo," *Informações Econômicas. Governo do Estado de São Paulo. Instituto de Economia Agrícola* 30, no. 1 (2000): 11, based on data given in table 1.

85. Globo Rural, http://revistagloborural.globo.com/Revista/Common/0,,ERT216287-18283,00.html, accessed February 11, 2017.

86. IBGE, SIDRA, table 74.

87. Joelma Cristina dos Santos, "Sistema agroindustrial do leite na região de Presidente Prudente–SP," MA thesis, Universidade Estadual Paulista, Presidente Prudentes, 2004, 51.

88. Sérgio Rangel Figueira, "Transformações na cadeia produtiva do leite—uma análise a partir das cooperativas," MA thesis, Universidade Estadual de Campinas, 1999, chap. 1.

89. Flávia Lopes Dionizio, "Qualidade do leite e impacto econômico de diferentes tipos de coletas e condições de transporte da fazenda à indústria," MA thesis, Universidade Federal de Minas Gerais, 2013, 15–19.

90. Paulo Roberto Scalco, "Identificação do poder de mercado no segmento de leite *in natura* e UHT," PhD thesis, Universidade Federal de Viçosa, 2011, 27.

91. Figueira, "Transformações na cadeia produtiva do leite," 2.

92. Data from Milkpoint, https://www.milkpoint.com.br/cadeia-do-leite/giro-lacteo/cooperativa-central-de-laticiniossp-e-a-primeira-a-exportar-13192n.aspx, accessed February 12, 2017.

93. Santos, "Sistema agroindustrial do leite na região de Presidente Prudente," 53.

94. Evandro Cesar Clemente, "Formação, dinâmica e a reestruturação da cadeia produtiva do leite na região de Jales-SP," MA thesis, Universidade Estadual Paulista, Presidente Prudente, 2006, 26–28.

95. IBGE, SIDRA, PMM, table 74.

96. IBGE, SIDRA, table 94.

97. Victor Hugo Junqueira, "O papel do estado na expansão do setor sucroalcooleiro na região de Ribeirão Preto," *Revista NERA* (Presidente Prudente) 19, no. 31 (2016): 56, table 1.

98. Daniel Alves de Aguiar, Wagner Fernando da Silva, Bernardo Friedrich Theodor Rudorff, Luciana Miura Sugawara, and Magog Araújo de Carvalho, "Expansão da cana-de-açúcar no estado de São Paulo: safras 2003/2004 a 2008/2009," paper presented at the Anais XIV Simpósio Brasileiro de Sensoriamento Remoto, Natal, April 2009, 12.

Chapter 4

1. Beginning in 1994 the IBGE adopted the classification system CNAE (Classificação Nacional de Atividades Econômicas), based on ISIC (International Standard Industrial Classification of All Activities) of the United Nations. The classification was updated in 2002. IBGE, *Classificação Nacional de Atividades Econômicas,* version 1 (Rio de Janeiro: IBGE, 2007). The A Comissão Nacional de Classificação (CONCLA) has the responsibility of updating the CNAE classification. See IBGE, CONCLA, https://concla.ibge.gov.br/concla.html, accessed November 15, 2019.

2. These are the Pesquisa Anual de Serviços (PAS) and the Pesquisa Anual de Comércio (PAC). For an analysis of these changes, see IBGE, Sínteses Históricas, Histórico dos Censo, https://memoria.ibge.gov.br/sinteses-historicas/historicos-dos-censos/censos-demograficos.html, accessed November 15, 2019.

3. This is the standard category name used by the US Bureau of Labor Statistics for what is called in Brazil "Servicos confecção e reparação"; see https://www.bls.gov/oes/2017/may/oes516052.htm.

4. The trade census presents sales and revenue data. In this case, we consider sales as the most important variable. In most services, the information refers to revenues and not sales. It is important to note that the variable is sales / revenue and not added value.

5. We combined the data for Rio de Janeiro and the Federal District in the tables, because the federal capital was a major center of services in general. Throughout the first half of the twentieth century, the state of São Paulo gradually overtook Rio de Janeiro in both industry and services despite the importance of the Federal District.

6. The Complementary Law no. 14, of July 8, 1973 created the Metropolitan Region of São Paulo (Região Metropolitana de São Paulo, RMSP). On the dynamics of the RMSP, see Regina Maria Prosperi Meyer, Marta Dora Grostein, and Ciro Biderman, *São Paulo Metrópole* (São Paulo: Edusp/Imprensa Oficial, 2004); Maria de Fátima Infante Araujo, "Trajetória econômica e espacial da metrópole Paulista," *São Paulo em Perspectiva* 7, no. 2 (1993): 29–37; Governo do Estado de São Paulo, *São Paulo no limiar do século XXI. Cenários da urbanização paulista. A região administrativa da Grande São Paulo*, 8 vols (São Paulo: Governo do Estado de São Paulo/Fundação SEADE, 1992); Maria

Irene de Q. F. Szmrecsányl, "A macro metrópole paulistana: 1950–2004," in Tamás Szmrecsányi, ed., *História econômica da cidade de São Paulo* (São Paulo: Editora Globo, 2005), 116–145.

7. On the ABC region, see Cecilia C. T. de Almeida, "O grande ABC paulista: o fetichismo da região," PhD thesis, FFLCH-USP, São Paulo, 2008; Jeroen Klink, "Regionalismo e reestruturação urbana: uma perspectiva brasileria de governança metropolitana," *Educação* (Porto Alegre) 32, no. 2 (2009): 217–226; Allen J. Scott, "Industrial Revitalization in the ABC Municipalities, São Paulo: Diagnostic Analysis and Strategic Recommendations for a New Economy and a New Regionalism," *Regional Development Studies* 7 (2001): 1–32; Angelo Marcos Queiroz Prates, "Reestruturação produtiva no Brasil dos anos 90 e seus impactos na Região do Grande ABC paulista," MA thesis, UNICAMP, Campinas, 2005.

8. There is a rich collection of studies on the state of São Paulo in the eight volumes of Governo do Estado de São Paulo, *São Paulo no limiar do século XXI.*

9. The industrial areas were initially installed in the lowland areas along the railroads, and from the 1950s onward, they began to move toward lands along the highways. Maria de Fátima Infante Araújo, "Os cem últimos anos na história da cidade e a formação da grande São Paulo," in Governo do Estado de São Paulo, *São Paulo no Limiar do Século XXI*, 6:28.

10. Censo Demográfico de 1980, volume 2, tomo 3, no. 1: 266.

11. Manuel Castells, *A sociedade em rede* (Rio de Janeiro: Paz e Terra, 2003); UNCTAD, *World Investment Report 2004: The Shift Towards Services* (New York: United Nations, 2004); Peter Dicken, *Global Shift: Mapping the Changing Contours of the World Economy* (New York: Guilford Press, 2000); Octavio de Barros and Fabio Giambiag, eds., *Brasil globalizado. O Brasil em um mundo surpreendente* (Rio de Janeiro: Elsevier, 2008); Gilberto Dupas, *Economia global e exclusão social* (São Paulo: Paz e Terra, 2000).

12. UNCTAD, *World Investment Report 2013, Global Value Chains: Investment and Trade for Development* (New York: United Nations, 2013), 122.

13. Harvey, when analyzing the so-called postmodern condition, understands that, parallel to the process of fragmentation of the production process, there were also significant changes at the consumption end, resulting in a notable increase in the use of services. David Harvey, *The Condition of Postmodernity* (Cambridge: Blackwell Publishers, 1992), 156.

14. IBGE, SIDRA, table 5938.

15. See the classification in https://concla.ibge.gov.br/busca-online-cnae.html?classe=45200&view=classe.

16. Altivo Roberto Andrade de Almeida Cunha, "Dimensões estratégicas e dilemas das Centrais de Abastecimento no Brasil," *Revista de Política Agrícola* XV, no. 4 (2006): 37–46. Also see Altivo Roberto Andrade de Almeida Cunha, "O sistema atacadista alimentar brasileiro: origens, destinos," PhD

thesis, UNICAMP, 2010; Altivo R. A. A. Cunha and Walter Belik, "Entre o declínio e a reinvenção: atualidade das funções do sistema público atacadista de alimentos no Brasil," *Revista de Economia e Sociologia Rura* 50, no. 3 (2012): 435–454.

17. CEAGESP (Companhia de Entrepostos e Armazéns Gerais de São Paulo) was established in 1969 by the fusion of two state companies: CEASA (Centro Estadual de Abastecimento) and CAGESP (Companhia de Armazéns Gerais do Estado de São Paulo). In 1997 the enterprise was turned into a federal company.

18. Governo Federal, https://www.ppi.gov.br/desestatizacao-da-ceagesp, accessed February 23, 2020.

19. São Paulo Turismo, http://cidadedesaopaulo.com/v2/atrativos/ceagesp/, accessed February 23, 2020.

20. Ministério da Agricultura, http://www.agricultura.gov.br/noticias/ceagesp-mudara-para-area-12-vezes-maior-a-atual-anuncia-governador-de-sp, accessed February 23, 2020.

21. For a complete list of the feiras (farmers markets) of São Paulo, see http://www9.prefeitura.sp.gov.br/secretarias/sdte/pesquisa/feiras/lista_completa.html.

22. A number of self-service stores had opened by the mid-twentieth century, but the first supermarket was opened in 1959 as Doceria Pão de Açúcar. Armando João Dalla Costa, *A importância da logística no varejo brasileiro: o caso Pão de Açúcar*, http://www.empresas.ufpr.br/logistica.pdf, 4, accessed December 10, 2017. Also see Umberto Antonio Sesso Filho, "O setor supermercadista no Brasil nos anos 1990," PhD thesis, Escola Superior de Agricultura Luiz de Queiroz, USP, 2003.

23. See Herbert S. Klein and Francisco Vidal Luna, *Feeding the World: Brazil's Transformation into a Modern Agricultural Economy* (Cambridge: Cambridge University Press, 2018).

24. Sesso Filho, "O setor supermercadista no Brasil nos anos 1990," 12; Denise Cavallini Ciryllo, *O papel do supermercado no varejo de alimentos* (São Paulo: Instituto de Pesquisas Econômicas, 1987), 198.

25. In 1975, Carrefour opened the first supermarket in the city of São Paulo. Regarding the consolidation process of supermarkets in this initial phase, see Cyrillo, "O papel do supermercado no varejo de alimentos."

26. Klein and Luna, *Feeding the World*, chap. 3.

27. Mariana Pires de Carvalho e Albuquerque, "Análise da evolução do setor supermercadista brasileiro: uma visão estratégica," MA thesis, Faculdade de Economia e Finanças IMBEC, Rio de Janeiro, 2007, 52.

28. Jony Lan, "A diversificação dos canais comerciais como fonte de vantagem competitiva em redes de supermercados no Brasil," MA thesis, Universidade Presbiteriana Mackenzie, São Paulo, 2010; Fernanda Bittencourt Pamplona, "Os investimentos diretos estrangeiros na indústria do varejo nos

supermercados no Brasil," MA thesis, Universidade Federal de Pernambuco, Recife, 2007; Ariel Wilder, "Mudanças no setor supermercadista e a formação de associações de pequenos supermercados," PhD thesis, Escola de Superior de Agricultura Luiz de Queiroz, Universidade de São Paulo, Piracicaba, 2003; PWC, "O setor de varejo e o consumo no Brasil. Como enfrentar a crise," January 2016, https://www.pwc.com.br/pt/estudos/setores-atividade/produtos-consumo-varejo/2016/pwc-setor-varejo-consumo-brasil-como-enfrentar-crise-16.html; Paulo Roberto do Amaral Ferreira, "O processo de globalização do varejo de massa e as lutas competitivas: o caso do setor supermercadista no Brasil," MA thesis, COPPEAD/UFRJ, Rio de Janeiro, 2013.

29. ABRAS (Associação o Brasileira de Supermercados), http://www.abras.com.br/economia-e-pesquisa/ranking-abras/os-numeros-do-setor/, accessed December 11, 2017.

30. See the useful overview by Elizabeth M. M. Q. Farina, "Consolidation, Multinationalisation, and Competition in Brazil: Impacts on Horticulture and Dairy Products Systems," *Development Policy Review* 20, no. 4 (2002): 441–457.

31. For an analysis of this question in the state of Rio Grande do Sul, see Vitor Francisco Dalla Corte, Sibele Vasconcelos de Oliveira, and Homero Dewesdas, "Market Concentration and Food Security in Developing Economies: Supermarket Power and Food Prices in the Brazilian State of Rio Grande do Sul," *Australian Journal of Basic and Applied Sciences* 9, no. 11 (2015): 1–7.

32. Semma Empresa de Shopping Centers, http://www.semma.com.br/historia-dos-shopping-centers-no-brasil/, accessed December 11, 2017.

33. The success of new shopping centers also depended on a basic change in rent charged to tenants. Leases specified that a store's tenant would pay a preestablished percentage of its sales as rent, which would allow potential investors to protect themselves against the losses caused by inflation, as well as to participate in the growing success of each mall, thus guaranteeing and increasing their financial return. Semma Empresa de Shopping Centers, http://www.semma.com.br/historia-dos-shopping-centers-no-brasil/, accessed December 11, 2017.

34. See ABRASCE, "Censo brasileiro de shopping centers," http://www.portaldoshopping.com.br/uploads/general/general_4b58c194fec5e617b0e01fc71487af24.pdf, accessed December 11, 2017; Bradesco, "Shopping center," DEPEC, June 2017, , accessed December 11, 2017; Fernando Garrefa, "Shopping centers, de centro de abastecimento a produto de consumo," PhD thesis, FAU/USP, 2007; Madalena Grimaldi de Carvalho, "A difusão e a integração dos shopping centers na cidade. As particularidades do Rio de Janeiro," PhD thesis, UFRJ, Rio de Janeiro, 2005; Silvia Catarina Araújo das Virgens, "Shopping center e a produção do espaço urbano em Salvador, BA," MA,

Universidade Federal da Bahia, Salvador, 2016; Charles Albert de Andrade, "Shopping center também tem memória: uma história esquecida dos shoppings centers nos espaços urbanos do Rio de Janeiro e de São Paulo nos anos 60 e 70," MA thesis, Universidade Federal Fluminense, Niterói, 2009.

35. ABRASCE (Associação Brasileira de Shopping Centers), https://abrasce.com.br/, accessed February 24, 2020. Despite the importance of these shopping mall projects in Brazil, they are modest compared to other countries. Gross leasable area per inhabitant is 1,872 m^2 in the United States, 1,127 m^2 in Canada, 590 m^2 in Australia, 303 m^2 in Japan, more than 200 m^2 in France, South Africa, and Spain, 81 m^2 in Mexico, and just 40 m^2 in Brazil.

36. Valor 1000, https://www.valor.com.br/valor1000/2019/ranking1000maiores, accessed November 30, 2019.

37. Banco Central do Brasil, "Estatística mensal por município," https://www.bcb.gov.br/estatisticas/estatisticabancariamunicipios, accessed November 30, 2019.

38. Francisco Vidal Luna, "São Paulo: a capital financeira do país," in Tamás Szmrecsányi, ed., *História econômica da cidade de São Paulo* (São Paulo: Editora Globo, 2005), 329–330.

39. On the financial sector and its consolidation in São Paulo, see Francisco Vidal Luna and Herbert S. Klein, *Brazil Since 1980* (Cambridge: Cambridge University Press, 2006), chap. 3; Luna, "São Paulo: a capital financeira do país," 328–355.

40. With high inflation, commercial banks sought to create extensive networks of branches to capture demand deposits, obtained without any remuneration. This increased costs but was offset by the inflationary tax obtained through demand deposits. In 1995, in order to anticipate the problems at this end of this system, the government created PROER, a program to stimulate bank restructuring and strengthen the national financial system in general; it was a great success.

41. Carlos Viana de Carvalho, "Relatório de economia bancária," Banco Central do Brasil, May 2019, https://www.bcb.gov.br/conteudo/home-ptbr/TextosApresentacoes/Apresentacao_REB%202018-2019_28_5_2019.pdf; also see Banco Central do Brasil, "Relatório de economia bancária 2018," https://www.bcb.gov.br/content/publicacoes/relatorioeconomiabancaria/reb_2018.pdf, accessed February 12, 2019.

42. In 1953 the so-called Cidade de Deus was created, to host the headquarters of Banco Bradesco and a village of employees. At that time, the region belonged to the municipality of São Paulo, but it was separated in 1962. Between Bradesco's headquarters in Cidade de Deus and São Paulo's former financial center, on Avenida Paulista, the distance is approximately 18 km.

43. For the purpose of calculating the representativeness of the city of São Paulo, we consider the amounts represented by Bradesco as generated in the

capital, as the bank's effective headquarters is in Osasco, which is completely integrated into the city of São Paulo. When the headquarters was created, that area, called Cidade de Deus, still belonged to the municipality of São Paulo.

44. Clarivate Analytics, "Research in Brazil," 54, https://www.capes.gov.br/images/stories/download/diversos/17012018-CAPES-InCitesReport-Final.pdf, accessed December 5, 2019.

Chapter 5

1. IBGE, SIDRA, table 1288, "População nos Censos Demográficos por situação do domicílio."

2. IBGE, SIDRA, table 1294, "Número de cidades e população nas cidades nos Censos Demográficos por tamanho da população."

3. IBGE, SIDRA, table 1287, "População dos municípios das capitais e percentual da população dos municípios das capitais em relação aos das unidades da federação nos Censos Demográficos."

4. IBGE, SIDRA, table 1287. It was not until 1960, when the metropolitan regional population of São Paulo reached 8.1 million, that it passed the metropolitan region of Rio de Janeiro, which then counted only 6.9 million persons. Ipeadata, Regional, População, http://www.ipeadata.gov.br/Default.aspx.

5. For the age data for São Paulo, see IBGE, Recenseamento Geral 1950, volume XXV, tomo 1: 1, table 1, calculated from individual year data and uncorrected for age bunching. For the age data for the nation, see CEPALSTAT, which has been corrected for such errors.

6. Sophisticated estimates mapping the fertility decline in all regions of Brazil stress that the "fertility transition began in small clusters of the South and Southeast before 1960 and gradually spread to the rest of the country over the next 30 years." Joseph E. Potter, Carl P. Schmertmann, Renato M. Assunção, and Suzana M. Cavenaghi, "Mapping the Timing, Pace, and Scale of the Fertility Transition in Brazil," *Population and Development Review* 36, no. 2 (2010): 292.

7. CELADE, "Brazil: Long Term Population Estimates and Projections 1950–2100" (2013 revision), https://www.cepal.org/celade/proyecciones/basedatos_BD.htm, accessed May 26, 2019; Fausto Brito, "Transição demográfica e desigualdades sociais no Brasil," *Revista Brasileira de Estudos Populacionais* 25, no. 1 (2008): 17, table 4; and IBGE, SIDRA, table 200.

8. IBGE, "Projeção da população por sexo e idade—Indicadores implícitos na projeção—2010/2060, [2018]," https://www.ibge.gov.br/estatisticas/sociais/populacao/9109-projecao-da-populacao.html?t=resultados, accessed June 5, 2019. Hereafter cited as IBGE, "Projeção da população" 2018.

9. It has been recently suggested that declining child mortality most likely influenced the decision to reduce fertility in the pre-oral-contraceptive period in most societies. See David Sven Reher, Glenn Sandström, Alberto

Sanz-Gimeno, and Frans W. A. van Poppel, "Agency in Fertility Decisions in Western Europe During the Demographic Transition: A Comparative Perspective," *Demography* 54, no. 1 (2017): 3–22.

10. Eduardo E. Arriaga and Kingsley Davis, "The Pattern of Mortality Change in Latin America," *Demography* 6, no. 3 (1969): 226.

11. Elza Berquó and S. M. Cavenaghi, "Demographic Evolution of the Brazilian Population During the Twentieth Century," in Daniel J. Hogan, ed., *Population Change in Brazil: Contemporary Perspectives* (Campinas: NEPO/UNICAMP, 2001), 15, table 3.

12. For European rates in 1930, see Francine Van de Walle, "Infant Mortality and the European Demographic Transition," in Ansley Johnson Coale, ed., *The Decline of Fertility in Europe* (Princeton: Princeton University Press, 2017), 212, table 4.2.

13. CELADE, *Boletim Demográfico* no. 74 (2004): 24, table 6.

14. The available infant mortality rates for urban populations show that in 1941 the urban infant mortality rate was 202 deaths per 1,000 live births, and in 1970 it was 109 deaths per 1,000 live births. See Joao Yunes, "Mortalité," in Elza S. Berquó and Candido Procopio F. de Camargo, eds., *La population du Brésil* (Paris: UN/CICRED, 1974): 52, table 26.

15. For national infant mortality rates, see IBGE, *Tábua completa de mortalidade para o Brasil—2017 Breve análise da evolução da mortalidade no Brasil* (Rio de Janeiro: IBGE, 2018), table 1, and for 2020, IBGE, "Projeção da população," 2018. It should be noted that this rate is still well above world standards: in 2010 the rate for Portugal was just 2.5 deaths per thousand live births. For this figure and other developed-world infant mortality rates in 2010, see CDC, "International Comparisons of Infant Mortality and Related Factors: United States and Europe, 2010," in *National Vital Statistics Reports* 63, no. 5 (2014), https://www.cdc.gov/nchs/data/nvsr/nvsr63/nvsr63_05.pdf.

16. SEADE, *SP Demográfico* 16, no. 4 (2016): 5, table 1.

17. IBGE, "Projeção da população" 2018.

18. IBGE, *Tábua completa de mortalidade para o Brasil—2017, Breve análise da evolução da mortalidade no Brasil*, 14, figs. 5 and 6, https://biblioteca.ibge.gov.br/visualizacao/livros/liv101628.pdf, accessed May 30, 2019.

19. For example, infectious diseases accounted for only 5% of the deaths in the state of São Paulo (and 7% of deaths among infants and children) in 2001. SEADE, Anuário Estatístico do Estado de São Paulo, 2001, quadro 25, accessed at http://www.seade.gov.br.

20. Some 30% of the deaths in São Paulo state in 2001 were due to heart disease, the biggest killer, followed by cancers, which accounted for another 15%. SEADE, Anuário Estatístico do Estado de São Paulo, 2001, quadro 25.

21. Cássia Maria Buchalla, Eliseu Alves Waldman, and Ruy Laurenti, "A mortalidade por doenças infecciosas no início e no final do século XX no Município de São Paulo," *Revista Brasileira de Epidemiologia* 6 (2003): 336–338.

22. Luana Junqueira Dias Myrrha, Cassio M. Turra, and Simone Wajnman, "A contribuição dos nascimentos e óbitos para o envelhecimento populacional no Brasil, 1950 a 2100." *Revista Latinoamericana de Población* 20 (2017): 45, table 1.

23. IBGE, SIDRA, table 364, "Número de óbitos registrados no ano por grupos de idade do(a) falecido(a), ano de ocorrência e sexo."

24. Anuario Estatistico de São Paulo, 2003, table 27, http://produtos.seade.gov.br/produtos/anuario/index.php?anos=2003&tip=ment&opt=temas&cap=2&tema=dem#1; for 2017, see IBGE, SIDRA, table 2684, "Óbitos, por ano de ocorrência, natureza do óbito, sexo, idade, local de ocorrência e lugar do registro."

25. SEADE, Histórico Demográfico do Município de São Paulo, table 25, found at http://smul.prefeitura.sp.gov.br/historico_demografico/tabelas.php.

26. *São Paulo, Annuário Demográphico, Anno XII, 1905*, 17 and table "Obitos por edade e sexo," 58–68.

27. IBGE, SIDRA, table 2684.

28. Rates of growth calculated from midyear population estimates of IBGE, found at Ipeadata, "População residente—1° de julho—Anual—Pessoa—IBGE Outras/Pop—DEPIS_POP."

29. Calculated from tables presented in CELADE, *Boletín Demográfico* no. 66 (July 2000).

30. CELADE, "Brazil: Long Term Population Estimates and Projections 1950–2100" (2013 revision).

31. CELADE, "Brazil: Long Term Population Estimates and Projections 1950–2100" (2013 revision). Also see Thomas William Merrick and Elza Berquó, *The Determinants of Brazil's Recent Rapid Decline in Fertility* (Washington, DC: National Academies Press, 1983), 20, table 2; and Joseph E. Potter, Carl P. Schmertmann, and Suzana M. Cavenaghi, "Fertility and Development: Evidence from Brazil," *Demography* 39, no. 4 (November 2002): 741. The estimate for 2020 comes from IBGE.

32. José Miguel Guzmán, "Introduction: Social Change and Fertility Decline in Latin America," in José Miguel Guzmán et al., *The Fertility Transition in Latin America* (Oxford: Clarendon Press, 1996), xxiii.

33. Luiz Antônio P. Oliveira and Celso Cardoso da S. Simões, "As informações sobre fecundidade, mortalidade e anticoncepção nas PNADs," *Livros*, 2015: 205, table 3.

34. UNFPA, *Fecundidade e dinâmica da população brasileira* (Brasília: UNFPA, 2018), 33; Elza Berquó, Regina Maria Barbosa, and Liliam Pereira de Lima, "Uso do preservativo: tendências entre 1998 e 2005 na população brasileira," *Revista de Saúde Pública* 42 (2008): 34–44.

35. Elisabeth Meloni Vieira, "A esterilização de mulheres de baixa renda em região metropolitana do sudeste do Brasil e fatores ligados à sua prevalência." *Revista de Saúde Pública* 28 (1994): 442, table 1, and 443, table 3.

36. Anibal Faúndes, Rosely Gomes Costa, Karla Simônia de Pádua, and Antero Marques Perdigão, "Associação entre prevalência de laqueadura tubária e características sócio-demográficas de mulheres e seus companheiros no Estado de São Paulo, Brasil," *Cadernos de Saúde Pública* 14 (1998): 51, table 1.

37. For age-specific fertility rates from 1933 to 1988, see Cláudia Júlia Guimarães Horta, José Alberto Magno de Carvalho, and Luís Armando de Medeiros Frias, "Recomposição da fecundidade por geração para Brasil e regiões: atualização e revisão," paper presented at the XI Encontro Nacional de Estudos Populacionais da ABEP, 2016, 6, table 3.

38. SEADE, *SP Demográfico* 15, no. 5 (2015): 13, table 6.

39. IBGE, Estatísticas do Registro Civil, 2002, volume 29, fig. 12, "Idade média ao casar—Brasil—1991/2002," and calculated for 1999 from IBGE, Estatísticas do Registro Civil, 1999, Casamentos, table 2.4, https://www.ibge.gov.br/estatisticas/sociais/populacao/9110-estatisticas-do-registro-civil.html?edicao=17071&t=downloads.

40. Calculated from IBGE, Estatísticas do Registro Civil, 2017, Tabelas de Resultados, Casamentos, Table 4.4.1, https://www.ibge.gov.br/estatisticas/sociais/populacao/9110-estatisticas-do-registro-civil.html?edicao=17071&t=downloads.

41. Calculated from IBGE, Estatísticas do Registro Civil, 2010, Casamentos, table 4.8, https://www.ibge.gov.br/estatisticas/sociais/populacao/9110-estatisticas-do-registro-civil.html?edicao=17071&t=downloads.

42. SEADA estimate accessed at https://www.seade.gov.br/em-sao-paulo-homens-casam-em-media-com-34-anos-e-mulheres-com-32/.

43. These 2030 estimates are in IBGE, "Projeção da população" 2018.

44. It should be noted that there are several other groupings of the state's municipalities based on education or health.

45. Juan Chackiel and Susana Schkolnik, "Latin America: Overview of the Fertility Transition, 1950–1990," in Jose Miguel Guzmán et al., *The Fertility Transition in Latin America* (Oxford: Clarendon Press, 1996), 4.

46. The data for 2020 are found in the 2018 projections from IBGE, "Projeção da população" 2018.

47. Ana Amélia Camarano and Ricardo Abramovay, "Êxodo rural, envelhecimento e masculinização no brasil: panorama dos últimos 50 anos," discussion paper no. 621, IPEA, Rio de Janeiro, 1998, 1. The authors point out that Brazil, like several other countries in Latin America, describes urban centers by administrative definition rather than size, which tends to underestimate the rural population.

48. IBGE, Estatísticas do Século XX, 2003, table "pop_S2T04."

49. Data for 1872–1972 from Maria Stella Ferreira Levy, "O papel da migração internacional na evolução da população brasileira (1872 a 1972)," *Revista de Saúde Pública* 8, supp. (1974): 71–73, table 1; data from 1820–1871 taken

from Directoria Geral de Estatistica, *Boletim Commemorativo da Exposição Nacional de 1908* (Rio de Janeiro, 1908), 82–85.

50. Thomas W. Merrick and Douglas H. Graham, *Population and Economic Development in Brazil, 1800 to the Present* (Baltimore: Johns Hopkins University Press, 1979), 125, table VI-4.

51. Rosana Baeninger, "São Paulo e suas migrações no final do século 20," *São Paulo em perspectiva* 19, no. 3 (2005): 87, table 1.

52. Marden Campos, "A migração para a região metropolitana de São Paulo no início do século XXI aspectos demográficos e familiares," *Anais do XXI Encontro Nacional de Estudos Populacionais*, 2018, 9, table 1.

53. IBGE, SIDRA, table 631.

54. IBGE, SIDRA, table 202.

55. Numbers generated from IBGE, SIDRA, tables 1294 and 1288.

56. Thus for example, between 1991 and 2002 the municipality of Belo Horizonte grew at only 1.1% per annum, while the towns surrounding the city and now making up the greater metropolitan area grew in the 1960s and 1970s at rates of 4.4% per annum. In 1991 these towns made up just 41% of the metropolitan regional population; eleven years later they made up half of the metropolitan population. Fundação João Pinheiro, *Perfil Demográfico do Estado de Minas Gerais 2000* (Belo Horizonte: Fundação João Pinheiro, 2003), 24, table 15.

57. Numbers generated from IBGE, SIDRA, table 202.

58. Fausto Brito and José Alberto M. de Carvalho, "As migrações internas no Brasil: as novidades sugeridas pelos censos demográficos de 1991 e 2000 e pela PNADs recentes," *Anais do XX Encontro Nacional de Estudos Populacionais*, 2016, 13, table 4.

59. Data taken from Brito and Carvalho. "As migrações internas no Brasil," 9, table 2.

60. The data for household and family size are from IBGE, Censo Demográfico, 1950, Série Nacional, volume 1: 286; IBGE, Censo Demográfico, 1960, Série Nacional, volume 1: 112; IBGE, Censo Demográfico, 1970, Série Nacional, volume 1: 206; IBGE, Censo Demográfico 2000—Resultados do universo, table 1.3.6; IBGE, Censo Demográfico 2010, Características da população e dos domicílios, resultado do universo, table 1.6.1; IBGE, Censo Demográfico 2010: famílias e domicílios resultados da amostra, table 1.1.3. The PNAD data for 1990, 2005, and 2015 are from IBGE, SIDRA, PNAD, tables 1940, 1948; also see José Eustáquio Diniz Alves and Suzana Cavenaghi, "Tendências demográficas, dos domicílios e das famílias no Brasil," *Aparte: Inclusão Social em Debate* 24 (2012): table 6; and Suzana Cavenaghi and José Eustáquio Diniz Alves, "Domicilios y familias en la experiencia censal del Brasil: cambios y propuesta para identificar arreglos familiares," *Notas de Población* [CEPAL] 37, no. 92 (2011): 33, cuadro 1; Arlindo Mello do

Nascimento, "População e família brasileira: ontem e hoje," paper presented at the XV Encontro Nacional de Estudos Populacionais, ABEP, 2006, 15, quadro 1.

61. For the urban rate in 1950 we have combined the urban and suburban populations. IBGE, Censo Demográfico, 1950, Série Nacional, volume 1: 280.

62. IBGE, SIDRA, table 382.

63. IBGE, SIDRA, table 668.

64. IBGE, SIDRA, Censo 2010, tables 3495 and 3521.

65. SEADE, "Histórico demográfico do Município de São Paulo," table 08, "Total de domicílios e no. médio pessoas/domicílio Município de São Paulo 1960 a 2000," http://smul.prefeitura.sp.gov.br/historico_demografico/tabelas.php.

66. IBGE, SIDRA, tables 156, 229, and 3145; IBGE, Recenseamento Geral 1970, Serie Nacional, volume 1: 232.

67. IBGE, SIDRA, table 385; IBGE, Síntese de indicadores sociais, 2014, table 5.1.

68. IBGE, Síntese de indicadores sociais, 2015, table 5.4.

69. IBGE, Síntese de indicadores sociais, 2005, table 5.5.

Chapter 6

1. IBGE, Censo Demográfico, 1950, Série Nacional, volume 1: 280.

2. Jusbrasil, "A trajetória do divórcio no Brasil: A consolidação do Estado Democrático de Direito," https://ibdfam.jusbrasil.com.br/noticias/2273698/a-trajetoria-do-divorcio-no-brasil-a-consolidacao-do-estado-democratico-de-direito, accessed November 26, 2017.

3. The constitution of 1988 was the act that finally recognized the legality of consensual unions. In article 226, paragraph 3, it declared: "the stable union between a man and a woman is recognized as a family entity, and the law should facilitate its conversion into marriage." And article 4 stated: "It is also understood as a family entity the community formed by any of the parents and their descendants." http://www.planalto.gov.br/ccivil_03/constituicao/constituicaocompilado.htm, accessed November 26, 2017. This was further amplified in 1996 in the so-called União Estável law (no. 9.278), which declared in article 1 that the state "recognized as a family entity, the lasting, public and continuous coexistence of a man and a woman, established with the objective of establishing a family." And in article 5: "all "property acquired by one or both of the cohabitants, in the course of a common-law marriage and for consideration, are considered the result of common work and collaboration, and will belong to both, . . . in equal parts, unless otherwise stipulated in written contract." http://www.planalto.gov.br/ccivil_03/leis/L9278.htm, accessed November 26, 2017. Also see Jamil Salim Amin, "A união estável no

Brasil a partir da constituição federal de 1988 e leis posteriores," MA thesis, Flroianopolis, Universidade Federal de Santa Catarina, 2001.

4. Regarding the rights of children born outside of a formal marriage, the big change came in 1977 with the recognition and inheritance rights of such children, which was further reinforced by the Constitution of 1988, which declared that "children, whether or not they are related to a formal marriage, or by adoption, will have the same rights and qualifications, and any discriminatory designation relating to parentage is prohibited (art. 227, § 6°)." Mafalda Lucchese, "Filhos—evolução até a plena igualdade jurídica," in *10 Anos do Código Civil Aplicação , Acertos, Desacertos, e Novos Rumos*, vol. 1 (Rio de Janeiro: EMERJ, 2013) (http://www.emerj.tjrj.jus.br/serieaperfeicoamentodemagistrados/paginas/series/13/volumeI/10anosdocodigocivil_231.pdf, accessed November 26, 2017.

5. The first microdata made available by the IBGE was for the census of 1960; for this reason this is the base year for most analyses based on the Ipums sample. Suzana M. Cavenaghi and José Eustáquio Diniz Alves, "Domicilios y familias en la experiencia censal del Brasil: cambios y propuesta para identificar arreglos familiares," *Notas de población* [CEPAL] 37, no. 92 (2011): 19.

6. IBGE, Estatísticas do Registro Civil, table 426, "Número de divórcios concedidos em primeira instância por grupos de idade da mulher e do marido na data da sentença."

7. As could be expected, the mean age of persons separating, for both sexes, was three years less than those getting a final divorce. IBGE, Estatísticas do Registro Civil, 2002, volume 29, fig. 14, "Idade média da população de 20 a 64 anos de idade, na data da separação judicial e divórcio—Brasil—2002."

8. IBGE, Estatísticas do Registro Civil, table 426, "Número de divórcios concedidos em primeira instância por grupos de idade da mulher e do marido na data da sentença."

9. IBGE, Estatísticas do Registro Civil, table 723, "Número de divórcios concedidos em primeira instância por número de filhos do casal."

10. IBGE, Síntese de Indicadores Sociais, 2002, 271. For the divorce rate in 2017, see Rodrigo da Cunha Pereira, "Divórcios aumentaram e casamentos estão durando menos," March 11, 2019, http://www.rodrigodacunha.adv.br/divorcio/.

11. Glaucia Marcondes, "Rompendo laços: perfil das separações judiciais e divórcios no Brasil (1984–2010)," in *Congreso de ALAP 2012*, vol. 5: 9, table 1.

12. IBGE, Síntese de Indicadores Sociais, 2002, 275 and 277, tables 10.3 and 10.5.

13. IBGE, table 5.1, "Taxa de nupcialidade, segundo as Grandes Regiões e as Unidades da Federação—1999/2008," https://ww2.ibge.gov.br/home/estatistica/populacao/condicaodevida/indicadoresminimos/sinteseindicsociais2010/default_tab.shtm, accessed June 14, 2019.

14. IBGE, Síntese de Indicadores Sociais, 2004, table 6.6.

15. IBGE, SIDRA, table 2995.

16. IBGE, Estatísticas do Século XX, table "População1986aeb-047." In 1981 the figure was just 17%; IBGE, Estatísticas do Século XX, table "População1984aeb-089."

17. IBGE, "Pessoas responsáveis pelos Domicílios Particulares Permanentes," http://www.sidra.ibge.gov.br/bda/popul/.

18. PNAD 2002, Síntese de Indicadores, 129, fig. 5.2, and IBGE, SIDRA, table 1942.

19. IBGE, SIDRA, table 1942.

20. Calculated from PNAD 2015.

21. IBGE, SIDRA, table 97.

22. See Luiz Guilherme Dacar da Silva Scorzafave, "Caracterização da inserção feminina no mercado de trabalho e seus efeitos sobre a distribuição de renda," PhD thesis, FEA/USP, 2004, chap. 2.

23. In Brazil all income transfers related to the Bolsa Família are exclusively given to the mother even if a spouse is present. Priscilla Albuquerque Tavares, "Efeito do Programa Bolsa Família sobre a oferta de trabalho das mães," paper presented at XVI Encontro Nacional de Estudos Populacionais, ABEP, 2008, 4–5.

24. IBGE, SIDRA, table 1134. The number of men assisting female heads of households in this census year is below that of the PNAD surveys of the years before and after, giving a ratio of 26% to 29% of female-headed households depending on the color/ethnicity of the women. The lower census figure may be due to the question that asked if there was a "compartilhamento da responsabilidade pelo domicílio com a pessoa responsável" (someone helping run the household with you); the higher PNAD figure may be due to the existence of male spouses who were not providing any significant support to the female head of household.

25. IBGE, Estatísticas do Registro Civil, table 426, "Número de divórcios concedidos em primeira instância por grupos de idade da mulher e do marido na data da sentença."

26. For 2015, IBGE, SIDRA, table 1695; for earlier periods, IBGE, Estatísticas do Registro Civil, table 426, "Número de divórcios concedidos em primeira instância por grupos de idade da mulher e do marido na data da sentença."

27. The number of divorces conceded in these years. See IBGE, SIDRA, table 5929.

28. IBGE, Síntese de Indicadores Sociais, 2002, 275 and 277, tables 10.3 and 10.5.

29. Calculated from PNAD 2015. For data from 1992 to 2008, see IETS, Análises dos Indicadores do PNAD, https://www.iets.org.br/spip.php?rubrique2.

30. Calculated from PNAD 2015.

31. For all workers, IBGE, SIDRA, Censo Demográfico 2010, Resultados do Universo—Características da População e dos Domicílios, table 3170; for workers in the formal sector, IBGE, SIDRA, table 3577; and calculations from PNAD 2015.

32. IBGE, *Estatísticas de Gênero*, 2014, 66, fig. 5.

33. For example Carvalho shows that the third largest source of income in families in the Southeast metropolitan regions were widows pensions (65)—following salaries and retirement pensions (18%) in 2011. Cleuseni Hermelina de Carvalho, "Bolsa família e desigualdade da renda domiciliar entre 2006 e 2011,"(MA thesis; PUC São Paulo, 2013) :127, table 29.

34. Medeiros and Costa, "Poverty Among Women in Latin America."

35. See Marcelo Medeiros and Joana Simões Costa, "Poverty among women in Latin America: feminization or overrepresentation?," working paper no. 20, International Poverty Centre, Brasília, 2006.

36. Ricardo Barros, Louise Fox and Rosane Mendonça, "Female-Headed Households, Poverty, and the Welfare of Children in Urban Brazil," *Economic Development and Cultural Change* 45, no. 2 (1997): 231–257. Their data is based on the PNAD survey of 1984.

37. Jorge A. Rodríguez Vignoli, "Cohabitación en América Latina: ¿modernidad, exclusión o diversidad?," *Papeles de Población* 10, no. 40 (2004): 97–145.

38. IBGE, Sidra, table 1942.

39. IBGE, Estatísticas do Registro Civil, 2002 (Rio de Janeiro: IBGE, volume 29), n.p, fig. 10, "Taxa de nupcialidade geral—Brasil—1991–2002"; IBGE, Síntese de Indicadores Sociais, 2002, 269–270.

40. IBGE, SIDRA, table 1134.

41. On the surprisingly high income and status of elderly women living alone see Fabio Roberto Bárbolo Alonso, "As mulheres idosas que residem em domicílios unipessoais: uma caracterização regional a partir do Censo 2010," *Revista Kairós Gerontologia, Revista da Faculdade de Ciências Humanas e Saúde* 18, no. 19 (2015): 106, table 3. This pattern of wealth of women living alone compared to similar aged women living in families can be seen in local studies as well. See, for example, Mirela Castro Santos Camargos, Carla Jorge Machado, and Roberto Nascimento Rodrigues, "A relação entre renda e morar sozinha para idosas mineiras, 2003," paper presented at the XII Seminário Sobre a Economia Mineira, 2006, 6–7 and table 1.

42. Alonso, "As mulheres idosas," 111, table 6.

43. Brazil, Estatísticas do Século XX,2003, table "pop_1965aeb-05.1."

44. IBGE, Sidra, Censo 2000, table 2097.

45. IBGE, Censo 1991, table 141; IBGE, PNAD, table 1187.

46. This in the census of that year 13% of women had 11 or more years of schooling, compared to only 11% of the men. IBGE, Sidra, Censo 1991, table 142.

47. IBGE, Estatísticas do Século XX, 2003, table "Educação1955aeb-05."

48. Kaizô Iwakami Beltrão and José Eustáquio Diniz Alves, "A reversão do hiato de gênero na educação brasileira no Século XX." *Anais* (2016): 10, Figure 1.

49. IBGE, Sidra, PNAD, table 1189; for 2016, see IBGE, PNAD, Indicadores Sociais, 2016, table 4.13, found at https://www.ibge.gov.br/estatisticas-novoportal/sociais/populacao/9221-sintese-de-indicadores-sociais.html?edicao=9222&t=downloads.

50. IBGE, PNAD, Indicadores Socias, 2016, table 4.14, found at https://www.ibge.gov.br/estatisticas-novoportal/sociais/populacao/9221-sintese-de-indicadores-sociais.html?edicao=9222&t=downloads.

51. IBGE, *Estatísticas de Gênero*, 2014, 96, fig. 22.

52. IBGE, SIDRA, census, table 616.

53. IBGE, Censo Demográfico, 1950, Série Nacional, volume 1: 8, table 9.

54. For a discussion of the demographic bonus in the Brazilian context, see José Eustáquio Diniz Alves, "Crise no mercado de trabalho, bônus demográfico e desempoderamento feminino," in Nathalie Reis Itaboraí and Arlene Martinez Ricoldi, eds., *Até onde caminhou a revolução de gênero no Brasil? Implicações demográficas e questões sociais* (Belo Horizonte: ABEP, 2016), 23.

55. Alves, "Crise no mercado de trabalho," 29.

56. Adriana Strasburg de Camargo Andrade, "Mulher e trabalho no Brasil dos anos 90," PhD thesis, Universidade de Campinas, 2004, 61, table 01.

57. IBGE, SIDRA, census, table 616; Alves, "Crise no mercado de trabalho," 27, for pre-1991 rates.

58. US Bureau of Labor Statistics, table 3. 3, "Civilian Labor Force Participation Rate, by Age, Sex, Race, and Ethnicity, 1996, 2006, 2016, and Projected 2026 (in Percent)," https://www.bls.gov/emp/ep_table_303.htm, accessed December 4, 2017. The BLS estimates for 2050 are at https://www.bls.gov/opub/ted/2007/jan/wk2/art03.htm, accessed December 4, 2017.

59. The OECD data are available for 2000–2016 at https://stats.oecd.org/Index.aspx?DataSetCode=LFS_SEXAGE_I_R, accessed December 5, 2017.

60. Simone Wajnman, "'Quantidade' e 'qualidade' da participação das mulheres na força de trabalho brasileira," in Nathalie Reis Itaboraí and Arlene Martinez Ricoldi, eds., *Até onde caminhou a revolução de gênero no Brasil? Implicações demográficas e questões sociais* (Belo Horizonte: ABEP, 2016), 46–47.

61. IBGE, *Estatísticas de Gênero*, 2014, 103, table 15; 104, fig. 28; 106, fig. 30.

62. Wajnman, "'Quantidade' e 'qualidade' da participação," 48–49.

63. On current industrial participation rates of women, see "Participação de mulheres no mercado de trabalho industrial cresce 14,3% em 20 anos," Agência de Notícias da Indústria, November 8, 2016, http://www.portaldaindustria.com.br/agenciacni/noticias/2016/11/participacao-de-mulheres-no

-mercado-de-trabalho-industrial-cresce-143-em-20-anos/, accessed November 30, 2017.

64. Amélia Artes and Arlene Martinez Ricoldi, "Mulheres e as carreiras de prestigio no ensino superior brasileiro: o não lugar feminino," in Nathalie Reis Itaboraí and Arlene Martinez Ricoldi, eds., *Até onde caminhou a revolução de gênero no Brasil? Implicações demográficas e questões sociais* (Belo Horizonte: ABEP, 2016), 89, quadro1.

65. IBGE, Sintese de Indicadores Sociais, 2016, table 5.15, https://www.ibge.gov.br/estatisticas-novoportal/sociais/trabalho/9221-sintese-de-indicadores-sociais.html?edicao=9222&t=downloads.

66. Noronha usefully defines the *carteira de trabalho*, or labor booklet, as "a sort of a 'labor ID' in which the employers are obliged to write down information about their wage, social security, hiring and firing dates and conditions, among other details. Therefore, the Labor Booklet tells the history of all formal jobs the worker has had and it is frequently used to show that the worker is a reliable citizen when he is hired for a new job or needs to get a loan, and that he deserves to be respected by the society." Eduardo G. Noronha, "Informal, Illegal and Unfair: Perceptions of Labor Markets in Brazil," *Revista Brasileira de Ciências Sociais* 18, no. 53 (2003): 111–129, http://socialsciences.scielo.org/scielo.php?pid=S0102-69092005000100009&script=sci_arttext&tlng=en.

67. This was first issued by the Vargas government in 1943 (decree-law no. 5.452, of May 1, 1943) and has been amended constantly through the years, with the latest amendment occurring in 2017 to include part-time workers' rights. See Marcelo Moura, *Consolidação das leis do trabalho*, 7th ed. (Salvador: JusPodivm, 2017), https://www.editorajuspodivm.com.br/cdn/arquivos/ca615420c19a66758beaf108395fe01b.pdf, accessed December 7, 2017.

68. IBGE, SIDRA, table 1916.

69. IBGE, Síntese de Indicadores Sociais, 2016, table 5.13, https://www.ibge.gov.br/estatisticas-novoportal/multidominio/genero/9221-sintese-de-indicadores-sociais.html?edicao=10739&t=downloads.

70. IBGE, *Estatísticas de Gênero*, 2014, 137, table 37.

71. Maria Cristina Aranha Bruschini, "Trabalho e gênero no Brasil nos últimos dez anos," *Cadernos de Pesquisa* 37, no. 132 (2007): 537.

72. For law 5859/72, see http://www.normaslegais.com.br/legislacao/trabalhista/lei5859_1972.htm.

73. For law 150/2015, see http://www.planalto.gov.br/ccivil_03/leis/LCP/Lcp150.htm.

74. The first of these anti-slavery laws was passed in the penal code of 1940 (art. 149), but it really became effective in the 1990s; it was revised only recently, in 2017. See https://www.jusbrasil.com.br/topicos/10621211/artigo-149-do-decreto-lei-n-2848-de-07-de-dezembro-de-1940.

75. Andrade, "Mulher e trabalho no Brasil," 62, table 03.
76. IBGE, SIDRA, table 1906.
77. IBGE, SIDRA, table 1908.

Chapter 7

1. UNU/WIDER World Income Inequality Database (WIID), "World Income Inequality Database WIID3.4, Released in January 2017," at https://www.wider.unu.edu/database/world-income-inequality-database-wiid34. For Brazil the latest 2006 PNAD survey gives 16% for the bottom 50% and 45% for the top 10 (IBGE, SIDRA, table 297).

2. WIID, table WID2a1. IPEA lists Brazil's top 10% as owning 47% of total income in 1981 and 46% in 2002. Ipeadata, "Renda—parcela apropriada por 10% mais ricos—(% renda total)."

3. Usually inequality studies in Brazil are based on PNAD (National Survey by Household Samples), which includes in the questionnaire income from work, pensions, retirement income, donations, transfers from social programs, rents, and interest from financial investment and dividends. IBGE, PNAD, "Dicionário de variáveis da PNAD 2015," https://ww2.ibge.gov.br/home/estatistica/populacao/trabalhoerendimento/pnad2015/microdados.shtm.

4. As a recent World Bank study concluded, "According to household surveys, the richest 10 percent of individuals receive between 40 and 47 percent of total income in most Latin American societies, while the poorest 20 percent receive only 2–4 percent. These differences are substantially higher than in OECD countries, Eastern Europe, and most of Asia. Moreover, the most distinctive attribute of Latin American income inequality is the unusually large concentration of income at the very top of the distribution. . . . Even the most equal countries in Latin America (Costa Rica and Uruguay) have significantly higher levels of income inequality." David de Ferranti, Guillermo E. Perry, Francisco Ferreira, and Michael Walton, *Inequality in Latin America: Breaking with History?* (Washington, DC: World Bank, 2004), Summary-3. For the latest Gini indices for Latin America, see fig. 2-3: 2-10.

5. Traditionally the studies on the distribution of income were made on the basis of the PNAD surveys, which have been carried out in Brazil annually since the mid-1970s. To these annual surveys were added the data from the decennial censuses. Recently several studies were done based on the annual income tax declarations. These are usually more accurate for the top of the income scale, and have resulted in studies showing higher ratios of concentration than were found for the PNAD and census-based studies alone.

6. Marcelo Medeiros and Pedro H. G. F. Souza, "A estabilidade da desigualdade no Brasil entre 2006 e 2012: resultados adicionais," *Pesquisa e Planejamento Econômico* 46, no. 3 (2016): table 1.

7. Medeiros and Souza, "A estabilidade," 20, fig. 2.

8. While comparisons are difficult due to changing tax collections, taxable rates, and estimates of gross income and wealth in earlier periods, a recent study suggest a relative stability of shares of total income for the top 1% going back to the 1930s. See Pedro H. G. F. Souza, "Top Incomes in Brazil, 1933–2012: A Research Note," December 11, 2014, http://dx.doi.org/10.2139/ssrn.2537026, accessed October 6, 2017.

9. Thomas Piketty, *Capital in the 21st Century* (Cambridge, MA: Harvard University Press, 2014). Also see Facundo Alvaredo, Anthony B. Atkinson, Thomas Piketty, and Emmanuel Saez, "The Top 1 Percent in International and Historical Perspective," *Journal of Economic Perspectives* 27, no. 3 (2013): 3–20; Branko Milanovic, "Global Inequality and the Global Inequality Extraction Ratio: The Story of the Past Two Centuries," *Explorations in Economic History* 48 (2011): 494–506.

10. Marc Morgan, "Extreme and Persistent Inequality: New Evidence for Brazil Combining National Accounts, Surveys and Fiscal Data, 2001–2015," working paper series, no. 12, World Wealth and Income Database, 2017, 47, table 2.

11. Recent data correlating income groups and years of schooling show that Brazil has consistently improved for all age groups over time in average years of schooling even for the bottom deciles of income. Nevertheless, income inequality levels have changed little. For education and income distribution data, see Ferranti et al., *Inequality in Latin America*, 419–20, 422, tables A22, A23, and A25. Also see the age breakdown in more detail in the supplementary educational/age and Gini index tables found at http://www.depeco.econo.unlp.edu.ar/cedlas/wb/.

12. Warren Dean, "Latifundia and Land Policy in Nineteenth-Century Brazil," *The Hispanic American Historical Review* 51, no. 4 (1971): 606–625.

13. Antonio Marcio Buiainai et al., "Sete teses sobre o mundo rural brasileiro," in Antônio Márcio Buainain et al., eds., *O mundo rural no Brasil do século 21, A formação de um novo padrão agrário e agrícola* (Brasília, DF: Embrapa, 2014), 1159–1182. On the recent development of Brazilian agriculture, see Herbert S. Klein and Francisco Vidal Luna, *Feeding the World: Brazil's Transformation into a Modern Agricultural Economy* (Cambridge: Cambridge University Press, 2018).

14. See Bastiaan Philip Reydon, "Governança de terras e a questão agrária no Brasil," in Antônio Márcio Buainain et al., eds., *O mundo rural no Brasil do século 21:A formação de um novo padrão agrário e agrícola* (Brasília: Embrapa, 20014), 736, table 3.

15. There are few specific studies on the transition of the freed slaves in 1888 and their immediate insertion in the labor market (either in the coffee plantations, in supplementary activities, or in subsistence agriculture) or their integration into urban life. On the sociological aspects of this transition, see the seminal work of Florestan Fernandes, *A Integração do Negro na Sociedade*

de Classes (São Paulo: Ática, 1978). See also Hebe Maria Mattos, *Das cores do silêncio* (Rio de Janeiro: Nova Fronteira, 1998).

16. CEPAL, Anuario Estadistica de America Latina, 1980, 102, table 35.

17. Censo 1950, volume 1, Serie Nacional, 90, quadro 47.

18. IBGE, Século XX, tables "Educação1960aeb-02.1" and "Educacao1990aeb15."

19. Helena Sampaio, Fernando Limongi, and Haroldo Torres, "Equidade e heterogeneidade no ensino superior brasileiro," documento de trabalho 1/00, NUPES-USP, n.d.; Maria Helena Guimarães de Castro, "Avaliação do sistema educacional brasileiro: tendências e perspectivas," INEP, Brasília, 1998; Nadir Zago, "Do acesso à permanência no ensino superior: percurso de estudantes universitários de camadas populares," *Revista Brasileira de Educação* 11, no. 32 (2006): 226–237; Nilson José Machado, "Qualidade da educação: cinco lembretes e uma lembrança," *Estudos Avançados* 21, no. 61 (2007): 277–294; José Goldemberg. "O repensar da educação no Brasil," *Estudos Avançados* 7, no. 18 (1993): 65–137; Simon Schwartzman, Eunice Ribeiro Durham, and José Goldemberg, "A educação no Brasil em perspectiva de transformação," Projeto sobre Educação na América Latina, São Paulo, June 1993, http://www.schwartzman.org.br/simon/transform.htm.

20. After the government spent years combating inflation by both orthodox and heterodox methods, the Plan Real obtained effective results; inflation has remained stable for ten years. Among the extensive literature in this subject are the following: João Sayad, "Planos Cruzado e Real: Acertos e desacertos," Seminários Dimac no. 30, IPEA, Rio de Janeiro, September 2000; Luiz Filgueiras, *História do Plano Real* (São Paulo: Boitempo Editorial, 2000); Aloizio Mercadante, ed., *O Brasil pós Real. A política econômica em debate*_(Campinas: UNICAMP, 1997); Fabio Giambiagi and Maurício Mesquita Moreira, *A economia brasileira nos anos 90* (Rio de Janeiro: BNDES, 1990); Maria da Conceição Tavares, *Destruição não criadora* (Rio de Janeiro: Record, 1990); Gustavo Franco, *O Plano Real e outros ensaios* (Rio de Janeiro: Editora Francisco Alves, 1995). Even the former minister of agriculture and planning in the military government, Delfim Netto, one of Brazil's most respected economists, said that the Real Plan was "a little gem. It was an important and practical contribution of the Brazilian economists who participated in it. Some of them had the experiences of other stabilization programs, but it was a new concept." Despite these accolades, he would emphatically criticize the appreciation of the national currency that occurred after its implementation. Ribamar Oliveira, "Delfim Netto: Plano Real acentuou redução da capacidade exportadora brasileira," *Jornal Valor Econômico*, June 29, 2014.

21. Rodolfo Hoffman and Regis Oliveira, "The Evolution of Income Distribution in Brazil in the Agricultural and the Non-Agricultural Sectors," *World Journal of Agricultural Research* 2, no. 5 (2014): 194, table 1.

22. Utilizing the estimates of the population given by IBGE, http://www.ibge.gov.br/home/estatistica/populacao/projecao_da_populacao/2013/default.shtm, accessed July 28, 2018, as well as the estimates of GDP published by the Banco Central in *Focus: Relatório do Mercado*, https://www.bcb.gov.br/pec/GCI/PORT/readout/R20180720.pdf, accessed July 20, 2018. For the 2019 estimate see World Bank at: https://data.worldbank.org/indicator/NY.GDP.PCAP.CD?locations=BR. Acessed December 2, 2021

23. See Edmar Bacha and Herbert S. Klein, eds., *Social Change in Brazil, 1945–1985: The Incomplete Transformation* (Albuquerque: University of New Mexico Press, 1989).

24. IETS/OPE Sociais, based on PNAD, table "PNAD—Séries Históricas—Pobreza—1990–2014," https://www.iets.org.br/spip.php?article406, accessed July 4, 2019.

25. IBGE, SIDRA, table 1860.

26. Kaizô Iwakami Beltrão, Francisco Eduardo Barreto de Oliveira, and Sonoê Sugahara Pinheiro, "A população rural e a previdência social no Brasil: uma análise com ênfase nas mudanças constitucionais," discussion paper no. 759, IPEA, Rio de Janeiro, 2000.

27. PNUD, Fundação João Pinheiro, IPEA, Atlas do Desenvolvimento Humano no Brasil, 2003.

28. Hoffman and Oliveira, "The Evolution of Income Distribution in Brazil 2014," table 2.

29. Brazil, Estatísticas do Século XX, 2003, table "trabalho1981aeb_01."

30. Carlos Antonio Costa Ribeiro and Maria Celi Scalon, "Mobilidade de classe no Brasil em perspectiva comparada," *Dados: Revista de Ciências Sociais* 44, no. 1 (2001): 53–96.

31. José Pastore, *Inequality and Social Mobility in Brazil* (Madison: University of Wisconsin Press, 1982), chap. 4.

32. Adalberto Cardoso and Edmond Préteceille, "Classes médias no Brasil: Do que se trata? Qual seu tamanho? Como vem mudando?," *Dados: Revista de Ciências Sociais* 60, no. 4 (2017): 999, table 2.

33. Pastore, *Inequality and Social Mobility*, 21.

34. Pastore, *Inequality and Social Mobility*, 32–33.

35. Carlos Antonio Costa Ribeiro and Maria Celi Scalon, "Mobilidade de classe no Brasil em perspectiva comparada," *Dados: Revista de Ciências Sociais* 44, no. 1 (2001): 66, table 4.

36. These data are from Carlos Antonio Costa Ribeiro, "Quatro décadas de mobilidade social no Brasil," *Dados: Revista de Ciências Sociais* 55, no. 3 (2012): 656, table 1.

37. Ribeiro and Scalon, "Mobilidade de classe no Brasil," table A, and Ribeiro, "Quatro décadas de mobilidade," table 1.

38. For an interesting discussion of these strategies, see Marcelo Medeiros, "O que faz os Ricos ricos: um estudo sobre fatores que determinam a

riqueza," PhD thesis, Departamento de Sociologia, Universidade de Brasília, 2003.

39. Carlos Antonio Costa Ribeiro, "Tendências da desigualdade de oportunidades no Brasil: mobilidade social e estratificação educacional," *Boletim, Mercado de Trabalho: Conjuntura e Análise* (IPEA) 23, no. 62 (2017): 656, table 1.

40. Pastore, *Inequality and Social Mobility*, 69, table 5.1.

41. For a detailed analysis of the PNAD 2015 survey, see Herbert S. Klein and Francisco Luna, *Brazil: A Modern Social History* (Cambridge: Cambridge University Press, 2020), chap. 7. A recent study by Torche and Ribeiro supports this idea of changing patterns of mobility in the pre- and post-1980s periods. They also stress the declining bonus given to education as more workers achieve equal levels of education. See Florencia Torche and Carlos Costa Ribeiro, "Pathways of Change in Social Mobility: Industrialization, Education and Growing Fluidity in Brazil," *Research in Social Stratification and Mobility* 28, no. 3 (2010): 291–307.

42. See Florencia Torche, "Unequal but Fluid: Social Mobility in Chile in Comparative Perspective," *American Sociological Review* 70, no. 3 (2005): 422–450; and Florencia Torche, "Intergenerational Mobility and Inequality: The Latin American Case," *Annual Review of Sociology* 40 (2014): 619–642.

43. The Amerindian population was 4% of the population in 1872 but only 0.4% in the census of 2010, and it was not counted in twentieth-century censuses until 1991. Equally, race was not listed in the census of 1920 and was dropped from the census of 1970.

44. Rafael Guerreiro Osório, "O sistema classificatório de 'cor ou raça' do IBGE," discussion paper no. 996, IPEA, Brasília, 2003. On intergenerational boundary-crossing among families, see Luisa Farah Schwartzman, "Does Money Whiten? Intergenerational Changes in Racial Classification in Brazil," *American Sociological Review* 72 (2007): 940–963.

45. For a very good review of the Brazilian sociological literature on this debate about racism, see Rafael Guerreiro Osório, "A mobilidade social dos negros brasileiros," discussion paper no. 1033, IPEA, Brasília, 2004.

46. IBGE, SIDRA, table 136; Censo Demográfico 1950, Série Nacional, volume 1: 69, table 39.

47. IBGE, SIDRA, table 262.

48. "In the 1990s, reflections on the demography of inequality emerged as a new object of study in the public health field . . . and leaders from the black movement began to question the relationship between racism and health, urging the public health administration to include the race/color category in the health information systems. This inclusion first took place in São Paulo City (Ordinance n. 696/90 7). In 1996, the color category was included in the Brazilian Ministry of Health's Mortality Information and Live-Births Information Systems (Ordinance n. 3,947/98 8)." Luis Eduardo Batista and Sônia Barros,

"Confronting Racism in Health Services," *Cadernos de Saúde Pública* 33 (2017): 1. See also Rubens de C. F. Adorno, Augusta Thereza de Alvarenga, and Maria da Penha Vasconcellos, "Quesito cor no sistema de informação em saúde," *Estudos Avançados* 18, no. 50 (2004): 119–123.

49. See Francisco Vidal Luna and Herbert S. Klein, *The Economic and Social History of Brazil Since 1889* (Cambridge: Cambridge University Press, 2014), chap. 4.

50. Estela Maria Garcia de Pinto da Cunha, "Condicionantes da mortalidade infantil segundo raça/cor no estado de São Paulo, 1997–1998," PhD thesis, Campinas Fac de Ciencias Medicias, 2001, 78, table 5.

51. It should be noted that the data for 1950 that appear in Charles H. Wood, José Alberto Magno de Carvalho, and Cláudia Júlia Guimarães Horta, "The Color of Child Mortality in Brazil, 1950–2000: Social Progress and Persistent Racial Inequality," *Latin American Research Review* 45, no. 2 (2010): 114–139, differ considerably from the estimates for 1950 given in Charles H. Wood and José Alberto Magno de Carvalho, *The Demography of Inequality in Brazil* (Cambridge: Cambridge University Press, 1988), 145, table 6.2. Also, it would seem that in this and many other aspects, the census of 1991 is not very reliable.

52. This study, however, did not control for age, so the higher white rates for classic degenerative diseases may be due to differences in life expectancy. See Luís Eduardo Batista, Maria Mercedes Loureiro Escuder, and Julio Cesar Rodrigues Pereira, "A cor da morte: causas de óbito segundo características de raça no Estado de São Paulo, 1999 a 2001," *Revista da Saúde Pública* 38, no. 5 (2004): 633, table 2.

53. Paulo Andrade Lotufo and Isabela Judith Martins Bensenor, "Raça e mortalidade cerebrovascular no Brasil," *Revista de Saúde Pública* 47, no. 6 (2013): 1201.

54. All of these indices of access to health care can be found at IBGE, SIDRA, Pesquisa Nacional de Saúde, https://sidra.ibge.gov.br/pesquisa/pns, and especially "Saúde de Mulheres" in volume 4 and volume 1. A more recent study has suggested that there are still some differences in prenatal care and hospital birth experiences between Blacks, Whites, and Browns. Maria do Carmo Leal, Silvana Granado Nogueira da Gama, Ana Paula Esteves Pereira, Vanessa Eufrauzino Pacheco, Cleber Nascimento do Carmo, and Ricardo Ventura Santos, "The Color of Pain: Racial Iniquities in Prenatal Care and Childbirth in Brazil," *Cadernos de Saúde Pública* 33, supp. 1 (2017): 2–17.

55. IBGE, SIDRA, table 1173.

56. PNAD, 2001, microdata, table 9.16.

57. IBGE, Síntese de Indicadores Socias, 2017, table 1.25, found in a separate appendix data set at https://www.ibge.gov.br/estatisticas-novoportal/sociais/populacao/9221-sintese-de-indicadores-sociais.html?edicao=9222&t=downloads, accessed July 7, 2019.

58. The figures were 86% to 79% for the 15–17 cohort and 30% to 23% for the 20–24 group. IBGE, Síntese de Indicadores Sociais 2004, table 11.4.

59. Ricardo Paes de Barros, Samuel Franco, and Rosane Mendonça, "Discriminação e segmentação no mercado de trabalho e desigualdade de renda no Brasil," discussion paper no. 1288, IPEA, Rio de Janeiro, 2017, 14.

60. Paes de Barros, Franco, and Mendonça, "Discriminação e segmentação," 8.

61. Ricardo Paes de Barros, Carlos Henrique Corseuil, Daniel Domingues dos Santos, and Sérgio Pinheiro Firpo, "Inserção no mercado de trabalho: diferenças por sexo e conseqüências sobre o bem-estar," discussion paper no. 796, IPEA, Rio de Janeiro, 2001, 4–5.

62. On the secular decline of differences—which has been faster in Brazil than in the USA—see Ana Carolina Giuberti and Naércio Menezes-Filho, "Discriminação de rendimentos por gênero: uma comparação entre o Brasil e os Estados Unidos," *Economia Aplicada* 9, no. 3 (2005): 369–383.

63. Maria Cristina Cacciamali and Guilherme Issamu Hirata, "A influência da raça e do gênero nas oportunidades de obtenção de renda—uma análise da discriminação em mercados de trabalho distintos: Bahia e São Paulo," *Estudos Econômicos* 35, no. 4 (2005): 774–785.

64. IBGE, Síntese de Indicadores Sociais, Uma análise das Condições da Vida da População Brasileira, 2016, table 4.14, found in a separate appendix data set at https://www.ibge.gov.br/estatisticas-novoportal/sociais/populacao/9221-sintese-de-indicadores-sociais.html?edicao=9222&t=downloads. The functionally illiterate were defined as those with no education or with primary school incomplete (sem instrução e fundamental incompleto).

65. IBGE, Síntese de Indicadores Sociais 2016, table 4.13, found in a separate appendix data set at https://www.ibge.gov.br/estatisticas-novoportal/sociais/populacao/9221-sintese-de-indicadores-sociais.html?edicao=9222&t=downloads.

66. IBGE, SIDRA, table 3899.

67. Claudia Cavalieri and Reynaldo Fernandes. "Diferenciais de salários por gênero e cor: uma comparação entre as regiões metropolitanas brasileiras." *Revista de economia política* 18, no. 1 (1998): 161, table 3.

68. IBGE, table 3.8, from Sintese de Indicadores Sociais 2020, https://www.ibge.gov.br/estatisticas/sociais/saude/9221-sintese-de-indicadores-sociais.html?=&t=o-que-e, accessed August 19, 2021.

69. PNAD 2016, table 4.8, "Proporção de estudantes de 15 a 17 anos de idade com distorção idade-série . . . ," https://www.ibge.gov.br/estatisticas-novoportal/sociais/populacao/9221-sintese-de-indicadores-sociais.html?edicao=9222&t=downloads.

70. Edward E. Telles, *Race in Another America: The Significance of Skin Color in Brazil* (Princeton: Princeton University Press, 2014): 176–177.

71. Carlos Antonio Costa Ribeiro and Nelson do Valle Silva, "Cor, educação e casamento: tendências da seletividade marital no Brasil, 1960 a 2000," *Dados: Revista de Ciências Sociais* 52, no. 1 (2009): 25.

72. José Luis Petruccelli, "Seletividade por cor e escolhas conjugais no Brasil dos 90," *Estudos Afro-Asiáticos* 23, no. 1 (2001): 40, table 9.

73. Ribeiro and Silva "Cor, educação e casamento," 27, table 3.

74. Ribeiro and Silva "Cor, educação e casamento," 8.

75. Telles, *Race in Another America*, chap. 8. The quote is from 205.

76. Overall, the rate of dissimilarity was 30, and went from 18 at the lowest economic strata to 36 at the highest (above 20 minimum salaries). See Danilo Sales do Nascimento França, "Raça, classe e segregação residencial no município de São Paulo," MA thesis, Universidade de São Paulo, 2010, 71–72 For other studies of income segregation, see Elvis Vitoriano da Silva, "Desigualdade de renda no espaço intra-urbano: análise da evolução na cidade de Porto Alegre no período 1991–2000," MA thesis, Universidade Federal do Rio Grande do Sul, 2011, 141. For a very detailed analysis of indices of isolation by income class in all the districts of a Southern town of 261,000 population, see Thayse Cristiane Severo do Prado, "Segregação residencial por índices de dissimilaridade, isolamento e exposição,com indicador renda, no espaço urbano de Santa Maria—RS, por geotecnologias," MA thesis, Universidade Federal de Santa Maria, 2012.

77. For the classic position, see Carlos A. Hasenbalg, Nelson do Valle Silva, and Marcia Lima, *Cor e estratificação social no Brasil* (Rio de Janeiro, Contracapa, 1999); Ricardo Henriques, "Desigualdade racial no Brasil: evolução das condições de vida na década de 90," discussion paper no. 807, IPEA, Rio de Janeiro, July 2001. For alternative arguments stressing nonracial factors inflencing the differences, see Pedro Ferreira de Souza, Carlos Antonio Costa Ribeiro, and Flavio Carvalhaes, "Desigualdade de oportunidades no Brasil: considerações sobre classe, educação e raça," *Revista Brasileira de Ciências Sociais* 25, no. 73 (2010): 77–100; and Carlos Antonio Costa Ribeiro, "Classe, raça e mobilidade social no Brasil," *Dados: Revista de Ciências Sociais* 49, no. 4 (2006): 833–873.

78. Carlos Antonio Costa Ribeiro and Maria Celi Scalon, "Mobilidade de classe no Brasil em perspectiva comparada," *Dados* 44, no. 1 (2001).

79. For two basic surveys of social mobility in this period, see Ribeiro and Scalon, "Mobilidade de classe no Brasil em perspectiva comparada"; Carlos Antonio Costa Ribeiro, "Quatro décadas de mobilidade social no Brasil," *Dados* 55, no. 3 (2012); Carlos Antonio Costa Ribeiro, *Estrutura de classe e mobilidade social no Brasil* (Bauru: EDUSC, 2007); Maria Celi Scalon, *Mobilidade social no Brasil: padrões e tendências* (Rio de Janeiro: Revan/IUPERJ-UCAM, 1999). See also the classic study by José Pastore, *Inequality and Social Mobility in Brazil* (Madison: University of Wisconsin Press, 1981), and its updated revision in

José Pastore and Nelson do Valle Silva, *Mobilidade Social no Brasil* (São Paulo: Makron, 2000).

80. IBGE, Síntese de Indicadores Socais 2017, tables 3.12 and 3.12a, https://www.ibge.gov.br/estatisticas-novoportal/multidominio/genero/9221-sintese-de-indicadores-sociais.html?&t=resultados.

81. Telles, *Race in Another America*, 140–145.

82. As Ribeiro has noted, "The main problem in the analysis of the intergenerational mobility of whites, browns, and blacks is that the first group tends to be overrepresented in the highest origin classes, and the last two groups in the lowest origin classes. This fact makes opportunities greater for whites than those for blacks and browns. Therefore, when analyzing the chances of mobility using only gross rates (percentages), we cannot separate the effect of the origin class from that of skin color." Ribeiro, "Classe, raça e mobilidade social no Brasil," 862.

83. Ribeiro, "Classe, raça e mobilidade," 862–866. As Osorio noted in his detailed study on income distribution, "Social origin is the principal factor explaining the reproduction of inequality, but its persistence is only made possible through the complement of discrimination." Rafael Guerreiro Osorio, "A desigualdade racial de renda no Brasil: 1976–2006," PhD thesis, Universidade de Brasília, 2009, 315.

Chapter 8

1. Caio Prado Jr., "A cidade de São Paulo, geografia e história." In Caio Prado Jr., *Evolução Política do Brasil e Outros Estudos* (São Paulo: Brasiliense, 1972), 91–139.

2. Prado, "A cidade de São Paulo, geografia e história."

3. On Japanese immigration to Brazil, see Henrique Gomes de Almeida. "Do Japão do Brasil: Trabalhadores japoneses em São Paulo (1908–1922)," MA thesis, Campinas, UNICAMP, 2012); Arlinda R. Nogueira, *Imigração Japonesa para a lavoura cafeeira Paulista: 1908–1922* (São Paulo: Instituto de Estudos Brasileiros, 1973).

4. Jader Tadeu Fantin, "Os Japoneses no Bairro da Liberdade-SP na primeira metade do século XX," MA thesis,São Carlos, FAU-USP, 2013.

5. The Japanese consulate estimates in 1988 that there were 366,000 Japanese in the capital, 500,000 in the RMSP and 887,000 in the State. https://www.sp.br.emb-japan.go.jp/itpr_pt/nipobrasileiro.html.

6. The area of the current ABC of São Paulo was separated from the city of São Paulo in 1889, when São Bernardo do Campo was established as an independent municipality. Later Santo André would be created by being separated from São Bernardo do Campo, and the same would happen with São Caetano, created in 1948. Both São Caetano and Santo André have CPTM

stations, formerly of the Santos Jundiai railroad line. In 1953, the municipality of Mauá was created after the dismemberment of the municipality of Santo André. In the area belonging to Mauá, a Petrobrás Oil refinery was installed. In 1960 the Municipality of Diadema was created, an area previously belonging to São Bernardo do Campo.

7. Opened in 1867, the São Paulo Railway became the major access route to the port of Santos. Through it flowed the entire production of coffee exported by São Paulo until 1937, when an alternative route was opened by the Estrada de Ferro Sorocabana. In 1940 it was taken over by the federal government, which later changed its name to Estrada de Ferro Santos Jundiaí. Subsequently, there was an integration of the federal railroads, forming the Federal Railway Network. In the 1990s, the Brazilian rail system was privatized. In the case of the former Santos Jundiai section, part was privatized for cargo operations and part was placed in the metropolitan railway complex, operated by the government of the state of São Paulo, through the Cia Paulista de Trens Metropolitanos (CPTM). The metropolitan train system operated by CPTM today has 7 intercity lines and 94 stations, is 270 km long, and carries 2.8 million passengers a day. See http://www.cptm.sp.gov.br/a-companhia/Pages/a-companhia.aspx. On the São Paulo Railway, also see http://www.metro.sp.gov.br/metro/licenciamento-ambiental/pdf/linha_18_bronze/eia/volume-iii/Arquivo-20.pdf, accessed March 1, 2020.

8. According to Lima, the decree-law no. 311, of March 2, 1938, determined that the headquarters of municipalities would be classified as cities and the headquarters of districts as towns. Thus the Brazilian territorial structure was organized primarily for political and administrative reasons, since cities and towns, in addition to being, respectively, the headquarters of municipalities and districts, also became the only urban spaces, whose limits were, from the beginning, determined by municipal laws. This law determined that municipalities would comprise one or more districts. The seat of the municipality would be called a city. The district would be called by the name of the respective headquarters and would have the category of town. In other words, within a municipality there would be an urban area called "city," and within each district, its urban area would be classified as a "village"or "town." See Maria Helena Palmer Lima, "A delimitação legal do espaços urbanos," in *Brasil: uma visão geográfica e ambiental no início do século XXI* (Rio de Janeiro: IBGE, 2016), https://biblioteca.ibge.gov.br/visualizacao/livros/liv97884_cap3.pdf, accessed January 3, 2020.

9. The "other activities" were considered services because they included credit institutions, insurance and financial transactions, trade and administration of real estate and securities, international organizations and foreign representations, activities not included in the other branches, and ill-defined or undeclared activities.

10. The census of de 2010 showed the population of the city of São Paulo with 904,424 "industrial goods and service production workers," or some 16% of the total worforce. In the RMSP there were 1,868,317 industrial workers, who represented 20% of all workers in the metropolitan region. IBGE, SIDRA, table 3591.

11. IBGE, Recenseamento Geral 1980, volume 1, tomo 4, no. 19: 65; IBGE, Sinopse Preliminar do Censo Demográfico—1991—São Paulo, 71; IBGE, SIDRA, table 2093.

12. IBGE, Sinopse Preliminar do Censo Demográfico—1991—São Paulo, 15.

13. Claúdia Antico, "Deslocamentos pendulares nos espaços sub-regionais da Região Metropolitana de São Paulo," http://www.abep.org.br/~abeporgb/publicacoes/index.php/anais/article/viewFile/1286/1250, accessed February 3, 2019.

14. In the 1980 census, the IBGE adopted the following definition for a "special dwelling sector," which would correspond to a favela: "formed by at least 50 households, most of them endowed with poor infrastructure and located on land that does not belong to the residents, generally known as favela, mocambo, stilt, invasion, maloca." IBGE, Sinopese preliminar do censo demografico, Recenseamento Geral 1980, pp. X and XX. The biggest criticism of urban planners regarding this definition is specifying a minimum number of 50 households. This limits areas that could be called favelas.

15. Nabil Georges Bonduki. "Origens da habitação social no Brasil," *Análise Social,* 29, no. 127 (1994): 729. On the development of the favelas in São Paulo, also see Jorge Paulino, "O pensamento sobre a favela em São Paulo: uma história concisa das favelas paulistanas," MA thesis, São Paulo, FAU/USP, 2007; Elisabete França, "Favelas em São Paulo (1980–2008). Das propostas de desfavelamento aos projetos de urbanização. A experiência do Programa Guarapiranga," PhD thesis, São Paulo, Universidade Presbiteriana Mackenzie, 2009; Suzana Pasternak. "São Paulo e suas favelas," *Pós. Revista do Programa de Pós-Graduação em Arquitetura e Urbanismo da FAUUSP* 19 (2006): 176–197; Suzana Pasternak, "Espaço e população nas favelas de São Paulo." *Anais* (2016): 1–17; Suzana Pasternak Taschner. "Moradia da pobreza: habitação sem saúde," PhD thesis, São Paulo, Faculdade de Saúde Pública, USP, 1982.

16. Pasternak, "São Paulo e suas favelas," 187.

17. IBGE, Sinopse Preliminar do Censo Demográfic, Recenseamento Geral 1980, volume 1, tomo 1, no. 8: 159–167. The census listed favelas by municipality, number of households and inhabitants, categorized by sex. There was a gender balance in the state and an average of 4.77 people per household.

18. These maps are found at https://www.prefeitura.sp.gov.br/cidade/secretarias/urbanismo/dados_estatisticos/info_cidade/habitacao/index.php?p=260286.

19. On the relationship between housing and health, see Taschner, "Moradia da pobreza: habitação sem saúde."

20. França, "Favelas em São Paulo (1980–2008)"; Rosana Denardi, "Políticas de Urbanização de Favelas: evolução e impasses," PhD thesis, FAU/USP, 2003; Thais Faraboli Pala, "Favela Nova Jaguaré: intervenções de políticas públicas de 1989 a 2011," MA thesis, Universidade Presbiteriana Mackenzie, 2011; Nelson Antonio Alesse, "Formam-se favelas e ganham importância no cenário urbano São Paulo: Heliópolis e Paraisópolis," MA thesis, FFLCH-USP, 2009; Educarp Pimental Pizarro. "Interstícios e interfaces urbanos como oportunidades latentes: o caso da Favela de Paraisópolis, São Paulo" (MA thesus, FAU/USP, 2014); Felipe de Freitas Moreira, "Heliópolis e as estratégicas de enfrentamento da cidade real," MA thesis, FAU/USP, 2017; Felipe de Freitas Moreira, "Heliópolis e a produção municipal de moradias populares em favelas," paper presented at the XVII ENAPUR, São Paulo, 2017, http://anpur.org.br/xviienanpur/principal/publicacoes/XVII.ENANPUR_Anais/ST_Sessoes_Tematicas/ST%205/ST%205.8/ST%205.8-04.pdf, accessed November 19, 2020.

21. Marcio Rufino Silva, "'Mares de prédios' e 'mares de gente': território e urbinzação crítica em Cidade Tiradentes," MA thesis, FFLCH USP, 2008; Ana Paula Alves de Lavos, "Sociabilidade em conjuntos habitacionais produzidos pelo estado: o caso da COHAB Cidade Tiradentes," MA thesis, São Carlos, Escola de Engenharia de São Carlos/USP, 2009; Simone Lucena Cordeiro. "Cidade Tiradentes e Cohab: moradia popular na periferia da cidade de São Paulo—projetos e trajetórias (1960–1980)," PhD thesis, São Paulo, PUC-SP, 2009.

22. Dieese, "Mulheres no mercado de trabalho da Região Metropolitanade São Paulo Março de 2019," https://www.dieese.org.br/analiseped/2019/2019pedmulhersao.html; Dieese, "A inserção das mulheres nos mercados de trabalho metropolitano," https://www.dieese.org.br/analiseped/2018/2018ApresentacaoMulherSintMet.html.

23. Paul Freston, "'Neo-Pentecostalism' in Brazil: Problems of Definition and the Struggle for Hegemony," *Archives de Sciences Sociales des Religions* 44, no. 105 (1999): 145.

24. These are estimates for all the world's countries from the Pew Religious Census of 2010, http://www.pewforum.org/2011/12/19/table-christian-population-in-numbers-by-country/, accessed October 22, 2017.

25. Historians of Protestantism in Brazil usually divide the movement into two groups, those religions introduced by immigrants (*protestantismo de imigração*) who brought their religion with them, and those introduced by missionaries from Europe or North America (*protestatismo de missão*). The first is primarily the German Lutherans, but almost all the other traditional Protestant religions were introduced either by immigrants or by missionaries coming from their home countries to minister to their nationals as well as seeking

Brazilian converts. IBGE has defined all of these traditional churches as missionary Evangelicals (*evangélicas de missão*). All introduced in the nineteenth century, they include the Lutherans (founded 1823 and the largest of these traditional churches), Presbyterians (founded in 1859), Methodists (1867), and Baptists (1882). Coming after 1900 are the Pentecostals (called by IBGE *evangélicas de origem pentecostal*), which have both missionary and indigenous origins. The first missionary-founded Pentecostal churches were the Congregação Cristã no Brasil (1910) and the Assembleia de Deus (1911); both are still the largest of the Pentecostal churches, and both were founded just a few years after the birth of the Pentecostal movement in 1906 in Los Angeles. This first wave of Pentecostal churches was followed by numerous immigrant, missionary, and finally native-founded Pentecostal churches throughout the twentieth century and into the twenty-first century. See Carl Joseph Hahn, *História do culto protestante no Brasil* (São Paulo: ASTE, 1981); Antonio Gouvêa Mendonça and Prócoro Velasques Filho, *Introdução ao protestantismo no Brasil* (São Paulo: Edições Loyola, 1990); and Paul Freston, "Protestantes e politica no Brasil: da constituente ao impeachment," PhD thesis, UNICAMP, 1993, 41.

26. Maria Bernadete Pita Guimarães, "Alcoolismo, pentecostalismo e família," PhD thesis, Universidade Federal Juiz de Fora, 2008. This is a theme found in many studies of Pentecostalism; see Ricardo Mariano, "Sociologia do crescimento pentecostal no Brasil: um balanço," *Perspectiva Teológica* 43, no. 119 (2011): 15. For detailed activities in relation to incorporation, women, and the family in the IURD church, see Patricia Birman, "Conexões políticas e bricolagens religiosas: Questões sobre o pentecostalism a partir de alguns contrapontos," in Pierre Sanchis, ed., *Feis e Cidadãos, percursos de sincretismo no Brasil* (Rio de Janeiro: EDUERJ, 2001), 59–86.

27. José Eustáquio Diniz Alves, Luiz Felipe Walter Barros, and Suzana Cavenaghi, "A dinâmica das filiações religiosas no Brasil entre 2000 e 2010: diversificação e processo de mudança de hegemonia," *REVER—Revista de Estudos da Religião* 12, no. 2 (2012): 160.

28. The poorly defined "neo-pentecostalism" movement refers to the Brazilian churches founded in the last quarter of the twentieth century. They supposedly stress exorcism (*libertação*), which includes elements of African Brazilian religions even though they reject these religions. R. Andrew Chesnut, "Exorcising the Demons of Deprivation: Divine Healing and Conversion in Brazilian Pentecostalism," in Candy Gunther Brown, ed., *Global Pentecostal and Charismatic Healing* (New York: Oxford University Press, 2011): 12, 18. These neo-pentecostal churches seem to be more secular in their teachings than the older Pentecostal churches and more hierarchical. See Ricardo Mariano, "Expansão pentecostal no Brasil: o caso da Igreja Universal," *Estudos Avançados* 18, no. 52 (2004): 123–124; Ricardo Mariano, "Efeitos da secularização do estado, do pluralismo e do mercado religiosos sobre as igrejas pentecostais," *Civitas* 3, no. 1 (2003): 111–125; and Patricia Birman, "Mediação

feminina e dentidades Pentecostais," *Cadernos PAGU* no. 6–7 (1996): 201–226. However, given the fluidity of the movement there is some debate about whether such a subgroup is as coherent as some propose. See Freston, "'Neo-Pentecostalism,'" 154–162.

29. As Freston has noted, "Founders of major pentecostal groups [in Latin America] include proletarians, independent artisans and lower middle-class white collar workers. Rare are the founders of higher social origin. Most pentecostal churches (unlike their historical counterparts) were founded either by Latin Americans who broke with an existing protestant denomination or by independent missionaries, and only rarely by a foreign pentecostal denomination." Paul Freston, "Evangelicals and Politics in Latin America," *Transformation* 19, no. 4 (October 2002): 272. As part of this process, the preachers of the largest of these movements, the Assemblea de Deus, opposed the creation of formal seminaries for most of the movement's early history. Bertone de Oliveira Sousa, "Entre a espera pelo céu e a busca por bem-estar," in Jérri Roberto Marin and André Dioney Fonseca, eds., *Olhares sobre a Igreja Assembleia De Deus* (Campo Grande: Editora UFMS, 2015), 51.

30. On the theology of the Pentecostals and their appeal to the poor, see Cecília Loreto Mariz, *Coping with Poverty: Pentecostals and Christian Base Communities in Brazil* (Philadelphia: Temple University Press, 1994); André Corten, *Pentecostalism in Brazil: Emotion of the Poor and Theological Romanticism* (New York: St. Martin's Press, 1999). On their role in the favelas and prisons, see Andrew Johnson, *If I Give My Soul: Faith Behind Bars in Rio de Janeiro* (New York: Oxford University Press, 2017), chap. 3.

31. On the evolution of this participation, see Taylor C. Boas, "Serving God and Man: Evangelical Christianity and Electoral Politics in Latin America," paper presented at the American Political Science Association annual meeting, Chicago, August 29–September 1, 2013, http://people.bu.edu/tboas/serving_god_man.pdf, accessed October 28, 2017; Ari Pedro Oro, "A política da Igreja Universal e seus reflexos nos campos religioso e político brasileiros," *Revista Brasileira de Ciências Sociais* 18, no. 53 (2003): 53–69. Reich and Santos argue that there are two basic forms of political participation by Pentecostals, as individuals and formally sponsored and promoted by their churches. The latter have been less successful, and have become involved in some of the major parliamentary scandals. Gary Reich and Pedro dos Santos, "The Rise (and Frequent Fall) of Evangelical Politicians: Organization, Theology, and Church Politics," *Latin American Politics and Society* 55, no. 4 (2013): 1–22. Finally, on their electoral success or lack thereof, see Fabio Lacerda, "Pentecostalism, eleições e reprentação política no Brasil contemporâneo," PhD thesis, USP, 2017.

32. https://congressoemfoco.uol.com.br/area/congresso-nacional/veja-quais-deputados-e-senadores-fazem-parte-da-bancada-evangelica/

33. From the pioneering work of Manuel Castells an important line of research has emerged that analyzes the new role played by cities in the globalized world, with new technologies and new production processes. São Paulo is usually included in this group of cities, which also includes London, New York, and Tokyo. J. V. Beaverstock, R. G. Smith, and P. J. Taylor, "A Roster of World Cities," *Cities* 16, no. 6 (1999): 445–448; P. J. Taylor, "Worlds of Large Cities: Pondering Castells' Space of Flows," *Third World Planning Review* 21, no. 3 (1999): iii–x. Several national studies seek to apply this methodology to the study of São Paulo. For an overview of the theme in Brazil, see Stamatia Koulioumba, "São Paulo: cidade mundial?," PhD thesis, FAU-USP, São Paulo, 2002; João Sette Whitaker Ferreira, "São Paulo: o mito da cidade-global," PhD thesis, FAU-USP, São Paulo, 2003; Milton Santos, *Técnica, espaço, tempo: globalização e meio técnico-científico informacional* (São Paulo: Hucitec, 1997), 151.

34. "Public administration, defense, and social security" comprises the administration of the state and economic and social policy; that is, public administration in general, and regulation of health activities, education, and cultural services, along with regulation of economic activities. These also include collective services provided by the administration (foreign affairs, defense, justice, public security, civil defense) and mandatory social security. This group of employed persons includes all the employees of the city of São Paulo (about 112,000), the employees of the government of the state of São Paulo working in the city, and the federal employees working in the city. In the case of the government of the state of São Paulo, there was an increase from 782,000 initially to 820,000 between 2002 and 2013. Then there was a systematic decrease until the number hit 697,000 in 2017. Atlas do Estado Brasileiro, http://www.ipea.gov.br/atlasestado/consulta/82, accessed December 7, 2019.

35. Bradesco has its administrative center in the city of Osasco, in the metropolitan area of São Paulo, a region fully integrated with the municipality of São Paulo.

36. Data from the Comissão de Valores Mobiliários.

37. BM&F, www.bmf.com.br.

38. See www.seade.gov.br/negocios/snpmr-v2.html.

39. See http://www.seade.gov.br/negocios/snpmr-v2.html.

40. São Paulo Convention Bureau, in Pesquisa e Diagnóstico Econômico do Turismo de Eventos na Cidade de São Paulo, www.spcvb.com.br, and Anuário Estatístico da Embratur, 2003, www.embratur.gov.br.

41. According to Stamatia Koulioumba, the city of São Paulo has 30,000 hotel beds, with the most recent large increase attributed to investments of foreign origin made during the 1990s. In addition, there is a big increase of hotels of international chains. Stamatia Koulioumba, "São Paulo: Cidade Mundial?," PhD thesis, FAU-USP, São Paulo, 2002, 174.

42. Cidade de São Paulo Saúde, *Relatório Anual de Gestão de São Paulo, SUS, 2018.* (São Paulo: Prefeitura Municipal de São Paulo, Secretaria Municipal de Saúde, 2019): 32; Prefeitura Municipal São Paulo, *Atlas da Saúde na Cidade de São Paulo* (São Paulo: PMSP/Via Pública, 2011); Eduardo Jorge M. A. Sobrinho and Paulo Fernando Capucci, "Saúde em São Paulo: aspectos da implantação do SUS no período de 2001–2002," *Estudos Avançados* 17, no. 48 (2003): 200–227.

43. Setor Saúde, https://setorsaude.com.br/16-hospitais-brasileiros-estao-entre-os-melhores-da-america-latina/, accessed December 3, 2019.

44. Regina Maria Prosperi Meyer, Marta Dora Grostein, and Ciro Biderman, *São Paulo Metrópole* (São Paulo: Edusp/Imprensa Oficial, 2004), 64.

45. The first corridor was built in the municipality of São Paulo in 1980 on the east side of the city. The original plan foresaw the construction of 280 km, but so far only 130 km have been completed.

Conclusion

1. Vol 1 was *Slavery and the Economy of São Paulo, 1750-1850.* Stanford: Stanford University Press, 2003; and vol 2 *The Economic and Demographic History of São Paulo 1850-1950.* Stanford: Stanford University Press, 2018

BIBLIOGRAPHY

Primary Materials

"A Fiat Automóveis inicia sua história em nosso País." https://docplayer.com.br/19143891-Fiat-automoveis-inicia-sua-historia-em-nosso-pais.html.

"Setor sucro-alcooleiro (complexo cana-de-açúcar) no território brasileiro," 2009. http://www.observatoriogeograficoamericalatina.org.mx/egal12/Geografiasocioeconomica/Geografiaespacial/60.pdf.

ABPA (Associação Brasileira de Proteína Animal). Annual Reports, 2015 and 2016.

AFDC (Alternative Fuels Data Center). "World Fuel Ethanol Production by Country or Region." https://afdc.energy.gov/, accessed February 8, 2017.

Alesp (Assembleia Legistativa do Estado de São Paulo). http://www.al.sp.gov.br/portal/site/Internet/.

ANFAVEA (*Associação Nacional de Fabricantes de Veículos Automotores*). Anúario da Indústria Automobilística Brasileira, 2019. São Paulo: Anfavea, 2019.

Anti-slavery laws: https://www.jusbrasil.com.br/topicos/10621211/artigo-149-do-decreto-lei-n-2848-de-07-de-dezembro-de-1940.

Banco Central do Brasil. "Focus: Relatório do Mercado." https://www.bcb.gov.br/pec/GCI/PORT/readout/R20180720.pdf.

Banco Central do Brasil. Estatística bancária mensal por município—ESTEBAN. https://www.bcb.gov.br/estatisticas/estatisticabancariamunicipios.

Banco Central do Brasil. *Relatório de inflação* 13, no. 3 (2011).

Banco Central do Brasil. *Relatório economia bancária 2018*. https://www.bcb.gov.br/content/publicacoes/relatorioeconomiabancaria/reb_2018.pdf

BM&F (Bolsa de Mercadorias e Futuros). www.bmf.com.br.

BNDES (Banco Nacional de Desenvolvimento Econômico e Social). Aeroespaço e defesa.

BNDES-Setorial, 2010 a 2018. https://www.bndes.gov.br/wps/wcm/connect/site/648bf519-e15e-41a0-a599a7cb4827be8a/BNDES_Setorial__A%26D_completo.pdf?MOD=AJPERES&CVID=mHlAmTY.

Brady Plan. https://www.bcb.gov.br/content/publicacoes/Documents/outras_pub_alfa/D%C3%ADvida_Externa_Brasileira_-_Segunda_Edi%C3%A7%C3%A3o_Revisada_Ampliada.pdf.

Brasil, Conselho do Desenvolvimento, *Relatório do Período 1956–1960*, tomo IV. Rio de Janeiro, 1960.

Carta ao Povo Brasileiro, June 22, 2002. http://www1.folha.uol.com.br/folha/brasil/ult96u33908.shtml.

CDC, National Center for Health Statistics. *National Vital Statistics Reports* 63, no. 5 (September 24, 2014).

CEDLAS (*Centro de Estudios Distributivos, Laborales y Sociales*). http://www.depeco.econo.unlp.edu.ar/cedlas/wb/.

CELADE (Comisión Económica para América Latina y el Caribe). "Brazil: Long Term Population Estimates and Projections 1950–2100" (2013 revision). https://www.cepal.org/celade/proyecciones/basedatos_BD.htm.

CELADE. "Brasil tasas de fecundidad y distribución relativa por edades, tasa global de fecundidad, y nacimientos anuales por edad de la madre segun quinquênios." http://www.eclac.cl/celade/proyecciones/intentoBD-2002.htm.

CELADE. *Anuario Estadistica de America Latina*, 1980.

CELADE. *Boletín demográfico* no. 66 (July 2000).

CEPALSTAT, ECLAC/CEPAL *[Economic Comission for Latin American and the Caribbean]*. found at https://estadisticas.cepal.org/cepalstat/WEB_CEPALSTAT/estadisticasIndicadores.asp?idioma=i

CESP (Companhia Energética de São Paulo). http://www.cesp.com.br/portalCesp/portal.nsf/V03.02/Empresa_Historia?OpenDocument.

Cidade de São Paulo Saúde, *Relatório Anual de Gestão de São Paulo, SUS, 2018*. São Paulo: Prefeitura Municipal de São Paulo, Secretaria Municipal de Saúde, 2010.

Citrosuco. http://www.citrosuco.com.br/nossa-empresa.html.

Clarivate Analytics. *Research in Brazil: A Report for Capes*. https://www.capes.gov.br/images/stories/download/diversos/17012018-CAPES-InCites Report-Final.pdf.

Clube do Fordinho. http://www.clubedofordinho.com.br/si/site/0058/p/Hist%C3%B3rico%20da%20Ford%20Brasi.

CNC (Confederação Nacional do Comércio, Bens, Serviços e Turismo). Endividamento e Inadimplência do Consumidor. http://www.cnc.org.br/sites/default/files/arquivos/analise_peic_janeiro_2015.pdf.

CNI (Confederação Nacional da Indústria). http://www.portaldaindustria.com.br/agenciacni/noticias/2016/11/participacao-de-mulheres-no-mercado-de-trabalho-industrial-cresce-143-em-20-anos/.

CNI. Nota Econômica. http://arquivos.portaldaindustria.com.br/app/conteudo_24/2015/02/20/526/Notaeconomica01-Competitividade.pdf.

CONAB (Companhia Nacional de Abastecimento). "Produtos da indústria sucroalcooleira comparativo de área, produtividade e produção safras 2018/19 e 2019/20." https://www.conab.gov.br/info-agro/safras/cana.

Concla (Comissão Nacional de Classificação). https://concla.ibge.gov.br/busca-online-cnae.html?classe=45200&view=classe.

Constitution of 1988. http://www.planalto.gov.br/ccivil_03/constituicao/constituicaocompilado.htm, accessed November 26, 2017.

CPTM (Companhia Paulista de Trens Urbanos). http://www.cptm.sp.gov.br/a-companhia/Pages/a-companhia.aspx.

Directoria Geral de Estatistica. *Boletim Commemorativo da Exposição Nacional de 1908.* Rio de Janeiro, 1908.

ECLAC (Economic Comission for Latin American and the Caribbean). CEPALSTAT. https://estadisticas.cepal.org/cepalstat/WEB_CEPALSTAT/estadisticasIndicadores.asp?idioma=i.

Embraer S.A. https://historicalcenter.embraer.com/br/pt/historia.

EMBRATUR (Instituto Brasileiro do Turismo). Anuário Estatístico da Embratur, 2003, http://www.embratur.gov.br/.

EMPLASA. https://emplasa.sp.gov.br/RMSP.

FGV CPDOC (Centro de Pesquisa e Documentação de Histórica Contemporânea do Brasil). Fábrica Nacional de Motores. http://www.fgv.br/CPDOC/ACERVO/dicionarios/verbete-tematico/fabrica-nacional-de-motores-fnm.

FGV CPDOC. First National Conference of Working Classes (I Conclat). August 1981, Confederação Geral dos Trabalhadores (CGT). http://www.fgv.br/cpdoc/acervo/dicionarios/verbete-tematico/confederacao-geral-dos-trabalhadores.

Fundação João Pinheiro. *Perfil Demográfico do Estado de Minas Gerais 2000.* Belo Horizonte, 2003.

Fundação SEADE. Anuário Estatístico do Estado de São Paulo, 2003.

Fundação SEADE. Histórico Demográfico do Município de São Paulo. http://smul.prefeitura.sp.gov.br/historico_demografico/tabelas.php.

Fundação SEADE. Mapa da Indústria Paulista. April 2019.

Fundação SEADE. *SP Demográfico.* Various years and issues.

Fundação SEADE. Anuário Estatístico do Estado de São Paulo, 2001.

Fut Pop Clube. https://futpopclube.com/tag/ranking-mundial-de-publico-nos-estadios/. Accessed June 11, 2017.

Globo Rural. http://revistagloborural.globo.com/Revista/Common/0,,ERT216287-18283,00.html.

GM Notícias. https://media.gm.com/media/br/pt/chevrolet/news.detail.html/content/Pages/news/br/pt/2015/jan/0126-1925.html.

Governo do Estado de São Paulo, São Paulo no Limiar do Século XXI. *Cenários da Urbanização Paulista. A região administrativa da Grande São Paulo.* 8 vols. São Paulo: Governo do Estado de São Paulo/Fundação SEADE, 1992.

Governo Federal, Brasil Maior. http://www.brasilmaior.mdic.gov.br/conteudo/128.

Greve do ABC. http://www.abcdeluta.org.br/materia.asp?id_CON=34.
History of CPDOC. https://www.fgv.br/cpdoc/acervo/dicionarios/verbete-tematico/forca-sindical.
IBGE (Instituto Brasileiro de Geografia e Estatística). Anuário Estatístico do Brasil 1939–1940, 1951.
IBGE. "Projeção da população por sexo e idade—Indicadores implícitos na projeção—2010/2060, [2018]." https://www.ibge.gov.br/estatisticas/sociais/populacao/9109-projecao-da-populacao.html?t=resultados.
IBGE. "BRASIL, Projeção da população por sexo e idade—Indicadores implícitos na projeção—2010/2060." https://www.ibge.gov.br/estatisticas/sociais/populacao/9109-projecao-da-populacao.html?t=resultados.
IBGE. "Pessoas responsáveis pelos domicílios particulares permanentes." http://www.sidra.ibge.gov.br/bda/popul/.
IBGE. "Projeção da população" 2018. https://www.ibge.gov.br/estatisticas/sociais/populacao/9109-projecao-da-populacao.html?=&t=downloads.
IBGE. Anuário Estatístico do Brasil. Various years.
IBGE. *As fundações privadas e associações sem fins lucrativos no Brasil, 2010.* Estudos & Estudos 20. Rio de Janeiro, 2012.
IBGE. Brasil Censo Demográfico 1950, Série Nacional, volume III, tomo 1 (Censo Industrial).
IBGE. Brasil Censo Demográfico 1950, Série Nacional, volume XXV, tomos 1 and 3.
IBGE. Brasil Censo Demográfico de 1950, Série Regional, volume XXV, tomos 1, 2, and 3
IBGE. Brasil, Censo Agrícola 1950, Série Nacional, vols. II and III.
IBGE. Brasil, Censo Agropecuário 2006, volume 2.
IBGE. Brasil, Censo Demográfico 1920.
IBGE. Brasil, Censo Demográfico 1950, Série Nacional, volume 1.
IBGE. Brasil, Censo Demográfico 2000—Resultados do Universo.
IBGE. Brasil, Censo Demográfico 2010, Caracteristicas da População e dos Domicílios, Resultado do Universo.
IBGE. Brasil, Censo Demográfico 2010, Famílias e Domicílios Resultados da Amostra.
IBGE. Brasil, Censo Demográfico de 1950, Série Regional, volume XXXV, tomo 1.
IBGE. Brasil, Censo Demográfico de 1960, Série Regional, volume 1, tomo xiii.
IBGE. Brasil, Censo Demográfico de 1980, volume 1, tomo 4.
IBGE. Brasil, Censo Demográfico de 1980, volume 2, tomo 3, parte 1.
IBGE. Brasil, Censo Demográfico de 1980, volume 3, tomo 2, parte 1.
IBGE. Brasil, Censo Demográfico de 1980, volume 4, no. 1 and no. 19.
IBGE. Brasil, Censo Demográfico de 1980, volume 5, no. 4 and no. 19.
IBGE. Brasil, Censo Demográfico de 1991.

IBGE. Brasil, Censo Demográfico, 1970, Série Nacional, volume 1.
IBGE. Brasil, Censo Industrial 1980, volume 1, tomo 2.
IBGE. Brasil, Censo Industrial de 1960, Série Nacional, volume III.
IBGE. Brasil, Censo Industrial, Comercial e de Serviços, 1950.
IBGE. Brasil, Estatísticas do Século XX, 2003.
IBGE. *Classificação Nacional de Atividades Econômicas*. Rio de Janeiro: IBGE, 2007.
IBGE. CONCLA (A Comissão Nacional de Classificação), https://concla.ibge.gov.br/concla.html.
IBGE. *Estatísticas de Gênero: uma análise dos resultados do Censo Demográfico 2010*. Estudos & Pesquisas 33. Rio de Janeiro: IBGE, 2014.
IBGE. *Estatísticas do Registro Civil, 1999, Casamentos*, https://www.ibge.gov.br/estatisticas/sociais/populacao/9110-estatisticas-do-registro-civil.html?edicao=17071&t=downloads.
IBGE. *Estatísticas do Registro Civil, 2002*, volume 29.
IBGE. *Estatísticas do Registro Civil, 2010, Casamentos*.
IBGE. *Estatísticas do Registro Civil, 2017, Tabelas de Resultados, Casamentos*.
IBGE. Estatísticas do Registro Civil.Sistema de Estatísticas Vitais. https://www.ibge.gov.br/estatisticas/sociais/populacao/9110-estatisticas-do-registro-civil.html?=&t=o-que-e.
IBGE. Pesquisa Anual de Serviços, volume 2, 2000.
IBGE. PNAD (Pesquisa Nacional por Amostra de Domicílios), 2015. Microdata.
IBGE. *PNAD, 2001: microdados*. Rio de Janeiro: IBGE, 2002. CD-ROM.
IBGE. PNAD, *Aspectos das Relações de Trabalho e Sindicalização, 2015*. Rio de Janeiro, 2017.
IBGE. PNAD, Dicionário de variáveis da PNAD, 2015. ftp://ftp.ibge.gov.br/Trabalho_e_Rendimento/Pesquisa_Nacional_por_Amostra_de_Domicilios_anual/microdados/2015/leia_me_PNAD_2015_20170517.pdf.
IBGE. PNAD, Indicadores Sociais, 2016. https://www.ibge.gov.br/estatisticas-novoportal/sociais/populacao/9221-sintese-de-indicadores-sociais.html?edicao=9222&t=downloads.
IBGE. Projeções da População 2018 (and of 2013). https://www.ibge.gov.br/apps/populacao/projecao/.
IBGE. Projeções da População do Brasil e Unidades da Federação por sexo e idade: 2010–2060. https://www.ibge.gov.br/estatisticas/sociais/populacao/9109-projecao-da-populacao.html?t=resultados.
IBGE. Século XX. Various tables. https://seculoxx.ibge.gov.br/.
IBGE. *Séries estatísticas retrospectivas*, volume 2, tomo 3. Rio de Janeiro, 1986.
IBGE. SIDRA (Sistema IBGE de Recuperação Automática), Censo Agro 2017.
IBGE. SIDRA, Censo Agrário 2006.
IBGE. SIDRA, Censo Demográfico 1991.

IBGE. SIDRA, Censo Demográfico 2000.
IBGE. SIDRA, Censo Demográfico 2010.
IBGE. SIDRA, PAM (Produção Agrícola Municipal).
IBGE. SIDRA, PAS (Pesquisa Anual de Serviço).
IBGE. SIDRA, PNAD (Pesquisa Nacional por Amostra de Domicílios).
IBGE. SIDRA, PNS (Pesquisa Nacional de Saúde).
IBGE. SIDRA, PPM (Pesquisa Pecuária Municipal).
IBGE. *Sintese de Indicadores Sociais*, 2001, 2002, 2004, 2016, 2017.
IBGE. Síntese de Indicadores Sociais. Various years and issues.
IBGE. *Sínteses Históricas, Histórico dos Censo*. https://memoria.ibge.gov.br/sinteses-historicas/historicos-dos-censos/censos-demograficos.html.
IBGE. Sintesis de Indicadores Sociais. https://www.ibge.gov.br/estatisticas/sociais/trabalho/9221-sintese-de-indicadores-sociais.html?edicao=9222&t=downloads.
IBGE. Sistema de Contas Nacionais.
IBGE. *Tábua completa de mortalidade para o Brasil—2017 Breve análise da evolução da mortalidade no Brasil.* Rio de Janeiro, 2018.
IBGE. *Tendências demográficas: uma análise da população com base nos resultados dos censos demográficos 1940 e 2000.* Rio de Janeiro, 2007.
IETS (Instituto de Estudos do Trabalho e Sociedade). Análises dos Indicadores do PNAD. https://www.iets.org.br/spip.php?rubrique2.
IETS (Instituto de Estudos do Trabalho e Sociedade). IETS/OPE Sociais, based on PNAD, table "PNAD—Séries Históricas—Pobreza—1990–2014." https://www.iets.org.br/spip.php?article406.
Igreja Metodista. http://www.metodista.br/midiareligiaopolitica/index.php/composicao-bancada-evangelica/.
ILO (International Labor Organization). ILOSTAT. https://www.ilo.org/ilostat/faces/oracle/webcenter/portalapp/pagehierarchy/Page3.jspx?locale=EN&MBI_ID=49.
INEP (Instituto Nacional de Estudos e Pesquisas). http://inep.gov.br/sinopses-estatisticas-da-educacao-superior.
Instituto Brasileiro de Direito da Família. "A trajetória do divórcio no Brasil: A consolidação do Estado Democrático de Direito" https://ibdfam.jusbrasil.com.br/noticias/2273698/a-trajetoria-do-divorcio-no-brasil-a-consolidacao-do-estado-democratico-de-direito, accessed 11/26/2017.
IPEA (Instituto de Pesquisas Econômicas Aplicadas). Atlas do Estado Brasileiro. http://www.ipea.gov.br/atlasestado/.
IPEA (Instituto de Pesquisas Econômicas Aplicadas). Ipeadata (macroeconomic/regional/social). http://www.ipeadata.gov.br/Default.aspx.
IPEA. Atlas do Desenvolvimento Humano no Brasil, 2003.
Ipums International. 5% sample of Brazilian Census 1960–1980. https://international.ipums.org/international-action/samples.

Jornal Valor 1000. March 3, 2020. https://www.valor.com.br/valor1000/2019/ranking1000maiores.

Lance. Pesquisa Lance/Ibope. http://www.lance.com.br/futebol-nacional/flamengo-segue-com-maior-torcida-mas-vantagem-para-timao-cai.html.

Luné, Antônio José Batista de, and Paulo Delfino da Fonseca. *Almanak da Provincia de São Paulo para 1873. Primeiro anno.* 1873.

MAPA (Ministério da Agricultura, Pecuária e Abastecimento). http://indicadores.agricultura.gov.br/agrostat/index.htm.

MDIC (Ministério da Economia Indústria, Comércio Exterior e Serviço). http://www.mdic.gov.br/index.php/comercio-exterior/estatisticas-de-comercio-exterior/series-historicas.

MDIC. Exportação Brasileira, São Paulo, Principais Productos, 2016. http://www.mdic.gov.br/comercio-exterior/estatisticas-de-comercio-exterior/balanca-comercial-brasileira-unidades-da-federacao.

Merce-denco. http://merce-denco.blogspot.com/2012/10/l-312-o-caminhao-que-deu-inicio-saga-da.html.

Milkpoint. https://www.milkpoint.com.br/cadeia-do-leite/giro-lacteo/cooperativa-central-de-laticiniossp-e-a-primeira-a-exportar-13192n.aspx.

Ministério da Fazenda. "Nota Técnica do Tesouro, Dívida Bruta do Governo Geral do Brasil." July 29, 2015. www.fazenda.gov.br/area-destaques/.../arquivo .

Ministério da Saúde. Cadernos de Informações de Saúde. http://tabnet.datasus.gov.br/tabdata/cadernos/cadernosmap.htm

Ministério de Ciência, Inovações e Comunicações. Plano de Ciência, Tecnologia e Inovação para Petróleo & Gás Natural. 2018.

Ministério do Trabalho. Bases Estatísticas RAIS and CAGED. http://bi.mte.gov.br/bgcaged/.

Ministério do Trabalho. Relação Anual de Informações Sociais, 2000.

Notícias Automotivas. https://www.noticiasautomotivas.com.br/listas-de-montadoras-de-veiculos-por-estado-no-brasil/.

O Globo. G1, January 11, 2020.

OCB (Organizações das Cooperativas Brasileiras). http://www.ocb.org.br/noticia/20916/unimeds-fazem-bonito-em-ranking-da-ans.

OECD. https://data.oecd.org/rd/gross-domestic-spending-on-r-d.htm.

OECD. https://stats.oecd.org/Index.aspx?DataSetCode=LFS_SEXAGE_I_R. Accessed December 5, 2017.

Operação Lava Jato. http://www.mpf.mp.br/grandes-casos/lava-jato/entenda-o-caso.

OS da Cultura. http://portal.mec.gov.br/index.php?option=com_docman&view=download&alias=49141-pceb010-16-pdf&category_slug=outubro-2016-pdf&Itemid=30192.

Petrobrás. http://www.petrobras.com.br/fatos-e-dados/refinaria-presidente-bernardes-completa-60-anos-de-atividades-em-cubatao.htm.

Petrobrás. http://www.petrobras.com.br/pt/nossas-atividades/principais-operacoes/refinarias/refinaria-capuava-recap.htm.

Plano Collor. Documentos. *Revista de Economia Política* 10, no. 3 (1990): 114–148. http://www.rep.org.br/pdf/39-9.pdf.

Portal Imprensa. http://www.portalimprensa.com.br/noticias/brasil/66895/pesquisa+do+ibope+aponta+que+tempo+dedicado+ao+esporte+na+tv+cresceu+53.

Prefeitura do Município de São Paulo. *Atlas da Saúde na Cidade de São Paulo.* São Paulo: PMSP/Via Pública, 2011.

Prefeitura do Município de São Paulo. Cidade de São Paulo Saúde, Relatório Anual de Gestão de São Paulo, 2018.

Prefeitura do Município de São Paulo. Demografia—Tabelas. https://www.prefeitura.sp.gov.br/cidade/secretarias/urbanismo/dados_estatisticos/info_cidade/demografia/index.php?p=260265.

Prefeitura do Município de São Paulo. Info Cidade. https://www.prefeitura.sp.gov.br/cidade/secretarias/urbanismo/dados_estatisticos/info_cidade/index.php/.

Presidência da República. II Plano Nacional de Desenvolvimento (1975–1979), quadro 1. http://www.biblioteca.presidencia.gov.br/publicacoes-oficiais/catalogo/geisel/ii-pnd-75_79.

R&D. The 2016 Global R&D Funding Forecast: Supplement to R&D Magazine. Winter 2016.

São Paulo Convention Bureau. Pesquisa e Diagnóstico Econômico do Turismo de Eventos na Cidade de São Paulo. www.spcvb.com.br.

São Paulo Railway. http://www.metro.sp.gov.br/metro/licenciamento-ambiental/pdf/linha_18_bronze/eia/volume-iii/Arquivo-20.pdf.

São Paulo. *Annuário Demográphico*, Anno XII. 1905

Saraiva, José Antonio. *Documentos com que o presidente de São Paulo Instruiu o Relatório da Abertura da Assembléa Legislativa Provincial no dia 15 de fevereiro de 1855*, São Paulo, 1855.

SEADE (Fundação Sistema Estadual de Análise de Dados). *BCD: Boletim da Directoria de Industria e Commercio*, various years and issues. https://bibliotecadigital.seade.gov.br/view/#2.

SEADE, "Causas de óbito segundo raça/cor e gênero no Estado de São Paulo," Revista de Saúde Pública, 39, no. 6 (2005): 987-988.

Secretaria da Cultura do Estado de São Paulo. Boletim UM—10 anos de parceria com OSs de Cultura—2004 a 2014.

Secretaria da Cultura. Boletim UM—Cultura em Números, São Paulo. January 2017.

Secretaria da Saúde do Estado de São Paulo. *As organizações Sociais de Saúde do Estado de São Paulo. A experiência da Secretaria da Saúde. – planejamento e mecanismos de acompanhamento, controle e avaliação.* http://www.saude.sp

.gov.br/resources/ses/perfil/gestor/homepage/auditoria/reunioes/organizacoes_sociais_de_saude_no_estado_de_sao_paulo.pdf.

Secretaria do Tesouro Nacional. http://www.tesouro.fazenda.gov.br/resultado-do-tesouro-nacional.

Setor Saúde. https://setorsaude.com.br/16-hospitais-brasileiros-estao-entre-os-melhores-da-america-latina/.

Sócio Torcedor. https://www.90min.com/pt-BR/posts/6076274-atualizado-os-10-clubes-que-lideram-o-ranking-de-socio-torcedor-no-brasil.

Toyota do Brasil. https://www.toyota.com.br/mundo-toyota/sobre-a-toyota/.

UNCTAD (United Nations Conference on Trade and Development). World Investment Report 2013.

UNCTAD. *Global Value Chains: Investment and Trade for Development.* NewYork : United Nations, 2013.

UNFPA (United Nations Populaton Fund, Brasil). *Fecundidade e dinâmica da população brasileira.* Brasília: UNFPA, 2018.

UNICA (União da Indústria de Cana-de-Açúcar). "Exportação anual de açúcar pelo brasil por estado de origem." http://www.unicadata.com.br/listagem.php?idMn=43.

UNICA. "Exportação anual de etanol por estado brasileiro (mil litros) 2012/13 to 2016/16." http://www.unicadata.com.br/listagem.php?idMn=23.

UNICA. "Frota brasileira de autoveículos leves . . . 2007–2015" at http://www.unicadata.com.br/listagem.php?idMn=55.

UNICA. "Histórico e Missão." http://www.unica.com.br/unica/?idioma=1.

UNICA. "Sugarcane, Ethanol and Sugar Production." http://www.unicadata.com.br/.

UNICA. http://www.unicadata.com.br/historico-de-producao-e-moagem.php?idMn=31&tipoHistorico=2.

UNICA. Various production tables for the period 1980/1981 to 2016/2017 by state. http://www.unicadata.com.br/historico-de-producao-e-moagem.php?idMn=32&tipoHistorico=4.

UNU/WIDER World Income Inequality Database (WIID). "World Income Inequality Database WIID3.4." January 2017. https://www.wider.unu.edu/database/world-income-inequality-database-wiid34.

US Bureau of Labor Statistics. "Civilian Labor Force Participation Rate, by Age, Sex, Race, and Ethnicity, 1996, 2006, 2016, and Projected 2026 (in Percent)." https://www.bls.gov/emp/ep_table_303.htm.

US Bureau of Labor Statistics. Estimates for 2050. https://www.bls.gov/opub/ted/2007/jan/wk2/art03.htm.

USDA, FAS (US Department of Agriculture, Foreign Agricultural Service). "2017 Sugar Annual Brazil." Report BR17001. April 28, 2017.

USDA, FAS. *Citrus Annual Brazil 2016.* Report BR16020. February 15, 2016.

USDA, FAS. *Citrus Annual Brazil 2019*.
USDA, FAS. *Citrus: World Markets and Trade*. January 2017.
USDA, FAS. *Citrus: World Markets and Trade*. July 2020.
Volkswagen. http://vwbr.com.br/ImprensaVW/page/Historia.aspx.
World Bank Group. *Doing Business 2020. Comparing Business Regulation in 190 Economies*. Washington, DC: World Bank, 2020.
World Bank. Gini Index. https://data.worldbank.org/indicator/SI.POV.GINI?year_high_desc=false.
World Bank. Open Data (data bank). https://data.worldbank.org/.

Secondary Sources

Abranches, Sérgio H. "Governo, empresa estatal e política siderúrgica: 1930–1975." In Olavo Brasil de Lima Jr. and Sérgio H. Abranches, eds., *As origens da crise: Estado autoritário e planejamento no Brasil*. São Paulo: Vértice, Revista dos Tribunais, 1987, 158–213.
Abreu, Marcelo de P., and Rogério L. Furquim Werneck. "Estabilização, abertura e privatização, 1990–1994." In Marcelo de P. Abreu, ed., *A Ordem do progresso: dois séculos de política econômica no Brasil*, 313–330. Rio de Janeiro: Elsevier, 2014.
Accorsi, Antonio Carlos. "Estado e grupos econômicos: a política de expansão rodoviária no Brasil a partir de 1930." MA thesis, EAESP/FGV, 1996.
Adorno, Rubens de C. F., Augusta Thereza de Alvarenga, and Maria da Penha Vasconcellos. "Quesito cor no sistema de informação em saúde," *Estudos Avançados* 18, no. 50 (2004): 119–123.
Adriano, Eduardo Ribeiro. *Organizações sociais de saúde. OSS*. Governo do Estado de São Paulo, São Paulo, October 2016. http://ses.sp.bvs.br/wp-content/uploads/2017/05/CGCSS-CCTIES_apresentado-na-reuni%C3%A3o-Holanda-201016_Dr.-Eduardo.pdf.
Affonso, José Roberto F. "ICMS: crise federativa e obsolescência." *Revista Direito GV* 14, no. 3 (2018): 986–1018.
Affonso, José Roberto F., et al. "Guerra fiscal do ICMS: organizar o desembarque." *Revista de Direito Internacional Econômico Tributário* (Brasília) 12, no. 1 (2017): 416–443.
Aguiar, Daniel Alves de, Wagner Fernando da Silva, Bernardo Friedrich Theodor Rudorff, Luciana Miura Sugawara, and Magog Araújo de Carvalho, "Expansão da cana-de-açúcar no Estado de São Paulo: safras 2003/2004 a 2008/2009." *Anais XIV Simpósio Brasileiro de Sensoriamento Remoto* (Natal, Abril 2009).
Aguirre, Basília Maria Baptista, and Fabiana da Cunha Saddi. "Uma alternativa de interpretação do II PND." *Revista de Economa Política* 17, no. 4 (1997): 79–98.

Alesse, Nelson Antonio. "Formam-se favelas e ganham importância no cenário urbano São Paulo: Heliópolis e Paraisópolis." MA thesis, FFLCH-USP, 2009.

Almeida, Cecilia C. T. de. "O grande ABC paulista: o fetichismo da região." PhD thesis, FFLCH-USP, São Paulo, 2008.

Almeida, Henrique Gomes de. "Do Japão do Brasil: Trabalhadores japoneses em São Paulo (1908–1922)." MA thesis, Campinas, UNICAMP, 2012.

Almeida, Mansueto. "O novo estado desenvolvimentista e o governo Lula." *Revista Economia & Tecnologia* 7 (2011): 68–89.

Almeida, Mansueto, Renato Lima-de-Oliveira, and Ben Ross Schneider. "Política industrial e empresas estatais no Brasil: BNDES e Petrobras." Discussion paper no. 2013, IPEA, 2014.

Almeida, Raquel F. de. "Políticas de conteúdo local e setor para-petróleo: uma análise comparativa Brasil e Noruega." MA thesis, Rio de Janeiro, COPPE/UFRJ, 2015.

Almeida, Rita, Nicole Amaral, and Fabiana de Felicio. *Assessing Advances and Challenges in Technical Education in Brazil*. Washington, DC: World Bank, 2015.

Alonso, Fabio Roberto Bárbolo. "As mulheres idosas que residem em domicílios unipessoais: uma caracterização regional a partir do Censo 2010." *Revista Kairós Gerontologia, Revista da Faculdade de Ciências Humanas e Saúde* 18, no. 19 (2015): 99–122.

Alvaredo, Facundo, Anthony B. Atkinson, Thomas Piketty, and Emmanuel Saez. "The Top 1 Percent in International and Historical Perspective." *Journal of Economic Perspectives* 27, no. 3 (2013): 3–20.

Alves, José Eustáquio Diniz. "Crise no mercado de trabalho, bônus demográfico e desempoderamento feminino." In Nathalie Reis Itaboraí and Arlene Martinez Ricoldi, eds., *Até onde caminhou a revolução de gênero no Brasil? Implicações demográficas e questões sociais*, 21–44. Belo Horizonte: ABEP, 2016.

Alves, José Eustáquio Diniz, Luiz Felipe Walter Barros, and Suzana Cavenaghi. "A dinâmica das filiações religiosas no Brasil entre 2000 e 2010: diversificação e processo de mudança de hegemonia." *REVER—Revista de Estudos da Religião* 12, no. 2 (2012): 145–174.

Alves, José Eustáquio Diniz, and Suzana Cavenaghi. "Tendências demográficas, dos domicílios e das famílias no Brasil." *Aparte: Inclusão Social em Debate* 24 (2012): 1–33.

Alves, Maria Helena Moreira. *Estado e oposição no Brasil (1964–1984)*. Petrópolis: Vozes, 1989.

Amaral, Taís Mahalem do, Marcos Fava Neves, and Márcia A. Dias de Moraes. "Cadeias produtivas do açúcar do estado de São Paulo e da França: comparação dos sistemas produtivos, organização, estratégias e ambiente institucional." *Agricultura São Paulo* 50, no. 2 (2003): 65–80.

Amin, Jamil Salim. "A união estável no Brasil a partir da constituição federal de 1988 e leis posteriores." MA thesis, Universidade Federal de Santa Catarina, 2001.

Andrade, Adriana Strasburg de Camargo. "Mulher e trabalho no Brasil dos anos 90." PhD thesis, Universidade de Campinas, 2004.

Andrade, Maria Lucia Amarante de, and Luiz Maurício da Silva Cunha. "O setor siderúrgico." BNDES. https://web.bndes.gov.br/bib/jspui/bitstream/1408/13314/1/BNDES%2050%20Anos%20-%20Hist%C3%B3rias%20Setoriais_O%20Setor%20Siderurgico_P.pdf.

Antico, Claúdia. "Deslocamentos pendulares nos espaços sub-regionais da Região Metropolitana de São Paulo, Paper Presented at the *XIV Encontro Nacional de Estudos Populacionais, ABEP, 2004*. http://www.abep.org.br/~abeporgb/publicacoes/index.php/anais/article/viewFile/1286/1250.

Araujo, Edson Gramuglia. "As centrais no sistema de representação sindical no Brasil." MA thesis, Faculdade de Direito da USP, 2012.

Araújo, Ernesto Henrique Fraga. *O Mercosul: negociações extra-regionais*. Brasília: Fundação Alexandre de Gusmão, 2007.

Araújo, José de Souza Pizarro e. *Memórias históricas do Rio de Janeiro*. Rio de Janeiro: Imprensa Nacional, 1945.

Araújo, Maria de Fátima Infante. "Os cem últimos anos na história da cidade e a formação da grande São Paulo." In Seade, *Cenários da urbanização paulista: a região administrativa da Grande São Paulo*. São Paulo: Fundação Seade 1992: 15-51

Araujo, Maria de Fátima Infante. "Trajetória econômica e espacial da metrópole paulista." *São Paulo em Perspectiva* 7, no. 2 (1993): 29–37.

Arbix, Glauco. "Políticas do desperdício e assimetria entre público e privado na indústria automobilística." *RBCSi* 17, no. 48 (2002): 109–129.

Ariz, Cecília L. "Missão religiosa e migração: 'novas comunidades' e igrejas pentecostais brasileiras no exterior." *Análise Social* 44, no. 1 (2009): 161–187.

Arriaga, Eduardo E., and Kingsley Davis. "The Pattern of Mortality Change in Latin America." *Demography* 6, no. 3 (1969): 223–242.

Artes, Amélia, and Arlene Martinez Ricoldi. "Mulheres e as carreiras de prestígio no ensino superior brasileiro: o não lugar feminino." In Nathalie Reis Itaboraí and Arlene Martinez Ricoldi, eds., *Até onde caminhou a revolução de gênero no Brasil? Implicações demográficas e questões sociais*, 81–94. Belo Horizonte: ABEP, 2016.

Asfora, Laila Federica. "Terceiro Setor: Organizações Sociais." MA thesis, PUC-RIO, Rio de Janeiro, 2012.

Averbug, André. "Abertura e integração comercial brasileira na década de 90." In Fabio Giambiagi and Maurício Mesquita Moreira, eds., *A Economia Brasileira nos Anos 90*, 43–84. Rio de Janeiro: BNDES, 1999.

Bacha, Edmar. "Moeda, inércia e conflito: reflexões sobre políticas de estabilização no Brasil." *Pesquisa e Planejamento Econômico* 18, no. 1 (1988): 1–16.

Bacha, Edmar, and Robert Greenhill. *150 anos de café*. São Paulo: Marcelino Martins & Johnston Exportadores, 1992.

Bacha, Edmar, and Herbert S. Klein, eds. *Social Change in Brazil, 1945–1985: The Incomplete Transformation*. Albuquerque: University of New Mexico Press, 1989.

Baeninger, Rosana. "Expansão, redefinição ou consolidação dos espaços da migração em São Paulo: análises a partir dos primeiros resultados do Censo 2000." *XIII Encontro da Associação Brasileira de Estudos Populacionais, ABEP, 2002*: 1–27.

Baeninger, Rosana. "São Paulo e suas migrações no final do século 20." *São Paulo em perspectiva* 19, no. 3 (2005): 84–96.

Bahia, Luiz Bias, and Edson Paulo Domingues. "Estrutura de inovações na indústria automobilística brasileira." Discussion paper no. 1472, IPEA, Brasília, 2010.

Ballestrin, Luciana Maria de Aragão. "Estado e ONG's no Brasil: acordos e controversias a propósito de direitos humanos (1994–2002)." MA thesis, Universidade Federal do Rio Grande do Sul, 2006.

Barat, José. "O setor transporte na economia brasileira." *Revista de Administração Pública* (Rio de Janeiro) 2, no. 4 (1968): 117–166.

Barata, Luiz Roberto Barradas, and José Dinio Vaz Mendes. *Organizações sociais de saúde: A experiência exitosa de gestão pública de saúde do Estado de São Paulo*. São Paulo: Secretaria de Saúde, 2007.

Barros, Daniel Chiari, Bernardo H. R. de Castro, and Luiz Felipe H. Vaz. "Panorama da indústria de autopeças no Brasil: características, conjuntura, tendência tecnológicas e possibilidade de atuação do BNDES." *BNDES Setorial* 42 (2015): 167–216.

Barros, Daniel Chiari, Bernardo H. R. de Castro, and Luiz Felipe H. Vaz. *Panorama Setorial 2005–2018. Automotivo*. BNDES, n.d. https://web.bndes.gov.br/bib/jspui/bitstream/1408/14155/1/Automotivo_P_BD.pdf.

Barros, Octavio de, and Fabio Giambiagi, eds. *Brasil globalizado: o Brasil em um mundo surpreendente*. Rio de Janeiro: Elsevier, 2008.

Barros, Octávio de, and Robson Rodrigues Pereira. "Desmistificando a tese da desindustrialização: reestruturação da indústria brasileira em uma época de transformações globais." In Octávio de Barros and Fabio Giambiagi, eds., *Brasil globalizado: o Brasil em um mundo surpreendente*, 299–330. Rio de Janeiro: Campus, 2008.

Barros, Ricardo Paes de, Carlos Henrique Corseuil, and Daniel Domingues dos Santos. "Consequencias de um novo padrão de inserção das mulheres no mercado de trabalho sobre o bem-estar na região metropolitana de São Paulo." In Lena Lavinas and Francisco León, eds., *Emprego feminino no Brasil: mudanças institucionais e novas interseções no mercado de trabalho*. CEPAL, División de Desarrollo Social, (2002).

Barros, Ricardo, Louise Fox, and Rosane Mendonça. "Female-Headed Households, Poverty, and the Welfare of Children in Urban Brazil." *Economic Development and Cultural Change* 45, no. 2 (1997): 231–257.

Barros, Ricardo Paes de, Samuel Franco, and Rosane Mendonça. "Discriminação e segmentação no mercado de trabalho e desigualdade de renda no Brasil." Discussion paper no. 1288, IPEA, Rio de Janeiro, 2017.

Basseto, Sylvia. "Política de mão-de-obra na economia cafeeira do Oeste Paulista (período de transição)." PhD thesis, FFLCH-USP, 1982.

Bastos, Estêvão, Kopschitz Xavier, and Patrícia Vivas da Silva Fontes. "Mercado de câmbio brasileiro e intervenções do Banco Central." IPEA, Brasília, September 2012.

Bastos, Pedro Paulo Zaluth, and Pedro Cesar Dutra Fonseca. *A era Vargas: desenvolvimento, economia e sociedade*. São Paulo: Editora da UNESP, 2012.

Batista, Luis Eduardo, and Sônia Barros. "Confronting Racism in Health Services." *Cadernos de Saúde Pública* 33 (2017).

Batista, Luís Eduardo, Maria Mercedes Loureiro Escuder, and Julio Cesar Rodrigues Pereira. "A cor da morte: causas de óbito segundo características de raça no Estado de São Paulo, 1999 a 2001." *Revista da Saúde Pública* 38, no. 5 (2004): 630–636.

Beaverstock, J. V., R. G. Smith, and P. J. Taylor. "A Roster of World Cities." *Cities* 16, no. 6 (1999): 445–448.

Belluzzo, Luiz Gonzaga. "Um novo estado desenvolvimentista?" *Le Monde Diplomatique Brasil* 3, no. 27 (2009). https://diplomatique.org.br/um-novo-estado-desenvolvimentista/.

Beltrão, Kaizô Iwakami, and José Eustáquio Diniz Alves. "A reversão do hiato de gênero na educação brasileira no século XX." *Anais* 2016: 125–156.

Beltrão, Kaizô Iwakami, Francisco Eduardo Barreto de Oliveira, and Sonoê Sugahara Pinheiro. "A população rural e a previdência social no Brasil: uma análise com ênfase nas mudanças constitucionais." Discussion paper no. 759, IPEA, Rio de Janeiro, 2000.

Benetti, Maria Domingues. "Endividamento e crise no cooperativismo empresarial do Rio Grande do Sul: análise do caso FECOTRIGO/CENTRALSUL—1975–83." *Ensaios FEE* (Porto Alegre) 6, no. 2 (1985): 23–55.

Benevides, Maria Victoria de Mesquita. *O governo Kubitschek. Desenvolvimento Econômico e Estabilidade Política*. Rio de Janeiro: n.p., 1977.

Berquó, Elza, and S. M. Cavenaghi. "Demographic Evolution of the Brazilian Population During the Twentieth Century." In *Population Change in*

Brazil: Contemporary Perspectives, 13–33. Campinas: NEPO/UNICAMP, 2001.

Berquó, Elza S., and Candido Procopio F. de Camargo, eds. *La population du Brésil.* Paris: UN/CICRED, 1974.

Bignon, Vincent, Rui Esteves, and Alfonso Herranz-Loncán. "Big Push or Big Grab? Railways, Government Activism, and Export Growth in Latin America, 1865–1913." *Economic History Review* 68, no. 4 (2015): 1277–1305.

Birman, Patricia, and David Lehmann. "Religion and the Media in a Battle for Ideological Hegemony: The Universal Church of the Kingdom of God and TV Globo in Brazil." *Bulletin of Latin American Research* 18, no. 2 (1999): 145–164.

Birman, Patricia. "Conexões políticas e bricolagens religiosas: questões sobre o pentecostalismo a partir de alguns contrapontos." In Pierre Sanchis, ed., *Feis e cidadãos, percursos de sincretismo no Brasil*, 59–86. Rio de Janeiro: EDUERJ, 2001.

Birman, Patricia. "Mediação feminina e identidades Pentecostais." *Cadernos PAGU,* no. 6–7 (1996): 201–226.

Bittencourt, Lúcio Nagib. "As organizações sociais e as ações governamentais em cultura: ação e política pública no caso do Estado de São Paulo." PhD thesis, FGV/SP, São Paulo, 2014.

Boarati, Vanessa. "A discussão entre os economistas na década de 1970 sobre a estratégia de desenvolvimento econômico II PND: motivações, custos e resultados." MA thesis, FEAUSP, São Paulo, 2003.

Boas, Taylor C. "Serving God and Man: Evangelical Christianity and Electoral Politics in Latin America." Paper presented at the American Political Science Association Annual Meeting, Chicago, August 29–September 1, 2013. http://people.bu.edu/tboas/serving_god_man .pdf.

Bonduki, Nabil Georges. "Origens da habitação social no Brasil." *Análise Social* 29, no. 127 (1994): 711–732.

Bonelli, Regis, and Renato Fonseca. "Ganhos de produtividade e de eficiência novos resultados para a economia brasileira." *Pesquisa e Planejamento Econômico* (Rio de Janeiro) 28, no. 2 (1998): 273–314.

Bonelli, Regis, and Pedro Malan. "Os limites do possível: notas sobre balanço de pagamento e indústria nos anos 70." *Pesquisa e Planejamento Econômico* 6, no. 2 (1976): 355–406.

Bonelli, Regis, and Samuel de Abreu Pessoa. "Desindustrialização no Brasil: um resumo da evidência." Discussion paper no. 7, FGV/IBRE, Rio de Janeiro, March 2010.

Bonelli, Regis, and Armando Castelar Pinheiro. "Abertura e crescimento econômico no Brasil." In Octavio de Barros and Fabio Giambiagi, eds., *Globalizado*, 89–124. Rio de Janeiro: Campus, 2008.

Brandão, Ramon de Lima. "O automóvel no Brasil entre 1955 e 1961: a invenção de novos imaginários na era JK." MA thesis, Universidade Federal de Juiz de Fora, 2011.

Brentani, Ricardo Renzo, and Carlos Henrique de Brito Cruz, eds. *Indicadores de ciência tecnologia e inovação em São Paulo 2010.* 2 vols. São Paulo: Fapesp, 2011.

Brito, Fausto. "Transição demográfica e desigualdades sociais no Brasil." *Revista Brasileira de Estudos Populacionais* 25, no. 1 (2008): 5–26.

Brito, Fausto, and José Alberto M. de Carvalho. "As migrações internas no Brasil: as novidades sugeridas pelos censos demográficos de 1991 e 2000 e pela PNADS recentes." *Anais do XX Encontro Nacional de Estudos Populacionais, 2016.*

Bruschini, Maria Cristina Aranha. "Trabalho e gênero no Brasil nos últimos dez anos." *Cadernos de Pesquisa* 37, no. 132 (2007): 537–572.

Buainain, Antonio Marcio, et al. "Sete teses sobre o mundo rural brasileiro." In Antônio Márcio Buainain et al., eds., *O mundo rural no Brasil do século 21, a formação de um novo padrão agrário e agrícola*, 1159–1182. Brasilia: Embrapa, 2014.

Buchalla, Cássia Maria, Eliseu Alves Waldman, and Ruy Laurenti. "A mortalidade por doenças infecciosas no início e no final do século XX no Município de São Paulo." *Revista Brasileira de Epidemiologia* 6 (2003): 335–344.

Búrigo, Fábio Luiz. "Finanças e solidariedade: o cooperativismo de crédito rural solidário no Brasil." *Estudos Sociedade e Agricultura* 1 (2013): 312–349.

Cacciamali, Maria Cristina, and Guilherme Issamu Hirata. "A influência da raça e do gênero nas oportunidades de obtenção de renda—uma análise da discriminação em mercados de trabalho distintos: Bahia e São Paulo." *Estudos Econômicos* 35, no. 4 (2005): 774–785.

Caderno MARE da Reforma do Estado. *Organizações Sociais.* 2 vols. Brasília, 1998.

Caldas, Aline Diniz Rodrigues, Ricardo Ventura Santos, Gabriel Mendes Borges, Joaquim Gonçalves Valente, Margareth Crisóstomo Portela, and Gerson Luiz Marinho. "Mortalidade infantil segundo cor ou raça com base no Censo Demográfico de 2010 e nos sistemas nacionais de informação em saúde no Brasil." *Cadernos Saúde Pública* 33, no. 7 (2017). http://www.scielo.br/scielo.php?script=sci_arttext&pid=S0102-311X2017000705007.

Calife, Flávio Estévez. "Duas escolas em confronto. A visão de Luiz Gonzaga Belluzo e Gustavo Franco em relação à inserção externa do Brasil nos anos 90." MA thesis, FGV/EAESP, 2000.

Camarano, Ana Amélia, and Ricardo Abramovay. "Êxodo rural, envelhecimento e masculinização no brasil: panorama dos últimos 50 anos." Discussion paper no. 621, IPEA, Rio de Janeiro, 1998.

Camargo, Candido Procópio Ferreira de, ed. *Católicos, protestantes, espíritas*. Petrópolis: Editora Vozes, 1973.

Camargos, Mirela Castro Santos, Carla Jorge Machado, and Roberto Nascimento Rodrigues. "A relação entre renda e morar sozinha para idosas mineiras, 2003." Paper presented at the XII Seminário Sobre a Economia Mineira, 2006.

Campos, Bruno Nascimento. "Tropas de aço: os caminhos de ferro no Sul de Minas (1875–1902)." MA thesis, Universidade Federal de São João del Rei, 2012.

Campos, Marcos Paulo. "Movimentos sociais e conjuntura política: uma reflexão a partir das relações entre o MST e o governo Dilma." *Revista Cadernos de Estudos Sociais e Políticos* 4, no. 7 (2015): 79–100.

Campos, Marden. "A migração para a região metropolitana de São Paulo no início do século XXI aspectos demográficos e familiares." *Anais do XXI Encontro Nacional de Estudos Populacionais, ABEP, (2018).*

Canabrava, Alice P. "Decadência e Riqueza." *Revista de História* (São Paulo) 100, no. 1 (1974): 335–366.

Canabrava, Alice P. "Uma economia de decadência: Os níveis de riqueza na Capitania de São Paulo, 1765/67." *Revista Brasileira de Economia* 26, no. 4 (1972): 95–123.

Cano, Wilson. "A desindustrialização no Brasil." *Economia e Sociedade* (Campinas) 21, special no. (December 2012): 831–851.

Cano, Wilson. *Desequilíbrios regionais e concentração industrial no Brasil, 1930–1995*. Campinas: Universidade Estadual de Campinas Instituto de Economia, 1998.

Cano, Wilson. *Raízes da concentração industrial em São Paulo*. São Paulo: Difel, 1977.

Caputo, Ana Cláudia, and Hildete Pereira de Melo. "A industrialização brasileira nos anos de 1950: uma análise da instrução 111 da Sumoc." *Estudos Econômicos* 39, no. 3 (2009): 513–538.

Cardoso, Adalberto, and Edmond Préteceille. "Classes médias no Brasil: Do que se trata? Qual seu tamanho? Como vem mudando?" *Dados: Revista de Ciências Sociais* 60, no. 4 (2017): 977–1023.

Cardoso, Fernando Henrique. "Condições sociais da industrialização: o caso de São Paulo." *Revista Brasiliense* 28 (1960): 31–46.

Cardoso, Fernando Henrique. *Mudanças Sociais na América Latina*. São Paulo: Difusão Européia do Livro, 1969.

Cardoso, Fernando Henrique, and Enzo Faletto. *Dependência e desenvolvimento na América Latina—ensaios de interpretação sociológica*. Rio de Janeiro: Zahar, 1970.

Cardozo, Soraia Aparecida. "Guerra fiscal no Brasil e as alterações das estruturas produtivas estaduais desde os anos 1990." PhD thesis, UNICAMP, 2010.

Carneiro, Ricardo. *Desenvolvimento em crise. A economia brasileira no último quarto do século XX*. São Paulo: Editora UNESP, 2002.

Carvalho, Carlos E. "As origens e a gênese do Plano Collor." *Nova Economia* (Belo Horizonte) 16, no. 1 (2006): 101–134.

Carvalho, Carlos E. "O fracasso do Plano Collor: erros de execução ou de concepção." *Economia* (Niterói, RJ) 4, no. 2 (2003): 283–331.

Carvalho, Carlos Viana de. "Relatório de economia bancária, Banco Central do Brasil," 2018. https://www.bcb.gov.br/conteudo/home-ptbr/TextosApresentacoes/Apresentacao_REB%202018-2019_28_5_2019.pdf.

Carvalho, Cleusení Hermelina de. "Bolsa família e desigualdade da renda domiciliar entre 2006 e 2011." MA thesis, PUC São Paulo, 2013.

Carvalho, Enéas Gonçalves de. "Globalização e estratégias competitivas na indústria automobilística: uma abordagem a partir das principais montadoras instaladas no Brasil." *Gestão & Produção* 12, no. 1 (2005): 121–133.

Carvalho, Thiago Franco Oliveira de. "Modernização agrícola e a região da alta mogiana paulista análise da expansão da produção de cana-de-açúcar em uma tradicional região cafeeira." MA thesis, Universidade Estadual Paulista Júlio de Mesquita Filho, Rio Claro, 2014.

Castells, Manuel. *A sociedade em rede*. Rio de Janeiro: Paz e Terra, 2003.

Castells, Manuel. *The Urban Question*. London: Arnold, 1977.

Castillo, Ricardo Abid. "Região competitiva e circuito espacial produtivo: a expansão do setor sucro-alcooleiro (complexo cana-de-açúcar) no território brasileiro." *Centro* no. 289.373,416 (2009): 543–310.

Castro, Antonio Barros de, and Francisco Eduardo Pires de Souza. *A economia brasileira em marcha forçada*. Rio de Janeiro: Paz e Terra, 1985.

Castro, Maria Helena Guimarães de. *Avaliação do sistema educacional brasileiro: tendências e perspectivas*. Brasília: INEP, 1998.

Cavalcante, Luiz Ricardo, and Fernanda Negri. *Trajetória recente dos indicadores de inovação no Brasil*. Discussion paper no. 1659, IPEA, Brasília, 2011.

Cavalcante, Pedro, ed. *Inovação e política públicas, superando o mito da ideia*. Brasilia: IPEA, 2019.

Cavalieri, Claudia, and Reynaldo Fernandes. "Diferenciais de salários por gênero e cor: uma comparação entre as regiões metropolitanas brasileiras." *Revista de Economia Política* 18, no. 1 (1998).

Cavenaghi, Suzana, and José Eustáquio Diniz Alves. "Domicilios y familias en la experiencia censal del Brasil: cambios y propuesta para identificar arreglos familiares." *Notas de Población* [CEPAL] 37, no. 92 (2011).

Cavenaghi, Suzana and Elza S. Berquó, "Perfil socioeconômico e demográfico da fecundidade no Brasil de 2000 a 2010,"in Suzana Cavenaghi and Wanda Cabella, eds., Comportamiento reproductivo y fecundidad en América Latina: una agenda inconclusa (Rio de Janiro/Brasilia: ALAP, 2014): 67-60.

Cechin, José. "A construção e operação das ferrovias no Brasil do século XIX." MA thesis, Instituto de Economia, UNICAMP, 1978.

Celli, Andressa. "Evolução urbana de Sorocaba." MA thesis, FAUUSP, São Paulo, 2012.

Cerqueira, Cézar Augusto, and Gustavo Henrique Naves Givisiez. "Conceitos básicos em demografia e dinâmica demográfica brasileira." *Livros* 2015: 13–44.

Chackiel, Juan, and Susana Schkolnik. "Latin America: Overview of the Fertility Transition, 1950–1990." In Jose Miguel Guzmán et al., *The Fertility Transition in Latin America*. Oxford: Clarendon Press, 1996.

Chaddad, Fabio Ribas. "Cooperativas no agronegócio do leite: mudanças organizacionais e estratégicas em resposta à globalização." *Organizações Rurais & Agroindustriais* 9, no. 1 (2011).

Chaddad, Fabio Ribas. *The Economics and Organization of Brazilian Agriculture: Recent Evolution and Productivity Gains*. Amsterdam: Academic Press, 2016.

Chesnut, R. Andrew. "Exorcising the Demons of Deprivation: Divine Healing and Conversion in Brazilian Pentecostalism." In Candy Gunther Brown, ed., *Global Pentecostal and Charismatic Healing*. New York: Oxford University Press, 2011.

Clemente, Evandro Cesar. "Formação, dinâmica e a reestruturação da cadeia produtiva do leite na região de Jales-SP." MA thesis, Universidade Estadual Paulista, Presidente Prudente, 2006.

Conejero, Marco Antonio, Eduardo José Sia, Mairun Junqueira Alves Pinto, Ricardo Kouiti Santos Iguchi, and Rafael Oliveira do Amaral. "Arranjos contratuais complexos na transação de cana à usina de áçucar e alcool: um estudo de caso no centro-sul do brasil." Paper presented at the XXXII Encontro da ANPAS, 2008, Rio de Janeiro. http://www.anpad.org.br/admin/pdf/GCT-D2072.pdf.

Cordeiro, Simone Lucena. "Cidade Tiradentes e Cohab: moradia popular na periferia da cidade de São Paulo—projetos e trajetórias (1960–1980)." PhD thesis, São Paulo, PUC-SP, 2009.

Corten, André, *Pentecostalism in Brazil: Emotion of the Poor and Theological Romanticism*. New York: St. Martin's Press, 1999.

Costa, Antonio Carlos Augusto da, Nei Pereira Jr., and Donato Alexandre Gomes Aranda. "The Situation of Biofuels in Brazil: New Generation Technologies." *Renewable and Sustainable Energy Reviews* 14 (2010).

Costa, Nilson do Rosário, and José Mendes Ribeiro. "Estudo comparativo do desempenho de hospitais em regime de organização social." FIOCRUZ/ENSP, Rio de Janeiro, 2005.

Costa, Valeriano M. F. "A dinâmica Institucional da Reforma do Estado: um balanço do período FHC." In *O estado numa era de reformas: os anos FHC* Brasília SEGES-MP 2002.

Coutinho, Luciano G., and Luiz Gonzaga Mello Belluzo. "Desenvolvimento e estabilização sob finanças globalizadas." *Economia e Sociedade* (Campinas) 7 (1996): 129–154.

Couto, Joaquim Miguel. "Entre estatais e transnacionais: O polo industrial de Cubatão." PhD thesis, Campinas, UNICAMP, 2003.

Croffot, Elizabeth, Eric Hayek, and Michael Paterra. "Charting International Labor Comparisons." The Conference Board, 2014. https://www.conference-board.org/publications/publicationdetail.cfm?publicationid=2715.

Cunha, Ana C. N. M. Fernandes da. "As organizações sociais de saúde na cidade de São Paulo e a efetivação do Direito Fundamental à Saúde." MA thesis, Faculdade de Direito-USP, 2016.

Cunha, Estela Maria Garcia de Pinto da. "Condicionantes da mortalidade infantil segundo raça/cor no estado de São Paulo, 1997–1998." PhD thesis, Campinas, Fac. de Ciências Médicas, 2001.

Cunha, José Marcos Pinto da. "Impactos da migração intercensitária em algumas características demográficas do Estado de São Paulo (1970–1980)." *Anais do X Encontro Nacional de Estudos Populacionais* (1988).

Daudat, Gabriel, and Luiz Daniel Willcox. "Indústria automotiva." BNDES. https://web.bndes.gov.br/bib/jspui/bitstream/1408/16241/1/PRCapLiv214167_industria_automotiva_compl_P.pdf.

Dean, Warren. *The Industrialization of São Paulo, 1880–1945*. Austin: University of Texas Press, 1969.

Dean, Warren. "Latifundia and Land Policy in Nineteenth-Century Brazil." *The Hispanic American Historical Review* 51, no. 4 (1971): 606–625.

Dedecca, Cláudio Slavadori, and José Marcos Pinto Cunha. "Migração, trabalho e renda nos anos 90: o caso da Região Metropolitana de São Paulo." Paper presented at the XIII Encontro da Associação Brasileira de Estudos Populacionais, Ouro Preto, Minas Gerais, Brasil, November 4–8, 2002.

Delfim Netto, Antonio. "Análise do comportamento recente da economia brasileira: diagnóstico." Mimeo, São Paulo, 1967.

Denardi, Rosana. "Políticas de urbanização de favelas: evolução e impasses." PhD thesis, FAU/USP, 2003.

Dicken, Peter. *Global Shift: Mapping the Changing Contours of the World Economy*. New York: Guilford Press, 2000.

Diniz, Eli. "Empresariado industrial, representação de interesses e ação política: trajetória histórica e novas configurações." *Politica & Sociedade* 9, no. 17 (2010): 106–109.

Diniz, Sarah Silveira, Marcia Regina Gabardo da Câmara, Marcelo Ortega Massambani, João Amilcar Rodrigues Anhesini, and Umberto Antonio Sesso Filho. "Análise espacial da produtividade da Laranja dos municípios do estado de São Paulo: 2002 a 2010." Paper presented at the 50 Congresso da SOBER 2012.

Dionizio, Flávia Lopes. "Qualidade do leite e impacto econômico de diferentes tipos de coletas e condições de transporte da fazenda à indústria." MA thesis, Universidade Federal de Minas Gerais, 2013.

Draibe, Sonia. *Rumos e metamorfoses. Estado e industrialização no Brasil: 1930–1960*. Rio de Janeiro: Paz e Terra, 1985.

Duarte, S. B. "Organizações sociais de cultura em São Paulo—desafios e perspectivas." Paper presented at the IV Congresso Consad de Gestão Pública, Brasília, May 2012.

Dulci, Otávio Soares. "Guerra fiscal, desenvolvimento desigual e relações federativas no Brasil." *Revista de Sociologia e Política,* no. 18 (2002): 95–107.

Dupas, Gilberto. *Economia global e exclusão social.* São Paulo: Paz e Terra, 2000.

Fantin, Jader Tadeu. "Os Japoneses no Bairro da Liberdade-SP na primeira metade do século XX." MA thesis, São Carlos, FAU-USP, 2013.

Faria, Antonio Augusto da Costa. "A Light e a utilização dos recursos hidrícos da Bacia do Tietê para a geração de energia elétrica." http://arquivos.ambiente.sp.gov.br/cea/2011/12/AntonioAugusto.pdf.

Faúndes, Anibal, Rosely Gomes Costa, Karla Simônia de Pádua, and Antero Marques Perdigão. "Associação entre prevalência de laqueadura tubária e características sócio-demográficas de mulheres e seus companheiros no Estado de São Paulo, Brasil." *Cadernos de Saúde Pública* 14 (1998): S59–S57.

Fausto, Boris. *A revolução de 1930: historiografia e história.* São Paulo: Editora Brasiliense, 1970.

Fernandes, Bernardo Mançano. "Contribuição ao estudo do campesinato brasileiro formação e territorialização do Movimento dos Trabalhadores Rurais Sem Terra—MST (1979–1999)." PhD thesis, USP, São Paulo, 1999.

Fernandes, Florestan. *A integração do negro na sociedade de classes.* São Paulo: Ática, 1978.

Fernandes, Rosangela Aparecida Soares, and Cristiane Márcia dos Santos. "Competitividade das exportações sucroalcooleiras no Estado de São Paulo." *Anais do 4° ECAECO [Encontro Científico de Administração, Economia e Contabilidade]* 1, no. 1 (2011).

Ferranti, David de, Guillermo E. Perry, Francisco Ferreira, and Michael Walton. *Inequality in Latin America: Breaking with History?* Washington, DC: World Bank, 2004.

Ferrari Filho, Fernando. "Análise de um motor do ciclo diesel operando no modo bicombustível: diesel/etanol." MA thesis, PUC, Rio de Janeiro, 2011.

Ferraz, Ivan Roberto. "Indicadores de desempenho das organizações sociais de cultura do Estado de São Paulo." MA thesis, PUC/SP, São Paulo, 2008.

Ferraz, Luciano. "Regime jurídico aplicável aos conselhos profissionais esta nas mão do Supremo." Consultor Jurídico. https://www.conjur.com.br/2017-mar-02/interesse-publico-regime-juridico-conselhos-profissionais-maos-stf.

Ferreira, Carlos Eugenio de Carvalho and Luciane Lestido Castiñeiras. "O rápido aumento da mortalidade dos jovens adultos em São Paulo, uma trágica tendência." *São Paulo em Perspectiva* 10 (1996): 34–41.

Ferreira, João Sette Whitaker. "São Paulo: o mito da cidade-global." PhD thesis, FAU-USP, São Paulo, 2003.

Ferreira, Vanessa de Lima. "Estratégia na relação com os fornecedores na indústria aeronáutica brasileira. O caso Embraer." MA thesis, São Paulo, Escola Politécnica da USP, 2010.

Figueira, Sérgio Rangel. "Transformações na cadeia produtiva do leite—uma análise a partir das cooperativas." MA thesis, Universidade Estadual de Campinas, 1999.

Figueiredo, Adelson Martins, Hildo Meireles de Souza Filho, and Luiz Fernando de Oriani Paullilo. "Análise das margens e transmissão de preços no sistema agroindustrial do suco de laranja no Brasil." *Revista de Economia e Sociologia Rural* 51, no. 2 (2013): 331–350.

Filgueiras, Luiz. *História do Plano Real.* São Paulo: Boitempo Editorial, 2000.

Firpo, Sérgio Pinheiro. "Inserção no mercado de trabalho: diferenças por sexo e consequências sobre o bem-estar." Discussion paper no. 796, IPEA, Rio de Janeiro, 2001.

Fishlow, Albert. "Algumas reflexões sobre a política brasileira após 1964." *Estudos Cebrap* 6 (1974): 6–65.

Fishlow, Albert. "Origens e consequências da substituição de importações no Brasil." *Estudos Econômicos* 2, no. 6 (1972): 7–75.

Florêncio, Sérgio Abreu e Lima. "Trajetória do Mercosul e mudança de paradigmas e de posições da política externa brasileira: começo virtuoso e crise recente—possíveis interpretações." Discussion paper no. 2125, IPEA, Rio de Janeiro, 2015.

Fonseca, Pedro Cezar Dutra, et al. "O Brasil na Era Lula: retorno ao desenvolvimentismo." *Nova Economia* 23, no. 2 (2013): 403–428.

Fonseca, Pedro Cezar Dutra, and Sérgio Marley Modesto Monteiro. "O estado e suas razões: o II PND." *Revista de Economia Política* 28, no. 1 (2007): 28–46.

França, Danilo Sales do Nascimento. "Raça, classe e segregação residencial no Município de São Paulo." MA thesis, Universidade de São Paulo, 2010.

França, Elisabete. "Favelas em São Paulo (1980–2008). Das propostas de desfavelamento aos projetos de Urbanização. A experiência do Programa

Guapiranga." PhD thesis, São Paulo, Universidade Presbiteriana Mackenzie, 2009.

Francisco, Vera Lúcia F. dos Santos, Celso Luis Rodrigues Vegro, José Alberto Ângelo, and Carlos Nabil Ghobril. "Estrutura produtiva da cafeicultura paulista." *Informações Econômicas SP* 39, no. 8 (2009): 42–48.

Franco, Angela. "Em tempos globais, um 'novo' local: a Ford da Bahia." *Caderno CRH* (Salvado) 22, no. 56 (2009): 359–380.

Franco, Gustavo. *O desafio brasileiro: ensaios sobre desenvolvimento, globalização e moeda*. São Paulo: Editora 34, 1999.

Franco, Gustavo. "A inserção externa e o desenvolvimento." *Revista de Economia Política* 18, no. 3 (1998): 121–147.

Franco, Gustavo. *O Plano Real e outros ensaios*. Rio de Janeiro: Editora Francisco Alves, 1995.

Freitas, Elizabeth Ponte de. "Por uma cultura pública: organizações sociais, Oscips e gestão pública não estatal na área da cultura." MA thesis, Universidade Federal da Bahia, 2010.

Freitas, Luiz Antonio Rossi de, and Oscar Bertoglio. "A evolução da avicultura de corte brasileira após 1980." *Economia e Desenvolvimento* 13 (2001): 100–135.

French, John D. *The Brazilian Workers' ABC: Class Conflict and Alliances in Modern São Paulo*. Chapel Hill: University of North Carolina Press, 1992.

Freston, Paul. "Evangelicals and Politics in Latin America." *Transformation* 19, no. 4 (2002).

Freston, Paul. "'Neo-Pentecostalism' in Brazil: Problems of Definition and the Struggle for Hegemony." *Archives de Sciences Sociales des Religions* 44, no. 105 (1999): 145–162.

Freston, Paul. "Protestantes e politica no Brasil: da constituinte ao impeachment." PhD thesis, UNICAMP, 1993.

Frias, Luiz Armando de Medeiros and Juarez de Castro Oliveira. "Níveis, tendências e diferenciais de fecundidade no Brasil a partir da década de 30." *Revista Brasileira de Estudos de População* 8, no. 1/2 (1991): 72–111.

Furtado, Celso. *Formação econômica do Brasil*. Rio de Janeiro: Paz e Terra, 1959.

Galvão, Jane. "Access to Antiretroviral Drugs in Brazil." *The Lancet* 360, no. 9348 (2002): 1862–1885. https://pubmed.ncbi.nlm.nih.gov/12480377/.

Garcia, Carmen de Jesus. "Uma análise das mudanças na estrutura industrial brasileira nos anos 90." MA thesis, UFRJ, 2001.

Garcia, Glaucia. "A história da fábrica da DKW Vemag." *São Paulo Antiga*. http://www.saopauloantiga.com.br/vemag-uma-fabrica-que-agoniza-no-tempo/.

Gargiulo, Flavio Riva. "Indústria de construção aeronáutica, o caso da EMBRAER: história e avaliação." MA thesis, FGV, 2008.

Gentile, Fabio. "O fascismo como modelo: incorporação da 'Carta del Lavoro' na via brasileira para o corporativismo autoritário da década de 1930." In *Dossie—pensamento de direita e chauvinismo na América Latina*, 84–101. http://www.uel.br/revistas/uel/index.php/mediacoes/article/view/19857.

Giambiagi, Fabio, and Lavinia B. de Castro. "Previdência social: diagnósticos e propostas de reforma." *Revista do BNDES* 10, no. 19 (2003): 265–292.

Giambiagi, Fabio, and Maurício Mesquita Moreira. *A economia brasileira nos anos 90*. Rio de Janeiro: BNDES, 1990.

Giuberti, Ana Carolina, and Naércio Menezes-Filho. "Discriminação de rendimentos por gênero: uma comparação entre o Brasil e os Estados Unidos." *Economia Aplicada* 9, no. 3 (2005): 369–383.

Gohn, Maria da Glória. *Movimentos sociais e redes de mobilizações civis no Brasil contemporâneo*. Petrópolis: Editora Vozes, 2010.

Goldemberg, José. "O repensar da educação no Brasil." *Estudos Avançados* 7, no. 18 (1993): 65–137.

Goldemberg, José, Suani Teixeira Coelho, and Patricia Guardabassi. "The Sustainability of Ethanol Production from Sugarcane." *Energy Policy* 36 (2008): 2086–2097.

Gomes, Sérgio B. V. *A indústria aeronáutica no Brasil. Evolução recente e perspectivas*. Brasília: BNDES, 2012. https://web.bndes.gov.br/bib/jspui/bitstream/1408/919/1/A%20ind%C3%BAstria%20aeron%C3%A1utica%20no%20Brasil_P-final_BD.pdf.

Gonçalves, José Sidnei. "Dinâmica da agropecuária paulista no contexto das transformações de sua agricultura." *Informações Econômicas SP* 35, no. 12 (2005): 65–98.

Gonçalves, Reinaldo. "Competitividade internacional e integração regional: a hipótese da inserção regressiva." *Revista de Economia Contemporânea* 5, special ed. (2001).

Governo do Estado de São Paulo. *São Paulo no limiar do século XXI*. 8 vols. São Paulo: GESP/SEADE, 1992.

Graef, Aldino, and Valéria Salgado. *Relações de parceria entre poder público e entes de cooperação e colaboração no Brasil*. Brasília: Editora IABS, 2012.

Graham, Richard. *Britain and the Onset of Modernization in Brazil 1850–1914*. Cambridge: Cambridge University Press, 1968.

Guedes, Clélia F. B. "Políticas públicas de estímulo à P&D: uma avaliação dos resultados do programa regulado pela Agência Nacional de Energia Elétrica—ANELL." MA thesis, Universidade de Brasília, 2010.

Guerra, Clarissa Battistella. "Gestão privada na saúde pública: um estudo empírico com hospitais sob contrato de gestão no Estado de São Paulo." MA thesis, INSPER, São Paulo, 2015.

Guimarães, Maria Bernadete Pita. "Alcoolismo, pentecostalismo e família." PhD thesis, Universidade Federal Juiz de Fora, 2008.

Guzmán, José Miguel. "Introduction: Social Change and Fertility Decline in Latin America." In Jose Miguel Guzmán et al., *The Fertility Transition in Latin America*. Oxford: Clarendon Press, 1996.

Hahn, Carl Joseph. *História do culto protestante no Brasil*. São Paulo: ASTE, 1981.

Hanley, Anne G. *Native Capital: Financial Institutions and Economic Development in São Paulo, Brazil, 1850–1920*. Stanford: Stanford University Press, 2005.

Haraguchi, N. "Patterns of Structural Change and Manufacturing Development." In J. Weiss and M. Tribe, eds., *Routledge Handbook of Industry and Development*, 38–64. Abingdon: Routledge, 2016.

Harvey, David. *The Condition of Postmodernity*. Cambridge: Blackwell Publishers, 1992.

Hasenbalg, Carlos A., Nelson do Valle Silva, and Marcia Lima. *Cor e estratificação social no Brasil*. Rio de Janeiro: Contracapa, 1999.

Henriques, Ricardo. "Desigualdade racial no Brasil: evolução das condições de vida na década de 90." Discussion paper no. 807, IPEA, Rio de Janeiro, July 2001.

Hira, Anil, and Luiz Guilherme de Oliveira. "No Substitute for Oil? How Brazil Developed Its Ethanol Industry." *Energy Policy* 37 (2009): 2450–2456.

Hoffman, Rodolfo, and Régis Oliveira. "The Evolution of Income Distribution in Brazil in the Agricultural and the Non-Agricultural Sectors." *World Journal of Agricultural Research* 2, no. 5 (2014): 192–204.

Holland, Marcio, ed, *Zona franca de Manaus, impactos, efetividade e oportunidades*. São Paulo: FGV EESP, 2019s. http://site.suframa.gov.br/assuntos/publicacoes/estudo_fgv_zfm_impactos_efetividade_e_oportunidades.pdf.

Horta, Cláudia Júlia Guimarães, José Alberto Magno de Carvalho, and Luís Armando de Medeiros Frias. "Recomposição da fecundidade por geração para Brasil e regiões: atualização e revisão." Paper presented at the *XI Encontro Nacional de Estudos Populacionais da ABEP, 2016*.

Hryniewicz, Roberto Romeiro. "Torcida de futebol: adesão, alienação e violência." MA thesis, Instituto de Psicologia da Universidade de São Paulo, 2008.

Iannone, Roberto Antonio. "A evolução do setor elétrico paulista." PhD thesis, FFLCHUSP, 2006.

Iglésias, Francisco. "Política Econômica do Estado de Minas Gerais (1890–1930)." V Seminário de Estudos Mineiros, UFMG, 1982.

Johnson, Andrew. *If I Give My Soul: Faith Behind Bars in Rio de Janeiro*. New York: Oxford University Press, 2017.

Junqueira, Victor Hugo. "O papel do Estado na expansão do setor sucroalcooleiro na região de Ribeirão Preto." *Revista NERA* (Presidente Prudente) 19, no. 31 (2016): 51–71.

Kakimoto, Sérgio Kenji. "Fatores críticos da competitividade da cadeia produtiva do ovo no estado de São Paulo." MA thesis, Universidade Federal de São Carlos, 2011.

Klein, Herbert S., and Francisco Vidal Luna. *Brazil, 1964–1985: The Military Regimes of Latin America in the Cold War.* New Haven: Yale University Press, 2017.

Klein, Herbert S., and Francisco Luna. *Brazil: A Modern Social History.* Cambridge: Cambridge University Press, 2020.

Klein, Herbert S., and Francisco Vidal Luna. *Feeding the World: Brazil's Transformation into a Modern Agricultural Economy.* Cambridge: Cambridge University Press, 2018.

Klink, Jeroen. "Regionalismo e reestruturação urbana: uma perspectiva brasileria de governança metropolitana." *Educação* (Porto Alegre) 32, no. 2 (2009): 217–226.

Koeller, Priscila, Renato B. Viotti, and André Rauen. "Dispêndios do governo federal em C&T e P&D: esforços e perspectivas recentes." *Radar* (Brasília) 48 (December 2016): 13–18.

Koulioumba, Stamatia. "São Paulo: cidade mundial?" PhD thesis, FAU-USP, São Paulo, 2002.

Kruger, Tania Regina, Simone Bihain Hagemann, and Aline Ayres Hollanda. "Organizações sociais e os serviços públicos de saúde em Santa Catarina." Paper presented at the Seminário Nacional de Serviço Social, Trabalho e Política Social, Florianópolis, UFSC, October 2015.

Lacerda, Fabio. "Pentecostalismo, eleições e representação política no Brasil contemporâneo." PhD thesis, USP, 2017.

Lamonier, Maria Lúcia. "Entre a escravidão e o trabalho livre. escravos e imigrantes nas obras de construção das ferrovias no Brasil no século XIX." *Economia* (Brasilia) 9, no. 4 (2008): 215–245.

Lamounier, Bolivar, and Rubens Figueiredo. *A era FHC. Um balanço.* São Paulo: Cultura Associados, 2002.

Lavos, Ana Paula Alves de. "Sociabilidade em conjuntos habitacionais produzidos pelo Estado: o caso da COHAB Cidade Tiradentes." MA thesis, São Carlos, Escola de Engenharia de São Carlos/USP, 2009.

Leal, Maria do Carmo, Silvana Granado Nogueira da Gama, Ana Paula Esteves Pereira, Vanessa Eufrauzino Pacheco, Cleber Nascimento do Carmo, and Ricardo Ventura Santos. "The Color of Pain: Racial Iniquities in Prenatal Care and Childbirth in Brazil." *Cadernos de Saúde Pública* 33, supp. 1 (2017). http://www.scielo.br/scielo.php?pid=S0102-311X2017001305004&script=sci_arttext&tlng=en.

Lessa, Carlos. "Estratégia de desenvolvimento, 1974–79: sonhos e fracasso." Tese de Professor Titular, UFRJ, Rio de Janeiro, 1978.

Lessa, Carlos. *Quinze anos de política econômica.* São Paulo: Brasiliense/UNICAMP, 1975.

Levy, Maria Stella Ferreira. "O papel da migração internacional na evolução da população brasileira (1872 a 1972)." *Revista de Saúde Publica* 8, supp. (1974): 49–90.

Liboni, Lara Bartocci, Luciana Oranges Cezarino, Michelle Castro Carrijo, and Rudinei Toneto Jr. "The Equipment Supply Industry to Sugar Mills, Ethanol and Energy in Brazil: An Analysis Based in Leading Companies and Key-Organizations of Sector and of LPA of Sertãozinho." *Independent Journal of Management & Production* 6, no. 4 (2015): 1070–1096.

Lima, Guilherme Gadonski de, Emerson Juliano Lucca, and Dilson Trennepohl. "Expansão da cadeia produtiva do leite e seu potencial de impacto no desenvolvimento da região noroeste rio-grandense." Paper presented of the 53rd Congresso da SOBER 2015, João Pessoa.

Lima, Heitor Ferreira, Morvan Dias de Figueiredo, Pereira Ignacio, Irmãos Jafet, Conde Matarazzo, Coronel Rodovalho, Roberto Simonsen, and Jorge Street. *Evolução industrial de São Paulo: esboço histórico.* São Paulo: Martins, 1954.

Lima, Marcos F. C., and Marconi Aurélio da Silva. "Inovação em petróleo e gás no Brasil: a parceria Cenpes-Petrobrás e Coppe-UFRJ." *Revista Sociedade e Estado* 27, no. 1 (2012): 97–105.

Lima, Maria Helena Palmer. "A delimitação legal do espaços urbanos." https://biblioteca.ibge.gov.br/visualizacao/livros/liv97884_cap3.pdf.

Limoncic, Flávio. "A civilização do automóvel: a instalação da indústria automobilística no Brasil e a via brasileira para uma improvável modernidade fordista, 1956–1961." MA thesis, UFRJ, 1997.

Locatel, Celso Donizete, and Fernanda Laize Silva de Lima. "Agronegócio e poder político: políticas agrícolas e o exercício do poder no Brasil." *Sociedade e Território* (Natal) 28, no. 2 (2016): 57–81.

Longhini, Tatielle M., et al. "Investimentos em inovação e sua influência na receita líquida de vendas. Uma análise com base dos dados do PINTEC." *BBR Brazilian Business Review* 15, no. 1 (2018): 1–16.

Longo, Luciene Aparecida Ferreira de Barros. "Uniões intra e inter-raciais, status marital, escolaridade e religião no Brasil: um estudo sobre a seletividade marital feminina, 1980–2000." PhD thesis, Belo Horizonte, Universidade Federal de Minas Gerais, 2011.

Lopreano, F. L. *Aspectos a atuação estatal de FHC a Dilma.* Discussion paper no. 2039, IPEA, Brasília, February 2015.

Lotufo, Paulo Andrade, and Isabela Judith Martins Bensenor. "Raça e mortalidade cerebrovascular no Brasil." *Revista de Saúde Pública* 47, no. 6 (2013): 1201–1204.

Loureiro, Alexandre Pinto. "O direito de greve do servidor público no Brasil diante do princípio do interesse público." MA thesis, Faculdade de Direito USP, 2009.

Loureiro, Maria Rita, Vinicius Macário, and Pedro Guerra. "Democracia, arenas decisórias e políticas públicas: o Programa Minha Casa Minha Vida." Discussion paper no. 1886, IPEA, Brasília, 2013.

Love, Joseph. *São Paulo in the Brazilian Federation, 1889–1937*. Stanford: Stanford University Press, 1980.

Love, Joseph, and Werner Baer, eds. *Brazil Under Lula: Economy, Politics, and Society Under the Worker-President*. Basingstoke: Palgrave Macmillan, 2009.

Lucchese, Mafalda. "Filhos—evolução até a plena igualdade jurídica." Available at http://www.emerj.tjrj.jus.br/serieaperfeicoamentode magistrados/paginas/series/13/volumeI/10 anosdocodigocivil_231 .pdf.

Luna, Francisco Vidal "Observações sobre os dados de produção apresentados por Muller." *Boletim de História Demográfica* 9, no. 24 (2002). http:// historia_demografica.tripod.com/pesquisadores/paco/pdf-paco/ar50. pdf.

Luna, Francisco Vidal. "São Paulo: A capital financeira do país." In Tamás Szmrecsányi, ed., *História Econômica da Cidade de São Paulo*, 328–355. São Paulo: Editora Globo, 2005.

Luna, Francisco Vidal, and Iraci del Nero da Costa. "Antecedentes históricos da via anchieta." *Suplemento Cultural do Estado de São Paulo*, ano II, no. 118 (1978): 14–16.

Luna, Francisco Vidal, and Herbert S. Klein. *Brazil Since 1980*. Cambridge: Cambridge University Press, 2006.

Luna, Francisco Vidal, and Herbert S. Klein. *The Economic and Demographic History of São Paulo 1850–1950*. Stanford: Stanford University Press, 2017.

Luna, Francisco Vidal, and Herbert S. Klein. *The Economic and Social History of Brazil Since 1889*. Cambridge: Cambridge University Press, 2014.

Luna, Francisco Vidal, and Herbert S. Klein. *Slavery and the Economy of São Paulo, 1750–1850*. Stanford: Stanford University Press, 2003.

Luna, Francisco Vidal, Herbert S. Klein, and William Summerhill. "The Characteristics of Coffee Production and Agriculture in the State of São Paulo in 1905." *Agricultural History* 90, no. 1 (2016): 22–50.

Lundberg, Eduardo. *Bancos oficiais e crédito direcionado—o que diferencia o mercado de crédito brasileiro?* No. 258, Central Bank of Brazil, Research Department, Brasília, 2011.

Machado, Adriano Henriques. "A influência dos setores católicos na formação do Partido dos Trabalhadores: da relação com os movimentos sociais à ideia de formar um novo partido." Paper presented at ANPUH—XXV Simpósio Nacional de História, 2009, Fortaleza. http://anais.anpuh.org/ wp-ontent/uploads/mp/pdf/ANPUH.S25.0956.pdf.

Machado, Humberto Fernandes. *Escravos, senhores e café. A crise da cafeicultura escravista do Vale do Paraíba, 1860–1888.* Niterói: Cromos, 1993.

Machado, Nilson José. "Qualidade da educação: cinco lembretes e uma lembrança. *Estudos Avançados* 21, no. 61 (2007): 277–294.

Maia, Rosane de Almeida. "Estado e industrialização no Brasil: estudo dos incentivos ao setor privado nos quadros do Programa de Metas do governo Kubitschek." MA thesis, FEA-USP, São Paulo, 1986.

Mariano, Ricardo. "Efeitos da secularização do estado, do pluralismo e do mercado religiosos sobre as igrejas pentecostais." *Civitas* 3, no. 1 (2003): 111–125.

Mariano, Ricardo. "Expansão pentecostal no Brasil: o caso da Igreja Universal." *Estudos Avançados* 18, no. 52 (2004): 121–138.

Mariano, Ricardo. "Sociologia do crescimento pentecostal no Brasil: um balanço." *Perspectiva Teológica* 43, no. 119 (2011), 11–36.

Mariotoni, Marili Arruda. "O desenvolvimento tecnológico do setor sucroalcooleiro no estado de São Paulo (1975–1985)." PhD thesis, Universidade Estadual de Campinas, 2004.

Mariz, Cecília Loreto. *Coping with Poverty: Pentecostals and Christian Base Communities in Brazil.* Philadelphia: Temple University Press, 1994.

Mariz, Cecília L. "Missão religiosa e migração: 'novas comunidades' e igrejas pentecostais no exterior." *Análise Social* 190 (2009): 161–187.

Marques, Maria Silva B. "O Plano Cruzado: teoria e prática." *Revista de Economia Política* 8, no. 3 (1983): 101–130.

Marques, P. V. "Contribuição ao estudo da organização agroindustrial: o caso da indústria de frango de corte no estado de São Paulo." *Scientia Agricola* 51, no. 1 (1994): 8–16.

Martinez, Maria R. E. "A globalização da indústria aeronáutica: o caso da Embraer." PhD thesis, Universidade de Brasília, 2007.

Martins, Renata. "Produção de amendoim e expansão da cana-de-açúcar na Alta Paulista, 1996–2010." *Informações Econômicas SP* 41, no. 6 (2011): 5–16.

Martins, Sônia Santana. "Cadeias produtivas do frango e do ovo: avanços tecnológicos e sua apropriação." PhD thesis, Fundação Getúlio Varas, São Paulo, 1996.

Martins, Sônia Santana, Ana Lúcia Lemos, Antônio de Pádua Deodato, Erica Salgado Politi, and Nilce M. S. Queiroz. "Cadeia produtiva do ovo no estado de São Paulo." *Informações Econômicas. Governo do Estado de São Paulo. Instituto de Economia Agrícola* 30, no. 1 (2000), http://www.iea.sp.gov.br/ftpiea/ie/2000/tec1-jan2000.pdf.

Matos, Carlos Alberto. "A Fenajufe e seus sindicatos: a CUT no poder judiciário federal e no ministério público da União." MA thesis, UNICAMP, 2002.

Mattei, Lauro. "Programa nacional para produção e uso do biodiesel no Brasil (PNPB): trajetória, situação atual e desafios." *BNB* [Banco Nordeste do Brasil] *Documentos Técnicos Científicos* 41, no. 4 (2010).

Mattoon, Robert H., Jr. "Railroads, Coffee, and the Growth of Big Business in São Paulo, Brazil." *The Hispanic American Historical Review* 57, no. 2 (1977): 273–295.

Mattos, Hebe Maria. *Das cores do silêncio.* Rio de Janeiro: Nova Fronteira, 1998.

Mattos, Marcelo Badaró. *Trabalhadores e sindicatos no Brasil.* São Paulo: Editora Expressão Popular, 2009.

Mattos, Odilon Nogueira de Matos. *Café e ferrovias: a evolução ferroviária de São Paulo e o desenvolvimento da cultura cafeeira.* São Paulo: Alfa-Omega, 1974.

McKay, Ben, Sérgio Sauer, Ben Richardson, and Roman Herre. "The Politics of Sugarcane Flexing in Brazil and Beyond." Transnational Institute Agrarian Justice Program Think Piece Series on Flex Crops and Commodities, no. 4, September 2014. http://repub.eur.nl/pub/77677/Metis_202533.pdf.

Medeiros, Marcelo. "O que faz os Ricos ricos: um estudo sobre fatores que determinam a riqueza." PhD thesis, Departamento de Sociologia, Universidade de Brasília, 2003.

Medeiros, Marcelo, and Joana Simões Costa. "Poverty Among Women in Latin America: Feminization or Overrepresentation?" Working paper no. 20, International Poverty Centre, Brasília, 2006.

Medeiros, Marcelo, and Pedro H. G. F. Souza. "A estabilidade da desigualdade no Brasil entre 2006 e 2012: resultados adicionais." *Pesquisa e Planejamento Econômico* 46, no. 3 (2016).

Medici, André, and Robert Murray. "Desempenho de hospitais e melhorias na qualidade de saúde em São Paulo (Brasil) e Maryland (EUA)." World Bank, Washington, DC, 2013.

Melo, Carlos Alberto Furtado de. *O governo Lula e o sistema político: inércia econômica, ativismo social e inação política—avaliando e buscando hipótese.* São Paulo: Insper, 2009.

Mendonça, Antonio Gouvêa, and Prócoro Velasques Filho. *Introdução ao protestantismo no Brasil.* São Paulo: Edições Loyola, 1990.

Menezes Filho, Naércio, Bruno Komatsu, Andrea Lucchesi, and Marcelo Ferrario. "Políticas de inovação no Brasil." Policy paper no. 11, Insper, São Paulo, August 2014.

Mercadante, Aloizio, ed. *O Brasil pós real. A política econômica em debate.* Campinas: UNICAMP, 1997.

Mercadante, Paulo. *Os sertões do leste. Estudo de uma região: a mata mineira.* Rio de Janeiro: Zahar, 1973.

"Mercado de consumo do futebol brasileiro." CNDL/SPC Brasil, September 2016.

Merrick, Thomas W., and Douglas H. Graham. *Population and Economic Development in Brazil, 1800 to the Present.* Baltimore: Johns Hopkins University Press, 1979.

Merrick, Thomas William, and Elza Berquó. *The Determinants of Brazil's Recent Rapid Decline in Fertility.* Washington, DC: National Academies Press, 1983.

Meyer, Regina Maria Prosperi, Marta Dora Grostein, and Ciro Biderman. *São Paulo Metrópole.* São Paulo: Edusp/Imprensa Oficial, 2004.

Milanovic, Branko. "Global Inequality and the Global Inequality Extraction Ratio: The Story of the Past Two Centuries." *Explorations in Economic History* 48 (2011): 494–506.

Modiano, Eduardo. "A ópera dos três cruzados: 1985–1989." In Marcelo de Paiva Abreu, ed., *A ordem do Progresso*, 347–386. Rio de Janeiro: Editora Campus, 1992.

Monbeig, Pierre. *Pioneiros e fazendeiros de São Paulo.* São Paulo: Hucitec-Polis, 1984.

Moraes, Márcia Azanha Ferraz Dias de. "O mercado de trabalho da agroindústria canavieira: desafios e oportunidades." *Economia Aplicada.* 11 (2007): 605-619.

Morceiro, Paulo César. *Desindustrialização na economia brasileira no período 2000–2011, abordagens e indicadores.* São Paulo: Cultura Acadêmica, 2012.

Morceiro, Paulo César. "A indústria brasileira no limiar do século XXI: uma análise da sua evolução estrutural, comercial e tecnológica." PhD thesis, FEA-USP, 2018.

Morceiro, Paulo César, and Joaquim José Martins Guilhoto. *Desindustrialização setorial e estagnação de longo prazo na manufatura brasileira.* São Paulo: Nereus, 2019.

Moreira, Felipe de Freitas. "Heliópolis e a produção municipal de moradias populares em favelas." Paper presented at XVII Enapur, São Paulo, 2017. http://anpur.org.br/xviienanpur/principal/publicacoes/XVII.ENANPUR_Anais/ST_Sessoes_Tematicas/ST%205/ST%205.8/ST%205.8-04.pdf.

Moreira, Felipe de Freitas. "Heliópolis e as estratégicas de enfrentamento da cidade real." MA thesis, FAU/USP, 2017.

Moreira, Maurício M. "Estrangeiros em uma econômica aberta: impactos recentes sobre a produtividade, a concentração e o comércio exterior." In Fabio Giambiagi and Maurício Mesquita Moreira, eds., *A economia brasileira nos anos 90*, 333–374. Rio de Janeiro: BNDES, 1999.

Morgan, Marc, "Extreme and Persistent Inequality: New Evidence for Brazil Combining National Accounts, Surveys and Fiscal Data, 2001–2015."

Working Paper Series no. 12, World Wealth and Income Database, 2017.

Morse, Richard. *From Community to Metropolis: A Biography of São Paulo, Brazil.* Gainesville: University of Florida Press, 1958.

Mota, Daniel Pestana. "CUT, sindicato orgânico e reforma da estrutura sindical." MA thesis, UNESP, Marília, 2006.

Moura, Alessandro. "Movimento operário e sindicalismo em Osasco, São Paulo e ABC Paulista: rupturas e descontinuidades." PhD thesis, UNESP, Marília, 2015.

Moura, Marcelo. *Consolidação das leis do trabalho,* 7th ed. Salvador: JusPodivm, 2017. https://www.editorajuspodivm.com.br/cdn/arquivos/ca-615420c19a66758beaf108395fe01b.pdf.

Mourad, Camila B. "Relação entre as atividades internas e externas no desempenho em inovação das empresas do setor industrial brasileiro: constatações baseadas em uma década de PINTE/IBGE." PhD thesis, Universidade de São Paulo, 2017.

Muller, Daniel Pedro. *Ensaio d'um quadro estatístico da província de São Paulo.* São Paulo: Governo do Estado de São Paulo, 1978.

Myrrha, Luana Junqueira Dias, Cassio M. Turra, and Simone Wajnman. "A contribuição dos nascimentos e óbitos para o envelhecimento populacional no Brasil, 1950 a 2100." *Revista Latinoamericana de Población* 20 (2017): 37–54.

Nascimento, Arlindo Mello do. "População e família brasileira: ontem e hoje." Paper presented at the XV Encontro Nacional de Estudos Populacionais, ABEP, 2006.

Nassif, André. "Há evidências de desindustrialização no Brasil?" *Revista de Economia Política* 28, no. 1 (2008): 72–96.

Naves, Rubens. *Organizações sociais—a construção do modelo.* São Paulo: Editora Quartier Latin, 2014.

Negri, Fernanda de, and Luiz R. Cavalcante. "Análise dos dados da PINTEC 2011." Nota Técnica no. 15, IPEA, Brasília, 2013.

Negri, Fernanda de. *Novos caminhos para a Inovação no Brasil.* Brasília: IPEA, 2018.

Negri, João Alberto de, and Mauro Borges Lemos. "Avaliação das políticas de incentivos à P&D e inovação tecnológica no Brasil." Nota Técnica, IPEA, Brasília, 2009.

Neto, Lira. *Getúlio Vargas.* 3 vols. São Paulo: Companhia das Letras, 2006–2014.

Neto, Sigismundo Bialoskorski, and Waldemar Ferreira Jr. "Evolução e organização das cooperativas agropecuárias paulistas na década de 90." Paper presented at the XLII Congresso da Sociedade Brasileira de Economia e Sociologia Rural, 2004.

Netto, Antônio Delfim. *O problema do café no Brasil.* São Paulo: IPE-USP, 1981.

Netto, José V. R., Lucio Bittencourt, and Pedro Malafaia. "Políticas culturais por meio de organizações sociais em São Paulo: expandindo a qualidade da democracia?" *Seminário Internacional de Políticas Culturais,* 2012: 1-16. http://culturadigital.br/politicaculturalcasaderuibarbosa/files/2012/09/Jose-Verissimo-Rom%C3%A30-Netto-et-alii.pdf.

Neves, Marcos Fava, Allan W. Grayb, and Brian A. Bourquard. "Copersucar: A World Leader in Sugar and Ethanol." *International Food and Agribusiness Management Review* 19, no. 2 (2016): 207–240.

Neves, Marcos Fava, and Vinícius Gustavo Trombin. "Mapping and Quantification of the Brazilian Citrus Chain." *Fruit Processing,* March/April 2012.

Neves, Marcos Fava, and Vinícius Gustavo Trombin, eds. *The Orange Juice Business: A Brazilian Perspective.* Wageningen: Springer Science & Business Media, 2012.

Ninaut, Evandro Scheidt and Marcos Antonio Matos. "Panorama do cooperativismo no Brasil: censo, exportações e faturamento." *Informações Econômicas SP* 38, no. 8 (2008): 43–55.

Nogueira, Antonio Carlos Lima, and Decio Zylbersztajn. "Coexistência de arranjos institucionais na avicultura de corte do estado de São Paulo." Working paper no. 03/022, USP–Faculdade de Economia, Administração e Contabilidade, Departamento de Administração, 2003.

Nogueira, Arlinda R. "Imigração japonesa para a lavoura cafeeira paulista: 1908–1922." PhD thesis, Instituto de Estudos Brasileiros, 1973.

Nogueira, Fernando Tadeu Pongelupe, and Danilo R. D. Aguiar. "Efeitos da desregulamentação na extensão e no grau de integração do mercado brasileiro de café." *Revista de Economia* 37, no. 3 (2011): 21–46.

Noronha, Eduardo G. "Informal, Illegal and Unfair: Perceptions of Labor Markets in Brazil." *Revista Brasileira de Ciências Sociais* 18, no. 53 (2003): 111–129. http://socialsciences.scielo.org/scielo.php?pid=S0102-69092005000100009&script=sci_arttext&tlng=en.

Nunberg, Barbara. "Structural Change and State Policy: The Politics of Sugar in Brazil Since 1964." *Latin American Research Review* 21, no. 2 (1986): 53–92.

Okie, Susan. "Fighting HIV—Lessons from Brazil." *New England Journal of Medicine* 354 (May 11, 2006): 1977–1981.

Oliveira, Juarez de Castro "Estimación de la Fecundidad en Brasil y en los Estados de Sao Paulo y Rio Grande do Norte en base a Datos Censales y de Registro de los Placimientos Vivos - 1980-." (CELADE, Documentos de Trabajo, Santiago, 1985).

Oliveira, Luiz Antônio P., and Celso Cardoso da S. Simões. "As informações sobre fecundidade, mortalidade e anticoncepção nas PNADs." *Livros,* 2015: 183–225.

Oliveira, Luiz Guilherme de. "A cadeia de produção aeronaútica no Brasil: Uma análise sobre os fornecedores da Embraer." MA thesis, UNICAMP, 2005.

Oliveira, Marcio de, Jr. "A liberação comercial brasileira e os coeficientes de importação—1990/95." Discussion paper no. 703, IPEA, Rio de Janeiro, 2000.

Oliveira, Ribamar. "Delfim Netto: Plano real acentuou redução da capacidade exportadora brasileira." *Jornal Valor Econômico*, June 29, 2014.

Olivo, Luis Carlos Cancellier de. *As organizações sociais e o novo espaço público.* Florianópolis: Editorial Studium, 2005.

Orenstein, L., and A. C. Sochaczewski. "Democracia com desenvolvimento: 1956–1961." In Marcelo de Paiva Abreu, ed., *A ordem do progresso,* 171–212. Rio de Janeiro: Editora Campus, 1992:

Oro, Ari Pedro. "A política da Igreja Universal e seus reflexos nos campos religioso e político brasileiros." *Revista Brasileira de Ciências Sociais* 18, no. 53 (2003): 53–69.

Osorio, Rafael Guerreiro. "A desigualdade racial de renda no Brasil: 1976–2006." PhD thesis, Universidade de Brasília, 2009.

Osório, Rafael Guerreiro. "A mobilidade social dos negros brasileiros." Discussion paper no. 1033, IPEA, Brasília, 2004.

Osório, Rafael Guerreiro. "O sistema classificatório de 'cor ou raça' do IBGE." Discussion paper no. 996, IPEA, Brasília, 2003.

Ossewaarde, Ringo, Andre Nijhof, and Liesbet Heyse. "Dynamics of NGO Legitimacy: How Organising Betrays Core Missions of INGOs." *Public Administration and Development* 28 (2008): 42–53.

Paiva, Eduardo Nazareth. "Fábrica Nacional de Motores (FNM): Historiando e considerando a ideia de um contra-laboratório na indústria automotiva brasileira." Paper presented at ANPUH—XXIII Simpósio Nacional de História, Londrina, 2005. https://anpuh.org.br/uploads/anais-simposios/pdf/2019-01/1548206371_9f108591a8d16592486497 11aac58ad2.pdf.

Pala, Thais Faraboli. "Favela Nova Jaguaré: intervenções de políticas públicas de 1989 a 2011." MA thesis, Universidade Presbiteriana Mackenzie, 2011.

Palma, José Gabriel. "Quatro fontes de desindustrialização e um novo conceito de doença holandesa." Paper presented at the Conferência de Industrialização, Desindustrialização e Desenvolvimento, Centro Cultural da Fiesp, São Paulo, 2005. https://macrododesenvolvimento.files.wordpress.com/2013/06/520-20quatro20fontes20_2_.pdf.

Pasternak, Suzana. "Espaço e população nas favelas de São Paulo." *Anais*, 2016: 1–17

Pasternak, Suzana. "São Paulo e suas favelas." *Pós. Revista do Programa de Pós-Graduação em Arquitetura e Urbanismo da FAUUSP* 19 (2006): 176–197.

Pastore, José. *Inequality and Social Mobility in Brazil.* Madison: University of Wisconsin Press, 1982.

Pastore, José, and Nelson do Valle Silva. *Mobilidade social no Brasil.* São Paulo: Makron, 2000.

Paula, Dilma Andrade de. "Estado, sociedade e hegemonia do rodoviarismo no Brasil." *Revista Brasileira de História da Ciência* (Rio de Janeiro) 3, no. 2 (2010): 142–156.

Paulillo, Luiz Fernando, ed. *Agroindústria e citricultura no Brasil: diferenças e dominâncias.* Rio de Janeiro: Editora E-papers, 2006.

Paulillo, Luiz Fernando, and Luiz Manoel de Moraes Camargo Almeida. "A coordenação agroindustrial citricola brasileira e os novos recursos de poder: dos políticos aos jurídicos." *Organizações Rurais & Agroindustriais* 11, no. 1 (2009): 11–27.

Paulino, Jorge. "O pensamento sobre a favela em São Paulo: uma história concisa das favelas paulistanas." MA thesis, São Paulo, FAU/USP, 2007.

Peláez, Carlos Manuel. "A balança comercial, a grande depressão e a industrialização brasileira." *Revista Brasileira de Economia* 2, no. 1 (1968): 15–47.

Peláez, Carlos Manuel. "As consequências econômicas da ortodoxia monetária, cambial e fiscal no Brasil entre 1889–1945." *Revista Brasileira de Economia* 25, no. 3 (1971): 5–82.

Peláez, Carlos Manuel. *História da industrialização brasileira. Crítica à teoria estruturalista no Brasil.* Rio de Janeiro: Apec, 1972.

Peláez, Carlos Manuel, and Wilson Suzigan. *História monetária do Brasil.* Brasília: Universidade de Brasília, 1981.

Pereira, Adriana Jimenez, and Lúcia Yasuko Izumi Nichiata. "A sociedade civil contra a Aids: demandas coletivas e políticas públicas." *Ciência & Saúde Coletiva* 16, no. 7 (2011): 3249–3257.

Pereira, Lia Valls. "Brazil Trade Liberalization Program."2006 http://citeseerx.ist.psu.edu/viewdoc/download;jsessionid=B99D9D94B14472D8DA1E43592 82B2C0D?doi=10.1.1.596.5279&rep=rep1&type=pdf.

Pereira, Luiz Carlos Bresser. *A construção política do Brasil: sociedade, economia e Estado desde a Independência.* São Paulo: Editora 34, 2014.

Pereira, Luiz Carlos Bresser. *Empresários e administradores no Brasil.* São Paulo: Brasilense, 1972.

Pereira, Luiz Carlos Bresser. "Inflação inercial e o Plano Cruzado." *Revista de Economia Política* 6, no. 3 (1986): 9–24.

Pereira, Luis Carlos Bresser. "Origens étnicas e sociais do empresário paulista." *Revista de Administração de Empresas* 4, no. 11 (1964): 86–106.

Pereira, Luiz Carlos Bresser, Nelson Marconi, and José Luís Oreiro. "Doença holandesa *Fórum de Economia da Fundação Getúlio Vargas,* 4,2007.". http://www.bresserpereira.org.br/papers-cursos/Cap.5-DutchDisease.pdf.

Perillo, Sonia, and Magaly Perdigão. "Cenários migratórios recentes em São Paulo." *Anais* 2016: 773–795.

Perissinotto, Renato Monseff. *Estado e capital cafeeiro em São Paulo (1889–1930)*. São Paulo and Campinas: Fapesp and UNICAMP, 1999.

Pestana, Paulo R. "A indústria do vidro." *BDIC* 1928, nos. 9 and 10: 199–202.

Petri, Kátia Cristina. "Terras e imigração em São Paulo: política fundiária e trabalho rural." *Histórica* no. 2 (2005). http://www.historica.arquivoestado.sp.gov.br/materias/anteriores/edicao02/materia01/.

Petrone, Maria Thereza Schorer, *A lavoura canavieira em São Paulo. Expansão e declínio (1765–1851)*, São Paulo: Difusão Européia do Livro, 1968.

Petrone, Pasquale. "A cidade de São Paulo no século XX." *Revista de História* 10, nos. 21–22 (1955): 127–170.

Petruccelli, José Luis. "Seletividade por cor e escolhas conjugais no Brasil dos 90." *Estudos Afro-Asiáticos* 23, no. 1 (2001): 5–28.

Piketty, Thomas. *Capital in the 21st Century*. Cambridge, MA: Harvard University Press, 2014.

Pinheiro, Armando Castelar. "A experiência brasileira de privatização: o que vem a seguir." Discussion paper no. 87, IPEA, Rio de Janeiro, 2002.

Pinheiro, Marcos Antonio Henriques. *Cooperativas de crédito: história da evolução normativa no Brasil*. 6th ed. Brasília: Banco Central do Brasil, 2008.

Pinto, Adolpho Augusto. *História da viação pública de São Paulo*. São Paulo: Governo do Estado, 1977.

Pinto, Céli Regina Jardim. "As ONGs e a política no Brasil: presença de novos atores." *Dados* 49, no. 3 (2006): 651–670.

Pires, Anderson José. "Café, finanças e bancos. Uma análise do sistema financeiro da zona da mata de Minas Gerais." PhD thesis, FFLCH-USP, 2004.

Pizarro, Eduardo Pimental. "Interstícios e interfaces urbanos como oportunidades latentes: o caso da Favela de Paraisópolis, São Paulo." MA thesus, FAU/USP, 2014.

Polo Industrial de Camaçari. *Plano Diretor*. Salvador: Secretaria da Indústria, Comércio e Mineração do Estado da Bahia, 2013.

Pompermayer, Fabiano M., Fernanda de Negri, and Luiz R. Cavalcante. *Inovação tecnológica no setor elétrico brasileiro. Uma avaliação do programa de P&D regulado pela ANEEL*. Brasília: Ipea, 2011.

Porto, Geciane S., and Caroline V. Memória. "Incentivos para inovação tecnologia: um estudo da política pública de renúncia fiscal no Brasil." *Revista de Administração Pública* (Rio de Janeiro) 53, no. 3 (2019): 520–541.

Potter, Joseph E., Carl P. Schmertmann, and Suzana M. Cavenaghi. "Fertility and Development: Evidence from Brazil." *Demography* 39, no. 4 (2002): 739–761.

Prado, Caio, Jr. "A cidade de São Paulo, geografia e história." In Caio Prado Jr., *Evolução política do Brasil e outros estudos*, 91–139. São Paulo: Brasiliense, 1972.

Prado, Caio, Jr. *História econômica do Brasil.* São Paulo: Brasiliense, 1945.

Prado, Thayse Cristiane Severo do. "Segregação residencial por índices de dissimilaridade, isolamento e exposição,com indicador renda, no espaço urbano de Santa Maria–RS, por geotecnologias." MA thesis, Universidade Federal de Santa Maria, 2012.

Prates, Angelo Marcos Queiroz. "Reestruturação produtiva no Brasil dos anos 90 e seus impactos na região do Grande ABC Paulista." MA thesis, UNICAMP, Campinas, 2005.

Rabuske, Irineu José, Paola Lucena dos Santos, Hosana Alves Gonçalves, and Laura Traub. "Evangélicos brasileiros: Quem são, de onde vieram e no que acreditam?" *Revista Brasileira de História das Religiões* 4, no. 12 (2012). http://periodicos.uem.br/ojs/index.php/RbhrAnpuh/article/view/30275/15877.

Rattner, Henrique. *Industrialização e concentração econômica em São Paulo.* Rio de Janeiro: Fundação Getúlio Vargas, 1972.

Rego, J. M. *Inflação inercial, teoria sobre inflação e o Plano Cruzado.* Rio de Janeiro: Paz e Terra, 1986.

Rego, Marcos Lopez, and José E. M. Faillace Jr. "O projeto de implantação da indústria automotiva no Brasil: por uma abordagem sob a ótica da Teoria dos Stakeholders." *O&S—Salvador* 24, no. 81 (2017): 216–236.

Reich, Gary, and Pedro dos Santos. "The Rise (and Frequent Fall) of Evangelical Politicians: Organization, Theology, and Church Politics." *Latin American Politics and Society* 55, no. 4 (2013): 1–22.

Reis, Daniel Aarãos, and Denis Rolland, eds. *Modernidades alternativas.* Rio de Janeiro: Ed. Fundação GetúlioVargas, 2008.

Resende, André Lara. "Estabilização e reforma." In Marcelo de Paiva Abreu, ed., *A ordem do progresso*, 213–232. Rio de Janeiro: Editora Campus, 1992.

Reydon, Bastiaan Philip. "Governança de terras e a questão agrária no Brasil." In Antônio Márcio Buainain et al., eds., *O mundo rural no Brasil do século 21: A formação de um novo padrão agrário e agrícola*, 725–760. Brasília: Embrapa, 2014.

Rial, Carmenl. "Neo-Pentecostals on the Pitch Brazilian Football Players as Missionaries Abroad." In Jeffrey D. Needell, ed., *Emergent Brazil: Key Perspectives on a New Global Power.* Gainesville: University of Florida Press, 2015.

Ribeiro, Carlos Antonio Costa. "Classe, raça e mobilidade social no Brasil." *Dados: Revista de Ciências Sociais* 49, no. 4 (2006): 833–873.

Ribeiro, Carlos Antonio Costa. *Estrutura de classe e mobilidade social no Brasil.* Bauru: EDUSC, 2007.

Ribeiro, Carlos Antonio Costa. "Quatro décadas de mobilidade social no Brasil." *Dados* 55, no. 3 (2012): 641–679.

Ribeiro, Carlos Antonio Costa. "Tendências da desigualdade de oportunidades no Brasil: mobilidade social e estratificação educacional." *Boletim, Mercado de trabalho: conjuntura e análise* (IPEA), April 2017.

Ribeiro, Carlos Antonio Costa, and Maria Celi Scalon. "Mobilidade de classe no Brasil em perspectiva comparada." *Dados: Revista de Sciências Sociais* 44, no. 1 (2001): 53–96.

Ribeiro, Carlos Antonio Costa, and Nelson do Valle Silva. "Cor, Educação e Casamento: Tendências da Seletividade Marital no Brasil, 1960 a 2000." *Dados: Revista de Ciências Sociais* 52, no. 1 (2009): 7–51.

Ribeiro, Helena, and Thomas Ribeiro de Aquino Ficarelli. "Queimadas nos canaviais e perspectivas dos cortadores de cana-de-açúcar em Macatuba, São Paulo." *Saúde Social* (São Paulo) 19, no. 1 (2010): 48–63.

Ricupero, Rubens. "Desindustrialização precoce: futuro ou presente do Brasil." *Le Monde Diplomatique* 80 (March 2014). https://diplomatique.org.br/desindustrializacao-precoce-futuro-ou-presente-do-brasil/.

Ricupero, Rubens. "Global Trends and Prospects" In UNCTAD, *Trade and Development Report, 2003: Capital Accumulation, Growth and Structural Change.* Geneva: UNCTAD, 2003.

Rodrigues, Iram Jácome. "Igreja e movimento operário nas origens do novo sindicalismo no Brasil (1964–1978)." *História, Questões & Debates* (Curitiba) 29 (1998): 25–58.

Rodrigues, Leôncio Martins. "As tendência políticas na formação das centrais sindicais." In Armando Boito, ed., *O sindicalismo brasileiro nos anos 80*, 11–42. Rio de Janeiro: Paz e Terra, 1991.

Rodrigues, Leôncio Martins. "Sindicalismo corporativo no Brasil." In *Partidos e sindicatos: Escritos de Sociologia Política*, 38–65. Rio de Janeiro: Centro Edelstein de Pesquisas Sociais, 2009. http://books.scielo.org/id/cghr3/pdf/rodrigues-9788579820267-04.pdf.

Rolnik, Raquel et al. "O Programa Minha Casa Minha Vida nas regiões metropolitanas de São Paulo e Campinas: aspectos socioespaciais e segregação." *Cadernos Metropolitanos* 17, no. 33 (2015): 127–154.

Rossi, José L., Jr., and Pedro C. Ferreira. "Evolução da produtividade industrial brasileira e a abertura comercial." Discussion paper no. 651, IPEA, Rio de Janeiro, 1999.

Rowthorn, Robert, and Ramana Ramaswamy. "Growth, Trade, and Deinstrialization." *IMF Staff Papers* 46, no. 1 (1999). https://www.imf.org/external/Pubs/FT/staffp/1999/03-99/pdf/rowthorn.pdf.

Saes, Alexandre Macchione. "A historiografia da industrialização brasileira." In *Anais do 3° Seminário Nacional de História da Historiografia.* Ouro Preto, 2009.

Saes, Flávio Azevedo Marques de. *As ferrovias de São Paulo, 1870–1940*. São Paulo: Hucitec-INL-MEC, 1981.

Saes, Flávio Azevedo Marques de. *A grande empresa de serviços públicos*. São Paulo: Hucitec, 1986.

Sakuramoto, Carlos, and Luiz Carlos DioSerio. "Indústria automobilística no Brasil: protagonista no palco de uma eminente transformação global." *Fórum de Inovação EASP*, 2015https://bibliotecadigital.fgv.br/dspace/bitstream/handle/10438/16340/Industria_automotiva_no_Brasil_Protagonista_no_palco_de_uma_eminente_transforma%c3%a7%c3%a30_global.pdf?sequence=1&isAllowed=y.

Sampaio, Helena, Fernando Limongi, and Haroldo Torres. *Equidade e heterogeneidade no ensino superior brasileiro*. NUPES-USP, Documento de Trabalho 1/00, n.d.

Sanchis, Pierre. "As religiões dos brasileiros." *Horizonte* 1, no. 2 (2009): 1–30.

Sano, Hironobu, and Fernandoo Luiz Abrucio. "Promessas e resultados da nova gestão pública no Brasil: o caso das organizações sociais em São Paulo." *Revista de Administração de Empresas* 48, no. 3 (2008): 64–80.

Santana, Leonardo Ferreira de. "Análise do desempenho dos serviços prestados através das organizações sociais de saúde no estado do Rio de Janeiro." MA thesis, FGV-RJ, Rio de Janeiro, 2015.

Santos, Ana Jacira dos. "As comunidades eclesiais de base no período de 1970 a 2000." PhD thesis, Universidade Federal do Rio Grande do Norte, 2002.

Santos, Angela M. M. M., and Caio M. A. Pinhão. "Polos automotivos brasileiros." BNDES, 1999. www.bndes.gov.br/bibliotecadigital.

Santos, Arthur Tranzola. "Abertura comercial na década de 1990 e os impactos na indústria automobilística." *Fronteira* (Belo Horizonte) 8, no. 16 (2009): 107–129.

Santos, Joelma Cristina dos. "Sistema agroindustrial do leite na região de Presidente Prudente–SP." MA thesis, Universidade Estadual Paulista, Presidente Prudentes, 2004.

Santos, Milton. *Metrópole corporativa fragmentada: o caso da São Paulo*. São Paulo: Secretaria de Estado da Cultura, 1990.

Santos, Milton. *Técnica, espaço, tempo: globalização e meio técnico-científico informacional*. São Paulo: Hucitec, 1997.

Sayad, João. "Planos Cruzado e Real: acertos e desacertos." Seminários Dimac no. 30, IPEA, Rio de Janeiro, September 2000.

Scalco, Paulo Roberto. "Identificação do poder de mercado no segmento de leite *in natura* e UHT." PhD thesis, Universidade Federal de Viçosa, 2011.

Scalon. Maria Celi. *Mobilidade social no Brasil: padrões e tendências*. Rio de Janeiro: Revan/IUPERJ-UCAM, 1999.

Schlesener, Anita Helena, and Donizete Aparecido Fernandes. "Os conflitos sociais no campo e a educação: a questão agrária no Brasil." *Cadernos de Pesquisa: Pensamento Educacional* 10, no. 24 (2017): 131–148.

Schwartzman, Luisa Farah. "Does Money Whiten? Intergenerational Changes in Racial Classification in Brazil." *American Sociological Review* 72 (2007): 940–963.

Schwartzman, Simon, Eunice Ribeiro Durham, and José Goldemberg. "A educação no Brasil em perspectiva de transformação." Projeto sobre educação na América Latina, São Paulo, June 1993. http://www.schwartzman.org.br/simon/transform.htm.

Scorzafave, Luiz Guilherme Dacar da Silva. "Caracterização da inserção feminina no mercado de trabalho e seus efeitos sobre a distribuição de renda." PhD thesis, FEA/USP, 2004.

Scott, Allen J. "Industrial Revitalization in the ABC Municipalities, São Paulo: Diagnostic Analysis and Strategic Recommendations for a New Economy and a New Regionalism." *Regional Development Studies* 7 (2001): 1–32.

Semeghini, Ulisses Cidade. "Campinas (1860 a 1980): agricultura, industrialização e urbanização." MA thesis, UNICAMP, 1988.

Semeghini, Ulisses Cidade. "A região administrativa de Campinas." In Fundação SEADE, *São Paulo no Limiar do Século XX*, 8:15–70. São Paulo: SEADE, 1992.

Sérgio B. V. Gomes, João A. Barcellos, and Nelson Tucci. "Embraer e Boeing vis-à-vis Airbus e Bombardier: Quais as implicações para o Brasil?" *Aeroespacial e Defesa/BNDES Setorial,* 47: 61–122.

Shapiro, Helen. "State Intervention and Industrialization: The Origins of the Brazilian Automotive Industry." *The Journal of Economic History* 49, no. 2 (1989): 448–450.

Shimizu, Ullisses Kazumi. "A influência da inovação no desempenho das firmas no Brasil." PhD thesis, Universidade Presbiteriana Mackenzie, 2013.

Silber, Simão. "Política econômica. Defesa no nivel de renda e industrialização no período 1929–1939." MA thesis, FEAUSP, 1973.

Silva, César Roberto Leite da, and Sérgio Antonio dos Santos. "Política agrícola e eficiência econômica: o caso da agricultura paulista." *Pesquisa & Debate. Revista do Programa de Estudos Pós-Graduados em Economia Política* 12, no. 2 (2001): 66–82.

Silva, Danielle Barbosa Lopes da. "O impacto da abertura comercial sobre a produtividade da indústria brasileira." MA thesis, FGV, 2004.

Silva, Elvis Vitoriano da. "Desigualdade de renda no espaço intra-urbano: análise da evolução na cidade de Porto Alegre no período 1991–2000." MA thesis, Universidade Federal do Rio Grande do Sul, 2011.

Silva, Haroldo José Torres da. "Estudo da viabilidade econômico-financeira da indústria de citros: impactos da criação de um conselho setorial." PhD thesis, Escola Superior de Agricultura Luiz de Queiroz, 2016.

Silva, Marcio Rufino. "'Mares de prédios' e 'mares de gente': território e urbanização crítica em Cidade Tiradentes." MA thesis, FFLCH USP, 2008.

Silva, Sérgio. *Expansão cafeeira e origens da indústria no Brasil.* São Paulo: Alfa-Omega, 1995.

Silva, Vanice M. da, Sheyla L. Lima, and Marcia Teixeira. "Organizações e fundações estatais de direito privado no sistema único de saúde: relação entre o público e o privado e mecanismos de controle social." *Saúde Debate* (Rio de Janeiro) 39, special no. (December 2015): 145–159.

Simonsen, Mario Henrique. *Inflação, gradualismo x tratamento de choque.* Rio de Janeiro: Apec, 1970.

Simonsen, Mario Henrique, and Roberto Campos. *A nova economia brasileira.* Rio de Janeiro: José Olympio, 1979.

Simonsen, Roberto. *Evolução industrial do Brasil e outros estudos.* São Paulo: Companhia Editora Nacional, 1939.

Singer, Paul. *A crise do "Milagre."* Rio de Janeiro: Paz e Terra, 1977.

Sobrinho, Eduardo Jorge M. A., and Paulo Fernando Capucci. "Saúde em São Paulo: aspectos da implantação do SUS no período de 2001–2002." *Estudos Avançados* 17, no. 48 (2003): 200–227.

Souza, Bertone de Oliveira. "Entre a espera pelo céu e a busca por bem-estar." In Jérri Roberto Marin and André Dioney Fonseca, eds., *Olhares sobre a Igreja Assembleia de Deus.* Campo Grande: Editora UFMS, 2015.

Souza, Pedro Herculano Guimarães Ferreira de "A desigualdade vista do topo: a concentração de renda entre os ricos no Brasil, 1926-2013," (Phd thesis, Brasilia, Universidade de Brasília, 2016)

Souza, Pedro Ferreira de, Carlos Antonio Costa Ribeiro, and Flavio Carvalhaes. "Desigualdade de oportunidades no Brasil: considerações sobre classe, educação e raça." *Revista Brasileira de Ciências Sociais* 25, no. 73 (2010): 77–100.

Souza, Pedro Herculano Guimarães Ferreira de "Top Incomes in Brazil, 1933–2012: A Research Note." December 11, 2014. http://dx.doi.org/10.2139/ssrn.2537026.

Spix, J. B., and F. P. von Martius. *Viagem pelo Brasil, 1817–1820.* 2 vols. Rio de Janeiro: Imprensa Nacional, 1938.

Stefani, Célia Regina Baider. "O sistema ferroviário paulista: um estudo sobre a evolução do transporte de transporte de passageiros sobre trilhos." MA thesis, FFLCH-USP, 2007.

Stein, Stanley J. "Aspectos do crescimento e declínio da lavoura de café no Vale do Paraíba 1850–1860." *Revista de História da Economia Brasileira* 1, no. 1 (1953).

Stein, Stanley J. *The Brazilian Cotton Manufacture: Textile Enterprise in an Underdeveloped Area, 1850–1950*. Cambridge, MA: Harvard University Press, 1957.

Stein, Stanley J. *Vassouras, a Brazilian Coffee County, 1850–1900: The Roles of Planter and Slave in a Plantation Society*. Princeton: Princeton University Press; 1985.

Suárez, Naila López Cabaleiro. *O modelo de gestão das organizações sociais de cultura em São Paulo*. São Paulo: FGV, 2011.

Sued, Ronaldo. *O desenvolvimento da agroindústria da laranja no Brasil: o impacto das geadas na Flórida e na política econômica governamental*. Rio de Janeiro: Fundação Getúlio Vargas, 1993.

Summerhill, William R. *Order Against Progress: Government, Foreign Investment, and Railroads in Brazil, 1854–1913*. Stanford: Stanford University Press, 2003.

Suzigan, Wilson, *Indústria brasileira. Origens e desenvolvimento*. São Paulo: Brasiliense, 1986.

Szmrecsányi, Tamás, and Eduardo Pestana Moreira. "O desenvolvimento da agroindústria canavieira do Brasil desde a Segunda Guerra Mundial." *Estudos Avançados* 5, no. 11 (1991): 57–79.

Szmrecsányl, Maria Irene de Q. F. "A macro metrópole paulistana: 1950–2004." In Tamás Szmrecsányi, ed., *História Econômica da cidade de São Paulo*, 116–145. São Paulo: Editora Globo, 2005.

Taschner, Suzana Pasternak. "Moradia da pobreza: habitação sem saúde." PhD thesis, Faculdade de Saúde Pública, USP, 1982.

Tavares, Maria da Conceição. "Auge e declínio do processo de substituição de importações no Brasil." In Maria da Conceição Tavares, *Da substituição de importações ao capitalismo financeiro*, 27–115. Rio de Janeiro: Zahar, 1973.

Tavares, Maria da Conceição. *Destruição não-criadora*. Rio de Janeiro: Record, 1990.

Tavares, Priscilla Albuquerque. "Efeito do Programa Bolsa Família sobre a oferta de trabalho das mães." Paper presented at the XVI Encontro Nacional de Estudos Populacionais, ABEP, 2008.

Taylor, P. J. "Worlds of Large Cities: Pondering Castells' Space of Flows." *Third World Planning Review* 21, no. 3 (1999): iii–x.

Teixeira, Ana Claudio Chaves. *Identidade em construção: as organizações não-governamentais no processo brasileiro de democratização*. São Paulo: AnnaBlume, 2003.

Telles, Edward E., *Race in Another America: The Significance of Skin Color in Brazil*. Princeton: Princeton University Press, 2014.

Torche, Florencia. "Intergenerational Mobility and Inequality: The Latin American Case." *Annual Review of Sociology* 40 (2014): 619–642.

Torche, Florencia. "Unequal but Fluid: Social Mobility in Chile in Comparative Perspective." *American Sociological Review* 70, no. 3 (2005): 422–450.

Torche, Florencia, and Carlos Costa Ribeiro. "Pathways of Change in Social Mobility: Industrialization, Education and Growing Fluidity in Brazil." *Research in Social Stratification and Mobility* 28, no. 3 (2010): 291–307.

Triner, Gail D. *Mining and the State in Brazilian Development*. London: Pickering & Chatto, 2011.

Troiano, Mariele. "Os empresários no congresso: a legitimação de interesses via audiências públicas." MA thesis, Universidade Federal de São Carlos, 2016.

Turchi, Lenita Maria, and José Mauro de Morais, eds. *Políticas de apoio à inovação tecnológica no Brasil*. Brasília: IPEA, 2017.

Uchoa, Martinho Prado. "A história da Cosipa." http://www.novomilenio.inf.br/cubatao/ch027.htm.

Udaeta, Rosa Guadalupe Soares. "As Hospedarias de Imigrantes em São Paulo." In *Anais do XVII Encontro Regional de História— O Lugar da História*. Campinas: ANPUH/SPUNICAMP, 2004.

UNCTAD. *World Investment Report 2004: The Shift Towards Services*. New York: United Nations, 2004.

Velasco, Licínio, Jr. *Privatização: mitos e falsas percepções*. Rio de Janeiro: BNDES, 1999.

Velloso, João P. dos Reis. "A fantasia política: a nova alternativa de interpretação do II PND." *Revista de Economia Política* 18, no. 2 (1998): 133–144.

Versiani, Flávio Rabelo, and Maria Teresa R. O. Versiani. "A industralização antes de 1930: Uma contribuição." *Estudos Econômicos* 5, no. 1 (1975): 37–63.

Vieira, Danilo Jorge. "Um estudo sobre a guerra fiscal no Brasil." PhD thesis, Campinas, UNICAMP, 2012.

Vieira, Danilo Jorge, André Eduardo S. Fernandes, and Nélio Lacerda Wanderlei. "A questão da guerra fiscal: uma breve resenha." *Revista de Informação Legislativa* (Brasília) 37, no. 148 (2000): 5–20.

Vieira, Elisabeth Meloni. "A esterilização de mulheres de baixa renda em região metropolitana do sudeste do Brasil e fatores ligados à sua prevalência." *Revista de Saúde Pública* 28 (1994): 440–448.

Vignoli, Jorge A. Rodríguez. "Cohabitación en América Latina: ¿modernidad, exclusión o diversidad?" *Papeles de Población* 10, no. 40 (2004): 97–145.

Villa, Marco Antonio. *Quando eu vim-me embora: História da migração nordestina para São Paulo*. Rio de Janeiro: Leya, 2017.

Villela, Aníbal, and Wilson Suzigan. *Política do governo e crescimento da economia brasileira, 1889–1945*. Rio de Janeiro: IPEA/INPES, 1973.

Wajnman, Simone. "'Quantidade' e 'qualidade' da participação das mulheres na força de trabalho brasileira." In Nathalie Reis Itaboraí and Arlene Martinez Ricoldi, eds., *Até onde caminhou a revolução de gênero no Brasil?*Belo Horizonte: ABEP, 2006 www.abep.org.br/publicacoes/index.php/ebook/article/view/2446/2401.

Werneck, R. L. F. "Alternância política, redistribuição e crescimento, 2003–2010." In M. P. Abreu, ed., *A ordem do progresso. Dois séculos de política econômica no Brasil*, rev. ed., 357–397. Rio de Janeiro: Elsevier, 2014.

Werneck, Rogério. *Empresas estatais e política macroeconômica*. Rio de Janeiro: Campus, 1987.

Wilkinson, John. *O setor sucroalcooleiro brasileiro na atual conjuntura nacional e internacional*. Rio de Janeiro: ActionAid, 2015.

Wolfe, Joel. *Autos and Progress: The Brazilian Search for Modernity*. New York: Oxford University Press, 2010.

Wolfe, Joel. *Working Women, Working Men: São Paulo and the Rise of Brazil's Industrial Working Class, 1900–1955*. Durham: Duke University Press, 1993.

Wood, Charles H., and José Alberto Magno de Carvalho, *The Demography of Inequality in Brazil*. Cambridge: Cambridge University Press, 1988.

Wood, Charles H., José Alberto Magno de Carvalho, and Cláudia Júlia Guimarães Horta. "The Color of Child Mortality in Brazil, 1950–2000: Social Progress and Persistent Racial Inequality." *Latin American Research Review* 45, no. 2 (2010): 114–139.

Wulfhorst, Ingo. "O Pentecostalismo no Brasil." *Estudos Teológicos* 35, no. 1 (1995): 7–20.

Ximenes, Assuero Fonseca. "Apropriação do fundo público da saúde pela organizações sociais em Pernambuco." PhD thesis, UFP, Recife, 2015.

Yunes, João, and Vera Shirley Carvalho Ronchezel. "Evolução da mortalidade geral infantil e proporcional no Brasil." *Revista de Saúde Pública* 8 (1974): 3–48.

Zago, Nadir. "Do acesso à permanência no ensino superior: percurso de estudantes universitários de camadas populares." *Revista Brasileira de Educação* 11, no. 32 (2006): 226–237.

Zangelmi, Arnaldo José, Fabrício Roberto Costa Oliveira, and Izabella Fátima Oliveira de Sales. "Movimentos, mediações e estado: apontamentos sobre a luta pela terra no Brasil na segunda metade do século XX." *Sociedade e Cultura* 19, no. 1 (2016): 133–141.

Zanini, Fabio. "Lula aceita fazer novo acordo com FMI." *Folha de São Paulo*, May 21, 2002.

Zimmermann, Beate, and Jurgen Zeddies. "International Competitiveness of Sugar Production." Paper presented at the 13th International Farm

Management Congress, Wageningen, The Netherlands, July 7–12, 2002. http://econpapers.repec.org/paper/agsifma02/.

Zimmermann, Gustavo. "A região administrativa de Sorocaba." In Fundação SEADE, *São Paulo no Limiar do Século XX,* 8:147–180. São Paulo: SEADE, 1992.

INDEX